Municipal Management Series

Management Policies in Local Government Finance

International
City/County
ICMA
Management
Association
icma.org

The International City/County Management Association (ICMA) is the professional and educational organization for appointed administrators and assistant administrators in local government. The mission of ICMA is to create excellence in local governance by developing and fostering professional local government management worldwide. To further this mission, ICMA develops and disseminates new approaches to management through training programs, information services, and publications.

Local government managers—carrying a wide range of titles—serve cities, towns, counties, councils of governments, and state/provincial associations of local governments. They serve at the direction of elected councils and governing boards. ICMA serves these managers and local governments through many programs that aim at improving the manager's professional competence and strengthening the quality of all local governments.

ICMA was founded in 1914, adopted its Code of Ethics in 1924, and established its Institute for Training in Municipal Administration in 1934. The institute provided the basis for the Municipal Management Series, popularly known as the "ICMA Green Books." By 1994, the institute had evolved into the ICMA University, which provides professional development resources for members and other local government employees.

ICMA's interests and activities include public management education; voluntary credentialing and standards of ethics for members; an information clearinghouse; local government research and development; data collection and dissemination; technical assistance; and a wide array of publications, including *Public Management* magazine, newsletters, management reports, and texts. ICMA's efforts toward the improvement of local government—as represented by this book—are offered for all local governments and educational institutions.

Contributors

J. Richard Aronson
Roy W. Bahl Jr.
Timothy J. Bartik
Edward J. Bierhanzl
Paul B. Downing
Mary H. Harris
William W. Holder
M. Corinne Larson
Paul A. Leonard
John L. Mikesell
Rowan A. Miranda
Vincent G. Munley

Wallace E. Oates
John E. Petersen
Arnold H. Raphaelson
Claire Lee Reiss
Leonard I. Ruchelman
Larry D. Schroeder
Eli Schwartz
Paul L. Solano
Khi V. Thai
Robert J. Thornton
Peter C. Young

Municipal Management Series

Management Policies in Local Government Finance

Fifth Edition

**Published
for the
ICMA University**

Edited by

**By the
International
City/County
Management
Association**

J. Richard Aronson
Lehigh University

Eli Schwartz
Lehigh University

International
City/County
Management
Association
icma.org

ICMA UNIVERSITY

ICMA Textbooks

Management Policies in Local Government Finance

Advanced Supervisory Practices

Budgeting: A Guide for Local Governments

Capital Budgeting and Finance: A Guide for Local Governments

Economic Development: Strategies for State and Local Practice

Effective Communication

The Effective Local Government Manager

Effective Supervisory Practices

Emergency Management

The Future of Local Government Administration: The Hansell Symposium

Human Resource Management in Local Government: An Essential Guide

Local Government Police Management

Managing Fire and Rescue Services

Managing Human Resources: Local Government Cases

Managing Local Economic Development: Cases in Decision Making

Managing Local Government: Cases in Decision Making

Managing Local Government Finance: Cases in Decision Making

Managing Small Cities and Counties

The Practice of Local Government Planning

The Practice of State and Regional Planning

Service Contracting: A Local Government Guide

Library of Congress Cataloging-in-Publication Data

Management policies in local government finance /
edited by J. Richard Aronson, Eli Schwartz. 5th ed.
    p. cm.
Includes bibliographical references and index.
  ISBN 0-87326-142-9
  1. Local finance. 2. Municipal finance. I. Aronson,
        J. Richard (Jay Richard), 1937- II.
Schwartz, Eli. III.   ICMA Training
Institute.
  HJ9105.M3 2004
  352.4 214 dc22

                                    2004011526

Printed in the United States of America

10 09 08 07 06 05 04

10 9 8 7 6 5 4 3 2 1

43062
04-108

Foreword

This fifth edition of *Management Policies in Local Government Finance* is published at a time of great stress for local government financial managers. The recent, precipitous loss of federal and state revenues has brought into sharp focus the need for sound local financial management. Restructuring of our economy, as globalization becomes a reality, is possibly the most visible challenge for local economies in the United States, but infrastructure needs and the sheer complexity of management in the twenty-first century contribute mightily to a high-risk environment that demands intelligence, foresight, decisiveness, and political acumen. The need for strong leadership in financial management has never been greater.

Management Policies in Local Government Finance joins two recent ICMA publications that address current financial management issues: *Evaluating Financial Condition: A Handbook for Local Government* and *Capital Budgeting and Finance: A Guide for Local Governments*. The two earlier books offer hands-on assistance and in-depth guidance in two important areas of management: financial trend monitoring and planning, and financing capital expenditure. In contrast, the volume in hand covers the entire spectrum of local government financial management. Its nineteen chapters offer the young manager a thorough grounding in all the principles of financial management and a review of policies and practices in use in local governments in the United States.

This book replaces the 1996, 1987, 1981, and 1975 editions of *Management Policies in Local Government Finance*, which in turn replaced *Municipal Finance Administration*, first published in 1937. For nearly seventy years, this book has been ICMA's basic reference for city and county managers, finance officers, budget officers, and planners. It serves as a core text in courses on finance in schools of public administration and in professional development training for future managers.

Like its predecessors, this edition focuses on management principles and practice while outlining the financial and economic context within which public financial management takes place at the local level. The contributors are all recognized authorities in their respective fields and bring their individual perspectives and experience to their chapters. Several changes distinguish this book from its predecessors: new chapters have been added in school finance, enterprise resource planning systems, cost-benefit analysis, and purchasing and risk management.

Part One explains the local government setting that makes financial management of towns, cities, and counties unique. A new chapter on public school finance places local revenue raising in context.

Part Two introduces the tools of financial management: forecasting, cost-benefit analysis, budgeting, accounting, and enterprise resource planning systems.

Part Three looks at revenue sources, including property and nonproperty taxes and user charges and fees, and Part Four addresses several responsibilities that fall within the finance director's portfolio and that merit attention in any local government: economic development, debt management, procurement, cash and investment management, risk and insurance management, public employee pension funds, and unions and labor management.

Management Policies in Local Government Finance has been prepared for the ICMA University, which was established to provide professional development opportunities for managers in local government. The ICMA University develops in-service training for local officials whose principal responsibilities are to lead, plan, direct, and coordinate the work of others.

ICMA is grateful to the editors, J. Richard Aronson and Eli Schwartz, for once again editing this volume, and to the many contributors who wrote individual chapters. Their biographies appear at the end of the book.

The editors wish to thank Rene Hollinger, secretary, Department of Economics, Lehigh University; and Rosemary Krauss, secretary, Martindale Center for the Study of Private Enterprise, Lehigh University, for their assistance.

ICMA staff members and former staff members who contributed to the present volume include Barbara H. Moore, director of publishing and information resources; Christine Ulrich, editorial director; Sandra F. Chizinsky and Jane Cotnoir, editors; Nedra James, publications assistant, and Dawn M. Leland, director of publications production. David S. Arnold, former editor of the Municipal Management Series, contributed substantially to the development of earlier editions on which this book is based.

Robert J. O'Neill Jr.
Executive Director
International City/County
Management Association

Contents

Figures

Part one:
The local
government setting

1

The finance function in local government

LEONARD I. RUCHELMAN

The finance manager, in performing the duties of the office, advises on revenue sources and budget expenditures; manages the collection and distribution of funds; and keeps an eye on demographic changes, economic conditions, and shifts in federal, state, and local fiscal relations. As advances in electronics, transportation, and communications reshape the nation's urban areas, dramatically changing the way that most Americans live and work, the economic, social, and intergovernmental context of local government administration is changing. The finance manager must be sensitive to such changes and must be prepared to respond through the effective management of scarce resources.

Thus, a first step for the local finance manager is to understand the setting in which fiscal responsibilities are carried out. This opening chapter considers the local government finance function within the context of urban development patterns, the legal and institutional framework, and local government structures. It also examines the organizational structures of financial administration and a range of approaches to financial decision making.

In 2002 there were nearly 88,000 governments in the United States. Of these, all but 51 were local governments: counties, municipalities, townships, school districts, or special districts. Table 1–1 shows that the number of local governments increased notably between 1987 and 2002 and that municipalities and special districts accounted for most of that increase. Table 1–2 offers a closer look at municipalities with populations of 2,500 or more.

The mayor-council form of government is dominant among the largest municipalities (those with populations of 250,000 or more), whereas the council-manager form is prevalent among small and medium-sized municipalities (those with populations between 2,500 and 99,999). Larger cities—those with populations of 100,000 or more—tend to be central cities constituting the regional core, whereas smaller and medium-sized municipalities tend to be located in outlying areas. The overall number of suburban communities is far greater than that of central cities, a pattern that reflects rapid suburban growth. Table 1–2 also shows that the nation's largest cities are no longer confined primarily to the Northeast and North-Central regions of the country; many are now located in the South and the West, areas that grew rapidly in the 1980s and 1990s.

Table 1–3 shows the cumulative distribution of counties in the United States. As the principal jurisdictions serving areas that are predominantly rural, most counties have populations under 50,000 and are independent of metropolitan areas. The Northeast has the fewest counties, primarily because this region of the country has a strong tradition of relying on towns and villages for service provision. The

Table 1–1 Number of governments in the United States.

Type of government	1987	2002
Total	83,237	87,900
U.S. government	1	1
State governments	50	50
Local governments	83,186	87,849
County	3,042	3,034
Municipal	19,200	19,431
Township/town	16,691	16,506
School district	14,721	13,522
Special district	29,532	35,356

largest counties—those with more than one million in population—tend to be on California's Pacific Coast.

The finance function in local government is carried out within a complex intergovernmental system in which policy is made and implemented on three levels: federal, state, and local. Within this system, local governments are the workhorses of domestic policy implementation. For example, not only do local

Table 1–2   Cumulative distribution of U.S. municipalities with a population of 2,500 or more.

	Population								
	2,500 and over	5,000 and over	10,000 and over	25,000 and over	50,000 and over	100,000 and over	250,000 and over	500,000 and over	Over 1,000,000
Total, all municipalities	7,091	5,118	3,246	1,429	650	247	68	31	9
Population group									
Over 1,000,000	9	9	9	9	9	9	9	9	9
500,000–1,000,000	22	22	22	22	22	22	22	22	—
250,000–499,999	37	37	37	37	37	37	37	—	—
100,000–249,999	179	179	179	179	179	179	—	—	—
50,000–99,999	403	403	403	403	403	—	—	—	—
25,000–49,999	779	779	779	779	—	—	—	—	—
10,000–24,999	1,817	1,817	1,817	—	—	—	—	—	—
5,000–9,000	1,872	1,872	—	—	—	—	—	—	—
2,500–4,999	1,973	—	—	—	—	—	—	—	—
Geographic region									
Northeast	1,934	1,435	878	317	108	33	8	4	2
North-Central	2,080	1,441	908	370	146	44	14	5	1
South	2,021	1,380	839	353	174	77	23	13	3
West	1,056	862	621	389	222	93	23	9	3
Geographic division									
New England	729	556	353	137	46	12	1	1	—
Mid-Atlantic	1,205	879	525	180	62	21	7	3	2
East North-Central	1,392	1,012	660	265	102	30	8	5	1
West North-Central	688	429	248	105	44	14	6	—	—
South Atlantic	855	592	382	166	84	34	9	4	—
East South-Central	439	308	169	56	22	12	3	2	—
West South-Central	727	480	288	131	68	31	11	7	3
Mountain	377	272	160	92	52	27	8	2	1
Pacific Coast	679	590	461	297	170	66	15	7	2
Metro status[a]									
Central	541	540	540	505	358	175	65	30	9
Suburban	4,152	3,203	2,087	801	285	72	3	1	—
Independent	2,397	1,375	619	123	7	—	—	—	—
Form of government[a]									
Mayor-council	3,089	1,993	1,167	481	230	96	39	21	5
Council-manager	3,453	2,721	1,851	894	405	144	27	9	4
Commission	145	112	73	26	9	6	2	1	—
Town meeting	338	236	108	6	—	—	—	—	—
Representative town meeting	63	56	47	22	6	1	—	—	—

Note: (—) indicates data not applicable or not reported.
[a]Totals for municipalities of 2,500 and over do not add
   to 7,091 because a few jurisdictions did not report
   this information.

governments provide basic public services such as elementary and secondary education, public health, public works, and public safety, but they also help to fulfill certain national domestic policy objectives such as homeland security and environmental protection (see Figure 1–1, which shows local government employment patterns by function). As shown in Figure 1–2, which compares the number of government employees in 1987 and 2001, local government has

Table 1–3   Cumulative distribution of U.S. counties with a population of 2,500 or more.

		Population								
	All counties	2,500 and over	5,000 and over	10,000 and over	25,000 and over	50,000 and over	100,000 and over	250,000 and over	500,000 and over	Over 1,000,000
Total, all counties	3,040	2,926	2,753	2,367	1,498	860	477	201	91	28
Population group										
Over 1,000,000	28	28	28	28	28	28	28	28	28	28
500,000–1,000,000	63	63	63	63	63	63	63	63	63	—
250,000–499,999	110	110	110	110	110	110	110	110	—	—
100,000–249,999	276	276	276	276	276	276	276	—	—	—
50,000–99,999	383	383	383	383	383	383	—	—	—	—
25,000–49,999	638	638	638	638	638	—	—	—	—	—
10,000–24,999	869	869	869	869	—	—	—	—	—	—
5,000–9,000	386	386	386	—	—	—	—	—	—	—
2,500–4,999	173	173	—	—	—	—	—	—	—	—
Under 2,500	114	—	—	—	—	—	—	—	—	—
Geographic region										
Northeast	190	190	189	184	175	130	86	45	19	3
North-Central	1,054	1,007	914	747	445	229	125	45	19	7
South	1,372	1,346	1,301	1,152	684	365	178	66	28	7
West	424	383	349	284	194	136	88	45	25	11
Geographic division										
New England	46	46	46	44	41	25	15	6	2	
Mid-Atlantic	144	144	143	140	134	105	71	39	17	3
East North-Central	437	436	433	407	298	165	94	33	15	5
West North-Central	617	571	481	340	147	64	31	12	4	2
South Atlantic	545	543	535	482	314	192	101	39	17	3
East South-Central	360	358	356	323	175	73	27	7	2	—
West South-Central	467	445	410	347	195	100	50	20	9	4
Mountain	276	245	215	159	93	54	32	14	7	2
Pacific Coast	148	138	134	125	101	82	56	31	18	9
Metro status										
Central	458	458	458	458	455	440	378	195	89	28
Suburban	341	339	338	331	283	177	68	6	2	—
Independent	2,241	2,129	1,957	1,578	760	243	31	—	—	—
Form of government[a]										
County commission	2,191	2,089	1,922	1,583	889	407	177	59	24	4
County council–administrator (manager)	370	364	363	349	287	212	142	69	36	14
County council–elected executive	478	473	468	435	322	241	158	73	31	10

Note: (—) indicates data not applicable.
[a]Total for all counties does not add to 3,040 because one jurisdiction did not report this information.

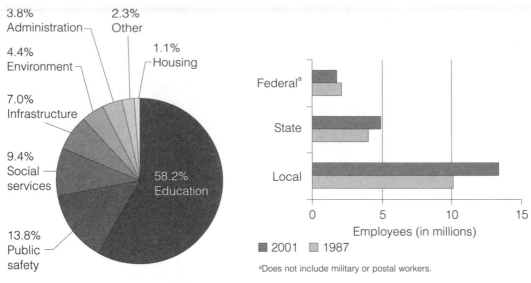

Figure 1–1   Local government employment by function, 2000.

Figure 1–2   Federal, state, and local government employees.

come to play an increasingly prominent role in meeting the needs of society; the number of federal employees actually decreased during the period shown in the figure.

In recent years, the already significant burdens on local government have been increased by growing demands for services and substantial reductions in federal aid to localities. Economic restructuring—a shift from an essentially goods-producing economy to a service-based economy—has also placed new pressures on local jurisdictions. Older central cities have been especially vulnerable to fiscal stress: as businesses and middle- and upper-income households continue to move to the suburbs in search of lower costs and better conditions, high concentrations of poorer households have been left behind, resulting in an increase in the need for social services and a decreasing capacity to pay for them. Other local jurisdictions, primarily in the West and Southwest, have been forced to commit substantial additional resources to infrastructure development and services to accommodate large increases in population.

The significance of fiscal stress first captured national attention in the late 1970s, when New York City approached financial collapse and Cleveland actually defaulted on its borrowings. During the 1980s, many jurisdictions, including Bridgeport, Connecticut; Philadelphia, Pennsylvania; and Orange County, California, continued to have great difficulty managing their finances. Although economic conditions appeared to improve during the 1990s, the new century seems to be ushering in another round of fiscal strain. In a survey conducted by the National League of Cities, chief financial officers were asked whether their city was better able to address its financial needs in the current fiscal year (2002) than in the preceding year (2001).[1] For the first time in nine years, more than half the respondents (55 percent) believed that their city was less able to meet financial needs in the current fiscal year (see Figure 1–3). This negative assessment on the part of local officials is consistent across cities of varying size, from different regions, and with different levels of taxing authority, and it represents a significant change in local fiscal health since 2000.

When fiscal conditions worsen, local governments pay a heavy price. Restricted by state law from borrowing to finance operating deficits, many local

Percentage of cities

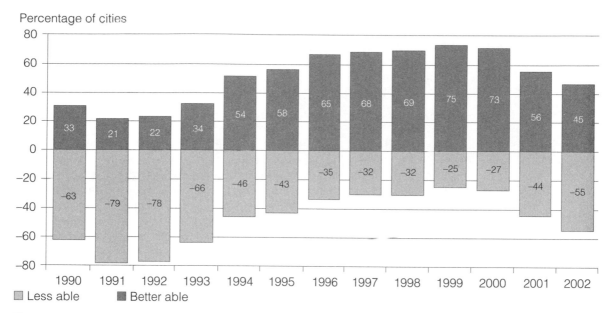

Figure 1–3   Percentage of cities that were "better able/less able" to meet their financial needs in the current year than in the previous year, 1990–2000.

governments are compelled to reduce services or defer maintenance of equipment and facilities. In addition, many draw on their reserve funds as an alternative to raising taxes and fees. Indeed, the ability to make do with less has come to be the basic measure of success for those who manage local government finance.

What adds urgency to this situation are the specialized needs—ranging from transportation to water supply to pollution control—of an urbanizing society. The spillover of local problems into neighboring jurisdictions has spawned ever more intricate arrangements among government agencies for the provision of services. Thus, the institutional arrangements that, taken together, make up the governmental context are another factor affecting financial management. These arrangements determine, for example, where the finance function is located, who shares in it, and what degree of coordination exists among the different jurisdictional components. Such matters can become quite complex in an intergovernmental system such as ours, in which service delivery often involves a multiplicity of federal, state, and local agencies. A basic concern is how well the institutional framework facilitates financial decision making for the efficient use of resources. In a democratic society, moreover, the institutional framework must also ensure equity and accountability.

In devising solutions to the problems of local financial management, it is important to recognize that there is no universal model applicable to all communities for all time. Instead, as this chapter demonstrates, communities draw from a variety of governmental and organizational arrangements to accommodate different social, economic, and political conditions. And as conditions change, arrangements tend to change as well. Communities subject to fiscal stress can be expected to undergo more extensive reform of financial management practices.

Finance managers play a major role in meeting the challenges of contemporary urban society. In the course of their work, they confront and respond to the internal demands of local finance management—budgeting, taxing, accounting, debt management, and related matters. Their job becomes especially difficult when expenditures outpace revenues. Under conditions of fiscal stress, paying bills requires a careful balancing of cash flow and creditors' demands; labor-management relations require more extensive negotiation on employee salaries and benefits; and budgeting becomes more politicized under the pressure of responding to funding requests from different agencies.

Patterns of urban development

As noted earlier, local government finance is significantly influenced by the larger environment. The finance function must thus be seen as a dynamic element subject to change: as conditions alter, methods of resource management that may once have been appropriate may cease to be appropriate. To respond swiftly and thoughtfully to changing local needs, the finance manager must first understand the factors in the external environment that shape those needs. This section provides a brief overview of the changing patterns of urban development in the United States; the next section examines the internal environment—the institutional context—within which financial decision making occurs.

From central-city concentration to suburban deconcentration

The United States transformed itself from a predominantly rural and agricultural nation into a predominantly urban and industrial nation within a relatively short time. With the exception of such East Coast cities as Baltimore, Boston, New York, and Philadelphia, few U.S. cities were highly developed before the mid-nineteenth century. Lacking cultural traditions as an integrating force, most American cities were put together hastily, without clear physical or social goals. Indeed, the dominant goals in the development of most cities were economic, and they varied by region. Most cities in the West and Midwest, for example, functioned primarily to coordinate the country's developing productive and commercial forces. In the West and Southwest, cities were oriented primarily toward the development of natural resources for mining and agriculture.

Technological advances in long-distance transportation and communication, as represented by the railroad and the telegraph, gradually linked small towns and large cities together into integrated systems. Cities were increasingly viewed as desirable places to live and work; and as cities became more accessible, more and more people and firms moved to them. The resulting increases in land values and congestion, however, soon led to an increase in the cost of living and doing business in cities.

After World War II, significant changes took place in the way communities developed. As automobiles and highways made cities more accessible to outlying areas, both people and businesses were able to use urban amenities without having to reside in the city. To take advantage of lower densities, growing numbers of households and firms began leaving the central city for the suburban hinterland. More recently, the development of new communications technologies—such as e-mail, the Internet, and wireless communications—has provided additional impetus for the spread of people and jobs across the urban landscape.

Figure 1–4 shows that as of 2000, approximately half the American population lived in the suburbs, compared with 31 percent in 1960 and 23 percent in 1950. While rural (nonmetropolitan) areas continue to lose population, the percentage of the population living in central cities hovers around 30 percent. However, the overall figures for central-city populations mask important differences between the relatively newer cities in the South and West that are ex-

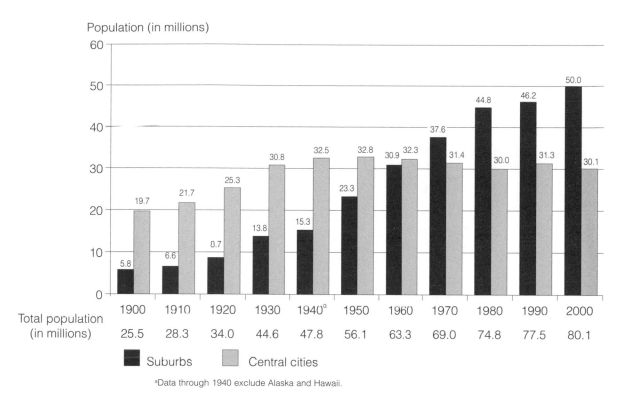

Figure 1–4   Percentage of U.S. population living in suburbs and central cities, 1900–2000.

Table 1–4   The ten fastest-growing U.S. metropolitan areas by rate of growth, 1990–2000.

Rank	Metro area	Population, 1990	Population, 2000	Numerical increase	Percentage increase
1	Las Vegas, Nevada–Arizona	852,737	1,563,282	710,545	83
2	Naples, Florida	152,099	251,377	99,278	65
3	Yuma, Arizona	106,895	160,026	53,131	50
4	McAllen-Edinburg-Mission, Texas	383,545	569,463	85,918	48
5	Austin–San Marcos, Texas	846,277	1,249,763	403,486	48
6	Fayetteville-Springdale-Rogers, Arkansas	210,908	311,121	100,213	48
7	Boise City, Idaho	295,851	432,345	136,494	46
8	Phoenix-Mesa, Arizona	2,238,480	3,251,876	1,013,396	45
9	Laredo, Texas	133,239	193,117	59,878	45
10	Provo-Orem, Utah	263,593	368,539	104,946	40

periencing growth (see Table 1–4) and the many older industrial cities in the East and Midwest that are experiencing decline (see Table 1–5).

As people and firms continue to move to the suburbs, central cities and suburban communities reveal important demographic differences. First, as noted earlier, large concentrations of poor people, many of whom are members of ethnic or racial minorities, remain in the cities. Table 1–6 shows that as of 2000, blacks and Hispanics made up 21 percent and 19 percent, respectively,

Table 1–5   Cities that lost more than 5 percent of their populations between 1990 and 2000.

City	Population, 1990	Population, 2000	Percentage change in population, 1990–2000
Cleveland, Ohio	505,616	478,403	−5.4
Washington, D.C.	606,900	572,059	−5.7
Toledo, Ohio	332,943	313,619	−5.8
Jackson, Miss.	196,637	184,256	−6.3
Lansing, Mich.	127,321	119,128	−6.4
Detroit, Mich.	1,027,974	951,270	−7.5
Birmingham, Ala.	265,968	242,820	−8.7
Dayton, Ohio	182,044	166,179	−8.7
Macon, Ga.	106,612	97,255	−8.8
Cincinnati, Ohio	364,040	331,285	−9.0
Pittsburgh, Pa.	369,879	334,563	−9.5
Syracuse, N.Y.	163,860	147,306	−10.1
Norfolk, Va.	261,229	234,403	−10.3
Buffalo, N.Y.	328,123	292,648	−10.8
Flint, Mich.	140,761	124,943	−11.2
Baltimore, Md.	736,014	651,154	−11.5
St. Louis, Mo.	396,685	348,189	−12.2
Hartford, Conn.	139,739	121,578	−13.0

Table 1–6   Distribution of whites, blacks, and Hispanics in central cities and suburbs.

Race	Year	All metropolitan statistical areas/primary metropolitan statistical areas	All central cities	Suburbs
White, non-Hispanic	1980	77.8	65.2	86.6
	1990	73.3	59.6	82.2
	2000	66.0	51.4	74.9
Black, non-Hispanic	1980	12.4	21.4	6.1
	1990	12.6	21.4	6.9
	2000	12.9	21.1	8.0
Other races, non-Hispanic	1980	2.4	3.0	2.0
	1990	3.9	4.9	3.3
	2000	6.8	8.3	6.0
Total Hispanic (all races)	1980	7.4	10.4	5.3
	1990	10.1	14.0	7.6
	2000	14.2	19.3	11.2

of central-city populations; the comparable figures for the suburbs are 8 percent and 11 percent. Second, as shown in Figure 1–5, central cities continue to have higher shares of low-income residents—around 18 or 19 percent, versus 8 or 9 percent in the suburbs. However, demographic patterns are also beginning to change in the suburbs, where the proportion of whites declined from 87 percent in 1980 to 75 percent in 2000.

Most significantly, in most of the nation's hundred largest cities, non-Hispanic whites are now in the minority. As shown in Figure 1–6, between 1990 and 2000, the non-Hispanic white population in those cities fell from 52 to 44 percent—a loss of about 2.3 million people.[2] The five largest cities alone—New York, Los Angeles, Chicago, Philadelphia, and Houston—lost nearly 1 million non-Hispanic white residents, and the Hispanic populations

Figure 1–5 Poverty rates in 2000 for central cities and suburbs in metro areas with populations over 500,000.

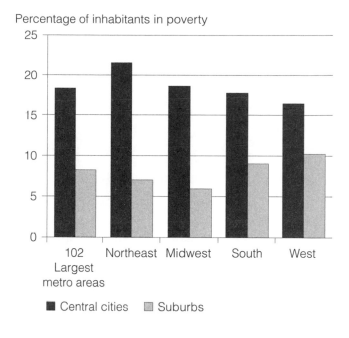

Percentage of inhabitants in poverty

■ Central cities ▨ Suburbs

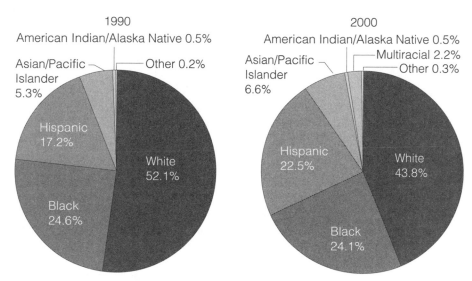

Figure 1–6 Shifts in the racial and ethnic mix in the top 100 U.S. cities, 1990–2000.

in these cities grew dramatically, from 17.2 percent in 1990 to 22.5 percent in 2000, representing approximately 3.8 million new Hispanic residents. Ten Texas cities together gained about 1 million Hispanics. During the same period, the Asian population increased by 1.3 percent and the black population remained relatively stable.

The implications of the increases in the Hispanic population are considerable. Changes in the demographic composition of city populations can affect their fiscal base. Census estimates from 1999 indicate, for example, that median annual income for Hispanic households was lower, by more than $14,000, than that of non-Hispanic white households.[3] Thus, a decline in the non-Hispanic white population is likely to reduce average household income in cities. In addition, cities with a significant influx of Hispanic residents must adapt services such as health care, public education, public safety, and recreation to the needs of a changing population.

Metropolitan regions

Population dispersion and the spread of development have focused attention on the metropolitan area as a geographic unit of analysis. First introduced in the 1950 U.S. Census, the metropolitan statistical area has been widely used by government agencies as the basis for data gathering and statistics. A metropolitan area is generally defined as a large urban center and its adjacent communities; these communities manifest a high degree of social and economic integration with each other and with the urban core.

Current U.S. Office of Management and Budget (OMB) standards provide for three levels of classification: metropolitan statistical areas (MSAs), primary metropolitan statistical areas (PMSAs), and consolidated metropolitan statistical areas (CMSAs). MSAs have either a city or a Bureau of the Census urbanized population of at least 50,000 and a total population of at least 100,000 (75,000 in New England). Each MSA has at least one central city and one central county and may include outlying counties with economic and social ties to the central core.

MSAs of more than one million inhabitants can be designated PMSAs. There are three criteria for PMSA designation: (1) there must be local support for separate recognition; (2) at least 65 percent of the area population must be urban; and (3) the percentage of residents commuting to jobs outside the county or counties must be less than 50 percent. PMSAs that have one million or more residents and are closely related socially and economically are designated as CMSAs—essentially, a supermetropolitan category. As of 1999, OMB had identified 258 MSAs, 18 CMSAs, and 73 PMSAs in the United States. In addition, there were 3 MSAs, 1 CMSA, and 3 PMSAs in Puerto Rico.[4]

In contrast to earlier times, when formal legal boundaries defined cities, it is now the outer contours of metropolitan areas that bear greater significance: the typical central city cannot be fully understood apart from the suburban environment to which it is organically linked.[5] Cities like Boston, Chicago, and Los Angeles lend their names to entire regions, to which they contribute only a portion of the population and jobs. Surrounding the urban core is a wide array of jurisdictions of varying sizes and complexity that, collectively, make up the suburban hinterland.

As shown in Table 1–4, metropolitan growth is still very high, especially in the Sun Belt: between 1990 and 2000, all of the ten fastest-growing metropolitan areas were located in the West or the South. Most notable is that the Las Vegas, Nevada–Arizona metropolitan area grew by 83 percent—from 852,737 in 1990 to 1,563,282 in 2000. Other large metro areas showing huge percentage gains are Austin–San Marcos, Texas, and Phoenix-Mesa, Arizona.

Among the largest metropolitan areas, Los Angeles had the biggest numerical gain in population: 1,842,116 people moved into the huge, five-county region. Not far behind were New York–New Jersey–Connecticut, with a gain of 1,650,216; Dallas–Fort Worth, with a gain of 1,184,519; and Atlanta, with a gain of 1,152,248. Overall, the ten metropolitan areas that were the largest as of 2000 were home to approximately 31 percent of the country's population.

As metropolitan areas have continued to expand, many have become linked into a vast urbanized complex called a megalopolis. French geographer Jean

Gottmann first identified this phenomenon in the 1950s, just as it was becoming evident along the northeastern seaboard of the United States:

We must abandon the idea of the city as a tightly settled and organized unit in which people, activities, and riches are crowded into a very small area clearly separated from its nonurban surroundings. Every city in this region spreads out far and wide around its original nucleus; it grows amidst an irregularly colloidal mixture of rural and suburban landscapes; it melts on broad fronts with other mixtures, of somewhat similar though different texture, belonging to the suburban neighborhoods of other cities.[6]

The region described by Gottmann—popularly referred to as Boswash—reaches from Maine to Northern Virginia and has approximately fifty million residents. It encompasses, in addition to Boston, major cities such as Baltimore, New York, Philadelphia, and Washington, D.C.; all the major cities in this megalopolis have come to serve as specialized economic subcenters. Other developing megalopolitan centers include the Florida peninsula, the lower Great Lakes, northern California, and southern California. These huge geographical clusters constitute an emerging form of urban development in America that will increase the scale and complexity of problems confronting local governments. Given the need to match local service jurisdictions with human settlement patterns, intergovernmental fiscal relations will become ever more critical.

Urban sprawl

As population and development continue to diffuse into the hinterland, huge chunks of open space (rural land) are being developed. In the 1990s, land consumption in the United States proceeded at twice the rate of population growth, and land is being consumed at a faster rate than ever before. As reported by the U.S. Department of Housing and Urban Development, land development between 1994 and 1997 averaged 2.3 million acres annually. Of the more than 9 million acres developed during those years, the overwhelming majority were outside metropolitan areas, in fringe suburbs or smaller towns and cities. The rate of land consumption in the 1990s was approximately twice that of the 1950s.[7]

The resulting type of development, commonly known as sprawl, is characterized by low density, wide gaps between development clusters, fragmented open space, and the absence of public spaces or community centers. Among the factors that encourage sprawl are heavy public investments in roads, water, and sewer lines; land use regulations that promote low-density, far-flung development; consumers' desire for rural lifestyles with large homes and large yards; the preference of business and industry for easy highway access and plenty of free parking; lower land prices (and often lower taxes) in peripheral areas; and advances in telecommunications.

Many people who are concerned about the quality of life have observed that sprawl has numerous negative effects—from traffic congestion, to air and water pollution, to the loss of productive farmland. But sprawl also creates significant economic costs, and one of the most serious is the unremitting increase in the demand for roads, utility lines, and service delivery to be extended to dispersed development. Such demands undermine local governments' ability to finance public services. Another economic effect is premature disinvestment in the buildings, facilities, and services of older urban centers.[8]

According to a *New York Times* analysis of census data, although sprawl continues unabated across the nation, its rate of growth varies along regional lines. From the percentage-of-change data shown at the bottom of Figure 1–7, it can be seen that suburban expansion slowed during the 1990s in every region of the

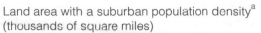

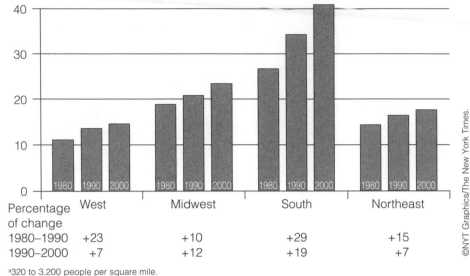

ª320 to 3,200 people per square mile.

Figure 1–7   Suburban growth by region, 1980–2000.

country except the Midwest.[9] What underlies this new trend is that as residents and businesses continue to move outward from central cities, they are beginning to encounter a variety of new constraints, including physical and topological barriers, ever-greater commuting distances, and the air and water pollution that accompany increased development.

In the West, suburban growth slowed considerably, from about 23 percent in the 1980s to about 7 percent in the 1990s: land and resources are simply not as available as they were in the past, which has led to increased infill development in existing cities and suburbs. Growth also slowed in the South, though not as extensively—from 29 to 19 percent. Because this region offers fewer natural barriers to growth, development can occur almost anywhere along transportation corridors; the result is unbroken chains of medium-density development that are hundreds of miles long. These population clusters are not located near great ports or waterways as in previous eras; instead, they are suburbs of interstate highways.[10] In comparison, the Midwest shows a minimal increase in suburban growth (from 10 to 12 percent), while the Northeast shows a decline (from 15 to 7 percent).

As long as the U.S. population continues to increase, the expansion of development into rural areas can be expected to continue. In light of the growing public awareness of the costs of sprawl, conservationists and slow-growth advocates are beginning to campaign for a smart-growth agenda at all levels of government. For the most part, however, states have become the focus of a smart-growth policy framework, which includes land use reforms designed to manage growth at the metropolitan fringe, and the use of state resources to preserve tracts of land threatened by sprawl. In addition, states have begun to steer infrastructure investment to older, built-up areas.[11] For example, under Maryland's Smart Growth Act of 1996, state permitting or funding for infrastructure and other facilities for new development projects is tightly restricted to older established areas and excludes less developed outlying areas. Similarly, Oregon has defined an urban growth boundary around the Portland metropolitan area, beyond which growth is severely restricted.

The new urban economies

Tables 1–7 and 1–5 show the cities that experienced substantial growth in the 1990s and those that experienced severe decline. Growing cities are primarily relatively new cities in the South and West; declining cities are primarily older cities in the East and Midwest. In attempting to understand what underlies these variations in urban growth, it is important to consider the special role of computers and communications technology, both as they have evolved over the past several decades and in their current effects on regional and local economies.[12]

Until recently, cities developed as centers of commerce largely because of the need for physical proximity among firms, suppliers, and customers. Such "clustering," as it is known, allowed for the efficient production and distribution of goods and services. Today, new technologies can transmit information cheaply, instantaneously, and at high volumes almost anywhere, making it possible for related economic functions to be physically separate. In practical terms, this means that firms do not need to be located near their suppliers or customers—or even near other units within the firm. And whereas cities previously served a multiplicity of functions, many have come to perform more specialized roles.

In *Urban Fortunes: The Political Economy of Space,* John R. Logan and Harvey L. Molotch explain that because some urban areas are better able to attract investment than others, urban economies reflect different growth patterns. Thus, urban places can be viewed as examples of different types.[13]

Table 1–7   High fliers: Cities that grew by more than 25 percent between 1990 and 2000.

City	Population, 1990	Population, 2000	Percentage increase in population, 1990–2000
Las Vegas, Nev.	258,295	478,434	85.2
Plano, Tex.	128,713	222,030	72.5
Scottsdale, Ariz.	130,069	202,705	55.8
Boise City, Idaho	125,738	185,787	47.8
Glendale, Ariz.	148,134	218,812	47.7
Laredo, Tex.	122,899	176,576	43.7
Bakersfield, Calif.	174,820	247,057	41.3
Austin, Tex.	465,622	656,562	41.0
Salinas, Calif.	108,777	151,060	38.9
Mesa, Ariz.	288,091	396,375	37.6
Durham, N.C.	136,611	187,035	36.9
Charlotte, N.C.	395,934	540,828	36.6
Santa Clarita, Calif.	110,642	151,088	36.6
Reno, Nev.	133,850	180,480	34.8
Phoenix, Ariz.	983,403	1,321,045	34.3
Overland Park, Kans.	111,790	149,080	33.4
Raleigh, N.C.	207,951	276,093	32.8
Chesapeake, Va.	151,976	199,184	31.1
Santa Rosa, Calif.	113,313	147,595	30.3
Irvine, Calif.	110,330	143,072	29.7
Winston-Salem, N.C.	143,485	185,776	29.5
Chula Vista, Calif.	135,163	173,556	28.4
Colorado Springs, Colo.	281,140	360,890	28.4
Arlington, Tex.	261,721	332,969	27.2
Salem, Ore.	107,786	136,924	27.0
Rancho Cucamonga, Calif.	101,409	127,743	26.0
Hayward, Calif.	111,498	140,030	25.6

One relatively new type of urban place that has evolved is the self-sustaining *center of innovation,* where research and development are ongoing, and continuous inputs of knowledge are far more important to the production process than they were in previous eras; many such centers are linked directly to global markets. Cities such as Austin and Arlington, Texas; Raleigh and Durham, North Carolina; and Phoenix and Mesa, Arizona, which are listed in Table 1–7, have succeeded in strategically positioning themselves to take advantage of opportunities being generated by new technology.

Links to research institutes and universities, good transportation and communication networks, and an educated workforce are important assets. Key high-tech sectors include electronics and telecommunications, biotechnology, aerospace, nuclear technology, and medical technologies.

Tourism and leisure playgrounds constitute another growth industry that has come to play an important role in shaping the urban landscape.[14] Thanks to new technical achievements—robotics, online videos, computer animation, virtual reality—fantasy environments are now available not only in theme parks but also in resort areas, gaming complexes, museums, and shopping malls. Las Vegas, the fastest-growing city in the nation (see Table 1–7), grew by more than 85 percent between 1990 and 2000. Although casino gambling remains the city's economic backbone, growing competition from other gaming cities has forced Las Vegas to market itself to a wider clientele by focusing more on family-oriented, theme-park-style entertainment—including fake volcanoes, fire-breathing dragons, and sound and light spectaculars. Equally significant are the Disney theme parks that opened in Anaheim, California, in 1955 and in Orlando, Florida, in 1971. Most growth in the theme-park industry occurred between the 1960s and the 1980s. The Disney Development Company's international operations include Tokyo Disneyland, which opened in 1983, and Disneyland Paris, which opened in 1992. Other high-tech prototypes that have garnered attention are Universal Studios' CityWalk mall, in Hollywood and Orlando, and the restructuring of New York's Times Square.

Underlying these theme-park ventures are real estate deals and large development projects. Architecture critic Ada Louise Huxtable elaborates as follows:

The theme park as opportunity for land development is one of the most lucrative of all investments. Ostensibly (and practically) the surrounding land is bought and held by the park's owners for expansion, including its own hotels and resorts. But the big payoff comes with office complexes, malls, housing developments, and other commercial construction, owned, operated, sold or leased, leased back, retained or disposed of by any number of elaborate real estate mechanisms.[15]

Table 1–7 also shows significant growth in Scottsdale, Arizona, which grew by 56 percent in the 1990s. Scottsdale is a well-to-do community that functions in two complementary ways—as a tourist center and as a *retirement center.* The aging of the U.S. population and the trend toward early retirement have contributed to a proliferation of such communities, which also include St. Petersburg and Sarasota, Florida, and the numerous Sun City developments in the West and Southwest. Las Vegas is also a prominent retirement center. Similarly, Reno, Nevada, continues to grow as both a tourist and a retirement center.

Where U.S. metropolitan areas once consisted of a dominant central city surrounded by a constellation of suburbs, these urban regions are now developing multiple centers, as the original, older central cities lose some of their dominance and the newer, satellite cities—which author Joel Garreau refers to as *edge cities*—increase in importance.[16] Most edge cities were first established in the 1950s, as suburban bedroom communities for central cities. Propelled by advances in transportation and communication, many of these communities gradually became economic entities in their own right. To the extent that residents of edge cities can identify a common center, it is typically the shopping mall. After a century of evolution, malls now contain post offices, hotels, counseling centers, and even amusement parks—all within a safe, clean environment that is protected from the elements. Among the most impressive of these centers is Tyson's Corner, in Fairfax County, Virginia, which boasts a rich mix of retail, office, hotel, and industrial space. Table 1–7 lists three California cities that emerged as full-blown edge cities in the 1990s: Bakersfield, outside Los Angeles; Hayward, outside San Diego; and Irvine, outside San Francisco.

Another type of city, the *headquarters city,* serves as the headquarters for major organizations, both public and private. On the face of it, such cities would seem indistinguishable from central cities, where banks, corporate headquarters, and such related organizations as law firms, accounting firms, and advertising agencies are concentrated. What sets headquarters cities apart, however, is that they are places where most of the leading global markets for commodities and investment capital, equities, and bonds can be found. In addition, they are the locations of the national and international headquarters of trade and professional associations. Table 1–7 lists two cities that are experiencing rapid growth as the sites of corporate headquarters: Charlotte, North Carolina, which is the second-largest banking center in the United States, and Boise City, Idaho, which is the largest city in the state and a hub of banking and commerce.

Fiber-optic networks and satellite communications systems have enabled firms to handle enormous volumes of financial and business transactions around the globe, creating *global cities,* which have emerged as strategic sites in the world economy. Decisions made in global cities such as New York, London, or Tokyo affect jobs, wages, and the economic health of locations throughout the world.[17] In North America, New York is the quintessential global city, followed by such second-tier cities as Chicago and Los Angeles. Houston, Miami, San Francisco, Toronto, Vancouver, and Washington, D.C., are viewed as third-tier cities in the global system.

Although all cities have their ups and downs, depending on general economic trends, types such as innovation centers and headquarters cities have succeeded in adapting to the opportunities being afforded by the new economies. In contrast, most of the declining cities listed in Table 1–5 lack all or some of the key features that would allow them to participate more fully in the national and global economies. For the most part, these are *older industrial cities* such as Baltimore, Birmingham, Cincinnati, Cleveland, Detroit, and Flint. As factories in these places continue to close down and manufacturing jobs are lost, residents of these cities move on to other places.

Such cities tend to lack the distinctive features of headquarters cities or of innovation centers that would allow them to control their own destinies: specifically, they depend on control centers that are located elsewhere, and they are expendable in the system of places: that is, any number of other places can carry out the functions they perform. As a consequence, older manufacturing cities of the Northeast and Midwest have been especially vulnerable to mergers and downsizing decisions made by distant companies with global interests.

What does the future hold? Most likely, the continued growth and proliferation of new types of cities. Those who are responsible for governing and managing these cities will confront a number of new questions. One very important question is how cities can adapt to change, given their different advantages and disadvantages. Where cities lack certain key features—such as an educated workforce, good research institutions, good transportation and communications, and a good quality of life—they are not likely to be able to participate effectively in the new global economy.[18]

With regard to small towns and rural counties, two forms of development are likely, in addition to their traditional role of serving agricultural interests. To the extent that they can maintain an ambience that typifies "small-town America," such places will be increasingly attractive to retirees and vacationers. In addition, as places where the cost of living is relatively low, they are likely to attract back-office operations (such as call centers and reservation centers) that have been spun off from central headquarters as an economizing strategy.

Ultimately, how well cities and counties are able to meet the challenges of the new century will depend largely on the quality and organization of their leadership, and the finance manager and his or her staff are key players in that leadership.

The legal and institutional context

It is the finance manager's role to respond to changing community needs within the context of complex legal, organizational, and institutional arrangements. In this section of the chapter, three vital aspects of the decision-making context—home rule, the intergovernmental system, and local government structure—are examined in detail.

The principle of home rule

According to the U.S. Constitution, the federal government and the states share sovereign power. Because this basic document contains no provisions defining their status, local governments possess no sovereignty and come into existence only at the will of the states. Thus, they have only those powers granted by the states. Local governments with home rule are subject to statutory and constitutional provisions that allow them to exercise powers of local self-government.

Municipal governments are legally established through a process of incorporation. Just as a business becomes incorporated so that its organizers may carry on certain legal and financial transactions on a basis other than that of individual responsibility, so a city, town, borough, or village is given legal status as a corporate body through a state-granted charter of incorporation. (Counties are, in contrast, administrative subdivisions of the state and are established to carry out state programs.) However, charters granted to private business corporations differ in many important respects from those granted to local governmental units.

Private and municipal charters　A private charter is essentially a contract between two parties: a business corporation and a state. It can be created, altered, or terminated only with the consent of both parties. In the case of a municipal charter, however, a state has full authority over the local government concerned unless the state has imposed limitations on itself through a constitutional amendment. Many state governments are therefore empowered to alter the major features of a municipal corporation whenever they wish to do so. For example, the state government can change the municipal corporation's powers, officers, jurisdiction, and requirements for carrying out such vital activities as borrowing money.

The second major difference between private and municipal charters is that a private business can do just about anything as long as it is not illegal and does not violate the rights of others. A municipality, on the other hand, can carry on only those activities expressly authorized by state law. If no state law expressly allows the holding of a lottery, for example, a community cannot authorize a lottery.

Dillon's Rule   Whenever there has been doubt about what a municipality can or cannot do, the courts have usually given local powers a very strict interpretation. In the late nineteenth century, Judge John F. Dillon gave a succinct summary of the approach taken by the courts. His characterization is known as Dillon's Rule:

It is a general and undisputed proposition of law that a municipal corporation possesses and can exercise the following powers and no others: First, those granted in express words; second, those necessarily or fairly implied in or incident to the powers expressly granted; third, those essential to the accomplishment of the declared objects and purposes of the corporation—not simply convenient, but indispensable. Any fair, reasonable, substantive doubt concerning the existence of power is resolved by the courts against the corporation, and the power is denied.[19]

Even though most states have adopted home rule guarantees enabling municipalities to exercise all powers of local self-government, the entity thus formed is still subject to the constitution and general laws of the state. Although home rule has permitted municipalities greater discretion in routine matters of an essentially local character, such as recreation and zoning, the scope of municipal activity has not been enlarged significantly. For the most part, state legislatures and administrative bodies across the nation have continued to exercise the broad supervisory authority expressed in Dillon's Rule. The limited development of municipal power is in marked contrast to the broad interpretation of the Constitution made by the U.S. Supreme Court, through which federal authority has expanded at the expense of that of the states.

Unfunded state mandates   Relying on their superior legal status, state governments have consistently used their legislative and regulatory powers to require local government to assume responsibility for new services. Although some of these mandates may be supported by local officials—particularly as a "cover" to implement unpopular programs—they often interfere with local priorities and with local management flexibility. Even more important, unfunded mandates impose costs that have to be paid from local revenues, and complying with a state mandate can mean that local officials risk incurring the anger of local taxpayers.[20]

Although most states require cost estimates of mandates imposed on localities, the estimates are often either inaccurate or ignored by state legislators. More effective than cost estimation is state reimbursement to cover the costs of mandates, which is required by about one-third of the states. Some states, however, manage to avoid the intent of this requirement by earmarking as reimbursement part of the funding already allocated as state aid to local government. In recent years, the overall number of new state mandates has decreased—a change that can be attributed to anti-mandate laws, which, in turn, were spurred by the negative publicity that mandates have received.[21]

State oversight of municipal finance   The role of the states in overseeing municipal finance provides yet another perspective on the limits placed on localities. Generally, the states limit municipal financial powers by determining how localities may tax, how much they may tax, how much indebtedness they may incur, and how they should manage their finances. Two explanations have been advanced for this high level of state control. According to the first theory, state officials share a pervasive skepticism about the ability of municipalities to manage their resources successfully. A second theory holds that states may not want municipalities to rely heavily on those tax sources that the states themselves wish to reserve for their own revenues.

State supervision of municipal government finance includes the following:

Defining standards for the performance of municipal government functions such as budgeting, accounting, and auditing

Limiting localities with respect to the amounts, types, and rates of debt, taxes, and expenditures

Coordinating the activities of municipal units to avoid unnecessary duplication and to ensure cooperation in carrying out various functions (e.g., requiring municipal officials to collect state taxes)

Taking over the fiscal management function during periods of municipal emergency

Ensuring that municipal governments comply with contracts entered into with state agencies.

The growing local tax burden has provoked periodic taxpayer rebellions and given rise to demands for state limitations on the taxing and spending powers of municipal governments. Faced with citizen demands for property tax relief, some states have imposed tax freezes and capped increases in assessment rates. Others have expanded homestead exemptions, and still others have shifted much of the burden of financing education from the property tax to other taxes, such as the sales tax. Since the early 1980s, there has been a big push to obtain tax relief by legalizing gambling. Many states permit sports gambling and betting on horse races or dog races. Close to half the states allow casino gambling in at least some of their cities, and gambling in some form is now found in every state but Hawaii and Utah.

The intergovernmental system

As noted earlier, the local government finance function occurs within a complex intergovernmental system. The relationships of the three levels of government—federal, state, and local—have changed significantly as the federal government has come to play an increasingly important role in state and local affairs. This change has been implemented largely through federal actions regarding grants and mandates.

Federal aid Federal grants-in-aid to state and local governments escalated rapidly in the early 1970s, peaked at 17 percent of total federal outlays in 1973 and 1978, and went into sharp decline in the 1980s. Under President Ronald Reagan's New Federalism, the national government shifted much of the domestic financial burden to state and local governments, reducing or eliminating federal grants for housing, education, mass transportation, and public works. The $4.6 billion general revenue-sharing program was terminated in 1986. As Figure 1–8 shows, federal grants began to rise in 1990, largely because of direct payments—known as entitlement grants—to individuals. By 1996, such grants made up 63 percent of all federal grants, nearly double their share in 1978. Most of such funding in the 1990s was directed to health-related entitlement programs such as Medicaid and Medicare. Aid to Families with Dependent Children (AFDC), another entitlement program, was converted in 1996 to a block grant known as Temporary Assistance to Needy Families (TANF), which turned greater fiscal and programmatic responsibility over to the states. In the near term, the change is designed to increase aid to the states and their localities; over the longer term, however, states and localities will bear nearly full responsibility for increases in welfare costs.

Figure 1–8   Federal grants-in-aid as a percentage of federal outlays, 1970–96.

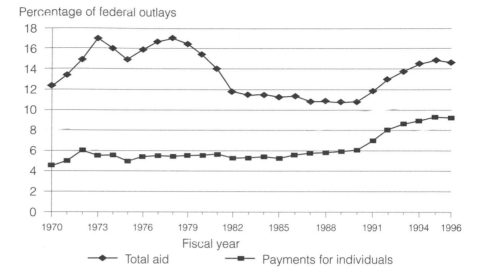

Whereas federal aid constituted about 27 percent of state-local spending in 1978, the level had fallen to 17 percent by 1989.[22] Federal dollars for such high-priority programs as wastewater treatment, low-income housing, public transit, and job training took big hits in the 1980s and 1990s. Although federal spending has since increased and, during the 1990s, made up about 22 percent of state-local spending, much of the increase has gone to state rather than local government. As of the late 1990s, close to 89 percent of federal aid went directly to the states.[23]

Unfunded federal mandates   At the same time that Washington has been cutting aid to local government, the pressures on local governments for services—from better schools, to more roads, to assistance for the homeless—have continued to rise. Pressure to spend also comes from the federal government itself: federal rules, regulations, and mandates often impose new responsibilities. Costly mandates have been imposed in areas such as air and water quality, solid waste, hazardous waste, transportation standards, labor management, and health care. "Specific congressional legislation that has created unfunded mandates includes the Americans with Disabilities Act, the Safe Drinking Water Act, and the National Voter Registration Act. By shifting much of the financial burden onto state and local governments, mandating has allowed federal officials to claim credit for taking action on issues while simultaneously reducing pressure on the federal budget."[24]

With the decline in federal aid in the 1990s, local governments increasingly turned to the states for assistance. State aid to local governments consists primarily of grants and shared taxes. Grants are typically targeted for specific programs in areas such as education or transportation. Most states, however, also provide unrestricted grants for general purposes. With regard to shared taxes, states serve as tax collectors and return all or a portion of the yield according to an allocation formula or on the basis of how the revenue originated. Sales, income, and gasoline taxes are state taxes that are usually shared. As with grants, states usually earmark much of the shared revenue for specific purposes: for example, localities may be required to spend their share of the state gas tax on highway or street improvement. Although state aid to localities varies from state to state and fluctuates over time, it is usually a major source of local revenue, contributing about 30 percent of all municipal and county revenue. Most state aid—about 60 percent—goes to independent school districts.[25]

State aid   Thanks to a vibrant national economy, the 1990s were, for the most part, a decade of revenue growth in the states; however, the new century has ushered in an economic downturn. As more and more states have difficulty balancing their budgets, state aid to local governments has declined, accentuating local fiscal stress.[26] Moreover, various studies report that local officials are generally critical of the loss of local autonomy, the lack of sufficient discretion to generate revenues, and the lack of state financial aid and technical assistance; and they are especially critical of the difficulties posed by unfunded mandates.[27]

Local government structure

The way that government is organized may be viewed as a product of evolving social values. Political scientist Herbert Kaufman has identified three core values that have had the greatest influence on the evolution of local government in the United States: (1) representativeness; (2) technical, nonpartisan competence; and (3) executive leadership.[28] Kaufman shows that at different periods in American history, each of these values has had a significant effect on the arrangement and organization of government. Moreover, all three continue to affect contemporary government practice.

What Kaufman characterizes as "the pursuit of representativeness" grew out of the Revolutionary period of American history. Rising antagonism between the colonies and the English monarch (represented by the colonial governors) generated deep-seated distrust of executive power. After 1776, executive rule—an unhappy reminder of the king's authority—was held in contempt. Citizens of the fledgling democracy deferred to their legislatures instead, believing them to be more representative of the public interest.[29] On the local level, elected councils assumed leadership responsibilities, and mayors were often reduced to little more than ceremonial figures.

With the inauguration of President Andrew Jackson in 1829, the value assigned to representativeness in national life intensified; what came to be known as Jacksonian democracy epitomized the anti-aristocratic feelings of the common citizen. During the Jacksonian era it was widely held that "any man was as good as another man"; the idea that a candidate for office should possess special qualifications for that office was frowned upon. And as the franchise was extended and elections became the primary mechanism for elevating candidates to office, the number of elected officials began to increase.

After the Civil War, the emphasis on representativeness began to erode as the country grew in size and complexity. The Industrial Revolution generated complex problems of governmental management—problems that were often beyond the capabilities of part-time, amateur council members. In the late nineteenth century, the demonstrable corruption of many urban elected officials and the role of the local party "boss" in dispensing patronage also undermined support for representativeness.

As the value of representativeness lost some of its luster, technical, nonpartisan competence began to take on greater value. By the beginning of the twentieth century, reformers had devised new governing procedures intended to serve as antidotes to the perceived excesses of the existing system. Civil service was introduced in some of the larger cities in an attempt to ensure the expertise of government workers, and multimember boards and commissions were created for the purpose of "taking politics out of government." Reformers believed that if a number of nonpartisan commissioners held long, overlapping terms of office, both special interests and party organizations would be denied effective influence. What they did not expect, however, was that the proliferation of both elective offices (dating from the Jacksonian era) and new boards and commissions would produce immense difficulties of coordination. The opportunity for special-interest groups and parties to sway decision making was not impeded but enhanced, and the public became increasingly confused by the complexity of governmental arrangements.

Consequently, during the 1920s and 1930s, reformers began to urge acceptance of a new set of doctrines to achieve integration and coordination in local government. Under the leadership of a strong executive, the number of independent administrative offices and agencies could be reduced. The reformers now believed that establishing clear lines of command under a mayor would reduce waste and improve accountability. Under these conditions, they argued, the mayor could be held accountable to the electorate for the administration of the government. This shift in attitudes gave mayors new powers to appoint and remove staff. In many jurisdictions, mayors were given authority to formulate and execute municipal budgets. (Budgets initiated and developed by a mayor or chief administrative officer are known as executive budgets.) In short, the value of executive leadership took on greater significance in response to the proliferation of administrative offices and agencies.

Municipal government

The relative weight accorded each of the core values of government—representativeness; technical, nonpartisan competence; and executive leadership—has played a major role in shaping governmental structures during different periods in American history. These values have also shaped the three formal models of local government that currently exist: mayor-council government, commission government, and council-manager government.

Mayor-council government   The two principal types of mayor-council government are the weak-mayor type and the strong-mayor type; many localities have variations that fall between these two forms. The weak-mayor form, with its roots in early U.S. history, reflects the value of representativeness. In this system, the mayor's power in administrative matters is limited in relation to that of the council—for example, the mayor has limited authority to appoint or remove staff or prepare the budget—and he or she may well be chief executive in name only. The weak-mayor form persists in many mayor-council localities, particularly in smaller communities where the value of representativeness continues to exert a strong influence.

Under the strong-mayor system, the council has less relative importance, and administrative powers are centralized in the hands of the executive. Historically, the strong-mayor form can be traced to the first model-city charter drafted by the National Municipal League in 1897. In addition to strengthening the role of the mayor, the charter recommended that ballots be shortened and that legislative powers be centralized in a unicameral city council to reduce institutional complexity and make government more accountable to the citizenry. Through the influence of the National Municipal League, the strong-mayor form of government began to take hold in the first decades of the twentieth century.

Responding to the growing administrative complexity of urban government, large cities such as Chicago, New Orleans, New York, and Philadelphia have assisted their mayors by providing them with chief administrative officers (CAOs). Subject to the will of the mayor, the CAO is expected to look after the details of interagency communication, budget preparation, personnel administration, and other management areas, thereby freeing the mayor to concentrate on policy matters.

The strong mayor, then, is an elected chief executive who prepares the budget, appoints and removes department heads and other principal officers, and is responsible for both the political and administrative functioning of the local government. Proponents of the strong-mayor form point to its political and administrative advantages. The strong mayor has a constituency that looks to him or her for leadership. At the same time, the mayor is held accountable to the constituency. Perhaps more important, proponents contend that the strong mayor is in a better position to manage conflict, particularly in very large cities characterized by diversity in their social and economic makeup and by intense competition between different groups.

By 2003, the council-manager form of government was the most prevalent form of municipal government structure, in force in 3,453 of those municipalities with a population of 2,500 or more (see Table 1–2). However, the mayor-council form was more popular in very large cities: of 31 cities with populations of 500,000 or more, 21 had the mayor-council form. In cities with populations of more than one million, 5 out of 9 had mayor-council governments.

Commission and town-meeting governments   The commission form of government stems from the values of representativeness and nonpartisanship. It originated in Texas, following the catastrophic hurricane of 1900, when the governor appointed five businessmen to administer the city of Galveston. This system of government allows a small number of commissioners—between five and seven—to be elected on a nonpartisan ticket referred to as "the short ballot." As a group, the commissioners are responsible for policy formation and legislation. Each commissioner also serves as the head of an administrative department; thus, in contrast with the mayor-council form, commission government places both administrative and legislative authority in the hands of the same officers.

Proponents of the commission plan view the short ballot as enhancing accountability because, in their view, it is easier for the electorate to exercise choice among a limited number of candidates for office. Critics, on the other hand, point to the dangers inherent in a government run by amateurs and subject to administrative fragmentation. However, the commission form has long since passed the peak of popularity that it enjoyed in the early decades of the twentieth century, and such discussion has become increasingly academic. By 2003, the commission form was in operation in only 145 municipalities—and was, in fact, less popular than the town-meeting form of government, which operated in 338 municipalities (see Table 1–2).

The town meeting, which is largely associated with the New England region, is a form of government derived from the value of representativeness. The roots of this form reach back into the colonial period, when it served to reinforce the democratic strivings that led to the Revolution. The town meeting today is of minor significance in the overall national picture of local government.

Council-manager government   The council-manager form of government shows the influence of all three values that have been discussed: representativeness, effected through an elected council as the policy-making body; nonpartisan, technical competence, implemented in most local governments through nonpartisan elections and through a professional manager who directs administration; and executive leadership, effected by a limited number of independent departments integrated into a chain-of-command structure headed by the manager.

In the council-manager plan, the council performs the legislative function. It appoints a manager, who, in turn, selects department heads and directs their activities. Where there is a mayor, his or her role is primarily ceremonial. In about one-half of the communities that have this form of government, the mayor is selected by the council from among its own membership; the remaining communities elect their mayor by popular vote.

Drawing on the experience of Staunton, Virginia—where, in 1908, pragmatic experimentation led to the creation of the post of general manager—Richard Childs, founder of the council-manager plan, formulated a system intended to separate policy making from administration. Childs drew on the experience of the commission form of government—notably its integrated structure and its nonpartisan, short ballot—and added the idea of a professional general manager, a concept derived from the business sector. In essence, the council would propose and the manager would dispose. In practice, as the council-manager form grew in popularity over the ensuing decades, this distinction was not always so clear-cut. The manager's powers—appointing and removing administrators, preparing and executing the budget, making recommendations to the council—imply that the professional manager does exercise some degree of influence on policy. Political scientists seem to agree that the most successful managers have always been formulators of policy, although this role must be exercised with great skill and delicacy.[30] The professional manager, after all, must always be aware that he or she serves at the pleasure of the council.

Supporters of the council-manager plan note that it allows for administrative and supervisory responsibility to be centralized in a single individual and that it emphasizes technical expertise. Critics contend that the plan may fail to generate effective political leadership, especially in larger, highly diverse cities with many competing interest groups. Professional managers, they argue, do not have the necessary political resources to mediate among contending political forces such as powerful unions, business interests, and racial or ethnic groups.

In recent years, the council-manager form of government has achieved widespread popularity. As noted earlier, by 2003 it was the form of government in 3,453 municipalities with populations of 2,500 or more. Although this form existed in only 9 of the 31 cities of 500,000 and over (the remainder being governed mostly by mayor-council systems), it was clearly the most popular form in cities of 25,000 and over. In this population range, 894 communities had adopted the council-manager plan, compared with 481 local governments with the mayor-council form and 26 communities with the commission form (see Table 1–2). Finally, it is important to note that even in local governments that are not officially organized according to the formal council-manager model, a position akin to that of the local government manager often exists.

County government

When the national government was formed, the framers of the Constitution did not provide for local governments. Instead, they left the matter to the states. County governments were brought into existence by early state constitutions, which created counties as administrative arms of the state that were responsible for certain basic services such as tax collection, law enforcement, judicial functions, record keeping, and the administration of elections. During the twentieth century, as the nation became more densely settled, the growing complexity of providing services created pressures that led to a restructuring of county government. Changes called for by reformers included increasing the autonomy of counties in relation to the states, allowing counties to raise revenue, and increasing the political accountability of county government. Counties began providing an ever-widening range of services—a trend that, along with greater autonomy, the increasing right to raise revenues, and enlarged accountability—continues apace today.

Forty-eight of the fifty states have operational county governments. Alaska and Louisiana call their county-type governments boroughs and parishes, respectively. Connecticut and Rhode Island are divided into geographic regions called counties, but these entities do not have functioning governments as defined by the U.S. Census Bureau.

Counties vary greatly in size and population—from 26 to 8,710 square miles (Arlington County, Virginia, and North Slope, Alaska, respectively) and from 140 to 9,213,513 in population (Loving County, Texas, and Los Angeles County, California, respectively). In 2003, counties with populations below 50,000 accounted for nearly three-fourths of all county governments (see Table 1–3).

County government takes three basic forms. Under all three, many administrative responsibilities are vested (either by state constitution or statute) in independently elected row officers such as clerk, coroner, sheriff, and treasurer.

Commission form   The distinguishing characteristic of the commission form of county government is that legislative authority (e.g., the power to enact ordinances and adopt budgets) and executive authority (e.g., the authority to administer policies and appoint county employees) are exercised jointly by an elected commission or board of supervisors. Table 1–3 shows that this is the predominant form of county government, found for the most part in relatively rural areas of less than 50,000 in population. The table also shows that the forms that provide for a strong executive who is separate from the commission or council predominate in larger counties (those with populations of 250,000 or more).

Council-administrator form   Under the council-administrator, or council-manager form, an elected county council appoints an administrator who serves at its pleasure. The administrator may be vested with a broad range of powers, including the authority to hire and fire department heads and to formulate a budget. Table 1–3 shows that this form predominates in the more populated counties, where the demand for services tends to be greater and where there is a special need for a professional manager.

County executive form   The separation of powers concept underlies the county executive system of governance. A county executive is the chief administrative officer of the jurisdiction and an elected official able to assert some degree of independence from the council. Typically, the executive has the authority to veto ordinances enacted by the county council (subject to possible override) and to hire and fire department heads. This form predominates in the larger counties, where the challenge of managing in a complex and relatively diverse political environment calls for strong executive leadership.

Organizing for financial administration

The remainder of this chapter discusses organizational models for financial administration and the essential characteristics of financial decision making in local government.

Financial administration and financial decision making are highly interrelated and may be difficult to distinguish in practice. Financial decision making generally occurs through the budget adoption process and encompasses policy decisions: specifically, what kinds and levels of revenues to collect and what kinds and levels of services to provide. Financial decisions include, for example, whether to cut back or to expand police, public works, or emergency services. Financial administration is the means of implementing these decisions—putting a tax or fee system in place, monitoring each department's expenditures, analyzing the cost-effectiveness of services. The tools of financial administration include forecasting, cost analysis, risk management, pension analysis, and auditing. These analytical tools should provide information about the resources and obligations of the government that set constraints on policy and decision making. For example, a disappointing revenue forecast may affect any number of allocation decisions.

The historical perspective

The drive to improve financial administration in the United States has been inextricably linked to the shifts in government organization and structure that have already been described. Thus, for example, when prevailing sentiment decreed that local government should be decentralized through the creation of multiple independent offices, administration of the financial functions underwent related structural changes. Similarly, when the strong-mayor and council-manager forms of government became popular, the hitherto fragmented functions of financial administration became more centralized.

The civic reform movement associated with the founding of the National Municipal League in 1894 was of significant influence in the ensuing years. Espousing the value of executive leadership, the league's model municipal code included a budget system that was to be directed by the mayor rather than by the city council. This concept was further developed by the New York Bureau of Municipal Research, established in 1906. The bureau viewed municipal budgeting as a major tool for achieving responsibility in government: budgeting would realize economies, eliminate dishonest practices, and set fixed and objective standards of accountability. Furthermore, with the chief administrator responsible for recommending revenue and expenditure levels, coordination of goals, programs, and services would be achieved. Encouraged by the strong support of business leaders who called for demonstrable economy and efficiency in government, many communities eventually adopted these budget proposals.

In subsequent decades, local and state governments began to upgrade and interrelate other important components of financial administration, such as accounting, auditing, purchasing, tax administration, and treasury management. Gradually, the idea emerged of a centralized finance department that would serve the chief administrator as a vital instrument of local government. By the mid-1920s, financial practices in American cities had undergone a fairly thorough reform and had come to include some version of a budget system.[31]

Currently it appears that where the value of representativeness prevails, certain fiscal offices—notably that of the treasurer and controller—are still independently elected. Where the value of nonpartisan, technical competence is strong, it is possible to find a variety of autonomous fiscal agencies, ranging from boards of tax appeal to boards of assessors. However, the idea of a fully integrated financial system under the chief administrator continues to win favor, even if its implementation varies.

The integrated system

A model city charter suggested by the National Civic League describes a fully integrated financial system.[32] In this model, the local government manager, appointed by the council, assumes overall responsibility for financial affairs. (In mayor-council government, the mayor—often with his or her principal administrative assistant—would perform an equivalent role.) As shown in Figure 1–9, a general organization chart for a finance department, the department is divided into five areas of control—accounts, budget, assessments, purchasing, and treasury. (In small local governments, the finance director, who is sometimes the manager, may be responsible for several of these functions.) The director of the finance department, often called the finance director or finance officer, is appointed by the local government manager and serves at the manager's pleasure; division heads, in turn, are appointed by the finance director.

Figure 1–9 also includes an independent outside audit, which should be distinguished from the pre-audit performed by the accounts division. The pre-audit is conducted before the payment of all claims and includes a daily check of all revenues and receipts. The independent audit, or post-audit (taking place after payment), ascertains whether any errors have been made or whether any illegal expenditures have occurred and serves as a check on executive officials. The objectivity of the independent audit would, of course, be in question if it were administered by staff from the same branch that had authorized the expenditures. Generally, therefore, an outside auditor is employed. In a small number of local governments, the audit function is carried out by an independently elected auditor or controller.

Figure 1–9
General organization
chart, department of
finance.

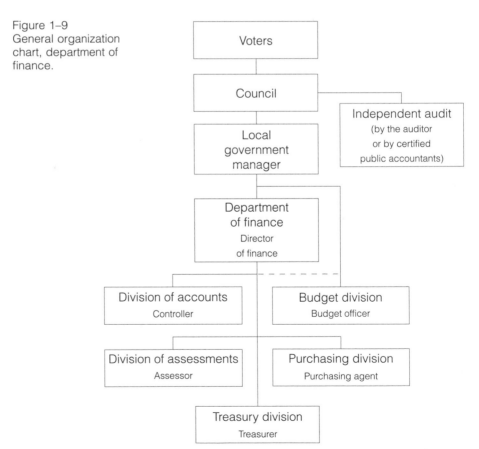

Note: The dotted line between the director of finance and the budget officer indicates that the latter is often primarily responsible to the chief administrator—and physically located in the finance department—to prevent the duplication of records. In many local governments, the finance director handles the budget.

Within this overall framework it is possible to delineate specific components of financial management. Figure 1–10 illustrates a possible division of responsibility for those components, which includes the positions of director of finance, controller, assessor, treasurer, purchasing agent, and budget officer.

Organization for financial administration tends to vary from community to community. Usually, the larger the community, the more specialized the organizational components that function within an integrated framework. Smaller communities are likely to be less specialized and to rely more on independent boards and elected officials. These organizational configurations are important not only because they influence how financial functions are carried out, but also because they help determine the nature of financial decision making.[33]

Director of finance As a department head, the finance director supervises and coordinates the administration of major financial services. As a managerial aide to the chief administrator (the manager or mayor), the director advises

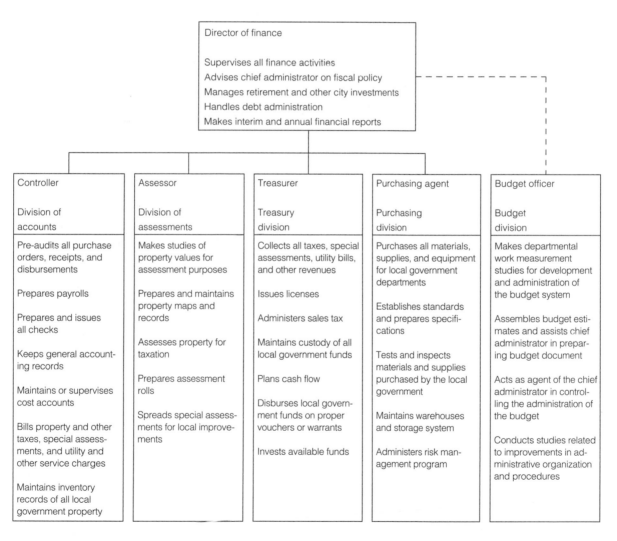

Director of finance

Supervises all finance activities
Advises chief administrator on fiscal policy
Manages retirement and other city investments
Handles debt administration
Makes interim and annual financial reports

Controller	Assessor	Treasurer	Purchasing agent	Budget officer
Division of accounts	Division of assessments	Treasury division	Purchasing division	Budget division
Pre-audits all purchase orders, receipts, and disbursements	Makes studies of property values for assessment purposes	Collects all taxes, special assessments, utility bills, and other revenues	Purchases all materials, supplies, and equipment for local government departments	Makes departmental work measurement studies for development and administration of the budget system
Prepares payrolls	Prepares and maintains property maps and records	Issues licenses	Establishes standards and prepares specifications	Assembles budget estimates and assists chief administrator in preparing budget document
Prepares and issues all checks		Administers sales tax		
Keeps general accounting records	Assesses property for taxation	Maintains custody of all local government funds	Tests and inspects materials and supplies purchased by the local government	Acts as agent of the chief administrator in controlling the administration of the budget
Maintains or supervises cost accounts	Prepares assessment rolls	Plans cash flow		
Bills property and other taxes, special assessments, and utility and other service charges	Spreads special assessments for local improvements	Disburses local government funds on proper vouchers or warrants	Maintains warehouses and storage system	Conducts studies related to improvements in administrative organization and procedures
Maintains inventory records of all local government property		Invests available funds	Administers risk management program	

Note: The dotted line between the director of finance and the budget officer indicates that the latter is often primarily responsible to the chief administrator—and physically located in the finance department—to prevent the duplication of records. In many local governments, the finance director handles the budget.

Figure 1–10 Detailed organization chart, department of finance, showing typical functions and activities.

on fiscal policy and other related concerns, such as debt and investment management. In some local governments the finance officer may also be the chief budget officer.

Accounts   After the council has adopted a budget for the forthcoming fiscal year, the division of accounts administers the budget through the pre-audit function. This division assures each department of permission to spend, within authorized guidelines. The division also keeps accounts, maintains inventory records of local government property, and furnishes financial information needed for the preparation of the next budget.

Assessments   In theory, assessment does not involve decision making; it is the mechanical application of state and local laws to the evaluation of property for tax purposes. In the uncompromising reality of contemporary local government, however, assessors often function as important decision makers who have some discretion in computing property values. Because assessments can thus be a matter of judgment, the local government usually establishes a board of appeals or a board of equalization to perform this function (unless the state provides a means of handling assessment appeals).

Treasury   The treasury division collects the taxes and pays out the monies that, taken together, are the lifeblood of local government. Payments cannot be made, however, until after the pre-audit and after certification by the controller. In many local governments the treasury is also empowered to issue licenses, administer sales taxes, and invest idle funds.

Purchasing   Most of the supplies, materials, and equipment for a local government are procured (and then stored) through the purchasing division. This division can thus achieve savings that are likely to accrue from large-scale, centralized purchasing, particularly if the government is large. The division can also administer quality-control procedures, specifying standards against which purchases are tested and inspected. In addition, the purchasing division is usually responsible for risk management. (For detailed discussions of purchasing and risk management in local government, see Chapters 15 and 17.)

Budgeting   The budget division occupies a position of paramount importance in the overall functioning of a municipality or county. Where an executive budget is in use, the head of the budget division usually becomes one of the principal aides to the chief administrator. Where the budget officer is not the director of finance, he or she is usually placed in the office of the chief administrator to ensure a direct line of communication. Because of the wealth of knowledge that is acquired in the course of preparing the budget, the budget officer may well know more about governing operations than any other local official, including the manager or mayor. The budget officer's expertise typically extends beyond purely fiscal concerns, and he or she often contributes to studies and proposals involving administrative organization and management planning. Once the budget has been approved by the council, the budget officer and budget staff assist the chief administrator in administering the budget. The budgeted amounts are turned over to the accounting division, which pre-audits expenditures.

Financial decision making

At the heart of the local government fiscal system is the decision-making process. It energizes and directs the system, and all administrators are expected to abide by its mandates. The finance officer must be viewed as both administrator and decision maker—roles that, for a number of reasons, are often inextricably related. First, information that the finance officer conveys to policy makers is largely contingent on his or her values or perspective. Second, the finance officer has knowledge of the financial resources available to policy makers. Third, it is not unusual for policy makers to take advantage of the finance office's expertise by requesting specific policy proposals. Fourth, and perhaps most important, policy makers are not able to take account of all contingencies in the formulation of policy; the more technical the subject, the more inclined they are to allow discretion to administrators during the implementation phase.

To perform effectively as a decision maker, the finance officer must understand the political and administrative system of which he or she is a part. The roles and responsibilities of the job are shaped by underlying social and economic conditions in the community as well as by formal rules established by government. The finance officer must also deal with representatives of other public agencies (federal, state, and local) and with interest groups, each of which has a special stake in the development and implementation of fiscal policies. In the effective performance of the finance function, responsiveness to the political context is just as critical as efficiency. Reconciling these two concerns can be very difficult in all areas of administration but is especially difficult in the financial area.[34]

Figure 1–11 shows the factors involved in financial decision making and their interrelationships. Social and economic conditions (box 1) refer to community needs and resources. Particularly important here is whether the community's resources are increasing or decreasing and whether changing needs are being met. For example, when the number of elderly dependents increases at the same time that average personal income declines, the community is faced with a growing demand for services for elderly people and a reduced capacity to raise revenues. Where there is severe economic decline, local government is not likely to be able to fund its programs at previous levels.

The formal authority structure (box 2) refers to the power legally granted to local officials through the home rule provisions of the local government charter and through state statutes that structure state-local relations. Particularly important here is the amount of authority conferred on local government to manage matters such as debt, taxes, and expenditures. The charter also

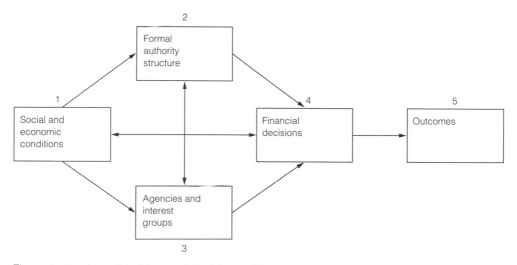

Figure 1–11 A model of financial decision making.

specifies the powers of the council, manager, mayor, and other officials relative to financial decision making: the executive initiation of the budget, the power to appoint or remove finance officers, and the power of review over the budget. The formal authority structure specified in the charter determines to what extent the implementation of financial functions is either integrated or dispersed within the financial management system. Another facet of the formal structure concerns how state and local laws define the division of labor among the different divisions that administer fiscal policies.

The third component of the model (box 3) includes other local government agencies as well as a range of interest groups—business organizations, labor unions, civic associations, and racial and ethnic groups. Some groups prefer to work alone in developing political strategies, but most are inclined to form coalitions as a way of strengthening their position. Local government agencies, which generally see themselves as being in competition with other agencies in the pursuit of their share of the funding pie, are usually very much a part of interest-group politics. In the course of requesting or defending budgetary allocations, it is not unusual for local government agencies to seek ties with client groups for support. Usually, as issues change, so will coalitions.

Ultimately, all these factors affect financial decisions (box 4) and outcomes (box 5). How decision makers respond to changing conditions and evolving needs is largely a reflection of who the decision makers are (e.g., whether they are appointed or elected officials), how they perceive their role, and the political and organizational environment in which they function.

Where political pressure from interest groups and governmental agencies is substantial and where decision makers have little or no professional orientation, decisions are likely to be based more on the need for political accommodation than on the criteria of effectiveness and efficiency. On the other hand, where political pressures are moderate and decision makers have strong professional backgrounds, decisions are more likely to reflect a more concerted effort to achieve effectiveness and efficiency through rational planning. More often than not, decision making lies somewhere between these two extremes.

While outcomes may be viewed as the results of decisions made by key actors, they also reflect the influence of social and economic conditions, the formal authority structure, and interest groups. Generally, outcomes are assessed on the basis of criteria such as efficiency, effectiveness, responsiveness, and equity. Efficiency refers to the level of resources required to deliver the desired level of services. Various polls indicate that in recent years, many citizens have come to believe that the cost of administering government has increased significantly but that the quality and quantity of public services have declined.[35] Effectiveness refers to the extent to which, cost aside, public services achieve the desired results. Responsiveness refers to how well government is able to meet the needs of particular groups in the community and whether it does so in a timely manner. Equity refers to the distribution of services to various sectors of the community, by income and neighborhood, for example. In many communities, residents of low-income minority neighborhoods complain that they tend to receive fewer services.

Incrementalism

Several models have been put forth that attempt to explain decision making as it occurs in different settings. In the incremental model, decision makers make small adjustments to existing policy rather than strive for broad or comprehensive change. In their search for solutions, decision makers often find that time and money constraints prevent them from identifying the full range of alternatives and their likely consequences. They also find it easier to obtain agreement among different interests when the proposal being considered varies only marginally from the previous arrangement. In the incremental model, decisions evolve through cautious steps based on what is already accepted as policy.[36] In essence, this means that the existing level of funds is accepted as the legitimate basis for future decisions; that is, next year's budget is based on this year's, as this year's budget was based on last year's.

Many social scientists are critical of the incremental approach, contending that incremental budgeting is likely to be based on percentages rather than on content. As Ira Sharkansky has observed, "The criteria employed by financial decision makers do not reflect a primary concern with the nature of the economy, the platforms of political parties, or articulated policy desires. . . . The criteria of financial decision makers are non-ideological and frequently non-programmatic."[37] Those who accept incrementalism argue that it is unavoidable in the real world of politics—particularly with regard to budget making, which lies at the core of the political process.[38] Defenders also contend that cost-benefit ratios for alternative policies cannot be accurately calculated where many diverse political, social, and economic values are at stake. Finally, defenders argue that at least for conventional, long-established services such as police and fire protection, incrementalism may function reasonably well in the short run.

Rational planning

Although the incremental model is useful for understanding the many constraints on decision making posed by the organizational environment, it has little to say about how to achieve efficiency through systematic analysis. The rational planning model, as illustrated in Figure 1–12, is the key here.[39] Under this model, the organization or individual

Recognizes a need

Defines the problem in light of this need

Identifies goals and objectives that reflect value preferences

Searches for and identifies different alternatives for achieving goals and objectives

Estimates costs and benefits for each alternative

Compares and ranks alternatives using the criterion of expected maximum benefits over least costs

Recommends the preferred alternative as a solution.

In recent years, as pressures for fiscal austerity have continued, the rational planning approach to financial decision making has received special emphasis. The rational planning approach, which views the budget as the optimal solution to the problem of allocating scarce resources, is exemplified by PPBS (planning-programming-budgeting system) and, more recently, by ZBB (zero-base budgeting). Derived from operations research, PPBS uses a long-term planning model to determine comprehensively the costs and benefits of expenditures on all program objectives. Variations of PPBS have been used by governmental bodies on all levels. In ZBB, every ongoing program and activity must be justified from the bottom up each year. A program that has been funded in the past will not necessarily be funded in the future; its value cannot be taken for granted. (PPBS and ZBB are discussed in more detail in Chapter 7 of this volume.)

Both PPBS and ZBB are useful concepts, but both have encountered strong obstacles to implementation. Some administrators have resisted adopting these

Figure 1–12   The rational planning model for decision making.

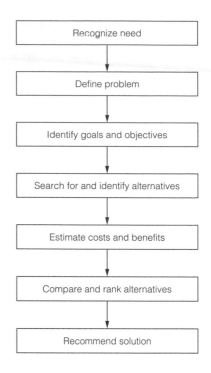

approaches because they view them as fads, others because they feel that so many budgeting approaches have been labeled PPBS or ZBB that the terms lack any real meaning. Still others criticize PPBS and ZBB in practice, citing the wide gap between the theoretical concepts and the constraints on local government practice. For example, changing budget-making procedures will not necessarily change the use to which the budget is put: relations between administrative agencies and the local governing body are such that a change desired by the local government manager or an agency head may not have high priority among council members, who represent different constituencies and have a different view of their professional role. Ultimately, however, the strongest obstacles to the implementation of PPBS and ZBB are bureaucratic:

The unwillingness of agency personnel to develop meaningful work units, to learn the skills of the cost-effectiveness analyst, to accept the system analyst into the decision-making circle, and the general unwillingness to change time-hallowed practices all militate against budget innovation. Additionally, lack of resources in the agencies reduced the likelihood of any kind of change.[40]

Although the PPBS and ZBB approaches have not been adopted widely, their many variations have made important contributions to what are known as "program budgeting" practices. Under these practices, the major actors in the budgetary process—the council, the chief administrator, the department heads, the program administrators, the finance and budget staffs, and major interest groups—are forced to deal with fiscal issues in relation to service levels and programs that are deemed likely to contribute greater efficiency.[41]

"Satisficing"

Political scientist Thomas D. Lynch has described "satisficing" as a mode of decision making in which decision makers develop their own criteria to determine acceptable alternatives for dealing with a given problem.[42] In other words, rather than consider the best possible alternative according to the criteria of maximum benefits and minimum cost, decision makers settle on an alternative that appears to be "good enough." Supporters of this approach point out that with deadlines to meet, it is often too time-consuming and expensive to collect all the necessary information about every possible alternative and its likely consequences. Thus, satisficing may be economically justifiable when the cost of gathering extra information is taken into consideration. Furthermore, proponents claim that rational planning requires a vision of the future, which is extremely difficult to achieve in a field where predictive capabilities are neither sophisticated nor very accurate. Consequently, decision makers may choose to satisfice—to be only as systematic and rational in their search for solutions as is feasible.

The role of the finance officer

What is the appropriate role of the finance officer in decision making? Because the role tends to vary with circumstances, there are no simple answers to this question. Lynch identifies four ideal types worthy of consideration: the true rational believer; the pure reactive person; the finance-wise person, or cynic; and the wise finance person.[43]

The true rational believer   The true rational believer tries to follow the rational planning approach outlined in Figure 1–12. Although this approach holds the most promise for achieving efficiency, the finance officer should be aware of its limitations as well. In many instances, the need to achieve political compromise among competing interests prevents public agencies from defining specific goals and objectives: agreement comes more easily where goals and objectives are not stated very clearly. Furthermore, an exhaustive examination of all alternatives and their likely consequences is usually not feasible. In the real world of public affairs, the budget calendar cannot wait until an analysis has been completed.

The pure reactive person   The pure reactive person defines the job of finance officer in very limited terms—namely, performing the formal requirements of the job description and responding to specific requests made by policy makers and ranking administrators. This individual provides technical information but does not see himself or herself as a decision maker. The hazard of this approach, according to Lynch, is that foolish mistakes can occur, particularly in the budget process. As Lynch explains, "The budget person has a unique vantage point and can often understand both the political actors' viewpoints as well as the workings of government. By merely reacting, the government loses the important insight of the budget expert. Thus more errors are likely to occur."[44]

The finance-wise person   The finance-wise person, or cynic, views government decisions as based entirely on political criteria. Such people are keenly aware of the trade-offs that occur among different interests in the course of negotiating decisions, and they believe that policy makers do not take information and advice from professional staff seriously. To corroborate this belief, they perpetuate stories of corruption and conflict of interest. While corruption and conflict of interest may characterize some government settings, this is not universally the case. Moreover, in recent years, citizens have made increasing demands for improved accountability in the public sector—including demands that decisions be based on concerns for productivity and efficiency rather than on narrowly political criteria.

The wise finance person The wise finance person recognizes that if government is to attain a high level of efficiency, both politics and expertise are crucial to the decision-making process. The sheer complexity of financial decision making demands that chief administrators and council members seek such financial expertise. The wise finance person recognizes the need for

Hard work

Mastery of detail

Honesty

Tight control over taxpayers' money

A rational approach to financial management

Adaptability to political exigencies

Informing and updating policy makers

Establishing trust

Discretion.

Conclusion

How local governments manage their finances depends on a number of factors, including urban settlement patterns, the legal and institutional context, the organizational structure, and the government's approach to financial decision making. Central to the functioning of a local government is the finance officer, who makes the fiscal system work. To perform successfully, a finance officer must not only understand the external and internal factors and trends that shape government processes but also come equipped with the knowledge and skills needed to contribute to and implement decisions.

These functions of the finance manager, and the stage on which he or she performs, are covered fully in this book. The chapters that follow elaborate further—from a theoretical as well as a practical perspective—on the local government setting, management tools, revenue sources, and financial management principles and techniques.

1 Michael A. Pagano, *City Fiscal Conditions in 2002* (Washington, D.C.: National League of Cities, 2002).

2 Brookings Institution, Center on Urban and Metropolitan Policy, *Racial Change in the Nation's Largest Cities: Evidence from the 2000 Census* (Washington, D.C.: Brookings Institution, April 2001).

3 Ibid.

4 U.S. Department of Commerce, Bureau of the Census, *Statistical Abstract of the United States: 2002* (Washington, D.C.: U.S. Government Printing Office, 2001), 908.

5 See L. C. Ledebur and W. R. Barnes, *All in It Together: Cities, Suburbs, and Local Economic Regions* (Washington, D.C.: National League of Cities, 1993).

6 Jean Gottmann, *Megalopolis: The Urbanized Northeastern Seaboard of the United States* (New York: Twentieth Century Fund, 1961), 5.

7 U.S. Department of Housing and Urban Development (HUD), *The State of the Cities 2000* (Washington, D.C.: HUD, 1997), 40, 41.

8 See Gregory D. Squires, ed., *Urban Sprawl* (Washington, D.C.: Urban Institute Press, 2002).

9 David Firestone, "The New Look Suburbs," *New York Times,* April 17, 2001, A1, A14.

10 Charles Jaret, "Suburban Expansion in Atlanta: 'The City without Limits,' " chap. 7 in Squires, *Urban Sprawl.*

11 Bruce Katz, *Smart Growth: The Future of the American Metropolis,* Case Paper 58 (London: Center for Analysis of Social Exclusion, London School of Economics, July 2002).

12 Leonard Ruchelman, *Cities in the Third Wave: The Technological Transformation of Urban America* (Chicago: Burnham, Inc., 2000).

13 John R. Logan and Harvey L. Molotch, *Urban Fortunes: The Political Economy of Space* (Berkeley and Los Angeles: University of California Press, 1987).

14 See Dennis R. Judd and Susan S. Fainstein, eds., *The Tourist City* (New Haven: Yale University Press, 1999).

15 Ada Louise Huxtable, *The Unreal America: Architecture and Illusion* (New York: New Press, 1997), 48.

16 Joel Garreau, *Edge Cities: Life on the New Frontier* (New York: Doubleday, 1991).

17 See Saskia Sassen, *The Global City: New York, London, Tokyo,* 2nd ed. (Princeton, N.J.: Princeton University Press, 2001); and *Cities in the World Economy,* 2nd ed. (Thousand Oaks, Calif.: Sage, 2000).

18 David Rusk, *Cities without Suburbs* (Washington, D.C.: Woodrow Wilson Press, 1993), 67.

19 John F. Dillon, *Commentaries on the Law of Municipal Corporations,* 5th ed., vol. 1 (Boston: Little, Brown, 1911), section 237.

20 See *State Mandates* (Washington, D.C.: National League of Cities, 1992).

21 David R. Berman, "State-Local Relations: Authority, Finances, Partnerships," in *Municipal Year Book 2001* (Washington, D.C.: International City/County Management Association, 2001), 65.

22 Center for the Study of the States, *State Fiscal Briefs* (Albany: Center for the Study of the States, Nelson A. Rockefeller Institute of Government, State University of New York, April 1998), 8.

23 Ibid.

24 Berman, "State-Local Relations," 62.

25 David R. Berman, "State-Local Relations: Authority, Finances, Cooperation," in *Municipal Year Book 2002* (Washington, D.C.: International City/County Management Association, 2002), 53.

26 See various commentaries on the squeeze on state and local budgets in *U.S. Mayor,* 3 February 2003.

27 See Anthony G. Cahill et al., "State Government Responses to Municipal Fiscal Distress: A Brave New World for State-Local Intergovernmental Relations," *Public Productivity and Management Review* 17 (spring 1994): 253–264; and Scott R. Mackey, *State Programs to Assist Distressed Local Governments* (Denver: National Conference of State Legislators, March 1993).

28 Herbert Kaufman, *Politics and Policies in State and Local Government* (Englewood Cliffs, N.J.: Prentice-Hall, 1963), chap. 2.

29 On the national level, the Articles of Confederation provided for no executive at all. Historians have held that the creation of a strong presidency at the Philadelphia Convention of 1787 may be attributable to the atypical leanings of the delegates, who happened to be strong nationalists.

30 See, for example, Stanley T. Gabis, "Leadership in a Large Manager City: The Case of Kansas City," *Annals of the American Academy of Political and Social Science* 347 (May 1963): 52–63; and Keith Mulrooney, ed., "Symposium on the American City Manager: An Urban Administrator in a Complex and Evolving Situation," *Public Administration Review* 31 (January/February 1971): 6–46. See also David R. Morgan and Sheilah S. Watson, "Policy Leadership in Council-Manager Cities: Comparing Mayor and Manager," *Public Administration Review* 52 (September/October 1992): 438–452.

31 Jesse Burkhead, *Government Budgeting* (New York: John Wiley and Sons, 1956), 14.

32 National Civic League, *Model City Charter,* 7th ed. (Denver: National Civic League, 1989).

33 See Robert L. Bland and Irene S. Rubin, *Budgeting: A Guide for Local Governments* (Washington, D.C.: International City/County Management Association, 1997).

34 See Irene S. Rubin, *The Politics of Public Budgeting: Getting and Spending, Borrowing and Balancing,* 3rd ed. (Chatham N.J.: Chatham House, 1997).

35 One example is the Gallup Poll of February 2001, "Mood of America," survey #GO 132067 (Wilmington, Del.: Scholarly Resources), 30.

36 See Charles F. Lindblom, "The Science of Muddling Through," *Public Administration Review* 19 (spring 1959): 79–88; and Aaron B. Wildavsky, *The New Politics of the Budgetary Process* (Glenview, Ill.: Scott, Foresman, 1988).

37 Ira Sharkansky, *Spending in the American States* (Chicago: Rand McNally, 1970), 13. See also Rubin, *Politics of Budgeting,* 127, 128.

38 Wildavsky, *New Politics.*

39 See John Dewey, *How We Think* (Boston: D.C. Heath, 1919); and Thomas D. Lynch, *Public Budgeting in America,* 3rd ed. (Englewood Cliffs, N.J.: Prentice-Hall, 1990), 18–22.

40 John Wanat, *Introduction to Budgeting* (North Scituate, Mass.: Duxbury Press, 1978), 105.

41 How cities adopt budget reforms such as PBB and ZBB is analyzed by Irene S. Rubin in "Budget Reform and Political Reform: Conclusions from Six Cities," *Public Administration Review* 52 (September/October 1992): 438–446.

42 The term *satisfice* was first used by Herbert Simon, who coined it by combining *satisfy* with *suffice.* See "Theories of Decision Making in Economics and Behavioral Science," *American Economic Review* 49 (June 1959): 262–264. See also Lynch, *Public Budgeting,* 19.

43 Lynch, *Public Budgeting,* 89–91.

44 Ibid., 90.

2 Fiscal structure in the federal system

WALLACE E. OATES

On a conceptual level, the federal model of government might be envisioned as a tidily organized structure characterized by a clearly recognized and constitutionally specified separation of powers among the different levels of government. Agencies at different levels would pursue their activities independently. In the late nineteenth century, James Bryce described such a federal system as "a great factory wherein two sets of machinery are at work, their revolving wheels apparently intermixed, their bands crossing one another, yet each doing its own work without touching or hampering the other."[1]

Federal systems, however, have evolved far differently. The public sector in the United States, Canada, and most other federal countries is a highly fragmented system of governmental units. These units function within the context of a constitution that defines only roughly the scope of responsibility and authority at different levels of government. The activities of the various levels of government in the modern federal system overlap and intertwine in such fundamental and complex ways that political scientists now characterize our age as one of "cooperative federalism." Some observers even contend that assigning functional responsibility among levels of government is a futile enterprise. As political scientist Michael Reagan puts it, "Those things are national and justify grant programs which the Congress *says* are national. The concepts of local and national interest are squishy at best."[2]

Despite the apparent chaos and absence of principle in the functioning of federal structures, the economic roles of different levels of government can and should be considered systematically. This chapter thus begins by exploring, from an economic perspective, the division of functions among levels of government in the United States, with some reference to the intergovernmental fiscal system in other federal countries. The literature on fiscal federalism has developed a number of insights into the design of multilevel fiscal systems. Drawing on this work, the second major section of the chapter provides an overview of the principles of fiscal design, with a particular focus on the importance of what are known as "hard budget constraints." A key fiscal instrument in intergovernmental finance is the transfer of revenues—intergovernmental grants—from higher to lower levels of government. In fact, such grants have come to play a basic role in modern fiscal systems. This chapter explores intergovernmental grants in some detail: their economic rationale, the economic principles underlying their design, and their role in the U.S. federal system. The two final sections place the discussion in this chapter in the context of the historical evolution of federal fiscal systems and offer some concluding observations on the current state of the debate on fiscal federalism in the United States and elsewhere.[3]

The division of functions

From an economic perspective, government has three functions: (1) stabilizing the economy at high levels of output and employment without creating excessive inflationary pressures; (2) establishing an equitable distribution of income; and (3) providing certain public goods and services directly and introducing regulations or incentives to correct for significant distortions in the market-determined allocation of resources. While these functions refer to the public sector as a whole, the peculiarly federal issue is the assignment of these functions to different levels of government.

Economic stabilization

The macroeconomic function of stabilizing the economy rests primarily with the central government, which controls the creation and destruction of money. If each local government had monetary control, there would be a powerful incentive to create new money to purchase goods and services from other jurisdictions, in lieu of raising money through local taxation. The result would be excessive creation of money and consequent rapid inflation.

Moreover, the limited scope for local countercyclical budgetary measures and the "openness" of regional and local economies severely constrain local fiscal policy. If, for example, a local authority were to undertake a general tax cut to stimulate the local economy, it would find instead that most of the newly generated spending would flow out of the jurisdiction in payment for goods and services produced elsewhere. There would be little ultimate effect on local employment levels.

In short, the absence of monetary prerogatives and the openness of regional and local economies suggest that the potential for effective macroeconomic stabilization is quite limited at lower levels of government. Nevertheless, states (and, to some extent, local governments) can undertake certain countercyclical measures. For example, they can use tax stabilization funds (sometimes called "rainy-day funds") to even out spending over the course of the business cycle: during expansionary periods, fiscal surpluses are used to build up reserves, which can then be drawn down during recessions. Ultimately, however, the central government, with its monetary and fiscal instruments, must assume primary responsibility for macroeconomic stabilization.

Income distribution

The income distribution function also requires the central government to play a major role. The national economic system substantially constrains the capacity of local governments to redistribute income. Because of the high degree of mobility of households and firms, one local government cannot, for example, tax a particular group significantly more heavily than it is taxed elsewhere without creating incentives for migration. An aggressive local program to reduce income inequality through subsidies for the poor and steeply progressive tax rates for the rich, for example, would lead higher-income households to leave and settle in jurisdictions where they would obtain more favorable fiscal treatment, and would lead poorer families to migrate into the community. A more equal distribution of income may result, but it would be created by the out-migration of the well-to-do and the in-migration of lower-income families. (Studies conducted in the United States have found significant migration of low-income households across states and metropolitan areas in response to differentials in welfare payments; some of these studies also suggest that these migration patterns have led state and local governments to hold down the levels of support payments.)[4]

The economic consequences of a mobile population were recognized explicitly under the Poor Laws in England.[5] Although the care of the poor (which dated back to pre-Elizabethan times) was designated as a local (parish) responsibility, this care extended *only* to the parish's own poor. Under the Law of Settlement and Removal, paupers from other parishes were deported, often quite cruelly. Without such strict "residency requirements" (which, incidentally, are now unconstitutional in the United States), an effective system of local relief for the poor would probably not have been feasible. Writing in the nineteenth century, the British economist Edward Cannan concluded that

measures adopted to produce greater equality are, however, exceedingly unsuitable for local authorities. The smaller the locality, the more capricious and ineffectual are likely to be any efforts it may make to carry out such a policy. It seems clearly desirable that all such measures should be applied to the largest possible area, and that subordinate authorities should be left to act, like the individual, for motives of self-interest.[6]

This is not to imply that local governments cannot redistribute income to any extent at all; they can and do. Nevertheless, the mobility of households and firms imposes substantial constraints on the character and level of local income-transfer programs and taxation. As a result, the central government must not only stabilize the economy but also assume primary responsibility for programs designed to distribute income more equitably. That responsibility, however, does not preclude an extensive role for localities in administering and operating income-transfer programs; it simply recognizes that levels of redistribution cannot vary widely among local jurisdictions and that localities cannot be expected to fund the bulk of redistributive programs from their own sources.

Provision of goods and services

It is the direct provision of public goods and services that provides lower levels of government with their basic economic rationale. Certain public goods, such as national defense, are intended to benefit all members of society, and the federal government is unquestionably the appropriate agent for providing such truly national public services. In contrast, many other services that provide collective benefits are primarily local. Refuse disposal and sewer systems, fire and police protection, libraries, and recreational resources are but a few examples. In these cases, a compelling argument can be made for the local provision of services based on local preferences; centralized control tends to result in more uniform levels of output across all jurisdictions—which, by restricting choice, can entail substantial losses in consumer well-being.

Econometric estimates of demand curves for various local public goods can measure the potential losses in consumer well-being when everyone is required to consume the same level of public services. Studies suggest that the magnitude of these losses can be quite substantial.[7] Wherever possible, then, levels of consumption should be adjusted to the preferences of individuals or groups of individuals. Because it is more sensitive to local consumers' preferences, the decentralized provision of services is most likely to achieve this goal.[8] As Alexis de Tocqueville observed, "In great centralized nations the legislator is obliged to give a character of uniformity to the laws, which does not always suit the diversity of customs and of districts."[9]

The economic literature on local finance during the past thirty years has emphasized the role of mobility in enabling consumers to realize gains from locally determined levels of public services. In 1956, Charles Tiebout introduced a model of local finance in which individuals seek a community that provides the level of public output best suited to their tastes.[10] The outcome closely resembles the market solution for private goods:

Just as the consumer may be visualized as walking to a private market place to buy his goods, the prices of which are set, we place him in the position of walking to a community where the prices (taxes) of community services are set. Both trips take the consumer to the market. There is no way in which the consumer can avoid revealing his preferences in a spatial economy. Spatial mobility provides the local public-goods counterpart to the private market's shopping trip.[11]

The Tiebout model thus envisions a system of local finance in which consumers sort themselves out according to their demands for public goods. As in the private market, individual consumers "purchase" their preferred basket of services according to their preferences and the cost of those services.

The Tiebout model entails a number of heroic assumptions—in particular, one of footloose consumers moving freely, and without cost, among localities and choosing a community of residence solely on the basis of fiscal considerations. Nevertheless, subsequent research suggests that the mobility model is useful. Numerous studies have found, for example, that local property values vary directly with the level of local services. People pay more for houses of the same size and quality in order to live in communities that provide such amenities as better schools and greater safety from crime.[12]

Such evidence should not come as a surprise. Households in the United States move with considerable frequency. The 2000 census, for example, found that nearly half the families sampled were not living in the same house as they had been in 1995. Surely the vast majority of these moves were not motivated primarily by fiscal considerations but by changes in employment or family status. Nevertheless, the process of choosing a new community in which to live is likely to involve serious consideration of local services and taxes. People who work in a metropolitan area, perhaps in the central city itself, have a wide range of choices among suburban communities in which to reside. The quality of local services—such as police protection and education—is likely to be a significant factor in this choice.

In assessing the implications of the literature on local finance, it is important to distinguish between the descriptive and the prescriptive. The mobility model isolates an important set of forces that have had a profound effect on the evolution of metropolitan areas. Families with high demands for public services tend to live in suburban communities with high levels of amenities; households with lower demands for public services tend to live in jurisdictions where the level or quality of services is lower. From a descriptive perspective, the mobility model can "explain" how metropolitan areas gradually develop into clusters of relatively small suburban communities, each with a relatively homogeneous population when compared with that of the urban area as a whole.

From a prescriptive point of view, however, things are somewhat more complicated. Purely in terms of consumer choice, the outcome described in the Tiebout model has real appeal. A variety of communities permits individual consumers to purchase the quantity of public services that they desire (as if they were purchasing private services, but with price taking the form of a local tax payment). But from a broader social perspective, the model raises some troubling issues. Because the demand for services is positively correlated with income, the "sorting-out" process tends to generate a system in which communities are effectively segregated by income group. Thus, the spectrum of communities that emerges ranges from high-income jurisdictions with high service levels to low-income jurisdictions with low service levels. While this outcome may not be objectionable to some, it runs counter to a general societal concern for equality—and to certain court decisions that reflect that concern. Whatever the implications of the potential tension between local choice and social justice, the mobility model illuminates a powerful set of forces that must be dealt with in the design of social and economic policy.[13]

An overview of federal fiscal structure

In a federal system, each level of government has its own set of expenditure functions and revenue sources. But there are typically important interrelationships within this multilevel structure. A local government, for example, will normally finance some part of its budget through its own taxes and user fees, another portion with funds from debt (bond) issues, and the remainder with grant monies (transfers) received from higher levels of government. The structure and workings of this interdependent system of public finance have important implications for the performance of the government sector in meeting its responsibilities. This section provides a brief overview of some important properties of a sound intergovernmental fiscal system.

A high level of public sector performance requires more than just a proper assignment of functions to the different levels of government. It also requires a coherent set of fiscal and regulatory institutions that embody incentives for effective policy making.[14] The basic idea, or "principle," here is that fiscal structure should provide a setting in which public officials at all levels have incentives to enact programs that provide overall benefits in excess of their costs. In particular, the system should not embody major avenues through which public decision makers can circumvent costs by introducing measures that benefit their jurisdictions at the expense of the polity elsewhere. Indeed, where this principle is violated, provincial, state, and local finance can become a destabilizing force in the economy.

The design of a sound fiscal system is a broad and complex issue. One critical element (especially for state and local levels of government) is what economists have come to call a "hard budget constraint."[15] Effective public decision making requires voters and public officials to weigh the benefits of proposed public programs against their costs. And if jurisdictions are to make proper fiscal decisions, one implication is that they must bear the cost of proposed extensions of public programs. If programs are financed from external sources, there may be little incentive to ensure that they are worth their cost. Thus, a well-developed system of state and local taxation and user fees, through which these levels of government can generate the necessary revenues to pay for the programs they choose, is of central importance in federal fiscal structure (see Chapters 10 through 12).

As will be clear from subsequent discussion, intergovernmental grants, if properly designed, have an important role to play in the fiscal system. But if intergovernmental grants dominate state and local revenue systems, then local governments are likely to turn to political channels to get additional funding from above, instead of relying on increases in own-source revenues. In fiscal parlance, the system must not embody fiscal bailouts, which undermine responsible and accountable budgetary decision making.

This does not, most assuredly, rule out an important role for systems of intergovernmental grants. But it suggests, as will be clear in subsequent sections, that such grants should be lump-sum in character (not expansible), so that state and local governments must finance extensions of public programs. The one exception, to be noted shortly, is where these programs provide spillover benefits to other jurisdictions. But aside from this special case, state and local officials must not have the prospect that increases in their budgets will be funded by an augmentation of the transfers they receive from above; increased spending must not be ratified by bailouts from higher levels of government.

This principle also suggests the need for limitations on debt finance (as will be discussed in Chapter 14). The issuance of bonds to finance state and local expenditures makes economic sense for investment in public infrastructure (capital projects); it provides a sensible way to spread out the payments for long-term projects over their useful life. Thus, most state and local governments turn to bond issues to finance the construction of major facilities such as large bridges or school buildings. But debt issues should not be available to finance deficits on current account.[16] Where such practices exist, public officials can enact programs that provide current benefits to the electorate but push the burden of paying for these programs onto future administrations and residents. Thus, it is for good reason that most state and local governments limit the use of debt finance to the funding of capital projects.

The principle of building hard budget constraints into the intergovernmental fiscal system implies some practical rules for the design of state and local revenue systems. Where these rules are ignored, fiscal and economic chaos can result. In recent years, some countries (largely developing nations) have failed to observe these precepts, with disastrous consequences. In Argentina, for example, provincial governments, knowing that the central government would bail them out through increased intergovernmental transfers, far outspent their current revenues. Moreover, to fill any further budgetary gaps, they simply sold provincial bonds to publicly owned banks. These practices were possible because provincial officials did not face effective budgetary constraints: they could spend as they liked—and did so, destabilizing the fiscal system and the national economy.

To ensure an appropriate set of incentives for public decision making, a well-designed system of intergovernmental finance thus requires careful attention to the roles of different levels of government and to the fiscal institutions themselves. Such a system also requires a reasonable balance between own-source revenue and intergovernmental transfers.

Intergovernmental transfers

De Tocqueville observed that "the federal system was created with the intention of combining the different advantages which result from the magnitude and the littleness of nations."[17] Economic analysis provides some support for his claim. A centralized authority is necessary to implement macroeconomic stabilization policy, to accomplish income redistribution, and to provide those goods and services whose benefits are national in scope. At the same time, the "littleness" of local fiscal jurisdictions offers compelling advantages in terms of tailoring the provision of certain public services to local tastes. Even in countries with unitary governments, there is considerable de facto budgetary choice at lower levels of the public sector. In an economic sense, government fiscal structure in all nations is "federal" because, to a greater or lesser degree, some budgetary discretion is exercised at several levels of the governmental system.

Although the assignment of functions outlined earlier can provide a framework for thinking about federal fiscal structure, it is a bit too neat and tidy. The macroeconomic and redistribution functions are not *solely* centralized responsibilities. State and local governments undertake some explicitly counter-cyclical and redistributive measures. Moreover, some services (e.g., education), although primarily of local interest, have important national dimensions or spillover effects. It is unclear how best to structure the provision of such services. As one observer of federal government has noted, "There is and can be no final solution to the allocation of financial resources in a federal system. There can only be adjustments and reallocations in the light of changing conditions. What a federal government needs, therefore, is machinery adequate to make these adjustments."[18]

The federal system has several levels, and there is often considerable uncertainty in determining which level of government should provide a particular service. The operations of federal, state, and local governments interact with and overlap one another to such a degree that it is often difficult to integrate the budgetary and other decisions of different public units into a coherent and consistent set of policies.

Federal governments have found intergovernmental grants to be a piece of "fiscal machinery" well suited to dealing with the continuing budgetary tensions among different levels of government. Grants function as a link among the budgetary structures of the different levels of government. They are highly flexible instruments, capable of assuming a number of different forms to promote varied objectives in the public sector, from the expansion of specific activities to the equalization of fiscal capacity; nearly all federal countries have come to place a heavy reliance on them.[19] In the United States, political scientist William Young contends that "the most powerful engine in the century for reshaping national-state relations has been the grant-in-aid system of national financing of state and local activities."[20]

Grants take two basic forms: conditional or unconditional (lump sum). A conditional grant is contingent on some specified behavior on the part of the recipient; the funds must be used in a particular way. Under matching grants, which are one type of conditional grant, the grantor agrees to pay some fraction of the unit cost paid by the recipient. Under one-to-one matching, for example, a locality receives one dollar in grant monies for each dollar it expends from its own funds, effectively cutting in half the cost of the service to the locality. Moreover, the only way the locality can increase its grant money is to increase its own spending. But conditional grants need not be matching grants: a conditional grant may be a fixed sum to be used for a specified purpose. Such nonmatching conditional grants do not have a direct price effect on local services; they simply provide a certain sum that must be spent for prescribed purposes. In contrast, unconditional—or lump-sum grants, as they are sometimes called—have no strings attached; the recipients are free to use the funds however they wish.[21]

The rationale for intergovernmental grants

Intergovernmental grants can serve a number of functions: they can alleviate external effects, equalize fiscal capacity, and, when they take the form of revenue sharing, promote fair and efficient taxation.

Alleviation of external effects Whenever the actions of one person (or group of people) impinge significantly on the welfare of others in the absence of any monetary compensation, there is potential for distortion in economic decisions. A classic example is the factory that spews forth damaging smoke, thereby imposing external costs on the neighboring laundry. In this case, the decision makers (the factory owners) have little incentive to take into account the external costs (the smoke damage) they generate. They do not pay for the clean air they "consume" in their production process as they do for the labor and materials they employ. Thus, the economic choices of the immediate decision makers fail to incorporate the full range of costs. In certain instances where the affected parties (in this example, the factory owners and the laundry owners) are able to come together and negotiate an agreement, voluntary private decisions can yield an efficient outcome.[22] However, because the voluntary resolution of problems that arise from external effects depends on a number of restrictive conditions, such as low negotiation costs, it is appropriate only to cases involving a small number of participants.[23] In cases involving larger numbers of participants, where voluntary resolution is more cumbersome, the more likely outcome is a distorted pattern of economic activity—in which the activities that generate external costs are carried on at excessively high levels, and the activities that include spillover benefits are carried on at excessively low levels.

External effects are not limited to decisions by private consumers or firms; the programs adopted by one local or state government may have important implications for the well-being of residents in other jurisdictions. A good system of roads in one locality, for example, serves travelers from elsewhere. Similarly, medical research funded in one state may produce new treatments of widespread interest. In such instances, a state or locality can hardly be expected to use its own resources to expand such activities to levels for which outsiders would be willing to pay if a payment mechanism existed. From the perspective of the federal government, the perfectly rational but myopic decisions of states and localities are a matter of serious concern when they affect programs that have important external benefits or costs.

As a representative of the national interest, the federal government could, in principle, simply take over the whole function and thereby "internalize" all associated costs and benefits. However, this response is often politically infeasible or simply unconstitutional. Even if it were a viable alternative, however, centralization is a cure that is often worse than the disease. Because state and local governments are in a position to fashion their programs according to the preferences of their constituencies, decentralized provision of public services can lead to a more efficient use of resources.

How, then, does the federal government influence state or local services that have external effects across jurisdictions, without at the same time preempting state and local governments? It employs conditional intergovernmental grants, which encourage the expansion of a particular service (e.g., medical research). However, if the goal is to encourage local spending for a particular program, the federal government must not only earmark the funds for that purpose but also ensure that the local government does not substitute the grant monies for local revenues that would otherwise have been spent on the service.

Even if a grant is conditional (in the sense that the recipient is required to use the monies for a prescribed function or program), it does not follow that the grant will increase spending for the function. For example, a locality that receives a grant to expand local police services might use these funds—especially in periods of rising budgets—to cover planned budgetary increases that would otherwise have been financed with locally raised revenues. The grant funds would, in effect, be available indirectly for use in other programs or, alternatively, for local tax cuts. In short, this "fungibility" of grant funds may allow states and localities to use conditional grants in the same way that they would employ monies with no strings attached, thereby frustrating the intent of the federal grant programs. (A special case occurs if a state or locality would have expended none of its own funds—or less than the sum of the grant—on the aided program. For example, "demonstration grants" may induce expenditures that would not have taken place without federal assistance.)

More generally, when both local and external benefits are involved, the appropriate form of grant is a matching grant. In theory, the grant terms should reflect the magnitude of the spillover effect. If, for example, two dollars of local expenditures generate one dollar of benefits for residents of other jurisdictions, then the granting government's share should be one-third (or one-to-two matching). This proportion would effectively induce the recipient to take account of the external benefits. In practice, it may be difficult to determine the precise ratio of local to external benefits, but the analysis provides some guidelines. For example, where the spillover benefits are considered large relative to local benefits, the grant program should offer relatively generous matching terms. The matching, incidentally, should be open-ended: the matching funds should be available to the recipient at whatever level of spending is selected. If matching is capped at a specified level of local expenditure, the grant ceases to reduce the cost to the local government and thus loses its ability to induce local spending.[24]

The U.S. federal government has made extensive use of matching grants for several programs with important spillover benefits. For example, federal matching grants to the states have supported the construction of a national network of highways. Federal agencies have also used matching grants for educational programs that have a clear national interest. The actual evolution of federal systems of intergovernmental grants will be examined later in this chapter, but these examples suggest that the economic principles of grant design can provide a rationale for the structure of some grant programs.

Fiscal equalization Federal systems of government have typically relied on intergovernmental grants to correct geographical inequities as well as to improve the allocation of resources. One rationale for these grants stems from geographical differences in fiscal well-being. In jurisdictions with relatively large tax bases and populations that require comparatively little in the way of social services, adequate service levels can be provided with relatively low tax rates. Areas with smaller tax bases may have significantly higher needs for services and comparatively high tax rates. Central governments in dozens of countries have attempted to use equalizing grants to decrease or eliminate such differences. The purpose of such grants is to enable each state or locality to provide a satisfactory level of key public services with a fiscal effort that is not discernibly greater than that of other jurisdictions. To achieve this goal, the central government bases the allocation of grant funds on the measured need and fiscal capacity of the lower levels of government. Thus, jurisdictions with populations requiring large public expenditures or with comparatively small tax bases (or with an unfortunate combination of the two) receive proportionately larger sums.

Three points concerning equalizing grants are worthy of special emphasis. First, because the intent is to equalize fiscal capacity, the appropriate grant form in this case is an unconditional grant rather than a matching grant, which would effectively lower the cost of services to each jurisdiction and thereby encourage increased spending. Although fiscal equalization grants should vary with a jurisdiction's need and fiscal capacity, they should not depend on the fiscal response of the jurisdiction.

Second, although equalizing grants may reduce fiscal disparities among *jurisdictions,* they are not an effective device for redistributing income among *individuals.* Typically, such grants will channel funds to poorer areas; but because most low-income areas have some wealthy residents and most high-income areas have some poor residents, transfers from rich to poor *areas* through the medium of equalizing grants are bound to have some undesired redistributive effects. That is, the wealthy in poor areas will receive benefits that they do not need, and the poor in wealthy areas will fail to receive the benefits that they do need. Unconditional equalizing grants are not a substitute for a national program designed to achieve an equitable distribution of income among individuals.

Third, the scope and design of equalizing grants should not overlook the powerful market forces that compensate automatically for some of the apparent inequities in a federal fiscal system. The case for equalizing grants is sometimes made in terms of the principle of horizontal equity: people in equal positions should be treated equally. At first glance, it would appear that a system of decentralized finance is likely to violate this principle because the size of the per capita tax base will vary from one jurisdiction to the next, and different tax rates will therefore be required to raise the same amount of revenue per person. A resident of a locality with a relatively large tax base may thus enjoy a lower tax rate and have a lower tax bill than his or her counterpart in a district with a smaller tax base. (This apparent source of inequity was, incidentally, one of the grounds for declaring the system of school finance in the state of New Jersey to be unconstitutional.)

However, where households are highly mobile, market forces can eliminate such horizontal inequities. Suppose, for example, that one jurisdiction has a notable fiscal advantage over others (e.g., a relatively large tax base or a lower cost of maintaining clean air because of a hilltop location). The mobility of households means that the value of such differences will be capitalized into local property values. Consumers will bid for places in the fiscally advantaged community until the increased price of property exactly offsets the fiscal gain. Thus, a person who is considering buying a house in a community with a relatively high tax rate will find that the high tax liability is approximately offset by the lower price of the property.[25]

Mobility, therefore, promotes the equal treatment of equals. Whatever fiscal advantages are enjoyed will be paid for in the form of higher actual (or imputed) rent; conversely, higher taxes will be offset by lower property prices. In the mobility model, horizontal equity tends to be self-policing, which suggests that significant horizontal inequities may be ironed out to some extent by market forces within the metropolitan economy. This may not be true, however, at the regional level, where obstacles to mobility may permit unequal treatment of equals to persist. Moreover, sudden changes in the fiscal position of a community can generate one-time gains or losses in property values.

Taxation and revenue sharing   A third basic rationale for intergovernmental grants is the need to establish an efficient and fair system of taxation for the public sector as a whole. There is some evidence that the federal tax system is more equitable and less distorting than state and local tax systems. The federal income tax, for example, is probably a good deal more progressive than state and local income, sales, and property taxes.[26] Moreover, taxes at the lower levels of government have a greater potential for distorting the flow of resources in the economy. The relatively high mobility of both goods and people across state and local boundaries implies that there may be much more sensitivity to state and local fiscal differentials than to those at national levels. For example, because federal taxes cannot be avoided by a change of location within the national economy, taxation at the federal level does not create direct incentives for locational distortions. At state and local levels, however, differentials in tax rates may chase capital from high-tax to low-tax jurisdictions, resulting in inefficiencies in resource allocation and a consequent reduction in output.

In addition, states and localities often shift a substantial portion of their tax burden onto residents of other jurisdictions. Taxing certain production activities in one jurisdiction, for instance, may result in higher prices, which are paid largely by outsiders. For example, the burden of taxation of Michigan's auto industry falls largely on purchasers of new automobiles nationwide. Similarly, areas that draw heavy tourist populations often meet many of their local tax needs through excise taxes on hotel and restaurant bills. And these are not isolated examples. Charles McLure, a leading expert on state and local finances, has estimated that, on average, state governments are able to export approximately 20 to 25 percent of their taxes to residents of other states.[27] The federal government, in contrast, has a greater opportunity to rely on fairer, more wide-reaching programs (such as progressive taxation and the national uniformity of tax rates) and thereby avoid the distortions in resource allocation generated by state and local tax differentials.

Finally, a greater reliance on centralized taxation provides some economies of scale in tax administration. Available data for the United States indicate that the cost of administering the federal individual income tax system amounts to only about 0.6 percent of the revenues received. At the state level, the administrative costs for income or sales taxes are typically 1 to 2 percent of revenues received.[28]

It would appear, then, that the equity and efficiency of the federal-state-local tax system as a whole might be improved by shifting more of the taxation function to the central government. However, as has been discussed previously, retaining state and local discretion over the size and composition of expenditures has important benefits. One way to retain state and local control is through revenue sharing, which substitutes federal for state and local taxation. In a sense, the federal government acts as a tax collector for states and localities, collecting tax revenues in excess of its own needs and distributing this excess in lump-sum form to state and local treasuries. The appropriate form for the transfer of such funds is the unconditional grant: since the purpose of these monies is to alter the overall revenue system rather than to encourage spending on particular functions (or spending in general), recipients should not be required to spend the funds as a condition for receiving them.

Careful attention must be paid, however, to the impact of revenue sharing. An implicit assumption in the foregoing discussion is that the central government can function as a tax collector for state and local governments without intruding on state and local expenditure prerogatives or creating perverse incentives for state and local budgetary decision making. But even if the transfers take an unconditional form, political pressures and opportunities can easily induce central agencies to use their fiscal leverage to achieve some of their own objectives. In the United Kingdom, for example, where local governments rely heavily on grants (primarily unconditional) from the center, there is widespread concern about the erosion of local autonomy. Likewise, in two federal countries, Australia and Canada, the heavy reliance of state or provincial governments on revenue transfers has, in the view of many observers, undercut the fiscal independence and performance of the recipients.

As discussed earlier, own-source revenues are critical if state and local officials are to face the hard budget constraints needed to provide the right kinds of fiscal incentives. Because an excessive dependence on central revenues can undermine the effectiveness of the entire fiscal system, the development of productive and sound systems of state and local taxation is of the greatest importance. Designing the fiscal system to achieve an appropriate balance between intergovernmental grants and a reliance on own-source tax revenues is a challenging and critical task.

Unconditional grants thus have two potential roles (within limits): fiscal equalization and an improved overall system of taxation. In practical terms, nothing prevents the public sector from pursuing both these objectives at the same time through a system of unconditional grants (revenue sharing) in which the size of the per capita grant varies with the fiscal characteristics of the jurisdiction. This approach has, in fact, been the standard practice in a large number of countries around the world.

The magnitude and structure of intergovernmental grants in the United States

During the past half-century, the growth in the size and complexity of the public sector has generated a striking expansion in the use of intergovernmental grants. Such transfers have provided a policy tool capable of promoting a number of quite different and important government objectives. As shown in Table 2–1, federal grants to state and local governments increased from about $3 billion in 1955 to almost $300 billion in 1999. This exaggerates the real growth in such transfers because it incorporates the effects of general inflation. But even after allowing for inflation, column 2 shows that, in constant 1996 dollars, federal intergovernmental grants increased nearly twentyfold from 1955 to 1999. This growth is also reflected in column 3, which shows that federal intergovernmental grants account for a growing share of federal spending: from 4.2 percent in 1955 to more than 13 percent by 1995.

Table 2–1 Intergovernmental grants in the United States, selected years.

Year	(1) Federal grants to state and local governments ($ in billions)	(2) Federal grants in constant 1996 dollars ($ in billions)	(3) Federal grants as a percentage of federal expenditures (%)	(4) Federal grants as a percentage of state-local revenues (%)	(5) Intergovernmental revenue as a percentage of local general revenues (%)
1955	3.1	15.7	4.2	8.5	26.3
1960	7.0	31.3	7.2	9.5	27.1
1965	11.1	46.3	8.5	11.4	28.4
1970	23.3	79.5	11.2	16.8	33.1
1975	49.6	122.9	14.5	22.6	38.8
1980	90.8	158.2	14.7	22.8	39.7
1985	107.2	144.8	10.4	17.2	34.3
1990	147.0	169.3	10.6	16.8	32.9
1995	233.4	237.8	13.7	20.1	34.2
1999	294.5	281.1	n.a.	20.1	34.4

n.a. = not available.

This expansion in the use of intergovernmental grants has not, however, been entirely continuous. Following a period of rapid growth throughout the 1970s, such grants actually declined in real terms during the early 1980s (see column 2). This decline resulted from the Reagan administration's New Federalism, a program of fiscal retrenchment that reduced federal support for state and local government. (New Federalism will be discussed in more detail in a later section of this chapter.) Growth in federal grants resumed, however, in the late 1980s and continued throughout the 1990s.

As column 4 indicates, state and local governments have become increasingly reliant on intergovernmental funds. By 1980, federal grants funded more than 20 percent of the spending of state and local governments (although this percentage declined somewhat in the ensuing decade). Local governments, for their part, have become even more dependent on intergovernmental transfers, and now receive more than 30 percent of their revenues in this form. The lion's share of these transfers comes not from the federal government but from the state level. State governments typically transfer substantial funds to their respective localities, largely for school finance. Beginning in the 1970s, a number of court rulings declared existing systems of school financing unconstitutional; as a result, the states have taken a more active role in financing public education, providing local school districts with large grants that have somewhat equalized school spending across high- and low-income districts. In addition to grants for education, state governments provide transfers to their local governments for highways, public welfare, and other programs.

Federal transfers support a wide variety of public programs. Table 2–2 shows the breakdown of federal grants by category of aid for fiscal year 2000. Two characteristics of these grants are worthy of note: first, the diversity of purposes to which grant funds are directed; second, the fact that a substantial portion of federal intergovernmental transfers is for income redistribution (including major portions of federal grants for health, income security, and social services). As discussed earlier, it is difficult for states, and especially for localities, to finance aggressive redistributive programs, so the federal government makes extensive use of intergovernmental transfers to assist lower-income households. Much of this aid takes the form of assistance for medical expenditures under the Medicaid program.

Certain federal grants provide a stimulus for state-local programs that confer benefits on residents of other areas. Federal grants for transportation and for

Table 2–2 Federal grants to state and local governments by function, 2000.

Function	Amount ($ in billions)
Health	124.8
Income security	63.2
Social services	42.1
Transportation	32.2
Community and regional development	8.7
Natural resources and environment	4.6
General government	2.3
Administration of justice	5.1
Energy	0.4
Other	1.2
Total	284.6

educational and training activities are good examples; the United States as a whole has an important interest in both a good system of national roadways and an educated electorate. By providing budgetary incentives, conditional intergovernmental grants enable state and local governments to address the broader interests of the citizenry.

In addition to its extensive system of conditional grants, in 1972 the United States instituted a modest program of general revenue sharing with state and local governments. But largely because of fiscal stringency at the federal level, revenue sharing was discontinued in the 1980s. In contrast, many other federal countries rely heavily on unconditional grants. In both Australia and Canada, for example, the central government acts as a revenue-raising agent for other levels of government, distributing to them large, unconditional sums.

The design and effects of intergovernmental grants

Thus far, this chapter has presented the economic principles of grant design and related them to the structure of the intergovernmental transfer system. A closer examination of the actual form of federal transfers to state and local governments, however, reveals a number of anomalies; this should not be too surprising, because the design and enactment of grant programs result, in part, from interactions between federal legislators, governors, local government officials, and various special-interest groups. Such interaction is frequently characterized by a certain tension: the grant administrator wants to pursue the agency's objectives by restricting the use of funds, and the recipient wants to minimize any strings attached to the monies. The grant program that finally emerges typically reflects some degree of compromise.

How consistent is the structure of grants with the economic criteria for grant design? As discussed earlier, external benefits across jurisdictions are a primary justification for intergovernmental grants. Matching grants—where the respective matching shares reflect the extent of the spillover benefit—are the appropriate vehicle for supporting state or local programs that have external effects. Yet from this perspective, certain characteristics of the federal grant system are quite puzzling. Under most matching grants, federal matching ceases at some modest level of local expenditure (the major exception being grants under the Medicaid program). Caps on matching funds mean that states and localities at maximum funding levels receive no inducement to undertake further expenditures; thus, they have no incentive to take into account the spillover benefits that their fiscal decisions generate. If state and local officials are to be induced to expand their fiscal commitment to programs that have spillover benefits, matching grants should be open-ended: their provisions should apply to any potential extensions of budgetary programs.

In the case of a number of programs, it would be difficult to justify the matching shares by the extent of external benefits. For example, the federal share of interstate highway construction was, for many years, 90 percent of cost, although it seems unlikely that 90 percent of the value of the interstate highways passing through a particular state accrues to out-of-state drivers. The benefits from sewage treatment systems are even more definitively local: neighboring jurisdictions may benefit in some instances, but hardly enough to justify the original federal share of 75 percent of construction costs. A review of federal grant programs reveals that most require either low (less than 50 percent) or no matching on the part of the recipient state or local government. The federal matching share for a variety of highway programs, for example, ranges from 75 to 100 percent.

Other aspects of grant design can also impair the effectiveness of a particular grant program. As various studies have shown, the failure to link grants directly to their intended purpose can seriously undercut their efficacy. One important example is the program under which the federal government provided several billion dollars in subsidies for the construction of new waste treatment plants to reduce water pollution. These subsidies supported only a specific technology (waste treatment) even where a less costly and more effective alternative existed. Moreover, by subsidizing only the *construction* of treatment plants, the program provided no incentive for the efficient *operation* of these facilities. One analysis found that in more than half of the plants studied, services were substandard either because of poor operating procedures or because the plants were not designed to treat the waste load that was delivered to them.[29] The program still exists, although the federal matching share has been reduced from 75 to 55 percent.

Any evaluation of federal grant programs must attempt to measure the actual effect of the programs on the decisions (budgetary and otherwise) of state and local officials. There have been some efforts in this direction, although general understanding of the effects of federal grants continues to be spotty. Despite considerable variation in estimates from one study to the next, most research suggests that federal grants have had a significant expansionary effect on state and local spending. In other words, grant monies have not been used simply to substitute for state and local tax revenues.[30] Moreover, the evidence supports the expectation that conditional grants generate a larger expenditure response (dollar for dollar) than do unconditional transfers, with high federal matching providing a greater stimulus than low federal matching.

In fact, intergovernmental grants, whether conditional or not, induce a surprising degree of budgetary expansion. Consider, for example, the case of an unconditional grant to a community. Because such a grant contains no explicit incentives for budgetary expansion, the community might be expected to treat these monies as a kind of windfall—a supplement to local income. In theory, if local officials are responsive to the preferences of their constituencies, it should make little difference whether the grant monies flow into the local government treasury or directly into the pockets of local residents. From this perspective, an unconditional intergovernmental grant could be regarded as a veil for a direct federal tax cut to individuals.[31]

The implication of the "veil hypothesis" is that the additional local public spending generated by one dollar of lump-sum grant monies should be approximately the same as would result from a one-dollar increase in private income in the jurisdiction: in both cases, the jurisdiction's aggregate income has risen by one dollar, so the increase in public spending should be about the same. However, empirical evidence suggests that this is not the case. Specifically, since the state and local sector currently accounts for 10 to 15 percent of gross domestic product, one might expect increases in private income to induce additional state and local expenditure on the order of 10 to 15 cents per dollar of additional income. The evidence indicates, however, that unconditional intergovernmental transfers induce additional local expenditures of 40 to 50 cents on the dollar. This finding has become known among economists as "the flypaper effect" (i.e., money sticks where it hits)—and has been the subject of much debate and varying interpretations. Generally, however, the effects of intergovernmental grants are clear: they induce sizable increases in spending by recipients.[32]

Unfunded mandates　The federal and state governments require local governments to perform certain activities. When the costs of carrying out such activities are not covered by funding from a higher level of government, the local government has an "unfunded mandate." An unfunded mandate might be thought of as a negative grant-in-aid: as with a grant, the higher level of government wants the local government to perform a function that provides spillover benefits to a wider area or jurisdiction. In the case of an unfunded mandate, however, the higher level of government is not paying the cost. Instead, the incentive for local government compliance is the risk of losing other funding.

In response to complaints from local governments, Congress passed the Unfunded Mandates Reform Act of 1995 (UMRA), which was designed to ensure that before enacting legislation, Congress would receive information about the potential direct costs of federal mandates. Under UMRA, the Congressional Budget Office (CBO) and congressional authorizing committees are required to report information about the costs of mandates included in proposed legislation. If the total direct costs of all mandates in a bill are above $50 million (in 1996 dollars, adjusted yearly for inflation) in any of the first five fiscal years in which the mandates are effective, CBO must provide an estimate of those costs (if feasible) and the basis of its estimate. Five years after the passage of UMRA, CBO reported a decrease in the number of bills with mandates over $50 million.

For example, in a review of a number of bills that were part of the Internet Tax Freedom Act, which would have prohibited the collection of some state and local taxes for a specified period, CBO found that, at some point during the first five years, revenue losses from the prohibition would exceed the statutory threshold. Congress responded by revising the act so that states that were currently collecting a sales tax on Internet access could continue to do so. CBO estimated that the revenue losses associated with this final version of the law would not exceed the UMRA threshold.

Nevertheless, unfunded mandates remain a major concern for local governments and an important intergovernmental issue, especially when local sources of revenue are scarce. Another issue is that many federal and state actions that local governments regard as unfunded mandates probably fall outside UMRA's narrow definition. For example, commenting on the failure of Congress to provide aid for local governments in early 2003, John DeStefano Jr., president of the National League of Cities and mayor of New Haven, Connecticut, said, "This latest blow comes on the heels of the latest orange homeland security alert—another unfunded mandate that costs cities millions of dollars per day in law enforcement and security costs without any relief from the federal government."

Sources: "A Review of CBO's Activities in 2002 under the Unfunded Mandates Reform Act," May 2003; "CBO's Activities under the Unfunded Mandates Reform Act, 1996–2000," May 2001, both available at www.cbo.gov; and John DeStefano Jr., "Congress Fails Cities: No Economic Stimulus for Local Governments," available at www.nlc.org.

Economic analysis provides a number of important insights into the design and workings of intergovernmental grants. To satisfy their intended objectives, such grants must take the appropriate form and provide the right incentives for state and local decision makers. Through careful evaluation of grant programs—in terms of both economic principles and evidence of actual effects—fiscal analysts can contribute in important ways to the evolution of a more effective system of intergovernmental transfers.

Historical trends in federal fiscal structure

The increasing reliance of state and local levels of government on intergovernmental transfers from the federal government raises a broader question: Does the expansion of such grants reflect a continuing tendency toward the centralization of fiscal structure? Over a century ago, de Tocqueville predicted that "in the democratic ages which are opening upon us . . . centralization will be the natural government."[33] Referring to the federal form of government in particular, Edward McWhinney has cited Bryce's Law, which holds that "federalism is simply a transitory step on the way to governmental unity."[34] In this view, a public sector that relies substantially on decentralized budgetary choice is unstable and will, over time, move toward more reliance on central government.

Although the next section will show that temporary departures from this trend occurred in the 1980s, a case can be made for the likelihood of centralization over the long term. Rising incomes, improved transportation, and new modes of communication link regions and localities in the modern nation-state ever more closely, fostering increased mobility and interdependence. As a result, decisions made in one part of the country affect other areas. For example, the services provided in one jurisdiction have an "option value" to people who currently reside in other areas and who may, at some future date, choose to move.[35] Clearly, certain basic features of economic growth promote increased centralization of government. As Michael Reagan has observed, "Many more problems today than in the past are national in the sense of being affected by developments elsewhere in the nation or having their own impact upon other parts of the nation."[36]

However, the case for the centralization thesis is far from ironclad. As the mobility model of local finance suggests, people seek out communities that provide the public services they want. From this perspective, improved transportation and mobility may permit the local public sector to perform its functions more effectively. Those who work in one part of the metropolitan area—often the central city—have easier access to a wide range of residential jurisdictions offering a varied menu of public services. Economic growth, then, can facilitate the congregation of people with similar demands for local public goods and, in this way, generate potentially powerful economic and political forces in support of a continued reliance on local budgetary choice. To the extent that local jurisdictions can cater to the particular demands of their own relatively homogeneous populations, there will be strong support for local government to play a major role within the public sector.

Some indices of fiscal concentration can (1) suggest whether reliance on central government is increasing or decreasing and (2) reveal the effect of affluence on centralization. But first, the ambiguities inherent in any measure of centralization should be acknowledged.[37] There is no single satisfactory measure of the "quantity" of decision-making power at each level of government; even if there were, it would be impossible to weight the roles of the federal, state, and many local governments to produce a single, unambiguous index of fiscal centralization. Nevertheless, certain summary measures may at least suggest tendencies in the vertical structure of the fiscal system.

Table 2–3 presents a historical profile of U.S. public expenditure in the twentieth century by level of government. The first four columns show absolute spending; the last three indicate percentage shares. The federal share of total public expenditures may be regarded as a kind of "centralization ratio" that reflects the extent of fiscal centralization in the United States.

A cursory examination of the table provides strong support for the centralization thesis. Between 1902 and 1985, the federal share of total spending rose from about one-third to almost two-thirds. The state share of total spending almost doubled, from about 11 to 19 percent. These increases in the federal and state shares came, by definition, at the expense of local governments, whose relative share of public expenditure fell from more than 50 to less than 16 percent. A strong trend toward fiscal centralization appears to characterize the twentieth century in the United States.

However, a closer look suggests an important qualification: after 1950, the federal share leveled off. Federal spending in 1995 as a percentage of total public expenditure was actually less than in 1950, and state and local shares likewise changed by only a few percentage points. Thus, although the first half of the twentieth century was characterized by a strong tendency toward fiscal centralization, that tendency seems to have weakened during the years between 1950 and 1995.[38] Data from other nations reveal similar trends. Studies of a number of countries—including Canada, France, Germany, Switzerland, and the United Kingdom—indicate that the central government's fiscal share declined after the middle of the twentieth century.[39]

The picture that emerges from the data is a fairly complex one, but it does not support any sweeping hypothesis of a pervasive and continuing tendency toward a more centralized fiscal structure. On the contrary, during recent decades the trend seems to have been, if anything, slightly in the opposite direction, indicating that local government is alive and well. The local share of total public spending has actually risen since 1980. This trend should not be too surprising: the local provision of certain services offers such important advantages that it seems quite unlikely that the local sector would simply wither away.

Although a simplistic version of the centralization thesis does not seem tenable in light of the evidence, the evolution of the public sector both in the United States and elsewhere nevertheless exhibits some intriguing elements. In particular, as the public sector grows as a whole, there seems to be a tendency to form new types of units and jurisdictions for public decision making. The

Table 2–3 Public expenditure by level of government, selected fiscal years.

Year	Total public expenditure ($ in billions)	Expenditure by level of government ($ in billions)			Percentage share (%)		
		Federal	State	Local	Federal	State	Local
1902	1.7	0.6	0.2	0.9	34.5	10.8	54.8
1913	3.2	1.0	0.4	1.9	30.2	11.6	58.3
1922	9.3	3.8	1.3	4.3	40.5	13.6	46.0
1932	12.4	4.3	2.6	5.6	34.3	20.6	45.1
1940	20.4	10.1	4.5	5.8	49.3	22.3	28.5
1950	70.3	44.8	12.8	12.8	63.7	18.2	18.1
1960	151.3	97.3	25.0	29.0	64.3	16.5	19.1
1970	333.0	208.2	64.7	60.1	62.5	19.4	18.1
1980	958.7	615.4	191.8	151.4	64.2	20.0	15.8
1985	1,581.1	1,030.2	305.8	245.1	65.2	19.3	15.5
1990	2,218.8	1,393.1	435.2	390.5	62.8	19.6	17.6
1995	2,835.4	1,705.1	630.0	500.3	60.1	22.2	17.6

governmental sector seems to be evolving into a more complex and highly specialized set of institutions, which take different forms in different countries. In the United States, the most dramatic manifestation of this trend is the rise of special districts (see Chapter 12). As Table 2–4 indicates, the number of special districts more than quadrupled between 1942 and 1997, reflecting increasing specialization in the public sector as most of the districts are single purpose. Moreover, the services provided by special districts are diverse and include highways, sewage disposal, housing, libraries, fire protection, natural resources, hospitals, and cemeteries. At the same time, however, the total number of governmental units has decreased significantly, primarily because of consolidations among smaller school districts and some small townships.

The creation of new governmental units has not, however, been limited to single-purpose public agencies. In fact, the public sectors in Western industrialized economies are continuously establishing new levels of government to cope with new demands. Metropolitan governments have been created in some urban areas in the United States, in Canada, and in several European urban centers. The goal is to integrate the fiscal decision making of suburban communities and the central cities that serve them. Similarly, the central government's inability to meet certain regional needs has led to the establishment of regional governments in Italy and Spain and to the creation of Scottish and Welsh assemblies in the United Kingdom. Economist Alan Peacock contends that in the United Kingdom, the "deviation in individual and group preferences from those reflected in the existing amount and pattern of government services has become more marked [and has resulted in] the growing demand for devolution."[40]

Moreover, the formation of new governments has not been restricted to the lower tiers. The jurisdiction of the European Union (EU), a totally new level of government, embraces most of Western Europe. It is not yet clear what the EU's ultimate range of responsibilities and powers will be, but the contrast between a newly created European level of government and the move toward devolution in certain member countries does suggest the diversity of pressures operating on the public sector.

The implications of these changes for the future of federal fiscal structure are not clear. However, any simplistic prediction of continuing centralization and the eventual extinction of local government seems highly unlikely and inconsistent with recent fiscal trends. Local government will continue to contribute to the functioning of the public sector. This prediction by no means implies a static view of local structure and its role in the federal system, for local government has shown itself quite capable of taking new forms in re-

Table 2–4   Number of governmental units in the United States, selected years.

| | | | | Type of government | | | | |
| | | | | Local government | | | | |
Year	Total	U.S. government	State government	Total	County	Municipal	Township and town	School district	Special district
1942	155,116	1	48	155,067	3,050	16,220	18,919	108,579	8,299
1952	116,807	1	50	116,756	3,052	16,807	17,202	67,355	12,340
1962	91,237	1	50	91,186	3,043	18,000	17,142	34,678	18,323
1972	78,269	1	50	78,218	3,044	18,517	16,991	15,781	23,885
1982	81,831	1	50	81,780	3,041	19,076	16,734	14,851	28,078
1992	85,006	1	50	84,955	3,043	19,279	16,656	14,422	31,555
1997	87,504	1	50	87,453	3,043	19,372	16,629	13,726	34,683

sponse to changing demands. It is interesting to speculate on the growing specialization that emerging forms and levels of government represent. The general growth of the public sector has no doubt made it feasible to increase the degree of specialization in government. There may be a principle for the public sector that parallels Adam Smith's famous dictum for the private sector: "The division of labour is limited by the extent of the market."

Fiscal federalism: Problems and prospects

In the 1980s, President Reagan undertook a determined effort at fiscal decentralization under his New Federalism program. The president believed that the federal government had become too intrusive into state and local fiscal matters and sought to return more authority and responsibility to the states and their local governments. In particular, he thought that the huge federal grant system had undercut state and local autonomy, and he therefore proposed major revisions to the federal system of intergovernmental grants. Under these revisions, not only were the levels of various grant programs reduced, but their forms were also restructured: certain specific grant programs—encompassing a wide range of domestic functions—were consolidated into a smaller number of more broadly defined block grants. Such block grants would allow state and local governments more discretion in their design of programs and in their use of the grant monies.[41] The New Federalism initiative met with mixed success; some parts of the program were enacted and other were not. Several block grant programs came into being that consolidated a myriad of smaller, more narrowly defined categorical grant programs for such functions as public health, substance abuse, and community and social service.

Some of the momentum established for fiscal devolution reached well into the 1990s. Most notably, in 1996, President Clinton signed into law a major reform of the U.S. welfare system that replaced the long-lived system of Aid to Families with Dependent Children (AFDC), based on federal matching grants to the states, with a new block grant program called Temporary Assistance for Needy Families (TANF). The new program, reflecting long-standing dissatisfaction with the AFDC program, gave the states wide-ranging discretion in the design and administration of programs to assist the poor. These were financed by large grants from the federal government with few strings attached.

One of the basic ideas embodied in welfare reform was "laboratory federalism." Proponents of reform contended that a more decentralized structure would allow the states to design a whole range of new programs—in other words, to experiment with policy alternatives, which would reveal much about what works and what does not. This was not a new idea. James Bryce, in his insightful study of the U.S. system of government in the nineteenth century, observed long ago that "federalism enables a people to try experiments which could not be safely tried in a large centralized country."[42] Better known is a statement made by Justice Louis Brandeis in the 1930s: "It is one of the happy incidents of the federal system that a single courageous State may, if its citizens choose, serve as a laboratory; and try novel social and economic experiments without risk to the rest of the country."[43] In fact, since the institution of new federal welfare legislation, the states have introduced an imaginative array of measures for addressing poverty, especially for moving people off the welfare rolls into productive jobs, that may well provide important general lessons for the design of such programs.

Both in the United States and abroad, there continues to be widespread interest in fiscal decentralization as a means of improving the performance of the public sector. In Europe, for example, the Maastricht Treaty for European Union explicitly adopts the "principle of subsidiarity," under which public policy is to be assigned to the lowest level of government with the capacity to achieve the objectives. In a similar spirit, many developing countries are moving toward fiscal decentralization in an effort to break the grip of central planning and to address more effectively the regional and local issues that arise in the course of economic and political development.[44] Finally, the transitional economies of Eastern Europe are undertaking determined efforts to create new constitutions and public sector institutions in which lower levels of government play a much greater role.[45]

A pervasive and contentious issue in the decentralization debate is that of economic competition among governments. (See Chapter 13 for a description of local economic development programs.) Economists have long recognized the beneficial effects of competition in the private sector, where it induces firms to produce the goods and services that people want and to do so at the least cost. But the effects of competition among state and local governments in a federal system are, in the view of some, less clear. In particular, certain public-finance economists have argued that state and local officials, in their eagerness to attract new business and create jobs, compete by holding down rates on state and local taxes, creating a "race to the bottom" that leaves their jurisdictions with underfunded and inadequate levels of public services.[46] Fear of such outcomes has led members of the EU to impose a floor on tax rates for the value-added tax.

However, other observers see competition among governments as a healthy phenomenon that constrains the public sector's tendency toward excessive growth and provides needed incentives for the efficient provision of public services. Public-choice economists Geoffrey Brennan and James Buchanan, for example, have argued that fiscal decentralization and the resulting competition help control the tendencies of central government toward monopolistic behavior and excessive budgetary growth.[47]

In support of such a view, Nobel laureate Gary Becker has claimed that "competition among nations tends to produce a race to the top rather than to the bottom by limiting the ability of powerful and voracious groups and politicians in each nation to impose their will at the expense of the interests of the vast majority of their populations."[48] But even more conventional models of public decision making with beneficent-minded public officials can produce results where such competition is efficiency-enhancing in the sense of providing the right kind of incentives for budgetary choices. This debate is far from settled, but it does have some important implications for the fiscal structure of the public sector.[49]

Summary

The fiscal structure of the federal system does not involve a clearly delineated separation of functions among levels of government. Nevertheless, economic analysis provides some insights into the appropriate roles for different levels of the public sector. It suggests that the central government must assume the major responsibility for macroeconomic stabilization of the economy, for the redistribution of income, and for the provision of certain public goods and services (such as national defense). Lower levels of government make their major contribution by providing public goods and services in ways that respond to the preferences and circumstances of their constituencies.

There is, however, inevitably some overlap in the workings of different levels of government. The intergovernmental grant system has proved to be a flexible and widely employed mechanism for integrating the operations and interests of different levels of government. Such grants are used to supply state and local governments with incentives to provide services that benefit those residing in other jurisdictions, to help equalize fiscal capacity among jurisdictions, and to achieve a more fair and efficient tax system. To perform their function effectively, grant programs must employ the form (e.g., conditional or unconditional, matching or nonmatching) that is needed to achieve the desired result. Moreover, grants must be limited in magnitude and scope so as not to undermine the fiscal decision making of the recipient governments.

During the first half of the twentieth century, the historical record of fiscal structure reveals a pronounced trend toward centralization of the public sector. The role of the central government during this period rose dramatically at the expense of the state and local sectors. However, evidence from several countries indicates that the trend toward centralization has leveled off since the 1950s and, in some instances, even reversed itself. There is, moreover, widespread interest around the globe—in Europe, in developing nations, and in the transitional economies of Eastern Europe—in fiscal decentralization as a means of promoting better decision making in the public sector. The challenge that remains is to align fiscal responsibilities with the appropriate levels of government and to develop fiscal institutions that embody the kinds of incentives that will improve the overall performance of the public sector.

1 James Bryce, *The American Commonwealth,* 3rd ed., vol. 1 (New York: MacMillan, 1901), 325.

2 Michael D. Reagan, *The New Federalism* (New York: Oxford University Press, 1972), 81.

3 For a survey and review of the fiscal federalism literature, see Wallace E. Oates, "An Essay on Fiscal Federalism," *Journal of Economic Literature* 37 (September 1999): 1120–1149.

4 For a description and discussion of these studies, see Charles C. Brown and Wallace E. Oates, "Assistance to the Poor in a Federal System," *Journal of Public Economics* 32 (April 1987): 307–330.

5 Geoffrey W. Oxley, *Poor Relief in England and Wales, 1601–1834* (North Pomfret, Vt.: David & Charles, 1974).

6 Edwin Cannan, *The History of Local Rates in England,* 2nd ed. (London: P. S. King & Son, 1912), 185.

7 See, for example, David Bradford and Wallace E. Oates, "Suburban Exploitation of Central Cities and Governmental Structure," in *Redistribution through Public Choice,* ed. Harold Hochman and George Peterson (New York: Columbia University Press, 1974), 43–90; and Michael Boss, "Economic Theory of Democracy: An Empirical Text," *Public Choice* 19 (1974): 111–115.

8 See the discussion of the decentralization theorem in Wallace E. Oates, *Fiscal Federalism* (New York: Harcourt Brace Jovanovich, 1972), 33–38, 54–63.

9 Alexis de Tocqueville, *Democracy in America,* vol. 1 (New York: Vintage Books, Alfred A. Knopf, 1945), 169.

10 Charles Tiebout, "A Pure Theory of Local Expenditures," *Journal of Political Economy* 64 (October 1956): 416–424.

11 Ibid., 422.

12 See, for example, Wallace E. Oates, "The Effects of Property Taxes and Local Public Spending on Property Values: An Empirical Study of Tax Capitalization and the Tiebout Hypothesis," *Journal of Political Economy* 77 (November/December 1969): 957–971. William Fischel describes how the benefits from local services and the burden of local taxes are capitalized into local property values. He goes on to show how such capitalization encourages efficient local decisions. See *The Homevoter Hypothesis:* *How Home Values Influence Local Government Taxation, School Finance, and Land-Use Policies* (Cambridge: Harvard University Press, 2001). For an alternative approach involving the study of fiscally induced migration patterns, see J. Richard Aronson and Eli Schwartz, "Financing Public Goods and the Distribution of Population in a System of Local Governments," *National Tax Journal* 26 (June 1973): 137–160.

13 For a useful and recent collection of studies that address these issues, see Wallace E. Oates, ed., *Property Taxation and Local Government Finance: Essays in Honor of C. Lowell Harriss* (Cambridge, Mass.: Lincoln Institute of Land Policy, 2001).

14 For an excellent set of studies that explore this theme, see Robert Picciotto and Eduardo Wiesner, eds., *Evaluation and Development: The Institutional Dimension* (Washington, D.C.: World Bank, 1998).

15 Ronald McKinnon provides an excellent discussion of the role of hard budget constraints in "Market-Preserving Federalism in the American Monetary Union," in *Macroeconomic Dimensions of Public Finance: Essays in Honor of Vito Tanzi,* ed. M. Blejer and T. Ter-Minassian (London: Routledge, 1997), 73–93.

16 This maxim does not apply in the same way to the central government. It is often important in times of recession to allow the central government budget to go into deficit on current account (financed by bond issues) in order to provide a needed macroeconomic stimulus to the economy.

17 De Tocqueville, *Democracy in America,* vol. 1, 168.

18 Kenneth C. Wheare, *Federal Government,* 4th ed. (London: Oxford University Press, 1963), 117.

19 Oates, *Fiscal Federalism,* chap. 3.

20 William H. Young, ed., *Ogg and Ray's Introduction to American Government,* 13th ed. (New York: Appleton-Century-Crofts, 1966), 62.

21 For an excellent description of grant forms and a study of their use in the United States, see Shama Gamkhar, *Federal Intergovernmental Grants and the States: Managing Devolution* (Cheltenham, U.K.: Edward Elgar, 2002).

22 Ronald Coase, "The Problem of Social Cost," *Journal of Law and Economics* 3 (October 1960): 1–44.

23 William J. Baumol and Wallace E. Oates, *The Theory of Environmental Policy,* 2nd ed. (Cambridge, U.K.: Cambridge University Press, 1988), chap. 2.

24 Oates, *Fiscal Federalism,* chap. 3.

25 For some findings on the capitalization of fiscal differentials into local property values, see Oates, "Effects of Property Taxes," and Aronson and Schwartz, "Financing Public Goods."

26 For a good summary of the evidence on the incidence of various taxes (i.e., who pays the taxes) in the United States, see Joseph A. Pechman, *Who Paid the Taxes, 1966–1985* (Washington, D.C.: Brookings Institution, 1985). As Pechman makes clear, any conclusions on overall tax incidence must be hedged by a number of important qualifications.

27 Charles McLure, "The Interstate Exporting of State and Local Taxes: Estimates for 1962," *National Tax Journal* 19 (March 1967): 49–77.

28 Harvey S. Rosen, *Public Finance,* 4th ed. (Boston: Irwin/McGraw-Hill, 1995), 348; and J. Richard Aronson and John L. Hilley, *Financing State and Local Governments,* 4th ed. (Washington, D.C.: Brookings Institution, 1986), 101.

29 See Allen V. Kneese and Charles L. Schultze, *Pollution, Prices, and Public Policy* (Washington, D.C.: Brookings Institution, 1975), chap. 3.

30 For a useful early survey of the empirical work on the budgetary impact of intergovernmental grants, see Edward M. Gramlich, "Intergovernmental Grants: A Review of the Empirical Literature," in *The Political Economy of Fiscal Federalism,* ed. Wallace E. Oates (Lexington, Mass.: Lexington Books, 1977), 219–240. For a more recent summary of work in this field, see Gamkhar, *Federal Intergovernmental Grants.*

31 For a formal presentation of the veil hypothesis, see David F. Bradford and Wallace E. Oates, "The Analysis of Revenue Sharing in a New Approach to Collective Fiscal Decisions," *Quarterly Journal of Economics* 85 (August 1971): 416–439.

32 For reviews and interpretations of the literature on the impact of intergovernmental grants, see Wallace E. Oates, "Federalism and Government Finance," in *Modern Public Finance,* ed. John Quigley and Eugene Smolensky (Cambridge: Harvard University Press, 1994), 126–151; and James Hines Jr. and Richard Thaler, "The Flypaper Effect," *Journal of Economic Perspectives* 9 (fall 1995): 212–226.

33 De Tocqueville, *Democracy in America,* vol. 2, 313.

34 Edward McWhinney, *Comparative Federalism,* 2nd ed. (Toronto: University of Toronto Press, 1965), 105.

35 On option value in local finance, see Burton Weisbrod, *External Benefits of Public Education* (Princeton, N.J.: Industrial Relations Section, Department of Economics, Princeton University, 1964).

36 Reagan, *New Federalism,* 77.

37 On this issue, see Oates, *Fiscal Federalism,* chap. 5.

38 Table 2–3 shows the shares of public expenditure by level of government; it is also possible to examine the respective shares of public *revenues,* which yields virtually identical findings. The federal share of public revenues grew rapidly during the first half of the twentieth century—from 39 percent in 1902 to a high of 72 percent in 1952—and then declined to 56 percent by 1995. See David Hoffman, ed., *Facts and Figures on Government Finance,* 36th ed. (Washington, D.C.: Tax Foundation, 2002), 170.

39 Werner W. Pommerehne, "Quantitative Aspects of Federalism: A Study of Six Countries," in Oates, *Political Economy,* 275–355.

40 Alan Peacock, "The Political Economy of Devolution: The British Case," in Oates, *Political Economy,* 51.

41 For an insightful treatment of the nature of block grants and their actual impact, see Gamkhar, *Federal Intergovernmental Grants.*

42 Bryce, *American Commonwealth,* 353.

43 Quoted in David Osborne, *Laboratories of Democracy* (Boston: Harvard Business School Press, 1988). For an illuminating examination of laboratory federalism in the context of U.S. welfare reform, see Craig Volden, "Entrusting the States with Welfare Reform," in *The New Federalism: Can the States Be Trusted?,* ed. J. Ferejohn and B. Weingast (Stanford: Hoover Institution Press, 1997), 65–97. See also Oates, "Essay on Fiscal Federalism," 1131–1144.

44 For an excellent study of fiscal decentralization in the developing world, see Richard Bird and Francois Vaillancourt, eds., *Fiscal Decentralization in Developing Countries* (Cambridge, U.K.: Cambridge University Press, 1998).

45 See Richard Bird, Robert D. Ebel, and Christine I. Wallich, *Decentralization of the Socialist State: Intergovernmental Finance in Transition Economies* (Washington, D.C.: World Bank, 1995).

46 One of the early proponents of this view was George Break, *Intergovernmental Fiscal Relations in the United States* (Washington, D.C.: Brookings Institution, 1967). For a more recent treatment, see John Wilson, "Theories of Tax Competition," *National Tax Journal* 52 (June 1999): 269–304.

47 Geoffrey Brennan and James Buchanan, *The Power to Tax: Analytical Foundations of a Fiscal Constitution* (Cambridge, U.K.: Cambridge University Press, 1980). The evidence on the actual effect of interjurisdictional competition on the growth of government is far from clear: see, for example, Wallace E. Oates, "Searching for Leviathan: An Empirical Study," *American Economic Review* 75 (September 1985): 748–757.

48 Gary Becker, "What's Wrong with a Centralized Europe? Plenty," *Business Week,* 29 June 1988, 22.

49 For a survey and assessment of this issue, see Wallace E. Oates, "Fiscal Competition and European Union: Contrasting Perspectives," *Regional Science and Urban Economics* 31 (April 2001): 133–145.

3 Public school finance

Mary H. Harris and Vincent G. Munley

In dollar terms, education from kindergarten through high school (K–12) is by far the single most important government service provided at the state and local levels. In the 2000–01 fiscal year, state and local government expenditures for education amounted to more than $400 million, or about 25 percent of total expenditures.[1] What is perhaps most striking about K–12 finance is the degree to which the institutions that govern the provision of school financing—for example, referenda and debt limitations—vary across the fifty states.

This chapter provides a historical view of school district expenditures at the elementary and secondary level since the 1960s and examines the sources from which local education authorities (usually referred to as school districts) derive their major revenues. The discussion focuses on the various financial and political characteristics of both state governments and school districts that are important for understanding the economics of school finance. Of particular importance are the programs that state governments use to disburse grants to local education authorities. These programs—and, in particular, the formulas used to determine the amount of funding that school authorities receive—have widely varying effects on the operating and capital expenditures of school districts.

Expenditure trends

Since the early 1960s, per-pupil expenditures for K–12 education have increased markedly, both in nominal terms and in constant dollars. For the United States as a whole, between the 1959–60 and the 1998–99 school years, these expenditures increased in real terms at an annual rate of 3.1 percent.[2] During the same time period, per capita gross domestic product (GDP) and median family income increased in real terms at annual rates of 2.4 percent and 1.9 percent, respectively.[3]

It is worth noting that for two of these three economic measures, growth patterns during the 1990s differed substantially from those of the previous three decades. For per capita GDP, the growth rate was almost exactly the same during the 1990s as during the period from 1960 through 1990.[4] The growth rate for median family income, however, accelerated from a rate of 1.7 percent from 1960 through 1990 to a rate of 2.7 percent during the 1990s.[5] The biggest change, however, was in the growth rate of spending per pupil, which slowed from 3.8 percent during the period from 1960 through 1990 to only 0.9 percent during the 1990s.[6]

Table 3–1 presents per-pupil expenditures, by state, for selected school years from 1959–60 through 1998–99. In the majority of states, per-pupil expenditures increased overall between 1989–90 and 1998–99, in keeping with their long-term trend. However, expenditures in eight states (Alaska, Arizona, Connecticut, Florida, Maryland, New Hampshire, Pennsylvania, and Vermont) were actually lower for the 1998–99 school year than they had been ten years earlier. (Table 3–2 shows, for each state, the pattern of change in school spending.)

Table 3–1   Per-pupil expenditures by state, selected school years (in constant 1998–99 dollars).

State	1959–60	1969–70	1979–80	1989–90	1998–99
Alabama	1,350	2,369	3,416	4,312	5,512
Alaska	3,059	4,890	10,020	10,926	9,209
Arizona	2,260	3,137	4,177	5,252	5,235
Arkansas	1,261	2,472	3,337	4,516	5,193
California	2,374	3,777	4,806	5,690	6,045
Colorado	2,218	3,214	5,131	6,117	6,386
Connecticut	2,442	4,143	5,129	10,156	9,620
Delaware	2,552	3,921	6,064	7,514	8,336
Florida	1,779	3,190	4,004	6,476	6,443
Georgia	1,419	2,561	3,445	5,539	6,534
Hawaii	1,817	3,661	4,921	5,765	6,648
Idaho	1,622	2,628	3,517	3,988	5,379
Illinois	2,455	3,961	5,482	6,632	7,676
Indiana	2,065	3,171	3,990	5,969	7,249
Iowa	2,059	3,677	4,931	5,770	6,548
Kansas	1,947	3,358	4,606	6,157	6,708
Kentucky	1,305	2,375	3,605	4,853	6,412
Louisiana	2,083	2,823	3,798	5,058	6,019
Maine	1,583	3,016	3,865	6,963	7,688
Maryland	2,199	4,000	5,506	8,132	7,865
Massachusetts	2,290	3,742	5,975	8,082	8,750
Michigan	2,325	3,937	5,596	7,187	8,142
Minnesota	2,381	3,936	5,059	6,441	7,159
Mississippi	1,153	2,182	3,526	4,009	4,871
Missouri	1,926	3,086	4,104	5,840	6,393
Montana	2,300	3,406	5,249	6,138	6,768
Nebraska	1,887	3,208	4,557	6,274	6,856
Nevada	2,410	3,352	4,426	5,335	5,934
New Hampshire	1,945	3,149	4,061	6,873	6,780
New Jersey	2,170	4,426	6,764	10,547	10,748
New Mexico	2,031	3,080	4,310	4,555	5,363
New York	3,145	5,779	7,338	10,447	10,514
North Carolina	1,329	2,667	3,718	5,559	6,088
North Dakota	2,053	3,004	4,070	5,429	5,820
Ohio	2,044	3,180	4,397	6,537	7,295
Oklahoma	1,744	2,633	4,083	4,546	5,684
Oregon	2,511	4,028	5,705	7,094	7,787
Pennsylvania	2,293	3,841	5,372	8,071	8,026
Rhode Island	2,315	3,882	5,513	8,252	9,049
South Carolina	1,232	2,668	3,713	5,289	6,003
South Dakota	1,942	3,005	4,043	4,835	5,613
Tennessee	1,333	2,466	3,466	4,748	5,521
Texas	1,861	2,719	4,060	5,378	6,161
Utah	1,806	2,728	3,511	3,581	4,478
Vermont	1,926	3,516	4,233	8,069	7,984
Virginia	1,536	3,083	4,175	6,054	6,129
Washington	2,354	3,987	5,443	6,093	6,595
West Virginia	1,447	2,918	4,070	5,651	7,176
Wisconsin	2,313	3,845	5,250	7,158	8,062
Wyoming	2,522	3,728	5,355	7,227	7,393
United States[a]	2,101	3,554	4,815	6,453	7,013

Note: Figures are based on average daily attendance.
[a]Figures in this row reflect the average of the state values, weighted on the basis of the number of pupils in each state.

Table 3–2 Percentage change in per-pupil expenditures, by state
(based on constant 1998–99 dollars).

State	1959–60 to 1969–70	1969–70 to 1979–80	1979–80 to 1989–90	1989–90 to 1998–99
Alabama	7.5	4.4	2.6	2.8
Alaska	6.0	10.5	0.9	−10.6
Arizona	3.9	3.3	2.6	0.0
Arkansas	9.6	3.5	3.5	1.5
California	5.9	2.7	1.8	0.6
Colorado	4.5	6.0	1.9	0.4
Connecticut	7.0	2.4	9.8	−0.5
Delaware	5.4	5.5	2.4	1.1
Florida	7.9	2.6	6.2	−0.1
Georgia	8.0	3.5	6.1	1.8
Hawaii	10.1	3.4	1.7	1.5
Idaho	6.2	3.4	1.3	3.5
Illinois	6.1	3.8	2.1	1.6
Indiana	5.4	2.6	5.0	2.1
Iowa	7.9	3.4	1.7	1.3
Kansas	7.2	3.7	3.4	0.9
Kentucky	8.2	5.2	3.5	3.2
Louisiana	3.6	3.5	3.3	1.9
Maine	9.1	2.8	8.0	1.0
Maryland	8.2	3.8	4.8	−0.3
Massachusetts	6.3	6.0	3.5	0.8
Michigan	6.9	4.2	2.8	1.3
Minnesota	6.5	2.9	2.7	1.1
Mississippi	8.9	6.2	1.4	2.2
Missouri	6.0	3.3	4.2	0.9
Montana	4.8	5.4	1.7	1.0
Nebraska	7.0	4.2	3.8	0.9
Nevada	3.9	3.2	2.1	1.1
New Hampshire	6.2	2.9	6.9	−0.1
New Jersey	10.4	5.3	5.6	0.2
New Mexico	5.2	4.0	0.6	1.8
New York	8.4	2.7	4.2	0.1
North Carolina	10.1	3.9	5.0	1.0
North Dakota	4.6	3.5	3.3	0.7
Ohio	5.6	3.8	4.9	1.2
Oklahoma	5.1	5.5	1.1	2.5
Oregon	6.0	4.2	2.4	1.0
Pennsylvania	6.8	4.0	5.0	−0.1
Rhode Island	6.8	4.2	5.0	1.0
South Carolina	11.7	3.9	4.2	1.3
South Dakota	5.5	3.5	2.0	1.6
Tennessee	8.5	4.1	3.7	1.6
Texas	4.6	4.9	3.2	1.5
Utah	5.1	2.9	0.2	2.5
Vermont	8.3	2.0	9.1	−0.1
Virginia	10.1	3.5	4.5	0.1
Washington	6.9	3.7	1.2	0.8
West Virginia	10.2	3.9	3.9	2.7
Wisconsin	6.6	3.7	3.6	1.3
Wyoming	4.8	4.4	3.5	0.2
United States	7.0	4.0	3.0	1.0

Note: Figures are based on average daily attendance.

Expenditures per pupil rise when school budgets increase at a faster rate than enrollments. During the 1960s, even though enrollment grew at an annual rate of 2.6 percent,[7] real per-pupil expenditures grew more rapidly. In the 1970s and 1980s, moderate growth in real per-pupil spending occurred while enrollments were actually declining. During the 1990s, enrollment once again increased, at an annual rate of 1.2 percent;[8] but, as noted earlier, growth in per-pupil expenditures declined during that decade to 0.9 percent. Thus, the greatest growth in per-pupil spending came from rapidly expanding budgets in the 1960s; during the 1990s, however, the growth rate for real expenditures was essentially the same as the growth rate of elementary and secondary enrollments.

Because the cost of providing a unit of education services of a standard quality varies across states, Table 3–1 may exaggerate the differences between states in the level and quality of such services. For example, teachers' salaries and class size are major elements in the cost of providing education services,[9] but average teachers' salaries vary across and even within states because of a number of factors: variations in the average wages across jurisdictions, with the result that teachers' salaries will vary accordingly; the strength of teachers' bargaining power relative to that of the hiring jurisdiction and other public employees; varying levels of experience and educational qualifications; and variations in local preferences for education. Other elements that go into the cost of education services, such as utilities, also vary in price across and within states and affect the cost of services.

School districts must channel funding into operating expenditures and capital outlays. Table 3–3 shows the breakdown by state for 1999–2000. Operating expenditures cover the daily operation of the schools, such as salaries, benefits, utilities, supplies, and insurance. The operating budget also typically includes annual repairs and maintenance of buildings and equipment, but does not usually include expenditures for new construction or extensive renovations. The funding for such capital outlays will be discussed later in this chapter.

Revenue trends

Traditionally, local taxes and state aid to school districts, rather than federal monies, have been the major sources of revenue for K–12 public schools. The share of public school funds provided by the federal government has typically ranged from 4 to 10 percent. Federal funds reached a maximum of 9.8 percent in 1978–80 and have, on average, declined since then.[10] While the combined state and local component of public school revenues has remained between 90 and 95 percent, the relative contributions from these two sources have changed. From 1959–60 to 1999–2000, the state share increased from roughly 39 to 50 percent of the total, while the locally raised share declined from roughly 57 to 43 percent (see Figure 3–1). The relative decline in local support is largely due to increases in state aid aimed at equalizing fiscal resources across school districts.

Although states in the aggregate contribute about 50 percent of public school revenues, there is substantial variation among states in the ratio of state to local revenue-raising responsibility. At one extreme is Hawaii, where state revenues provide more than 85 percent of funds for the single statewide school system. At the other end is New Hampshire, where the state provides only 9 percent of public school revenues. Table 3–4 presents data by state for the distribution of K–12 public school revenues by level of government.[11] The table shows that the aggregate trend toward greater reliance on state funds holds true for better than two-thirds of the states, and that the largest concentration of states that run counter to this trend is in the Southeast.

Table 3–3   School district expenditures by state, 1999–2000.

State	Operating expenditures ($)	Percentage of total	Capital expenditures ($)	Percentage of total	Total
Alabama	4,266,675	87	663,903	13	4,930,578
Alaska	1,182,144	86	184,546	14	1,366,690
Arizona	4,333,171	85	768,425	15	5,101,596
Arkansas	2,473,705	94	146,666	6	2,620,371
California	38,918,421	87	5,849,441	13	44,767,862
Colorado	4,404,617	85	782,711	15	5,187,328
Connecticut	5,004,650	93	369,278	7	5,373,928
Delaware	928,022	92	79,176	8	1,007,198
Florida	14,015,580	83	2,792,662	17	16,808,242
Georgia	9,179,227	86	1,520,834	14	10,700,061
Hawaii	1,247,539	91	115,972	9	1,363,511
Idaho	1,283,575	89	153,472	11	1,437,047
Illinois	14,700,330	86	2,467,748	14	17,168,078
Indiana	6,891,491	89	841,171	11	7,732,662
Iowa	3,271,730	90	353,405	10	3,625,135
Kansas	2,963,326	93	206,141	7	3,169,467
Kentucky	3,890,034	88	515,109	12	4,405,143
Louisiana	4,293,656	91	414,669	9	4,708,325
Maine	1,605,582	92	143,112	8	1,748,694
Maryland	6,364,133	89	760,810	11	7,124,943
Massachusetts	8,451,566	94	533,702	6	8,985,268
Michigan	13,561,716	88	1,866,666	12	15,428,382
Minnesota	6,299,355	87	901,829	13	7,201,184
Mississippi	2,518,217	86	421,075	14	2,939,292
Missouri	5,746,904	88	756,817	12	6,503,721
Montana	982,492	94	57,419	6	1,039,911
Nebraska	1,854,375	88	243,866	12	2,098,241
Nevada	1,880,148	81	428,541	19	2,308,689
New Hampshire	1,397,541	91	130,011	9	1,527,552
New Jersey	13,855,416	91	1,320,024	9	15,175,440
New Mexico	1,877,656	88	255,735	12	2,133,391
New York	29,292,023	90	3,266,115	10	32,558,138
North Carolina	7,690,395	85	1,385,226	15	9,075,621
North Dakota	662,527	89	81,274	11	743,801
Ohio	13,112,226	90	1,378,528	10	14,490,754
Oklahoma	3,542,361	93	286,261	7	3,828,622
Oregon	3,871,479	91	391,189	9	4,262,668
Pennsylvania	14,386,952	89	1,851,099	11	16,238,051
Rhode Island	1,324,635	98	30,587	2	1,355,222
South Carolina	4,123,825	85	716,110	15	4,839,935
South Dakota	726,219	83	144,296	17	870,515
Tennessee	4,944,404	87	743,326	13	5,687,730
Texas	24,697,690	84	4,719,976	16	29,417,666
Utah	2,144,710	89	270,172	11	2,414,882
Vermont	869,156	96	39,112	4	908,268
Virginia	7,810,638	89	1,011,384	11	8,822,022
Washington	6,455,036	86	1,048,059	14	7,503,095
West Virginia	2,100,766	94	129,872	6	2,230,638
Wisconsin	6,806,843	88	958,597	12	7,765,440
Wyoming	685,155	91	70,579	9	755,734

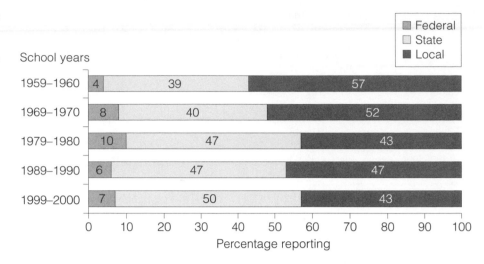

Figure 3–1   Revenues of public school districts by source, selected school years.

Revenue sources for state funds

It is commonplace for state governments to derive some of the funds that are distributed to local school districts from one or more dedicated revenue sources. Examples of earmarked taxes, from which all or part of the proceeds flow to local schools, include a statewide property tax; selected excise taxes; insurance premium fees;[12] federal forest and mineral lease receipts; coal, oil, and gas extraction fees; lottery proceeds; and interest from a permanent school trust fund.

Although such earmarked revenues are an important source of funds for many state aid programs, legislative appropriations from the general fund are the single most important component of the state share of public school revenues: in the majority of states, such appropriations account for more than 80 percent of total state aid; and in many states, they constitute the sole source of state-generated revenues.[13] Moreover, even in states where dedicated receipts are substantial, supplemental appropriations from the general fund are important.

Fiscal independence and referendum requirements

The U.S. Census Bureau defines independent school systems as "school districts that are administratively and fiscally independent of any other government."[14] According to this definition, in thirty-one states all public schools are independent, and in fifteen states some districts are independent while others are not. Hawaii has a single system dependent on the state government. In most other states with dependent school systems, the systems are dependent on a county or municipal government.[15] Schools in North Carolina and Maryland are dependent solely on municipal governments. In Alaska, the majority of districts are dependent on municipal governments, although some districts in sparsely populated areas of that state are dependent solely on the state government. The variety of organizational structure is perhaps most pronounced in Maine, where some school districts are independent, others are dependent on municipal governments, and still others (in sparsely populated areas) are dependent solely on the state government.

Table 3–5 lists the number of independent and dependent school districts by state according to two sources: the American Education Finance Association

Table 3–4   Share of federal, state, and local funding of public schools, by state, selected periods.

State	1959–60 Federal	State	Local	1979–80 Federal	State	Local	1999–2000 Federal	State	Local
Alabama	8.1	69.3	22.6	12.6	69.0	18.4	9.1	61.6	29.3
Alaska	17.9	50.0	32.1	13.0	70.2	16.9	13.8	61.0	25.2
Arizona	6.8	39.5	53.7	11.1	41.6	47.3	10.0	43.2	46.8
Arkansas	8.0	47.7	44.3	14.5	53.0	32.5	10.2	57.8	32.0
California	3.6	42.7	53.7	8.7	71.2	19.1	8.6	59.3	32.1
Colorado	5.7	19.9	74.4	6.1	41.0	52.9	5.1	42.5	52.4
Connecticut	3.0	26.8	70.2	6.1	31.5	62.5	4.0	39.0	57.0
Delaware	2.2	78.9	18.9	13.0	64.7	22.3	7.4	64.3	28.3
Florida	2.2	57.7	40.1	11.0	55.2	33.7	7.9	50.3	41.8
Georgia	11.1	62.8	25.1	11.8	57.6	30.6	6.7	49.1	44.2
Hawaii	13.6	69.9	16.5	12.5	85.2	2.4	9.8	87.8	2.4
Idaho	5.8	33.2	61.0	9.5	55.0	35.5	7.1	61.5	31.4
Illinois	2.7	18.9	78.4	12.8	41.2	46.0	7.2	30.1	62.7
Indiana	3.1	29.8	67.1	6.9	56.1	37.0	5.0	52.5	42.5
Iowa	2.9	12.1	85.0	6.7	42.2	51.0	5.6	50.5	43.9
Kansas	5.3	21.5	73.2	6.9	43.3	49.8	6.1	61.6	32.3
Kentucky	4.7	44.9	50.4	12.5	69.7	17.8	9.2	61.8	29.0
Louisiana	2.4	67.7	29.9	14.8	54.4	30.8	11.5	50.4	38.1
Maine	4.0	30.6	65.4	9.6	48.9	41.5	7.5	45.9	46.6
Maryland	6.9	36.4	56.7	8.0	40.2	51.8	5.5	39.5	55.0
Massachusetts	2.0	20.5	77.5	6.5	36.3	57.2	5.0	42.1	52.9
Michigan	2.8	43.8	53.4	7.4	42.7	49.9	7.1	64.7	28.2
Minnesota	2.7	38.2	59.1	6.1	56.6	37.3	5.0	57.6	37.4
Mississippi	9.2	52.4	38.4	24.1	53.1	22.8	14.0	54.9	31.1
Missouri	4.8	30.5	64.7	9.7	36.7	53.6	6.5	39.0	54.5
Montana	3.7	25.4	70.9	8.4	49.3	42.2	11.3	44.9	43.8
Nebraska	4.3	4.3	91.4	7.9	18.2	73.9	6.9	37.1	56.0
Nevada	9.4	56.4	34.2	8.6	58.5	32.9	4.6	32.4	63.0
New Hampshire	4.6	5.3	90.1	5.1	6.8	88.1	4.0	8.9	87.1
New Jersey	1.5	24.1	74.4	4.1	40.4	55.5	3.7	41.3	55.0
New Mexico	15.2	69.4	15.4	16.6	63.4	20.0	13.4	72.5	14.1
New York	1.2	39.3	59.5	5.0	40.6	54.4	6.0	42.2	51.8
North Carolina	4.7	68.3	27.0	15.2	62.4	22.3	6.9	68.7	24.4
North Dakota	1.7	31.3	67.0	7.7	46.5	45.7	13.0	40.3	46.7
Ohio	2.8	30.3	66.9	7.7	40.6	51.6	5.8	42.1	52.1
Oklahoma	7.2	42.2	50.6	11.8	43.8	44.4	9.1	60.2	30.7
Oregon	4.5	29.5	66.0	9.9	35.5	54.6	7.0	56.8	36.2
Pennsylvania	1.8	50.2	48.0	8.5	45.0	46.5	6.0	38.2	55.8
Rhode Island	4.0	18.1	77.9	5.9	38.8	55.4	5.6	41.6	52.8
South Carolina	5.8	70.9	23.3	14.9	56.8	28.3	8.2	52.1	39.7
South Dakota	5.3	8.6	86.1	13.9	20.8	65.3	10.5	35.9	53.6
Tennessee	3.7	54.0	42.3	14.0	48.3	37.7	8.8	47.2	44.0
Texas	4.6	49.9	45.5	11.0	50.1	38.9	8.5	42.4	49.1
Utah	5.3	41.9	52.8	7.8	54.0	38.2	7.0	61.1	31.9
Vermont	0.8	23.1	76.1	7.7	28.0	64.2	5.8	74.4	19.8
Virginia	9.5	36.5	54.0	9.5	40.9	49.6	5.2	33.8	61.0
Washington	5.7	61.1	33.2	8.6	70.8	20.6	6.8	64.6	28.6
West Virginia	4.2	54.2	41.6	10.6	60.1	29.3	8.5	62.7	28.8
Wisconsin	2.9	21.3	75.8	5.5	37.6	56.8	4.6	53.4	42.0
Wyoming	5.7	45.7	48.6	6.6	29.6	63.8	7.4	52.3	40.3

Note: Because of rounding, detail may not add to 100.

Table 3–5   Status of school districts by state.

State	Source: American Education Finance Association, 1998–99		Source: U.S. Department of Commerce, Bureau of the Census, 1997	
	Independent	Dependent	Independent	Dependent
Alabama	0	128	127	0
Alaska	0	53	0	53
Arizona	222	6	231	10
Arkansas	310	0	311	0
California	988	0	1,069	60
Colorado	176	0	180	0
Connecticut	0	166	17	149
Delaware	19	0	19	0
Florida	67	0	95	0
Georgia	180	0	180	0
Hawaii	0	1	0	1
Idaho	113	0	114	0
Illinois	897	0	944	0
Indiana	294	0	294	0
Iowa	375	0	394	0
Kansas	304	0	324	0
Kentucky	176	0	176	0
Louisiana	66	0	66	0
Maine	86	199	98	195
Maryland	0	24	0	41
Massachusetts	0	361	85	253
Michigan	555	0	584	89
Minnesota	350	0	360	2
Mississippi	152	0	164	4
Missouri	525	0	537	0
Montana	460	0	362	0
Nebraska	604	0	681	0
Nevada	17	0	17	0
New Hampshire	1	176	166	10
New Jersey	575	0	552	76
New Mexico	89	0	96	0
New York	677	5	686	36
North Carolina	2	115	0	175
North Dakota	231	0	237	0
Ohio	611	0	666	0
Oklahoma	547	0	578	0
Oregon	198	0	258	0
Pennsylvania	500	1	516	0
Rhode Island	0	36	4	32
South Carolina	59	27	91	0
South Dakota	176	0	177	0
Tennessee	0	138	14	126
Texas	1,042	0	1,087	0
Utah	40	0	40	0
Vermont	252	0	279	0
Virginia	0	137	1	134
Washington	296	0	296	0
West Virginia	55	0	55	0
Wisconsin	426	0	442	4
Wyoming	48	0	56	0

(AEFA) and the U.S. Census Bureau. Note that for some states, the sources differ in both the number of school districts listed and the classification of districts as independent or dependent. For example, for California, the AEFA reports 988 independent school districts and the Census Bureau reports 1,069 independent and 60 dependent school districts. For Massachusetts, the AEFA reports 361 dependent school districts and the Census Bureau reports 85 independent and 253 dependent school districts. It seems likely that these differences in classification stem from different definitions of fiscal independence.

The most important aspect of school system independence is a district's ability to determine the amount of local revenues to be raised for education. Typically, this involves establishing the tax rate that will be levied on each allowable tax base. State constitutions or legislative provisions, in turn, usually specify what revenue sources local jurisdictions, such as school districts, are allowed to tax.

In the case of dependent school districts, locally raised revenue is appropriated to the school district from the general fund of the municipal government on which the district is dependent. Thus, the school district must solicit funds from the same budget that supports police and fire protection, sanitation, parks and recreation, health and hospital services, and other functions.

There are, of course, several checks on the ability of independent school systems to raise local revenues. The first and most obvious is the ability of voters to elect school board members or, in the case of appointed school boards, to elect the public officials responsible for appointments. The leverage, of course, is that voters can vote out officials who do not operate according to their desires.

Referendum requirements create an even more direct form of voter control over local school taxing and spending decisions. Referendum requirements may apply to school districts' operational or capital spending, or both. Thirty-four states have provisions for referendum input into the operating budget process, although the exact nature of these provisions varies considerably. In some cases, referendum approval of each year's budget is required; in other cases, a referendum is necessary only if the budget requires a tax increase; and in still other cases, a referendum is required only for tax levies above a certain rate. In Maine, New Jersey, and Rhode Island, certain classifications of school districts have referendum requirements and others do not. In South Carolina, establishing referendum requirements is a local prerogative.

Figure 3–2 (page 70) summarizes state referendum requirements for operating and capital spending. Referendum requirements for capital spending come into play when school districts borrow funds through the issue of bonds, a process described in more detail later in this chapter.

In some states, the fiscal autonomy of local school districts is constrained by constitutional or statutory provisions that limit tax rates, spending levels, or increases in annual spending. As with referendum requirements, the nature of these limits varies considerably among the states that have them. Perhaps the most well known case is California, where Proposition 13 limits both the local property tax rate and the annual increase in property tax assessments, effectively transferring to the state the responsibility for raising additional tax dollars for public schools. Similarly rigid limitations have had the same effect in Nevada and New Mexico.

Indiana, Kansas, and New Jersey have a distinctive approach to limiting increases in per-pupil spending. In these states, the amount by which any district may increase spending depends on the district's current expenditure level. Although there are variations in the restrictions, the general policy allows districts with lower expenditure levels to increase spending by a greater amount

	Capital expenditures	Operational expenditures
Alabama	Simple majority on bonds	Tax levy above specified millage rate
Alaska	None	None
Arizona	Simple majority on bonds	Tax levy above specified millage rate
Arkansas	Simple majority on second-lien bonds	None
California	None	Two-thirds vote to levy special taxes for bond debt
Colorado	Simple majority on bonds, millage	Tax levy above specified millage rate
Connecticut	None	Annual budget
Delaware	Simple majority on bonds, millage	Tax increases
Florida	Simple majority on mill levies above 2 mills	Tax levy above specified millage rate, bond debt
Georgia	Simple majority on bonds	Tax levy above specified millage rate
Hawaii	None	None
Idaho	Two-thirds majority on multiyear levy	Tax levy above specified millage rate
Illinois	Simple majority on bonds	Bonds
Indiana	Simple majority on bonds	None
Iowa	None	None
Kansas	None	Tax increases, bonds
Kentucky	None	Tax levy above specified millage rate
Louisiana	None	Tax increases, bonds
Maine	Simple majority on bonds	Budgets for small districts, bonds
Maryland	None	None
Massachusetts	Simple majority on bonds	Tax levy above specified millage rate
Michigan	Simple majority on bonds, up to 7-mill levy	Tax levy above specified millage rate, tax increase
Minnesota	Simple majority on bonds	Tax levy above specified millage rate
Mississippi	60 percent approval on bonds	Tax increase greater than 10 percent above the specified millage rate
Missouri	Simple majority on bonds	Two-thirds vote on tax increases
Montana	Simple majority on bonds	Budget increases based on formula
Nebraska	None	None
Nevada	None	None
New Hampshire	Two-thirds majority on bonds	Annual budget, bonds
New Jersey	None	Annual budget for most school districts
New Mexico	Simple majority on bonds	None
New York	None	Annual budget
North Carolina	None	None
North Dakota	Simple majority on mill levies of up to 20 mills annually	Tax levy above specified millage rate
Ohio	None	Tax levy above specified millage rate
Oklahoma	None	State tax rate increases
Oregon	None	Tax increases
Pennsylvania	Simple majority on bonds	None
Rhode Island	None	Annual budgets for small districts
South Carolina	Simple majority on bonds	Varies by district
South Dakota	None	Tax levy above specified millage rate
Tennessee	None	None
Texas	Simple majority on bonds	Tax rate increases
Utah	None	Tax increases
Vermont	Simple majority on bonds	Annual budget, bonds
Virginia	None	None
Washington	Simple majority on bonds	Special levies
West Virginia	Simple majority on bonds	None
Wisconsin	Simple majority on bonds	Annual tax levy, bonds
Wyoming	None	None

Figure 3–2   Referendum
requirements for
bond issues by state,
1998–99.

than districts with higher expenditure levels. Over time, this form of limitation on spending increases should work to bring about greater equality in per-pupil spending across districts.

Revenue sources for locally raised funds

In states where districts have independent taxing authority, the ad valorem property tax is by far the most important source of locally raised revenue for schools. It accounts for more than 80 percent of total local revenues in most cases,[16] and in some states it is the sole tax base on which districts may impose their own levy. In addition to being applied to all nonexempt real estate, this tax often covers personal property, such as automobiles and boats; moreover, it applies in some cases to financial instruments, such as personally held mortgages.

Two features of the property tax are particularly noteworthy in the context of public school finance. The first, discussed earlier, concerns the various constitutional and statutory limitations that, in some states, restrict the ability of independent districts to set or raise property tax rates. The second is the marked differences in assessment practices and tax rate schedules, both within and between states.

Where they have independent taxing authority, school districts raise revenue from a variety of nonproperty tax sources, including local sales taxes, individual income or wage taxes, occupation taxes, motor vehicle license fees, severance taxes, interest income, and a share of the proceeds from court fines. However, these revenues constitute only an infra-marginal source of funds for school spending and cannot replace the property tax as the major source of revenue. In some cases school districts collect nonproperty tax revenues directly; in other cases they share the revenues with another local government. In cases where the state government sets the tax rate (e.g., for local sales taxes), school districts do not have any control over the level of revenues raised.

Identifying the sources of funds for school spending is more complicated in the case of dependent school districts. Because these districts rely on appropriations from local governments, the link between local tax dollars and school spending may be disguised. Analysis of the expenditure decisions of dependent school districts requires explicit consideration of two factors: (1) the potential trade-off between spending on schools and on other local public services and (2) the manner in which all funds, including intergovernmental aid, are allocated through the local public fisc. Funding issues are more complicated for dependent school districts because total state funding must be allocated across a range of functions (including police, fire, and roads, for example, as well as schools) and cannot be determined by the school district itself. However, because property taxes are the single most important source of revenue for municipal governments in most states, the discussion of state aid programs that follows treats them as the primary source of funds in the spending decisions of dependent, as well as independent, school districts.

State aid programs

As noted earlier, a significant trend in K–12 public school finance over the past forty years is the marked increase in the relative share of revenues provided by state governments. During the 1960s and, especially, the 1970s, most states not only increased their level of funding but also altered the way in which they disbursed funds to local school districts. These shifts began as a result of a series of state court cases; the most well known of these was *Serrano v. Priest,* in California. The plaintiffs in these cases argued that because school finance relied so heavily on property taxation, children in districts with low property wealth per pupil were denied access to educational resources—and hence educational opportunities—that were comparable to those enjoyed by children who lived in communities with greater property wealth. (Critical to this argument, of course, is the assumption that there is a direct relationship between the quality of education and school spending per pupil.)

Determining the appropriate standard by which to measure the degree of equity in educational opportunity across school districts is difficult both conceptually and operationally.[17] On conceptual grounds, should the pursuit of equity entail public policies that provide more resources to poor districts while restraining wealthy districts from providing above-average education? Or should the pursuit of equity simply ensure the provision of additional resources to poor districts? On operational grounds, if fiscal equity is measured by actual expenditures, should these expenditures be cost-adjusted to take into account differences in urban versus rural areas, or differences in teacher salaries? Resolving these issues has proved a difficult task for both academic researchers and educational policy makers.

The many court challenges (which had varying outcomes, depending on state constitutional provisions) have prompted widespread legislative activity. The result has been an increased emphasis, in state aid allocation formulas, on the equalization of per-pupil spending across districts. State aid programs designed to promote equitable spending across school districts fall into two broad classifications: foundation programs and power-equalization programs (see Figure 3–3).

Foundation programs

Foundation programs establish a state-guaranteed minimum level of expenditure per pupil. A state may fully fund this level of expenditure, or it may require each district to contribute a share. Where a local share is required, the amount generally depends on the district's wealth. Most foundation programs use property value per pupil as the measure of wealth; the local share is the amount of revenue that would have been raised from the property tax if the rate were uniform throughout the state.

According to this criterion, the tax effort required to support the local share of the foundation spending level is the same in each district, regardless of property wealth per pupil. Because the state contribution equals the difference between the foundation expenditure and the local share, state aid is greater for less wealthy districts, where taxing at the statewide rate generates a smaller local contribution. In most states with foundation programs, districts may augment the minimum level of spending with additional locally raised revenues.

Power-equalization programs

Power-equalization programs guarantee that each district will have the ability to generate the same revenue per pupil from a given tax rate, regardless of the size of the district's tax base. Each district sets its own local tax rate. If the revenues raised locally from this levy do not yield an amount per pupil that equals the guaranteed level, the state provides the difference.

Power-equalization programs come in two common forms: guaranteed tax base and guaranteed tax yield. Since, for any property tax levy, the yield equals the rate times the base, specifying either the yield or the base at any given tax

Figure 3–3 State funding programs for capital and operational aid, 1998–99.

	Capital funding	Operational funding
Alabama	Flat grant/guaranteed yield	Foundation
Alaska	Flat grant	Foundation
Arizona	Foundation (NLE)	Foundation
Arkansas	Foundation (RLE)	Foundation
California	State bonds	Foundation/flat grant
Colorado	Foundation (RLE)	Foundation
Connecticut	Percentage equalization	Foundation
Delaware	Percentage equalization	Flat grant/equalization
Florida	Foundation (RLE)	Foundation
Georgia	Percentage equalization	Foundation/equalization
Hawaii	Full state funding	Full state funding
Idaho	None	Foundation
Illinois	Percentage equalization	Foundation/flat grant
Indiana	Flat grant	Guaranteed tax base
Iowa	None	Foundation
Kansas	Percentage equalization	Foundation
Kentucky	Flat grant	Foundation
Louisiana	None	Foundation
Maine	Percentage equalization	Foundation
Maryland	Percentage equalization	Foundation
Massachusetts	Percentage equalization	Foundation
Michigan	None	Foundation
Minnesota	Percentage equalization	Foundation
Mississippi	Flat grant	Foundation
Missouri	None	Foundation
Montana	Percentage equalization	Foundation
Nebraska	None	Foundation
Nevada	None	Foundation
New Hampshire	Flat grant	Foundation
New Jersey	Percentage equalization	Foundation
New Mexico	Power equalization	Foundation
New York	Percentage equalization	Foundation/percentage equalization with ceiling and flat grant
North Carolina	None	Foundation
North Dakota	None	Foundation
Ohio	Power equalization	Foundation
Oklahoma	None	Foundation
Oregon	None	Foundation
Pennsylvania	Percentage equalization	Foundation
Rhode Island	Percentage equalization	Foundation
South Carolina	Flat grant	Foundation
South Dakota	None	Foundation
Tennessee	Foundation (RLE)	Foundation
Texas	Guaranteed yield	Foundation with guaranteed yield
Utah	Percentage equalization	Foundation
Vermont	Flat grant	Flat grant with guaranteed yield
Virginia	Flat grant	Foundation
Washington	Percentage equalization	Full state aid
West Virginia	Funding available	Foundation
Wisconsin	Guaranteed tax base	Guaranteed tax base
Wyoming	None	Foundation

Notes: NLE indicates that no local effort is required.
RLE indicates that a local effort is required.

rate effectively establishes the other. Thus, the two programs are functionally equivalent.

In implementing a power-equalization program, two important policy elements must be addressed. The first is whether the program requires recapture. This issue arises in the case of wealthy districts where the amount of revenue generated at a given tax rate exceeds the amount guaranteed under the state aid program. Under a recapture provision, such a district must remit to the state any excess revenue generated. This money is then used, together with state funds, to provide aid to districts where locally raised revenues fall short of the state guarantee.

For a power-equalization program to truly equalize revenue-raising potential, regardless of differences in local wealth, a recapture provision is necessary. Thus, a program with a recapture provision is sometimes referred to as a "pure" power equalization program.[18] However, recapture provisions tend to be unpopular among the residents of wealthier districts. As a result, and undoubtedly for political reasons, wealthy districts are commonly allowed to retain all locally raised revenues; for districts that raise less than the guaranteed amount of revenue at a given tax rate, the state alone makes up the difference.

The second policy decision that must be addressed is whether to impose a limit on the extent to which the state aid program will augment local spending increases. From the perspective of a receiving district, a power-equalization program constitutes a matching grant where the matching rate depends on how far the amount of local revenue raised at a given tax rate falls short of the program guarantee. Districts with less wealth per pupil, for which the state must provide a greater percentage of the total revenue raised at any tax rate, receive a higher matching rate. As a result, the cost of raising an additional dollar of expenditure per pupil is the same for all districts.[19]

Under an open-ended matching program, no limit exists on the tax rate—and hence the total expenditure per pupil—to which the state subsidy applies. Under a closed-end matching program, a limit is imposed on the amount of expenditure to which the matching rate applies. The rationale for imposing such a cap is to limit the exposure of state budgets to the decisions of local school districts.

Other forms of state aid

Three other classifications of state aid are worth noting, although none is as widely used as the foundation and power-equalization programs.

Flat grants   State aid on a flat-grant basis provides a set dollar amount per some measurement unit (e.g., number of pupils in daily attendance, full-time equivalent employees) for each school district in the state. Such programs do not take into consideration the fiscal capacities of individual school districts.[20] When states adopted new programs to pursue greater equity in spending across school districts, flat-grant programs were often replaced by foundation programs or power equalization.

Percentage equalization   Under a percentage-equalization program, each district receives a certain amount of aid per pupil (or per instructional unit) that is calculated to give relatively more aid to districts with less fiscal capacity. This program can take several forms: in some cases, at least a certain level of expenditure is required; in others, no particular level of local effort is required.

Generally, percentage-equalization programs operate as the functional equivalent of either a foundation or a power-equalization program.[21]

Full state funding Hawaii has a single statewide school district funded from the state budget. The American Education Finance Association (AEFA) also classifies Washington State as providing full state funding.[22]

State aid classifications

Aid to local school districts in most states consists of a basic instructional aid program (operational) plus categorical aid for a variety of special purposes (e.g., capital funding). The AEFA classifications presented in Table 3–5 are determined on the basis of both capital and operational funding.

There are two important observations regarding state aid programs that are not directly observable from Table 3–5. First, for programs based on per-pupil expenditures, the total amount of state aid that a district receives is equal to the amount of state aid per pupil, multiplied by the number of pupils. However, states use a variety of techniques to measure the number of pupils. Two popular measures are average daily membership (ADM) and average daily attendance (ADA). ADM is an approximate measure of average total enrollment throughout the academic year, while ADA includes only pupils who are present on the day or days when measurement occurs. Thus, for purposes of determining total state aid, ADA penalizes districts with high rates of absenteeism.[23]

Second, state aid programs commonly include provisions designed to address special circumstances. For example, to assist rural districts, additional aid may be awarded on the basis of low population density; to assist urban districts, additional aid may be awarded on the basis of high population density. Another reason for such provisions is to provide relief for districts experiencing rapid increases or declines in enrollments. In some instances, such special provisions are contained in the basic state aid program—for example, as a factor in the determination of a foundation expenditure level. In other instances, these provisions are implemented through special categorical grants that supplement the basic program. In yet other instances, special circumstances are addressed through hold-harmless provisions.[24] Another frequent use of hold-harmless provisions is to provide a minimum flat grant per pupil to wealthy districts that would otherwise not qualify for any aid under a foundation or power-equalization program.

This discussion of the diversity in the structure of state aid programs suggests an extraordinarily important conclusion: extreme caution must be exercised when comparing, across states, the level of support that states provide for K–12 education.

Local bond issues

A capital expenditure project typically begins with a decision to expand or enhance the physical facilities of the school district. The next step generally involves initiating a bond issue to raise the required local revenue. As the district prepares to issue a bond, it must decide whether to have it rated by an independent bond-rating agency. Because these agencies charge a fee to conduct bond ratings, the district must undertake a cost-benefit analysis in order to make this decision.

The stated purpose of the rating is to indicate to potential bond buyers how great the risk is that the district will default on future payments. In practice, the bond market uses the rating to determine the creditworthiness of the district, and this information, in turn, influences the yield (interest rate) at which the bond offering can be issued. The report (or lack thereof) of a rating agency thus plays a significant role in determining the final yield on the bond issue. (For more on bonds, see Chapter 14 of this volume.)

Once a bond has been rated, the school district must determine whether to improve the bond rating by purchasing bond insurance. Again, because there is a premium charged to cover this guarantee, this determination also requires a cost-benefit analysis. The bond-insurance companies are key players in this part of the process, and they evaluate the districts in a different way than do the rating agencies.[25] (See Chapter 14 for a general discussion of bond insurance.)

Summary

This chapter has reviewed a number of important aspects of financing for elementary and secondary school districts. Over the past forty years, two trends stand out: an overall increase in per-pupil expenditures and a growing role for states in the provision of school funding. Nevertheless, generalizations about typical school financing arrangements are difficult. For example, because costs vary so greatly between and even within states, it is difficult to make meaningful comparisons of per-pupil expenditures. Similarly, states are subject to vastly differing requirements with respect to the property tax, which remains the principal source of funding for education, and to the provision of equal educational opportunity.

1 U.S. Department of Commerce, Bureau of the Census, "Summary of State and Local Finances by Level of Government: 2000–01," table 1, available at www.census.gov.

2 U.S. Department of Education, National Center for Education Statistics, *Digest of Education Statistics 2002* (Washington, D.C.: U.S. Department of Education, November 2001), table 168.

3 U.S. Department of Commerce, Bureau of Economic Analysis, "Percent Change from Preceding Period in Real Gross Domestic Product," table 1.1.1, available at www.bea.doc.gov; and U.S. Department of Commerce, Bureau of the Census, *Historical Income Tables,* "Type of Family by Mean and Median Income: 1947 to 2001," table F-7, available at www.census.gov/hhes/income/histinc/f07.html.

4 Bureau of Economic Analysis, "Percent Change from Preceding Period," table 1.1.1.

5 Bureau of the Census, "Mean and Median Income."

6 National Center for Education Statistics, *Digest of Education Statistics 2002,* table 168. Conclusions about the effect of increased spending on educational output must be made with caution, however. A substantial portion of the new resources devoted to school spending has been directed at providing greater educational opportunity for targeted groups, such as students with disabilities or special needs. Such programs often incur significant costs that do not necessarily have a large impact on the average scores of standardized national tests.

7 Ibid., table 3.

8 Ibid.

9 A pooled, cross-sectioned, time-series regression revealed that interstate variations in teachers' salaries and in the ratio of teachers per enrolled pupil explain, statistically, 85 percent of the variation in current expenditures per pupil in average daily attendance across states and over time. See Vincent G. Munley, *The Structure of State Aid to Elementary and Secondary Education* (Washington, D.C.: U.S. Advisory Commission on Intergovernmental Relations, December 1990).

10 National Center for Education Statistics, *Digest of Education Statistics 2002,* table 157.

11 Because of differences in the way that states report contributions for employee benefits—particularly pension plans, social security, and Medicare—it is necessary to interpret Figure 3–1 with some caution. For example, some states include state funds contributed for teachers' benefits as part of total state aid to local school districts while other states do not. This reporting difference could have a noticeable impact on the distribution of state-local shares in the figure because for some states that count benefit contributions as part of total state aid, such contributions account for more than 20 percent of total aid.

12 Some states require insurance companies to pay them a small premium for the ability to underwrite policies in that state.

13 Catherine C. Sielke et al., eds., *Public School Finance Programs of the United States and Canada: 1998–99,* National Center for Education Statistics no. 2001309 (Washington, D.C.: U.S. Department of Education, 2001).

14 U.S. Department of Commerce, Bureau of the Census, *Government Organization,* 1987 Census of Governments, vol. 1, no. 1 (Washington, D.C.: U.S. Government Printing Office, 1989), xii.

15 For an extended discussion of how dependent school districts are organized, see Bureau of the Census, *Government Organization.*

16 Sielke et al., *Public School Finance.*

17 For an excellent, detailed discussion of the complex issues involved in assessing equity in school finance,

see Robert Berne and Leanna Stiefel, *The Measurement of Equity in School Finance* (Baltimore: Johns Hopkins University Press, 1984), especially chap. 2.

18 See, for example, Robert P. Inman, "Optimal Fiscal Reform for Metropolitan Schools," *American Economic Review* 68 (March 1978).

19 Except in the absence of a recapture provision, where the cost is lower for wealthy districts.

20 Richard Salmon et al., eds., *Public School Finance Programs in the United States and Canada: 1986–1987* (Sarasota, Fla.: American Education Finance Association, 1988), 5.

21 See Munley, *Structure of State Aid,* 48.

22 Salmon et al., *Public School Finance Programs.* According to the AEFA, "If the government provided a high level of total revenue receipts (over two-thirds) coupled with fiscal equalization programs that deducted much of the remaining local revenue from state allocations, the states employing such programs were classified as fully state funded." Nevertheless, both the AEFA and the U.S. Census Bureau classify all of Washington's school districts as independent because they are permitted to issue bonds for capital expenditures (see Table 3–5).

23 Another element that some states factor into aid calculations is the relative cost of educating students at various grade levels. To reflect such differences in cost, states may multiply the number of pupils by a weighted average, such as 0.5 for kindergarten, 1.0 for elementary school, and between 1.0 and 1.5 for secondary school.

24 Hold-harmless provisions typically place a limit on the percentage increase (or decrease) in the amount of aid that a district receives from one year to the next.

25 For more on debt funding for school districts, see Mary H. Harris, "Bond Ratings and Bond Insurance: Market and Empirical Analysis for School Districts," *Developments in School Finance, 2001–2002,* NCES no. 2003-403 (Washington, D.C.: Institution of Education Sciences, U.S. Department of Education, June 2003). Also see Mary H. Harris and Vincent G. Munley, "The Sequence of Decisions Facing School District Officials in the Bond Rating Process: A Multistage Model," *Journal of Education Finance* 28, no. 1 (summer 2002): 75–96. For a full discussion of all aspects of debt financing, see A. John Vogt, *Capital Budgeting and Finance: A Guide for Local Governments* (Washington, D.C.: International City/County Management Association, 2004).

Local government expenditures and revenues

Roy W. Bahl Jr.

How should local governments set their budget priorities? Budget decisions are ultimately political. But well before the council determines final budget choices, a great deal of hard economic analysis will have been undertaken.

This chapter is about the analytic framework for setting local government budget priorities. It begins with a review of the possible criteria for choosing a revenue and expenditure structure, and then describes the fiscal choices that U.S. state and local governments actually make. Finally, the chapter considers the pressures that local government fiscal planners will face in the coming years.

The fiscal roles of government

In his classic book *The Theory of Public Finance,* the economist Richard Musgrave laid out a set of considerations for those who make decisions about how to raise and spend the public's money.[1] In Musgrave's view, three key concerns drive budget decisions, and the trade-offs among these concerns determine the nature of the budget. The first is allocation: What services will be provided? The second is distribution: Who will benefit from new services, and who will pay for them? The third is economic development: What levels of income and job growth are required? Local government financial planners—finance officers, budget officers, and chief administrators—might begin their evaluation of alternative fiscal actions by considering each of these three issues.

Allocation

The most important fiscal role of local government is to decide on the level and mix of taxes and expenditures that best match the needs and preferences of the local population. That local governments take this allocation function seriously is evidenced by the wide variety of choices they actually make. For example, in Arizona, the share of local government expenditures devoted to education is 36 percent in Tucson but 46 percent in Yuma; in Pennsylvania, the share of local expenditures for police is 2.9 percent in the Reading metropolitan area but 5.6 percent in Philadelphia.[2] Average effective property tax rates also vary widely: for example, the effective tax rate on a primary residence with a value of $80,000 is a little over 1 percent in metropolitan Phoenix but about half as much in metropolitan Denver.[3] Underlying such variations are a number of other important choices, such as whether to hire more firefighters or pay current firefighters a higher wage; whether to provide refuse collection or to contract out the service; whether to purchase a CAT scanner or a school bus.

In making such choices, local government officials and managers can be guided by three general criteria: (1) economic efficiency, (2) technical efficiency, and, when jurisdictions or interests overlap, (3) net social benefit. Usually, there are good justifications for most expenditure programs, and local officials are forced to make difficult trade-offs: as will be discussed later in this section, this compels local government officials to clearly identify their priorities.

Economic efficiency　Ideally, the price that each citizen pays for public services should equal the value of those services to that citizen. Thus, economic efficiency requires that government fiscal decisions match local preferences for public services. In other words, the government should try to deliver the package of government services and taxes that the population wants. But how does the government know what local citizens want? A number of factors can affect the "preferred" package: Syracuse requires more snow removal than does St. Petersburg, which requires more services for elderly residents. Cleveland and Buffalo must maintain an aging stock of public capital, whereas growing cities in the South and West must allocate more funds to the development of new infrastructure. Large cities must address mass-transit problems that small cities may not share.

Public service packages also vary with the peculiar preferences of the local population. New York residents have historically preferred a relatively large government sector, a progressive tax system, and substantial support for public education; Florida residents prefer a smaller public sector, no individual income tax, and a smaller allocation for public education. In some states, these differences are actually legislated: Hawaii laws ensure, for example, the fiscal dominance of the state government over localities, whereas New York laws assign a relatively greater fiscal role to local government.

If allocation decisions are to meet the criterion of economic efficiency, local government decision makers need to recognize citizens' preferences. This task may seem easy, since voters make their wishes known through school budget votes, bond referendum votes, and general elections. Even citizen surveys might be used to help make budget allocations. Nevertheless, local officials can easily misread a community's preferences—and, in any case, voters may have mixed views on what they want or may be unable to reveal their preferences on every issue (e.g., there is no separate vote on the police budget). In addition, preferences change. Two surveys of public opinion on taxes conducted by the Advisory Commission on Intergovernmental Relations (ACIR) offer an interesting example. When respondents were asked, in 1972, which tax was the least fair, 45 percent named the property tax and 19 percent the federal income tax. When the same question was asked in a 1993 survey, 26 percent of respondents named the property tax and 36 percent the federal income tax.[4] Finally, preferences may be difficult to read because voters are sometimes irrational in their expectations: they often demand *both* lower taxes and better public services.

Technical efficiency　Technical efficiency refers to the provision of services at least cost. Local officials can take a number of actions to lower the cost of operations:

Increase the productivity of workers (through training, revised job rules, or new management and work procedures)

Improve long-range planning

Substitute capital for labor

Reduce interest costs on local debt

Capture economies of scale in service delivery

Contract with private organizations for service delivery.

But however attractive each option may be, none is without its social or economic price. Productivity improvement, for example, is especially appealing because it arouses little political opposition (who could oppose a more productive public sector labor force?). But improved productivity may result in the elimination of "excess" public workers. Although decreasing the size of the workforce may help the budget, it may harm the local employment situation and may prove to be a politically unattractive policy.

Examples of improved planning include establishing a schedule for maintenance of the capital stock and instituting a multiyear fiscal planning model. In the long run, such actions can significantly improve the efficiency of government operations and probably reduce the unit cost of services provided, but a significant outlay may be necessary to establish and maintain the planning effort.

Examples of substituting capital for labor are computerization, newer police cars and fire trucks, less labor-intensive refuse collection systems, and the relocation of certain public facilities, such as fire stations. Although all these actions may be cost savers, they also imply a substantial initial capital outlay.

Actions that lead to a higher bond rating or improve the marketability of a bond issue can reduce interest costs. A local government can increase the attractiveness of an issue by dedicating a portion of general revenue to debt repayment, purchasing bond insurance, or gaining a state government guarantee or bank letter of credit.[5] However, these actions also entail costs: a dedicated revenue stream weakens the general fiscal base available for other purposes, and bond insurance is purchased for a fee. Moreover, many local governments cannot, in fact, easily take advantage of such enhancements: a state guarantee is only as good as the inherent creditworthiness of that state, and the value of a bank letter of credit is tied to the credit rating of the bank that issues it. Thus, only local governments that have access either to a creditworthy state government or to a bank with a high credit rating are in a position to employ these cost reduction measures.

Economies of scale can be realized by expanding the geographic area over which a public service is delivered. These economies are a principal reason that regional and consolidated service districts are common for certain services, such as water and sewers, hospitals, parks, and physical planning. However, even though regional service provision usually lowers unit costs, it also entails some loss of local control and, consequently, leads to more difficulty in satisfying local preferences.

Finally, privatization of public services can improve technical efficiency. Refuse collection is the most commonly mentioned example, but numerous other services are amenable to private delivery. On the one hand, turning a service over to the private sector can relieve the local government of some responsibility, and competition among contractors may increase the overall quality of service. On the other hand, in the case of services that have a broad social purpose, privatization may impose a substantial social cost if it reduces the level of output. Moreover, it is by no means certain that all services can be delivered less expensively by the private sector. In addition to the payment of contractors' fees, private contracting involves extensive government administration and monitoring.[6]

Net social benefit   Local decisions may impose costs or confer benefits on other jurisdictions. For example, a community may overuse water from the local river, depriving adjacent communities of an adequate supply; unbridled growth in a suburban community may increase the number of commuters to the central city, placing an undue burden on central-city services; and the failure or inability to provide adequate primary and vocational education in one community may lead to crime in another. When such externalities, or spillover effects, are involved, local officials should consider net social benefit, not just the needs and interests of their particular constituency. Nevertheless, the decisions of local officials are usually based on what is in the best interests of their constituents, not on what is of the greatest benefit to society.

Policy makers typically respond in one of three ways to the spillover problem: (1) the federal or state government may either coerce or induce local governments to provide the "right" amount of a public service; (2) local governments may engage in some form of intergovernmental contract to compensate one another for external social costs incurred or benefits received; (3) a local government may expand its service boundaries so as to "internalize the externalities."

Trade-offs   Local government officials, even if guided by sound economic reasoning, face some difficult choices in allocating services. Economic efficiency is best served by units of government that are small enough to allow preferences to be taken into account. In fact, one economist has suggested that a theoretically ideal arrangement for metropolitan governance would consist of many different local governments offering different packages of public services and taxes.[7] In this consumer-sovereign world, consumer-residents could "vote with their feet" by choosing a community whose tax and public service package best matched their own preferences.

In contrast, considerations of technical efficiency and net social benefit seem to argue for less emphasis on local preferences and greater emphasis on the larger governmental unit. Thus, technical efficiency and net social benefit become arguments for areawide consolidation of some services, for metropolitan governance, and for regional tax sharing. The trade-off is that in exchange for reduced unit costs and equitable handling of spillover effects, residents may be required to relinquish some local control over their service package. A particularly bothersome problem is that of unfunded mandates. In this case, the higher-level government (state or federal) might impose some restrictions on local governments to accommodate the regional or national interest. The mandate might take the form of an environmental protection program, or worker safety initiatives, or even school lunch programs. Sometimes the higher-level government mandates these programs but does not provide the necessary funding; hence, local resources are at risk and the local budget process is circumvented.

Distribution

Distribution is another major fiscal role of local government. How should the benefits and burdens of local budgets be divided among residents? Economics and history have shown that because people are relatively free to move across local boundaries, local governments cannot successfully use transfer payments to redistribute income. This does not mean, however, that local government officials should abandon all involvement whatsoever in income redistribution. After all, local governments collect a significant portion (18 percent) of all taxes and make a significant portion (27 percent) of all expenditures; they are thus in a position to have a substantial impact on the relative well-being of lower-income families.

One of the three major ways local governments can affect the distribution of real income is by choosing *where* to deliver services. For example, a city might decide that in lower-income areas it will increase the frequency of refuse collection, establish neighborhood health clinics, provide special park facilities, or improve police protection. Such decisions can provide, in effect, a subsidy to low-income neighborhoods. (Note that such decisions can be made even after the overall size of the budget has been settled.)

The second way that local governments can affect the distribution of real income is in their choice of services to be delivered. Most local governments have enough discretion to choose among programs that benefit different economic groups: low-income residents, for example, tend to benefit most from social services; all residents benefit from environmental protection programs; and middle- and upper-income residents are likely to benefit from programs that reduce traffic congestion or improve airports. In some cases, it is possible to predict which choices will primarily benefit the low-income population. In other cases—such as choosing between spending more for social services (e.g., subsidized housing and welfare) and devoting the funds to economic development programs that may produce more jobs—the final distributional effects are not as clear. The debate on such issues is endless, and there are no easy guidelines.

The third way that local governments can affect income distribution is through the revenue side of the local budget: that is, through the levy of property, income, and sales taxes, and through the system of user charges. A local government can decide, for example, what proportion of local transit system expenditures will be financed by fares and what proportion by local general revenues. It should be emphasized, however, that decisions about what kinds of taxes to levy and how to structure those taxes are often made at the state level. For example, the state government decides whether circuit breakers can be used to grant elderly and low-income residents property tax relief, whether local governments can levy local sales or income taxes, and whether food, medicine, and clothing will be included in the sales tax base.

Economic development

Budget planners often ask whether their local government can use fiscal policy to promote economic development. How this question is answered depends on who is asked. Virtually every local government has some sort of development agency dedicated to promoting local job growth. Officials from this agency will point to the many instruments that the local government has available to lower the cost of doing business for prospective firms: although the most obvious incentive is lower taxes, local governments may also offer nontax incentives such as subsidized construction costs, land assembly, and special education programs.

Those who research these questions, however, are skeptical about the positive fiscal impacts of incentive programs. Study after study has shown that factors such as location, energy costs, and the availability of a skilled labor supply are far more important in location decisions than are local tax and expenditure policies. The current consensus seems to be that fiscal incentives have some positive impact but that it is likely to be small and to be most effective in helping local governments compete with other localities within the same region.[8] (But even this tempered enthusiasm for incentives does not apply to every type of incentive; researchers are particularly skeptical, for example, about programs such as enterprise zones.)[9]

It is difficult to develop a prescriptive guideline that would fit every community. Local officials usually try to do what they are most capable of doing: creating an economic development program that best fits local circumstances. Even if in the final analysis, for example, tax concessions are deemed unimportant, local government officials are very aware that other communities offer such incentives. Because failing to implement tax concessions signals that the climate is "hostile" to development, these and other incentives may be necessary defensive actions.

Ultimately, decisions about the nature and extent of economic development efforts are yet another fiscal choice. How much is a local government willing to charge its current citizens, in the form of higher taxes or lower levels of public service, to provide tax incentives for economic development? The answer to this question depends on local officials' evaluation of a number of factors: the probability that the fiscal incentive will work; the need for jobs in the local area; the likelihood that the new jobs will go to local residents; and the potential effect of any new industry on local government costs and revenues. (For a detailed discussion of economic development issues, see Chapter 13 of this volume.)

Expenditures

How do local governments actually spend their funds? How much do they spend, and what patterns are "average" or "normal"? To what extent are allocation, distribution, and economic development objectives served?

The magnitude of local expenditures

An examination of expenditure patterns reveals that local governments play an important and distinctive role in the American system of fiscal federalism. As shown in Table 4–1, local governments account for more than 28 percent of all government expenditures. They also play the primary role in delivering education services, accounting for nearly three-fourths of all government expenditures on education. Local governments are much less involved in the provision of health services and income security; as the table illustrates, little of the income redistribution that occurs through transfer payments takes place at the local level.

Table 4–2 shows the distribution of expenditures by U.S. local governments. The first column shows how local government resources are distributed according to object and function—for example, 13.7 percent for capital outlay and 1.4 percent for assistance and subsidies. The bottom panel of the table shows the distribution of local government expenditures by function. More than 40 percent of local government resources are allocated to education services; no other function comes close. The remaining columns in that panel show how these totals are divided among municipalities, counties, and special districts. It is not surprising that special districts, which include school districts, also account for more than 40 percent of total local government spending—more than the percentage accounted for by either municipalities or counties.

Table 4–3 shows selected indicators of trends in local government expenditures between 1992 and 2000. Per capita expenditures by local governments—the average amount that local governments spend per person—increased significantly during the period covered in the table. However, the local gov-

Table 4–1   Local government share of all government expenditures, 2001.

Expenditure category	Total (in billions of $)	Local government share (%)
Education	519	73.6
Health[a]	658	3.0
Income security[b]	814	4.4
Total[c]	2,847[d]	28.4

[a] Including Medicare.
[b] Including social security.
[c] Excluding defense.
[d] Including functions not shown separately.

Table 4–2 Local government expenditures, 1996–97.

Expenditures	Distribution of total local government expenditures by object and by function (%)	Distribution of total government expenditures by type of government (%)		
		Municipalities[a]	Counties	Special districts[b]
Total by object[c]	100.0	36.1	23.7	41.5
Current operations	77.6	33.4	22.8	43.8
Capital outlay	13.7	40.8	17.9	41.3
Assistance and subsidies	1.4	23.1	76.9	—
Interest on debt	5.4	41.0	23.5	35.4
Insurance benefits and repayments	1.9	78.1	19.3	—
Total by function[c]	100.0	33.0	26.1	42.5
Education services	42.9	10.8	8.9	81.1
Transportation	6.2	56.5	32.7	11.6
Social services	13.3	19.8	47.4	12.6
Public safety	10.4	58.9	18.2	3.1
Environment and housing	11.1	14.6	7.0	5.4
Administration	5.4	23.7	37.2	0.0
Interest on general debt	4.9	40.3	28.2	31.5
Other and unallocable	5.6	63.8	36.6	—

Notes: Figures such as those shown in the table are available from the Census of Governments, which is compiled in the "2" and "7" years. The table reports data from the 1997 volume.
Because of rounding, detail may not add to totals.
(—) indicates that data are unavailable.

[a] Includes townships.
[b] Includes school districts.
[c] Some expenditures could not be allocated by function; hence, the allocations across local governments by object and by function do not apply to the same total amounts.

Table 4–3 Trends in local government revenues, expenditures, and employment.

	1992	1996	2000
Local government own-source revenues			
Per capita	$1,416	$1,654	$1,915
As a percentage of gross national product (GNP)	5.7	5.6	5.5
As a percentage of state government revenues[a]	82.3	79.9	75.9
As a percentage of total government revenues[a]	21.7	21.9	20.6
Local government direct expenditures			
Per capita	$2,565	$2,963	$3,502
As a percentage of GNP	10.4	10.0	10.0
As a percentage of state direct expenditures[b]	131.2	129.4	130.2
As a percentage of total government expenditures[b]	26.1	27.4	29.2
Local government employment			
Per 10,000 population	377.4	382.1[d]	392.9
As a percentage of total government employment[c]	59.4	61.2	62.3

[a] From own sources.
[b] After intergovernmental transfers.
[c] Including the military.
[d] This figure is for 1997.

ernment sector (whether measured in terms of revenues raised or expenditures made) has not increased in importance relative to GNP since 1992. Local government expenditures have more or less kept pace with state government expenditures, but locally raised revenues have not kept pace with state-raised revenues. The last row of the table shows that local governments continue to account for more than half of all public employment in the United States.

Determinants of local expenditures

The level and mix of local government expenditures are determined by myriad economic and demographic factors. Some of these (e.g., federal and state policies) are largely beyond local government control. Others, such as the performance of the local economy, are not easily influenced, in the short run, by local policy. But local government officials still have a great deal of choice: depending on their preferences and those of voters, they can raise taxes or lower service levels; alter the service mix; or change the compensation program for local government employees.

The job of local fiscal planners is to identify the determinants of public spending, estimate their potential effects on local budgets, and present the available fiscal choices to the public. These tasks can be accomplished most effectively if the local finance officer has a framework within which to consider the factors that determine the level and mix of items in the government budget.

The determinants of local government spending can be thought of within a demand-supply framework. After all, each year's budget is an attempt by local officials to balance demand (the quantity and quality of public services local residents would like to have at any given "tax price") and supply (the quantity and quality of services the local government will provide at given levels of revenue, or "tax prices"). In addition to demand and supply, certain other external factors—a national or regional recession, for example—can influence expenditure levels.

Demand factors   The demand for public services, as expressed in community preferences, is affected by four major factors: (1) population shifts, (2) national economic performance, (3) the relative price of services, and (4) changes in income level. Each of these factors will affect the demand for public services and, ultimately, the growth of local government expenditures. However, because the precise effect of these and other factors varies from one locality to another, it is impossible to make an unambiguous statement about their influence on the growth of public expenditures. Much depends on local preferences, the persuasiveness of local politicians, and the ability of local officials to inform citizens of the choices available to them. The task of local government fiscal planners is to try to anticipate changes in "tastes" for local public goods and then to take them into account in the multiyear budgeting of expenditures.

Population shifts   A community's preferences for public service may shift with a change in the size and composition of the population. In the South and Southwest, for example, rapid in-migration has brought new populations with new demands. In general, higher-growth areas face increasing public service demands and rapidly escalating budgets. The arrival of new industries and the annexation of adjoining areas create pressure to expand local infrastructure, thus increasing the debt burden. Accommodating "growing pains"—such as traffic congestion, pollution, strains on the water supply, and inadequate work-force development—can be quite expensive, and at least some of the burden falls on local governments. Moreover, newly arrived companies and higher-income in-migrants often demand improvements in the educational system and other public services; such factors may lead the cost of managing and maintaining the local government to increase at a faster rate than the population.

National economic performance   Although state government expenditures are more sensitive to the national business cycle than local government expenditures, the performance of the national economy can nevertheless have a significant effect on the level and mix of local public services. The prolonged economic expansion of the 1990s brought increases in real local expenditures and real revenues raised. Likewise, the recession of the early 2000s had a dampening—even disastrous—effect on the budgets of some local governments. In times of recession, local government expenditures related to unemployment and poverty automatically rise, while the local revenue base grows slowly. Local government decision makers are then forced into a tough corner: balance the budget by cutting services or by raising taxes. In times of inflation, local government expenditures are driven up, principally because of local government employees' demands for increased compensation. During the 1990s and early 2000s, inflation rates remained low, so there was little inflationary pressure on local spending; nor were there inflationary increases in the tax base, however.

Relative price   A change in the relative price of a public service will cause a change in the quantity demanded. It stands to reason that if the price of government-provided services increases relative to the price of privately provided services, citizens will reduce their demand for the higher-priced services. A change in the relative price of publicly supplied goods is only half the story, however. The other half is the extent to which local governments *respond* to changes in relative prices. A great deal of research on public sector behavior indicates that the governmental response to increases in the price of inputs is not very great. For instance, when the wages of public employees increase, local governments do not appear to cut back public employment in proportion to those increases.[10]

The relative price of public goods can also increase if the price of government services outpaces the growth of the local tax base. For example, the fact that the local property tax base often fails to increase at the same rate as personal income or inflation effectively reduces the purchasing power of local government revenues. Thus, higher rates of inflation can slow the growth of real local government expenditures, especially in older cities where property values are relatively stable and relatively little new construction is under way.

Community income   As their incomes increase, citizens want more and better services from local governments, such as better schools, better parks, and better road maintenance. Research has shown that many public services are "income elastic": that is, demand increases with growth in income, but at a disproportionately high rate. When local government fails to respond to this increased demand for higher-quality services, some families may search for alternative methods of buying the services (e.g., sending their children to private schools, making private security arrangements, or buying bottled drinking water). Private purchase of services may, in turn, dampen citizens' enthusiasm for participation in the improvement of local governance. On the other hand, public efforts to provide improved services may be costly, may require a tax increase, and may give rise to negative public sentiment.

While it is clear that local officials must plan a budgetary response to anticipated increases or decreases in community income, the appropriate response will vary with local circumstances. For example, certain types of income growth are less likely than others to cause growth in public expenditures. Substantial increases in welfare-related transfer payments and social security benefits, for instance, do not yield the same amounts of local tax revenues as other sources of income and therefore may not provide the same stimulus to local public expenditures. Similarly, increased income in the hands of retirees is not likely to bring about the same demand for increased school spending as increased income in the hands of younger families. In addition, the budgetary response will vary with the source of the income change: some changes in local income, for example, are brought on by federal government action; examples include changes in the amount of federal grants, in federal income tax rates, or in the deductibility of state and local government taxes under the federal income tax. The deductibility of the property tax from federal taxable income, for example, effectively lowers the local property tax burden and gives local governments more room to increase their property tax rate. This kind of tax break is very much like an increase in community income and is likely to call forth a response from local government fiscal planners.

Supply factors   The level of local government expenditures is also determined by supply factors, which affect the cost of providing a given level of public service. Among the most important of these factors are labor and capital costs, economies of scale, indexation, long-term costs associated with capital investments, and employee productivity, all of which can raise or lower the relative cost of local government services over time. Although some of these factors are uncontrollable, others can be affected by policy actions. Local government fiscal planners must monitor these supply factors and, if necessary, consider cost-saving service-delivery options. As with demand factors, the single most important thing that local officials can do is to anticipate and plan for cost changes through long-range fiscal planning.

Costs of labor and capital   If the wages paid to local government workers increase more rapidly than those paid to workers in general, the relative price of local government goods may be driven up. Similarly, expenditures can grow if the price that local governments pay for capital rises more quickly than the price that other users pay. Between 1983 and 1991, the average compensation paid to a state or local government worker increased at a faster rate than the average compensation paid to a private sector worker and outpaced increases in the consumer price index.[11] The pattern reversed itself in the 1990s, when the pay of state and local government workers increased less rapidly than that of private sector workers.[12]

Economies of scale   Through economies of scale, local governments can reduce the unit cost of producing higher levels of service. But the means of capturing economies of scale—city-county consolidation, annexation, metropolitan government, areawide special districts—are often difficult to sell to voters. Politically feasible opportunities to capture such economies are generally limited to public utilities and other hardware-type services; planning efforts can also sometimes be consolidated to realize economies.

Indexation   Some welfare and medical services—and even some collective bargaining contracts—are indexed, which means that the unit expenditures rise automatically with the rate of inflation. Local expenditures in these areas rise accordingly. Although most social services are state responsibilities and affect the state government budget, any resulting state budget difficulties might be passed on in the form of reduced state allocations to local governments.

Long-term capital commitments   The long-term, recurrent cost commitments that grow out of capital projects are an important and often neglected source of growth in expenditures. Building an auditorium today will lead to debt service requirements tomorrow, as well as to maintenance and operating costs for the new capital facility. Fiscal planning includes debt service but often underestimates maintenance costs. As local governments respond to the increasing demand for infrastructure improvements, these long-term expenditure commitments will become even more important.

Employee productivity   Local government activities are labor-intensive, and for many services there is relatively little opportunity to increase productivity by substituting capital for labor. Public workers may nevertheless receive increases in salary and benefits that parallel those received in the goods-producing private sector, where such increases are often related to real productivity gains. The inevitable result, it has been argued, is that government claims an increasing share of private sector income.[13] Although it may be an oversimplification, this basic concept is useful. If local government remains labor-intensive and oriented more toward people than toward products, and if technological improvements and productivity gains are tied to capital, then the relative cost of delivering a given quantity and quality of a service-oriented output will tend to increase over time.

Other external factors   Events that are entirely beyond local government control—a national or regional recession or the closure of a military base or a local plant, for example—can have a major effect on both the level of fiscal resources available to the local government and the level of expenditures for programs such as unemployment compensation and public assistance. (Even though public assistance and unemployment compensation are state-level expenditures, they have implications for local governments because they affect the pool of funds available for intergovernmental transfers.) External factors can also create uncertainty, and therefore more caution, on the part of state and local government officials—which can lead, in turn, to much lower spending levels.

A good case in point is the nationwide financial conservatism that arose after New York City's 1975 financial collapse; another is the zeal for fiscal limitations that arose after California's passage of Proposition 13, which set stringent limits on the use of the property tax. It is reasonable to assume, in fact, that state and local budgetary decisions are still guided largely by a spirit of fiscal conservatism. Between the mid-1970s and the early 2000s, increases in state and local government expenditures were modest. In 1975, three years before Proposition 13, state and local expenditures were equivalent to 12.2 percent of gross domestic product (GDP). By 2001, this share stood at 12.8 percent.[14] More recent data, from the National League of Cities 2001 survey of city government financial conditions, indicate that even in the face of a declining economy, city year-end cash balances continued to increase.[15]

Other external factors influencing the level and growth rate of local government expenditures are higher-level government policies, such as state and federal mandates and court-imposed school financing requirements. Federal fiscal policy can be another significant influence. Although state and local government expenditures have, since the early 1980s, increased along with income, federal grants as a share of GDP have remained about constant. Depending on how much of the federal transfer is passed through by the states, the onus for local financing may be increasingly shifted to local governments.

Nor are local governments exempt from the impact of federal and state tax policies. The 1986 changes in the federal marginal tax rate and the elimination of the sales tax as a federal income tax deduction lowered the value of deductions to taxpayers who itemize, thus increasing the "price" of state and local government expenditures. Other federal tax adjustments, such as the elimination of taxes on dividends and capital gains, could also burden local budgets if the state governments pass on their losses. Finally, state legislative decisions, many of which concern the property tax, can significantly compromise the local government tax base. In the short run, local officials can do little more than plan to absorb the effects of these external changes.

Revenues

Local governments receive revenues from user charges, taxation, intergovernmental transfers, and borrowing. While there is no one best revenue structure, some general principles can guide the fiscal planner in designing the optimum mix of taxes and other revenue sources for financing local government services.

The appropriate assignment of revenue sources depends on the expenditure responsibilities of the local government:

User charges are the most efficient revenue instrument for services whose benefits accrue primarily to those who consume the service. User charges are appropriate, for example, for financing public utilities, public transit, and certain roads and bridges.

Local taxes are the best source of revenue for local services when benefits accrue to the entire local population and individual pricing cannot be applied. Examples are general administration, traffic control, street lighting, and police and fire services.

State or federal intergovernmental transfers should contribute to the financing of functions—such as public assistance, health, and education—that create substantial spillover benefits for neighboring jurisdictions. Purely local financing (i.e., user charges or taxes) would lead provision of these services to fall short from a regional or national perspective.

Borrowing is an appropriate source of financing for long-lived capital investments.

These guidelines are based on economic efficiency, which is not the only value that may influence a local financing system: there are also equity, political, legal, and administrative concerns. For example, although user charges may be an efficient way to finance most of the costs of a local transit system, a larger general-revenue subsidy may be justified on the grounds of reducing the burden on low-income families, who are the most dependent on public transit. Higher local taxes or a reduction in expenditures may be the most appropriate way to finance a recurrent budgetary shortfall, but emergency aid from a higher-level government or a drawdown from local asset balances often turns out to be more politically acceptable.

Designing a local tax system

Five criteria are typically considered in structuring a revenue system: yield, equity, neutrality, administrative ease, and political feasibility. Only the first three of these criteria—those related to the economics of taxation—will be discussed here. (Administrative and political considerations are no less important, but these topics are far afield from the main concerns of this chapter.)

Although each of these criteria is important in evaluating every tax, policy makers must recognize that there is no perfect tax. Not every tax will be equitable, yield adequate revenues, and be free of heavy administrative costs. When designing a tax system, policy makers should focus on the whole rather than on the individual parts, consider the trade-offs involved, and select a tax structure that will, in its aggregate effects, come closest to meeting the desired criteria.

Yield   The most important goal in structuring a tax is to raise adequate revenue. In fact, local taxes can be thought of as a general charge for the provision of local government services. To cover the costs of these services, the tax base must be broad enough to allow rates to be set at feasible levels. One can think of any number of "desirable" objects of taxation whose base is simply too small to generate an adequate revenue flow—industrial polluters, luxury jewelry, or gourmet food purchases. To raise significant funds from such bases, the nominal tax rates would have to be unrealistically high. The alternative is to search for broader bases, such as aggregate consumption, earnings, and property wealth. Unfortunately, states often deny local governments access to these bases or limit the rate that can be applied.

In addition to having a broad base, a tax should have adequate elasticity: that is, tax revenues should grow sufficiently to cover expenditures and should not require annual discretionary adjustments in the rate or base.[16] What is the right level of elasticity? It depends on the anticipated growth rate of expenditures. If expenditures respond proportionately to local income growth, revenues should as well. If elasticity is too low, local officials will be forced either to cut expenditures or to seek voters' approval for a rate increase; this is commonly the case with school budgets in areas where growth in property values has not kept pace with expenditure needs. However, if elasticity is too high, the tax burden will automatically rise each year, which could conceivably generate voter dissatisfaction; some observers think that the high elasticity of the local property tax in California helped precipitate Proposition 13. Moreover, higher elasticity may also imply that revenues will be less stable over the course of the business cycle. Historical data indicate that since the early 1980s, state and local governments' own-source revenues have grown slightly faster than GDP, but this is partly attributable to discretionary changes in the tax rate and the tax base.

Elasticity is of particular concern in relation to the property tax. The base of the property tax has the potential to grow with income and to keep pace with local demand for public expenditures. For example, if an area draws in-migrants and new businesses, and if the valuation process captures the resulting increases in property values, then property tax revenues can be quite buoyant, as has been the case in some fast-growing cities and suburbs. However, if the local economy is not growing, or if the assessment process fails to capture increases in property values, then growth in income and in the demand for local expenditures can significantly outpace growth in the property tax base. Moreover, in many cities, the loss of private sector manufacturing and service jobs has taken many high-value properties off the tax roll. In many cases, urban economies have gained employment in governmental, educational, or nonprofit institutions, but the fact that these entities are nontaxable dampens the growth of the nonresidential tax base. (To obtain support for the cost of direct services, such as police and fire protection, some localities negotiate payments in lieu of taxes from exempt institutions.)

Yet another problem is political resistance to increases in the tax rate that are designed to make up for slow growth in the base. Since the passage of Proposition 13 in California, the property tax has not grown as a percentage of total GDP—even when the definition of revenue growth takes all discretionary changes into account. In fact, over the long run, state discretionary actions have dramatically reduced the taxation of assets such as business machinery, equipment, and inventories, thereby reducing the potential growth of the property tax.[17] Moreover, there is a continuing popular movement in the United States to roll back the level of property tax burdens. It would thus be fair to speculate that property tax revenues will not automatically keep pace with income growth. If recent history is any guide, local fiscal planners may have to look elsewhere for a revenue source that will provide the necessary elasticity.

What can local governments do to increase the elasticity of their tax base? Several steps can be taken, including regularly revaluating the property tax base; levying piggyback sales and income taxes where permitted by the state; and periodically adjusting those sales taxes and user charges that are not levied on an ad valorem base. (Such adjustments are necessary in order to account for the increased value of the consumption that underlies the tax or user charge; when a tax or charge is levied on a specific basis—for example, per motor vehicle—revenues will increase as the number of motor vehicles increases but not as the *value* of motor vehicles increases.) Other ways to broaden the tax base are to limit local tax exemptions and to negotiate in lieu payments from exempt institutions.

Realistically, for many local governments the key to revenue health lies in the state capitol. Successful lobbying of state legislatures for innovative measures such as regional financing, the authority to levy sales and income taxes, better-formulated state intergovernmental transfers, and the suspension of property tax rollbacks may be the one action that is most likely to contribute to local government fiscal health.

Equity   Equity, or fairness, in taxation can mean several things. User charges are fair according to the benefits-received principle: they charge the beneficiaries for services received (a bus fare and a water-meter charge are examples). However, these charges might be viewed as unfair in that they do not take into account the user's ability to pay: everyone riding the bus pays the same fare, regardless of income. An alternative to the benefits-received principle is to tax citizens according to their ability to pay, but this raises the issue of vertical equity: Do those with a greater ability to pay bear a greater tax burden?

Most concern about the equity of local tax systems has centered on the issue of regressivity. If lower-income families pay a greater percentage of their income in taxes, the taxes are considered regressive. As other chapters of this book will point out, however, firm conclusions about the vertical equity of local taxes are not easily reached. For example, the property tax on rented residential units, viewed by many as regressive, is probably divided between renters (in the form of higher rents) and landlords (in the form of a lower return on their investment). To the extent that landlords bear part of this burden—and the evidence suggests that they do—the property tax may actually be *progressive,* because higher-income taxpayers pay a higher percentage of their income in property taxes.[18]

Yet another aspect of fairness in taxation is horizontal equity: are equals treated alike? Variations in assessments on homes of similar value are a form of horizontal inequity that draws particularly strong objections. Many communities attempt to measure the fairness of their assessment practices by estimating the ratio of assessment dispersion, and many states have faced challenges to the classification practices associated with the property tax, particularly with regard to the differential treatment of residential and nonresidential properties.[19]

What equity goals can local governments realistically attain through their revenue structures? Because the base of local income taxes is not sufficiently broad, nor the rate structure sufficiently graduated, it is unlikely that local governments can achieve significant progressivity through their income tax systems. Since the local government tax structure (property and sales taxes) is approximately proportional—that is, the tax rate remains constant across all income classes—local governments might concentrate on making these taxes as horizontally fair as possible by, for example, striving for maximum equality in property tax assessment ratios. In general, income redistribution might best be left to the state and federal tax systems. Local governments might accomplish more in the way of income redistribution by approaching the problem through the expenditure side of the budget.

Neutrality   The neutrality principle in tax design holds that the tax structure should distort economic choices as little as possible: in other words, the tax system should not markedly affect decisions about location, employment, or consumption. In theory, there are some taxes—such as lump-sum land-value taxes—that do not affect economic choices; but in practice, most taxes do affect economic behavior. Local sales taxes might affect the choice of where a family shops; local income taxes might affect the choice of where a firm locates; and property taxes can influence the decision to hold wealth in the form of real property or in some other form.

Local government fiscal planners should design their tax systems with neutrality in mind. The general rules are as follows: (1) avoid those distortions that seem most harmful and (2) resist the temptation to fine-tune the local tax structure to achieve non-revenue-related goals.

With respect to the neutrality of taxes, local government officials are likely to face three important issues. The first is differential tax rates among neighboring or competing jurisdictions. Many analysts and policy makers believe that people and businesses will travel short distances to save on their tax bills. And many local governments fear, probably with some legitimacy, that differences between sales tax rates in contiguous communities will cause consumers to shop across jurisdictional lines; similarly, cities worry that the imposition of a commuter tax might draw businesses to a nearby suburb that does not have such a tax. Thus, the strategies of neighboring jurisdictions are almost inevitably a factor to be considered in making decisions about local taxes—and, in fact, empirical research on U.S. counties indicates that tax mimicking does occur.[20]

A second, related issue is the use of tax incentives to attract jobs. There is considerable debate about the extent to which business location choices within metropolitan areas are influenced by variations in the level and types of taxation. Even if tax subsidies do not make much of a difference overall, they may still have to be granted for defensive purposes—that is, as a competitive measure. Tax incentives do introduce distortions, however, and fiscal planners should recognize these. Preferential tax treatment for incoming firms effectively pushes the burden of financing the incremental expenditures onto the remainder of the tax base. A fair question for the local fiscal planner to ponder: Should new firms be taxed at a lower rate than existing firms?

The third important issue concerns the practice of assessing both land and capital improvements for property tax purposes, a practice that penalizes investment in structures. A tax on land value, in contrast, yields equal revenue without rewarding or penalizing structural investments. The desire to remove some of the disincentives to property improvements has led many countries and a handful of U.S. cities to tax buildings at a lower rate than land.[21]

It is a generally accepted principle of good local taxation that a community should not export its tax burdens to residents of other communities. When taxes are exported, the price of local services appears to be quite low (because the cost is, in effect, being subsidized by residents of other communities), and the taxing jurisdiction may be induced to overspend. Thus, although a tax that is largely exported may be a "dream tax" for local politicians, it is not good public policy.

The use of exported taxes is restricted by two factors: direct prohibition by the state and the ability of businesses to relocate to avoid high taxes. Although some local governments do effectively export tax burdens—through taxes on hotel occupancy and business property, and through special taxes aimed at tourists, for example—it would be better public policy to try to capture only the increased costs that can be attributed to the use of services by nonresidents.

Local government revenue structures

How do local governments structure their finances? As shown in Table 4–4, in 2001 U.S. local governments raised about 18 percent of all government revenues and nearly all property tax revenues. They also raised 15 percent of general sales tax revenues and nearly half of all user charges. With respect to income taxes, however, local governments are small players in comparison to the federal and state governments. Table 4–5, which shows the distribution of local government revenues by source, indicates that local governments depend on intergovernmental assistance, primarily from state governments, for about 47 percent of their current revenues, and on property taxes for about one-third of their current revenues.

These averages, however, reflect a wide variation in practice. States grant local governments varying degrees of control over sales and income taxes, and local governments vary in their rate and base structures and in the mix of taxes levied. Thirty-four states allow at least one of their local governments to levy a sales tax, although a rate ceiling is usually imposed.[22] Local government use of income taxes is much more limited. However, income and sales taxes are not insignificant sources of revenue for cities and counties, and have been increasing in importance in recent years.[23]

Table 4–4 Government revenues by source, 2001.

Government revenues	Total federal, state, and local revenues (in billions of $)	Local revenues as a percentage of total government revenues
Property taxes	257	97.1
General sales taxes[a]	408	15.0
Income taxes	1,219	1.6
Other taxes[b]	298	8.3
User charges	84	49.5
Total own-source revenues[c]	2,266	17.5

[a] Includes excises.
[b] Includes miscellaneous general revenue.
[c] Excludes social security contributions and state government contributions for social insurance.

Table 4–5 Distribution of local government revenues by source, 2001.

Revenue category	Percentage of total
Current revenues	100.0
Intergovernmental transfers	47.2
From federal government	2.6
From state government	44.6
Own-source revenues	52.8
Property tax	33.2
Income tax	6.2
Sales tax	8.1
Other	5.3

Because of the degree of variation in practice, it is difficult to construct a general profile of local government tax structures. Some generalizations are possible, however. Local sales taxes tend to follow their respective state structures: flat rates and a base that usually excludes housing, food, and most services. Local income taxes tend to be flat rate. Finally, the property tax, the major local revenue source, dominates the local tax structure.

The outlook for local finances

Local governments face a number of opportunities and uncertainties. Because many of the important influences on local budgets will be "uncontrollables," there will be a premium on efficient fiscal planning. The following are some of the important factors that will shape local government budgets:

National economic performance

Regional shifts in population and economic activity

Demographic changes, such as the changing age structure of the population

Voter resistance to higher taxes and government regulation

Level of unfunded or inadequately funded mandates.

National economic performance

The performance of the national economy is a major determinant of the fiscal health of state and local governments. If national economic growth is strong, revenue growth will be strong and there will be less likelihood of reductions in federal aid and less need for welfare-related expenditures. In times of recession, local governments feel the pinch of slower growth in revenues and increased pressure to protect vulnerable populations, and state and federal governments have less wherewithal to provide assistance. The business cycle is a major influence on local governments' financial condition.

The 1990s were years of strong economic expansion and relatively little discussion of local fiscal problems. Revenue growth kept pace with income growth in most of the country, federal aid at least held steady as a share of total national output, and real expenditures of local governments increased. The recession of the early 2000s reversed that rosy picture, and speculations about the future are characterized by a great deal of uncertainty. How might this uncertainty play out in the fiscal decisions of local governments?

One likely outcome is for local governments to hold larger precautionary financial balances, spend less, and levy higher taxes than they would in a more stable economic environment. State and local governments may shy away from commitments to long-term programs or new activities and may attempt to reduce the proportion of uncontrollable expenditures in their budgets. Even in the booming 1990s economy, many cities drew heavily on current revenues and accumulated balances to finance capital facilities, a pattern that suggests a spirit of conservatism on the part of local fiscal planners even in times of growth.[24] But conservative fiscal behavior in the aftermath of a recession will be very difficult because many important programs were curtailed during the downturn, capital expenditures and maintenance were deferred, and the compensation rates of local government employees probably increased slowly, if at all. In the coming years, fiscal planners will play a particularly crucial role in evaluating budgetary choices.

Uncertainty has a greater effect on the finances of some local governments than on those of others. Local governments whose revenues cover their obligations by only a small margin, and perhaps those whose credit ratings are lowest, may take the most conservative fiscal stance. Cities that are growing or that are financially stronger can afford to gamble somewhat more: first, their natural economic growth will probably offset most errors; second, such cities are likely to have greater reserves on which to draw. However, as many local governments in the South and West learned during the early 2000s, continued growth is not a certainty. The stereotypes of the booming Sun Belt and the decaying Rust Belt are much less valid than they were in the 1980s.

Regional shifts

During the 1960s and 1970s, per capita personal income across states converged significantly, but there has been little convergence since that time.[25] Shifts in personal income within states, moreover, have had varying fiscal implications for local governments. Many formerly rich states, for example, have had to increase their efforts to bring their budgets into line with new, relatively lower levels of economic output. In many states, particularly those in older industrial regions, this retrenchment could mean continued reductions in government services. In New York State, for example, per capita personal income was 18 percent above the national average in 2000, but per capita expenditures were 40 percent above the national average.[26] Given that the state's long-term income growth has been lower than the national average, retrenchment would seem inevitable.

In growing regions, where some of the less-developed public sectors are located, fiscal adjustments of a different type will be called for. Local governments in the South and West will face more pressure to deal with rural poverty—and, in response to the pressures of a growing population, will also be compelled to expand infrastructure, improve school and health care systems, deal with water shortages, and ameliorate environmental problems. Per capita income in Georgia, for example, was about 6 percent below the national average in 2001, but per capita state and local government expenditures were about 9 percent below the national average.[27] Moreover, because Georgia's income growth has been above the national average, the state and local governments are under pressure to increase spending.

In short, fiscal planners in both growth and nongrowth areas will face challenges. Many high-growth localities will have difficulty keeping pace with the demand for infrastructure and will be forced to consider borrowing against their future to resolve the issue. Low- or slow-growth localities, lacking the strong growth against which to borrow and trying to support existing services with a tax base that is less than vigorous, will face an even more difficult problem. Either way, there will be a premium on effective long-term fiscal planning.

Demographic changes

Those who plan local government budgets must also stay abreast of anticipated changes in the level and makeup of the population. Just how large and powerful these changes can be was one of the most striking realizations of the 1990s. In fact, the combined effects of the birth rate and immigration made growth during that decade the greatest in U.S. history. The fastest-growing areas during this period were "edge cities" that accepted the spillover populations from nearby metropolitan areas.

The changing composition of the population is of great importance for many local government budgets, as are the changes in the labor force that are likely to result.[28] The coming years will see continued growth in the share of women, Hispanic Americans, and Asian Americans in the labor force. The proportion of people over fifty-five will also continue to increase.

These demographic changes will almost certainly call for adjustments in local government budgets. Certainly, politicians will recognize shifts in voting power and will respond to the demands of new interest groups. The expenditure side of local budgets will respond as well to the increasing proportion of women and immigrants (many of whom do not speak English) in the labor force, and to the needs of a growing retiree population. The revenue side of local government budgets will also be affected. On the one hand, the population increase among those aged forty-five to sixty-four, a productive age group, may suggest some increase in taxable capacity. On the other hand, growth in the retirement-age population may dampen revenue growth, since retirees earn less taxable income and spend less on housing and taxable consumer goods. In addition, many states have given older residents preferential treatment under the property tax and individual income tax. Fiscal planners developing medium-term budget projections must take all these demographic factors into account.[29]

A particular problem facing some local governments is a heavy concentration of poor families. As of 2000, the incomes of about 12 percent of U.S. residents were below the poverty line. But the concentration of low-income residents varied widely among states—from less than 8 percent in New Hampshire to more than 19 percent in New Mexico—and such variations are likely to be even wider among local governments.[30]

Fiscal planning to deal with financially distressed families is a particularly difficult job. Meeting the needs of the poor will impose a substantial cost on many local governments, but increased tax rates to finance services for lower-income residents have proven difficult to sell to voters. Moreover, heavy concentrations of poor families often go hand in hand with a weak tax base. Nor can economic growth alone solve the problem: as the 1980s and 1990s showed, rising metropolitan-area incomes alone are not adequate to raise the relative status of the poor.[31] The task of addressing unacceptable income disparities will remain on the desks of local government fiscal planners.

Tax limitations

A good local government fiscal planner will recognize the constraints created by context. One such constraint may be a strong "no-tax" culture. Despite the fact that the United States has one of the lowest levels of taxation of any industrial country, and notwithstanding recognized deficiencies in public services, American politicians continue to push for tax controls, if not reductions. State and local government own-source revenues were equivalent to 7.9 percent of GDP in 1980 and to 8.8 percent in 1999.[32] Although state and local government expenditures have, since the early 1980s, increased along with income, federal grants as a share of GDP have remained about constant. A local government fiscal plan that relies on significant tax hikes to finance a larger local government sector may be a tough sell.

The late 1970s saw the beginning of a series of legal actions to roll back property tax rates and limit future tax increases. The movement to limit taxes and expenditures focused on certain features of local government that many citizens found objectionable: too much property tax, too much welfare expenditure, and perhaps too little work on the part of the public sector.

Some state governments have formalized control over taxes through legal limitations on taxing and spending. About two-thirds of the states now limit municipal spending or taxing, and most states limit property tax levels in one way or another. Researchers are divided, however, about whether it is indeed the tax-limitation movement that has restrained the growth in property tax revenues or whether local voters have simply found the tax too objectionable. In

1960, the property tax accounted for 3.0 percent of GDP; in 2001, it accounted for 2.4 percent.[33]

Unfunded mandates

Unfunded mandates are another important external influence on local government budgets. These arise when the state or federal government (1) stipulates a particular activity (such as homeland defense) or a particular level of service (such as that for Medicaid programs) that is beyond what is currently covered in the local budget, and (2) fails to provide sufficient funds to support the mandated activity. The Unfunded Mandates Reform Act, passed by Congress in 1995, gives the Congressional Budget Office the task of providing information on, and tracking trends in, unfunded mandates.

Mandates can be an important—and positive—public policy measures. They may require local governments to expand public services to better account for spillover effects on other jurisdictions, as in the case of environmental protection, or they may redirect local priorities toward activities that are in the national interest, as in the case of school lunches. Mandates may also be introduced to ensure uniformity within the state in the delivery of some essential service. Mandates may derive from the federal or state government, or from the courts.

Although there may appear to be very good reasons for higher-level governments to mandate certain local government activities, mandates can nevertheless pose significant problems. When a mandate is not funded, the required activity must be supported by locally raised revenues. But with their limited ability to raise revenues, local governments may be hard-pressed to respond, and the net effect of the mandate may be to displace other local expenditures. Thus, local preferences for budgetary allocations may be overridden by mandates from higher-level governments. Moreover, all mandates are accompanied by a compliance cost: the local government must administer the mandated program.

The federal government has moved in recent years to reduce the burden of unfunded mandates on state and local governments, but these efforts have failed to eliminate the problem of displaced local government priorities. Moreover, because the benefits and costs are rarely studied before a mandate is issued, the net benefits of the program and the net impact on the local government usually remain unknown.[34]

Mandates place a special burden on local government fiscal planners. While planners are not likely to be successful at gaining repeal of a mandate, or even heading one off, they may be able to put a reasonable estimate on the cost of the program. It is also incumbent on fiscal planners to determine how best to meet the increased costs associated with mandates.

Conclusion

Local fiscal planners need a framework within which to evaluate budget choices. The context in which decisions must be made changes so rapidly that there is a risk of falling into a pattern of ad hoc decisions and failing to adhere to a fiscal strategy. For example, the context that characterized much of the early and mid-1990s—economic growth and even excess revenues—had transformed into one of revenue shortfalls and a struggling national economy by the end of the decade. Health care costs and environmental problems continued to pose challenges, but the unemployment rate and the attendant social-welfare needs moved to the foreground. Faced with a changing context, fiscal planners might recommend different budgets, but they should also continue to consider the trade-offs made in the services being provided, the impacts on different groups in the local population, and the effects on the competitiveness of the local economy.

1 Richard A. Musgrave, *The Theory of Public Finance: A Study in Public Economy* (New York: McGraw-Hill, 1959).

2 U.S. Department of Commerce, Bureau of the Census, *Statistical Abstract of the United States: 2002* (Washington, D.C.: U.S. Government Printing Office, 2001), sec. 8.

3 Utah Foundation, *Property Taxes in Utah and the Fifty States,* Research Report No. 644 (Salt Lake City: Utah Foundation, July 2001).

4 Advisory Commission on Intergovernmental Relations (ACIR), *Changing Public Attitudes on Governments and Taxes* (Washington, D.C.: U.S. Government Printing Office, 1985), 1; and ACIR, *Changing Public Attitudes on Governments and Taxes* (Washington, D.C.: U.S. Government Printing Office, 1993), 1.

5 John Mikesell, *Fiscal Administration,* 5th ed. (Orlando, Fla.: Harcourt Brace and Company, 1999), chap. 14.

6 Ronald C. Fisher, *State and Local Government Finance,* 2nd ed. (Chicago: Irwin, 1996), chap. 7.

7 Charles M. Tiebout, "A Pure Theory of Local Expenditures," *Journal of Political Economy* 64 (October 1956): 416–424.

8 Katharine Bradbury, Yolanda Kodrzycki, and Robert Tannenwald, "The Effects of State and Local Public Policies on Economic Development: An Overview," *New England Economic Review* (March/April 1997): 1–12.

9 Joseph Cordes and Nancy Gardner, "Enterprise Zones and Property Values: What We Know (or Maybe Don't)," in National Tax Association, *Proceedings of the 94th Annual Conference on Taxation* (Washington, D.C.: National Tax Association, 2002), 279–287.

10 Roy Bahl, Marvin Johnson, and Michael J. Wasylenko, "State and Local Government Expenditure Determinants: The Traditional View and a New Approach," in *Public Employment and State and Local Government Finance,* ed. Roy Bahl, Jesse Burkhead, and Bernard Jump (Cambridge, Mass.: Ballinger Publishing, 1980), chap. 3.

11 Computed from data in *Survey of Current Business,* various years.

12 Albert E. Schwenk, "Compensation Cost Trends in Private Industry and State and Local Governments," *Compensation and Working Conditions* 4, no. 3 (fall 1999): 13.

13 This thesis was developed by William Baumol in "The Macroeconomics of Unbalanced Growth: The Anatomy of Urban Crisis," *American Economic Review* 57 (June 1967): 415–426.

14 Based on data in Bruce Baker, "Receipts and Expenditures of State Governments and of Local Governments, 1959–2001," *Survey of Current Business* 83, no. 6 (June 2003): 36–53.

15 National League of Cities (NLC), *City Fiscal Conditions in 2001* (Washington, D.C.: NLC, 2001).

16 Most analysts measure the elasticity of a tax system in relation to income. The revenue–income elasticity of a tax is the percentage change in revenues (net of any discretionary changes) associated with each 1 percent change in personal income.

17 Dick Netzer, "Will the Property Tax Become an All-But-Forgotten Relic of an Earlier Fiscal Age?" *State Tax Notes,* 7 July 2003, 30–37.

18 See Henry J. Aaron, *Who Pays the Property Tax? A New View* (Washington, D.C.: Brookings Institution, 1975).

19 The common measure is the coefficient of intra-area dispersion; that is, the mean of the absolute values of the deviations of assessment-sales ratios around their median, divided by the median.

20 Helen F. Ladd, "Mimicking of Local Tax Burdens among Neighboring Counties," *Public Finance Quarterly* 20, no. 4 (October 1992): 450–467.

21 Roy Bahl, "Land Value Taxation in Third World and Transition Countries," in *Land Value Taxation in Contemporary Societies,* ed. Dick Netzer (Cambridge, Mass.: Lincoln Institute of Land Policy, 1998).

22 National Conference of State Legislatures, *Critical Issues in State-Local Fiscal Policy: A Guide to Local Option Taxes* (Denver: Foundation for State Legislatures and National Conference of State Legislatures, November 1997).

23 Therese McGuire, "Alternatives to Property Taxation for Local Governments," *State Tax Notes,* 15 May 2000, 1715–1723.

24 Michael Pagano, "Municipal Capital Spending during the Boom," *Public Budgeting & Finance* 22, no. 2 (summer 2002): 1–20.

25 G. Andrew Bernat, "Convergence in State Per Capita Personal Income," *Survey of Current Business* 81, no. 6 (June 2001): 36–48.

26 Computed from data in Bureau of the Census, *Statistical Abstract: 2002,* table 422.

27 Ibid.

28 Mitra Toossi, "A Century of Change: The U.S. Labor Force, 1950–2050," *Monthly Labor Review* (May 2002): 15–28.

29 For a good discussion of the changing age distribution of the population, see U.S. Department of Commerce, Bureau of the Census, "National Population Projections Summary Tables," 13 January 2000, available at www.census.gov/population/www/projections/natsum-T3.html. For a good discussion of the budgetary implications of these changes, see Sally Wallace, "Changing Times: Demographic and Economic Changes and State and Local Government Budgets," in *State and Local Finance under Pressure,* ed. David Sjoquist (Cheltenham, U.K.: Edward Elgar, 2003), 31–59.

30 Bureau of the Census, *Statistical Abstract: 2002,* table 673.

31 David Sjoquist, "The Atlanta Paradox: Introduction," in *The Atlanta Paradox,* ed. David Sjoquist (New York: Russell Sage Foundation, 2000), 1–15.

32 Computed from data in Baker, "Receipts and Expenditures," 36–53.

33 Ibid.

34 Mikesell, *Fiscal Administration,* chap. 13.

Part two:
Management tools

5 Forecasting local revenues and expenditures

LARRY D. SCHROEDER

During the second half of the 1990s, local economies in most regions of the nation were experiencing fairly consistent growth, and inflation was being held in check. These conditions, however, had changed dramatically by 2001, particularly in the wake of the events of September 11. By 2002, many local economies were suffering from recession: state and local government revenues were falling and, in many instances, spending needs were increasing, especially in the areas of health care and social services.

Revenue and expenditure forecasting offer no magical solutions for the fiscal crises that face local governments from time to time. Forecasts that extend beyond a single fiscal year can, however, help local governments avoid at least some of the difficulties associated with economic fluctuations. Moreover, such forecasts can support policy decisions that are likely to have a positive impact on future revenues, expenditures, or both.

All local governments engage in forecasting, whether they use highly complex models or more simple techniques. Some local governments, for example, undertake cash flow projections to protect themselves from short-term cash shortages.[1] Predicting cash flow needs is fiscally prudent because if cash is *not* needed, it can be invested in money-market instruments that will yield interest returns for periods as short as one day. The annual budget is also a forecasting exercise. Some jurisdictions, instead of focusing only on the next fiscal year, undertake medium-term forecasts, projecting revenues and expenditures two to five years into the future. For particular public policy decisions—for example, a land development project, an annexation proposal, or a transportation project—local governments may estimate longer-term (beyond five years) impacts on fiscal conditions.

This chapter emphasizes medium-term forecasting techniques, but the general principles apply to shorter- and longer-term projections as well. The first major section provides an overview of long-range forecasts, which are used to identify general fiscal trends. Medium-range forecasting techniques are then considered in detail, as are the data requirements for both revenue and expenditure forecasting. The next two sections of the chapter describe how local governments use forecasts to deal with projected shortfalls and how forecasts are implemented. The concluding section offers a look at administrative and political issues associated with forecasting.

Long-range forecasting

Long-range forecasting techniques focus primarily on the long-term health of the local economy—which will, in turn, affect the fiscal condition of the local government. The techniques that local government analysts use to carry out such a review nearly always rely heavily on past trends in local fiscal and economic indicators.[2] Used successfully, these techniques can provide early warning that something is amiss.

When planning a long-range forecast for a community, the fiscal analyst should first assess the past and present state of the local economy and examine recent trends among the following factors, each of which can affect taxpaying capacity and service demands: population (including composition by age, skills, and education), income structure, and local employment mix. In addition, the analyst should identify especially important features of the local economy and note any significant changes in them. For example, budget analysts in Bexar County, Texas (near San Antonio), create a "local economic outlook" to accompany their long-term financial forecast. Because of the large number of defense facilities located in the area, a recent version of the outlook considered possible changes in U.S. defense policies; because of the county's close economic ties to Mexico, the outlook also considered the possible future course of the Mexican economy.[3]

The four brief sections that follow discuss the principal techniques that are used to describe the local economic base.[4]

Population projections

Anticipated population is an important determinant of the future of a local economy. The number of people living and working in a jurisdiction will significantly influence both the revenue base and the need for local public services. Although the U.S. Census Bureau creates state- as well as national-level population projections, it does not provide substate projections. State governments, however, recognizing the potential importance of such projections for planning purposes, produce their own population projections, either through state offices or through support units in state universities.[5] Although most local governments use projections created by others, larger cities and counties may have the expertise to produce their own population forecasts; Fort Worth, Texas, for example, does its own population projections.

The methods used by each state office or university unit may differ and will rely on a variety of assumptions about fertility, mortality, migration, and other factors that can influence future population growth. The level of detail included in projections may also vary. Some projections include only aggregate population figures, whereas others provide demographic breakdowns. California's and Utah's population projections, for example, include breakdowns by age, sex, race, and ethnicity;[6] Utah's projections include information on county employment as well. Before using projections developed outside the locality, the analyst will want to find out what assumptions underlie the estimates.

Location quotient analysis

Although population is important, it is only one characteristic of the local economy. Location quotient analysis is a popular analytical technique used to obtain an understanding of the local economy's industrial composition.[7] Briefly, location quotients compare the importance of a given industry in the local economy with the importance of that industry in the nation as a whole (i.e., local employment in the industry divided by total local employment, versus national employment in the same industry divided by total national employment). If a locality has relatively greater numbers of employees in a given industry than does the nation as a whole, its location quotient for that industry is greater than 1, and the locality can be regarded as specializing in that industry. Specialization is not, in and of itself, good or bad: it may mean, for example, that the locality should consider diversifying its industries to help protect against the boom-and-bust pattern that characterizes some industries; on the other hand, specialization may help attract complementary industries to the area.

Location quotients can also be used to project the changes in total employment and population that may be associated with increases or decreases in employment in particular industries. Although a detailed treatment is beyond the scope of this chapter, this analytical technique is based on the idea that, to the extent that an industry location quotient for a locality exceeds 1, that industry must be "exporting" its products outside the region.[8] But other, "non-export" employees—such as teachers, barbers, lawyers, and retail clerks—are necessary to support the export-oriented employment. Employment increases or decreases in exporting industrial sectors will therefore have a multiplier effect on total employment, which will likely alter total population. Population changes, in turn, will affect the local tax base as well as the demand for public services.[9] The finance analyst can use such information first to determine whether a fiscal crisis is on the horizon, and then to choose a course of action to prevent or mitigate such a crisis if necessary. Location quotients can also be used to forecast output by industry—which, in turn, provides input for revenue-forecasting models.[10]

Shift-share analysis

Location quotients provide information about a local economic base for a given point in time, whereas shift-share analysis attempts to describe how, over time, local employment (classified by industry) has changed in relation to national employment.[11] Shift-share analysis considers such changes from three different perspectives: (1) how much local employment would have grown had it increased at the same rate as national employment; (2) the growth (or decline) in local employment in an industry, given that industry's rate of growth nationally relative to total national employment; and (3) the degree to which local employment within an industry grew as rapidly as employment within that industry grew throughout the nation. The second factor permits the analyst to determine whether local employment is dominated by relatively slow-growth industries, in which case decision makers may try to attract industries with brighter long-range futures. The third factor reveals whether a local industry is competitive with other areas of the country. If it appears to be in an unfavorable competitive position, decision makers can determine how and why this situation may have developed and devise strategies to improve it.[12]

Shift-share analysis is primarily a descriptive analytical technique; it does not explain the underlying causes of change.[13] Although these causes may in fact lie outside the powers of local decision makers (e.g., a declining regional population or pressures that have made local wages noncompetitive), local policies may nevertheless succeed in altering the competitive balance. Tax breaks, special services to new industries, or aggressive promotion of the area may yield positive results.[14] In any event, shift-share analysis can be an important step in initiating a long-range planning process.

Fiscal impact analysis

Because neither location quotient analysis nor shift-share analysis can be used to obtain explicit, long-range projections for local fiscal conditions, a third technique—fiscal impact analysis—is used. The rationale underlying fiscal impact models is that as the size and composition of the population shift, as income levels and distribution change, and as land use patterns vary, revenues and expenditures will change accordingly.

Although any land use may require new capital investment to provide streets and sewer and water service, infrastructure requirements are likely to differ for commercial and residential land uses, as will demand for public services such as police and fire protection. Moreover, even within the same general land use category, fiscal impact will vary with the specific type of use. For example, housing may take the form of apartments, condominiums, or single-family detached houses. Population density (including the number of school-age children), income levels, and public service costs will differ for each form of housing. Taxes, and thus the revenue yield, will also vary depending on both the general and the specific category of land use.

If the effects of different population groups, income groups, and land uses on government revenues and expenditures can be roughly calculated, then the budgetary effects of zoning policies can be projected under alternative policy scenarios. Furthermore, because development may require a different time schedule for each type of land use, the flow of revenues and expenditures—including debt financing—can be forecast and compared.[15] Policy makers could then use such projections when reviewing current zoning classifications or petitions for zoning changes. Fiscal impact analysis can also be used to estimate the net fiscal effects of government incentives for new businesses or expansions of existing businesses.

Fiscal impact analysis recognizes that new developments will affect public expenditures because new capital equipment, as well as both labor and non-labor inputs, will probably be required. In some localities, these additional expenditures are passed on to developers (and ultimately on to the purchasers of the property) in the form of development impact fees. These fees, which constitute a revenue source for the local jurisdiction, are used to offset the additional public expenditures associated with the development. Estimating appropriate development impact fees is not unlike estimating expenditures for fiscal impact models.[16]

Models such as shift-share analysis, economic base studies, and fiscal impact analysis are all amenable to computerization. A number of commercial firms provide such software and training or can carry out such analysis under contract.

Fiscal impact analysis focuses primarily on the long-range effects of public policies, rather than on the shorter-range effects of changes in economic conditions. Thus, although the fiscal impact models could be tailored for use in

---

A fiscal impact model for economic development   In Utah, the Governor's Office of Planning and Budget has constructed a fiscal impact model capable of estimating the economic and net fiscal effects of a proposed economic development scenario. The model consists of five components:

An input-output-based economic model that allows forecasters to estimate how changes in employment and output in one industry will affect other industries

A demographic model that links changes in expected employment to changes in population

An expenditure model that estimates changes in expenditures associated with changes in population

A revenue model that links changes in employment to state and local government revenues

A financial model that discounts the expected flows of future expenditures and revenues to the present and allows the users to see, in present value terms, the total net revenue implications of an economic development project.

Source: Governor's Office of Planning and Budget, Demographic and Economic Analysis Section, "Utah State and Local Government Fiscal Impact Model," Working Paper Series 94-3 (June 1994), available at www.governor.state. ut.us/dea/publications/fim/94-3.pdf.

---

two- to five-year budget forecasts, the techniques described in the following section are more likely to be appropriate for shorter-range projections.

Medium-range forecasting

Failure to plan for periods longer than the traditional budget year often results in "management by crisis" and hasty remedies, such as tax increases and emergency cutbacks in expenditures.[17] By anticipating future budgetary problems, medium-range forecasting can help avert the emergencies that all too often characterize public sector financial management. Longer-term financial planning can have the additional benefit of convincing bond-rating agencies that the local government does not focus exclusively on short-term issues.

Medium-range forecasts generally focus on anticipated revenues and expenditures two to five years into the future. Although the projections may reveal future surpluses, such forecasts are principally used to project fiscal gaps, or revenue shortfalls. Given a set of assumptions, forecasters project revenues and expenditures independently. If the projections suggest that revenues will fall far short of expenditures, policy decisions can be made to balance the two sides of the budget. It is imperative, however, for those who make and use forecasts to realize that projections are not inalterable prophecies but guides to be adjusted as necessary. When steps are taken to eliminate the fiscal gap, actual revenues and expenditures should not and will not be the same as those originally forecast. The final figures do not reflect "errors" in the initial forecast but simply document the fact that the forecasting effort has effectively aided the management process.

Medium-range forecasting can also help with policy decisions that have fiscal implications extending beyond the current budget period. For example, the

---

Alternative scenarios in a forecast document The forecast document prepared for Bexar County, Texas, includes the following passage:

Forecasts are not predictions! Forecasts are projected end results that may occur based upon stipulated assumptions. . . . [C]hange the assumptions and the end results will change. The value of forecasts is that they allow policy makers to anticipate potential issues and take a proactive stance, enabling greater success when mitigating problems and maximizing opportunities.[1]

To assist decision makers, the document includes both a Baseline General Fund Forecast and a Short Term Issues General Fund Forecast. The first is based on the assumption that only mandated expenditures and expenditures previously authorized by decision makers will be undertaken during the five-year projection period. The second includes the costs of initiatives that local decision makers *may* choose to fund in the upcoming budget.

For example, in the forecast prepared before the 2002–03 budget, the Baseline General Fund Forecast showed a surplus in the general fund through 2003–04 and relatively small deficits for 2004–07. The Short Term Issues General Fund Forecast, however, which included the costs of certain proposed policy decisions (including a performance-based pay program, an upgrade of computer software, and the civilianization of some positions in the sheriff's office), projected substantial deficits beginning in fiscal year 2002–03 and even larger deficits in the future, unless steps were undertaken to increase revenues.

[1]Planning and Resource Management Department, Bexar County, Texas, *Long Range Financial Forecast and Strategies, FY 2002–03 through 2006–07* (San Antonio, Tex.: July 2002), 1. The entire document is available at www.co.bexar.tx.us/prm/CDROM/cdrom.htm.

fiscal implications of multiyear labor contracts and state or federal grants will reach well into the future. Expenditures for capital projects also extend beyond the current budget year. Capital debt service charges are the most obvious of the associated longer-term expenditures, but capital projects may also require incremental operating and maintenance expenses over the life of the investment. Analyzing the implications of these longer-range costs is a particularly important function of medium-range forecasts.

The remainder of this section focuses on the four principal techniques used to project revenues and expenditures from two to five years into the future; each can also be used in the preparation of the annual budget.[18] The methods differ primarily in complexity. In general, there is a trade-off between the effort and cost involved in assembling a forecast and the amount and accuracy of the information obtained: the simpler methods require less data, less time to produce—and, possibly, less expertise on the part of the forecaster. The more complex methods take longer and are more costly, but they can incorporate the effects of a larger number of factors, are more amenable to systematic analysis, and are likely to provide more useful information for considering particular policy choices. The size of the community, the sensitivity of its revenues and expenditures to economic conditions, and the complexity of its fiscal problems will also influence the choice of technique.

Expert or judgmental forecasts

Few generalizations can be made about expert forecasts—other than that the key to success is finding the appropriate expert. Because successful judgmental forecasting requires an in-depth understanding of revenue systems, the experts are generally drawn from within the local government. For example, experienced local finance officers can probably develop reasonably accurate estimates of future revenue streams without the aid of a formalized, explicit model.

Rather than rely on a single expert, some localities use a panel whose members are familiar with the local economy. In Chesterfield County, Virginia, for example, a panel that includes local business leaders, the chief economist from the Federal Reserve Bank of Richmond, economists from state agencies, and top county management meets semiannually to discuss future economic trends and the likely course of revenue flows.[19] The estimated cost of such an event is only about $200, and the resulting revenue projections are not appreciably less accurate than those yielded by the more complex models that the county had used previously. Furthermore, the approach appears to have had both internal and external benefits. Elected county officials view the projections as more realistic, and local business leaders have gained a greater understanding of the fiscal issues faced by the county.

Expert forecasting has a number of drawbacks, however. First, it may be difficult to determine, after the fact, why a forecast was correct or incorrect. Second, experts have difficulty estimating the effects of external factors or discretionary policy changes. Third, the approach is probably less accurate in the case of longer-term projections. Finally, if the projections depend on the expertise of a single forecaster, the "model" is lost if the forecaster leaves. Nevertheless, the low cost of the approach is an important advantage.

Time-series techniques

Some revenues and expenditures can be projected through time-series, or time-trend, techniques, which use past values as the basis for future estimates. The longer the history of the revenue or expenditure variable, the stronger the basis for the use of time-series techniques. Time-series techniques differ greatly in their complexity and data requirements; this discussion is limited to the simpler approaches.

Time-series techniques generally ignore factors other than time in projecting the future. The assumptions that are used to project time-dependent relationships may vary, however: (1) the variable will change next year by the same absolute amount that it changed during the previous year; or (2) the rate of growth will be the same in the future as it was in the immediate past. For example, if property taxes grew by 7 percent during the previous period, one simple approach is to forecast that they will grow by 7 percent during each subsequent period. (It is important to note that a constant absolute increase in a series implies a *slowing* growth rate: as the base of a series increases, a constant absolute increase represents a lower *relative* change in the variable. So, for example, if a person weighs 100 pounds, a gain of 5 pounds constitutes a 5 percent— 5/100—weight increase, whereas for a person who weighs 200 pounds, a gain of 5 pounds constitutes only a 2.5 percent—5/200—increase.)

Which of the alternative assumptions is used will depend primarily on past patterns, since time-series techniques assume the continuation of past trends. To determine which alternative seems best, the analyst can plot the previous values of the revenue or expenditure against time—that is, with time measured on the horizontal axis. For example, a history of nearly equal annual increments during the past several years (i.e., data points that approximate a straight line) would provide strong evidence for an assumption of constant absolute growth. If, on the other hand, the plotted points appear to follow a nonlinear path concave from above, a constant growth *rate* may be the more reasonable assumption.

The appropriateness of assuming a constant growth rate for a given variable can be easily tested by determining past annual growth rates for the variable. These rates are determined as follows:

$$g_t = [(V_t - V_{t-})] \, 100, \tag{1}$$

where

g_t = the percentage growth rate in the variable
V = the variable
t = the period of time.

Thus, if property taxes yielded $5.1 million in 2002 and $5.3 million in 2003, the annual growth rate was 4.5 percent. If each period from 1996 through the present yields similar rates—in the range of 3.5 to 4.5 percent, for example— a 3.9 or a 4 percent annual growth rate might be assumed in forecasting the future.

Although time-trend analysis is likely to be easily grasped by decision makers and can be useful for deriving quick, relatively short-range forecasts, it will never predict a turning point: regardless of what may occur in the local economy, time-trend analysis will project only increases or decreases throughout the projection period.

Other time-series models are also available for forecasting.[20] Some are quite simple and rely on averages of the past values for a variable; others, such as weighted-average forecasts, which give more weight to recent values of the variable and less weight to values from the more distant past, are a bit more complicated. Still other models (e.g., the ARIMA model) are even more complex, but these are not used for local government forecasting as extensively as econometric models (discussed in a later section of this chapter).[21] Two factors may account for the relative lack of popularity of the more complex time-series models among local government forecasters: one is the complexity of the models and the need for more extensive data, and the other is the limitations of the pure time-series approach, which cannot take into account the effects of economic or policy variables.[22]

Deterministic techniques

Unlike time-trend forecasts, in which time is the only variable used to project revenues or expenditures, deterministic techniques allow for other variables as well. The most common deterministic technique is the use of a preestablished formula. For example, if a city knows it will obtain $900 per pupil in state education aid, total aid can be determined by multiplying $900 by the projected school enrollment.

Deterministic forecasting is especially useful for the expenditure side of the budget. For example, school district policy may require that no more than 30 students be assigned to a single teacher. If it is anticipated that 1,000 new residents will include 150 school-age students, and that all will be enrolling in the public schools, then a deterministic estimate of the number of teachers who must be hired is 5 (150 students divided by 30). If an analysis of personnel positions shows that, on average, 40 support personnel (administrators and staff) are required for every 100 teachers in the school system, then the additional 5 teachers projected would require an additional 2 support personnel (5 teachers times 0.4 support personnel per teacher). This technique is, of course, similar to that used in many fiscal impact models.

Implicit in these examples are assumptions that should be examined before proceeding with the deterministic approach. One assumption concerns the level

---

A deterministic revenue-estimation model In Prince William County, Virginia, deterministic models are the primary technique for estimating local revenues. Since the county's population has been increasing and is expected to continue to do so, many of the revenue projections are based on the expected increase in the number of housing units (along with other factors that might affect a specific revenue source). For example, to estimate local sales tax revenues for 2002–06, the county assumed that current sales tax revenues per housing unit would remain constant; it then used projected increases in the number of housing units to project total sales tax revenues in terms of current dollars. These results were then inflated by projected changes in the consumer price index to derive nominal estimates of future revenues. The county used a similar approach to project revenues from taxes on the use of wired telephone service, mobile telephone service, and electric and natural gas utilities. Since the consumer utility taxes are based on

the quantity of the utility service used (e.g., kilowatt-hours of electricity consumed) rather than on the dollar amount of expenditures, the assumption was made that additional housing units and additional businesses would serve as appropriate drivers for revenues from these utilities, with no need to adjust for anticipated changes in the prices of utility services. The forecast reflects, however, changing tastes in the types of phone services being used. In the 1990s, additional wired phone lines were being installed for Internet access and fax machines, and to provide private lines for various members of a family; these trends have recently been replaced by rapid increases in the number of mobile phones. Judgmental approaches were used to project different rates of increase for these two types of phone service.

Source: Prince William County, Virginia, Finance Department, "Fiscal Year 2003–2007 Projections of General County Revenue" (February 26, 2002), available at www.co.prince-william.va.us/finance/pdf/Revenues/revised03-07.pdf.

of service being provided; another concerns the combination of resources required to produce that service. The assumption that there will be one teacher for every thirty students, for example, implies that the level of service will be held at the specified level. Similarly, the projection for support personnel assumes that the ratio of support personnel to teachers is inflexible.

Another assumption concerns the use of averages. The projection in the example was based on averages (40 support personnel *per* 100 teachers), even though the projections were in terms of 5 additional, or *marginal,* teachers. In some instances, projections of marginal changes may be more reasonable if they are not assumed to be the same as the existing average. For example, even though a city may currently have one fire station for every 15,000 residents, an anticipated influx of 1,000 new residents may not require any change in the number of fire stations and any addition of personnel to staff them. If, however, most of these new residents are expected to locate in an area that is already only minimally served, it may be necessary to build, equip, and staff an additional fire station. In this instance, the expenditures associated with one additional fire station would be projected even though the average (one station per 15,000 residents) would call for only 0.07 stations.

Still another issue is the usefulness of the deterministic approach for communities with declining populations. Although local governments are likely to hire more public employees in response to population growth, the assumption that the workforce will be reduced proportionately in response to population decline may be less realistic. In any case, both forecasters and policy makers should carefully examine each of the assumptions behind the forecasts.

Econometric forecasting

Econometric forecasting combines economic principles with statistical techniques, making it possible for the analyst to consider the simultaneous effects of several variables on a revenue or expenditure stream. Conceptually somewhat more complex than deterministic forecasting, econometric forecasting is capable of yielding more useful information to both the forecaster and the policy maker.

Regression techniques: A multistep process   The most common econometric approach is to forecast the revenue or spending series using statistical regression analysis techniques (see the sidebar on page 112). The approach generally entails several steps: (1) determining, for each revenue or expenditure item, which variables are good candidates to be used as "independent," or causal, variables to explain past and future changes in that revenue or expenditure; (2) obtaining historical data on the revenue and expenditure series and on the independent variables; (3) estimating the statistical relationship between the dependent variable and the independent variables; (4) obtaining projections of future values of the independent variables so that they can be used to forecast future values of the dependent variables; and (5) inserting these projected future values of the independent variables into the estimated regression equation to derive an estimate of the dependent variable. (Since revenue forecasts are more amenable to econometric forecasting than are expenditures, the examples are restricted to revenues.)

First, for a particular revenue source, one or more independent variables are hypothesized. Because economic theory is more likely to result in relationships that will hold true in the future, economic theory, rather than eclectic or empirical approaches, should be used to choose the independent variables. For example, economic theory suggests that income, relative prices, preferences, and number of consumers are variables that affect the demand for taxable

Linear regression analysis Linear regression analysis is a statistical technique that allows an investigator to estimate how one variable, called a *dependent variable,* is related to one or more other variables, termed *independent variables.* For example, one might expect that a local government's sales tax revenues (the dependent variable) would be related to the personal incomes of local residents and to the rate of the local sales tax relative to that in neighboring jurisdictions (the independent variables). Through regression analysis, past values for the dependent and independent variables can be used to estimate how changes in the independent variables would affect or be related to changes in the dependent variable. Such relationships can then be used to forecast future changes in the dependent variable on the basis of expected changes in the independent variables.

Most introductory statistics textbooks contain at least a couple of chapters on regression techniques. For a simple explanation of the rudiments of linear regression analysis and the interpretation of results, as well as a discussion of some major issues associated with the technique, see Larry D. Schroeder, David L. Sjoquist, and Paula Stephan, *Understanding Regression Analysis: An Introductory Guide* (Beverly Hills, Calif.: Sage, 1986).

consumer goods, which, in turn, determines sales tax revenues. An analyst using an empirical approach, in contrast, would use statistical regression techniques to estimate various relationships between the dependent variable—that is, the revenue series—and different independent variables, and then use whatever independent variables provide the "best fit" to the historical data. But the historical relationship may have been a fluke: the relationships that held during periods of rapid inflation, for example, may be inapplicable during periods in which prices remain relatively stable. If an empirical approach is used, the forecaster should carefully consider how realistic the resulting relationship seems as well as what it implies.

Second, forecasters should consult internal records for all historical data pertaining to a particular revenue source.[23] They must ensure, however, that the data truly reflect what they purport to measure and that data compilation methods were consistent during the entire period. For example, minor revenue sources such as service fees or charges may not have been reported consistently in the past. To the extent possible, forecasters should adjust the data to yield a series that most closely reflects the current definition of the revenue source. (This aspect of forecasting is described in more detail later in this chapter.) At this point, lack of data on the variables suggested by economic theory may require the substitution of proxy variables. For example, many local governments cannot obtain reliable time-series data on local income and must therefore use county, state, or national income data as a proxy.

Third, the forecaster will determine a statistical relationship among variables, preferably using linear regression analysis.[24] In linear regression analysis, the dependent variable, *Y,* is specified as a linear function of the independent variables:

$$Y = a + b_1 X_1 + b_2 x_2 + \cdots + b_k X_k, \tag{2}$$

where

$X_1, X_2, \ldots X_k = K$ different independent variables
$a, b_1, b_2, \ldots b_k =$ parameters to be estimated using regression techniques.

For example, in forecasting local sales taxes (*ST*), the analyst may specify that these revenues depend on real personal income (*I*), the consumer price index (*CPI*), and the population of the community (*POP*). The regression equation to be estimated is

$$ST = a + b_1I \quad b_2CPI \quad b_3POP. \tag{3}$$

Least squares regression analysis finds numerical estimates of a, b_1, b_2, and b_3.

An even simpler formulation would hypothesize that local sales taxes are a linear function of local income. The hypothetical values of these two variables have been plotted on the graph shown in Figure 5–1. Each point on the graph represents the observed values of the two variables in one year. Least squares regression then finds the *unique* line that passes through these points and *minimizes* the sum of the *squared* vertical distances between the line and all observed pairs of values. This unique line can be expressed algebraically as

$$ST = a + bI, \tag{4}$$

where

a = the "intercept term" or the value of *ST* when *I* equals zero
b = the slope of the line.

The slope can be interpreted as the change in *ST* associated with each unit change in *I*. For example, if the analysis yields the result

$$ST = 16.221 + 0.013I, \tag{5}$$

the implication is that for each $1.00 increase (or decrease) in income, sales tax revenues are estimated to increase (or decrease) by $.013. (The 16.221 term has no reasonable interpretation since it suggests positive tax revenues even with an income of zero; a nonzero intercept is necessary to ensure that the least-squared-distance criterion is satisfied.)

Instead of assuming that each additional dollar of income is associated with a constant absolute change in revenues, an alternative but still simple technique is to rely on estimates of revenue *elasticities*. Elasticities, which measure the percentage change in revenue associated with a percentage change in the independent variable, are especially useful because they only require projections of the rate of growth for an independent variable (e.g., income); it is not necessary to make forecasts about the absolute growth of that variable. For example, if the income elasticity for a revenue source is estimated to be 0.95, a jurisdiction that anticipates local incomes to increase by 4 percent would

Figure 5–1   Least squares regression analysis.

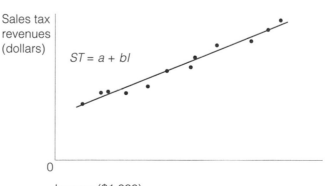

estimate its revenues to increase by 3.8 percent (0.95 × 4). For its revenue forecasts, Utah's fiscal impact model for state and local governments relies on estimates of the elasticity of revenues in relation to earnings.[25]

Regression estimates of elasticities are quite straightforward and rely on logarithmic transformations of both the independent and dependent variables. (Spreadsheet programs include functions that compute the logarithm of a variable.) Mathematically, the change in the logarithm of a variable is the same as a percentage change in the variable. Therefore, if the logarithm of the dependent variable (i.e., a tax revenue series) is regressed on the logarithm of the independent variable (such as personal income), the resulting slope coefficient can be interpreted as the ratio of the percentage change in the dependent variable relative to a percentage change in the independent variable; in other words, the coefficient is a direct estimate of the income elasticity of the revenue source.

Forecasters using regression analysis must keep several features of the technique in mind. Most often, revenue equations include two or more independent variables in place of the single variable used in equation (4). In such cases, the individual regression coefficients are estimates of the change in the dependent variable associated with a one-unit change in the particular independent variable, *with the remaining independent variables held constant.* The sign on the coefficient indicates whether the two variables tend to vary in the same or in opposite directions. Consider the following example of a multiple regression equation of the form specified in equation (3):

$$ST = 10.315 + 0.011I \quad 1.614CPI \quad 3.215POP. \tag{6}$$

These results imply that even if prices (*CPI*) and population (*POP*) remain constant, each $1.00 increase in real income is estimated to result in an increase of $0.011 in sales tax revenues. That the two variables are expected to move in the same direction follows from the plus sign (+) on the coefficient of income (I).

As noted in the discussion of elasticities, logarithmic transformations of variables can also be used in regression analysis to represent nonlinear relationships between variables. Another technique often used in econometric models is to specify that the value of the dependent variable (the one on the left-hand side of the equal sign) depends on the value of one or more independent variables in the previous period. These two concepts are illustrated in the following equation:

$$ln(CIG) = 5.33 + 1.007 \, ln(CIGR) + 0.970 \, ln(ILAG), \tag{7}$$

where

   $ln(CIG)$ = the natural logarithm of cigarette taxes
   $ln(CIGR)$ = the natural logarithm of cigarette tax rates
   $ln(ILAG)$ = the natural logarithm of real personal income, with a lag of one
       year.[26]

The equation implies that, with cigarette tax rates constant, a 1.0 *percent* increase in lagged real income is associated with a 0.970 *percent* increase in cigarette tax revenues. Lagged variables are appropriate when taxpayers are not expected to respond immediately to changes in variables such as income or prices. Although these transformations (and others) are extremely useful, the analyst should consider carefully whether the chosen equation makes theoretical and practical sense.

Regression analysis yields other statistics that can be used to judge the final results. One of these is the coefficient of determination (R^2), which can take on any fractional value from 0 to 1. Higher R^2 values suggest a closer fit between the observed points and the regression equation—which suggests, assuming that the relationship will hold in the future, that a more accurate forecast is likely to result. Another statistic, the estimated standard error of the regression coefficient, can be used to test whether a particular independent variable is statistically related to the dependent variable (i.e., whether the regression coefficient is equal to zero). The estimated standard error is especially important when the regression results are used to analyze policy questions that focus on a particular independent variable.

The cigarette tax example may be used to illustrate these two statistics. A complete reporting of the regression results shows

$$ln(CIG = 5.33+ 1.007\,ln(CIGR + 0.970\,ln(ILAG \qquad (8)$$
$$(1.26\ (\ 0.172 \qquad (\quad 0)163$$

$$R^2 = 0.965$$

where the number below each regression coefficient is its estimated standard error and the coefficient of determination is 0.965. The latter statistic means that more than 96 percent of the variation in the natural logarithm of cigarette taxes can be attributed to variation in the two independent variables. Thus, it appears that these variables offer a good "explanation" of cigarette tax revenues.

The estimated standard errors in equation (8) suggest that changes in each of the independent variables are significantly related to changes in the dependent variable. If the estimated standard error on the *ILAG* variable had been found to be as large, for example, as 0.6 rather than 0.163, there would have been insufficient evidence to conclude that changes in the natural logarithm of *ILAG* were significantly related to changes in the natural logarithm of *CIG*. Thus, even if real incomes increase, there would not be sufficient statistical evidence to conclude that cigarette tax revenues would respond.

The fourth step in the use of regression techniques occurs after the final equation has been chosen. The analyst must then forecast values for each independent variable for the projection period. This step may produce errors in the projections because the resulting forecast for the dependent variable (the final step) is based on variables that are forecasts themselves and therefore subject to forecasting error.

Advantages and disadvantages of econometric forecasting   The econometric, or statistical, approach to forecasting has advantages and disadvantages compared with expert, time-trend, and deterministic techniques. An econometric model bases projections on behavioral relationships that have a theoretical foundation and that can be evaluated by the user of the forecast—an attribute missing in expert forecasts. Simple time-trend techniques, such as that shown in equation (1), forecast that revenues or expenditures will continue to increase or decrease as they have in the past, with no possibility of changing direction. Regression techniques, on the other hand, have no such limitations.[27] For example, if real income were to fall, the cigarette tax equation in (7) would project decreases in revenues. Unlike their deterministic counterparts, statistical techniques can be used to test whether an observed relationship between variables is, in fact, statistically significant. For example, an analyst may believe that there is a link between income in a jurisdiction and the amount of revenues collected from fines. Statistical techniques provide a means of determining whether the link is sufficiently stable to justify forecasting revenues from fines on the basis of local income projections.

Purely deterministic approaches usually include only one causal variable (e.g., population), whereas the statistical regression approach uses several independent variables simultaneously. Thus, it is possible to estimate the effect that a change in one independent variable (e.g., tax rate) will have on revenues while holding the other variables (e.g., real income) constant—an especially useful feature for policy analysis. Alternatively, all the independent variables can be altered simultaneously to estimate the net effect of such changes on the dependent variable.

A major disadvantage of the statistical approach is cost. Choosing appropriate forecasting equations and developing estimates from them usually requires training in economics and statistics, which is less likely to be important for time-trend and deterministic techniques. Because regression analysis calls for more data than the alternative techniques do, data collection can also be costly.

Although the results derived from the statistical approach can be evaluated systematically, the forecasts may contain errors. In fact, each of the five steps in regression analysis contains potential for error: the equation may be improperly specified (i.e., the choice of independent variables may be incorrect); the data may not be appropriate for the intended use; the estimate may create particular statistical difficulties; and the values of the independent variables used to generate the econometric forecasts may themselves be in error.[28]

Analysts often find that no single technique is most appropriate for forecasting all revenue and expenditure streams; instead, a combination of techniques is generally most desirable (see the accompanying sidebar). Those revenue streams that are most sensitive to fluctuations in the local economy are best forecast using statistical techniques. Time-trend or expert projections may be most appropriate for revenues that are either insensitive to local economic conditions or so unstable that no underlying causal relationship can be specified.

Revenue forecasting techniques used by local governments Surveys of local governments have consistently shown that although most municipalities use a variety of forecasting techniques, judgmental forecasting is the most common method used for revenue forecasts. Trend analysis is generally the second-most-used technique.

A 1989 survey of 290 municipal finance officers found that approximately 82 percent of respondents used judgmental techniques and 52 percent used trend analysis.[1]

Analysis of a 1999 survey of 319 municipalities found that 94 percent of respondents used judgmental techniques to project property tax revenues, and that among jurisdictions that projected sales tax revenues, 96 percent used trend analysis.[2]

Analysis of a 1999 survey of 531 municipal finance officers revealed that more than 91 percent of responding jurisdictions used judgmental or expert-based techniques to forecast at least one type of revenue and that nearly that many (89.9 percent) used trend analysis to project at least one type of revenue.[3]

All three studies found that econometric methods are less commonly used: the proportion of respondents using such techniques ranged from approximately 20 to approximately 33 percent.

[1]Jane McCollough, "Municipal Revenue and Expenditure Forecasting: Current Status and Future Prospects," *Government Finance Review* (October 1990): 38–40.
[2]Marilyn Rubin, Nancy Mantell, and Michael Pagano, "Approaches to Revenue Forecasting by State and Local Governments," *Proceedings of the Ninety-Second Annual Conference of the National Tax Association* (Atlanta, Ga.: National Tax Association, October 1999), 205–221.
[3]Changhoon Jung, "Revenue Estimation Practices and Budget Process in Municipal Governments," paper presented at the fourteenth annual meeting of the Association for Budget and Financial Management, Kansas City, Mo., October 2002.

Expenditures are best forecast using some variant of the deterministic approach to ensure that they are realistic and amenable to policy analysis. Thus, before undertaking a forecasting project, the analyst should consider carefully the revenues and expenditures to be forecast, the characteristics and costs of the various techniques, and the needs of the jurisdiction.[29]

Revenue and expenditure forecasting: Applications and data requirements

This section describes how the four forecasting techniques just discussed are applied to revenue and expenditure forecasting. The section closes with a discussion of potential problems in working with internal and external data—for example, taking account of historical changes in revenues and expenditures and obtaining timely, reliable information from external sources.

Revenue forecasting

When analyzing the effects of specific policies or economic changes on revenue structure, the three types of revenue to consider are local tax revenue, local nontax revenue, and intergovernmental revenue. No single projection technique is necessarily most appropriate for all these revenue sources. Whichever approach is selected, separate (i.e., disaggregated) forecasting of each revenue source is recommended. Disaggregated projections include only those independent variables considered theoretically important to the revenue source in question and allow more extensive analysis of the source of errors in the forecast. The aggregated approach, which lumps together the various revenue sources, introduces a hodgepodge of data that can result in a distorted or potentially misleading analysis.

Tax revenues   Most tax revenues are sensitive to fluctuations in the local economy. Econometric forecasting is the most useful method for examining the effects of such changes. The first step is to specify the independent variables to be used in the regression equations. The purchasing power of the community, as measured by income (or some proxy thereof), is generally the most critical variable and the one most likely to be used by local governments that forecast revenues.[30]

Choosing a measure of income can be problematic, however, because few sources provide timely local income data. The Bureau of Economic Analysis (BEA) of the U.S. Department of Commerce publishes estimated income data for counties, but the data are available only after a lag of at least one year. The lack of up-to-date income data means that the analyst cannot use the most recent revenue data in a regression equation that uses personal income as an independent variable. Since many local governments can obtain historical revenue data only for the past fifteen years or so, omitting the most recent observations means that a considerable amount of relevant information will be lost. In addition, county data may not be appropriate for a municipality whose boundaries do not coincide closely with those of the county, or for a wealthy enclave in a relatively poor county. However, in the case of revenues such as the retail sales tax, if many of the taxable expenditures in a municipality are made by people who live in an overlapping county or by residents of adjacent counties, county-level income data may be the most relevant. States sometimes provide income estimates, at least at the county level, on a more timely basis than BEA, but the sources and definitions used to create the state data must be carefully reviewed. For example, data derived from state income tax returns may be based on a definition of income that differs considerably from that of the Commerce Department. Transfer payments, including both social security income and unemployment compensation, are likely to be excluded from the state data, although these income sources are included in BEA's income estimates. On the other hand, realized capital gains are included in state data but excluded by BEA. Because transfer payments are an important component of the community's overall purchasing power, excluding them from the income measure can yield inaccurate results, particularly if such payments constitute differing proportions of total income over time.

Even if local income data are available, it is still necessary to project future income in order to obtain revenue forecasts. Local econometric models available from commercial firms are one possible source of such projections, but these are generally county-level models and are likely to require relatively expensive subscriptions to the forecasting service. Another alternative is a state-level econometric model built by a state agency or university. If none of these alternatives is available, it may be necessary to construct a model based on national income projections (which are easily accessible) that links local economic variables to the national economy. In this approach, national income projections are used to forecast local income, and the resulting projections are then incorporated into the revenue equations.

Another approach, which involves using national income as an independent variable in the regression equation, works well as long as local patterns of change in income track national patterns closely. However, not all local economies experience exactly the same pattern of recessions and expansions as the rest of the nation. For example, manufacturing industries are generally more vulnerable to economic cycles than are consumer-oriented or service-based industries. Consequently, communities with an economic base that consists primarily of manufacturing may lead the nation in decline, whereas communities with service-based economies may be more resistant to a national recession. A forecaster choosing among various options for obtaining projections must first have a good understanding of the local economic base.

If national income data (which encompass the effects of changes in national population) are to be used in the tax equation, they should be adjusted to reflect relative changes in local population. To the extent that the local population grows more rapidly (or slowly) than the national population, changes in the local population can stimulate (or retard) the growth of the revenue source. One solution is to transform the data into per capita terms and then multiply the resulting forecast of per capita revenue by the projections for the local population. A second solution is to use local population directly in the forecasting equation. Both approaches require local annual population data as well as population forecasts; the sources discussed earlier in the chapter can provide the data to create the necessary estimates and projections.

The property tax, an important revenue source for many localities, can be difficult to project using an econometric model, principally because of the discretionary nature of assessment administration.[31] Unless assessed values are revised frequently to reflect current market conditions, simple time-trend techniques or expert methods may be superior to econometric models—and, in fact, these techniques are the most popular among the majority of municipalities.

Where assessed values do change to reflect fluctuations in the market, the property tax base generally responds positively to economic conditions, although perhaps not in all neighborhoods. Possible variables for use in property tax equations include income, prices, population, and measures of local building activity. Furthermore, the forecaster can choose between projecting the property tax base (to which an assumed tax rate can be applied to estimate revenues) or projecting the total tax revenues directly. Projecting the base may be more informative because it illustrates for policy makers the different tax yields associated with alternative tax rates.

Where assessment practices are such that new properties are the prime source of growth in the property tax base, new building activity should be used as the primary independent variable. If appropriate data are not available, projected population changes may be used as a proxy variable.

Nontax revenues   Forecasts of nontax revenue sources such as fines, interest, user charges, and fees often require a variety of projection techniques. Econometric techniques may be appropriate for some of these revenues. Certain fees may be closely related to economic activity (e.g., sewer connections and building activity), in which case assumptions similar to those used for projecting taxes can be applied.

Fairly accurate forecasts of nontax revenues can often be obtained through simple time-trend projections, deterministic approaches, or estimates from experts. For example, fees from such activities as the sale of maps by the planning department can be most accurately projected by planning department staff. Nevertheless, department-level forecasters must be given a set of assumptions on which to base the projections, and these assumptions should be consistent with those underlying other revenue and expenditure projections.

One of the most complex nontax revenue sources to project is interest income, primarily because of the difficulties in forecasting both the liquid-asset position of the local government and short-term interest rates. In such cases, projections based on expert opinion (e.g., that of a finance officer) will often be as effective as econometric projections. Even commercial econometric models have difficulty projecting a series as volatile as short-term interest rates, particularly when much of the change derives from the policies of the Federal Reserve.

Intergovernmental revenue   Because intergovernmental aid and grants are often important revenue sources for local government, they must be projected to obtain accurate predictions of total revenues. The primary determining variables for intergovernmental revenue are political decisions made at higher levels of government; thus, the forecaster may find it helpful to seek expert opinions on particular types of intergovernmental aid. State or federal legislators, for example, may be in a position to provide useful information on the likelihood that major grant programs will be continued or terminated. Deterministic methods can also be used if, for example, the grant program ties revenues to a local demographic variable such as population or student enrollments.

One commonly used assumption is that the dollars derived from intergovernmental grants will remain constant over the forecast period; this is the assumption used by Hennepin County, Minnesota, in its five-year financial projections for 2002–06. A less conservative approach assumes that grant funds will rise at the rate of inflation; a more conservative approach assumes that aid programs scheduled to be phased out during the forecast period will not be renewed and that funding levels for other grants will remain constant. Some observers have pointed out that categorical federal grants impose major hidden costs—namely, the expenditures necessary to keep a project in operation after it is begun. Forecasting that takes explicit account of operating and maintenance expenditures should determine whether the activity funded by the categorical grant is really a worthy project in an environment of fiscal constraint.

Expenditure forecasting

The deterministic approach, based on accounting identities, seems to work best for expenditure forecasting. Expenditures are classified by type of spending (e.g., personnel, materials, and debt service) and then projected according to a consistent set of assumptions about service levels, productivity, and prices. Although projections of some disaggregated expenditures may be amenable to econometric techniques, it is unlikely that a local government will find the benefits of a full-scale econometric model to be worth the cost.

The deterministic approach outlined here starts with a disaggregation of expenditures (1) by agency, department, or program and (2) by object (e.g., labor or materials). This spending breakdown can be further divided into units within agencies or departments (e.g., uniformed and nonuniformed personnel within police departments) and by sub-objects within objects (e.g., utilities or contractual expenditures within nonpersonnel expenditures). The forecast of these detailed expenditures can be as fine as desired, or at least as fine as the accounting or management system allows.

The following five sections discuss the general categories of expenditure.

Personnel expenditures   Total labor cost can be divided into direct labor expenditures and fringe benefits. Cost projections are made by functional area

---

Examples of assumptions for deterministic forecasting   Deterministic forecasting requires a set of assumptions regarding future prices and policies. The following examples are adapted from the six-year financial forecast prepared for the city of Eugene, Oregon, in 1999.

The consumer price index (CPI) will continue to rise slowly, at a rate of 2.75 percent per year, during the six-year projection period. However, sensitivity analysis was also carried out under the assumption that inflation would rise to 3 percent in FY02, increase by 0.25 percent each year, and reach 4 percent in FY06.

Health benefits were assumed to rise at faster rates than general prices. Specifically, a 6 percent annual increase was assumed.

A 3 percent cost-of-living adjustment was assumed for FY01; future increases were projected to increase at the same rate as the CPI.

The state Public Employee Retirement System biennially adjusts the city's required contribution rate. Based on a consultant's report to the city, the required contribution rate was increased from 13.91 percent to 15.91 percent of employee wages and salaries.

Since the population of Eugene has been increasing, a "growth factor" was included in the forecasts to account for future increases in services and costs that are expected to outpace inflation. The FY01 forecast included $1.25 million for the growth factor and an additional $750,000 for each subsequent year.

As new parks are added to the city's inventory, additional maintenance costs will be required. The additional annual costs of about $500,000 would be phased in over the three-year period from FY02 to FY04.

Since, during 1998, the city council had reduced the desired level of contingency revenues from $600,000 to $400,000, the smaller amount was assumed for the six-year projection period.

The forecast also included the fiscal implications of a city council policy specifying that the unappropriated ending fund balance would equal two months of operating expenses. Because operating expenses were projected to increase during the projection period, the level of unappropriated balances would have to increase proportionately.

Source: Adapted from City of Eugene, *General Fund Six-Year Financial Forecast, FY01 through FY06* (Eugene, Ore.: Department of Administrative Services, November 1999).

(e.g., budget unit, department, or program) and are based on the relatively homogeneous groups of employees (e.g., uniformed officers or professional staff) within that functional area. If this level of detail is impossible to achieve or deemed unnecessary, the approach can be applied to less disaggregated amounts, such as total personnel spending by department or program.

A straightforward accounting-identity approach shows that the wage rate multiplied by the number of employees equals the direct cost of labor, which can be represented as

$$L_t = W_t N_t, \tag{9}$$

where

L = labor costs
W = the wage or salary level of employees in a functional area
N = the amount of labor
t = the year under review.

Thus, the projections of direct labor expenditures (L_t) require forecasts of wage levels (W_t) and number of employees (N_t) throughout the projection period.

Derivations of projected employment levels are considered first. The amount of a particular type of labor employed depends on numerous factors, including the level of service, the local population, the productivity of the labor, and the wage for this type of labor relative to prices and to wages for other types of labor.

Expenditure projections are generally made using a baseline assumption of service levels. The usual assumption, a "constant-service-level budget," suggests that no discretionary changes in service levels are built into the forecasts. In practice, however, there seems to be little agreement about what constant service means. In communities where the population is increasing, for example, constant service level is often interpreted to mean that employment in the functional area will increase proportionately. This assumption may be reasonable for direct-service functions such as police and fire, but it may be less applicable when projecting the service level of staff functions.

Legislated changes in service levels should be factored into labor usage projections. Such changes may be mandated by higher levels of government or may result from local policies. If productivity improvements are foreseen, possible reduction of the labor force should also be factored into the forecast.[32] The sidebar on page 122 illustrates how Hennepin County, Minnesota, has attempted to incorporate service requirements, labor productivity, and labor costs into its five-year financial projections.

Estimates of the effect on employment of local population changes, legislated changes, productivity, and capital projects can be calculated in at least two ways. In one approach, the estimates are centralized (e.g., within the office of the local government manager or budget officer). Although this method may yield more consistent estimates because it is based on uniform assumptions, it increases the chances of overlooking major changes, such as scheduled state-mandated expenditures of which the central office may be unaware. Under the second approach (illustrated in the sidebar about Hennepin County), departments or budget units project personnel needs. Department administrators must take this task seriously and not use the projections simply as an opportunity to compile a wish list of projects. The central forecasting unit must review departmental projections to ensure that they are realistic and consistent with the assumptions that underlie the forecast.

Wage levels should also be considered in projecting labor expenditures. The most common approach is to use the same set of assumptions for all local

Projecting personnel expenditures   Hennepin County, Minnesota, projects personnel expenditures by first asking departments to forecast their workload for the projection period. These projections are based on assumed increases in population and service needs. The forecasters then assume that labor productivity will increase by approximately 2 percent annually (this figure is based on national data on private sector productivity increases rather than on estimates of changing productivity in the county). In a growing area, these two factors would partially offset each other.

Base-year expenditures are adjusted first by these two factors and then by assumed increases in wages, which consist of two parts: a 3 percent per year cost-of-living adjustment plus a 1.5 percent increase associated with merit pay increases. A further adjustment assumed that the employer's share of contributions to the Public Employees' Retirement Association and the employer's share of health costs would also each increase by 0.375 percent annually.

Source: Hennepin County, Minnesota, "Five-Year Financial Projections, 2002–2006" (April 1, 2001), available at www.co. hennepin.mn.us/obf/02-06finproj.htm.

government employees. One method assumes that wages will increase at the same rate as prices—that is, that real wages will remain constant. An alternative method assumes that increases in wages will lag behind price increases by one year. Whatever assumption is used, the forecaster should analyze historical changes in wages to justify the choice. Moreover, whenever wage changes are based on projected price changes, the price projections should be consistent with the macroeconomic assumptions used on the revenue side of the forecast, to ensure that the revenue and expenditure forecasts will be comparable.

Yet another approach to projecting wage levels simply assumes that wages will not change; this is the assumption used in the expenditure forecast created by Bexar County, Texas. One rationale for this assumption is that, at least when the forecast is produced, no policy decision has yet been reached regarding future wage and salary levels; hence, the assumption is in keeping with the philosophy that the forecast should reflect only policies that are in place. The model can then be used to explicitly reveal the longer-term spending implications of alternative wage policies. A second rationale for assuming no change in wage levels is to maintain confidentiality about the locality's strategies for collective bargaining.

Direct wages and salaries constitute the bulk of labor expenditures, but the cost of fringe benefits, particularly health insurance, is becoming increasingly important. The major fringe benefits, in addition to various insurance expenditures, are retirement contributions and the employer's share of social security payments. Retirement contributions and social security payments are likely to be related directly to the wage bill (total direct labor expenditures), whereas insurance expenditures usually depend on the number of people employed. Social security (employer) contribution rates can be assumed with reasonable certainty and multiplied by the projected levels of wages. If the local government does not have a self-administered retirement program, projections of retirement contribution rates may be obtained from the retirement system that administers the local government's retirement program. The analyst must be aware, however, of the actuarial assumptions that go into these projections and determine whether they are consistent with other components of the forecast.

Other benefits to be considered by the forecaster are fringes such as vacation and sick leave. If these benefits are projected to increase, and service levels and productivity are projected to remain constant, additional personnel may have to be hired. One way to account for changes in fringe benefits is to use full-time equivalents or labor hours, rather than the number of workers on the payroll, as the measure of labor in equation (9).

The deterministic forecasting method is, of course, particularly amenable to computerization using a common spreadsheet program. Computerization makes it especially easy to determine the implications of alternative assumptions about the number of employees, wages and benefits, or both. The Michigan Municipal League has developed a model that compares spending under various assumptions.[33]

Other current expenditures   Other expenditures include a multitude of items ranging from stationery and gasoline to contractual services. As with labor expenditures, some degree of disaggregation can be used to project the costs of supplies, materials, and equipment. That is,

$$Q_t = P_t Q_t, \tag{10}$$

where

- O = other current expenditures
- P = price
- Q = the quantity of materials projected to be purchased
- t = the fiscal year in which the expenses are incurred.

The degree to which these expenditures are disaggregated depends on the desired level of detail, the local government's ability to disaggregate materials into relatively homogeneous groups of goods, and the availability of price indexes for the different types of supplies. Under the assumption that the quantity of materials will change in proportion to changes in employment levels, projected changes in the quantities of materials are usually tied to projected changes in staffing. The lack of availability of disaggregated price indexes is generally the primary obstacle to a full disaggregation of current expenditures. For many categories of goods used in governmental production, no good price indexes exist; thus, either proxy variables or judgmental opinions are used to project these prices. The principal proxy variables for projecting prices include the producer price index, the consumer price index, and the components thereof.

Transfer payments   Although transfer payments to particular segments of the population, such as physically disabled or visually impaired residents, are not part of the budgetary responsibility of most municipalities, they can be critical parts of a county's budget. For jurisdictions that do have responsibility for such payments, trend or econometric projection techniques would be the most appropriate. For example, the caseloads of social-welfare programs probably increase when local economic activity slows. Techniques similar to those used to project tax revenues would apply in these instances; that is, predicted caseloads would be multiplied by an assumed or mandated level of payment.[34]

Debt service   Debt service—interest and debt retirement—can be one of the easiest expenditures to forecast. If no change in the overall level or composition of the debt is projected over the relevant time period, future debt service is known with certainty. It is more likely, however, that debt will increase in the course of implementing the long range capital plan, in which case the analyst must make assumptions about the structure and interest rates associated with the new debt. The cost of servicing short-range debt and bond or tax anticipation notes must also be forecast. Projections from a cash management model, together with interest rate forecasts obtained from external sources, can be used for these cost estimates. Again, assumptions about interest rates should be consistent with those used to project interest earnings on the revenue side of the forecast.

Capital projects scheduled for completion may affect the required level of labor and other current inputs associated with the new project. These, too, must be incorporated into the expenditure projections. For example, if a new recreation center is supposed to open in 2005, projections made in 2003 should include the operating and maintenance costs for the center from 2005 through the end of the projected period.

Interfund transfers   Local governments that focus their forecasts on the general fund must project transfers to and from this fund. For example, general-fund revenues are sometimes used to subsidize expenditures financed from other, separate funds. Such transfers may simply be forecast judgmentally.

If the details of the fiscal activity of all funds are forecast, interfund transfers (based on current policies concerning such transfers) can be built into the overall forecast. For example, it may be common practice for a community to transfer into the general fund all excess revenues obtained from a sewer fund. In that case, forecasted revenue surpluses in the sewer fund can be projected as a source of revenue to the general fund.

Internal data

Both econometric and time-trend techniques require historical data. A series of ten to fifteen years is best for obtaining reasonable results, but available data are not always reported consistently across the entire period. Two major problems inherent in working with historical information are changes in definitions and changes in the rates and bases of revenue sources.

Although major revenue sources are usually reported consistently over time, the same is not always true of minor revenue sources. Revenue from various fees, for example, may have been reported separately during some periods but aggregated in available financial records during others. Thus, to create a consistent time series, the forecaster must either combine the disaggregated amounts or, for the times that the amounts were reported as a single number, attempt to disaggregate the series. The first approach is easier but sacrifices information; the second approach requires more effort but may be more accurate.

Accounting for discretionary changes in the rate or base of a tax (especially the major tax revenue sources) creates a more complex problem. For example, a particular tax may have yielded $1 million in revenue for two or three years, after which the yield suddenly increased to $1.5 million. A 50 percent increase suggests that either the tax rate was increased or the tax base was broadened. To attribute such a change in revenues to changes in the economic or demographic variables used in the regression equation would be misleading and lead to biased results. Thus, it is necessary to "clean" the data series of the consequences of purely administrative or policy changes.

The various methods available for this cleaning operation essentially factor out the effects of discretionary changes by estimating what the revenues would have been without the changes.[35] Because such endeavors require both substantial investigation of the bases and rates of revenue sources and considerable computational effort, many forecasters opt to clean only the major revenue series.[36]

The difficulty involved in obtaining clean data suggests why statistical techniques do not work well for expenditure forecasts. Historical changes in expenditures nearly always arise from a combination of external factors (such as price increases) and internal policy changes (such as the addition of new police officers). To attribute all previous variations in spending to external economic factors, as would be assumed if expenditures were regressed on economic variables, would confuse the effects of the economic variables with the effects of policy initiatives. On the other hand, to clean these expenditure series for all such policy changes would be extremely difficult—and unlikely to yield forecasts any more useful than those produced under a deterministic approach.

External data

External data generally do not require cleaning, but they do raise certain issues. The most serious problem in the use of externally collected data is the difficulty of obtaining reliable, up-to-date information. Since the federal government does not, at least on a timely basis, provide detailed annual data for local governments, proxies are often necessary. Thus, as noted earlier, county-level economic data published by the federal government may be used as a proxy for economic conditions in a municipality.

State agencies such as the labor department, the tax or revenue department, and the commerce department may have useful information pertaining to local jurisdictions. Local firms, chambers of commerce, banks, and universities may also have considerable information on a locality, and may even have economic forecasting units that can make data or projections available to the budget forecaster. In addition, major national econometric forecasting firms can provide many of the independent variables required for econometric revenue forecasting, as well as access to the expertise of a staff of forecasters. Of course, subscriptions to obtain such services are expensive, costing several thousand dollars a year.

Often, local governments use forecasted data produced by national forecasting firms even without formal subscriptions to their services. Business publications such as the *Wall Street Journal* and *Business Week,* for example, report the projections of national income, gross national product, and inflation made by the major forecasting companies. National projections are also available from the Congressional Budget Office and the Office of Management and Budget, each of which produces five-year forecasts of the national economy. These forecasts include projections of national income and prices in alternative scenarios based on differing assumptions about the general rate of growth.[37] As noted earlier, some local governments find it useful to assemble a group of local experts to discuss the future of the local economy. Not only can such a group provide the local government with useful information, but it can also provide all group members with a better understanding of the fiscal issues faced by the locality.

Given the variety of macroeconomic forecasts available, the analyst should be aware that while econometric forecasts tend not to vary greatly in their final projections, different forecasters may use different assumptions. For example, a forecaster who assumes that a major strike by the teamsters' union will dampen the overall growth rate of the economy during a portion of the upcoming year may project lower growth rates than a forecaster who assumes that the strike will be settled quickly. Similarly, since each may be based on different assumptions, using national income projections from one model and price projections from another would create inconsistencies that could lead to forecasting errors.

Federal data sources   The federal government compiles many kinds of statistical data. Among the most important for financial analyses are those covering income, population, the labor market, and prices.

The principal agency that collects income data is the Bureau of Economic Analysis (BEA) of the U.S. Department of Commerce. The *Survey of Current Business,* published monthly by this bureau, includes estimates of national income, personal income, and the gross national product. Periodically, BEA also publishes income estimates for states, counties, and other areas within states. In addition to print publications, BEA offers CD-ROM versions of personal income and employment estimates for counties and metropolitan areas since 1969; data can also be downloaded from the BEA Web site: www.bea.gov.

The Bureau of the Census, also within the Department of Commerce, is the primary source of population data at the federal level. While the decennial census presents detailed demographic information for localities, the primary source of small-area data on an annual basis is Series P-25 of the Current Population Reports, *Population Estimates and Projections.* Approximately seventy reports are issued annually, including estimates of county populations and projections of state populations. Census data can also be accessed from the Web at www.census.gov.

The Bureau of Labor Statistics (BLS) of the U.S. Department of Labor compiles labor market and price information. The *Monthly Labor Review* contains nationwide data on labor market conditions, including those on employment, unemployment, earnings, and prices. The *Handbook of Labor Statistics* (Bulletin 2340) is a compilation of historical data collected by BLS; detailed definitions of the measures are provided in the *BLS Handbook of Methods* (Bulletin 2414). On the Web, the BLS home page is www.bls.gov.

A final problem that can arise when statistical relationships are estimated concerns possible disparities between the fiscal year of the local government and the time period covered by the external data (which is usually the calendar year). For example, if the 2003 fiscal year (FY03) runs from July 1, 2002, to June 30, 2003, and the data used for the independent variables are defined for calendar years, the results may differ depending on whether the statistical model uses independent variables from calendar year 2002 or 2003 as the determinants of FY03 revenues. Since many economic decisions involve time lags, it is probably more reasonable to assume that FY03 revenues are a function of the economic data from calendar year 2002. It is crucial, of course, that the staff collecting the data be aware of how the time period will be defined by those who will prepare the data for analysis.

Reporting and using projections

Given the projections of revenue and expenditures, the forecaster can construct a table or chart that compares the absolute levels of each for the entire forecast period. Since it is not uncommon for forecasters to use conservative assumptions regarding revenue and liberal assumptions regarding spending, forecasters often project revenue shortfalls. It is important for the forecaster to make clear, however, that these are not *predictions;* they are simply intended to serve as a warning that, without a change in policies, such deficits might arise.

Multiyear forecasts are generally produced before elected officials have determined budget priorities. In Kansas City, Missouri, for example, the five-year financial forecast was presented to the city council in October 2001. Relying on the projections in the forecast, on other studies, and on the city's broad long-term plans (including the strategic plan), the council set a number of priorities that were to be incorporated into the 2002–03 city budget, which was finally adopted in late March 2002.

The multiyear forecast projected 5.8 percent annual growth in expenditures and 2.7 percent annual growth in revenues. To at least partially offset the anticipated shortfalls, the council made a number of cuts and revenue enhancements for the 2002–03 budget (electing, for example, to reduce the budgeted fund balance from 8 to 5.3 percent of budgeted expenditures). Even so, shortfalls were still projected for fiscal years 2003–04 and 2004–05, meaning that the council would again face difficult decisions.

The forecast may also suggest policy alternatives designed to prevent the projected deficits. For example, a forecaster could indicate what increases in the property tax rate would be necessary to close the projected gaps. Or the forecast might propose policy changes that would help balance the budget. (The sidebar on Bexar County, Texas, on page 107 of this chapter, illustrates this use of the multiyear financial forecast.) Once the baseline projections are complete, a range of budgetary forecasts can be produced on the basis of alternative assumptions about important variables, such as the rate of inflation or the growth rate of the local economy.[38]

Multiyear forecasts can also be useful for capital budgeting. For example, Prince Georges County, Maryland, has adopted a formal policy that caps annual debt service expenditures for all county debt at 10 percent of annual revenues. The county uses its multiyear revenue forecast to determine the absolute number of dollars represented by the 10 percent cap; this figure can then be used to determine whether the debt service on proposed debt-financed projects will be in danger of exceeding the cap.

Building a forecasting model

Creating a revenue and expenditure projection model is not particularly difficult and certainly not beyond the capabilities of most local governments, but it does require thought and planning, appropriate data, and the time to assemble the data and construct the model. Nearly all experienced forecasters recommend, however, that when initiating a model-building effort, one should start at a simple level and attempt to make the model more complex only after gaining some experience.

The increased availability of microcomputers that have the capacity to handle spreadsheet programs and statistical analysis simplifies the overall task. Once the data are assembled, it is not difficult to produce deterministic expenditure forecasts using spreadsheet programs. Base-year spending (by function, object, or both) can be inserted into the program and then "rolled forward," using whatever assumptions the forecaster chooses regarding future levels of inputs and their prices. Statistical packages, as well as the popular spreadsheets available for personal computers, usually have regression analysis capabilities that can be used for econometric revenue forecasting. Given the widespread availability of computer resources, probably the greatest effort required to complete the initial forecast will go into collecting data from both inside and outside the governmental unit.

Administrative and political issues in forecasting

In addition to technical matters, forecasters should consider administrative and political issues when evaluating the feasibility of a forecasting project.[39]

Administrative issues

Among the administrative issues that may arise are (1) the role of the chief administrator, (2) the assignment of responsibility for the forecasts, and (3) presentation of the projections.

Role of the chief administrator   The chief administrator (mayor or local government manager), the finance officer, and the planning director are not likely to undertake the actual forecast, yet their role in forecasting is far from passive. The chief administrator, for example, must determine the most appropriate type of forecast to undertake, a decision that demands a thorough understanding of the forecasting process: he or she must be able to evaluate forecasting needs in relation to financial resources, determine the availability of data, and coordinate available staff.

The role of the chief administrator is probably most important when expenditure forecasts are based on data submitted by department heads. Compiling projections of labor and nonlabor costs under a set of assumptions and mandates that are likely to affect the department can be time-consuming. If department heads believe that their projections are not likely to be used or that the chief administrator has little interest in the final product, they may be unwilling to devote much effort to the process. However, if the chief administrator encourages the staff, conducting a systematic review of what is likely to occur over the next two to five years enables department heads to be more forward-thinking—to develop longer-range perspectives on the operations of their departments. Moreover, reviewing the overall projections for the locality may help the chief administrator develop a broader perspective on the entire organization. One basic requirement does persist, however: all those involved in forecasting must recognize that it is a tool, not a panacea—a means, not an end. Armed with this understanding and with sustained professional commitment and involvement, chief administrators, department heads, and their staffs can ensure that forecasting works effectively and efficiently to shape public policy.

Responsibility for forecasts   Responsibility for forecasts may fall to a variety of offices, depending on the organizational structure. In most local governments, however, forecasts originate in the budget office, since budget personnel are most intimately involved with the flow of expenditures and with the operations of individual departments.[40] Revenue projections, on the other hand, can be made either by the budget office or by a tax-oriented department, such as finance. Finance-office staff generally have the expertise necessary to clean data series; they are also likely to have experience projecting different revenue series for individual budget years.

A division of effort between the budget office and the finance office may be the least costly way to produce a forecast, but it raises some potential management issues. Because the revenue and expenditure projections are to be compared, both sets of projections should be based on a single set of assumptions about the course of the local economy. The chief administrator must see to it that the necessary coordination occurs.

Another management issue concerns the use of internal staff or outside consultants to produce the forecast. Although consultants are likely to have greater technical expertise, they may lack an intimate understanding of the local government's financial or organizational structure. Furthermore, constructing a model should be more than just a once-a-year exercise that produces a single set of numbers. Creating the forecast within the organization is most likcly to encourage its ongoing use as a management tool.

Presentation of projections   The chief administrator should be responsible for presenting the forecasts effectively. It is crucial to go beyond a simple description of projected revenues and expenditures. Readers of the forecast should be told the assumptions under which the budgetary projections are made—assumptions about the future of the local economy, the revenue structure, the costs of services, and service levels. Especially if a revenue shortfall is being projected, the rationale for the entire exercise should be presented in readily understandable language. Although the forecast document should make it clear that the local government will not necessarily resort to deficit financing to address the shortfall, it should indicate that some action will be taken (or at least planned) to avoid the problem. Some local governments go one step further and specify in the forecast document exactly what actions can be taken in the near term to avoid a deficit. Some combination of tax increases, increases in governmental aid, and expenditure cutbacks can then be used to balance the budget.

Graphic presentations can be particularly useful in conveying the results. Simple line charts—showing the past several years of revenues and expenditures along with the projected levels of each—are especially effective. The same information can also be effectively translated into bar graphs, which allow the user to easily see the extent of any projected fiscal gaps. If the forecast document includes alternative policy scenarios (e.g., projected revenues and expenditures with and without a major capital project, or with alternative wage policies for public employees), these results can be presented in both tabular (i.e., numerical) and graphic form. Since, however, highly complex graphs with too many scenarios included in the same display can be confusing, such presentations should be avoided.

Political issues

Like nearly all governmental activities, the forecasting process is shaped by its political context. Is the forecast intended to be a reference for the chief administrator, or is it intended to inform policy making? In the first case, the forecast might be considered an internal document; in the second case, it is a public document. Publicizing the forecast can have both negative and positive effects.

Some may view a forecast of a fiscal crisis as an indication of poor management or poor political leadership, a perception (especially if highlighted by the press) that could damage public confidence in the local government. On the other hand, making forecast results public can also be beneficial. In a collective bargaining environment, for example, a published projection of fiscal problems may lower the expectations and demands of unionized employees. Furthermore, while a projected revenue shortfall can create negative publicity, voters may be impressed when policy makers respond to the projections with informed decisions based on the forecast. Bond-rating organizations are also favorably impressed with forecasting as a management technique. Thus, even when fiscal problems are projected, the fact that a forecast was produced suggests that the local government is attempting to stay on top of its financial problems and is better equipped to handle them. Finally, some local governments use projections of fiscal problems to lobby for more aid from higher levels of government.[41]

Conclusion

The models of financial forecasting described in this chapter all feed into the budget-making process to be discussed in Chapter 7. The various techniques used for medium-range forecasting vary in data requirements, cost, and accuracy; the choice of method should be made only after a complete study of the costs and potential benefits. Most important, it must be remembered that forecasting is more than a technical exercise: its success depends on the cooperation, commitment, professionalism, and encouragement of both management and policy makers.

1   For a discussion of the basics of cash management, see Chapter 16 of this volume.

2   A review of many of these indicators is found in J. Richard Aronson, *Municipal Fiscal Indicators* (Washington, D.C.: Office of Policy Development and Research, U.S. Department of Housing and Urban Development, 1980). Specific guidelines for carrying out one such analysis can be obtained in Sanford M. Groves and Maureen Godsey Valente, with revisions by Karl Nollenberger, *Evaluating Financial Condition: A Handbook for Local Government,* 4th ed. (Washington, D.C.: International City/County Management Association, 2003).

3   See Planning and Resource Management Department, Bexar County, Texas, *Long Range Financial Forecast and Strategies, FY 2002–03 through 2006–07* (San Antonio, Tex.: July 2002), available at www.co.bexar.tx.us/prm/CDROM/cdrom.htm.

4   For an overview of economic modeling applicable to local government, see Ronald John Hy, "Economic Modeling and Local Government," *International Journal of Public Administration* 20, no. 8/9 (1997): 1447–1467. The volume contains ten additional papers focusing on various aspects of local economic forecasts.

5   Some examples of such forecasting units are the Bureau of Business Research at the University of Nebraska, Lincoln; the State Demographic Center at Minnesota Planning, an agency of the state government; and the Demographic and Economic Analysis Section of the Governor's Office of Planning and Budget in Utah. Many of these projections can be downloaded directly from the Web.

6   See California State Department of Finance, Demographic Research Unit, "County Population Projections with Age, Sex, and Race/Ethnic Detail, July 1, 1990–2040 in 10-Year Increments" (December 1998), available at www.dof.ca.gov/HTML/DEMOGRAP/Proj_age.htm.

7   Most urban and regional economics textbooks provide detailed discussions of how to compute and use location quotients. See, for example, John P. Blair, *Urban and Regional Economics* (Homewood, Ill.: Richard D. Irwin, 1991); and Wilbur Maki and Richard W. Lichty, *Urban Regional Economics: Concepts, Tools, and Applications* (Ames: Iowa State University Press, 2000).

8   As shown in Robert W. Gilmer, "Identifying Service-Sector Exports from Major Texas Cities," *Federal Reserve Bank of Dallas Economic Review* (July 1990): 1–16, "exporting industries" are not limited to physical products. Large cities, for example, can be "exporters" of services such as air transportation.

9   For further detail concerning the derivation and use of employment multipliers in the course of conducting local economic base studies, see Blair, *Urban and Regional Economics;* and Maki and Lichty, *Urban Regional Economics.*

10 San Francisco has used such methods to project revenues. See Stephen J. Agostini, "Searching for a Better Forecast: San Francisco's Revenue Forecasting Model," *Government Finance Review* (December 1991): 13–16.

11 Shift-share analysis is described thoroughly in Maki and Lichty, *Urban Regional Economics.*

12 Shift-share techniques can also be used to analyze competitiveness in relation to the global economy. This use of the technique (based on state-level data) is described in Cletus C. Coughlin and Patricia S. Pollard, "Comparing Manufacturing Export Growth across States: What Accounts for the Differences?" *Federal Reserve Bank of St. Louis Review* (January/February 2001): 25–40.

13 Shift-share analysis can be used to forecast future employment, but the technique generally must rely on the assumption that national increases in employment are the principal drivers of changes in local employment. For a forecasting model that combines shift-share analysis with the time-series techniques discussed later in this chapter, see J. A. Kurre and B. R. Welles, "Forecasting the Local Economy Using Time-Series and Shift-Share Techniques," *Environment and Planning A* 21 (June 1989): 753–770. The combination of the two approaches makes the model more complex than simple shift-share analysis; however, the additional complexity can improve the accuracy of the forecast.

14 Local economic development programs are considered more fully in Chapter 13 of this volume.

15 For a thorough discussion of the techniques associated with such studies, see Robert W. Burchell and David Listokin, in collaboration with Robert W. Lake et al., *The Fiscal Impact Handbook: Estimating Local Costs and Revenues of Land Development* (New Brunswick, N.J.: Center for Urban Policy Research, 1978). See also the user-oriented handbook that accompanies this book, Robert W. Burchell, David Listokin, and William R. Dolphin, *The New Practitioner's Guide to Fiscal Impact Analysis* (New Brunswick, N.J.: Center for Urban Policy Research, 1985).

16 For a discussion of how impact fees can be estimated and projected into the future, see Janet M. Kelly, "Development Impact Fees: Modeling Future Growth and Economic Development in a South Carolina Community," *International Journal of Public Administration* 20, no. 8/9 (1997): 1599–1617.

17 Analysis of a nationwide sample of counties showed that those that were experiencing fiscal stress were more likely to undertake formal revenue forecasting; furthermore, such counties tended to use models that were more complex than those used by counties that were not experiencing stress. See Susan A. MacManus and Barbara P. Grothe, "Fiscal Stress as a Stimulant to Better Revenue Forecasting and Productivity," *Public Productivity Review* 12 (summer 1989): 387–400.

18 The many books that have been devoted to forecasting methods provide more detail on the use of

these methods, especially in business situations. See, for example, Spyros G. Makridakis, Steven C. Wheelwright, and Rob J. Hyndman, *Forecasting: Methods and Applications,* 3rd ed. (New York: John Wiley & Sons, 1998). Econometric forecasting methods are detailed in Robert S. Pindyck and Daniel L. Rubinfeld, *Econometric Models and Economic Forecasts,* 4th ed. (Boston: Irwin/McGraw-Hill, 1998). Another very useful source is the *Principles of Forecasting* Web site maintained by Prof. Scott Armstrong, available at www-marketing.wharton.upenn.edu/forecast/.

19   James J. L. Stemaier and Martha J. Reiss, "The Revenue Forum: An Effective Low-Cost, Low-Tech Approach to Revenue Forecasting," *Government Finance Review* (April 1994): 13–16.

20   For a discussion of these techniques, see Pindyck and Rubinfeld, *Econometric Models,* chaps. 14–18.

21   There are some exceptions in the literature. For example, Aman Khan, "Forecasting a Local Government Budget with Time-Series Analysis," *State and Local Government Review* (fall 1989): 123–129, demonstrates how, despite relatively few observations (thirty-seven), the Box-Jenkins ARIMA technique yielded reasonable forecasts of general-fund revenues for the city of Miami. A more recent review of time-series techniques is Carmen Cirincione, Gustavo A. Gurrieri, and Bart van de Sande, "Municipal Government Revenue Forecasting: Issues of Method and Data," *Public Budgeting & Finance* 19 (spring 1999): 26–46. Drawing on data from monthly, bimonthly, and quarterly nontax general-fund revenues for six different Connecticut municipalities, the authors illustrate the use of seventeen different time-series techniques. Their findings suggest that if municipalities retain data at least bimonthly, relatively simple time-series models can prove useful to forecasters.

22   Thomas Fullerton Jr., "A Composite Approach to Forecasting State Government Revenues: Case Study of the Idaho Sales Tax," *International Journal of Forecasting* 5, no. 3 (1989): 373–380, illustrates how econometric and ARIMA forecasts can be used in combination.

23   Wilpen Gorr discusses how local governments can use database management systems to retain data on changes in tax rates, definitions of tax bases, or other special events, thus ensuring the protection of historical information crucial to accurate forecasting. See "Use of Special Event Data in Government Information Systems," *Public Administration Review* 46 (November 1986): 532–539.

24   It is beyond the scope of this chapter to provide details on the statistical aspects of regression analysis. Introductory statistics and econometrics books can provide such background. See, for example, James T. McClave, P. George Benson, and Terry L. Sincich, *Statistics for Business and Economics,* 8th ed. (Upper Saddle River, N.J.: Prentice Hall, Inc., 2001). For texts that are more oriented to the public sector, see Kenneth J. Meier and Jeffrey Brudney, *Applied Statistics for Public Administration,* 5th ed. (Fort Worth, Tex.: Harcourt College Publishers, 2002); and Evan M. Berman, *Essential Statistics for Public Managers and Policy Analysts* (Washington, D.C.: CQ Press, 2001).

25   See Governor's Office of Planning and Budget, Demographic and Economic Analysis Section, "Utah State and Local Government Fiscal Impact Model," Working Paper Series 94-3 (June 1994), available at www.governor.state.ut.us/dea/publications/fim/94-3.pdf.

26   This equation was in fact used to project cigarette taxes in San Diego. See City of San Diego Financial Management Department, *Long Range Planning: Revenue Project Model, FY 1979–84* (San Diego, Calif.: February 1978).

27   The more complex time-series models—such as ARIMA models—do project cycles in long-term trends and do not, therefore, suffer from this limitation.

28   The variety of statistical problems that arise in econometric projections are beyond the scope of this chapter but are discussed in nearly all econometrics books. See, for example, Pindyck and Rubinfeld, *Econometric Models;* and Damodar N. Gujarati, *Basic Econometrics,* 4th ed. (Boston: McGraw-Hill, 2003). For practical discussions of the difficulties of forecasting, see Michael Siegel, "Forecasting in the 90s: It's Not Like It Used to Be," *Government Finance Review* 8 (April 1992): 40–41; or Susan A. MacManus, "Forecasting Frustrations: Factors Limiting Accuracy," *Government Finance Review* 8 (June 1992): 7–11.

29   The use of the various techniques by local governments is the topic of Jan McCollough, "Municipal Revenue and Expenditure Forecasting: Current Status and Future Prospects," *Government Finance Review* 6 (October 1990): 38–40; and John P. Forrester, "Multi-Year Forecasting and Municipal Budgeting," *Public Budgeting & Finance* 11 (summer 1991): 47–59.

30   For an example of an econometric model for Wichita, Kansas, see J. D. Wong, "Local Government Revenue Forecasting: Using Regression and Econometric Forecasting in a Medium-Sized City," *Public Budgeting and Financial Management* 7 (fall 1995): 315–335. The paper includes specifications of forecasting equations for seven different local taxes plus transit fares; each of the equations includes real per capita personal income as one of the variables.

31   For an example of how an econometric model can be used to project property taxes, see Terri A. Sexton, "Forecasting Property Taxes: A Comparison and Evaluation of Methods," *National Tax Journal* 40, no. 1 (March 1987): 47–59.

32   Productivity increases are, unfortunately, more easily posited than measured because of the difficulty of measuring outputs. For a discussion of the issues associated with measuring productivity in state and local governments (and for annual productivity indexes for selected services), see Bureau of Labor Statistics, *Measuring State and Local Government Labor Productivity: Examples from Eleven Services,* Bulletin 2495 (Washington, D.C.: U.S. Department of Labor, June 1998).

33   See Mark Bottley and John Kaczor, "An Automated Five-Year Financial Model: Application in Michigan Cities," *Government Finance Review* (August 1997): 46–48. The model, as illustrated in the article, includes the revenue side of the budget as well as the capital budget. All aspects of the local fisc are linked within a single spreadsheet.

34   A projection model for welfare caseloads is discussed in Robert D. Plotnick and Russell M. Lidman, "Forecasting Welfare Caseloads: A Tool to Improve Budgeting," *Public Budgeting & Finance* 7 (autumn 1987): 70–81.

35   For discussions of different methods of cleaning revenue series, see Roy Bahl, *Alternative Methods for Tax Revenue Forecasting in Developing Countries* (Washington, D.C.: Fiscal Affairs Department, International Monetary Fund, 1972); Robert Harris, *Income and Sales Taxes: The 1970 Outlook for States and Localities* (Washington, D.C.: Council of State Governments, 1966); and A. R. Prest, "The Sensitivity of the Yield of Personal Income Tax in the United Kingdom," *Economic Journal* 72 (September 1962): 576–596.

36   Regression forecasting techniques provide another method for cleaning revenue series via "dummy" independent variables. Such variables take on the value of zero before a revenue rate (base) is changed, and a value of 1 after the change is made. The technique is especially useful when only one or two major administrative changes have been made in a tax source. For discussion of the dummy-variable technique, see McClave, Benson, and Sincich, *Statistics for Business and Economics,* or Gujarati, *Basic Econometrics.*

37   For a comparison of the forecasting accuracy of the CBO and OMB models, see Congressional Budget Office, "CBO's Economic Forecasting Record: A Supplement to *The Budget and Economic Outlook: An Update*" (November 2002), available at www.cbo.gov/showdoc.cfm?index=3980&sequence=0.

38   Forecasters must have a good understanding of measures of economic activity. See, for example, Office of the Texas Comptroller of Public Accounts, "Economic Indicators: Vital Signs Monitor Economy's Health," *Government Finance Review* 7 (December 1991): 17–19; and Donald Levitar, "How to Read the Economy: A Primer," *Government Finance Review* 9 (April 1993): 25–27.

39   These issues are discussed in more depth in Larry Schroeder, "Local Government Multi-Year Budgetary Forecasting: Some Administrative and Political Issues," *Public Administration Review* 42 (March/April 1982): 121–127.

40   In "Multi-Year Forecasting," John P. Forrester reports that budget and finance officers themselves produce the forecasts in a majority of the 170 cities he surveyed.

41   The possible politicization of state revenue forecasts (and their accuracy) is the topic of Stuart I. Bretschneider, Wilpen L. Gorr, Gloria Grizzle, and Earle Klay, "Political and Organizational Influences on the Accuracy of Forecasting State Government Revenues," *International Journal of Forecasting* 5, no. 3 (1989): 307–319; and Glenn Cassidy, Mark S. Kamlet, and Daniel S. Nagin, "An Empirical Examination of Bias in Revenue Forecasts by State Governments," *International Journal of Forecasting* 5, no. 3 (1989): 321–331.

Cost-benefit analysis and the capital budget

J. RICHARD ARONSON AND ELI SCHWARTZ

Cost-benefit analysis is the essence of economic reasoning. Only by comparing benefits and costs can a decision maker determine whether an activity should be undertaken. In the private sector, where the goal is to maximize profit, cost-benefit analysis involves translating benefits and costs into cash flows, and projects are undertaken when the present value of the net cash inflow is positive. Employing cost-benefit analysis in the public sector is more complicated. There, the goal of the decision maker should be to maximize welfare, a concept that is considerably broader and more complex than is the maximization of profit. Often, local government analysts must estimate the value of benefits and costs that are indirect and intangible or that may be external to the community. In such circumstances, cost-benefit analysis is a matter of art as well as science.

Cost-benefit analysis is particularly important when it comes to evaluating the capital budget. The capital budget itemizes the local government's planned outlays for long-term public projects—such as roads and bridges, public buildings, utility systems, and recreational and cultural facilities—and explains how the jurisdiction plans to finance them. Although the current, or operating, budget is subject to regular scrutiny, the capital budget is all too often an afterthought. Yet a well-thought-out capital budget and capital improvements program (CIP) may be crucial to a jurisdiction's long-term financial and economic health.

This chapter examines the major steps in preparing a capital budget or CIP: selecting and evaluating the projects to be undertaken, forecasting the community's fiscal resources, and projecting the effect of alternative financing methods on the operating budget. The chapter shows in detail how to calculate the net present value (NPV) of a project's benefits so that the NPV can be compared with the project's costs; how to organize and construct a fiscal-resource study on the basis of projected revenues and expenditures; and how to select a financing method for capital needs. The chapter includes a brief discussion of pass-through financing, which involves using the local government's credit to support socially desirable projects sponsored by nongovernmental organizations or programs.

The capital budget

Capital expenditures may be defined as outlays for the construction or purchase of facilities that are expected to provide benefits and services over a considerable period of time. Current (or operating) expenditures, in contrast, are made for items or services that are consumed in a short time. Moreover, when compared with expenditures for items in the operating budget, capital expenditures are usually relatively large.

The definition of a capital expenditure may vary with the size of a community and its budget: in a small locality, for example, patrol cars may be part of the capital budget; in a large city, patrol cars may be purchased annually under a regular appropriation in the operating budget. Even in a large city, however,

Examples of cost-benefit analysis
The fact that the value of the common social benefits of certain activities or services is difficult to calculate is perhaps the major reason that the activity has been given to the public sector. Nevertheless, some stalwart attempts have been made to apply cost-benefit analysis to particular activities. For example, if one were to attempt to evaluate the costs and benefits of expanding the police force, the costs would be those associated with training, equipping, managing, and compensating the men and women added to the force; the benefits would include the decrease in crime-related losses; the decrease in insurance costs; the increase in tourism brought about by a safer environment; and a "shadow price" that residents would be willing to pay for greater personal security. If the benefits exceed the costs, the program is worthwhile.

Shadow pricing has been employed to evaluate the benefits of parks and other public areas. What is the entry fee for private recreational areas? What might people pay to make trips to the countryside? What is the increase in real estate values for properties within reasonable access to the park? These values may be placed against the cost of maintaining the park.

Some broad areas under the purview of the states or the federal government, including safety and environmental regulations, have been subject to cost-benefit analysis. The benefits of such regulations are diffuse and widespread, and must be calculated in social-welfare terms. In the case of a regulation reducing the emission of acid-content smoke, for example, the costs would be those associated with enforcement (for the government) and those associated with compliance (for the private sector). The benefits would include the populace's enjoyment of cleaner environment, air, and water; specifically environmental benefits; and the value of longer life expectancies and lower medical costs. Although local finance officers are unlikely to be directly involved in the formulation of such regulations, it is important for them to understand the associated costs and benefits, particularly with respect to local industries.

---

the operating budget should distinguish between regular operating expenses and recurring expenditures for small capital items. (Recurring outlays for capital items such as desktop computers should be given special attention in evaluating current expenditures, even though the appropriation is part of the operating budget rather than the capital budget.)

Selecting and evaluating capital projects

Because the capital budget involves relatively large projects meant to serve the community for some time, its components should be analyzed carefully. Although requests for capital projects may originate from diverse sources—operating departments, administrative officers, the planning commission, or ad hoc citizens' committees, for example—responsibility for the analysis and evaluation of capital expenditure requests should be centralized.

Decisions on capital projects should generally be made by the planning department, under the direction of the chief administrator. On the basis of information garnered from economic base studies, land use reports, and population studies, the planning department, with direct assistance from the finance department, should conduct an economic and financial evaluation of each proposed project and determine which projects should be included in the capital budget that will be submitted to the governing body. Determining the selection, sequence, and timing of the projects in the CIP is not the sole responsibility of the finance officer, but the finance department should be instrumental in quantifying the economic benefits relative to the costs—that is, in quantifying the desirability of the proposed projects.[1]

Using economic base, land use, and population studies

Capital budgeting rests on a foundation of economic base studies, land use reports and maps, and population and migration studies, which provide the basis for projecting fiscal resources, assessing need, and identifying the most productive and viable capital projects. Local planning commissions often conduct such studies.

Economic base studies include data on various aspects of local industries, such as size, location, and employment levels. Such studies also include an economic history of the local government; an analysis of economic development trends, particularly with respect to the arrival of new industries; forecasts of local employment levels, wage levels, and construction activity; and a forecast of the future locations of economic activity in the area. Land use studies can be used to determine the amount of land available for various kinds of future development: they show population density and include an inventory of industrial, residential, recreational, commercial, and vacant land. Population studies detail current population characteristics and income levels and provide data on human resources. Because population studies provide data on age classes, they make it possible to project the size of the future labor force, the demand for schools, and the demand for facilities for older citizens. Migration studies indicate where people live and where they are likely to move.

To ensure that the types of data collected answer specific questions, the makers of the capital budget should be involved in the design of all these studies. On the capital expenditure side of the budget, the budgeters may want answers to the following types of questions: What industries are developing? What support will these industries need in the way of streets, docks, fire control equipment, or other government facilities? If the migration and land use studies indicate that the population is moving to new areas, what new facilities will be needed in the way of schools, transportation, parks, and recreation? If the local government wants to discourage migration—from older to newer parts of the area, for example—what improvements might slow such migration? Because the capital budget relies on the available resources of the locality, the economic base studies should try to identify trends in operating expenditures for social services, public safety, and general government programs, given forecasted changes in population and land use patterns.

For the revenue side of the budget, a similar set of questions might be asked: What are the likely growth rates and growth patterns for various parts of the local economy? Will an analysis of this growth provide enough information to estimate future tax sources? For example, will the value of downtown property decline? Will a decline in the property tax base be offset by growth in revenue from the earned-income tax? Is the population moving toward local vacant land that is likely to be developed and added to the tax base? Can it be assumed that future growth of the property tax base will be slower or faster than in the past? Chapter 5 deals with methods of handling these questions.

Cost-benefit analysis

At least in theory, the identification of worthwhile capital investments or projects is a straightforward matter. A public project is desirable when the present value of its estimated flow of benefits, discounted at the community's cost of capital, equals or exceeds the project's cost. The standard criteria used for making this determination are NPV and the internal rate of return.

Although present-value analysis of capital projects can be complicated, it is not the calculations themselves that are difficult; rather, it is the task of estimating benefits and costs and determining the appropriate discount rate. Nevertheless, present-value analyses of projects are worthwhile: even if some of the variables must be best-guess estimates, the exercise will still improve the evaluation of the economic desirability of many capital projects.

Net present value and internal rate of return

As shown in the sidebar on the opposite page, NPV is obtained by subtracting the initial outlays on the project from the gross present value of its benefits (PV_B); the gross PV_B is calculated by discounting the benefits at the community's weighted average interest rate. In other words, the stream of net future benefits is quantified, and each year's return is discounted to obtain its present value; the sum of present values is then compared with the immediate outlay on the project. If the sum of the present values of the benefit flows exceeds the outlay, the project should be accepted, assuming that no project serving the same function has a higher NPV. The internal rate of return is the rate that brings the present value (PV) of the benefit flow into equality with the initial outlay. If the internal rate of return exceeds the community's interest rate, the project is desirable, assuming that there is no suitable, alternative project with a higher NPV.

Figure 6–1 shows an example of the mechanics of capital-project evaluation. The project illustrated would be accepted because at a "community cost of capital" of 10 percent, the PV of the estimated stream of benefits is $7,156,650, or $1,156,650 in excess of the project's cost of $6,000,000. Thus, the projected rate of return on the project is higher than the 10 percent discount rate.

Project analysis in practice

Although simple in theory, decision making about public investments is much less so in practice. A number of factors complicate efforts to evaluate projects according to their benefits and costs; of these, the most important are (1) the intangibility of benefits, (2) spillover benefits, and (3) the community's discount rate. Other issues that can add complexity to the evaluation process include inflation, conflicting criteria, the necessity of quantifying full costs, and the determination of project size. Finally, there are broad external pressures—budget constraints, the temptation to delay repairs or renovations, and the tendency to focus on the short term—that can affect project evaluation.

Net present value and internal rate of return   The mathematical formula for obtaining the net present value (NPV) of a project is generally

$$NPV = PV_B - I$$

$$PV_B = \frac{B_1}{(1 + I)} + \frac{B_2}{(1 + I)^2} + \cdots$$
$$+ \frac{B_n}{(1 + I)^n} + \frac{S_n}{(1 + I)^n},$$

where

   B = the annual flow of the estimated benefits
   n = the forecasted economic life of the project in years
   S_n = the scrap value or remaining value of the project at the end of its economic life in year n
   i = the appropriate discount or interest rate for the community

I = the cost of the project, including start-up costs.

The equation for the internal rate of return is formally similar to that for NPV:

$$I = \frac{B_1}{(1 + I)} + \frac{B_2}{(1 + I)^2} + \cdots$$
$$+ \frac{B_n}{(1 + I)^n} + \frac{S_n}{(1 + I)^n}.$$

However, in this case, I (the investment cost of the project) is given, and the equation must be solved to find r (the rate of return that makes the present value of the benefits equal to the outlay, I. When $r > i$ (the cost of capital), the project is acceptable. However, if two alternative, substitutable projects differ in the size of the internal rate of return and in the amount of NPV, the project with the higher NPV is preferable.

Figure 6–1 Sample calculation of the net present value of a capital project.

Year	Investment cost of project ($)	Estimated net annual undiscounted benefits ($)	Discount rate (where cost of capital = 10%) $= \dfrac{1}{(1.10)^n}$	Present value of benefits ($)
0	6,000,000			
1		1,000,000	0.9091	909,100
2		2,500,000	0.8264	2,066,000
3		3,000,000	0.7513	2,253,900
4		1,500,000	0.6830	1,024,500
5		1,000,000	0.6209	620,900
6		500,000	0.5645	282,250
Total	6,000,000	9,500,000		7,156,650

Net present value = $1,156,650

Note: The n in the equation stands for the number of years in the future.

Intangibility of benefits   The benefits of a project are often intangible. Although the goals or utility of a public park, for example, may be clear (recreation, fresh air, light for adjoining properties, and beauty for visitors), such benefits often reside in shared social values—in a sense of what is "good" for the general welfare of the citizenry; thus, they are not easily expressed in monetary terms. (Of course, the existence of common social values is the major reason for assigning activities to the government sector.)

Even when benefits are difficult to quantify in monetary terms, the analytic techniques described earlier can still be used, albeit in reverse, by posing the following questions: Given the cost of a proposed project and the community's discount rate, what flow of annual benefits would justify the cost of this project? Does this flow of annual benefits, even though not exactly measurable, appear reasonable or attainable? If so, the project is desirable.

A concept known as *shadow pricing* is another way of getting at some estimate of the value of benefits. For example, how much will people pay to use *private* lakes, parks, and preserves? What is the average private outlay for vacations, scenic trips, and outdoor leisure pursuits? What are the outlays for private lawns, landscaping, and gardens? These activities, each of which has a price, provide benefits similar to those provided by a park.

Of course, estimating benefits becomes somewhat easier when public services are sold to the public rather than distributed free of charge: by paying for a service, consumers indicate how much they value it. However, even under these conditions, a public facility may provide some common social benefits that cannot be captured in the price.

Spillover benefits   Accounting for the spillover effects to neighboring jurisdictions is another difficulty in quantifying benefits. If, for example, a jurisdiction builds a sewage treatment plant, some of the benefits (e.g., cleaner downstream waters) may accrue to other communities in the area. If these external benefits can be measured, should some of their value be included in the determination of benefits? Perhaps a portion should be, because enlightened self-interest often brings a rebound reward. In financially tight times, however, it is difficult to be purely altruistic. The strong argument in favor of grants-in-aid from higher levels of government is that these grants compensate a community for some of the costs of undertaking projects whose benefits spill over to citizens of other localities.

The community's discount rate   Determining the community's discount rate (or time-preference rate)—that is, the rate of interest that should be used to discount the stream of benefits from a public project—is another difficulty in evaluating the costs and benefits of a capital project. At first glance, the borrowing rate of the local government might seem appropriate. But because the interest on local government debt is generally exempt from federal income taxation and because payment is generally backed by the taxable wealth of the entire community, the explicit rate on municipal issues is the lowest of all market interest rates. This low explicit rate is unlikely to reflect the true social cost of capital to the community.

Because governmental debt is a prior charge on the community's wealth, potentially ranking above all other obligations, an increase in debt imposes a "risk charge" on all the income streams or wealth in the community. The burden of this risk charge can raise the cost of capital (i.e., the necessary rate of return) required on all new and renewable capital investments. Thus, when analyzing the economic desirability of investing in public projects, local officials should account for this additional imputed burden by raising the presumptive discount rate accordingly. An approximation of the true social discount rate might be a rough, weighted average of the interest costs on local government bonds and the yields on other solid financial claims, such as mortgages and high-grade bonds.

Inflation   Because capital outlays are forward-looking by their very nature, inflation complicates the evaluation of capital projects. On the one hand, forecasted inflation raises the expected dollar value of future benefits, creating an apparent increase in the present value of the capital project that may lead decision makers to undertake a more expansive program. On the other hand, a rise in the inflation rate leads to a rise in the current nominal rate of interest in the money and capital markets, reducing the present value of future benefits. Under equilibrium conditions (and assuming all estimates are accurate), these factors should roughly cancel each other out, leaving the real value of any project unchanged. Unfortunately, inflation may also weaken the economic fiber of the community and make it difficult to find the resources to support public programs over time.

Conflicting criteria   The two standard criteria described earlier, NPV and internal rate of return, will indicate whether a single capital project is acceptable, but they may give conflicting signals when mutually exclusive projects that serve the same function are ranked. In the case of projects that show higher internal rates of return but lower NPV, ranking projects by NPV is the correct economic decision because NPV indicates the highest level of net benefits.

Rankings based on NPV and internal rate of return may conflict because of differences in the shape of the benefit flow over time, the investment size, or both. However, when rankings conflict, the project with the highest NPV—which indicates the highest total level of net benefits for the community—is always the most worthwhile. The maximization of net benefits is the proper criterion for choosing between mutually exclusive projects that serve the same function.

Full costs   In calculating the costs of a capital project, local officials sometimes overlook the long-range costs of owning and maintaining the asset—the "full-life" costs. These costs are overlooked because capital and operating budgets are generally developed separately.

The operating costs involved in using some assets change over time. In many cases, the cost of operating and maintaining an asset may increase as it ages; however, the cost of operating the existing asset may nevertheless be lower than the full cost of replacing it with a new project; and in other cases, the full cost of investing in a replacement may be lower.[2]

Project size   Many projects show a decreasing average cost per unit of capacity when more capacity is added to the base. Thus, for example, once the outlays on items such as planning, engineering, machinery, labor, and land acquisition for a road are complete, the cost of an additional lane, while considerable, is minimal when compared with the fundamental fixed costs of the basic construction. In a growing economy, therefore, there are often excellent economic reasons to add lanes beyond the current level of need or demand.

How far should local governments go in building capacity beyond current needs? The answer to this question involves estimating the growth rate of demand to determine (1) when the new capacity will be needed, (2) what the carrying costs (maintenance and interest) will be on the capacity installed now, and (3) the cost of constructing the added capacity in the future. If the combined costs of (1) installing the extra capacity now and (2) the compounded carrying costs (between now and the time that the additional capacity will be needed) are lower than the estimated cost of constructing the extra capacity in the future, then the additional capacity should be put in now. If the current cost of the additional capacity, plus the periodic carrying costs, plus interest on the total is greater than the estimated cost of constructing the additional capacity in the future, the local government should wait until the extra capacity is needed.[3]

External pressures   Several practical considerations affect the selection of capital projects. The arbitrary constraint of a fixed budget for capital expenditures, for example, may force decision makers to select less efficient projects or to delay implementing worthwhile improvements. If economically desirable projects cannot be undertaken because of a tight budget, public officials should attempt to persuade the public to accept a larger budget, as long as it is consistent with current and future debt obligations. Before pressing this case, however, local officials must be certain that all the costs and benefits have been counted and that the assumed discount rate is not too low. If it is not feasible to accommodate all worthwhile, noncompeting projects in the short term, the second-best solution is to ensure that those projects selected within the budget limit show the highest combined NPV.

One temptation that capital planners would do well to avoid is the tendency to fund new projects and to delay the repair or renovation of existing facilities. Local governments often defer maintenance or replacement because doing so is a relatively painless way to reduce expenditures and ease financial strain in the short term. Deferring maintenance and repair, however, can create short-term hazards and costs and lead to larger capital expenditures in the future. Maintenance and repair should not be ignored in the formulation of the capital budget: in many instances, such activities show the highest NPV of benefits.

Another proviso that should be kept in mind in constructing the capital budget is that the object of the capital planner is to increase the wealth and improve the welfare of the jurisdiction and its population, not just to better the position of the public treasury. An improvement that will produce increased revenues over the long term may impose immediate, short-run costs on the local budget; thus, there may be pressure to give up such a project. It is to be hoped that such difficulties will not lead the capital planner to ignore the wider, long-term social benefits of a project.

Forecasting fiscal resources and responsibilities

The forecast of financial resources and responsibilities, which provides the essential fiscal framework for the capital program, is one of the most important components of the capital budget. The forecast's major function is to project, under the existing fiscal structure, future net available fiscal capacity—that is, the potential funds that may be used either for direct capital expenditures or for service charges on additional debt incurred to finance capital improvements. Thus, the projection of fiscal resources and responsibilities encompasses normally anticipated revenues, normal expenditures, and existing debt service obligations. The financial impact of the desired capital improvements—given their estimated costs, the timing of construction starts and outlays, and the funds that may be available through grants from other governmental units—is measured against this projection. This analysis reveals the resources that will be available under the existing tax structure and prepares the community for any fiscal adjustments that may be required. It also indicates how much of the capital budget can be supported directly from current revenues, how any necessary bond financing can be serviced, and what tax increase (if any) will be required. Generally, the fiscal forecast, which is useful as a planning tool, should extend for five or six years.

A fiscal forecast can be conveniently summarized in a master table that presents projections of major revenue sources and major expenditure items. Figure 6–2 is a sample of such a forecast (see page 143).

To forecast recurring revenues and operating expenditures, it is necessary to separate their components into readily definable major categories. Data on these categories can be subjected to trend analysis or to one of the more sophisticated forecasting methods described in Chapter 5. Whatever forecasting method is used, however, the forecasts should not be made on a purely mechanical basis: the budget maker should interview local government staff to see whether any special factors are likely to cause deviations from past trends and relationships. Some parts of the capital budget itself may influence revenue trends. (For example, improved traffic flows could raise property values and thereby increase the revenue from the property tax.) However, unless there are strong local characteristics that may cause deviations from national patterns, the projections should be consistent with overall national trends in local government finance and with developments in the national economy.

To the extent possible, the forecaster should adjust the revenue and expenditure projections for inflation. To some degree, the rate of price increases may already be accounted for, insofar as historical trends reflect the rate of past inflation. Moreover, if inflation increases nominal costs and expenditures, it is also likely to increase the dollar amount of potential revenues. However, inflation can complicate the financing of local government activities because not all costs and revenues run parallel. Thus the effect of inflation may not be consistent across all costs and revenues, making forecasts more difficult.

Users of the fiscal forecast section of the capital budget should be aware of two underlying assumptions. First, the local government will undertake no new major operating functions in the period under review. (Note, however, that even if this were not the case, the budget would still be useful because it would give an estimate of future fiscal resources that might be available for any new functions.) Second, the revenue forecasts are based on existing taxes and tax rates. This assumption is necessary because the existing tax structure is the basis for estimating both (1) the additional revenue that might be obtained through an increase in current taxes and (2) the level of activity and services that the local economy can support.

To summarize, constructing the fiscal forecast necessitates three steps:

1. Analyzing past revenue data to develop a forecast of normal recurring future revenues
2. Analyzing past expenditure data to develop a forecast of normal recurring future expenditures
3. Comparing projected revenues and operating expenses against available fiscal resources, on the basis of the local government's current revenue structure.

The formal CIP is based on forecasts of the local government's fiscal resources. Usually, additional funds will be necessary to finance the program. If so, the budget maker should present alternative financial plans that indicate the timing and fiscal impact of raising these funds through various combinations of debt and tax increases. This step will be discussed in detail later.

Forecasting revenues

Much of the following discussion is based on the trend analysis method of forecasting. (Chapter 5 outlines other forecasting techniques; the capital improvements planner should use those statistical tools and methods best suited to the problems at hand.) Under the trend-analysis method, past revenue data are used to project future revenues. Projections should be based on current tax rates and applied to a forecast level of growth for the existing tax base. As noted earlier, current rates are used because the purpose of the forecast is to determine what changes in rates, if any, will be necessary to finance future capital projects.

In analyzing past trends, it is important to distinguish between the effects of economic growth and the effects of past legislated or structural changes in the tax system. For example, revenue increases could have been caused by a rise in new construction, an increase in tax rates, a change in assessment levels, or the institution of a new tax. Trends for combined revenues may also be misleading if the returns from specific taxes are growing at different rates. A relatively stable total revenue trend, for example, might encompass a slow decline in revenue from a major tax source and a concomitant increase from a new tax source. If the trends for the two taxes are analyzed separately, however, and the results are then combined, the analyst may find, for example, that after a brief period of stability, total revenues may be expected to start climbing significantly.

To ensure that an analysis of past revenue trends is useful, the analyst should keep the following points in mind:

The major revenue sources in past operating budgets should be classified under consistent headings. If budget classifications have changed, past revenue classifications should be made consistent with current ones.

As a major source of local government revenue, the property tax is worth considerable study. In analyzing property tax revenue, the forecaster should not overemphasize the trend in the total levy; the growth in the assessment base is the most significant variable in the forecast. Thus, a sudden jump in the assessment base should lead to further questioning. The jump may have resulted from an increase in the assessment ratio (e.g., from 40 to 60 percent) rather than from true economic growth. In projecting property tax revenues, the land use study and detailed analysis and knowledge of the local area can prove very useful. Whether any major developments are pending, how much land is still open for development and improvement, and whether any significant amount of property might be taken off the rolls in the future should also be considered.

A newly instituted tax requires careful analysis: if the base-year revenues do not represent a full fiscal year, the growth rate of revenues for a new tax may be overestimated. Moreover, the first years after the imposition of a tax may show rapid growth in revenue, some of which may be caused by improvement in administration as the local government becomes accustomed to the tax. Such growth is not likely to continue indefinitely at the same rate.

Any recent changes in patterns should be taken into account. Assume, for example, that during the past ten years, the overall compound rate of revenue growth for a local earned-income tax was 6 percent. However, during the first six years of the observed period, the annual growth rate was about 7 percent, and during the last four years, the rate decreased to about 5 percent. The projected annual rate might be set at 5 percent or even slightly lower.[4]

Forecasting expenditures

Like revenues, expenditures are forecast primarily by means of trend analysis, and the same care in classification and handling of the data is required. Before expenditures can be forecast, individual outlays must be grouped into workable categories, operating expenditures must be separated from any recurring capital expenditures that may be made from the general fund, and service charges on existing debt must be isolated.

Past expenditures are analyzed to identify trends for each major component and to determine the relationships between components. Where these trends and relationships appear to be consistent with general economic patterns, they are used to develop the forecast. (However, in many cases, the more complex methods cited in Chapter 5, such as linear regression analysis, may be preferable to simple trend-extrapolation techniques.) As in the case of revenue analysis, local government staff should be questioned about significant deviations from past trends so that they can identify any special, nonrecurring factors that may have affected the data.

In making expenditure projections, the analyst must apply informed judgment to the following issues, which parallel those on the revenue side:

Budget classifications may have changed in the time period under review. If they have, the existing budgetary classification should be used and past data arranged to conform to current usage.

For new government functions, the rate of expenditure growth may be quite high in the early years and then decline once the function has become established. The projections should take these secondary factors into consideration.

For totally new functions, there may be no record of past expenditures; consequently, they should be given a separate line in the forecast. The expenditure estimates for such functions will have to be based on interviews with staff members and on the judgment of the analyst. Regression models are often useful in such cases. The forecast amount and the rate of growth can also be compared with figures obtained from similar local governments that have already instituted the function.

The framework of the fiscal-resource study

How might the fiscal aspect of the capital planning budget be worked out? This section describes some of the specific factors that enter into the construction of the fiscal-resource study.

Figure 6–2 shows the projection of fiscal resources for a hypothetical local government for six years. The base year, 2005, is the current operating year. Row 1 shows the projected operating revenues for the next six years (excluding any grants from other governments that are to be used for capital improvements). Row 2 shows the projected level of operating expenditures. Row 3 is the difference between current revenues and expenditures. Rows 4 and 6

Figure 6–2 Fiscal projections for the general fund and the capital budget (in thousands of $)

	2005	2006	2007	2008	2009	2010	2011
(1) Projected operating revenues	6,000	6,500	7,000	7,300	7,700	8,000	8,400
(2) Less projected operating expenditures	5,000	5,800	6,300	6,600	7,000	7,300	7,700
(3) Gross cash flow	1,000	700	700	700	700	700	700
(4) Debt service[a] on existing obligations	500	500	350	300	250	200	150
(5) Gross funds flow after debt service charges	500	200	350	400	450	500	550
(6) Less projected recurring capital expenditures	200	300	350	400	450	500	500
(7) Net available funds[b]	300	(100)	0	0	0	0	50
(8) Less proposed major capital expenditures	1,000	1,000	1,000	500	500	0	0
(9) Net new financing required[c]	700	1,100	1,000	500	500	0	(50)

[a] Interest plus amortization.
[b] Parentheses indicate deficit.
[c] Parentheses indicate surplus.

show service charges on existing debt and the expenditures for recurring capital items such as police cars, computers, and sanitation equipment—items that are subtracted to produce row 7, the local government's projected annual net cash flow. This amount may be used (1) to help finance new capital projects and (2) to help cover the service charges on additional debt obligations that may be floated to finance the capital budget. Row 8 shows the proposed capital expenditures and row 9 the net new capital funds that will be required to finance the capital budget. Row 9 does not show, however, the full fiscal impact of the budget over time; to do so would require extrapolating the impact of the bond financing plan on the local government's tax structure. (Extrapolations showing the effect of the bond financing plan are discussed in more detail later in this chapter.)

Supporting data

The figures summarized in Figure 6–2 are derived from more detailed analyses and forecasts illustrated in Figures 6–3 through 6–7. In Figure 6–3, which shows the components of the overall revenue projections in row 1 of Figure 6–2, each major revenue item is projected separately for each year. Figure 6–4, in turn, is a breakdown of the components of the forecast of real estate tax revenues, a major item in most local budgets.

A similar analysis is undertaken for expenditures: thus, Figure 6–5 shows recurring capital expenditures and major operating expenditures. Each of these should be forecast separately to obtain the projection shown in row 2 of Figure 6–2. The recurring capital expenditures may be broken down further into the categories shown in Figure 6–6. Existing debt service (see Figure 6–7) is relatively easy to forecast because it is a projection of the already obligated annual interest charges and amortization on the existing debt.

Figure 6–3 Projected operating revenues (in thousands of $).

Year	Real estate taxes	Personal property taxes	Fines	User charges	Federal and state grants	Miscellaneous	Total
2005	4,500	300	100	370	700	30	6,000
2006	4,680	300	100	665	725	30	6,500
2007	4,867	300	100	953	750	30	7,000
2008	5,062	300	100	1,033	775	30	7,300
2009	5,264	300	100	1,206	800	30	7,700
2010	5,475	300	100	1,270	825	30	8,000
2011	5,694	300	100	1,426	850	30	8,400

Figure 6–4 Projected real estate taxes (in thousands of $).

Year	(A) Assessed value ($)	(B) Existing millage	(C) Levy ($) (C = A × B)	(D) Collections ($)	(E) Collection as a percentage of levy (E = D ÷ C)
2005	230,750	20	4,615	4,500	98
2006	238,776	20	4,776	4,680	98
2007	248,316	20	4,966	4,867	98
2008	259,590	20	5,192	5,062	98
2009	265,859	20	5,317	5,264	99
2010	279,337	20	5,587	5,475	98
2011	290,510	20	5,810	5,694	98

Year	Operating expenditures							Total recurring capital expenditures	Total operating and recurring capital expenditures
	Administrative	Judicial	Corrections	Welfare	Health and hospital[a]	Miscellaneous	Total		
2005	1,000	610	550	2,500	90	250	5,000	200	5,200
2006	1,040	634	560	2,750	566	250	5,800	300	6,100
2007	1,082	660	570	3,025	713	250	6,300	350	6,650
2008	1,125	686	580	3,328	731	150	6,600	400	7,000
2009	1,170	714	590	3,660	716	150	7,000	450	7,450
2010	1,217	742	600	4,026	665	50	7,300	500	7,800
2011	1,265	772	600	4,429	584	50	7,700	500	8,200

[a] A new hospital wing will be completed as of 2006.

Figure 6–5   Projected operating expenditures and recurring capital expenditures (in thousands of $).

Figure 6–6   Projected recurring capital expenditures from the general fund (in thousands of $).

Year	Administrative	Judicial	Corrections	Welfare	Miscellaneous	Total
2005	100	10	30	58	2	200
2006	150	10	30	108	2	300
2007	150	10	40	148	2	350
2008	200	10	40	148	2	400
2009	200	10	50	188	2	450
2010	250	10	50	188	2	500
2011	250	10	50	188	2	500

Figure 6–7   Service charges on existing debt, at 6 percent interest (in thousands of $).

Year	Balance outstanding as of 31 December	Debt retirement	Interest	Rounded total debt service
2005	1,876	387	113	500
2006	1,489	411	89	500
2007	1,078	285	65	350
2008	793	252	54	300
2009	541	218	32	250
2010	323	181	19	200
2011	142	142	9	150

The schedule of capital improvements

After the fiscal-resource study has been developed, the next phase in the construction of the capital budget involves detailing the costs of the capital projects for the next six years. The projected capital budget should be summarized in a table. Although the format can vary, this table should include the following (see Figure 6–8):

A complete list of major capital improvements.

Estimates of the total cost of each improvement.

Outside sources of financing, such as state or federal grants and private gifts. (The difference between the total cost of a project and the available grants is the net burden that must be borne by the fiscal capacity of the local government.)

The scheduling of construction starts and annual expenditures. (In most cases, the expenditures for a project will be spread over a number of years.)

Figure 6–8   Schedule
of capital improve-
ments projects
(in thousands of $).

Project	2005	2006	2007	2008	2009	2010	2011
Home for elderly citizens, addition and reconstruction	1,500	1,500	1,500	0	0	200	200
Less grants	1,000	1,000	1,000	0	0	200	200
Net cost to jurisdiction	500	500	500	0	0	0	0
Prison improvements	200	100	100	0	0	0	0
Recreation	0	0	0	300	300	0	0
Street improvements	700	700	700	200	200	0	0
Less grants	400	300	300	0	0	0	0
Net cost to jurisdiction	300	400	400	200	200	0	0
Summary: Projects' gross cost	2,400	2,300	2,300	500	500	200	200
Less total grants	1,400	1,300	1,300	0	0	200	200
Net cost to jurisdiction	1,000	1,000	1,000	500	500	0	0

The optimal timing of local government debt issues is a special problem in finance, and it depends on interest rate levels and trends and on the spread between municipals and short-term U.S. government bonds. The local government can often realize savings by floating all the bonds immediately and investing the proceeds in Treasury issues until they are needed, since the rate on tax-free municipals is generally lower than the yield on Treasury issues.

Determining financing needs

On the basis of the fiscal-resource study, the analyst can determine the financial requirements of the capital budget. According to row 7 in Figure 6–2, the net funds available to support new projects total $300,000 in 2005. By 2006, this figure is expected to turn into a deficit of $100,000. For 2007 through 2010, the plan is for the budget to be in balance. A modest surplus of $50,000 is projected for 2011.

Assuming that the local government follows through with its capital program, row 9 shows the required new financing: $700,000 in 2005 and $1,100,000 in 2006. The requirements of the program taper off to $500,000 in 2008 and 2009. There are no new large projects or requirements for funds for 2010, and a surplus of $50,000 is projected for 2011. The total capital financing required from 2005 through 2011 equals $3,800,000.

Evaluating financing options

The next step in capital budget preparation is to devise a financial plan and show how it will affect the local government's tax structure. The two basic approaches to financing capital programs are pay-as-you-go (or pay-as-you-acquire) and pay-as-you-use. In practice, many plans incorporate elements of both models.

Pay-as-you-go financing

In the past, many writers on local finance advocated pay-as-you-go financing as a way to save on interest charges. Pay-as-you-go meant that the local government would allocate a significant portion of operating revenues each year to a capital reserve fund. The monies in this fund would be used for annual capital improvements or saved until they were sufficient for large projects. In any case, regular capital allocations from the operating budget would be used to smooth out budget allocations for capital expenditures and eliminate the need for bond financing. Because the local government would save the interest charges that would have been incurred on the debt, the absolute amount of payments for any given capital program would be lower over time than if the program had been financed through bonds. Pay-as-you-go carried the cachet of "good planning" and was adopted by many communities.

However, pay-as-you-go financing creates certain difficulties in both theory and practice. For this financing method to function well, capital projects must be evenly spaced over time (i.e., large projects must be relatively rare). But only in large jurisdictions are capital projects likely to average out over time—and even there, the capital program is likely to be "lumpy," occasionally demanding heavy outlays. Under strict pay-as-you-go financing, some projects have to be delayed until the necessary funds can be accumulated. In the meantime, the community may be denied a very desirable facility, or a vital part of a total system (e.g., a road link or a docking facility) may have to be postponed, with a resulting loss to the local economy. Moreover, if public funds are accumulated for future expenditure, the local government has essentially taken over a savings function for its citizens. The citizens might have uses for these funds that would generate higher returns than the interest the government can earn while waiting to build a project.

Moreover, if the population is relatively mobile, pay-as-you-go financing is not equitable. For example, some citizens of a given jurisdiction may contribute heavily to capital improvements—but before they have had a chance to enjoy them, they may move to a different area and have to start paying for capital improvements all over again. Conversely, a new resident moving into a community that has completed the bulk of its capital program will enjoy the use of the facilities without having contributed to their financing. Pay-as-you-go financing also runs counter to principles of intergenerational equity. Older families will be taxed immediately to pay for capital facilities that may last long past their lifetimes, whereas the use and enjoyment of these facilities will accrue to younger people who may have made very little payment on them.

Pay-as-you-use financing

The pay-as-you-use method avoids most of the problems of pay-as-you-go plans. In its pristine theoretical form, pay-as-you-use financing means that every long-term improvement is financed by serial debt issues with maturities arranged so that the retirement of debt coincides with the depreciation of the project. When the project's useful life finally ends, the last dollar of debt is paid off. If a replacement facility is desired, it should be financed by a new bond issue tailored in the same manner. Under pay-as-you-use, each cohort pays for its own capital improvements. No one is forced to provide free goods for a future generation or to finance facilities for a jurisdiction in which he or she may not continue to live; nor will new members of the community reap where they have not sown. Thus, ideally, all long-lived projects should be financed by debt that is retired over the course of the project's life.

The weight of the theoretical analysis is in favor of pay-as-you-use financing. In fact, even the major argument for pay-as-you-go financing—the savings on total interest costs over time—is erroneous. It ignores the private time value of money and the fact that the local government's interest costs are generally lower than those of the rest of the financial market. In any case, over the years, increasing constraints on their fiscal resources have forced most local governments to abandon pay-as-you-go budgets.[5]

Debt financing

It is useful to set up the financing plan to show the project's anticipated effect on the local millage rate and on the community's financial position and credit rating. Figure 6–9 shows the fiscal effects of the pay-as-you-use financing plan, which relies entirely on debt financing. Of course, the financing plan simply provides a guideline; determining the feasibility of the proposed capital program is the responsibility of local decision makers.

The financing plan   Under the financing scheme shown in Figure 6–9, the community issues debt to cover its net new financial requirements. Row 1 shows the timing of debt issues to coincide with capital expenditures. Row 2, the debt amortization requirement, must be based on the issue length of serial bonds (normally fifteen to twenty-five years). Interest payments, calculated at an average rate, are shown in row 3. Row 4 (the sum of rows 2 and 3) presents the total debt service on the new bonds. Generally, under pay-as-you-use programs, the millage rate (or equivalent taxes) would remain relatively constant for the first year or so; afterward, the increasing service charges on the net debt would necessitate an increase in the millage rate. Nevertheless, the variations in tax rates are not onerous. One of the main advantages of debt financing is that it allows a relatively smooth budgetary transition. Row 7 shows the millage rate rising from a base of 20.0 mills to 21.7 mills in 2009. Thereafter the millage rate decreases in small annual increments.

Feasibility of debt financing   When bond financing is used, the community's debt-carrying capacity must be analyzed. Figures 6–10 and 6–11 show the basic factors used to measure the projected debt of the capital program against the local government's carrying capacity. (See Chapter 14 for addi-

Figure 6–9   The effect of the capital financing plan on the local millage rate.

	2005	2006	2007	2008	2009	2010	2011
(1) New debt required to finance the capital budget (nearest $100,000)[a]	700	1,100	1,000	500	500	—	—
(2) Amortization of debt (15-year issues) (nearest $100,000)	47	120	187	220	253	253	253
(3) Interest (6% on outstanding balance) (nearest $100,000)	42	105	158	177	194	178	163
(4) Funds needed for service charges on new debt (nearest $100,000)	89	225	345	397	447	431	416
(5) Additional mills required (to the nearest tenth)[b]	0.4	0.9	1.4	1.5	1.7	1.5	1.4
(6) Approximate revenue increase (nearest $100,000)	92	215	348	389	452	447	407
(7) Total millage	20.4	20.9	21.4	21.5	21.7	21.6	21.4

Note: Table assumes a pay-as-you-use, 100 percent debt financing plan. The current millage rate is 20.0.
[a] From row 9 of Figure 6–2.

[b] Estimated by dividing the amount in row 4 by the assessed value shown in column A of Figure 6–4.

tional discussion of these factors.) Column C of Figure 6–10 shows the ratio, or percentage, of outstanding general fund debt to the true (i.e., market) value of taxable property. Column E shows the total of the old and projected new debt. Column F shows the ratio of total projected debt to the value of the local property tax base. The general rule of thumb for local government debt is that the ratio of funded debt to true property value should not exceed 10 percent. The hypothetical case is well within this rough guideline.

Another measure of debt capacity is the ratio of debt service charges to current revenues. The framework for forecasting this ratio is shown in Figure 6–11. Column C gives the ratio of existing debt service charges to projected revenues. Column E shows the combined service charges on the old and projected new debt. Municipal bond analysts assume that a ratio of less than 20 percent of debt service charges to revenues is reasonable. If a debt plan were adopted, it would be important to determine whether the peak debt service charges would exceed

	(A) Existing debt outstanding as of 31 December[a] ($)	(B) True value of assessable property[b] ($)	(C) Debt outstanding as a percentage of true valuation (C = A ÷ B)	(D) Projected new debt as of 31 December[c] ($)	(E) Projected total debt outstanding ($) (E = D + A)	(F) Projected outstanding debt as a percentage of true valuation (F = E ÷ B)
2005	1,876	384,583	0.5	700	2,576	0.7
2006	1,489	397,960	0.4	1,753	3,242	0.8
2007	1,078	413,860	0.3	2,633	3,711	0.9
2008	793	432,650	0.2	2,946	3,739	0.9
2009	541	443,098	0.1	3,226	3,767	0.9
2010	323	465,561	0.1	2,973	3,296	0.7
2011	142	484,183	0.0	2,720	2,862	0.6

[a] From Figure 6–7.
[b] Based on Figure 6–4, assuming that the ratio of assessed to market value is approximately 60 percent in this jurisdiction.
[c] Based on Figure 6–9, assuming that each new debt issue is amortized in equal amounts over fifteen years.

Figure 6–10   Projected debt and true value of assessments (in thousands of $).

	(A) Service on existing debt[a] ($)	(B) Projected revenue[b] ($)	(C) Debt service as a percentage of projected revenue (C = A ÷ B)	(D) Projected service on new debt[c] ($)	(E) Projected service on total debt ($) (E = A + D)	(F) Projected debt service as a percentage of projected revenue (F = E ÷ B)
2005	500	6,000	8.3	89	589	9.8
2006	500	6,500	7.7	225	725	11.2
2007	350	7,000	5.0	345	695	9.9
2008	300	7,300	4.1	397	697	9.5
2009	250	7,700	3.2	447	697	9.1
2010	200	8,000	2.5	431	631	7.9
2011	150	8,400	1.8	416	566	6.7

[a] From Figure 6–7.
[b] From Figure 6–3.
[c] From Figure 6–9.

Figure 6–11   Debt service and projected revenue (in thousands of $).

this level. Again, the hypothetical case appears to be acceptable: debt service as a percentage of projected revenues is forecasted to peak in 2006 at 11.2 percent and to decline thereafter.

User charges and revenue bonds

In the hypothetical capital budget, the funds to be raised for debt service were to come from general taxation. This is the appropriate source of funds when (1) the benefits of a project accrue to the community as a whole; (2) it is impossible to measure the precise amount of benefits accruing to particular individuals; or (3) it is impossible to exclude anyone from using or enjoying the services provided. A new city park would be an example of such a project.

The benefits generated by some kinds of capital investments, however, accrue more directly to individual users; in such cases, the government can charge users for these services: examples include admission fees for the use of a swimming pool or toll charges to cross a bridge. Revenue bonds, with interest and amortization covered by user charges, may be the appropriate method of financing such facilities. Given the necessity of containing government expenditures and the frequent resistance to increases in broad-based taxes, use of revenue bonds is likely to continue to expand in the future.

If a capital improvement is to be financed fully by revenue bonds, the projected revenues should cover the maintenance and operating costs of the facility as well as the interest and service charges on the bonds, probably with some margin of safety.

Sometimes a project provides benefits beyond those that the fees of the immediate users can be expected to support. For example, a recreational facility in a poor neighborhood may provide social-welfare benefits to the broader population that exceed the revenues the facility may generate. For a socially worthwhile project to be economically feasible, the flow of benefits (including those for which there is no charge), discounted at the social cost of capital, should equal or exceed the total outlay on the project. To the extent that there are community common benefits, the project may be partly financed with general debt, or partially subsidized through a service charge from the general fund.

Although a user charge system can provide the basis for efficient economic decision making, it is often criticized on the grounds of equity. Because user charges will generally have more impact on the budgets of lower-income residents than on the budgets of higher-income residents, such charges can prevent lower-income residents from taking full advantage of local government services. Moreover, the services provided by government are those that are not fully supplied by the private sector; the community may have social reasons to encourage the consumption of certain services by people who could not afford to purchase them in the private market. Thus, by their nature, a significant number of government services must be subsidized by the community as a whole. The challenge to the public official is to find the optimal balance between efficiency in the supply of public services and equity among citizens.

Tailoring debt to the long-term costs of the project

If a project is financed with a serial bond issue, the maturities can be designed so that the total of (1) the service charges on the debt and (2) the facility maintenance costs (excluding the variable operating costs) is reasonably flat over the life of the project. Such an arrangement is another application of the general rule that each group of users should pay the same level of capital costs over time.

Figure 6–12 illustrates a debt service schedule designed to keep total debt service charges relatively stable. The project in this example costs $15 million, is expected to last fifteen years, and carries an average interest rate of 5 percent. As the figure shows, the repayments of principal are higher in later years but interest charges are lower: total debt service payments are thus relatively constant over the life of the project.

Optimally, the full costs of financing and maintaining the project should be constant for each generation of users. Thus, if maintenance costs are projected to rise over the life of the project, capital costs should be tailored to fall over time. Moreover, since debt service is only a portion of the total capital cost borne by taxpayers, it is important to ensure that facility maintenance costs are also taken into account in the schedule of capital costs. In the example shown in Figure 6–13, repairs, modifications, and maintenance costs are estimated to be $250,000 in year 1, but to increase by $50,000 per year to a total of $950,000 in year 15. In this case, a flat repayment of principal, in the amount of $1 million per year, best equalizes total annual capital costs. Thus, as shown in the figure, total capital costs, including major repairs and maintenance, are constant, an arrangement that spreads the financial burden equitably. Early users,

Figure 6-12 Constant total debt service (in thousands of $).

Year	Amortization of principal (15,000)	Interest (5%)	Total debt service
1	700	750	1,450
2	700	715	1,415
3	800	680	1,480
4	800	640	1,440
5	900	600	1,500
6	900	555	1,455
7	900	510	1,410
8	1,000	465	1,465
9	1,100	415	1,515
10	1,100	365	1,465
11	1,100	310	1,410
12	1,200	255	1,455
13	1,300	195	1,495
14	1,300	130	1,430
15	1,300	65	1,365

Figure 6-13 Constant debt service and maintenance costs (in thousands of $).

Year	Amortization of principal (15,000)	Interest (5%)	Total debt service	Maintenance and repair	Total capital cost
1	1,000	750	1,750	250	2,000
2	1,000	700	1,700	300	2,000
3	1,000	650	1,650	350	2,000
4	1,000	600	1,600	400	2,000
5	1,000	550	1,550	450	2,000
6	1,000	500	1,500	500	2,000
7	1,000	450	1,450	550	2,000
8	1,000	400	1,400	600	2,000
9	1,000	350	1,350	650	2,000
10	1,000	300	1,300	700	2,000
11	1,000	250	1,250	750	2,000
12	1,000	200	1,200	800	2,000
13	1,000	150	1,150	850	2,000
14	1,000	100	1,100	900	2,000
15	1,000	50	1,050	950	2,000

who have the advantage of using new, efficient equipment and facilities, pay somewhat heavier debt service charges; later users are compensated for the declining efficiency of the installation with lower debt financing costs.

Pass-through financing

In the 1980s, a spate of what were known as "pass-through financing" bond issues involved local government finance officers and planning officials in some very sophisticated financial dealings. As noted in Chapter 14, the Tax Reform Act of 1986 considerably restricted, by state, the total quantity of such issues and the types of projects whose financing would qualify for tax exemption. Nevertheless, local debt—with interest and service charges wholly or partially supported by the underlying activity—can still be used to provide financial aid to a considerable number of properly qualified activities.

In a pass-through, the state or local government lends its credit and tax-free status to some other institution or private enterprise without taking responsibility for the final outcome. For example, if a nonprofit hospital wished to finance an expansion of its facilities, the local government would float bonds for the necessary amount and turn the funds over to the hospital. There may be a small reserve fund held back to help repay the debt; nevertheless, the indenture would clearly state that neither the local government nor the state was in any way pledged to repay the bonds.

Local governments considering entering into pass-through financing schemes should meticulously check the credit of the basic beneficiary and the probability that the repayment plan will be fulfilled. Having lent the local government's name to the transaction, local officials may find that their jurisdiction will not escape the moral obligation to repay the debt in the event that the primary borrowers default.

One type of pass-through financing, subsidized mortgage schemes, involves selling tax-free bonds and then lending the money to institutions (e.g., banks and savings and loan associations) engaged in financing private mortgages for housing. These institutions can re-lend the money only to qualified, low-income home buyers at a lower rate than the free market would dictate. Housing finance bonds essentially favor subsidized borrowers over other borrowers. As long as tax-free bonds may be used for such purposes as subsidized private mortgages, it is probably competitively advantageous for any single locality to make use of the device, although it is probably not helpful for the country as a whole, since the net effect is to reduce available credit and raise the interest rate on the issue of regular bonds. Excessive use of the tax exemption causes taxes to increase on other types of returns and income.

The capital budget and the fiscal plan

Economic and fiscal factors determine a local government's capital budget and fiscal plan. The fiscal plan must compare benefits with costs. The initial step is to implement rules for selecting capital projects. This involves quantifying benefit flows, applying the concept of NPV, and using an appropriate estimate of the community's cost, or discount rate. Only projects that show a positive NPV and a positive benefit-to-cost ratio should be put into the CIP.

The second step is to forecast the fiscal capacity of the local government. Will the predicted growth of local revenues and wealth be sufficient to carry the service charges on the debt that will be incurred to finance the capital improvements? Although measuring fiscal capacity is considered an independent test and, indeed, is based on more objective data than the estimate of the benefits used to determine the NPV, the two tests are related: if the project is economically desirable, then one way or another it should generate sufficient social wealth to finance its associated carrying costs.

In the case of revenue bonds, which are becoming increasingly prevalent, the projected level of user charges is substituted for the estimate of community benefits. The flow of revenue must cover repair and operating costs and return a sufficient amount to cover the interest charges and the amortization of debt.

The third step is to select a financing method. On the grounds of equity, long-term debt is the optimal method for financing long-lived local capital projects. This view further implies that the debt issue should be tailored to the useful life of the project. If bonds are to be retired at the same rate as the capital is worn out, serial bonds should be used, and the periodic amount of bonds retired should be correlated to the reduction in the economic value of the project over time. (When this approach is implemented properly in a purely governmental accounting system, there is no need to use depreciation.)

Serial bond financing facilitates intergenerational equity because, in each time period, those who receive the benefits pay the equivalent of the user costs. The current generation is not required to reduce its income in order to transfer wealth to the future, which would occur if current taxes were used to pay for the capital improvement. Similarly, when serial bond financing is used, future generations are not left with the burden of retiring a balloon payment at the end of the asset's life.

The problem of equity between new residents and out-migrants is analogous to that of intergenerational equity. When local debt is properly used, new residents enjoy the benefits of the community assets and take up the financing burden in their taxes; out-migrants have already paid for their share of capital use during their residency.

Although it is naturally informed by financial considerations, the CIP cannot be considered only in financial terms. The objective of the capital program is to provide sufficient social capital to enable the local government to maintain a viable economic base and to provide worthwhile benefits or amenities for the well-being of its citizens. The final test of a successful program is that at the end of the planning horizon, the community shows improvement in indicators of social benefits, private wealth, economic activity, health, education, and quality of life.

1   For more on capital budgeting, see A. John Vogt, *Capital Budgeting and Finance: A Guide for Local Governments* (Washington, D.C.: International City/County Management Association, 2004).

2   Karl Nollenberger, ed., *Evaluating Financial Condition: A Handbook for Local Government* (Washington, D.C.: International City/County Management Association, 2003), 152.

3   Eli Schwartz, "Social Cost of Capital and Public Investment," *Journal of Finance* (March 1970).

4   See J. Richard Aronson and Eli Schwartz, "Forecasting Future Revenues," *Management Information Service (MIS) Report* (July 1970); "Forecasting Future Expenses," *MIS Report* (November 1970); and "Capital Budget Finance," *MIS Report* (February 1971).

5   J. Richard Aronson and John L. Hilley, *Financing State and Local Governments,* 4th ed. (Washington, D.C.: Brookings Institution, 1986), chap. 9.

7 Budgeting

PAUL L. SOLANO

A public budget—a financial plan prepared for a given fiscal period—is an instrument that allows government officials to allocate monies for personnel, goods, and services to achieve politically determined goals. This chapter examines the fiscal and accounting context of budgeting, the charactcristics of capital budgeting, the role of the budget in attaining goals, budgetary control, the budget cycle, dimensions of multiyear budgeting, and the types of budgets adopted by local governments.

Fiscal and accounting context

Local government budgeting takes place in a legal, political, and organizational setting that differs substantially from that of the private sector.[1] Budgeting practices are established and constrained by state law, accepted standards, and local ordinances and traditions. The generally accepted accounting principles (GAAP) that have been sanctioned by the Governmental Accounting Standards Board (GASB) provide the authoritative description of governmental budgetary practices and the accounting requisites for budgeting.[2]

Scope and content of budgets

A local government budget specifies the types and amounts of resources that are expected to be available for financing a level of estimated expenditures required to provide government programs and services. The budget is generally broken down into an operating budget, which shows expenditures for the current period (typically a fiscal year), and a capital budget, which shows the financial plans for long-term capital improvements, facilities, and equipment. The two budgets may be consolidated for certain purposes. The consolidated budget indicates the amount of total estimated revenues available for the current period and the amount of new dcbt to be incurred for projects in the capital budget.

In most local governments, the initial responsibility for budget formulation rests with the chief administrator (local government manager or mayor), who submits a proposed budget to the governing body for legal approval. The governing body generally has the power to revise the chief administrator's revenue and expenditure estimates, but an elected chief administrator may have the power to veto the entire budget or specific items. After the governing body approves the proposed budget through a budget ordinance, the newly adopted budget becomes a legally binding document for the manager or mayor to administer.

The period for which a budget is authorized spans a fiscal year that may correspond to the calendar year or to some other twelve-month pcriod, most commonly July 1 to June 30. Some local governments use multiyear budgets, most commonly biennial budgets, which span two years. In most annual reports, revenue and expenditure figures are presented as follows: (1) for the prior fiscal year, actual revenues and expenditures versus the budgeted figures; (2) for the current fiscal year, estimated revenues and expenditures; and (3) for the next fiscal year, proposed revenues and expenditures. The budget document for a typical consolidated budget summarizes the financial plans for all funds and shows expenditures either by department or by object of expenditure (see Figure 7–1).

Funds and budget types

Most government budgets include a number of subbudgets set up for individual funds within a fund accounting system (see Chapter 8).[3] A fund is an in-

	(1) Prior FY Budgeted $, 2004–05	(2) Prior FY Actual $, 2004–05	(3) Prior FY $ Variance favorable (unfavorable)[a]	(4) Current FY Budgeted $, 2005–06	(5) Next FY Proposed $, 2006–07
Revenues					
(1) Taxes	35,435,160	35,483,880	48,720	36,154,120	39,330,960
(2) Licenses and permits	13,253,400	13,926,920	673,520	15,319,640	16,851,600
(3) User charges and fees	1,476,600	1,345,960	(130,640)	1,480,560	1,628,600
(4) Intergovernmental revenue	4,330,920	4,224,200	(106,720)	4,646,640	5,111,280
(5) Special assessments	2,722,680	2,748,200	25,520	3,023,440	3,325,320
(6) Miscellaneous revenue	1,684,240	1,608,880	(75,360)	1,769,760	1,946,320
(7) Total revenues	58,903,000	59,338,040	435,040	62,394,160	68,194,080
Expenditures (by department)					
(8) General government	1,434,760	1,434,280	480	1,472,240	1,754,960
(9) Health	2,406,160	2,403,760	2,400	2,445,840	2,765,120
(10) Welfare	7,969,040	7,956,720	12,320	8,375,840	9,637,360
(11) Public safety	8,531,560	8,716,200	(184,640)	9,042,220	10,242,080
(12) Education	15,934,480	16,317,280	(382,800)	17,163,360	18,162,520
(13) Sanitation	5,998,520	6,272,120	(273,600)	6,306,880	7,307,560
(14) Highways and streets	12,979,320	13,173,200	(193,880)	13,466,160	14,945,640
(15) Recreation and cultural	3,608,440	3,564,760	43,680	3,578,840	3,699,240
(16) Total expenditures	58,862,280	59,838,320	(976,040)	61,851,380	68,514,480
(17) Excess of revenues over/(under) expenditures, or budget surplus (deficit)	40,720	(500,280)[b]		542,780[c]	(320,400)[d]
(18) Cumulative amount available for appropriations (or unreserved fund balance) from prior fiscal year	1,034,640	1,034,640		534,360[e]	1,077,140[f]
(19) Unreserved fund balance to be used for appropriations	320,400[g]				

[a] The variance shown in column 3 is the difference between the budgeted figures shown in column 1 and the actual figures shown in column 2.

[b] Actual budget deficit ($500,280), which is covered by the unreserved fund balance of $1,034,640 (line 18, column 1).

[c] Estimated budget surplus.

[d] Proposed budget deficit ($320,400) to be financed from the unreserved fund balance of $1,077,140 (line 18, column 5).

[e] Unreserved fund balance of $1,034,640 from prior fiscal year (line 18, column 1) minus budget deficit of $500,280 (line 17, column 2) in prior year.

[f] Current-year surplus of $542,780 (line 17, column 4) plus $534,360 (line 18, column 4).

[g] The amount of the available (unreserved) fund balance used to cover the budgetary deficit of $320,400 (line 17, column 5), shown formally here as a source of revenues to partially finance estimated expenditures. A deficit is intentionally incurred to use up some of the unreserved fund balance, which is considered to be too large.

Figure 7–1   Sample consolidated budget for all funds, fiscal year (FY) ending June 30.

dependent fiscal entity with assets, liabilities, reserves, a residual balance (also known as equity), and revenues and expenditures for undertaking activities. Funds may be expendable, meaning that authorization through appropriation for revenue collection and spending expires at the end of the fiscal period; or nonexpendable, or revolving, meaning that spending beyond the fiscal year is allowed without reauthorization—that is, without new appropriation. GASB recommends, where the scale of government warrants, the use of eleven different types of funds, which can be grouped into three broad categories—governmental funds, proprietary funds, and fiduciary funds. Governmental funds are to be operated under fixed budgets and proprietary funds under flexible budgets; depending on their nature and purpose, fiduciary funds may be operated under either fixed or flexible budgets.

Governmental funds   Most local government activities are conducted through governmental funds, of which five types are recommended by GASB. Each local government has one general fund but may have more than one of the other fund types (see Figure 7–2):

1. The general fund, a single entity that supports all services (e.g., police, fire, welfare) not assigned to other funds.
2. Special-revenue funds, which provide services financed from specifically designated revenues (e.g., recreation may be financed by fees earmarked for such use).
3. Capital projects funds, which obtain resources from long-term debt and intergovernmental grants and are used to acquire major assets that have a useful economic life greater than one year.
4. Debt service funds, which receive (1) monies transferred from other funds and (2) resources from taxes, from intergovernmental grants, or from the proceeds of bond issues that have been refunded. Debt service funds are used to pay the principal and interest on the government's long-term, general-obligation debt (municipal bonds).
5. Permanent funds, which finance continuing activities with resources (e.g., interest from endowments for a cemetery, library, or museum) that (1) are legally restricted to earnings derived from a safeguarded principal and (2) can be used only for programs that benefit the government or its citizens (i.e., cannot be used to benefit individuals, private organizations, or other governments).

Each governmental fund has a separate, fixed budget according to which the governing authority approves appropriations that authorize the spending of specific dollar amounts on particular items. Additional expenditures cannot be made without authorization. Under a fixed budget, appropriated funds are expendable because the authorization for spending expires at the end of the fiscal period. The budgetary transactions of managers can be easily tracked since the budget allows the governing authority to determine whether the appropriated monies were spent on the designated items and whether expenditures were kept within the stipulated amounts and time periods.

Figure 7–3 summarizes a typical balance sheet and budget for a governmental fund. The balance sheet shows (1) assets—what is owned by the fund; (2) liabilities—what is owed by the fund; and (3) the fund balance, which is the difference between the assets and the liabilities. That part of the fund balance that has been set aside for contingencies and potential liabilities is referred to as the reserves, or the reserved fund balance. If assets exceed liabilities plus reserves, the result is a positive unreserved fund balance, or a fund surplus, as shown in the figure; if assets are less than liabilities plus reserves, the result is a fund deficit, or negative unreserved fund balance. The accounts shown on the

	Governmental funds				
	General	Special revenue	Capital projects	Debt service	Permanent
Component funds	General fund	School aid Library book purchase City hospital emergency services State gasoline tax (roads)	Solano School Building Aaron Medical Center Street and road construction; Brams Bridge Storm-sewer construction	General improvements Nora Hospital Linn High School	Myrna Arts Endowment Alexis Park Facilities
Major resources	Property taxes Sales taxes Licenses and permits Intergovernmental grants	Property taxes Sales taxes Earmarked taxes Intergovernmental grants Charges	Intergovernmental grants Proceeds of general-obligation bond sale	Taxes Intergovernmental grants Proceeds of refunded bond issue	Contributions Interest on investment
Major expenditures	Personnel services Materials Supplies Contractual services Equipment	Personnel services Materials Supplies Contractual services Equipment	Construction contracts Engineering services	Retirement of bond principal Retirement of bond interest	Personnel services Materials Supplies Contractual services Equipment

Figure 7–2   Fund structure of local governments.

Figure 7–3   Structure and operations of balance sheet and budgetary accounts of expendable funds.

Balance sheet
June 30, 2004

Assets	
Cash	$3,120,000
Taxes receivable	874,000
Accounts receivable	904,000
Due from other funds	570,000
Inventory	440,000
Total assets	$5,908,000
Liabilities	
Vouchers payable	$2,500,000
Contracts payable	1,560,000
Due to other funds	420,000
Fund equity	
Reserves	$760,000
Fund balance	668,000[a]
Total fund equity	$1,428,000
Total liabilities and fund equity	$5,908,000

[a]Ending fund balance, 2004 ($668,000), plus budget surplus, 2005 ($250,000), equals ending fund balance, 2005 ($918,000). This amount could be made available for appropriation in the 2006 budget.

Proprietary funds		Fiduciary funds			
Enterprise funds	Internal service funds	Public pension trust	Investment trust	Private-purpose trust	Agency
City water and sewer Refuse collection	Motor pool Equipment replacement	Teachers' annuity Managerial employees' retirement	County cash management	College tuition savings	Liquor-tax collection (for schools) Lottery funds (for aid to elderly residents)
User charges	User charges	Contributions Interest on investments	Contributions Interest on investments	Contributions Interest on investments	Taxes Intergovernmental grants
Operating expenses Personnel services Contractual services Materials, supplies Depreciation Utilities Nonoperating expenses Fees Interest Rents	Operating expenses Personnel services Contractual services Materials, supplies Depreciation Utilities	Loans Transfers	Benefit payments	Benefit payments	Transfers

Actual budget
Fiscal year ending June 30, 2005

Revenues	
Taxes	$12,272,000
Licenses	810,000
Intergovernmental transfers	2,604,000
Charges	1,664,000
Total revenues	$17,350,000
Expenditures	
Personnel services	$8,890,000
Materials and supplies	990,000
Contracts	4,100,000
Capital outlays	3,120,000
Total expenditures	$17,100,000
Surplus (deficit)	$250,000[a]

Balance sheet
June 30, 2005

Assets	
Cash	$6,040,000
Taxes receivable	874,000
Accounts receivable	1,236,000
Due from other funds	798,000
Inventory	810,000
Total assets	$9,758,000
Liabilities	
Vouchers payable	$5,960,000
Contracts payable	1,920,000
Due to other funds	388,000
Fund equity	
Reserves	$572,000
Fund balance	918,000[a]
Total fund equity	$1,490,000
Total liabilities and fund equity	$9,758,000

balance sheet are affected by budgetary transactions: revenues increase assets, and expenditures reduce liabilities or may increase reserves.

As is evident from the budget portion of the figure, if revenue collections exceed expenditures for the fiscal period, the result is a budget surplus, which increases the fund balance; if expenditures are greater than collected revenues, the result is a budget deficit, which decreases the fund balance. The unreserved fund surplus can be used to cover a budgetary deficit or to finance the expenditures of a subsequent budgetary period (see Figure 7–1).

Proprietary funds   Two types of funds—enterprise funds and internal service funds (ISFs)—can be used when a government engages in activities that are analogous to private commercial operations (see Figure 7–2). Enterprise funds account for electric utilities, water and sewer systems, and other public services financed through user charges. ISFs account for the activities of governmental entities that provide services (e.g., purchasing and data processing) to other governmental units in return for fees that cover the cost of operations.

The main purpose of these business-like organizations is to provide services to consumers at a price that will cover both the current cost of operations (expenses) and the purchase and maintenance of necessary capital assets. Net income (revenues less expenses) or net loss at the end of the fiscal period either adds to or reduces the fund's residual equity, which is formally referred to as the net assets of the fund. Three components of net assets are reported: (1) those that are invested in capital assets, net of related debt; (2) those that are restricted; and (3) those that are unrestricted (see Figure 7–4). Unreserved, or unrestricted, funds can be used to cover an operating deficit in the current fiscal year.

Because the level and quality of the services provided are determined by a flexible budget rather than by a fixed budget, proprietary funds have a degree of flexibility that is not found in governmental funds. Although expenses are fixed for each unit of service (e.g., ten cents per gallon of water), total bud-

Figure 7–4   Structure and operations of net assets and operating (budgetary) accounts of proprietary funds.

Net assets June 30, 2004		
Assets		
Current		$2,618,000
Restricted		2,212,000
Property, plant, equipment		32,668,000
Less accumulated depreciation	$356,000	
Net property, plant equipment		32,312,000
Total assets		$37,142,000
Liabilities		
Current payables		$3,822,000
Long-term debt		21,304,000
Total liabilities		$25,126,000
Net assets		
Invested in capital assets, net of (less) debt[a]		$11,008,000
Restricted for debt service		605,000
Unrestricted		403,000[b]
Total net assets[c]		$12,016,000

geted spending will vary according to the anticipated demand for service. In the case of particularly large or complex enterprises, effective and efficient management may require the preparation of budget estimates based on several levels of consumer demand.

In the case of proprietary funds, when expenditures rise (because of increased production to satisfy demand), revenues also increase; this is not true of governmental funds. Moreover, capital outlays and long-term debt transactions of proprietary funds are not accounted for in separate funds but within the proprietary fund itself. Because governmental commercial entities are supposedly self-sustaining, budgetary authority is nonexpendable, or revolving; that is, authorization for collecting revenue and incurring expenses neither lapses at the end of the fiscal period nor requires renewal at the beginning of the next. Since budgetary authorization is continuous, conformity with budgetary estimates is not an issue; the governing body's main concern, instead, is operational performance, as reflected by the earning of adequate net income. Thus, the budget is a major tool for planning and evaluating operational efficiency in response to different levels of demand.

Fiduciary funds In the operation of a fiduciary fund (see Figure 7–2), the government acts as a custodian, receiving resources and distributing them to individuals, private and public entities, and other funds to finance specific, designated activities. GASB has specified four types of funds to pursue fiduciary objectives.

One type, an agency fund, is established for custodial purposes without any formal trust agreement being made with the government. This type of fund may be used to collect and distribute revenues (e.g., state lottery proceeds) shared by several governments or may be designed to receive grants (e.g., state revenue-sharing grants) to be held temporarily for distribution to the appropriate jurisdictions. Because agency funds merely transfer resources, budgeting to establish financial accountability is unnecessary.

Actual budget: Revenues, expenses, and change in net assets Fiscal year ending June 30, 2005	
Operating revenues	
Billings	$1,336,000
Charges	128,000
Nonoperating revenues	
Rents	16,000
Interest	14,000
Total revenues	$1,494,000
Operating expenses	
Personnel	$260,000
Contracts	40,000
Depreciation	540,000
Other	36,000
Total operating expenses	$876,000
Net income (loss)	$618,000[b]

Net assets June 30, 2005		
Assets		
Current		$3,144,000
Restricted		3,018,000
Property, plant, equipment		36,002,000
Less accumulated depreciation	$410,000	
Net property, plant, equipment		35,592,000
Total assets		$41,754,000
Liabilities		
Current payables		$4,326,000
Long-term debt		26,280,000
Total liabilities		$30,606,000
Net assets		
Invested in capital assets, net of (less) debt[a]		$9,312,000
Restricted for debt service		815,000
Unrestricted		1,021,000[b]
Total net assets[c]		$11,148,000

[a] Capital assets less (accumulated depreciation + outstanding principal of related debt). In 2005, $36,002,000 − ($410,000 + $26,280,000) = $9,312,000.

[b] Ending unrestricted net assets, 2004 ($403,000), plus net income, 2005 ($618,000), equals ending unrestricted assets, 2005 ($1,021,000). This amount could be made available for spending in the 2006 budget.

[c] Total net assets = total assets − total liabilities.

The other three types of fiduciary funds are investment trust funds, pension (and other employee benefit) trust funds, and private-purpose trust funds. Investment trust funds are government-sponsored financial arrangements that may take several forms. In one arrangement, the resources of separate governments are pooled in an investment portfolio that benefits all participants according to their invested amounts. When the sponsoring government is not a participant, the arrangement is generally referred to as an external investment pool; an example would be a state investment pool for which only local governments are eligible. If the sponsor is a participant, the fund is called a mixed investment pool. In a second arrangement, the sponsoring government holds separate investment accounts for individual governments. Because the assets and earnings are distributed in varying amounts to the participants, a flexible budget would be a useful means of recording the activities of these types of funds.

The largest local government trust funds are public pension (and other employee benefit) funds. Of these funds, pension funds are the most sizable; they hold (1) pension contributions from the government and its employees and (2) the earnings on those contributions. Whether both the principal and income or only the income of the fund is expendable depends on the enabling legislation for the pension system. Because pensions are awarded to individuals or families on the basis of stated criteria, flexible budgeting is necessary. Where a pension plan provides nonpension benefits, such as postemployment health care, the requisite nonpension resources must be accounted for in a separate employee benefit fund.

Private-purpose funds have three characteristics: (1) they are used to account for resources that are not associated with pension or investment trust funds; (2) the sponsoring government does not have any financial commitment to the funded activities; and (3) specific individuals, private organizations, and other governments are the beneficiaries of the activities. State-sponsored (but not publicly financed) tuition savings plans are an example. Again, because participants' benefits vary, a flexible budget would be appropriate.

Fiscal practices

Institutional forces have produced considerable variation in fund structures and budgets among local governments. State constitutions and statutes, as well as local government charters and laws, may place requirements on revenue collection and spending and specify how revenues and expenditures must be accounted for. A local government may, for example, be required to establish trust funds to transfer state grant monies to schools within its jurisdiction. According to local ordinance, a portion of local property taxes may have to be set aside in a capital projects fund to finance particular services, such as street repairs. In addition, as indicated in Figure 7–5, a single service may be financed from more than one fund. For instance, current expenditures for public safety (salaries and supplies) could be provided through the general fund, while the construction of the station house could be subsumed under a capital projects fund, and repairs to traffic-control equipment could be supported through special-revenue funds supported by earmarked sales taxes.

Fund structure A fund structure facilitates financial accountability by restricting the expenditure of separate resources—current revenues, borrowed monies, assets, and residual balances (e.g., fund balances, net assets)—to those purposes that have been legally authorized. The fund structure reflects political choices about the types of services that should be provided and how they should be financed. Because fund structures determine who bears the benefits and costs of services, they also embody policy decisions about the

Function	General fund ($)	Special-revenue fund ($)	Capital projects fund ($)	Debt service fund ($)	Enterprise fund ($)	Trust or agency fund ($)	Total estimated expenditures ($)[a]
General government	1,377,780			134,960		242,220	1,754,960
Health	1,560,060	401,860	803,200				2,765,120
Welfare	3,204,240	6,433,120					9,637,360
Public safety[b]	5,854,260	1,827,300	2,560,520				10,242,080
Fire department	1,932,460	595,440	1,263,460				
Inspection	619,460	101,200					
Investigation	310,240						
Fire and rescue	1,002,760	494,240	1,263,460				
Police department	3,921,800	1,219,860	1,297,060				
Investigation	482,640						
Traffic	503,520		182,420				
Patrol	2,935,640		1,514,640				
Personnel services	1,987,280						
Salaries	1,622,440						
Wages	96,400						
Sick pay	84,360						
Social Security	184,080						
Materials	568,320						
Office supplies	66,500						
Uniforms	44,220						
Gasoline and oil	263,200						
Heating and power	142,400						
Telephone service	52,000						
Equipment	180,040	1,219,860					
Communications		441,320					
Weapons	20,360	322,220					
Automobiles		456,320					
Furniture	159,680						
Contractual services	200,000						
Youth clubs	200,000						
Capital outlays			1,514,640				
Construction			1,051,120				
Patrol cars			463,520				
Education	12,265,100	1,685,340	4,212,080				18,162,520
Sanitation	1,272,060	1,330,780	2,695,440		2,009,280		7,307,560
Transportation	3,307,100	7,704,060	3,934,480				14,945,640
Recreation	3,316,500		382,740				3,699,240
Total expenditures	32,157,100	19,382,460	14,588,460	134,960	2,009,280	242,220	68,514,480

[a] Total estimated expenditures for the eight categories shown here by source of funding are taken from the consolidated budget shown in column 5 of Figure 7–1.

[b] Although not shown here because of space limitations, other functions would be similarly classified by department, organization, objects, and items.

Figure 7–5   Consolidated line-item budget by fund: Proposed expenditures.

economic efficiency and equity of local governmental activities. In some localities, for example, water or sewer services are operated through utility or enterprise funds as self-sustaining, fee-for-service, commercial operations. Such an arrangement (1) fosters efficiency, because payment for consumption is more in line with the costs of service provision, and (2) enhances horizontal equity, because every user is treated the same way (i.e., pays the same price for the same number of service units). In other municipalities, where water services are supported solely by property taxes and financed through the general fund, efficiency is compromised because usage is not tied directly to how much households pay for consumption; moreover, depending on the amount of property taxes that they pay, some users are effectively overcharged and others undercharged for the same level of water consumption. In still other municipalities, separate utility enterprises are partially subsidized by monies from the general fund or special-revenue funds, so that users do not pay the full cost of service. Such an arrangement creates inefficiency because users underpay in relation to how much they consume; it also creates inequity because general taxpayers are transferring income to service users. Finally, where charges exceed the costs of the services provided by an enterprise, "excess" revenues may be transferred to other funds, in which case users of the utility are effectively subsidizing other governmental activities.

Because accounting for a number of different revenue-producing services in the general fund is likely to obscure the relationship between costs and prices, services that directly benefit identifiable property owners (e.g., sidewalk installation, trash collection) are generally accounted for in individual funds. So that resources are allocated more efficiently and costs are distributed more equitably, it is desirable to finance such activities through special taxes, fees, charges, or assessments (see the accompanying sidebar).

Even though separate funds can substantially facilitate fiduciary accountability, GASB has noted that a proliferation of funds and fund types can complicate the budget process and produce administrative inefficiency and organizational rigidity.[4] Such difficulties can be avoided in several ways. First, all funds should have the same budget cycle. Second, the fund structure should be simplified whenever possible, as long as it remains adequate to the scope and nature of fiscal activities. For example, smaller municipalities consolidate revenue and expenditure activities into a few governmental funds, and many local governments record trust or fiduciary activities, debt service, and capital outlays as major accounts within the general fund. Third, even where numerous funds exist, steps can be taken to prevent the budget process from becoming overly complex. Enterprise funds do not have to be (and, in practice, are generally not) budgeted extensively because the primary legislative concern is to oversee the enterprise's financial performance. And because management of fiduciary funds is regulated by governmental policy, custom, or donors' legal stipulations, budgetary decision making is not needed. Fourth, integrating the individual budgets of each fund into two comprehensive budgets—the annual operating budget and

---

Accounting for special-assessment funds When local governments undertake capital improvements that directly benefit specific property owners, they may use special assessments to cover all or part of the cost of the improvements. Revenues from such levies then go into a special-assessment fund, which is used to finance outlays for the improvements. Creating a correspondence between those who benefit from a service and those who pay for it is a means of enhancing economic efficiency.

In 1987, the Governmental Accounting Standards Board declared that special-assessment funds should not be included in the financial statements presented in accordance with the reporting standards outlined in gener-

ally accepted accounting principles.[1] While special-assessment funds may still be operated for legal and contractual purposes, their activities must be reported in other governmental and proprietary funds that are consistent with the nature of the special-assessment activity. For example, if a sewer and water line for a new housing development had been financed by levies on the new home owners, the levies could be recognized in a special-assessment fund to ensure their proper use, but the official financial reports of the city or county would record the relevant transactions in a capital projects fund.

[1]Governmental Accounting Standards Board, *Accounting and Financial Reporting for Special Assessments,* Statement No. 6 (Chicago: Government Finance Officers Association, 1987).

the capital budget—allows greater coordination in fiscal and economic planning and thus minimizes the degree of oversight that managers and the governing body must engage in during the course of the budget process.[5] Together, the operating budget and the capital budget form the government's consolidated (or what is commonly referred to as the "current") budget, for the current fiscal year, as shown schematically in Figure 7–6.

Operating and capital budgets The annual operating budget is a financial document specifying expenditures for personnel services; materials and supplies; contractual services; and other resources needed to conduct local government operations for the fiscal year. The operating budget aggregates the individual budgets of the general fund, special-revenue funds, debt service funds, and permanent funds—and, if they are budgeted, proprietary and fiduciary funds as well.

The capital budget, on the other hand, covers outlays for the acquisition of major capital (i.e., fixed or long-lived) assets to be purchased from restricted monies, current resources, or debt. Capital assets include land and improvements to it, buildings and their improvements, machinery, equipment, and other tangible items that have a useful life longer than a single fiscal year. However, many minor and short-lived capital assets—such as furniture, fixtures, and small equipment—are budgeted as current expenditures in the general fund, special-revenue funds, or permanent funds.

The capital budget is the first year of the capital improvements program (CIP), which is the government's capital-facilities planning document. The CIP schedules projects over a five- to ten-year period, provides the economic justification for them, projects the interest and debt amortization (i.e., the schedule of periodic interest and principal payments on borrowed monies) required to finance the projects, and shows the effect of debt service on the operating budget.

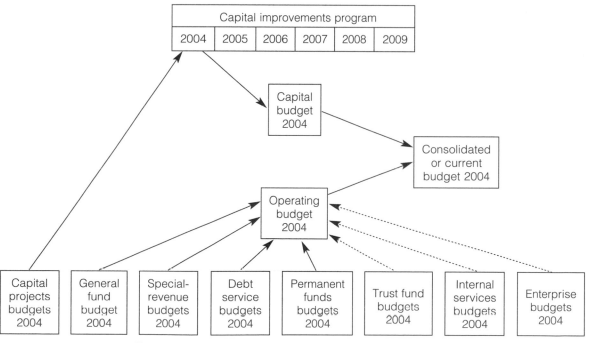

Note: A broken line (- - - -) indicates that the budget may not be integrated into the operating budget.

Figure 7–6 Consolidated budget and its components.

Only activities financed by capital projects funds, which are governmental funds, should be included in the capital budget. As will be discussed later in this chapter, unless legal requirements dictate otherwise, the capital outlays of proprietary funds should not be included in the capital budget.

The preparation and implementation of operating and capital budgets entail some different processes. The next two sections describe each type of budgeting.

Capital budgeting

The overarching goal of capital budgeting is to facilitate the economic viability and development of the community.[6] To continue to deliver services at current levels as economic growth occurs and to create the assets that will facilitate future economic growth, communities invest in fixed assets—that is, capital projects. Achieving these goals requires (1) fiscal planning, in which projects are proposed, evaluated, and selected for inclusion in the CIP (a process that is referred to as "programming projects"), and (2) approval of the financing of the current-year projects in the CIP.

Effective capital budgeting is founded on a community needs assessment. Such an assessment includes an economic and social profile that has at least three components: (1) an economic-base analysis of commercial activities and employment, (2) an inventory and evaluation of land use and existing infrastructure, and (3) analyses of demographic data (population profiles, housing characteristics, and demand for various types of services). This economic and social profile then becomes the basis for (1) forecasts of growth and change in the population and in the local economy, (2) projections of the fiscal resources that will be required under differing economic conditions, and (3) an evaluation of the status of available fixed assets. (Chapter 5 discusses forecasting in detail.)

The second major step in the preparation of the CIP is the identification and evaluation of potential capital projects. Capital improvements may involve rehabilitating, replacing, expanding, or adding fixed assets. Before being included in the CIP, projects should be evaluated for their economic and social impacts. A rigorous evaluation can be obtained through cost-benefit analysis (discussed in more detail in Chapter 6). This approach assigns estimated monetary values to a project's potential benefits and costs over the course of its expected useful life; these estimates are then discounted to determine the net present value (NPV) of a project. A positive NPV indicates that the project's value to the community is greater than the financial and social burden that would be required to undertake it.

If governments relied solely on cost-benefit analysis, which is a strictly economic criterion, they would obtain clear rankings based on the net gain associated with each project under consideration. But because political criteria are at work as well, decisions about the CIP are rarely made on the basis of cost-benefit analysis alone. Generally, priorities are set by a CIP committee, which can be made up of any combination of managers, members of the governing body, citizen representatives, and technical experts. The committee's decisions, in turn, take into account the views of the local government manager and department heads, the governing body, and citizen advisory groups. Views on the CIP can be solicited through formal meetings of government officials or through open public hearings in which citizens comment directly on the capital projects plan. In some jurisdictions, the CIP committee (or a group of elected officials and high-level managers) uses an established rating system to determine the rank and timing of capital projects.

Because the CIP is a plan, it does not require the approval of the governing body, but the governing body does vote on the priorities when it approves the capital budget. The CIP should be updated every year to show which projects are already on line and which projects will be started in the current year (and therefore need funding through the capital budget).

During the preparation stage of the capital budget, neither content nor process is guided by GASB. Under common practice, however, the capital budget includes the following for each project: a statement of purpose; a multi-year implementation schedule; anticipated expenditures, by year; the time frame required for completion; the sources and amount of financing; and the impact on the operating budget. The central budget office takes the essential step of determining whether the local government has the fiscal capacity to finance the proposed capital expenditures. To make this determination, the budget office projects capital expenditures (on the basis of cost estimates provided by engineering firms) and then compares those projections with the forecasts of the government's overall fiscal resources and expenditures.

Resources are forecast under varying assumptions regarding revenue sources, types of taxes and fees, intergovernmental grants, and debt obligations. Government-wide expenditure forecasts are important because they specify the amount of future spending called for in the operating budget, assuming prevailing services and program requirements, as well as the spending commitments that new or expanded capital assets will require under the operating budget. (A new fire station, for example, would produce additional spending on personnel and supplies.)

Together, the resource and expenditure forecasts provide the fiscal constraint on the capital budget: they determine what level of current resources will be available for capital projects once the spending requirements of the operating budget have been met. The level of available resources defines, in turn, the extent to which forecasted surpluses in the operating budget (which occur when revenues are greater than current expenditure commitments) can be used to finance capital projects, and how much debt can be supported to pay for proposed capital projects.

Two methods can be employed, solely or in combination, to finance the capital budget. Under the pay-as-you-go (or pay-as-you-acquire) approach, capital outlays are funded from current resources of the operating budget and from reserves held in the general and special-revenue funds. The pay-as-you-use approach entails debt financing, which means that capital outlays are funded with the proceeds from the sale of municipal bonds.

To use the pay-as-you-go method, a government must accumulate sufficient funds over time to spend on the selected projects; by doing so, it presumably avoids the interest costs on debt. But by waiting to accumulate the funds to undertake important projects, a local government may miss out on the economic gains that could have been achieved, through judicious capital investment, in the meantime. Moreover, during the accumulation period, citizens lose the use of their money, which could perhaps have been used more productively. If the community's population is relatively mobile, pay-as-you-go may also be inequitable; households that have made a contribution may move before the project is even undertaken, and once the project is completed, new residents may receive benefits without having contributed. Finally, if current residents are compelled to fund projects that will be used by subsequent residents who did not pay, pay-as-you-go can create intergenerational inequities.

Pay-as-you-use can overcome the inefficiencies and inequities associated with pay-as-you-go. Bond issues can be sold with a serial structure in which maturities (the expiration dates of the bonds) are arranged so that debt retirement corresponds to the depreciation of the acquired asset, in such a way as to reflect the value received by the users of the capital. (For more information on financing methods, see Chapter 14.)

When debt financing is used, interest and principal must be paid out of current revenues; thus, the impact of these payments on the operating budget must be determined. Both principal and interest payments should be recorded as transactions in the debt service funds. Monies for these payments are transferred from the general fund, from special-revenue funds, or from capital projects funds.

If bonds are sold, the proceeds are deposited in the capital projects funds, along with designated intergovernmental grants and current resources from other governmental funds. Separate capital projects funds should be established for each large project to account for the resources required to finance that project. As progress is made on a capital project, expenditures are paid out of the appropriate capital projects fund. When a project is complete, the fund is terminated and the remaining resources are transferred to debt service funds.

The capital outlays for proprietary funds should be excluded from the government's capital budget and the CIP. Enterprises and internal service organizations are "closed," self-sustaining, decision-making units. Decisions about investment in the fixed assets of these business-like activities are based on two assumptions regarding capital outlays, which are generally financed through borrowing in the form of municipal bond sales. First, the charges for the services produced through the use of capital assets will generate sufficient revenue to pay the interest costs charged for the borrowed monies. Second, depreciation expenses will be incorporated into service charges to reflect the contribution of capital assets to service production. When a fixed asset is acquired, its original value (purchase price) is amortized over its useful economic life, and the resulting depreciation values are recorded as current expenses for the fiscal year.

Budgeting for goal attainment: The operating budget

Whatever their fund structures, local governments can employ an annual consolidated budget, as shown in Figure 7–5, that will substantially determine both the efficiency and equity of the social outcomes of governmental actions. Efficiency concerns the relationship between the social value of the outcomes produced through budgetary actions and the social value of the costs required for budgetary implementation. Equity entails judgments about the fairness of social outcomes. Because social outcomes result in gains or losses for different individuals (e.g., members of various economic groups or age cohorts), budgetary actions inevitably affect the distribution of well-being among citizens; for example, government-financed activities can be used to affect income distribution. Similarly, budgeting can also be designed to promote more efficient social outcomes.

It is sometimes argued that the use of cost-benefit analysis to evaluate projects is inappropriate because managers need to take into account not only economic criteria but also potentially conflicting political and social criteria. If, however, cost-benefit analyses are conducted appropriately, they will, in fact, reflect gains or losses in social welfare. Purely political judgments, in contrast, tend to reflect the influence of local interest groups and may not express the preferences and values of the public at large.

Although a comprehensive, normative theory of public budgeting has not been developed to guide governments in their pursuit of efficient outcomes, a seminal paper by B. Verne Lewis suggests that the economics of resource allocation, although somewhat abstract and limited, can yield a prescriptive and theoretical basis for governmental budgeting.[7] The economic principles of cost-benefit analysis offer a somewhat more systematic embodiment of the economics of resource allocation.[8] In the model of budgetary decision making that follows, the principles of rational decision-making theory and cost-benefit analysis are integrated into traditional budgetary structures and processes.[9]

A rational budget-decision model

The economic theory of budgeting is a rational approach to the budgetary process in the sense that means (incremental costs or inputs) are explicitly tied to—and supposedly produce—certain ends (outcomes or benefits). Public budgeting can promote economic efficiency by allocating resources to those programs and services that (1) generate greater net benefits, in accordance with residents' preferences and valuations, than any other alternative and (2) result in incremental benefits that are greater than the incremental costs. Whether budgetary decisions enhance efficiency can be judged against three criteria that are linked to net benefits:

Intersector efficiency. The incremental spending on any government activity should yield more net benefits to society than would be obtained if the resources had remained in the private sector.

Interprogram efficiency. When resources must be allocated among competing government programs, they should be used to finance the one that produces the greatest net benefits.

Intraprogram efficiency. Within each program, the goal should be to maximize the net benefits from any expenditure increment. For example, if a given amount of money can be spent on personnel and materials for in-house service delivery or on contracting out, the choice of alternative depends on which one provides the greatest net benefits.

Because human limitations, organizational and fiscal structures, and governmental processes create obstacles to the rational attainment of goals through budgeting, the rational budget-decision model is difficult to implement. The practical approach to budgetary analysis that follows can help local governments achieve identified goals while taking such restrictions into account.

The chief administrator's role

To ensure that the budget process results in the most efficient use of resources, the chief administrator must (1) organize the budget units along programmatic lines that relate to organizational goals; (2) establish funding levels to guide budget units in preparing their alternatives; and (3) approve the alternatives (which are presented in the form of various funding levels for programs) selected by budget units. The three sections that follow discuss each of these decision points.

Program structure   The budget must yield meaningful data that will allow the chief administrator and governing body to see how the budget units propose to use the funding they receive to achieve organizational goals. A program budget format can facilitate the evaluation of goal achievement.[10] In this format, government activities are organized according to programs, so that the budget units that plan and undertake those activities can be held solely responsible for pursuing clearly defined goals. As shown in Figure 7–7, a program format can have three or more levels.

At the highest level in the program structure are the broad functional areas that reflect the basic needs and purposes of the government. Each functional area has its own goals. The next level in the program structure consists of distinct program categories aimed at specific goals. At the next level are pro-

Functional areas	Program categories	Program subcategories	Program elements

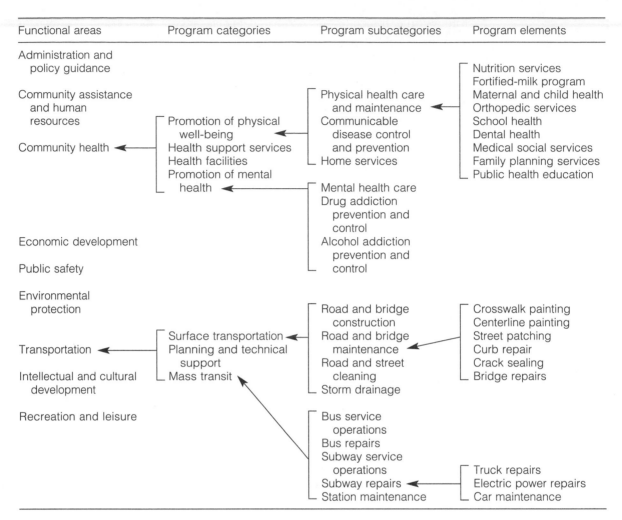

Figure 7–7   Sample program budget format.

gram subcategories, which identify one or more services that are designed to meet the particular needs of a defined clientele or that have other characteristics in common. The services undertaken at the program subcategory level are the responsibility of the budget units. Subsumed under the program subcategories are program elements, the main building blocks of the program structure. As discussed later, the program elements are activities undertaken by the organizational and administrative entities that budget units use to achieve specific outcomes. In summary, the activities undertaken at the lower levels of the program structure (e.g., in the program element and program subcategories) are the means of achieving the ends associated with the higher levels of the structure (e.g., program categories).

Figure 7–8 shows the structure of a program for the promotion of physical well-being. Note that each level in the structure includes specific program statements that describe—in the form of goals, objectives, and outputs—the results expected from the activities conducted at each level. (Because of space limitations, only two program elements are shown.) Together, the program structure and program statements describe the scope and purposes of program activities; at each phase of the budget process, the program structure and the program statements would accompany the actual and estimated expenditures

Figure 7–8   Sample program structure and program statements.

Functional area: Community health
Goal: To provide freedom from debilitating disease and illness for all residents

Program category: Promotion of physical well-being
Goal: To provide the necessary mechanisms and facilities for treatment and prevention of physical illness and diseases

Program subcategory: Physical health care and maintenance
Goal: To decrease the incidence of physical illness among city residents
Objectives: Decrease in the number of infant mortalities
                  Decrease in the number of maternal deaths
                  Decrease in the number of children suffering from nutritional deficiency
                  Decrease in the number of adults with specific illnesses
                  Decrease in the number of children with specific illnesses

Program element: Maternal and child health services
Outputs: Number of doctor's visits by indigent pregnant women for prenatal care
                  Number of doctor's visits by indigent children between birth and three years of age

Program element: School health
Outputs: Number of polio vaccine inoculations for children in grades one through three
                  Number of physical examinations of children in all grades with even numbers

for each program. As discussed in the next section, the program statements and the various levels of the program structure are critical to the budget analysis process that produces expenditure estimates.

For every functional area, managers are assigned at each level of the structure; the level of authority they exercise over lower-level units corresponds to their degree of responsibility for the performance of those units. In this decentralized system, higher-level managers oversee the activities of lower-level units, but lower-level managers have the authority and discretion to conduct the activities of their units as they see fit and are held accountable for their unit's performance, which is measured in accordance with the unit's achievement of stated objectives. Although all managers have budgetary decision-making authority, managers at each level of the program structure have somewhat different responsibilities in the budget-making process: budget preparation and implementation occur at the program subcategory and program-element levels, whereas the functional areas and their program categories are the major focus of analysis and policy.

When we refer to "the programs" of government for which direct budgetary actions are undertaken, it is the program subcategories that are at issue. A program is conducted by a budget unit that is directed by a program (or budget-unit) manager. Each program (i.e., program subcategory) is a combination of program elements, which are separate organizational units that undertake all the activities required to produce an identifiable and distinct output or set of outputs.[11] The outputs of a program element indicate the level of services that is expected to produce the achievement of program objectives.

Under a program format, each program element is an independent cost center because its staff members engage in the analysis of, and undertake decision making for, various mixes of objects of expenditure to determine their impact on outputs. Thus, a program element is a budget decision point. And because a single manager (a program-element manager) supervises the budgetary analysis and the implementation of activities produced by the selected mix of inputs, program elements are also responsibility centers. Responsibility centers are thus coterminous with cost centers.

The program manager is responsible for the preparation of spending estimates and the implementation of the budget unit's approved program budget. The program budget consists of expenditures for various combinations of program elements, which make up a program. As program elements are mixed in number, scope, or composition, they become separate program designs that can be used to pursue specific goals (measured as objectives). When a budget unit creates various program designs on the basis of the different funding levels stipulated by the chief administrator (as discussed later in this section), the result is a range of program alternatives. These alternatives are evaluated at each funding level for their contribution to program objectives and benefits (i.e., objectives are assigned monetary values that are referred to as benefits, as will be discussed more extensively later in this section). The alternatives are then submitted for budget approval by higher-level managers.

If program goals are measured as benefits, program managers can determine intraprogram efficiency—that is, the combination of program elements that has the greatest effect on goal attainment. Moreover, if benefits are measured at the program, or program subcategory, level, higher-level managers can allocate resources among competing programs to ensure greater interprogram efficiency.

Because most local governments are organized along departmental rather than program lines, responsibility centers do not necessarily mesh with cost centers, and the financial connections between programs and budget units can be complex. For example, a single program that provides prenatal care may be carried out by two separate divisions located in different departments: the welfare division of the social services department may identify and screen potential patients, and a division of the health department may actually provide the care. Similarly, a single department may use one division to undertake several programs: the department of public works may collect refuse, maintain streets, and repair bridges through its division of public roads.

Just as most local governments are organized along departmental rather than program lines, most remain wedded to the line-item budget, which appropriates funds for commodities to be purchased by units that perform multiple activities rather than by subunits that produce separate and distinct outcomes. Bringing an existing organizational structure into alignment with a program budget format—that is, restructuring the local government—is complicated and can be quite costly, particularly in the case of large jurisdictions. In addition, vested interests among departments and their client populations can present substantial political obstacles. And even if reorganization is workable, the structure would have to be adapted periodically to reflect changing goals.

One way of addressing the discrepancy between the line-item budget and a program structure is to create a crosswalk that links line-item departmental appropriation accounts to program categories, subcategories, and elements (see Figure 7–9 on pages 174–175).[12] The expenditures of the separate departmental subunits, or responsibility centers, that contribute to each specific output can be aggregated into cost centers (i.e., program elements).[13] Thus, all resources that are likely to contribute to a distinct objective and yield distinct benefits can be placed in a separate program subcategory. Producing such a cross-classification of accounts requires a sophisticated and costly accounting system; nevertheless, it reveals the explicit links between government activities (program elements) and desired goals and thus increases awareness of the relationship between the costs and benefits of government actions. Moreover, as discussed later in this section, combining program elements into programs will require the appointment of a program manager who will exercise authority and have responsibility over the various subunits that produce the program.

Funding levels   Once a program structure has been established, the chief administrator must establish funding levels for the preparation of program alternatives. For example, he or she should direct each budget unit to submit program spending proposals at several levels above and below the current funding level (e.g., 80, 90, 100, 110, and 120 percent). The number of funding levels should be limited; otherwise, the budget unit would have to examine so many alternatives that the quality of the analysis may suffer. Funding intervals should be large enough (e.g., 5 or 10 percent) so that the resources to be added or withdrawn can be expected to measurably influence progress toward goals. (If funding intervals are too small, budget units will be reluctant to perform extensive analyses in order to obtain insignificant additional resources.)

To prepare program alternatives, program managers and their analysts evaluate, for each funding level, the expected benefits of various combinations of program elements. The development of program alternatives also requires program-element managers to determine, for each funding level, the various outputs that each program element can produce, given various mixes of inputs (objects of expenditure in the form of delivery options). When a new program is under consideration, the program manager must be able to demonstrate that the money required to finance the program will yield more benefit than if it had been left in the private sector. Once a new program can be justified in this way, various funding levels can be analyzed for their effect on the program's goals.

The fact that the resources encompassed by the total budget may not be available for spending on all programs complicates the determination of funding levels and the selection of programs. For example, the chief administrator and the budget units do not have the discretion to move monies out of special-revenue funds and divert them to other programs; these funds receive earmarked revenues that must be spent on particular activities, such as roads and streets, or library building maintenance.[14] (If earmarked revenues are consistently larger than the resulting expenditures, it may be more beneficial to reduce them—in effect, to leave them in the private sector. Similarly, matching grants that commit the local government's own resources to programs that are deemed less beneficial than programs that are not eligible for grants should be neither pursued nor accepted.)

Approval of alternatives   Finally, the chief administrator should choose program alternatives, starting with those that promise the largest net benefits at given funding levels and continuing until the available resources are exhausted. Priority ranking can be used to determine which program alternatives will receive funding. (Priority ranking also plays an important role in zero-base budgeting, which will be discussed later in this chapter.) Under priority ranking, program goals are first translated into quantifiable objectives, which are then assigned "prices"—monetary values that indicate their anticipated benefits. Such quantitative information is desirable because it gives decision makers a better grasp of the relative value of programs in achieving community goals.

If program objectives are transformed into benefits, administrators at every level are tightly constrained in ranking alternatives. Figure 7–10 on page 176 illustrates the ranking process. First, at the budget-unit level, each program manager evaluates various program designs (i.e., mixes of program elements) to determine the level of net benefits (the difference between incremental costs and incremental benefits) that will be generated at each prescribed funding level (see step 1). Second, the program manager selects the program design for each funding level that generates the highest net benefits (see step 2). Third, for each functional area (e.g., health, public safety), higher-level managers rank, in descending order, the separate alternatives of any programs under their responsibility, according to the value of the net benefits that would be produced

Departmental line-item budget format	Program structure				
	Promotion of physical well-being (program category)				
	Physical health care and maintenance (program subcategory)				
	Nutrition services	Public health education	Maternal and child health	School health	Dental health
Health department					
Division of hospitals			X		
Personnel services			X		
Supplies			X		
Contracts					
Equipment			X		
Capital outlays			X		
Other					
Division of health care	X			X	X
Personnel services	X			X	X
Supplies				X	X
Contracts					
Equipment				X	X
Capital outlays					
Other					
Division of public health					
Personnel services					
Supplies					
Contracts					
Equipment					
Capital outlays					
Other					
Social service department					
Division of aging	X				
Personnel services	X				
Supplies	X				
Contracts					
Equipment					
Capital outlays					
Other					
Division of disability services					
Personnel services					
Supplies					
Contracts					
Equipment					
Capital outlays					
Other					
Division of assistance	X		X		
Personnel services	X		X		
Supplies	X				
Contracts					
Equipment					
Capital outlays					
Other					
Total estimated expenditures					

Figure 7–9   Crosswalk of a program structure and a line-item format: Assigning the contribution of the health and social services departments to various program subcategories.

Program structure					
Promotion of physical well-being (program category)					
Physical health care and maintenance (program subcategory)				Control and prevention of communicable diseases (program subcategory)	
Orthopedic services	Medical social services	Family planning services	Fortified-milk program	Communicable disease control	Chronic disease control
X	X	X		X	X
X	X	X		X	X
X	X	X		X	X
	X	X		X	X
X		X		X	X
		X	X	X	X
		X		X	X
	X				
X	X	X			
X	X	X			

Step 1: Generation of program designs at the budget-unit level

Alternative funding levels (percentage of prior year's budget)	Estimated net benefits of alternative program designs (in millions of $)[a]								
	Fire protection (FP)			Employment opportunity (EO)			Home health care (HHC)		
	FP_1	FP_2	FP_3	EO_1	EO_2	EO_3	HHC_1	HHC_2	HHC_3
90	4.0	8.4	7.5	10.1	9.9	9.8	10.2	10.9	11.0
100	5.5	7.5	6.9	9.2	8.9	9.8	10.2	10.9	11.0
110	5.4	6.4	6.6	8.5	8.1	8.3	8.6	8.8	9.3
120	4.0	5.5	5.8	7.2	7.0	6.9	7.6	7.5	8.1

[a] Estimated additional net benefits are defined as incremental benefits less incremental costs generated by moving from one level of funding to the next.

Step 2: Selection of alternatives by the program manager

Alternative funding levels (percentage of prior year's budget)	Chosen alternatives (net benefits, in parentheses, are in millions of $)		
	Fire protection (FP)	Employment opportunity (EO)	Home health care (HHC)
90	FP_2 (8.4)	EO_1 (10.1)	HHC_3 (11.0)
100	FP_2 (7.5)	EO_1 (9.2)	HHC_3 (11.0)
110	FP_2 (6.4)	EO_1 (8.5)	HHC_3 (9.3)
120	FP_2 (5.8)	EO_1 (7.2)	HHC_3 (8.1)

Step 3: Ranking and selection of program alternatives by the chief administrator

Rank, in descending order of net benefits	Program alternative (net benefits, in parentheses, are in millions of $)	Incremental budget cost ($)[a]	Cumulative budget cost ($) (budget constraint = $27,800,000)[b]
1	HHC_3 at 90% (11.0)	10,890,000	10,890,000
2	HHC_3 at 100% (11.0)	1,210,000	12,100,000
3	EO_1 at 90% (10.1)	7,650,000	19,750,000
4	HHC_3 at 110% (9.3)	1,210,000	20,960,000
5	EO_1 at 100% (9.2)	850,000	21,810,000
6	EO_1 at 110% (8.5)	850,000	22,660,000
7	FP_2 at 90% (8.4)	2,970,000	25,630,000
8	HHC_3 at 120% (8.1)	1,210,000	26,840,000
9	FP_2 at 90% (8.4)	330,000	27,170,000
10	EO_1 at 120% (7.2)	850,000	28,020,000
11	FP_2 at 110% (6.6)	330,000	28,350,000
12	FP_2 at 120% (5.8)	330,000	28,680,000

[a] The initial cost of a program at the lowest funding level is the program's incremental cost.

[b] Budget constraint: maximum amount of funds available for expenditure in the fiscal year.

Figure 7–10   The process of ranking alternatives.

by the alternatives (not shown in the figure). Finally, at the highest level, when the functional areas of the program structure have been ranked separately, the chief administrator simply ranks all the alternatives, in descending order, according to the value of their net benefits (see step 3). Funding is then assigned to alternatives in accordance with the rankings until the accumulated costs of the selected alternatives reach the limit of the budget.

In the absence of quantitative information, which provides a uniform basis for comparison, managers subjectively assign value to various alternatives. The dangers of subjective evaluation are twofold. First, subjective evaluations give the ranking process a veneer of objectivity that can then be used to support choices made for political purposes. Second, without objective information on the benefits of various alternatives, decision makers risk misallocating resources. In the long run, the local government's credibility may be damaged if it is perceived as failing to allocate resources in a way that effectively responds to community needs.

To avoid the dangers of subjective evaluation, managers must strongly encourage, if not require, estimates of the monetary value of the impacts of program alternatives, even in cases where benefits are difficult to measure. If benefits are not easily quantified, the estimate should be accompanied by an explicit justification and an explanation of the problems encountered in making the estimate. All estimates of benefits should be accompanied by data on objectives and on unit costs where relevant.

Budgetary analysis by the budget unit

Clearly, the preparation of a proposed budget (which takes the form of ranked program alternatives) for consideration by the chief administrator and the governing body requires careful analysis by the budget units. This section outlines the major steps of budgetary analysis: determining service needs; setting goals, objectives, and targets; identifying clientele and assessing demand; evaluating alternatives; presenting estimates; and planning the workload.

Determining service needs The first step in budgetary analysis requires both quantitative and qualitative data on the scope of community needs and problems.[15] First, quantitative (hard) data on social, economic, demographic, and physical conditions should be collected on a regular basis; data interpretation should be guided by contemporary literature in economics, sociology, psychology, and public finance. Second, qualitative information on community conditions should be obtained through surveys that ask citizens' opinions of the quality and effectiveness of service. These survey findings can be supplemented by information obtained during meetings with civic groups or in other public forums.

Setting goals, objectives, and targets Once needs have been identified, the next step is to develop goals and objectives that explicitly link the budget to those needs. To be effective, goals and objectives should be the product of a collective decision-making process involving citizens' groups, governmental operating units, the budget office, and the chief administrator. Goals can be set and clarified through a number of mechanisms, including public hearings, governmental committees, focus groups, and meetings with citizen advisory groups.

Goals are normative, value-laden statements that describe the intended results that will be sought in response to a particular need.[16] Objectives are specific, quantifiable measures that indicate progress toward goals (see Figure 7–11). Objectives do not describe a means or a process but a desirable, measurable end. For example, the goal of a public safety department might be to protect people and property against criminal activities. One of the objectives in support of that goal might be to reduce the crime rate by 12 percent. And one means (or alternative) of achieving that objective might be to enhance community policing by assigning additional foot patrols that can work with citizens to identify and alleviate local conditions that contribute to crime. Outputs, sometimes referred to as end products, contribute to the achievement of objectives and are often expressed as the number of services that program elements provide.

Several objectives may be required in support of a single goal, and in some cases the objectives may conflict. A goal to improve traffic conditions, for

Figure 7–11 Examples
of goals, objectives,
and outputs.

Functional area: Public safety
Program category: Environmental security
Program subcategory: Fire protection
  Goal
      To protect commercial and residen-
      tial units against personal injury,
      loss of life, and property damage
      caused by fire
  Objectives
      To reduce by 20% the amount of fire
      damage to property in both resi-
      dential and commercial units
      To reduce by 50% the loss of life
      caused by fires
      To reduce by 60% personal injuries
      caused by fires
      To reduce by 60% the medical costs
      of fire-related injuries
  Outputs
      Number of responses to fires
      Number of ambulance responses
      Number of fires investigated
      Number of housing units inspected

Functional area: Economic development
Program category: Community assistance
Program subcategory: Employment
    opportunities
  Goal
      To provide unemployed residents
      and employed residents whose in-
      comes are below the poverty level
      with opportunities to attain ade-
      quate family income
  Objectives
      To enable 70% of unemployed youth
      to obtain full-time summer jobs
      To enable 60% of unemployed adults
      to gain full-time employment at
      wages that are above the poverty
      level
      To enable 40% of employed adults
      whose incomes are below the
      poverty level to gain full-time
      employment at wages that are
      above the poverty level
  Outputs
      Number of workers trained
      Number of jobs developed
      Number of job placements for adults
      Number of job placements for youths

example, may have as its objectives (1) to reduce by twenty minutes the travel time from point A to point B and (2) to reduce traffic accidents by 40 percent. If widening the roadway were the means selected to achieve the first objective, faster-moving vehicles on the renovated road might increase the accident rate, thus compromising the second objective. Assigning monetary value to objectives is one way to resolve such conflicts. The choice of alternatives can then be based on the maximum net incremental benefit derived when the dollar losses of one objective are weighed against the dollar gains of the other.

Because goals and objectives are often unlikely to be realized within a short time, targets are used to specify interim results that indicate the partial realization of an objective.[17] For instance, for the objective of a 12 percent reduction in crime, an interim target could be "to reduce crime rates by 2 percent every six months." For each objective there may be numerous targets, each of which contributes, over time, to a given goal. Targets should be selected on the basis of an evaluation of alternatives—that is, by determining which combination of inputs will yield the greatest net benefits for given costs. The numerical value of an objective (e.g., a 12 percent reduction in crime) cannot be chosen until alternative means of achieving the objective have been evaluated. The numerical value chosen reflects the cumulative value of the targets that relate to that objective.

Targets are an inherent part of planning.[18] Establishing short-term targets directs the efforts of budget units toward their long-term purposes. Clear targets allow program managers to monitor progress toward goals and to make organizational and financial adjustments where necessary. Furthermore, establishing targets and objectives enables program managers, higher-level managers, and the chief administrator to evaluate the performance of subordinates and hold them accountable for the management of programs under their direction. Finally, the chain of goals, objectives, and targets can reduce duplication by revealing common threads that run through different programs and budget units.

Identifying clientele and assessing demand   Many government programs—those dealing with crime, air pollution, traffic congestion, and traffic safety, for example—are intended to address concerns that affect much or all of the entire population; thus, these programs serve a heterogeneous clientele. However, where the intended beneficiaries are a readily identifiable group, the objectives should reflect specific information about the target population. In the case of an assistance program for needy elderly residents, for example, an objective should specify the benefit and identify the group that is to receive it: "All elderly households with annual incomes of $15,000 or less will receive one free hot meal five days a week."

Knowledge of the target population and of the conditions that affect that population provides a basis for estimating demand and potential workload—which, in turn, can be built into the needs assessment and used to monitor program effectiveness. Determining the size and characteristics of the target population is necessary because even within a single population, clients may have different socioeconomic characteristics and thus may be able to obtain varying levels of benefit from government services. Once the various segments, or subgroups, of the target population have been identified, a monetary value must be assigned to the benefits that would accrue to each segment.

Numerous economic methodologies (e.g., cost savings, time saved, loss of life and limb, and pricing mechanisms) can be used to measure costs and benefits.[19] For example, one measure of the benefits of free meals provided to needy elderly residents might be the estimated savings on the costs of groceries, which would have varying impact depending on income level and marital status. Similarly, the monetary benefits of a program to relieve traffic congestion would vary according to the distance traveled, the cost of travel (e.g., fuel, oil, public transit fees), the value of travel time, and the loss of income for road users with various income levels. Figure 7–12 shows some possible measures of the benefits provided by fire protection and employment-opportunity programs. Admittedly, measuring benefits is problematic for some government activities, which makes interprogram efficiency somewhat difficult to judge.

Evaluating alternatives   Measurement problems aside, benefits that can be produced by a program depend on the chosen alternatives. Conceptually, alternatives are proposals that link resources with targets, objectives, and benefits. In practice, alternatives are various combinations of program elements, at various funding levels (specified by the chief administrator), that are intended to realize identified objectives. For each alternative, resources are proposed in the form of estimated expenditures for the purchase of personnel services, supplies, and other items necessary to carry out the program.

Identifying alternatives   To achieve intraprogram resource efficiency, the budget analyst must identify the program design (i.e., mix of program elements) that will yield the greatest net benefit for each level of funding. Determination of the most beneficial program design involves a number of considerations.

Because limited resources are available for the evaluation of alternatives, program managers must exercise judgment about which options are worthy of consideration. Thus, in most cases, only a moderate number of alternatives will be analyzed. In fact, given the complexity and amount of information needed to evaluate each alternative, full-scale analysis should be undertaken

	Objective	Benefit	Benefit measure
Fire protection	Reduction in property damage	Value of property damage prevented from occurring	Assessed market value of property destroyed and/or cost of repairing and restoring damaged property
	Reduction in deaths	Value of lives saved	Income that would have been lost by potential victims in accordance with their occupations
	Reduction in personal injury	Value of injuries prevented	Income that would have been lost by potential victims in accordance with their occupations
	Reduction in medical injury	Value of medical costs saved	Medical costs avoided
Employment opportunity	Youth summer employment	Additional income gained	Earnings from employment
	Full-time employment of formerly unemployed residents	Additional income gained	Difference between job earnings and unemployment compensation payments
	Full-time employment of employed residents with poverty-level incomes	Additional income gained	Difference between earnings from previous job and new job

Figure 7–12   Examples of objectives, benefits, and benefit measures.

before the implementation of new programs and only periodically thereafter. (Because an annual budget allows only a limited time for analysis—an issue discussed later in this section—in-depth evaluation of programs may be more compatible with multiyear budgeting.)

The selection of alternatives for analysis will be determined, in large part, by the analyst's understanding of the causal relationships between social factors and the end products reflected in the objectives. Knowledge of causal relationships allows the budget analyst to determine which factors can be affected by programs and which are outside governmental control. In some cases, however, theoretical knowledge and empirical evidence about causal relationships are so limited that the budget analyst can exercise only subjective judgments about the effects of program elements on targets and objectives.

If there is considerable doubt as to whether any selected program design will further the attainment of goals, the budget analyst has at least two options. In the submitted budget estimates for various spending levels, the analyst can indicate that program implementation carries a high risk of failure. Alternatively, the budget analyst can state that, given the ambiguity surrounding the outcomes that can be produced by various alternatives, money should not be allocated for the program.

The predicted causal relationships should guide the selection of activities—that is, program elements—that are likely to produce the desired outputs. These results are a product of the expenditures for which the budget-unit manager requests an allocation. Thus, the program elements (the funded activities) become cost centers. However, as explained earlier, in the line-item budget format used by many local governments, cost centers and responsibility centers are not necessarily coterminous. If this is the case, the objects of expenditure for separate responsibility centers must be aggregated into cost centers, as shown in Figure 7–13. A program coordinator—or, better yet, a program manager—should be assigned to direct the program's organizationally separate activities. To enhance program coordination, higher-level managers and the chief administrator should formally designate a program manager and inform

Cost centers		Responsibility centers		
Activity	Nature of workload	Organizational unit or subunit	Objects of expenditure	Estimates ($)
Administration	Supervision of program	Alcohol abuse division, health department	Personnel Supplies Overhead	90,000 6,000 12,000
Alcohol clinic	Medical care	Outpatient treatment services, hospital department	Personnel Supplies Rent Equipment	210,000 240,000 360,000 390,000
	Counseling	Social work division, human resources department	Personnel Supplies Overhead	108,000 6,000 24,000
Halfway houses for men	Provision of living quarters	Alcohol abuse division, health department	Personnel Contracts	66,000 90,000
	Counseling	Social work division, human resources department	Personnel Supplies Overhead	132,000 6,000 30,000
Halfway houses for women	Provision of living quarters Counseling	Alcohol abuse division, health department Social work division, human resources department	Personnel Contracts Personnel Supplies Overhead	96,000 60,000 84,000 6,000 18,000
Driving while intoxicated	Counseling	Social work division, human resources department	Personnel Supplies Overhead	30,000 6,000 6,000
Total budget estimate for program				2,076,000

Figure 7–13   Cost centers and responsibility centers in a program for the prevention and treatment of alcohol addiction.

all units that contribute to the program's objectives how they will be funded and what their financial and programmatic responsibilities will be.

Working together, the program manager and the manager of each responsibility center can determine the composition (the mix of objects of expenditure and activities) of each program element by analyzing the various combinations of inputs that can be purchased by each budget unit.

The objects of expenditure can be mixed to yield any of the following major delivery options: in-house delivery, contracting out, grants and subsidies, vouchers, and volunteers. These delivery options can be used alone or in combination to produce the expected outputs of the program element. For example, the health department's division of social work, which is responsible for substance-abuse counseling, might consider a number of delivery options, alone or in combination: increasing its own counseling staff; contracting with a private, nonprofit organization to provide counseling; and increasing the number of referrals to volunteer groups, such as Alcoholics Anonymous. For any program element, the "best" mix of inputs is the one that meets the criterion of economic efficiency—where, within the constraints of allowed funding levels, the incremental costs generate the greatest net benefits.

Spillover effects   In considering alternatives, the budget analyst must be aware that once a program alternative is implemented, its effects may spill over to nontargeted groups. For example, a widened roadway may be intended to save drivers travel time and reduce the number of car accidents. If the improved road also drives up the value of neighboring land and houses, that would be an unintended benefit to a nontargeted group. Similarly, if neighborhoods are destroyed to make way for the road, there are unintended spillover costs: even if residents are compensated for the market value of their properties, their lives may be adversely affected. The value of these unintended benefits or costs should be calculated in the evaluation of each alternative; benefits or costs that cannot be assigned a monetary value should still be described qualitatively.

Trade-offs   In the comparison of benefits associated with various alternatives, budget-unit managers can make trade-offs among various factors such as timeliness, responsiveness, level of service, and quality of materials. These trade-offs can increase or decrease the cost of alternatives and should therefore be incorporated into the benefit calculations. For example, a possible trade-off in a meal program for needy elderly residents would be to reduce the quality of the food and use the cost savings to serve a larger number of program participants. The response time of police and fire departments can be viewed similarly. While quicker response time may produce increased benefits in public safety, it may require additional costs in the form of personnel, equipment, and capital facilities.

Unquantifiable benefits   When benefits cannot be measured satisfactorily, program alternatives can be assessed for their potential to further objectives. In the case of a single objective, the best program design is the alternative that yields the greatest incremental gain in the direction of achieving the objective. For goals with multiple objectives, intraprogram efficiency is more difficult to determine because the trade-offs may be identifiable but not quantifiable. Consider, for example, a program to alleviate traffic congestion by widening a roadway and thus permitting travel at higher speeds: higher speeds will save time, but unless a monetary value can be assigned to the various multiple objectives (thus transforming them into benefits), how can the reduction in travel time be weighed against the cost of deaths, personal injuries, and property damage that may occur as a consequence of the higher speeds?

Moreover, trade-offs among programs—that is, interprogram efficiency—pose a problem because the objectives are not comparable in value. Consequently, the chief administrator may be compelled to choose, subjectively, between additional funding for recreational activities and additional funding for disease control. Judgments about intersector efficiency are also problematic. While it may be easy to assess the extent to which a program alternative can further one or several objectives, such an assessment does not indicate whether the benefit of furthering those objectives is of greater value than the losses that will be incurred when resources are extracted from the private sector to finance the alternative.

Unit cost   When the impacts of governmental activities cannot be expressed as measurable objectives, unit costs can sometimes be used as a limited guide in the evaluation of program alternatives.[20] It is important to note, however, that just as some governmental objectives do not lend themselves to quantifiable measures, some end products of governmental activities are not readily measurable; thus, it may not be possible to determine unit costs for them. Moreover, unit costs have other limitations as measures of efficiency, which will be discussed later in this section.

Operationally, unit cost is simply total cost divided by total output (see Figure 7–14). In principle, unit cost can be calculated for the individual cost cen-

Two-worker truck		One-worker truck		Contracting out	
Input mix	Cost ($)[a]	Input mix	Cost ($)[a]	Input mix	Cost ($)[a]
10 trucks	1,000,000	6 trucks	960,000	Contract	1,912,000
20 personnel	1,200,000	6 personnel	432,000	Supervision	40,000
Truck service	100,000	Truck service	80,000	Overhead	8,000
Supervision	80,000	Supervision	80,000		
Overhead	40,000	Overhead	32,000		
Total cost	2,420,000		1,584,000		1,960,000
Total output (tons collected)	8,000,000		8,000,000		8,000,000
Unit cost (cost/output)	0.30 cents/ton		0.20 cents/ton		0.25 cents/ton

[a]Cost estimation should entail the discounting of out-lays to present values over the period covering the useful life of the equipment.

Figure 7–14   Unit cost of three alternatives for refuse collection.

ters of a program as well as for the entire program. All expenditures (including depreciation and inventory) accrued in the fiscal year should be allocated, through a cost-accounting system, to the appropriate cost centers. When the cost centers are combined, they should produce either an identifiable and measurable workload or outputs that indicate the furtherance of a program goal and are directed toward a homogeneous clientele.[21] For example, unit cost could be determined for trash collection if the activity is considered to further the goal of a clean urban environment. However, separate unit cost measures should be calculated for residential and commercial trash collection if the characteristics of these two types of service differ substantially.

Presumably, unit cost measures the technical efficiency of governmental activity: decreasing costs reflect improved productivity. It is therefore sometimes argued that because lower costs imply a greater achievement of program goals, alternatives can be evaluated in terms of unit costs. However, a budgetary analysis that equates unit cost with economic efficiency has several limitations.[22] First, some declines in unit cost result from decreases in quality, not from improved productivity. Using less expensive materials to construct roads, for example, might reduce short-term governmental expenditures but might also increase the need for road repairs and cause more damage to automobiles, thus increasing long-term costs for both government and the private sector. Second, some outputs are not valid measures of program goals. For example, the number of tons of garbage collected is not, by itself, an indicator of the cleanliness of neighborhoods and streets: unit cost for trash collection is therefore of limited use in measuring progress toward the goal. Third, unit cost is not always a reliable index of program results. For instance, unit costs for programs directed at alleviating a social harm or correcting detrimental conditions (e.g., disease, crime, pollution) may rise, not fall, as the social problem decreases in severity.

When unit cost is considered a suitable indicator of goal attainment, a number of technical issues must still be addressed. First, a program design with the lowest unit cost does not necessarily have the lowest possible unit cost: the cost should be compared with the unit cost for similar activities undertaken by other governments and by private sector firms. Second, since inflation may affect costs from one fiscal year to the next, unit costs to be compared over time must be adjusted according to the appropriate price indexes.

Clearly, unit cost is of limited value as a decision tool. In the realm of intra-program efficiency, unit cost is problematic because lower costs may actually reflect a lower level of goal achievement. As a measure of intersector efficiency, lower unit cost may indicate improved productivity, but it does not reveal whether the value of the governmental activity is greater than the cost incurred to produce it. Finally, unit cost cannot be used to assess interprogram efficiency because decreases in unit costs among various programs do not indicate which programs produce a greater net value for society.

Presenting estimates   For each program, expenditure estimates for program alternatives should be prepared for the various funding levels specified by the chief administrator. These estimates should show the incremental benefits expected to result from changes in the proposed spending for the program elements. As noted earlier, if the appropriation structure is based on a line-item budget, the expenditure estimates should be cross-referenced (see Figure 7–9). Information should also be provided on any connections between the budget unit's proposed actions and the activities of other governmental units. Finally, the budget estimates should show financing sources for the proposed program alternatives.

Planning the workload   The final task in budget analysis is the preparation of management action and workload plans for the budget unit. As critical linkages between program resources and objectives, these plans should be multiyear and correspond to the expected length of the program's existence (i.e., the life cycle of the program). However, to discourage budget units from presenting unrealistic long-term projections, the schedule of proposed future actions beyond the budget year should be tied to continued funding at levels specified by the central budget office.

The workload plans should stipulate the goals and objectives of the program; guideposts (in the form of targets) indicating progress toward objectives; the resource levels needed to reach the targets; and a timetable of actions to be undertaken and completed. The description of each action should specify (1) the work unit responsible for executing the required activities, (2) the amount of work to be completed to meet deadlines, (3) the proposed use of resources, and (4) estimated obligations or encumbrances and expenditures. A management action and workload plan helps program directors focus on goal attainment and allows higher-level managers to hold program directors accountable for achieving agreed-upon objectives. Moreover, such a plan, with its benchmarks for assessing progress toward goals, provides a basis for establishing a managerial monitoring system.

Summary: Budgeting for goal attainment

The rational theory of budgeting is integrated and holistic because regardless of the level of resource allocation (intersector, interprogram, intraprogram), it applies the same principle of efficiency, which focuses on the incremental costs and benefits associated with alternative uses of revenues. Because costs and benefits cannot always be precisely quantified, the theory is not always easy to apply; nevertheless, it is valid on its own terms because it provides (1) a sound method of evaluation when costs and benefits can be quantified and (2) a qualitative framework for judgment when costs and benefits cannot be quantified but decisions must still be made. In other words, cost-benefit analysis is an organized thought process as well as a technical tool for implementing budget theory.

The practical difficulties of applying the prescriptive, rational theory of budgeting furnish a partial foundation for an alternative theory of public budgeting: incrementalism, or successive limited comparisons. Incrementalism describes how, in practical terms, the budget process is often actually conducted. Under the incremental approach, the number and types of alternatives that can be considered is hindered significantly by the conservative political and organizational nature of budgeting. Alternatives are chosen and evaluated according to their acceptability to decision makers; decision-making criteria are derived, in turn, from the need to reach consensus among interested parties and participants in government policy making. Decisions are thus the product of conflict between budget makers and clientele and among budget makers themselves, and are often arrived at through bargaining, negotiation, and similar strategies.

Budgetary control: A trade-off of purposes

The general purpose of budgetary control is to ensure that governmental funds are directed most effectively to their designated goals. While goal attainment is the central purpose of budgeting, government officials are also responsible for ensuring that public funds are used for legally sanctioned purposes. Both management and financial controls are used to realize the aims of budgetary control.

This section of the chapter considers some of the issues that arise in determining how much control is desirable and what types of control will best meet the local government's needs. The sections that describe the budget cycle, later in this chapter, also cover procedures, practices, and actions that can affect management and financial control.

Financial control

The purpose of financial control is to limit expenditures to the items, activities, and amounts specified in the appropriations. Thus, financial control is a means of addressing actual or potential fraudulent behavior. Fraud can be defined as intentional deception for the purpose of misappropriating monies, goods, or services. The misappropriation can take the form of theft or embezzlement (defalcation). Financial control depends significantly on fund accounting (discussed previously), accounting for budgetary transactions, and a range of procedures designed to prevent and detect fraudulent actions. Most financial control is internal to the government and originates in the executive branch; it may also involve, to a lesser extent, the governing body.

The four phases of the budget cycle are preparation, adoption, implementation, and evaluation. Controls for the prevention of fraud should be central during the preparation, adoption, and implementation phases. Controls for detection should play a prominent role during the implementation and evaluation phases. Financial transactions should be regularly monitored so that if there are indications of fraud, corrective action—and, if necessary, additional preventive action—can be taken. External control, implemented through audits conducted by independent outside agencies, is exercised during the evaluation phase of the budget cycle.

Management control

Waste can be defined as failure to employ resources in the least costly way consistent with the attainment of goals. Although waste differs from fraud in that it is not illegal, its effect is similar: like fraud, waste creates economic inefficiency by diverting governmental resources from their intended purposes. Management control mechanisms designed to ensure that governmental activities are linked closely to the achievement of specified objectives can provide substantial protection against waste. In fact, management control is built into the rational decision-making model outlined earlier in this chapter.

Management control mechanisms to protect against waste are central during the preparation, adoption, and implementation phases of the budget cycle. In the preparation phase, internal accountability, one of the foundations of budgetary control, helps to ensure that resources are used efficiently to promote goals.

During the preparation phase, management control (i.e., accountability) requires the development of goals that are consistent with citizens' values and preferences; adoption of a program format; and evaluation of alternatives in relation to incremental costs and benefits. During the adoption phase, this framework should be supported by compatible (i.e., lump sum) general appropriations approved by the governing body. During the implementation phase, management control is achieved through granting managers appropriate discretion over funds.

Management control mechanisms to detect waste are also central to the implementation and evaluation phases. During implementation, program activities are monitored to assess progress on objectives. In the evaluation phase, programs are analyzed to determine how much progress toward goals has been made under the direction of each manager; such assessments may be either internal or external.

Financial and management control: Striking a balance

The use of budgetary controls to prevent and detect fraud and waste raises a number of considerations. First, controls carry costs—both direct costs (from the expenditure of funds) and opportunity costs (because funds used to implement control mechanisms are not available for services). Second, and concomitantly, because the amount of fraud and waste that might occur in the absence of financial and management controls is unknown, determining the optimal balance—where the cost of control does not exceed the value of the harm deterred—is highly problematic. Third, financial control and management control often conflict.

Effective financial control requires centralization of authority by the chief administrator and the budget office; detailed prescriptions and circumscriptions regarding inputs and managerial actions; prior approval of resource use; extensive documentation both for resource use and for the activities of managers and their staff; and substantive judgments by higher-level managers regarding program implementation. These conditions make it difficult for managers and their subordinates to respond flexibly and creatively to changing service needs.

In contrast, management control generally requires authority to be decentralized to the departmental or program level, an arrangement that gives managers considerable leeway in designing and implementing their programs and allows for only limited scrutiny by upper-level decision makers. (The chief administrator and the budget office would still hold managers accountable for program activities by periodically assessing—at least annually—progress toward goals.) Because the devolution of authority to program managers reduces fiscal accountability in the preparation, adoption, and implementation phases of the budget, the chief administrator and finance officer must determine where to strike the balance between management control, which facilitates the achievement of goals, and financial control, which protects against the illegal use of resources.

The budget cycle

Four major players are involved in the budget cycle: the chief administrator, the governing body, the budget units, and the clientele affected by the goods and services provided by the government.[23] The clientele may be the public at large or groups of citizens whose welfare may be improved or worsened by budgeting decisions. The complex interactions among these institutional players are determined by organizational structure and budget procedures, which vary with population, scale of services, and form of government.[24] However, the basic phases and characteristics of the budget cycle are still applicable.[25]

As noted earlier, the budget cycle for a fiscal year has four phases: (1) preparation, when the budget units and the chief administrator estimate their resources and expenditures; (2) adoption, when the chief administrator's budget estimates are submitted to the governing body for approval; (3) implementation, when the adopted budget is executed during the fiscal year; and (4) evaluation, when implementation is assessed. These phases are common to the budgets of every fund and apply to line-item, performance, program, and zero-base budgeting. As shown in Figure 7–15, the budget cycle reaches beyond the fiscal year for which the budget is adopted and implemented. Moreover, budget cycles for separate fiscal years overlap.

Preparation

The preparation phase is initiated and completed by the chief administrator.[26] During this phase, the budget units create initial spending estimates, which they submit to the chief administrator. Final estimates of both revenues and expenditures are then made by the chief administrator, who submits them to the governing body. Because these estimates are accompanied by a statement of how policy goals are to be achieved, the preparation stage should include planning and programming for service delivery.

During budget preparation, the following internal procedures are essential to maintaining financial control over appropriated funds and thus preventing fraud:

Major fiscal functions—the collection and custody of revenues and the expenditure of funds—should be segregated.

Staff who are responsible for resource commitments and for making payments should be assigned exclusive authority to do so.

Guidelines for maintenance and use of records and supporting documentation should ensure that the purposes of and authorization for transactions are appropriately recorded and that transactions follow the proper sequence.

Procedures for the recruitment, hiring, and promotion of personnel should be established.

Central purchasing should have regulations that (1) require competitive bidding for purchases and (2) are designed to safeguard the quality and quantity of purchased goods and services.

Revenue and expenditure forecasts The central budget office must prepare estimates of the resources that are available for the budget year. The budget

Figure 7–15 Annual budget cycle for fiscal year (FY) 2005.

	July 1	Months of FY	June 30
FY 2004		Preparation of FY 2005	Adoption of FY 2005
FY 2005	Implementation of FY 2005		
FY 2006	Evaluation of FY 2005		

office forecasts the monies likely to be collected under the existing revenue structure and then adds any unreserved surpluses that may be available from various funds. The chief administrator, in cooperation with the budget officer, then estimates the total allowable expenditures, which reflect expected changes in population and social and economic conditions. Finally, an assessment of the local government's future fiscal condition, combined with the revenue forecast, is used to determine the additional long-term debt that can be incurred in the budget year.

If the estimated revenues are lower than the estimated expenditures, the resulting budgetary deficit can be avoided by cutting spending, raising additional revenues, or drawing upon unreserved fund balances. If estimated revenues exceed estimated expenditures, the predicted budgetary surplus can be used to expand services, reduce revenue levies, or create a reserve for contingencies. Too large a surplus poses several problems: first, it can lead to political criticism if citizens believe that they are being taxed excessively; second, it may be an indication of waste or of poor intersector resource efficiency (too much money being extracted from the private sector for public purposes).

Revenues and expenditures should be forecast for each month of the budgetary year so that cash flow requirements can be predicted. Because many tax receipts are not collected in the beginning of the fiscal year, revenues may be temporarily insufficient to cover cash needs. The chief administrator must decide on the amount and timing of short-term borrowing (e.g., tax-anticipation notes) to cover revenue insufficiencies. However, he or she should make a considerable effort to (1) retire nontax and tax-anticipation notes at the end of each fiscal year and (2) avoid using short-term debt to finance a continuing deficit. A sound budget rule is that current expenditures should be financed by current revenues. The unwillingness of local elected and appointed officials to live within their fiscal means can eventually damage a local government's credit rating.

Call for budget-unit spending estimates   The next step in the preparation phase is the call for budget-unit spending estimates and for estimates of such obligations as interest or principal payments due on outstanding indebtedness and pension payments. All budget units receive (1) a set of instructions describing how budget forms are to be completed and (2) a schedule that lists all the decision steps and deadlines that lead up to budget adoption. The chief administrator may also issue a policy statement that details the expected fiscal situation and describes the local government's position (e.g., as one of retrenchment or expansion). The chief administrator may, in addition, supply information on economic, financial, and social trends (e.g., price levels, pay policies) that will affect the cost of programs.

Two features of the "budget call" can further the attainment of goals. First, the chief administrator can require that budget-unit estimates be compatible with a program structure as well as with an objects-of-expenditure format. Budget estimates prepared under a program format allow the chief administrator and the governing body to more easily identify program costs, make policy judgments, and evaluate program performance. Second, the chief administrator can stipulate the processes by which budget analyses are to be conducted and the amounts of financing that can be requested. As suggested earlier, budget units should be required to submit alternative budgets—that is, estimates that link incremental spending amounts to incremental program benefits.

Several other options are available to chief administrators for the call for budget estimates.[27] Open-ended budgeting yields a bottom-up flow of estimates: budget units simply submit any amount deemed essential to execute their activities. Unfortunately, this approach presents two problems. First, higher-level managers have little knowledge of specific program activities and are therefore not in a position to assess the effect of spending cuts if spending levels have to be lowered. Second, a single estimate does not provide decision makers with enough information to judge the relative value of all programs within and across budget units.

Another option is to establish a fixed ceiling for the budget units' estimates. In this top-down approach to budgeting, higher-level managers judge the validity of the financing demands without information on the needs and likely performance of the various programs. In effect, executive judgment supersedes the expertise of budget-unit staff. Moreover, the fixed ceiling encourages budget units to request the maximum allowable funding. As is the case with open-ended budgeting, the estimates do not permit comparisons between programs to determine whether some monies could be allocated more efficiently.

Still another option is to require the budget units to submit, along with their single budget estimates, a ranked list of activities that could be eliminated if funding were unavailable. Again, however, such lists would not permit the chief administrator to compare the relative value of lower-priority items among different budget units.

Review of spending requests After the budget units conduct their budgetary analyses, their requests are forwarded to the budget office to be reviewed for mathematical accuracy and compliance with instructions. The budget-office analysts evaluate the appropriateness of the requests by examining audits and other reports on the budget units' past performance. Budget-unit managers are then given the opportunity to defend their expenditure recommendations. At the same time, the budget office should update its estimates of appropriable resources to reflect any significant changes since the initial forecast. The estimates of both the budget office and the budget units are then sent to the chief administrator, who must make trade-offs among programs to arrive at final decisions on funding. As noted earlier, decisions about trade-offs are more likely to be resource efficient if they are based on estimates that specify, for each funding level, projected incremental net benefits, progress toward the realization of objectives, or changes in unit cost.

Preparation of the budget document After completing the evaluation, the chief administrator writes a budget message, and the proposed budget document is prepared for the governing body. The budget message presents information on past and current trends and describes the chief administrator's major programmatic emphasis for the coming fiscal year. The budget document contains the following:

Summaries of the estimated receipts and outflows for all funds, and projections of the expected status of the funds at the beginning and end of the fiscal year

Estimates of the revenues and expenditures—by budget unit, according to the chosen format—for the consolidated budget

Separate revenue and spending estimates for the operating and capital budgets

A statement describing the current cash position of the government and the cash flow requirements for the budget year

A statement of the estimated level of short-term borrowing, and the anticipated repayment schedule for the fiscal period.

The governing body should also receive a draft of the property tax levy ordinance and a draft of the budget ordinance—which, if approved, transforms the proposed budget into the legally adopted budget of the local government. If the chief administrator presents a budget with a program format, which links effectiveness measures to alternative funding levels, the focus of the governing body shifts from maintaining financial control over input costs to making the best possible allocation of resources to achieve governmental goals.

Adoption

The second phase of the budget cycle involves the governing body's review of the chief administrator's proposed budget. Adoption entails the legal approval of both expenditures and financing authority.

Authorization   Some revenues (e.g., interest on investments) accrue without current legal authorization, and the collection of some taxes (e.g., licenses, fees, sales and income taxes) stems from past legislative approvals. But the right to levy property taxes must be authorized for every budget period. Similarly, the governing body must authorize certain current revenues, short-term borrowing, and long-term borrowing (i.e., municipal bonds). Requests for capital outlays may be submitted in the form of separate capital budgets for each capital projects fund; as a capital budget compiled from the capital improvements fund; or as separate items, depending on the budget format, in the operating budget. To safeguard the collected monies, the financing authorization should direct bond proceeds to particular capital projects funds.

To authorize spending by budget units, the governing body passes a budget ordinance that specifies appropriations for expendable funds (i.e., governmental funds and some trust funds). Appropriations are not needed for proprietary funds or for some fiduciary funds since they are self-sustaining, but integrating these funds into the budget process is desirable because it increases financial control over governmental resources.

Through the budget ordinance, departments are granted new authority, during the budget year, to make financial commitments in the form of contracts, purchase orders, and salary obligations.[28] As these commitments are made, an encumbrance is charged against the pertinent appropriation so that the required amount of money is reserved for expenditure when the commitments are fulfilled. Encumbered monies are those that have been committed but not spent; unencumbered monies are those that have not yet been committed. Additional commitments—and concomitantly, additional spending—can come only from unencumbered monies. With the completion of a commitment, the applicable encumbrances are canceled, and the value of the fulfilled commitment is charged against the appropriation as an expenditure. The amount of an appropriation that has been spent is the expended portion; the remainder—or the unexpended portion—is made up of encumbered and unencumbered monies.

Types of appropriations   In any given year, the governing body can establish three types of appropriations, with varying degrees of financial and management control: lapsing, continuing, and implied.[29] Most appropriations are lapsing, which means that any unexpended portions of the appropriations, both encumbered and unencumbered, expire at the end of the budget year and are unavailable for the next year's expenditures. Although, for most local governments, authorization for all unexpended funds, including encumbrances, expires at the end of the fiscal year, the government will honor commitments made during the budget year. Such commitments, however, must be charged against the appropriations of the following year. This activity is undertaken by the budget office, which maintains a reserve-for-encumbrances account that continues beyond the end of the budget year. If encumbrances are carried over, the chief administrator and the governing body are informed, through the reserve-for-encumbrances account, of the need to appropriate resources in the following year to cover past commitments.

For activities that require several years to complete (e.g., capital construction projects), continuing appropriations are employed. In some cases only the encumbered portions of the unexpended monies are carried over to the following year, and the remaining unexpended authorizations lapse. This carry-over is handled by the budget office, which reduces the unreserved fund balance of the pertinent funds and establishes an appropriation fund-balance account that is equivalent to the value of the nonlapsing encumbrances. These changes are recorded on the balance sheet, which informs the chief administrator and the governing body that only the unreserved fund balance can be appropriated and that some of the equity of a fund is legally committed.

Because the budget office has established an appropriation fund-balance account, further approval to finance the expenditures in the following years—so as to meet obligations incurred in the prior year—is not needed. For other continuing appropriations, authorization for all unexpended balances, including encumbrances, is carried over to the next budget year. As in the prior case, the unreserved fund balances of the relevant funds are reduced to account for the amounts carried over.

Finally, some appropriations—most commonly, debt interest and principal redemption—are implied each year through initial authorizing legislation.

Unfortunately, when managers know that unexpended appropriations (both encumbered and unencumbered) are scheduled to lapse, they may try to avoid losing the unexpended appropriations by engaging in ill-considered spending before the end of the fiscal year. Thus, efforts to maximize financial control through lapsing appropriations can actually provide an incentive for the inefficient use of resources. This result is less likely if funds are authorized through the following year; managers can then be confident that monies will be available when needed. Making funds available over time thus promotes greater efficiency in the use of resources and is consistent with the degree of program planning that is necessary for goal attainment. Linking resources to the achievement of objectives enhances managerial control.

Lump-sum appropriations are another means of trading off some financial control in the interest of attaining goals. Lump-sum appropriations authorize monies for a stated purpose, budget unit, or category of expenditure without providing detailed specifications for their use. The managers of the budget units awarded the appropriations are given the authority to spend the budgeted monies on those items and activities that they deem most valuable. However, as discussed in the section on budget implementation, such discretion requires the approval of the chief administrator. Since the point of appropriations is to provide resources to pursue program goals, this kind of financial flexibility allows decision makers to maximize program effectiveness by adapting inputs to changing conditions. While lump-sum appropriations require the governing body to relinquish stringent financial control, strong financial accountability can still be retained during budget implementation through the exercise of financial, managerial, accounting, and reporting controls, both external and internal. These controls can also foster managerial responsibility for the effectiveness of budget-unit activities.

Supplemental appropriations can also be granted. These appropriations authorize spending above the amount sanctioned by a budget unit's initial appropriation. Budget-unit managers can submit requests for supplemental appropriations to the budget office and the chief administrator, who evaluate the requests and determine the amounts to be transmitted to the governing body for approval. The requests for additional spending may be approved in the form of continuing or lapsing appropriations and may carry lump-sum or detailed expenditure authorization.

Implementation

The third phase of the budget cycle, implementation of the adopted budget, involves management of both revenues and expenditures.

Revenues   Financing program activities requires that resources be obtained either from current revenues or from borrowing. To ensure that cash will be available to pay expenses, the local government must establish policies and procedures that (1) promote prompt revenue collection, (2) minimize revenue delinquencies and nonpayments, and (3) foster quick deposit of revenue in government bank accounts to maximize interest income.

To meet these goals, the budget office should compare the monthly revenue, expenditure, and cash forecasts made in the preparation phase with the actual figures. If revenue shortfalls seem imminent, the chief administrator has several options: (1) improve revenue collection, (2) raise additional revenues, (3) reduce expenditures (a task that is easier and more efficient if alternative funding levels were specified during the preparation phase), (4) draw from a reserve-for-contingency account, or (5) use short-term borrowing.

Expenditures   On the expenditure side of the budget, the chief administrator has two responsibilities, which are executed by his or her staff—particularly the budget office. First, encumbrances and expenditures must be monitored to determine whether monies are being used in accordance with appropriations.[30] Second, it is necessary to ensure that spending is directed to those items and activities that contribute to program objectives. The extent to which these two responsibilities conflict and require trade-offs depends on the nature of the appropriations, the budget format (program or line-item), and the chief administrator's perspective on managerial responsibility.

The chief administrator can initiate preventive expenditure controls by requesting budget units to submit allotments, allocations, or both. An allotment controls the rate of spending authorized by an appropriation; an allocation controls the specific use of the monies appropriated. Since the appropriation bill generally does not specify when expenditures are to be made during the fiscal year, the chief administrator can divide an appropriation into bimonthly, monthly, or quarterly time segments: each allotment determines the limit of a budget unit's legal authority to incur obligations and make expenditures within the stated time frame.

In the case of detailed appropriations that restrict spending to specified amounts on particular authorized objects, making an allotment is the only step a chief administrator need take in order to retain financial control over the rate of spending. In the case of lump-sum appropriations, which allow managerial discretion in spending, the chief administrator can make allotments but must first designate the use of the appropriated monies through allocations, which may establish tight or loose financial control over spending. The chief administrator has the authority to permit or restrict a manager's spending on the items and activities sanctioned through lump-sum appropriations. For example, if the local fire department were given lump-sum authorization for all non-personnel goods and services, the chief administrator could simply confirm this discretion through a lump-sum allocation and then periodically allot the appropriation for the year. On the other hand, if the transportation department has a lump-sum appropriation for highway expansion, the chief administrator could maintain control by stipulating that spending must or must not entail purchases of certain personnel services, materials, or equipment.

If allotments are used to spread appropriation authority over the fiscal year, overspending can be forestalled, short-term borrowing can be minimized, and the need for supplemental appropriations can be avoided. However, budget-unit managers may be legitimately concerned about whether their programs will receive enough resources on a timely basis to deliver services as needed. Although no complete solution to this problem exists, the chief administrator is better able to make decisions about allotments if budget units have prepared workload plans that reflect service demands, the impact of various input mixes on the achievement of objectives, or both.

Allotments should not be uniform across budget units or within a program. Demand may vary seasonally—in education and public works, for example—and workloads may change as programmatic actions and external factors bring about increases or decreases in client populations. For example, the timing of equipment needs may vary for many programs, and some programs, such as recreation, need equipment earlier in the fiscal year than other programs. If allotments are established at more frequent intervals (e.g., bimonthly or monthly, rather than quarterly), program managers are more likely to have sufficient flexibility to respond to changing needs.

Monitoring The chief administrator can exert financial control through other budgetary accounting practices, all of which are designed to allow monitoring of the budget implementation process: allotment-expenditure ledgers, pre-auditing procedures, budget-office reports on allotments, and management action and workload plans.

With an allotment-expenditure ledger, as shown in Figure 7–16, the chief administrator and the budget office can monitor the use of funds authorized during each allotment period. First, the budget office records the approved allotments and allocations in the appropriate allotment-expenditure ledger in

Allotment for June 1999			City of Springfield			Function: Organization: Agency: Activity: Character: Object:		Health Department of Environmental Protection Bureau of Pollution Control Drainage and spraying Current expenses Materials and supplies	
			Encumbrances ($)			Expenditures ($)			
Date	Item	No.[a]	(1) Issued	(2) Completed	(3) Balance	(4) Amount	(5) Total expenditure	(6) Total allotment	(7) Unencumbered allotment balance
6/01	Allotment							150,000	150,000
6/02	Detergent	1	7,800		7,800				142,200
6/03	Uniforms	2	4,800		12,600				137,400
6/04	Detergent	1		7,800	4,800	7,800	7,800		137,400
6/04	Chemicals	3	84,000		88,800		7,800		48,600
6/06	Office	4	13,200		102,000		7,800		35,400
6/08	Chemicals	3		84,000	18,000	84,000	91,800		35,400
6/28	Uniforms	41	5,400		23,400		91,800		12,000[b]
6/30	Closing entry							(12,000)[b]	

[a]Number assigned to items as they are encumbered and unencumbered.
[b]This amount may be impounded by the chief administrator since it has not been encumbered by the agency.

Figure 7–16 Sample allotment-expenditure ledger.

accordance with the specification of appropriations. The ledger is opened with the amount allotted for the time period (column 6), and this amount is carried over to column 7 to show an unencumbered allotment balance available for spending. When a commitment is made through a contract or purchase order, the amount of the obligation is recorded as an encumbrance (column 1); the unencumbered allotment balance is then reduced by the value of the encumbrance, reflecting the new (and lower) amount available for expenditures and encumbrances. After a commitment is fulfilled, the pertinent encumbrance is canceled and expenditures are made. At any time, the ledger shows the value of the allotted funds that have been expended (column 5) and the value of the allotted funds that are encumbered for future payments (column 3). When these two figures are added together and then subtracted from the value of the allotment (column 6), the result is the unencumbered allotment balance (column 7)—the amount that the manager has available for further commitments.

Control over allotments can be further strengthened through pre-auditing procedures that require budget-office approval before obligations are incurred by the budget unit. Such procedures require that all commitments be submitted for review in the form of written documents such as purchase orders, requisitions, and contracts. Pre-auditing permits the budget office to determine whether uncommitted funds are available and whether the proposed commitments and the methods of meeting them are legally consistent with the allotment authorizations and relevant statutes.

A voucher system affords both the budget-unit manager and the budget office additional opportunity to scrutinize expenditures. Under this system, the budget unit must submit a voucher to the budget office to obtain approval for disbursements for completed commitments. This document verifies that the goods and services have been received, that the prices are consistent with the original commitment, that the expenditure can be charged to the allotment, and that the allotment has not been exceeded. Vouchers create a paper trail that can be used later to conduct a financial audit (discussed later in this section) that can detect fraud.

Periodic reports on the use and status of allotments, which can be issued by the budget office, are another means of strengthening financial control. Such reports include, for each allotment, information on encumbrances, expenditures, and available balance, and they should be distributed to budget-unit managers on a frequent and timely basis so that the managers can determine the amount and type of resources that are available and can take corrective action when funds are insufficient. Unless monthly allotment reports are distributed considerably before the end of the monthly allotment period, corrective action will be ineffective or obviated.

If a program format is adopted, or is adapted to a line-item budget, program implementation can also be facilitated by management action and workload plans, which were described previously. To monitor progress toward program goals, program managers can compare actual with targeted performance levels and can determine whether the activities deemed necessary for program effectiveness are being accomplished in accordance with the planning schedule.

Program managers should undertake such performance monitoring frequently (e.g., bimonthly or monthly), and staff engaged in delivering the program should, in addition, prepare periodic reports on the progress toward goals. The program manager should take the staff reports into account when evaluating program activities but should first assess their validity. If performance is inconsistent with programmatic plans (i.e., if targets are not being met in accordance with planned activities), the program manager can implement prompt corrective measures to prevent further diversion of resources from program goals. In addition, the program manager should submit the same performance reports to higher-level managers (e.g., the budget office) and to the chief administrator to enable them to assess progress toward program goals. If the program manager, the higher-level managers, and the chief administrator agreed upon the original management action and workload plans, the program manager can be held responsible for achieving the program targets of the budgetary year.

Accountability can be further enhanced by the compilation and publication of an annual report summarizing program accomplishments in relation to each program's specified objectives. Both periodic and annual performance reports can provide a basis for evaluating supplemental appropriation requests and budget estimates for the next year.

Problems in implementation Budget implementation does not always go as smoothly as planned, especially when the costs of inputs change and service demands increase. There are two ways to deal with such circumstances: through a reserve-for-contingency account (if the reserve is legally available for such use) or by means of a supplemental appropriation requested through the chief administrator. Additional authorizations should be avoided unless they are based on additional generation of revenues: authorizations that are not linked to revenues represent deficit spending or lead to drawdowns on unreserved fund balances.

Excessive reliance on either short-term borrowing or supplemental appropriations can be avoided through executive impoundment of the budget unit's unencumbered allotment balance at the end of each allotment period. This action prevents the balance from being carried over to the next allotment period and limits spending authorization in the next allotment period to the amounts specified in the original allotment schedule. The impounded balances can then be allocated to reserve accounts that are consistent with the original appropriations. For example, if a detailed appropriation stipulated that monies be used by a specific budget unit for a particular object of expenditure, a reserve fund can be established only in accordance with the specified purpose. If the budget unit requires additional money for the object covered by the reserve fund, a request can be made to the chief administrator for an amount from the appropriate reserve fund. On the other hand, if a lump-sum appropriation has been granted for an entire department, program, or activity, a reserve fund could be set up to correspond to the wide authorization of the appropriation, even though the expiring allotment balances had been allocated for particular objects. Thus, if the request is approved by the chief administrator, monies released from the reserve fund could be employed for any goods or services covered by the lump-sum appropriation.

Evaluation

The evaluation phase of the budget cycle is characterized by the exercise of both external and internal budgetary controls. External control is exerted through audits that are generally conducted by an independent public accounting firm. Internal control is exerted by the chief administrator through the budget office. There are two types of audits—financial and performance audits—each of which subsumes two separate categories of audits.[31] All audits are conducted under two sets of standards: (1) the generally accepted auditing standards established by the Auditing Standards Board of the American Institute of Certified Public Accountants, and (2) Government Auditing Standards (also known as the Yellow Book), a publication prepared under the auspices of the U.S. General Accounting Office and the comptroller-general of the United States.[32]

Financial audits Financial audits (or attest audits) are undertaken to exercise financial control over governmental operations. The first type of financial audit, a financial statements audit, is conducted by an independent accounting firm and is designed to provide assurances that (1) the government's financial statements are prepared in conformity with GAAP and authoritative financial reporting standards and (2) all material facts are disclosed. The second type of financial audit, a financial-related audit (also referred to as a compliance audit), can be completed internally or externally and is aimed primarily at detecting fraud. In the course of such an audit, financial records are investigated to certify the legality of expenditures, the proper recording of receipts, the correct operation of revenue and expenditure controls, and the accuracy and reliability of financial statements.

Performance audits Detecting fraud becomes a secondary concern in performance audits, where the focus of evaluation shifts from financial to management control. The purpose of a performance audit is to determine whether program and budget-unit managers are using resources efficiently and effectively. The first type of performance audit, an economy and efficiency audit (also known as a management or operational audit), entails determining (1) whether a governmental unit is achieving economy and efficiency in its service delivery (as measured by financial service costs) and (2) whether managerial and administrative practices are the cause of any inefficiencies.

The second type of performance audit, a program results audit, consists of a threefold evaluation. First, it entails determining the extent to which a governmental unit has achieved program objectives. Second, the audit assesses the effectiveness of the alternatives that were employed. Third, the audit determines whether the program has been implemented in compliance with applicable laws and regulations.

Performance auditing is an increasingly common means of (1) determining whether program goals are being attained and (2) ensuring that those entrusted with the management of public services and programs are held accountable for the achievement of organizational objectives. Performance auditing is also consistent with GASB's movement toward the development and use of service effort and accomplishment measures (SEA).[33] GASB-commissioned studies of various service functions, including police and public works, have yielded three types of SEA measures: (1) service effort (measures of inputs or of resources used), (2) service accomplishment (measures of outputs or quantity of service units produced, and outcomes or the impact of services), and (3) service efforts in relation to accomplishments (efficiency, or cost per unit of output, and effectiveness, or cost of achieving outcomes). While SEA measures are not included in GAAP (because of lack of consensus on what measures should be reported), the measures are strongly indicative of a general movement toward the principles of the rational budgeting model of goal attainment.

Summary: The budget cycle

In the course of the budget cycle, many accounting and budgeting mechanisms are used to increase managers' financial control over appropriated resources. In some instances these controls are so strict that they can actually hinder the achievement of program goals. Nevertheless, it is possible to maintain financial accountability while also providing managerial flexibility.

A program structure encourages the chief administrator, managers at all levels, and the governing body to examine activities in relation to community needs.

Defining program elements (or cost centers), goals, and objectives and determining benefits or unit costs help decision makers in budget units understand the relationship between inputs and the impact of activities.

Lump-sum appropriations and allocations allow program managers more discretion to adapt programs to changing conditions.

Strategic planning and budgetary analysis Strategic planning, a structured form of analysis that originated in the private sector, can facilitate goal-attainment budgeting. When government officials engage in strategic planning, they focus on the government's mission and attempt to establish clear connections between that mission and the organizational resources, structures, and processes that are used to achieve it. This rational approach is similar to that applied in goal-attainment budgeting and program budgeting.

Under a strategic planning approach, a chief executive and his or her principal administrators (department and agency managers) meet on a regular basis to clarify the government's mission, define its goals, and establish measures for objectives. They then evaluate alternatives for achieving the objectives, determine the resources needed to implement them, and select priorities. The annual budget is used to allocate resources according to the identified priorities. In subsequent years, performance is assessed with respect to objectives, and priorities are readjusted as necessary.

The infusion of strategic planning into government decision making has some drawbacks. First, the planning process is time-consuming: various plans are presented in detail, reviewed, and modified—activities that may draw decision makers away from other important tasks. Second, because of changes in political leadership, governmental goals may change more rapidly than those in the private sector, and priorities may therefore require frequent reassessment and revision over the long term.

One way to address this problem is to take a more limited approach that focuses on the government's mission at one point in time. A chief executive using this strategy would provide budget units with policy guidance before the preparation of their budget requests. The guidance would indicate the priorities for the coming year—that is, which proposals are likely to be received positively by the current administration. Budget units would then engage in extensive budgetary analysis and submit detailed program evaluations as part of their budget estimates. Because such analysis requires a considerable commitment of time on the part of both the budget office and budget-unit personnel, a government using an annual budget should give priority to budgetary analysis of programs that reflect administratively sanctioned priorities; other selected programs should be periodically subjected to extensive budgetary analysis to avoid overburdening budget-unit personnel and taking time away from implementation of the current-year budget. A local government that opts to use strategic planning as a decision tool should consider adopting a multiyear budget, which makes more time available for extensive budgetary analysis.

Sources: John M. Bryson, *Strategic Planning for Public and Nonprofit Organizations: A Guide to Strengthening and Sustaining Organizational Achievement*, rev. ed. (San Francisco: Jossey-Bass, 1999); Jack Koteen, *Strategic Management in Public and Nonprofit Organizations: Managing Concerns in an Era of Limits*, 2nd ed. (Westport, Conn.: Praeger, 1997); Roy T. Meyers, *Strategic Budgeting* (Ann Arbor: University of Michigan Press, 1994); Jack Rabin, Gerald Miller, and W. Bartley Hildreth, eds., *Handbook of Strategic Management*, 2nd ed. (New York: Marcel Dekkor, 2000), Alan Walter Steiss and Emeka O. Cyprian Nwagwu, *Financial Planning and Management in Public Organizations* (New York: Marcel Dekker, 2001); Robert D. Lee Jr. and Ronald W. Johnson, *Public Budgeting Systems*, 6th ed. (Gaithersburg, Md.: Aspen Publishers, Inc., 1998).

Appropriations, allocations, and allotments can be tied to performance factors (e.g., targets, unit cost) rather than to objects of expenditure. This connection permits higher-level managers to hold program managers accountable for program outcomes.

Budget reports should pertain to objectives and workloads and deal only secondarily with expenditure items. This approach to reporting provides a basis for evaluating program managers' achievement of program goals.

Pre-audits of a budget unit's expenditures should be restricted to checking the availability of authorized spending balances. This restriction allows program managers the flexibility to more effectively respond to changes in conditions.

Program managers should have considerable power to re-allot funds to adapt to changing program needs.

All these suggestions entail some shift in control from the budget office to the budget units. Although centralizing control in the budget office can prevent budget units from overspending appropriations and incurring deficits, it is the program managers who have the greatest understanding of, and experience with, the substantive issues of service delivery. If the budget office imposes burdensome financial controls and becomes involved in program decisions, program managers may lose their initiative and take less responsibility for program activities. A better alternative is (1) to shift the role of the budget office from pre-audit to post-audit evaluation and (2) to hold program managers accountable not only for effectiveness and efficiency but also for financial control. The system for rewarding good managers—and for removing ineffective ones—is then linked to the budget and to the attainment of program goals.

Multiyear budgets

The preceding section on the budget cycle was presented within the context of an annual (one-year) budget.[34] Local governments can also employ multiyear budgets, which incorporate estimated revenues and expenditures for two or more years. The biennial (two-year) budget is the most common form of multiyear budget. Currently, nineteen states have biennial budgets—a decline from 1940, when forty-four of the forty-eight states had biennial budgets. On the local level, the number of municipalities that use biennial budgets is increasing.[35]

The budget cycle

The budget cycles for an annual and a biennial budget differ not only in the length of time covered by the budget but also in the nature of the budgetary process. As illustrated in Figure 7–17, each two-year span of the biennial budget includes an "on" year (or base year) and an "off" year; it is during the on year that substantial time is allocated to budget preparation. Like an annual budget, a biennial budget is prepared during the year prior to implementation. The first year of implementation is the off year, which provides the time frame for extensive budgetary analysis. The second year of implementation is spent preparing for the next biennial budget.

Budget implementation entails application of the same management and financial controls outlined in the discussion of the annual budget: apportionments, allocations, allotments, workload planning, and monitoring. In the second year of implementation, the first year of a biennial budget could be subjected to financial and program audits, if required by the governing body. While the stages of the budget cycle are parallel and the processes are generally similar for all biennial budgets, the adoption of budget estimates varies with the form of budget, as discussed in the next section.

Figure 7–17 Biennial budget cycle for fiscal year (FY) 2005.

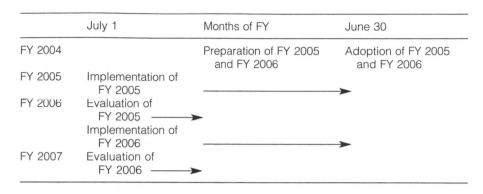

	July 1	Months of FY	June 30
FY 2004		Preparation of FY 2005 and FY 2006	Adoption of FY 2005 and FY 2006
FY 2005	Implementation of FY 2005	⟶	
FY 2006	Evaluation of FY 2005 ⟶		
	Implementation of FY 2006	⟶	
FY 2007	Evaluation of FY 2006 ⟶		

Forms of biennial budgets

Three forms of biennial budgets are used.[36] If the local government employs a traditional biennial budget, estimated revenues and expenditures are provided separately for two consecutive years, and the governing body either adopts two separate annual budgets at the same time or adopts a single budget for the two-year period. In the first case, the surplus remaining at the end of the first fiscal year would be returned to the appropriate governmental funds; in the second case, any surplus remaining at the end of the first fiscal year could be used in the next year without additional legislative approval. If the local government employs a rolling biennial budget, budgets for two consecutive years are prepared at the same time, but each budget is adopted separately, in the year of its implementation. That is, one budget is approved in the first year, and the second budget is approved in the second year. The third type of biennial budget is a biennial financial plan, which is merely an expansion of an annual budget. Under this arrangement, an annual budget is compiled for the first year and submitted with an appended financial plan for the second year. The annual portion is formally adopted, establishing authority for spending and revenue collection; the financial plan is not legally sanctioned and can be changed before it is formally approved and implemented in the second year.

How effective biennial budgets are as decision-making tools depends on the local government's fiscal and economic environment. Because they require two-year forecasts, both traditional and rolling biennial budgets require stable economic conditions, stability in expenditures and revenues, and accurate projections, with little disparity between predicted and actual values. Unless these conditions exist, a biennial financial plan is more appropriate: because it is an extension of the annual budget, it does not require a firm commitment of resources.

Advantages and disadvantages

Governments that opt to use multiyear budgets obtain fiscal advantages but also encounter decision-making limitations. One advantage of a biennial budget is that because budget preparation is undertaken only every other year, proportionally less time is allocated to preparation over the course of the two-year budget period. This advantage is somewhat offset, however, by the fact that the budget-office and budget-unit staff must devote a larger part of the on year to preparation; in addition, because of the time allocated to preparation, less time is available for the implementation of an ongoing budget. The increased workload for the first year of the biennial budget may also create stress among the participants in the budget preparation process.

A second advantage of multiyear budgeting is that it can produce a more policy-oriented budgetary process—one that is consistent with goal-attainment budgeting. In the off year, government officials can move away from the detailed, line-item approach and focus on programmatic goals. Confining preparation to the on year also means that more time can be spent on budgetary analysis during the off year. The budget office can improve its oversight of program performance and engage in more program monitoring. For budget units, a multiyear budget creates greater opportunity for long-range planning, program analysis, and program evaluation—specifically, more intensive (albeit less frequent) reviews of major programs and more attention to capital budgeting.

Third, it has been argued that multiyear budgeting can improve long-range and strategic planning because it requires, during the on year, multiyear forecasts of revenues and expenditures. Such forecasts could enable government officials and program decision makers to gain a better understanding of the community's future needs and demands and to assemble the fiscal capacity to meet the predicted challenges. (On the other hand, long-range projections could also be undertaken for annual budgets if the government provided the necessary resources for multiyear forecasting.)

Finally, multiyear budgeting can reduce the politicization of the budgetary process if local elections occur in the off year of the budget.

Among the potential disadvantages of biennial budgeting is decreased flexibility: because the off year is a full two years into the future, it may be difficult to predict revenues, expenditures, and potential outside influences that far ahead. Thus, biennial budgets may limit the local government's ability to respond to change.

Budgetary approaches

The previous sections have focused on two of the sometimes conflicting purposes of public budgeting: goal attainment and financial control. A third purpose of budgeting is managerial productivity, which is concerned with the cost efficiency of government services.[37] The different budgetary approaches used in local governments reflect variations in the political importance of these three purposes. Financial control is typically associated with the line-item budget, goal attainment with both program budgeting and planning-programming-budgeting systems (PPBS), and managerial productivity with both performance budgeting and zero-base budgeting (ZBB). Other budget reforms and innovations are variations of these approaches.[38] Because there is considerable diversity in practice, the discussion that follows describes each budgetary approach in its "ideal" form.

Line-item budgeting

The line-item budget was, for all practical purposes, the only budgetary approach employed by local governments until the 1950s and is still the predominant form. Developed in response to the substantial governmental corruption that prevailed at the turn of the twentieth century, the line-item budget was designed to ensure the financial accountability of public officials.[39] Under a line-item budget, financial control is exerted mainly through an objects-of-expenditure format that designates the types of inputs to be purchased. Generally, the objects are classified by character—current items (operating costs), long-term items (capital outlays), and past services (debt service). The separate organizational units and subunits are usually required to submit their expenditure estimates in accordance with these objects-of-expenditure classifications, as shown in Figure 7–5.

Because line-item budgets are fixed budgets with monies appropriated only for a particular time period, most commonly one year, the discretion of the chief administrator is limited, and can be limited even further through detailed appropriations. Appropriations may be approved for different classes of expenditure (personnel services, supplies), for different subclasses (wages, salaries, travel, overtime, office supplies), or even for specific items (compensation for individual positions, supplies of pencils and paper). The governing body also exerts financial control by setting overall spending limits and by conducting financial audits of the executive branch.

The major responsibility for exercising financial control during the preparation and implementation phases rests with the chief administrator. However, decision making—on the part of the chief administrator, the budget office, and the operating units—is uncoordinated. The chief administrator initiates the budget cycle by informing the budget units of the general policy orientation and the spending guidelines. Budget units prepare estimates independently for the services for which they are responsible and request spending for particular objects; estimates may be open-ended or subject to a fixed ceiling, depending on the approach chosen by the chief administrator. After the governing body adopts the budget, the chief administrator secures control over implementation by specifying allotments for the funded objects and pre-auditing expenditures to ensure that they are in accordance with allotments or appropriations. The budget office authorizes encumbrances and spending only for those items that fall within the scope of applicable allotments and may refuse expenditures if they are not deemed suitable for the service. Bimonthly or monthly financial reports confirm that spending is in accordance with legal requirements and highlight trends that could potentially interfere with the achievement of a balanced budget.

Because information is organized according to inputs, budgetary analysis focuses on what is purchased rather than on the role of government actions in achieving goals. Program elements are not coordinated with each other for the purpose of achieving goals; evaluation of alternatives is not encouraged; and the budget estimates submitted to the chief administrator do not contain information on intersector or intraprogram efficiency. There is no incentive for such analysis because the chief administrator's budget allocations are not based on the identification of the most efficient alternatives.

Since, in a strict line-item approach, budget units do not provide information on what is to be accomplished with the requested expenditures, the chief administrator and the governing body cannot determine whether a service is being provided effectively, or even efficiently. The chief administrator has no criteria for evaluating funding requests because he or she does not know what is to be lost or gained by increasing or decreasing expenditures. Thus, rational trade-offs among services are impossible; the chief administrator must make subjective judgments on service effectiveness and arbitrarily cut spending on particular objects. The line-item approach assumes that the chief administrator has greater expertise on service issues than the budget-unit managers.

Performance budgeting

Performance budgeting originated in the late 1940s, with the report of the Hoover Commission on federal government budgeting. Performance budgeting was viewed as a means of improving the management of service delivery; central to this view was the idea that cost efficiency should be the principal indicator of managerial effectiveness.[40] Under a performance budgeting approach, a program budget format (entailing a slightly different terminology) is adapted to the existing organizational structure. Government activities are divided into major functions, each of which encompasses a number of programs that further goals. Programs, in turn, are made up of a number of activities, each of which is undertaken by a separate performance unit. A unit may be an entire department, a division, or a work group, and any one unit may be responsible for more than one activity. Each activity must yield an identifiable output, sometimes referred to as an end product, and each output is produced by a mix of objects of expenditure.

The initiative in budget preparation lies with the performance unit. Output measures are developed for each activity of a performance unit. The performance-unit manager considers different mixes of objects of expenditure entailing different costs (expenses) and different levels of output, and then selects the alternative that yields the lowest unit cost. To obtain a budget estimate for the activity of the performance unit, the performance-unit manager estimates the number of required units of output and multiplies it by the chosen unit-cost figure. Along with the budget estimate, the performance-unit manager submits a narrative statement that (1) describes how each activity furthers the unit's assigned goals, (2) outlines the tasks to be performed in carrying out each activity, (3) demonstrates how the appropriations will facilitate each activity, and (4) sets forth a workload plan that (a) specifies guideposts for units of output to be accomplished during the budget year and (b) schedules the type and amount of work to be undertaken to reach the guideposts.

Since budget estimates are based on unit cost, management, administration, and other overhead costs are distributed among the various activities undertaken by the performance unit, to ensure that spending authorizations will cover the entire costs of the unit's operations. In addition, pre-auditing by the budget office is limited to checking allotment or appropriation balances and does not include evaluation of the suitability of encumbrances. This restraint on executive oversight allows performance-unit managers to exercise discretion in conducting activities and gives them primary responsibility for service provision. Managerial accountability can be reinforced by a performance reporting system, which is maintained by the budget office. The budget office monitors the activities of a performance unit by collecting data on outputs and comparing these data with the guideposts in the workload plan. Monthly reports enable performance-unit managers to adjust the timing, quantity, or mix of inputs to keep the unit on track in relation to the guideposts. Finally, performance audits can be used to foster managerial accountability.

Performance budgeting has several weaknesses. First, as noted earlier in this chapter, unit costs are not always meaningful indicators of progress toward goals. Second, because a program format is superimposed on the existing organizational structure, cost centers may not correspond to responsibility centers; that is, the various activities assigned to performance units may not include all the organizational actions that contribute to a particular output. As a result, total costs may not be compiled accurately, and unit costs may therefore be inaccurate. Third, because benefits are not measured, there are no indicators of inter-sector efficiency. Fourth, because unit cost does not indicate the net value yielded by each program, interprogram efficiency cannot be determined. Thus, a chief administrator who needs to decide how to distribute increments of available funding among competing activities cannot make that decision on the basis of the net benefits that would be gained or lost.

Program budgeting

The most elaborate form of program budgeting, PPBS, was initiated by the federal government in the early 1960s and has been adopted, in scaled-down form, by many state and local governments.[41] The program budgeting process is more centralized than other approaches: the chief administrator designates goals, thus providing explicit guidance at the preparation phase. On the basis of the goals, a program structure is designed to prescribe how the goals will be achieved organizationally (see Figure 7–7). Under a program format, all alternatives, both existing and potential, that could contribute to the achievement of goals are systematically examined. The alternative with the greatest net benefits for a given cost becomes the basis of the program's budget request.

The budget units analyze and evaluate the alternatives within the context of long-range planning. Consequently, multiyear plans are prepared along with the budget estimates. These plans describe how resources will be used to meet specified targets over the life of the program. The chief administrator receives one funding request for each program element. Funding is awarded according to the greatest net benefits—or, if benefits cannot be calculated, the greatest gains in the achievement of objectives. While the chief administrator makes funding choices, he or she also reviews the three- to five-year revenue and expenditure forecasts, prepared by the budget office, to identify future revenue needs.

When funding requests for the chosen program alternatives are submitted to the governing body, the budget is authorized through lump-sum and continuing appropriations so that program managers have the flexibility to mix objects of expenditure, as long as spending is compatible with long-range planning goals. Similarly, while appropriations must be allotted to ensure consistency with revenue flows, the chief administrator's allocations to program elements are lump sum, to mirror the appropriations. To further protect program managers' discretion, pre-audit controls are restricted to determining available unencumbered balances. Chief administrators can hold program managers accountable for spending by (1) comparing the targets in the program's multiyear plan with achievement of objectives and (2) undertaking program results audits to assess program effectiveness. Using their multiyear plans, managers can adjust program activities in response to changes that affect targets or workload requirements.

A program budget creates a number of difficulties.

1. Goals are hard to formulate and define.
2. Goals are subject to change, and the program structure must be changed in response.
3. For many goals, it is impossible to obtain objective measures of benefits.
4. The systematic evaluation of alternatives is subject to human limitations and time and cost constraints.
5. Although cost-benefit analysis of program alternatives can enable the chief administrator to determine intersector and intraprogram efficiency, it does not provide adequate information about interprogram efficiency: a single budget request does not offer a basis for reducing or expanding a program in relation to the overall size of the budget.

Zero-base budgeting

Zero-base budgeting (ZBB) originated in the private sector and gained popularity with the advent of the Carter administration in 1972.[42] The ZBB approach arose from concern about the cost efficiency of government services. Under ZBB, outputs are the basis for assessing the usefulness of an activity, and budget preparation and approval are focused on the effect of financing increments. Alternative funding levels (based on financing increments) are used to set priorities among activities.

The first step in ZBB is to establish decision units—organizational sub-units, each with a designated manager who has responsibility and authority over specific sets of activities. Unlike other approaches to budgeting, ZBB is not identified with a particular budget format. If a program format is adopted, the program elements will be the decision units. Most commonly, however, under ZBB, decision units are simply grafted onto the existing objects-of-expenditure format: a department or division can thus encompass more than one decision unit.

In the second step, decision units prepare a number of decision packages, one for each alternative funding level. Each package identifies the mission and goals of the unit, outlines different ways to deliver the services, and describes the benefits of each alternative. Generally, the decision-unit manager selects the option that provides the greatest gain in outputs. In most cases, packages have three different funding levels (most commonly, the minimum, current, and improved levels), which are stated in terms of percentages above and below current-year funding (e.g., 90, 100, and 110 percent).

The minimum level is the amount of funding needed to keep the activities viable. However, because the precise funding level required for viability is so difficult to determine, in practice the minimum funding level is generally set at 80, 85, or 90 percent of current funding. Current funding is usually defined as 100 percent of last year's expenditures; improved funding would be defined as more than 100 percent of the previous year's spending.

The third step in ZBB is to rank the decision packages. First, higher-level managers rank the packages of the decision units under their authority; these ranked packages are then ranked by the chief administrator. The rankings by the managers and chief administrators are based on their judgments about the additional gains that can be made at each funding level. The chief administrator selects the packages to be funded by starting with the highest-ranked package and continuing until the expenditure total equals the maximum allowable spending for the budget. This total budget, with its ranked packages, is then submitted to the governing body.

Several factors must be considered when ZBB is employed. First, in order to ensure that decision-unit managers have sufficient flexibility to adapt to changes that affect cost and output levels, appropriations and allocations should be lump sum, and executive pre-audits should be limited to checking unencumbered balances. Second, because the system does not provide for the measurement of costs and benefits, the chief administrator and governing body cannot judge intersector or interprogram efficiency. Third, because the system does not require a program structure, decision makers cannot conduct coherent analyses of alternatives. Finally, since activities in several decision units may contribute to the same output, authority over services is diffused.

Conclusion

The line-item budget, the most popular approach to local government budgeting, is easier to prepare and implement than performance, program, or zero-base budgets. Although these other approaches have an advantage over the line-item budget in that they shift the focus of public budgeting from financial control to goal attainment, they require—at least in their pure forms—large amounts of paperwork and administration; considerable supervisory time; and high accounting, information, and analysis costs. This level of complexity and expense is unnecessary for small local governments. Since the 1950s, however, many local governments have implemented variations on performance, program, or zero-base budgeting; others have incorporated into line-item budgeting some of the concepts embodied in the alternative approaches.

Neither these adaptations, however, nor the "ideal" forms of performance, program, or zero-base budgeting integrate all the major elements required for pursuing the basic purpose of public budgeting: the efficient attainment of governmental goals. This integration does occur with the rational budget model described earlier in the chapter, which combines major elements of program budgeting and zero-base budgeting. However, the rational budget model entails the same administrative costs and difficulties associated with other non-line-item approaches, and it also brings its own set of disadvantages—specifically, measurement obstacles and difficulty in obtaining the amount and type of information needed for analysis. As a consequence, the model must be adjusted in practice, but those adjustments may impair one of its principal advantages: the ability to determine intersector, interprogram, and intraprogram efficiency.

The rational budget model also necessitates various fiscal and accounting practices that decentralize decision-making authority, moving it from the chief executive to the program managers. As was noted earlier in the chapter, allowing program managers more discretion can improve goal attainment but requires the chief administrator and financial staff to relinquish significant control. The chief administrator nevertheless continues to exercise long-term policy and fiscal control through a system of accountability: managers are held responsible for achieving the outcomes they have explicitly identified as the expected results of their programs. Although it has drawbacks—including diminished financial control and the significant costs of administration, analysis, and implementation—the rational budget model is the most effective approach for realizing goals that reflect public preferences and values.

1 Much of the discussion in this section is based on the following sources: Government Finance Officers Association of the United States and Canada (GFOA), *Governmental Accounting, Auditing, and Financial Reporting* (Chicago: GFOA, 2002); Robert J. Freeman, Craig D. Shoulders, and Edward S. Lynn, *Governmental and Nonprofit Accounting: Theory and Practice,* 7th ed. (Englewood Cliffs, N.J.: Prentice Hall, 2002); and Earl R. Wilson, Susan C. Kattelus, and Leon E. Hay, *Accounting for Governmental and Non-Profit Entities,* 12th ed. (Boston: McGraw-Hill/Irwin, 2001). See also John L. Mikesell, *Fiscal Administration: Analysis and Applications for the Public Sector,* 5th ed. (Fort Worth, Tex.: Harcourt Brace College Publishers, 1999); and Alan Walter Steiss and Emeka O. Cyprian Nwagwu, *Financial Planning and Management in Public Organizations* (New York: Marcel Dekker, 2001), chap. 2.

2 The authoritative sources on these matters are GFOA, *Governmental Accounting,* often referred to as GAAFR, or the Blue Book.

3 GFOA, *Governmental Accounting,* chap. 2.

4 Ibid.

5 Ibid., chaps. 2 and 16.

6 For an analysis of capital budgeting, see Steiss and Nwagwu, *Financial Planning,* chaps. 8 and 9; Robert L. Bland and Wes Clarke, "Budgeting for Capital Improvements," chap. 26 in *Handbook of Government Budgeting,* ed. Roy T. Meyers (San Francisco: Jossey-Bass, 1999); Gerasimos A. Gianakis and Clifford P. McCue, *Local Government Budgeting: A Managerial Approach* (Westport, Conn.: Praeger/Quorum, 1999), chap. 7; David C. Nice, *Public Budgeting* (Belmont, Calif.: Wadsworth/Thomason Learning, 2002), chap. 8; and B. J. Reed and John W. Swain, *Public Finance Administration,* 2nd ed. (Thousand Oaks, Calif.: Sage, 1997).

7 The two classic writings on the theory of public budgeting are V. O. Key Jr., "The Lack of a Budgetary Theory," *American Political Science Review* 36 (1940): 138–144; and B. Verne Lewis, "Towards a Theory of Budgeting," *Public Administration Review* 12 (winter 1952). See also Aaron Wildavsky, *The New Politics of the Budgetary Process* (Glenview, Ill.: Scott Foresman, 1988).

8 Robert J. Brent, *Applied Cost-Benefit Analysis* (Cheltenham, U.K.: Edward Elgar Publishing, 1996); Anthony Boardman et al., *Cost-Benefit Analysis: Concepts and Practice,* 2nd ed. (Upper Saddle River, N.J.: Prentice Hall, 2001).

9 Some of the classic works on public decision making that relate to governmental budgeting are Charles E. Lindblom, "The Science of Muddling Through," *Public Administration Review* 19 (spring 1959): 79–88; David Braybrooke and Charles E. Lindblom, *A Strategy of Decision Making: Policy Evaluation as a Social Process* (New York: The Free Press, 1970); and Herbert A. Simon, *Administrative Behavior,* 2nd ed. (New York: The Free Press, 1965).

10 See Robert D. Lee Jr. and Ronald W. Johnson, *Public Budgeting Systems,* 6th ed. (Gaithersburg, Md.: Aspen Publishers, 1998).

11 A seminal article on cost and responsibility centers is Francis E. McGilvery, "Program and Responsibility Cost Accounting," *Public Administration Review* 28 (March/April 1968): 148–154. See also Lee and Johnson, *Public Budgeting Systems;* and Steiss and Nwagwu, *Financial Management,* chap. 3.

12 C. West Churchman and A. H. Schainblatt, "PPB: How Can It Be Implemented?" *Public Administration Review* 29 (March/April 1969): 178–189.

13 McGilvery, "Cost Accounting"; Steiss and Nwagwu, *Financial Planning,* chap. 3.

14 Sometimes earmarked revenues can provide more benefits to the community if the scope of earmarking

is widened to target particular social problems or community needs: for example, gasoline taxes could be used to alleviate traffic congestion not only through the construction of additional roads but also through the development of mass transit; library "taxes" could be used to purchase books as well as to maintain library buildings.

15 Steiss and Nwagwu, *Financial Planning;* and Nice, *Public Budgeting.*

16 David N. Ammons, *Municipal Benchmarks: Assessing Local Performance and Establishing Community Standards,* 2nd ed. (Thousand Oaks, Calif.: Sage, 2001); Harry P. Hatry, *Performance Measurement: Getting Results* (Washington, D.C.: Urban Institute Press, 1999); Richard C. Kearney and Evan M. Berman, *Public Sector Performance: Management, Motivation, and Measurement* (Boulder, Colo.: Westview Press, 1999).

17 Lee and Johnson, *Public Budgeting Systems.*

18 Lee and Johnson, *Public Budgeting Systems;* Ammons, *Municipal Benchmarks.*

19 For example, see Boardman et al., *Cost-Benefit Analysis;* Brent, *Applied Cost-Benefit Analysis;* and Robert J. Brent, *Cost-Benefit Analysis and Healthcare Evaluations* (Cheltenham, U.K.: Edward Elgar Publishing, 2003).

20 For the classic discussion of the use of unit cost in public budgeting, see Jesse L. Burkhead, *Government Budgeting* (New York: John Wiley & Sons, 1956), chaps. 5–7. See also Wilson, Kattelus, and Hay, *Accounting,* chap. 13; Ammons, *Municipal Benchmarks;* Hatry, *Performance Measurement;* and Kearney and Berman, *Public Sector Performance.*

21 Wilson, Kattelus, and Hay, *Accounting,* chap. 13.

22 Ibid.

23 Thomas D. Lynch, *Public Budgeting in America,* 3rd ed. (Englewood Cliffs, N.J.: Prentice Hall, 1990), chaps. 2 and 5. See also Wildavsky, *New Politics.*

24 For a compilation of theoretical arguments about the ways in which local government institutions and political processes might influence the level and type of government spending, taxation, and budget allocations, see Dennis C. Mueller, *Public Choice II* (Cambridge, U.K.: Cambridge University Press, 1989), chaps. 3–5. See also James J. Gosling, *Budgetary Politics in American Governments,* 3rd ed. (New York: Routledge, 2002); and Irene Rubin, *The Politics of Budgeting: Getting and Spending, Borrowing and Balancing,* 3rd ed. (Chatham, N.J.: Chatham House Publishers, 1997).

25 Freeman, Shoulders, and Lynn, *Nonprofit Accounting,* chaps. 3–4; Wilson, Kattelus, and Hay, *Accounting,* chaps. 2–5.

26 For a detailed discussion of budget preparation, see Robert L. Bland and Irene Rubin, *Budgeting: A Guide for Local Governments* (Washington, D.C.: International City/County Management Association, 1997).

27 Lewis, "Theory of Budgeting."

28 Freeman, Shoulders, and Lynn, *Nonprofit Accounting,* chaps. 3–6; and Wilson, Kattelus, and Hay, *Accounting,* chaps. 4–5.

29 Wilson, Kattelus, and Hay, *Accounting,* chaps. 2–5.

30 Freeman, Shoulders, and Lynn, *Nonprofit Accounting,* chaps 5–6; and Wilson, Kattelus, and Hay, *Accounting,* chaps. 4–5.

31 What is known as a single audit encompasses both a financial and a performance audit; single audits allow or require local governments, depending on the amount of federal assistance received, to have one audit performed to meet the needs of all federal grantor agencies, instead of having separate audits conducted on a grant-by-grant basis.

32 U.S. General Accounting Office, *Government Auditing Standards: 2003 Revision,* available at www.gao.gov/govaud/yb2003.pdf.

33 GFOA, *Governmental Accounting,* chap. 17.

34 This discussion is drawn from the following literature: Barry Blom and Salomon Guajardo, "Multiyear Budgeting: A Primer for Finance Officers," *Government Finance Review* 16 (February 2000): 39–43; Jerry McCafferty, "Features of the Budgetary Process," chap. 1 in *Handbook of Government Budgeting,* ed. Roy T. Meyers (San Francisco: Jossey-Bass, 1999); Andrea Jackson, "Taking the Plunge: The Conversion to Multiyear Budgeting," *Government Finance Review* 18 (August 2002): 24–27; and Steven M. Chapman, "Implementing Multiyear Budgeting in the City of Moreno Valley, California," *Government Finance Review* 14 (December 1998): 38–39.

35 McCafferty, "Budgetary Process."

36 Blom and Guajardo, "Multiyear Budgeting."

37 The major work on the history of public budgeting is Allen Schick, "The Road to PPB: The Stages of Budget Reform," *Public Administration Review* 26 (December 1966): 243–258.

38 Nice, *Public Budgeting;* Gianakis and McCue, *Local Government Budgeting.*

39 Schick, "Road to PPB"; Nice, *Public Budgeting;* Gianakis and McCue, *Local Government Budgeting.*

40 Burkhead, *Government Budgeting,* chaps. 5–7.

41 See Schick, "Road to PPB"; and Lee and Johnson, *Public Budgeting Systems.*

42 The seminal works on the topic are Peter A. Phyrr, "The Zero-Base Approach to Government Budgeting," *Public Administration Review* 37 (January/February 1977): 1–8; Robert N. Anthony, "Zero-Base Budgeting Is a Fraud," *Wall Street Journal,* 27 April 1977; Allen Schick, "Zero-Base Budgeting and Sunset: Redundancy or Symbiosis?" *The Bureaucrat* 6 (spring 1977); and Allen Schick, "Road from ZBB," *Public Administration Review* 38 (March/April 1978). See also Mikesell, *Fiscal Administration,* chap. 4; Nice, *Public Budgeting;* and Gianakis and McCue, *Local Government Budgeting.*

Financial accounting, reporting, and auditing

WILLIAM W. HOLDER

Local government financial management differs from private business practice in a number of major ways. A private firm is relatively free to operate in the economic arena, and its operations, revenues, and costs can vary considerably—for example, if the firm suddenly decides to take advantage of a new market opportunity. Governments, on the other hand, are generally more limited in the activities in which they can engage, the markets they can exploit, and the resources they can access. For example, laws, regulations, and budgets that have the force of law limit the expenditure of public monies. Bonds and other long-term debt instruments generally cannot be issued without appropriate legal authority frequently requiring a vote of the populace. Furthermore, although a government may have the right to levy and collect taxes, that ability is also limited by law. These differences have resulted in significant differences in the financial reporting for each type of organization. The reporting model for business enterprises is focused primarily on financial performance measures, whereas financial reporting for governments is affected more profoundly by the legal framework in which public organizations operate.

The budget is the heart of administering public resources, and governmental accounting is central to the budget-making process. Past accounting records furnish important data for the revenue forecasts used to construct the budget; these records also assist with expenditure forecasts by providing a fix on the costs of such standard operations as police and fire protection and street cleaning and maintenance. Accounting records also furnish data on debt and debt service charges and serve as a basis for estimating the local government's capacity to finance additional capital improvements. Finally, accounting reports provide timely information indicating when the budget plans are going amiss, when capital funds are being diverted to operations, when expenditures are outrunning revenues, and when the local government is incurring financial obligations beyond its fiscal capacity.

This chapter describes in detail the specific governmental accounting techniques that are used to monitor, control, and report on the sources and uses of financial resources. In particular, it addresses the changes that have been brought about as the result of *Statement of Governmental Accounting Standards (GAS) No. 34,* which added accrual accounting and aggregated presentations to the traditional financial reporting model used by state and local governments, and which required governments to supplement their basic financial statements with discussion and analysis.[1] While much of the traditional, fund-based, modified accrual system of financial reporting used by government entities remains, the changes required by *GAS No. 34* represent a virtual revolution in financial reporting.

Financial and management reporting play central roles in local government financial management. As will be discussed later in this chapter, financial statements provide information on budgetary and fiscal compliance, funds flow, and liquidity.[2] Administrators use this information to plan and evaluate operations as well as to comply with the requirements of a variety of regulatory and granting authorities. Modern computer technology—with its convenience, storage capacity, and quick, flexible access to data—is a great aid to efficient decision making.

This chapter also addresses auditing. Traditionally, auditing has focused primarily on financial and compliance issues. But it is now clear that the audit function holds substantial promise for local government managers attempting to improve overall efficiency and effectiveness. In fact, a broad definition of auditing is particularly useful in governments—where direct profit motive is, by necessity, usually lacking.

Auditing can also provide a powerful tool for preventing and detecting various types of fraud, including defalcations and other thefts of government resources. The audit function can assist managers in identifying weaknesses in internal control structures so that timely corrective action may be taken; it can also detect specific instances of wrongdoing, thereby facilitating the recovery of any losses and limiting the continuation and repetition of such activities.

Underlying the accounting, reporting, and auditing concepts described in this chapter are standards and techniques accepted by the profession for managing finances responsibly. The first two sections of this chapter present those standards and describe the users of financial reports.

Evolution of accounting and reporting standards

On the basis of tradition and best practices, the accounting profession has developed a set of principles—referred to collectively as GAAP (generally accepted accounting principles)—to guide financial reporting.

Generally accepted accounting principles are primarily conventional in nature. They are the result of decisions; they represent the consensus at any time as to how the financial accounting process should operate and how financial statements should be prepared from the information made available through the financial accounting process.

Inasmuch as generally accepted accounting principles embody a consensus, they depend heavily on notions such as "general acceptance" and "substantial authoritative support," which have not been and probably cannot be precisely defined. There is concurrence, however, that the notions of "general acceptance" and "substantial authoritative support" relate to the propriety of the practices, as viewed by informed, intelligent, and experienced accountants in the light of the purposes and limitations of the financial accounting process.[3]

The accounting profession in the United States has followed this rationale in creating bodies capable of establishing GAAP (see the accompanying sidebar, which describes the organizations that set accounting standards). Beginning in the 1930s, standards and practices representing GAAP for state and local governments were developed by the National Council on Governmental Accounting (NCGA) and by the predecessor committees sponsored by the Government Finance Officers Association (GFOA). Since 1984, the Governmental Accounting Standards Board (GASB) has been recognized as the authoritative organization for setting financial accounting and reporting standards for state and local governments. The first authoritative pronouncement made by GASB recognized and adopted all existing authoritative literature that had been published by the defunct NCGA. Therefore, until altered by GASB, NCGA statements and interpretations continue to define GAAP for state and local governments. In 2002, an audit guide dealing, in part, with state and local government financial accounting practices was issued by the American Institute of Certified Public Accountants (AICPA), which has been active in formulating such standards since 1974.

GASB is made up of seven members (currently, one full-time and six part-time), experts in governmental accounting and financial reporting who are supported by research and administrative staffs. Under this structure, emerging

Sources of state and local government accounting principles   The organization that is primarily responsible for establishing, reviewing, and changing accounting standards for state and local governments is the Governmental Accounting Standards Board (GASB). The standards established by this group provide for uniform accounting and financial reporting for citizens, the bond market, state and federal granting agencies, and public accounting companies.

GASB was created to replace another long-standing organization, the National Council on Governmental Accounting (NCGA), which had been operating since 1934, originally as the National Committee on Municipal Accounting. The NCGA was made up of twenty-one part-time volunteer members from local, state, and federal governments and the academic and private sectors and operated with the financial support of the Government Finance Officers Association (GFOA).

Generally accepted accounting principles (GAAP) were established by the NCGA in its 1968 publication *Governmental Accounting, Auditing, and Financial Reporting.* This publication was superseded by NCGA Statement 1, *Governmental Accounting and Financial Reporting Principles,* which was published in 1979. Following Statement 1, six additional statements, eleven interpretations, and one concepts statement were issued by the NCGA before that organization was replaced by GASB. In 1980, GFOA published *Governmental Accounting, Auditing, and Financial Reporting,* which was not an authoritative statement but an interpretation of NCGA Statement 1. GASB has codified all existing NCGA pronouncements and has issued two statements of governmental accounting concepts, forty-one statements of governmental accounting standards, and six interpretations; its staff has issued two technical bulletins.

The American Institute of Certified Public Accountants (AICPA) influences accounting principles for state and local governments, particularly through its *Audits of State and Local Governments,* an industry accounting and auditing guide published by the AICPA State and Local Government Committee, most recently in 2002.

The Financial Accounting Standards Board (FASB), a standard-setting body for the private sector and another source of generally accepted accounting principles, also influences state and local governments and their independent auditors. *GASB Codification,* for example, requires that government proprietary funds follow GAAP that are applicable to business enterprises. The AICPA's *Audits of State and Local Governments* also provides state and local governments with some guidance on accounting and financial reporting.

State and local government accounting practices are also influenced by federal accounting and reporting requirements for grant programs and by state laws covering state and local government financial reporting.

GASB is a separate and independent accounting standards board established to set standards of accounting for governments. The organization has a full-time staff and represents a broad range of public and private sector groups that are concerned with state and local government accounting standards. In addition, the Financial Accounting Foundation provides oversight and fundraising for GASB, and the Governmental Accounting Standards Advisory Council (GASAC), a group of up to twenty or more members, advises GASB on a wide range of issues.

issues can be addressed more quickly, due process established more readily, and research conducted more efficiently and directly than was possible under the NCGA, which was made up of twenty-one part-time members who had little technical or administrative support.

In addition to adopting all existing authoritative NCGA statements and interpretations, GASB has issued forty-one statements of governmental accounting standards, two statements of governmental accounting concepts, and six related interpretations. It is an axiom of good accounting that financial accounting and reporting should be tailored to the goals and objectives of different users, and financial statements should reflect those differences. By specifying the various types of reports to be prepared by governments, GASB's recent pronouncements indicate support for the principle of tailoring financial reports to users' needs. Some of the reports specified by GASB are described in this chapter.

Users of accounting, reporting, and auditing information

Government accounting systems provide data to many users—categorized here as external, internal, and internal/external—whose varied information needs should be anticipated and met to the fullest extent possible. Financial reporting, which can be thought of as the transmission of economic data about an organization to concerned individuals and institutions, is a complex communication form. Ultimately, the overriding criterion for the success of financial communication is the usefulness of the information provided, not the adherence of the reporting process to established standards.

External users

External users include suppliers, interested citizens, long- and short-term creditors, and many others transacting business with the local government or its agencies. External users need financial information because they have, or expect to have, a direct financial interest in the operations and financing of the local government. But because they function outside the government, external users lack the authority to prescribe the nature, timing, content, or extent of the financial information they receive. The accounting profession established GAAP (1) so that external users can be assured that similar economic events are accorded similar accounting treatments, (2) to ensure that relevant and reliable financial information is being transmitted, and (3) to provide for a common understanding of published financial statements.

Internal users

Internal users are the managers and administrators who are responsible for planning, organizing, executing, and reviewing the operations and strategies of the local government. These users need diverse types of financial information to prepare forecasts and budgets, to control expenditures, and to apply various techniques, such as cost-benefit analysis, to the decision-making process.

Unlike external users, most internal users have access to a large amount of financial information and are familiar with the assumptions and practices underlying that information. Some of the information may be in the form of published external financial statements, but much of it is not included in the external reports prepared in conformity with GAAP. Most of the financial information internal users need is obtained through features and functions of the accounting system other than those that supply external users with information: local government management requires different and more detailed information than is provided by financial statements that are designed to conform to GAAP.

Although most reports to decision makers and managers are prepared on a recurring basis, the accounting and reporting systems must also be flexible enough to meet unique reporting demands. For example, managerial accounting and analytical techniques commonly applied in business enterprises—such as activity-based costing, flexible budgeting, standard costing, and variance analysis—have recently become more prevalent in governmental operations. Although these techniques are not yet as robust and advanced in their application as might be desirable, their benefits in governmental administration seem clear. They require, however, relatively sophisticated and flexible reporting capabilities.

Internal/external users

A third category of users includes those who are not directly involved in day-to-day operations but who have significant authority over the local government, such as granting authorities, local or state legislative bodies, closely related governmental units, and other significant providers of resources. Such entities may require compliance reports to show that grant funds were properly used and may set specifications for the information they seek. Nevertheless, the reporting task may not be excessively onerous: once established, the requirements for the reports tend to remain constant for relatively long periods.

Another category of internal/external users includes those, such as legislative staff and citizens' groups, who analyze and distill information from financial reports and then pass it on to legislators or the public. Unlike external users, such groups need not rely completely on the application of professional standards to determine what information they can obtain; they have at least some ability to determine the nature and extent of the financial information they receive.

The fund basis of accounting and reporting

To a person familiar only with business accounting and reporting practices, governmental accounting represents a radical change. Business enterprises prepare GAAP-based reports for the total organization, not for the separate parts; state and local governments have historically prepared more narrowly focused reports. GASB defines a fund as

a fiscal and accounting entity with a self-balancing set of accounts recording cash and other financial resources, together with all related liabilities and residual equities or balances, and changes therein, which are segregated for the purpose of carrying on specific activities or attaining certain objectives in accordance with special regulations, restrictions, or limitations.[4]

The fund basis of accounting recognizes that most governmental assets are not fungible—that is, available for purposes other than those budgeted—and that records of budgetary compliance are an exceptionally important part of the stewardship responsibility of government. Fund accounting and reporting is necessary (1) to ensure that resources are applied to their designated use and (2) to demonstrate compliance with the various legal and budgetary constraints affecting government. In *GAS No. 34,* released in 1999, GASB recognized that government-wide information is necessary to ensure that the users of financial statements are adequately informed about a government's overall financial circumstances. Thus, if a government's financial statements are asserted to be in conformity with GAAP, its annual financial report must now provide both fund-specific and government-wide information. Accordingly, in addition to financial statements for major funds, *GAS No. 34* requires two government-wide financial statements to be prepared: the statement of net assets and the statement of activities. These statements provide information about the entire government but include separate reports covering the following:

Governmental activities: the traditional activities undertaken by governments, including police and fire protection, education, and other services that are not provided on a fee-for-service basis

Business-type activities: services provided in exchange for a fee; examples include toll roads and certain health care services

Component units: governmental organizations, such as development corporations and city colleges and universities, that are legally separate from the government that established them.

The statement of net assets contains information on (1) all government resources (i.e., assets) that meet certain recognition and display criteria, (2) all government obligations (i.e., liabilities) that meet certain recognition and display criteria, and (3) the government's net assets (i.e., all equity held in the form of assets). Although various standards currently define recognition and display criteria for specific types of assets and liabilities, GASB intends, through future projects, to better define the general criteria for the display and measurement of governmental assets and liabilities. The statement of activities also provides information about revenues (the resources obtained to finance the provision of services) and expenses (the costs of providing those services). The difference between revenues and expenses provides insight into the relationship between the resources being raised to provide services and the costs of those services.

A local government's comprehensive annual financial report (CAFR) is also required to include financial statements presented on a fund basis. GASB distinguishes among major fund types and requires all funds to be classified and reported in the government-wide financial statements in one of three separate fund categories: governmental, proprietary, or fiduciary.

Governmental funds

The five types of governmental funds are the general fund, special-revenue funds, capital projects funds, debt service funds, and permanent funds.

1. The general fund is normally the most significant fund of a local government. It accounts for all resources not otherwise devoted to specific activities, and it finances many basic local government functions, such as general administration and police.
2. Special-revenue funds account for the receipt and expenditure of revenues that have been earmarked for specific activities. For example, a municipality with a special property tax levy for parks might have a park fund, which records receipts and expenditures related to parks.
3. Capital projects funds account for the acquisition of long-lived capital facilities, which may be financed through bond issues, grants-in-aid, or transfers from other funds. This type of fund, which is most closely related to the capital budgeting process, is limited to accounting for receipts and expenditures on capital projects. Any bond issues will be serviced and repaid through debt service funds.
4. Debt service funds account for the interest and principal on general long-term debt. If single-maturity bonds have been issued that call for the establishment of a bond redemption fund, a debt service fund accounts for the accumulation of monies to be used to retire the bonds.
5. Permanent funds account for resources that are legally restricted so that earnings they generate may be used only to support operating activities.

The financial statements required for governmental funds consist of (1) the balance sheet and (2) a statement of revenues, expenditures, and changes in fund balances.

Proprietary funds

The two types of proprietary funds are enterprise funds and internal service funds (ISFs). Enterprise funds account for business-type activities supported largely by user charges. Generally, local government activities such as police and fire protection are financed by taxes and other fixed or restricted revenue sources, and expenditures are controlled by various budgetary processes. Certain business-type activities of governments, however, such as local utilities, golf courses, swimming pools, and toll bridges, are operated so that the costs incurred can be recovered through user fees. To ensure that the user fees are adequate to maintain the service, accounting for such activities is focused on matching revenues to expenses. Because of the differences in revenue sources and in operating and financing objectives, accounting and reporting practices for proprietary activities differ from those for standard governmental activities.

ISFs are similar to enterprise funds except that the services are not rendered to the public but to other governmental units within the same jurisdiction. Departments such as local government garages, central purchasing offices, and even office buildings have been placed under ISFs, both to account for the costs of the services they provide and to encourage economy in the use of those services. If, for example, a central photocopying machine is financed out of a single line item in the budget and is available free to all departments, department heads have little incentive to economize on use of the machine. This is not true, however, if a central duplicating department charges other departments on the basis of use.

Financial statements for proprietary funds consist of (1) the statement of net assets; (2) the statement of revenues, expenses, and changes in the net assets of the fund (or fund equity); and (3) the statement of cash flows.

Fiduciary funds

Fiduciary funds are composed of trust and agency funds and account for assets held for others or for nontax resources held under specific trust instructions. For example, taxes collected for (and to be forwarded to) other governmental units are accounted for in agency funds. Generally, the most important local government fiduciary funds are those associated with retirement systems. Financial statements for fiduciary funds consist of (1) the statement of fiduciary net assets and (2) the statement of changes in fiduciary net assets.

Budgetary accounting and control

GASB literature encourages every governmental unit to adopt an annual budget; it also states that the accounting system should provide the basis for appropriate budgetary control and that a comparison of budgeted with actual expenditures should be provided in the appropriate financial statements. Often, the budget itself is entered into the general ledger, which makes it part of the formal accounting system.

Government budgets represent a mandate for making as well as limiting expenditures, although expenditures may of course be subject to revision if economic or operating circumstances change significantly. Budgeted revenues are referred to as estimated revenues or anticipated assets, and budgeted expenditures are referred to as appropriations or anticipated liabilities. Formal budgets exist for almost all funds and fund types, but at the end of the budgetary period, budget-to-actual comparison reports are usually prepared only for the general and special-revenue funds.

Accounting for governmental funds

Because budgetary compliance is of such great significance in managing governmental activities and because expenditure overages may, if allowed to accumulate, endanger the fiscal health of the whole local government, techniques have been developed to help ensure conformance with budget specifications. Two such techniques are encumbrance accounting and equity reserves.

Encumbrance accounting   Administrators must know how much of an available appropriation is already committed to the acquisition of goods or services. As in commercial accounting, an expenditure and its related liability should be recognized only when the governmental unit incurs an obligation that must be paid. However, once a manager or department head reports an intent to purchase a particular object—even before incurring a definite liability—an encumbrance of funds should be recorded.

Encumbrance accounting is especially desirable for governmental funds in which a maximum expenditure limit is set for each budgetary period (usually a year) because the technique provides early warning if expenditures begin to approach the limit. It also ensures that no unexpected liabilities that must be paid from the current year's budget will emerge after the end of the year. In such a case, a reported encumbrance indicates a lingering commitment.

Encumbrances are often recorded as estimates on the basis of quotes from manufacturers. Expenditures reflect the actual amounts paid. Even though encumbrances appear in the accounting records, they should not be reported in the financial statements as expenditures or liabilities; they are entered instead as reductions in the unreserved fund balance. The reserve-for-encumbrances account should be reported as a reservation of the fund balance committed to a particular future expenditure. This practice is, of course, consistent with the nature of encumbrances and enhances the representational faithfulness of the financial statements. Thus, the local government's fund balance should not show a positive balance unless encumbrances have been accounted for. If an encumbrance lapses (i.e., if the proposed expenditure is never completed), the amount in the reserve-for-encumbrances account should be returned to the unreserved portion of the fund balance account.

The importance of a proper encumbrance system cannot be overemphasized. If administrators do not record encumbrances for orders and commitments, they may be appearing to stay within their budget, but these obligations then become a burden on the next period and may prematurely exhaust that period's appropriation. (For example, some administrators may encourage suppliers to delay rendering goods or services until the next budget period, in order to create the appearance that expenditures for the current year are within budgeted limits.) The payments due on later bills may be delayed again and again, and the deferred payments can eventually constitute a large—and not fully recognized—floating debt.

Nevertheless, one of the problems of budgetary control is that most governmental units are eager to use up their unencumbered balances at the end of the fiscal year, particularly if the unused appropriation is set to expire. This eagerness can lead to a rush of purchase orders in the last days of a fiscal period for items not needed to support current operations. To prevent this type of abuse, the local government manager should examine closely the outstanding encumbrances at the end of the year and, if necessary, cancel them.

Equity reserves   Equity reserves are net resources that can be used only for restricted purposes. Keeping track of equity reserves is a means of achieving budgetary control. In the balance sheet for a governmental fund, the unreserved fund balance should reflect the residual equity that is available for future commitment and expenditure. In the equity section of a fund's balance sheet, the funds in the reserve-for-encumbrances account are not available for expenditure; they reflect the estimate of the resources that have been committed to a particular objective. It is often necessary to create other reserve accounts in order to ensure the accurate reporting of the uncommitted fund balance. For example, when cash is expended to acquire supplies, any unused supplies are shown as assets in the fund's financial statements. But because the supplies are not expendable, it is necessary to reduce the expendable assets portion of the fund's unreserved equity by establishing a reserve for inventory. Figure 8–1 illustrates the structure of a balance sheet for a governmental fund. Figure 8–2, a sample operating statement for the general fund, illustrates the structure of revenues, expenditures, and changes in fund balance for a governmental fund.

Accounting for proprietary funds

When a local government enterprise is run on a fully independent, self-supporting basis, the financial accounting and reporting practices parallel those found in business enterprises. Because proprietary funds must cover all operating costs through user charges, an income determination/capital maintenance accounting model is employed. Such an accounting model measures expenses rather than expenditures. An expenditure reflects the cost of acquiring a good or service. An expense represents, in addition, the expiration of the value of the good or service acquired through the expenditure.

The balance sheets of proprietary funds differ from those of governmental funds in at least two significant ways. First, plant assets (e.g., property, plant, and equipment) used to render services are reported as fund assets, less an allowance for accumulated depreciation. Second, long-term debt incurred by a proprietary fund is reported as a liability of that fund rather than as a liability of the local government as a whole.

For proprietary funds, an income statement that matches revenues and expenses is necessary to report the results of operations. Reporting for proprietary funds also calls for a cash flow statement displaying the receipt and disbursement of cash. This statement summarizes cash flows in four categories: operating activities, investing activities, and two types of financing activities. Because

Assets			Liabilities and fund equity	
Cash		$15,000	Liabilities	
Short-term investment (at cost;			Accounts payable	$10,000
market value 123,000)		120,000	Payroll taxes payable	2,000
Property taxes receivable	$35,000		Total liabilities	12,000
Less allowance for				
uncollectible taxes	3,000	32,000	Fund equity	
Due from other funds		1,500	Reserve for encumbrances	7,000
Inventory of supplies		10,000	Reserve for inventory of	
			supplies	10,000
			Undesignated fund balance	149,500
			Total fund equity	166,500
Total assets		$178,500	Total liabilities and equity	$178,500

Figure 8–1   General fund balance sheet, Trojan City, 31 December 2003.

Classification	Budget ($)	Actual ($)	Actual over-(under-) estimated ($)
Revenues			
Taxes	240,000	290,000	50,000
Licenses and permits	30,000	36,000	6,000
Intergovernmental revenue	120,000	90,000	(30,000)
Charges for services	40,000	45,000	5,000
Fines and forfeitures	6,000	9,000	3,000
Miscellaneous	4,000	10,000	6,000
Total revenues	440,000	480,000	40,000
Expenditures (current)			
General government	45,000	41,000	4,000
Public safety	100,000	98,000	2,000
Highways and streets	60,000	60,000	0
Sanitation	40,000	39,000	1,000
Health	20,000	18,000	2,000
Welfare	30,000	25,000	5,000
Culture and recreation	16,000	13,200	2,800
Education	14,000	12,600	1,400
Capital outlay	75,000	75,000	0
Debt service	25,000	25,000	0
Total expenditures	425,000	406,800	18,200
Excess of revenues over expenditures	15,000	73,200	58,200
Fund balance (beginning of year, January 1)	76,300	76,300	58,200
Undesignated fund balance (end of year, December 31)	91,300	149,500	76,400

Figure 8–2   General fund operating statement.

proprietary funds require recognition of all expenses, it is also necessary to account for fixed assets and their depreciation. To properly match the cost of the asset with the revenue it helps to generate, the cost of a fixed asset (which represents an expenditure of resources at the time of acquisition) must be allocated over the estimated life of the asset. A statement of net assets should also be prepared to communicate information about the resources and obligations of the fund at a particular point in time.

ISFs, which render services to other units of government, should employ the same accounting practices used for proprietary funds. One objective of ISFs should be to break even—to cover costs with the fees earned for services rendered. This objective brings profit-oriented incentives for efficiency and effectiveness into the conduct of governmental operations. In fact, a GASB statement requires all accounting standards applicable to business enterprises to be applied to proprietary-type funds (1) as long as the standards were published on or before December 1, 1989, and (2) unless the standards conflict with or contradict GASB standards.[5] Standards that apply to business enterprises and that were published after November 30, 1989, *may* be applied to proprietary-type funds unless they conflict with GASB pronouncements.

Accounting for fiduciary funds

Accounting and reporting for fiduciary funds should follow either governmental or proprietary practices. For example, if a tax agency fund is used to collect and remit sales taxes for several different levels of government, then the operating and reporting emphasis is on strict accountability for the inflow and outflow of monies. However, if the fiduciary fund is designed to break even, then the income determination/capital maintenance accounting model should be employed.

Other financial reporting

To more fully inform the users of financial statements, GASB now requires supplements to the financial statements that have been discussed so far. Specifically, *GAS No. 34* calls for "management's discussion and analysis," which summarizes the government's financial status and operating results and highlights important financial issues, such as trends or significant events that occurred during the year. In addition, GASB now requires certain information about defined-benefit pension plans sponsored by the government and a statistical section dealing with the demographics and other characteristics of the government and the jurisdiction.

Management accounting and reporting

Management accounting and reporting involves the capture, retention, summary, and display of the information that is used by local government administrators to plan, control, and evaluate the operations for which they are responsible. At the heart of such a system is "responsibility accounting," an approach to management that holds people and programs accountable only for those conditions under their direct influence or control.

One of the principal goals of financial control is to reduce both the likelihood and the potential damage of fraud, including defalcations and deliberately misstated financial statements. Accounting systems generally include features, such as divisions of responsibility, that are designed to prevent employees from perpetrating or concealing such acts. For example, the employee who reviews incoming invoices and approves them for payment should not be the same one who prepares, signs, and transmits checks; the employee who is responsible for receiving and depositing cash receipts should not also have access to the records related to accounts receivable.

Determining and evaluating the costs associated with various activities is central to a well-designed management accounting system. Such costs can then be compared to those for prior periods, to standard or estimated costs, or to the costs for alternative means of achieving the same ends.

Cost determination   Cost determination is central to measuring the economic effort needed to undertake a certain activity. For most of the business-type activities of local government, cost determination primarily involves reclassifying the expense data (expired cost data) that are generated routinely for financial reporting—that is, transferring costs from a general responsibility center to a function or activity center that provides direct services to citizens. This process may be accomplished manually, using relatively simple work sheets, or by computer.

Cost determination for activities that are conducted with resources drawn from the general fund is more difficult and requires additional procedures. Data prepared for financial reporting purposes (i.e., on an expenditure basis) must be converted into data prepared on an expense or cost basis and must be presented in a form that is useful for management reporting purposes. In addition, the expense or cost data must be reclassified to the functional areas that benefited from the expenditures. Because a single government function may be financed and accounted for through several funds, data from several funds may need to be considered. For example, the cost of maintaining public roads and streets may be financed partly from a special gasoline-tax revenue fund and partly from the general fund.

Cost accounting, cost finding, and cost evaluation (which is discussed in detail in a later section of this chapter) are useful procedures for rationally allocating resources and evaluating the efficiency and economy of particular government functions.[6] Cost accounting is the continuous and routine process of capturing, analyzing, classifying, and summarizing cost data within the confines and control of a single accounting system. Results are reported to users on a regular basis. *GASB Codification,* in defining cost accounting, notes that cost accounting assembles and records "all the elements of cost incurred to accomplish a purpose, to carry on an activity or operation, or to complete a unit of work or a specific job."[7] Cost finding, a less formal method of determining costs, may be undertaken on an occasional basis for special purposes.

The total cost of any product or service generally has three components:

Direct materials: the cost of items used directly in the production of a good or service (e.g., asphalt in a street-paving project)

Direct labor: the salaries and other personnel costs related directly to a product or service (e.g., wages for employees working on a street-paving project)

Overhead: the indirect costs associated with the production of a good or service (e.g., employee benefits).

Accounting records are often available for determining the first two components (although, as noted earlier, the data may be reported in several funds). Determining overhead costs, however, may involve substantially greater effort. Analysts attempting to allocate overhead costs to particular projects or services encounter two major problems. First, cost data may be unavailable. If, for example, the cost of the machinery used to pave a street is unknown, surrogates for depreciation (e.g., use allowances) may have to be adopted that approximate the cost expiration or value of use during a period of time. Second, costs that benefit more than one project may be difficult to identify, and allocating such costs may require sophisticated techniques. For example, because fringe benefits such as employee pension costs may be paid from the general fund, they are not necessarily tracked separately or easy to find. It is essential to ensure that all expenses relating to a given activity are allocated to that activity; if such expenses are not considered, the full cost may be understated. Cost-finding techniques may be useful in such situations.

Of the several methods used to resolve these two problems, one—internal service funds (ISFs)—is used in general-purpose financial reporting as well.[8] State and local governments use ISFs to account for the provision of goods and services by one government department (the provider) to others (the consumers). These services are set up like business enterprises but are operated by one government office for other government entities on a fee-for-service basis.

In the professional literature, most discussion of ISFs focuses on the departments that provide the services rather than on those that consume them. But consuming departments and organizations are also a legitimate focus of attention. The use of space in a local government building provides a good illustration. If the building is accounted for through the general fixed assets group of accounts, and building expenses (such as utilities and maintenance) are paid through the general fund, then the local government lacks any means of charging departments for the building space they occupy. This arrangement has two consequences: first, the full costs of operating the various departments are understated; second, because building space is treated essentially as a "free good," departments have no incentive to make efficient use of existing space and tend to ask for additional space without considering its cost. Accounting for building space through an ISF, in contrast, creates an incentive for departments to use only as much space as is efficient for operations. The establishment of an ISF brings a number of additional advantages: (1) full cost information for each user department is generated as a routine bookkeeping function; (2) the real cost of operating each department, including space, is easier to determine; and (3) the property manager is held accountable for the quality and financial success of building operations, which helps meet the goals inherent in responsibility accounting.

Regardless of the methods used to capture cost information, cost determination is only the beginning. A full understanding of the operating and financial characteristics of various activities requires not only cost determination but also careful cost evaluation.

Cost evaluation Whenever a set of costs can be related to an activity, performance and output should be assessed from the perspectives of efficiency and economy. Standards established during planning and forecasting will be useful for such evaluations.

The evaluation of performance usually calls for costs to be classified as either fixed or variable. Fixed costs remain constant, in total, across a range of activity levels, whereas variable costs change with the activity level. Building rent, for example, remains constant under the current lease regardless of what the building is used for. The total cost of fuel, in contrast, changes with the amount of vehicle use and the market price of fuel. Within a given range of activity levels, variable costs per unit of activity tend to remain constant, but fixed costs per unit of activity change as activity levels change—decreasing as output increases and increasing as output decreases. However, because of the limited capacities of any facility, production cannot be expanded indefinitely; thus, capacity establishes the ceiling of activity levels to be considered.

Under static, line-item budgeting, the traditional method for controlling expenditure levels, expenditure lines reflect a single, constant level of activity. Although revisions may be made as necessary in the course of the budgetary period, a maximum expenditure level is established and expenditures are compared with this figure regardless of any discrepancies between actual activity levels and the estimates underlying the original budget. This method is unsatisfactory, however, for program evaluation and management control.

An improvement on traditional budgeting is the flexible budget, which is designed for many levels of activity rather than for one single level. Allowing expenses or expenditures to vary facilitates the evaluation of the financial aspects of an operation because it allows comparisons between estimated and actual costs at a given activity level.

Three separate and distinct steps are necessary to set up flexible budgeting procedures.

1. Before the operating period begins, a static budget is prepared on the basis of a relevant measure of anticipated future activity.
2. After the operating period ends, a flexible budget is developed on the basis of the *actual* activity level during the past operating period. (When the original static budget is tailored to a flexible budget, it is essential to take into account the distinction between fixed and variable costs.)
3. Actual expenses are then compared with the amounts allowed in the flexible budget. Any significant disparity should be analyzed to determine the need for corrective management action.

The evaluation of the disparities between the flexible budget and actual costs is called variance analysis. Variance analysis can take many forms, and the types of analysis described in the following paragraphs will not necessarily be appropriate for all situations. At least three types of variance should be considered:

Spending. A spending variance is the difference between actual costs and those predicted in the flexible budget. The fixed costs assumed in this type of variance analysis are the same as those in the static budget because they are not, by definition, expected to change with the activity level. Analysis of a spending variance is concerned only with the difference between expected and incurred costs at the actual activity level.

Usage. Usage (or volume) cost variances reflect the economies or diseconomies of use that result when the same total fixed costs are spread over greater or fewer units of activity. For example, if the activity level is higher than that anticipated in the static budget, then each unit of activity absorbs a smaller fixed cost. An analysis of usage variance identifies the economic impact of using a facility more or less extensively than was originally anticipated.

Efficiency. Analyzing efficiency (i.e., determining time variance) means comparing the actual number of hours required to accomplish the activity with the number of hours anticipated in the flexible budget. For example, if the flexible budget indicates that it should take 100 hours to process one million gallons of sewage but 120 hours were actually required, the time variance will be unfavorable. The variance is then translated into dollars so that the economic consequences will be clear.

Variances demonstrate only the degree of departure from management plans. They are red flags that indicate the need for further study. Once detailed variance analyses have been conducted, the next step is to determine the underlying causes of the variances. Spending variances, for example, may be caused by a rate of inflation that is higher than expected and may thus represent a forecasting deficiency rather than an operational problem. Efficiency variances may occur when the activities undertaken are more wide ranging or complicated than anticipated and may thus indicate not poor management but the need to allocate additional resources. At times, a careful analysis of unfavorable variances may reveal that the level of performance was actually higher than anticipated. In general, the combination of flexible budgeting and detailed variance analysis provides a powerful tool for evaluating performance.

In sum, management accounting techniques provide a dynamic basis for predicting, understanding, and controlling operations. Employed wisely, such controls can provide early warning of adverse economic and operational circumstances. Static budgets, although useful for some purposes, cannot provide the data necessary to evaluate governmental efficiency and effectiveness. The management practices recommended here are designed not as substitutes for but as supplements to standard budgeting. They are designed to ensure (1) compliance with laws and regulations, (2) legal control of expenditures, and (3) financial reporting in conformity with GAAP.

Compliance reporting

Local government accounting and reporting systems should be capable of providing specified information to a variety of regulatory or granting authorities. A local government developing an accounting system must take such reporting needs into account to ensure that the system will make it possible to meet all financial, managerial, and compliance reporting requirements.

Accounting reports to granting or regulatory authorities are designed to demonstrate that specific and restricted resources have been applied to the performance of specified functions or activities. Although many of the general aspects of financial and managerial reporting may apply to compliance reporting as well, there are several notable differences. For example, granting agencies frequently reimburse the recipient government for costs necessarily incurred in administering the grant program; but, under the terms of the grant, such allowable or refundable costs may be defined in such a way that special cost-finding techniques are required. It is thus important to identify all the costs that are related to a grant program and to establish a cost-accounting system capable of capturing data that conform to the grant provisions.

Grant provisions often require matching contributions from the recipient government. Whereas cash, supplies, or services are often easily identified, other contributions made by the local government, especially certain in-kind contributions, may be more difficult to trace. For example, the depreciation of equipment used in a program may qualify as a matching contribution. Labor expended on a grant-funded program may also qualify as a matching contribution even if employees do not devote all their time to the program. Careful accounting records and sound allocation practices will help ensure the reimbursement of all allowable costs for matching contributions.

Auditing

There are three principal types of audits: financial audits, single audits, and performance audits.

A financial audit determines whether the financial reports of an audited entity are presented fairly and whether the governmental unit has complied with applicable laws and regulations. Financial auditing is primarily concerned with detecting errors and fraud in the financial statements; errors are defined as unintentional misstatements, and fraud is defined as intentional misstatements. The category of fraud includes defalcations—deliberate alterations of financial statements and unlawful depletion of resources. An audit conducted in accordance with professional standards provides reasonable assurance that errors and fraud will be detected and reported. In addition, because financial audits require the auditors to consider the entity's internal control structure as it relates to assertions made in the financial statements, any significant shortcomings in the system are likely to be identified. Management can then take action to correct the identified deficiencies, thereby reducing the organization's vulnerability to both errors and fraud.

The Single Audit Act of 1984 (as amended) was a major step toward providing uniform, entitywide audits of governmental recipients of federal financial assistance. In essence, this act requires single audits of all governmental recipients of federal funds that exceed $300,000 in any fiscal year. Each single audit has two general objectives:

1. To determine whether the financial statements present fairly and in accordance with GAAP (1) the local government's financial position and results of operations and (2) the schedule of expenditures for federal awards
2. To determine whether the local government is in compliance with applicable laws and regulations with respect to expenditures of federal awards.

Generally, single audits focus more closely on the expenditure of grant resources than do other types of audits.

Performance audits are of two types: economy and efficiency audits and program audits. Economy and efficiency audits determine whether the governmental unit is acquiring, protecting, and using its resources economically and efficiently and whether it has complied with laws and regulations on matters of economy and efficiency. Program audits determine the extent to which desired results are being achieved and analyze related compliance issues.[9]

The use of performance auditing is increasing, but generally accepted standards for conducting audits with a broad scope have not yet been established at the level of detail that is applicable to financial and compliance audits. Before establishing audit programs and objectives, local government managers should consider carefully both the potential benefits and the limitations of performance auditing.

Modern auditing techniques are capable of both addressing compliance and providing valuable management tools for asset control and project evaluation. Although independent external auditors are available to provide evaluations on a contract basis, it is often desirable to maintain an internal audit department as well. However, because internal auditors are local government employees, it is important to establish controls to ensure the independence and competence of the internal audit department and the quality of the audits it conducts. Figure 8–3, which summarizes the provisions of the government auditing standards published by the U.S. General Accounting Office (GAO), may be useful as a self-evaluation guide for local governments establishing an internal audit function.

Summary

Accounting and reporting systems for state and local governments, like the information systems used in commerce and industry, must be capable of meeting many diverse requirements and operational reporting objectives. With GAAP as

---

General standards

Auditor qualifications
1. Continuing education requirements
2. Staff knowledge and skills

Independence
1. Personal impairments (e.g., official or personal relationships or biases such as political convictions)
2. External impairments (e.g., restrictions on the scope of work or time allowed)
3. Organizational independence
   a. Internal auditors: Audit organizations outside the staff or line management function of the unit under audit.
   b. External auditors: Elected auditors and those appointed by legislative bodies

Due professional care
1. Compliance with governmental auditing standards
2. Sound judgment

Quality control
1. Presence of internal quality control program
2. Participation in external quality control program

Fieldwork standards

Audit planning
1. Communication (between auditor and entity being audited, regulators, and others)
2. Auditor follow-up on findings from prior audits

Fraud, illegal acts, and other noncompliance
1. Auditor understanding of possible fraud and applicable laws and regulations

2. Due care in pursuing indications of fraud, illegal acts, or other noncompliance with laws and regulations
3. Forms of noncompliance other than illegal acts (e.g., violations of contracts and grant agreements)

Internal controls
1. Safeguarding of assets
2. Control over compliance with laws and regulations

Working papers
Sufficient to support knowledgeable review of evidence gathered and significant conclusions and judgments

Financial-related audits
1. American Institute of Certified Public Accountants standards
2. Follow-up and documentation

Reporting standards

Reporting on compliance with generally accepted government auditing standards

Reporting on compliance with laws and regulations

Reporting on internal control over financial reporting
1. Written reports on financial statements, internal control, and compliance
2. Scope of audit performed
3. Fraud, illegal acts, and other noncompliance
4. Deficiencies in internal control

Privileged and confidential information

Report distribution

Figure 8–3   Subjects covered by the U.S. General Accounting Office audit standards.

their underlying framework, accounting and reporting systems should assist in external decision making; provide operational information to management; provide adequate internal accounting controls to monitor expenditures; and demonstrate compliance with the budget and with various laws, regulations, and grant requirements. The usefulness of accounting data is limited only by the imagination and creativity of the information users and the reporting capabilities of the system. It is essential that accounting professionals determine the information needs of the users so that an effective system that is responsive to those needs can be designed.

Budgetary accounting practices strengthen the controls over expenditures from governmental funds. Encumbrance accounting and the use of equity reserves support other budgetary control measures, helping to ensure compliance with the budget and with laws and regulations. Cost accounting and cost finding represent valuable tools for government managers attempting to evaluate performance. Accounting control tools such as flexible budgeting and variance analysis are being adopted by more and more local government units. The development of user-friendly computer systems capable of amassing and holding tremendous amounts of data should give financial managers increasing control over financial operations and aid in the identification of uneconomic activities.

The rise of intergovernmental financial activity has required more sophisticated reporting systems. Intergovernmental grants, contracts, and other resource transfers necessitate special-purpose compliance reports and have led to higher standards of accountability.

Finally, the increased use of performance auditing has complemented traditional financial and compliance auditing to make the audit function more valuable to local government managers. Audits that report on the efficiency and economy of operations as well as on program effectiveness have become popular as government officials respond to tighter budgetary constraints. Audits conducted in accordance with GAO standards provide support for decisions on resource allocations and program funding. The results of such audits are useful in communicating the quality of management to taxpayers and bondholders.

1   See Governmental Accounting Standards Board (GASB), *Statement of Governmental Accounting Standards No. 34: Basic Financial Statements—and Management's Discussion and Analysis—for State and Local Governments* (Norwalk, Conn.: GASB, 1999).

2   Budgetary compliance refers to the government's adherence to the legally adopted budgets that govern its spending. Fiscal compliance refers to the government's adherence to other laws and regulations that may limit expenditures—for example, laws that prohibit the use of governmental funds for the acquisition of alcoholic beverages.

3   Marshall S. Armstrong, "Some Thoughts on Substantial Authoritative Support," *Journal of Accountancy* (April 1969): 50.

4   Governmental Accounting Standards Board (GASB), *National Council on Governmental Accounting Statement No. 1* (Norwalk, Conn.: GASB, 2002), para. 16.

5   Governmental Accounting Standards Board (GASB), *Accounting and Financial Reporting for Proprietary Funds and Other Governmental Entities That Use Proprietary Fund Accounting, Statement of Governmental Accounting Standards No. 20* (Norwalk, Conn.: GASB, 1993).

6   At least four specific steps are necessary: (1) activity identification—the selection of a meaningful measure of productivity for a project; (2) cost identification—the isolation of costs incident to conducting the activity identified in step 1; (3) cost and activity data accumulation—the capture, retention, and reporting of information specified in steps 1 and 2; and (4) evaluation—the analysis of the data to uncover the relationship between the outputs measured in step 1 and the inputs measured in step 2. This chapter concentrates on steps 2 and 4.

7   Governmental Accounting Standards Board (GASB), *GASB Codification* (Norwalk, Conn.: GASB, 2003), app. B.

8   For example, see Robert J. Freeman, Harold H. Hensold, and William W. Holder, "Cost Accounting and Analysis in State and Local Governments," in *The Managerial and Cost Accountant's Handbook,* ed. Homer A. Black and James D. Edwards (Homewood, Ill.: Dow Jones–Irwin, 1979), 794–839.

9   U.S. General Accounting Office, Controller General of the United States, *Government Auditing Standards* (Washington, D.C.: U.S. Government Printing Office, 2002).

Enterprise resource planning systems

ROWAN A. MIRANDA

Information technology (IT) is the single greatest factor facilitating change in the administration of modern government organizations. Since the early 1980s, new technologies have transformed nearly every aspect of public management and service delivery. Technology improves organizational productivity by increasing efficiency in transaction processing and promoting collaboration across business units. The current generation of information systems is having an immense impact on the internal business processes of government and on the ways in which public agencies communicate, collaborate, and transact business with external parties.

Advances in IT have changed financial management systems in several notable ways. Compared with the previous generation of systems, financial systems today can accomplish a much broader range of functions. Modern systems are also implemented and maintained differently from systems of the past. In the 1970s and 1980s, when a government installed an IT system, the software was often customized (i.e., the software manufacturer's code was rewritten) to fit existing business processes. But the expense and complexity of rewriting computer code made systems costly to maintain and difficult to upgrade. As software vendors developed new releases, many governments faced the choice of either customizing each new release or skipping the upgrade releases altogether, which guaranteed system obsolescence.

Modern systems, by contrast, are designed to resist obsolescence (at least as long as the software company is in business) because systems are installed "plain vanilla," with little or no customization, and upgraded approximately every two years to keep pace with new technology.

Yet another important difference is that today's systems are positioned to exploit the opportunities provided by the Internet to improve financial processes and reduce transaction costs for citizens, suppliers, and employees. In particular, the Internet has allowed the reengineering of paper-based processes in many areas (e.g., procurement, accounts payable) that have historically given government a reputation for duplication and red tape. Governments are also providing Web-based services in response to rising expectations from citizens, who conduct more and more of their personal business electronically. In essence, financial systems are expected to serve as the backbone for digital government strategies. It is the integration of "back-office" administration and "front-office" service delivery that is motivating governments to replace older financial systems with enterprise-wide software solutions.

This chapter discusses the state of the art of the technology that local governments of all types and sizes use to perform financial management and administrative tasks. It begins by examining how and why the financial systems of the past evolved into the more comprehensive systems of today. The chapter then describes the major components of a typical enterprise resource planning (ERP) software package (e.g., general ledger, accounts payable, procurement) and the technology architecture that serves as the platform for integration and process improvement.

How should governments go about procuring a new system? A needs assessment, which local governments use to determine if there is a business case for system replacement, is a key ingredient of systems planning. If the needs assessment determines that system replacement is appropriate, the local government then confronts a bewildering array of products and services. Thus, the next section of the chapter covers the system acquisition process, including requirements definition, vendor evaluation, and contract negotiations. The chapter then covers the next major challenge, system implementation, in detail. Finally, the last section of the chapter considers to what extent the new generation of information systems can guide the improvement of local government operations in general, and financial management in particular.

The evolution of financial systems

Journal entries, purchase orders, vendor payments, timekeeping, payroll checks, and grant billing are all examples of tasks that, without the use of technology, would overwhelm governments. The first computerized systems used by governments in the 1970s and 1980s—software systems that ran on mainframe computers—were designed to automate the repetitive aspects of many administrative tasks and to facilitate basic reporting on financial performance. Since the financial system had to exchange data with other administrative functions (e.g., to extract payroll data from a human resource application), computer code, or "interfaces," provided a bridge that allowed data to be transmitted from one system to another.

Many of the original financial systems were custom built to serve the particular processes of each government. Once they had been built, governments found it difficult to rewrite the code to facilitate new processes or to embrace improvements in technology. As "off-the-shelf" commercial packages came into vogue, system development became less expensive (in comparison to custom-built applications), but the available software still had two disadvantages: rigidity and proprietary technology. As governments purchased and built more systems (e.g., time and attendance, vendor registration, asset management) to address the limitations of the main financial system, the entire computing environment fragmented, and it became necessary to design even more interfaces so that the off-the-shelf packages could exchange data with each other.

Legacy systems had a number of disadvantages: first was their rigidity and proprietary nature, which led to widespread end-user dissatisfaction. Second, in older systems, transactions had to be aggregated and processed all at once—an approach known as batch processing. In contrast to systems that provide "real-time" information, batch processing requires decision makers to rely on data that are neither timely nor complete. Third, a considerable amount of time passed before users were notified that their transactions were error free and had been accepted by the system. Finally, legacy systems made it difficult to access and share information, could not maintain transaction histories, offered rudimentary budget controls and inflexible budget formats, provided weak audit trails and drill-down capabilities, led to the proliferation of conflicting information, and created year-end closing difficulties. A key improvement in modern systems is that transaction processing and information access (e.g., query capability) occur on an online, real-time basis.

With the personal computer revolution of the 1980s, government users took matters into their own hands and addressed some of their needs through low-cost spreadsheet and database software. Unfortunately, department- or agency-specific systems soon littered the government landscape with applications that did not "speak" to one another, further fragmenting information access and compartmentalizing business processes. Since centralized support for all these systems was impractical, individual departments and users slowly wrested control of applications development away from central IT. Government IT budgets were consumed by the effort involved in maintaining a fragmented technology environment: multiple software products that were manufactured by different software vendors, that relied on diverse technology platforms, and that were embedded with inconsistent business processes.

The need to consolidate information, link business processes and functions, and arrest the development of departmental systems in favor of a single "enterprise" system gave rise to a new generation of software: enterprise resource planning systems. In ERP, *enterprise* connotes that the software has an organization-wide impact; *resource* indicates that the system focuses on the management of both financial and nonfinancial resources; and *planning* implies that, in contrast to the retrospective focus of most accounting systems, the system seeks to shape an organization's strategic decision making.[1] ERP software products connect financial (e.g., accounting, budgeting) and nonfinancial (e.g., human resource, fleet management) applications through a common relational database, user-friendly interface, and embedded processes designed to tie functions together seamlessly.

The components of enterprise resource planning systems

Traditional financial systems handled core accounting, budgeting, procurement, and payroll-related functions. All other administrative software (e.g., human resources, fleet management) was typically either custom built using raw programming code or manufactured by a vendor other than the financial system vendor. Interfaces were used to make the entire computing maze work; thus, an upgrade (either to the main financial system or to a stand-alone system) often necessitated a redesign of the interfaces. If the interface was based on batch processing, data could not be accessed by one function from another on a real-time basis. ERP systems not only integrate areas outside of finance but also offer new applications in other areas, such as operations management, supply-chain management, and human resources (see Figure 9–1). This section of the chapter describes the major components of an ERP system.

Financial management applications

Financial management applications include the general ledger; budget preparation software; accounts payable; accounts receivable; procurement; project accounting; payroll and time-and-attendance; fixed assets; and grants management.

General ledger The main accounting and budget control functions in an ERP system are conducted through the general ledger (GL). As the repository of accounting transactions, the GL is arguably the single most important module in an ERP system.

The GL is used to produce the major financial reports issued by local governments: the comprehensive annual financial report (CAFR), the single audit, and interim financial reports. An important feature of the GL is a flexible chart of accounts (COA) that (1) categorizes accounting transactions (e.g., assets, liabilities, fund equity, revenues, and expenses), (2) facilitates costing by program and activity, and (3) permits mass account changes (e.g., a restatement of financial results such as might be required by a government reorganization). Real-time validation of journal entries, which permits immediate verification of batch and journal totals, is another useful feature. Other capabilities include

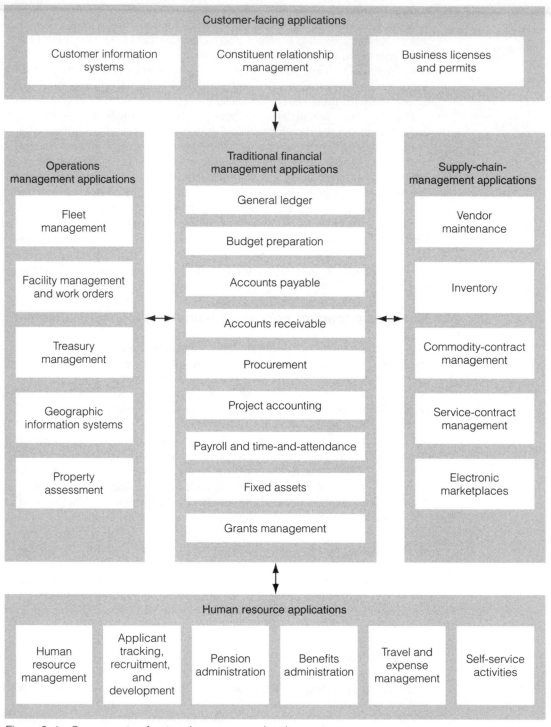

Figure 9–1   Components of enterprise resource planning systems.

cost allocations; accounting for different fund types; drill-down features, which permit end-users to reach the source document that supports a journal entry; and audit trails, which make it possible to view the entire history of changes to a record in the database.

Public sector ERP packages provide budget control as a feature within the GL module. Basic budget control includes appropriation control, allotments, and budget tracking by project or grant. Sophisticated systems allow the user to set (1) encumbrance and pre-encumbrance controls, (2) tolerances for transactions (e.g., to permit an invoice that exceeds the encumbrance level by 3 percent), and (3) custom controls at different organizational levels (e.g., at the division level for parks, at the station level for police). Budget modules also permit multiyear budgeting, allow spending authority to be linked to revenue collections, and support activity-based budgeting. Transactions that "hit" the GL must pass through "budget checking," which validates the availability of funding before an obligation is incurred.

The GL is typically installed first; other modules are then plugged onto it. Since nearly all financial modules require the GL, it is generally not an optional module. For example, a purchase order can result in an encumbrance and a reservation of fund balance. Integration of the database allows the procurement module to instantly update the GL (although other transaction details—such as item, vendor, and contract number—are relevant to the procurement function only).

Budget preparation   In many ERP software products, technology for budget preparation is still in its infancy. Part of the reason is that many public sector ERP products are derived from software originally developed for commercial use. Since commercial budgeting practices differ significantly from those in the public sector, budgeting modules rarely meet public sector needs. Instead of examining what budget modules actually do, the next sections describe some of the functionality that budgeting technology is expected to achieve as products improve.

Automated financial control   Budgeting technology is expected to serve as the main vehicle for spending control. Budgetary control at the transaction level typically rests in the GL module. But a broader concept of budgetary control includes the ability to analyze costs, monitor budget execution, and provide position control, all of which would require the budget system to interact with the GL and human resource (HR) modules.[2]

Budget development   Budget development refers to the "painful" side of budgeting: developing budget forms, managing budget versions, amalgamating budget requests, validating calculations, and accessing historical data. Budgeting technology should ease the staff burden and overhead costs of budget development. In particular, budgeting technology should permit the automated "self-assembly" of information submitted by stakeholders across the enterprise, which will ease the development of the budget document itself.

Planning and forecasting   Planning and forecasting are basic administrative functions. A fundamental tenet of administration holds that it is desirable to anticipate change in the organizational, economic, or political environment and to assess its impact on the level and allocation of resources. Budgeting technology permits the forecasting of revenues and expenditures and facilitates planning by projecting the impact of current programs on future budgets.

Analysis and reporting   An organization's transactional history is an important resource for planning and budgeting. Budgeting technology should facilitate data analysis and information access, making it possible to deliver high-quality reports that are closely tailored to the needs of diverse user groups. Once a data warehouse of budgetary information is developed, it is easier to make use of advanced capabilities such as performance measurement.

Collaboration   Budgets that minimize the input of stakeholders lack credibility. Budgeting technology should accommodate top-down goal setting, bottom-up feedback, and collaboration on an enterprise-wide basis. By allowing a large number of staff to provide input, budget preparation that takes advantage of Web technology can help reconcile competing interests.

In recent years, the use of business intelligence (BI) and online analytical processing (OLAP) software has improved the capabilities of ERP systems in the area of budgeting. Budget applications permit users to analyze historical budget data, develop "what-if" scenarios (e.g., *X* increase in salaries will have *Y* impact on benefit costs), and conduct financial forecasts. It is fair to state that the more sophisticated the budgeting approach, the greater the benefits of integration provided by ERP software.

Accounts payable   The accounts payable (AP) module is used to process invoices and record liabilities. Baseline functionality includes shared vendor master files, 1099 processing, liquidation of associated encumbrances, and automated bank reconciliation. AP systems permit users to establish tolerances (e.g., 3 percent over encumbrance), perform electronic data interchange (EDI), and evaluate receipt settlement; they also facilitate the use of procurement cards. Some systems also permit four-way matching (requisition, purchase order, invoice, and receiver document) and allow suppliers to review payment status.

The AP module often requires the GL to be installed for proper checking and updating of budgetary spending authority. Enhanced AP features will also require the installation of the procurement and accounts receivable module.

Accounts receivable   The accounts receivable (AR) module is used to record receivables, recognize revenue, track the status of payments received, and analyze delinquent accounts. Just as the AP module requires a vendor master file, the AR module relies on a master customer table. Typical features include the preparation of customer statements, maintenance of customer sales history, revenue budget updating, and the reduction of receivables upon payment. Most systems can handle internal charges and cash transfers, electronic fund transfers (EFTs), pooled cash accounting, and modified accrual for intergovernmental grants. Invoicing may be included with this module or may be provided in a separate billing module. Most AR modules are general in nature and cannot support detailed needs for property tax, income tax, or utility billing functions. The AR system also requires the GL to be installed for proper checking and updating of revenue budgets.

The billing subsystem of AR is used to process bills and to generate invoices and dunning letters on overdue invoices. This module is sometimes packaged with AR or can come separately. Common features include billing cycle establishment, bill consolidation, invoice creation, and bill adjustments. Billing systems can (1) group invoices by zip code to support bulk mailing, (2) produce itemized bills, and (2) support electronic billing. Like the AR module, the billing subsystem is general in nature and is not always suited to specialized requirements for taxes and utilities.

Procurement   Most traditional financial systems include basic procurement functionality. Advanced capabilities—referred to collectively as supply-chain management (discussed later)—are available primarily in high-end ERP systems.

A transaction within the procurement module affects many other modules in a system, including GL, AP, fixed assets, and inventory. Integration permits an automated procure-to-pay process. Common features include the online requisition and creation of purchase orders, blanket releases, maintenance of contract items, inventory replenishment, use of approved supplier lists, and enforcement of budgetary encumbrances.[3] Leading-edge procurement systems offer electronic catalogs and provide features that streamline the procurement process by making it paperless. Some systems have features that permit contract management, bid package development, and bid tabulation. Finally, some systems permit the distribution of expenses across multiple departments, programs, or other cost center categories.

Project accounting   Project accounting consists of project budgeting, funding-source management, and project management. The project accounting module is used to help manage internal projects and capital projects. Project activity is recorded by current budget year and over the life of the project. Usually, projects are linked to a funding source, such as a bond or grant, and project appropriation is based on the availability of funds. Although most systems will allow users to establish annual project budgets, project finances can also be subdivided into tasks and activities. Projects recorded within the system can be used across funds, departments, and business units (e.g., a capital project may require charges to multiple funds and/or departments). The most sophisticated project accounting systems have built-in project management capabilities. Users can alter or change project budgets and allocations by changing activities on the project management chart.

The project accounting module often requires the GL to be installed for proper checking and updating of budgets. Since the project management capabilities of the ERP system may be too basic, a third-party project management software package (i.e., a package not manufactured by the ERP vendor) may be warranted, depending on the needs of the government.

Payroll and time-and-attendance   The payroll and time-and-attendance modules are used to enter timesheets and produce paychecks, employee tax reports, and 1099 forms for vendors. Payroll and timekeeping are usually separate modules, and governments often enter time manually into the payroll system instead of using a timekeeping application.

Automatic deposit and manual check-writing capabilities are typical features of payroll modules. Sophisticated payroll modules can use information on employee deductions (e.g., pension contributions, tax withholding) to set up AP transactions and to produce garnishment checks. After each pay cycle, the payroll module sends accounting information to the GL for posting (i.e., each department or program is charged with its share of the salary costs). The payroll module usually requires basic HR components to be installed so that employee data (e.g., salaries, years of service) can be accessed.

The data used to calculate payroll and produce payroll checks are generally fed from the HR management and timekeeping modules to the payroll module. Although the time and attendance module is not part of every ERP application, it is critical to a payroll system. Since most of their resources are spent on salaries and wages, governments are starting to use online time entry to improve cost accounting. A timekeeping system should be tightly integrated with the payroll system, and should allow employees to independently enter time worked and leave time. Because the data can be reviewed, updated if necessary, and approved without rekeying, this arrangement obviates duplicate entry of data to generate paychecks. Another major benefit of an automated timekeeping system is that because pay and work rules are configured in the system—and are therefore uniformly applied to all employees, rather than being subject to the interpretation of payroll clerks and supervisors—fewer corrections need to be made.

Fixed assets   As its name implies, the fixed-assets module is used to record information about an entity's physical assets. Information that is often recorded includes serial number, location, description, insurance information, cost, and replacement cost. Fixed-asset transactions such as transfers, additions, deletions, and damages are also recorded in the system. The system allows accountants to maintain depreciation information and to apply different depreciation methods to each asset. In sophisticated systems, rules for defining a fixed asset can be set so that any transaction in the procurement or AP module triggers a transaction in the fixed-asset module. Other features include schedule reminders, electronic imaging, electronic tagging, and inventory integration. The fixed-asset module usually requires the GL to be installed.

Grants management   The grants management module is used to record grant activity, draw-downs in funds, information about the grantor, who applied for the grant, and when the grant was awarded. These systems will also flag underspending and the anniversary dates of applications.

Grants management software allows a grant to be set up as a funding source for a single project or multiple projects. Other features include the ability to record expenditures and related activity by period or over the life of the award. To make optimal use of the grants management module, the GL and the project accounting, AP, AR, and procurement modules usually need to be in place.

Human resource applications

The human resource function encompasses HR management (e.g., storage of employee data); applicant tracking, recruitment, and development; pension and benefits administration; travel and expense management; and certain activities that are handled by employees and managers on a self-service basis. The HR modules are almost always implemented at the same time as the payroll module. Many management questions (e.g., "What is the cost of program *X?*") require that the HR and financial modules be integrated; ERP systems provide such integration.[4]

Human resource management   The HR management component of the HR module is used to record personnel information from job application to retirement.[5] This component can be used to record basic demographic data, addresses, emergency contacts, budget data (e.g., salary, wages), and department assignments.

Some systems include features that can (1) read résumés and automatically enter pertinent information into applications, (2) provide employees with e-mail notification of certain important dates (e.g., benefits elections, training), and (3) assist with position control. The HR management component of the HR module is used to record the most comprehensive personnel information and, like the GL, is generally treated as the central module to which other components are linked.

Applicant tracking, recruitment, and development   The applicant tracking, recruitment, and development component of the HR module is designed to facilitate the hiring and training of the organization's workforce. The component provides for rules-based budget control and has the capability to create and monitor personnel requisitions; manage all applicant data; track applicants' progress through the hiring chain; and, upon the hiring of an applicant, convert applicant information into a new employee record in HR. Employee development is handled by components that collect information needed for education, skills tracking and matching, career planning, succession planning, organizational charting, and performance evaluations.

Employee development is an important link between individual and organizational goals. Web platforms can further streamline the recruitment process and provide extensive capabilities to manage the recruitment process and track recruitment costs.

Pension administration   Pension administration is the function responsible for the delivery of pension benefits and the accumulation and investment of the long-term assets needed to finance those benefits. The core pension administration software knits together the collection of employer and employee contributions, the tracking of employee service credits, and the payout of benefits at retirement. Pension administration software can also be used to design the pension plan, track contributions, and invest assets.

Some pension plans overlay the core pension administration module with customer relationship management (CRM) software to manage the many telephone (and, increasingly, e-mail and Web) inquiries about plan benefits and the attendant peak workloads.

Benefits administration   The benefits administration component of the HR module handles benefit-plan enrollment and administration, and employee benefit communication. The component is also used to set up employee benefit plan data. Advanced systems can (1) record benefits for each family member of an employee, (2) record COBRA (Consolidated Omnibus Budget Reconciliation Act) benefits, and (3) track information related to HIPAA (Health Insurance Portability and Accountability Act) requirements. Proper functioning of the benefits administration component requires employee data and benefit plans to be linked; thus, the HR module must be installed.

The benefits administration function has been significantly improved by Web platforms that permit employees to select and change benefit packages.

Travel and expense management   The travel and expense management component of the HR module improves transaction-processing efficiency and financial control by managing the entire life cycle (e.g., planning, accounting, and payment) of travel-related expenditures. Baseline functionality includes the accounting, taxation, and payment elements of employee travel and expense management.

Information captured by the accounting component is passed along to the AP module for reimbursement processing. The integration of the travel and expense management component with the rest of the ERP system provides multiple ways to reimburse employees; provides managers with greater detail regarding travel-related costs (including analysis of expenses by category, such as vendor, expense type, employee, and division); and permits efficient processing of forms from initial entry through reimbursement.

Self-service activities   As governments shift away from paper-based processes, incorporating self-service into a comprehensive system reduces the burden on employees, managers, and HR staff alike. In addition to being user-friendly and readily accessible (e.g., via a desktop Web browser or a central kiosk), self-service features provide opportunities to directly engage participants in business processes (e.g., obtaining reimbursement for travel, making changes to personnel data, selecting benefits, enrolling in training). And through that engagement, both employees and managers are, in effect, collaborating with the organization to make those processes more efficient for all parties.

Supply-chain-management applications

The procurement function has been a feature of traditional financial systems for some time. As is clear from the five sections that follow, ERP systems now provide software for a government's entire supply chain.

Vendor maintenance   The vendor maintenance component of the supply-chain-management module consists of a comprehensive vendor file that can be shared throughout the organization. The component allows an organization (1) to identify vendors for reporting and analysis and (2) to track basic vendor information (e.g., address, telephone number, taxpayer identification number, type of organization, products or services supplied, minority or disadvantaged business status). The integration of the comprehensive vendor file with the procurement module allows analysis of buying patterns by vendor, department, and type of purchase.

Inventory   The inventory component of the supply-chain-management module allows managers to track inventory, automate inventory replenishment, and record inventory usage. Items are usually assigned an inventory number, lot number, and location. The inventory component is typically fed information from the procurement and AP modules. Using these data and user-defined rules, the inventory component can create first-in-first-out (FIFO) and last-in-first-out (LIFO) valuations. Some systems can automatically generate inventory count sheets, place orders to replenish supplies, and record images of items. A fully integrated inventory system will also include inspection capabilities for all organization-wide purchases, bar-coding functionality, and inventory cycle counting. For proper checking and updating of budgetary spending authority for inventory disbursements, the inventory component works best when the GL, procurement, and AP modules are installed.

Commodity-contract management   Contract-management components allow users to track commodity contracts from the bid process through contract execution. For example, these components can track the information both in the main contract header and in the detail lines of a contract. (The main contract header includes the contract number, contract dates, the name of the contractor, and other similar information; the detail lines provide information about individual commodities and the prices for each commodity.)

Contract-management software also assigns legal terms and conditions to contracts, and offers the ability to track delivery and billing provisions. When integrated directly with vendor and commodity files, contract-management software enables an organization to prevent departments from making piecemeal purchases at higher prices outside negotiated agreements.

Service-contract management   A service-contract management component allows the organization to track all activities related to open-ended contracts for services such as landscaping, equipment repair, construction, and architectural design. Such systems usually have the capability to track contract start and end dates, contract expirations, maintenance scheduling, and details of specific activities. They can also provide cash flow analysis and revenue recognition and allocation. In most ERP systems, the service-contract management component is integrated with project management and work order modules to schedule and authorize jobs.

Electronic marketplaces The emergence of electronic commerce offers many opportunities for increased efficiency and the reform of government procurement. Electronic marketplaces, one approach to increasing efficiency, allow governments to make purchases from predefined lists of vendors that may provide traditional bids or auction bids. In recent years, some firms have launched B2B (business-to-business) electronic marketplaces, which interface with the procurement and supply-chain-management components of ERP systems and can generate up-to-the-minute prices. Bidding on government contracts can be an expensive undertaking, but electronic marketplaces reduce transaction costs by promoting competition and broadening access to government bidding opportunities.

Operations management applications

Operations management applications include fleet management, facility management and work orders, treasury management, geographic information systems, and property assessment.

Fleet management The fleet management module tracks vehicles and equipment, parts inventory, parts processing, and work-order processing. A fully integrated system may also include fuel-supply management, driver licensing, accident tracking, and vehicle risk management. In many governments, responsibility for fleet management is spread across departments; modern fleet management systems provide the informational foundation to coordinate fleet operations.

Facility management and work orders Facility management modules are similar in concept to fleet management systems but focus on buildings and other physical facilities. The modules track the resources that are used to complete different work routines on various physical assets. Work on facilities is usually requested by internal customers and is then assigned to technicians for completion. If the facilities management module is integrated with the AR and GL components of the ERP, work-related transactions will automatically generate interdepartmental billings.

Work-order modules allow an organization to track work effort at a summary or detailed level, beginning with the initiation of the work, continuing through resource assignment and inspection, and ending with the completion of the work and the reporting of resource use. Once a specific job is authorized, managers can assign the appropriate staff to complete it. In integrated systems, resource assignment is completed through the use of other modules (e.g., HR for labor, inventory for supplies, and fixed assets for equipment). When the work is complete, work-order systems allow for the work to be tracked in time increments (usually hours or days) and on the basis of system-defined tasks and activities.

Treasury management Treasury management—which is essentially cash management, broadly conceived—involves four tasks: the collection of revenue, the investment of assets, the management and coordination of revenue outflows and disbursements, and the management of banking relations. Investment is thus a core treasury function and must be handled by software that tracks outflows and disbursements.

The revenue collection module handles the activities involved in maximizing the government's revenue intake. The main objectives of revenue collection are to accelerate collections, minimize revenue loss, and establish a secure, documented process that ensures strong internal controls over all cash management activities.

The treasury module generally handles the processing of revenues taken in through cash drawers or lockboxes. The treasury module can have direct feeds to the GL and AR modules. When used with third-party cash-register software products, the treasury module can produce cash tapes and unlock cash drawers. Typical features of the treasury module include on-screen cash control totals, live links to AR, reconciliation by cashier, and the ability to accommodate cashier change-outs.

Geographic information systems   Geographic information systems (GIS) are technologies that link multiple data sources (e.g., demographic, economic, health, infrastructure) to geography. By allowing users to track characteristics that are linked to geographic areas, GIS supports a broad range of local government functions such as land use planning, disaster planning, and demographic analysis.

In the ERP arena, GIS is being used to improve operations management. For example, GIS can provide financial data about a geographic element, such as the total cost of repairing a particular road segment. Advanced GIS functions permit citizens to initiate work-order requests by clicking on maps on a local government's Web site. Citizens can point and click graphics (e.g., streetlights, stormwater drains) on a street map and initiate jobs for government departments.

Property assessment   ERP systems do not typically include tax assessment or tax collection modules. Instead, ERP systems are expected to interface with such systems. (Tax assessment software systems are often referred to as CAMA systems, for computer-assisted mass appraisal.) Because property assessment rules and tax exemptions vary widely across governments, these applications are commonly customized. Although it seems logical to integrate tax collection into ERP systems, business rules governing penalties, seizures, and payments are often unique to the individual local government; thus, tax collection software is likely to remain outside the domain of most ERP products.

Increasingly, taxpayers are using the Internet to inquire about the assessed value, payment status, and assessment criteria of properties.

Customer-facing applications

Customer-facing applications include customer information systems, constituent relationship management technology, and business licenses and permits. By reducing the transaction costs of interactions between citizens and the government, customer-facing applications enable government agencies to be more citizen-friendly.

Customer information systems   Customer information systems (CIS) are software modules that measure usage, conduct billing, and account for revenue for utilities and solid-waste collection. Although such systems have traditionally been focused on properties (because service was delivered to a location rather than to a customer), modern systems are more customer oriented because deregulation has served as a driving force in software development. To permit analyses of service terminations and the application of penalties, the CIS modules are usually integrated with the GL and the AR subsidiary ledger.

Constituent relationship management Improving service and reducing transaction costs are the goals of most governments' digital initiatives, and constituent relationship management (CRM) technology is critical to such efforts. CRM systems enable local governments to manage contacts with citizens through a variety of channels (e.g., phone, walk-in, e-mail) and in a variety of contexts (e.g., complaint tracking, case management). Call centers permit government staff to interact with citizens and customers in a number of formats; for public agencies, automated call centers are a particularly attractive feature of CRM modules. By enabling staff to quickly and easily involve supervisors or field personnel, automated escalation features help achieve prompt resolution of problems. CRM is generally integrated with the GIS, billing, and work-order modules of the ERP system.

Business licenses and permits The business licenses and permits module supports many of the code enforcement functions performed by local governments. From initiating and managing the building permit process to supporting site inspections for fire and public safety, business licenses and permits software helps track, analyze, and bill for regulatory tasks.

So that property uses can be mapped against zoning criteria, the business licenses and permits module is generally integrated with the GIS. To ensure the consistency and timeliness of accounting data and to avoid duplicate data entry, summary information on the collection of fees, fines, and permits is often integrated with the GL.

Technology architecture

Technology architecture is the most important determinant of the overall value an organization will gain from the purchase of an information system. Because systems based on aging standards are likely to face premature obsolescence, it is important for governments to understand the underlying technology of the software products they buy. This section describes the major technology considerations associated with ERP systems.

Architecture choices

There are three principal considerations in the selection of technology architecture: proprietary versus open-source and open-standards technologies; mainframe versus distributed processing; and Web-based versus Web-enabled architecture.

Proprietary versus open-source and open-standards technologies Governments today are moving away from proprietary technologies toward open-source and open-standards technologies. Proprietary technologies are privately owned and developed, and their owners restrict their use. Open-source software is distributed with the source code freely available so that users can customize it as needed. The term *open standards* refers to widely accepted and supported standards that are set by recognized organizations or the commercial marketplace. Modern ERP systems tend to rely on open-source or open-standards technologies, which means that systems can run on a broad range of hardware, operating systems, and databases.

Mainframe versus distributed processing Legacy financial systems often relied on a single mainframe or minicomputer that was linked to personal computers or dumb terminals (i.e., terminals that rely on another computer to process data). But because mainframe-based financial systems were rigid, were expensive to maintain, and relied on proprietary hardware and operating systems, most governments gradually shifted both ERP and other major enterprise applications to a distributed-processing, or client-server, environment. Under the distributed-processing model, the code for the ERP software application and all processing functions resides on an application server and on the many personal computers throughout the organization, and the data reside on a database server.

Although governments achieved better system performance with distributed processing than they had with mainframes, the many components of the technology architecture made the distributed-processing environment difficult to support. As a result, ERP software products are moving back to a reliance on centrally maintained servers. This shift has been made possible by improvements in programming languages and in the processing power of servers. Nevertheless, Web-based architecture, discussed in the next section, is the state of the art in technology architecture for ERP systems.

Web-based versus Web-enabled architecture　Web-based applications can be accessed only through an Internet browser. Typically, the older applications in proprietary languages are rewritten from scratch, using a modern programming language. As shown in Figure 9–2, a common database housed on a server serves as the foundation for all applications, and the entire system is made available to users via a Web server. When an application is Web enabled, only select portions of the product suite are browser based. In a Web-enabled ERP system, for example, employee self-service might be available in a browser-based format, but the GL might not be.

The main benefits of Web-based applications are that they can be made available to many users (inside the organization via an intranet, and outside the organization via an extranet or the Internet) and that the user interface is intuitive (user-friendly). These two advantages make it easy to add new applications and new users, and to train users. Since there is no software code on the client, the application can be accessed through many different vehicles (e.g., kiosks, mobile devices, laptops). Because Web-based applications allow hardware replacement cycles to be extended, require less maintenance, and foster centralized administration of security, it is often argued that such applications result in a lower total cost of ownership.

Although it is true that for large and complex organizations, Web-based architecture is often the only practical way to install an ERP system, Web-based systems are still expensive and are associated with some performance problems. For small and medium-sized jurisdictions, there are affordable, client- or server-based solutions that have a few Web-enabled self-service modules (e.g., benefits administration, vendor self-service) that, taken together, are likely to meet a government's needs.

Architecture components

The architecture components of ERP systems include hardware, a network operating system, database software, graphical user interface, development tool sets, data warehouse software, workflow features, and security features.

Hardware　Most ERP software products work on multiple hardware platforms. The following list describes the basic types of hardware needed.

Application server. This server, often referred to as the enterprise server, runs business software applications.

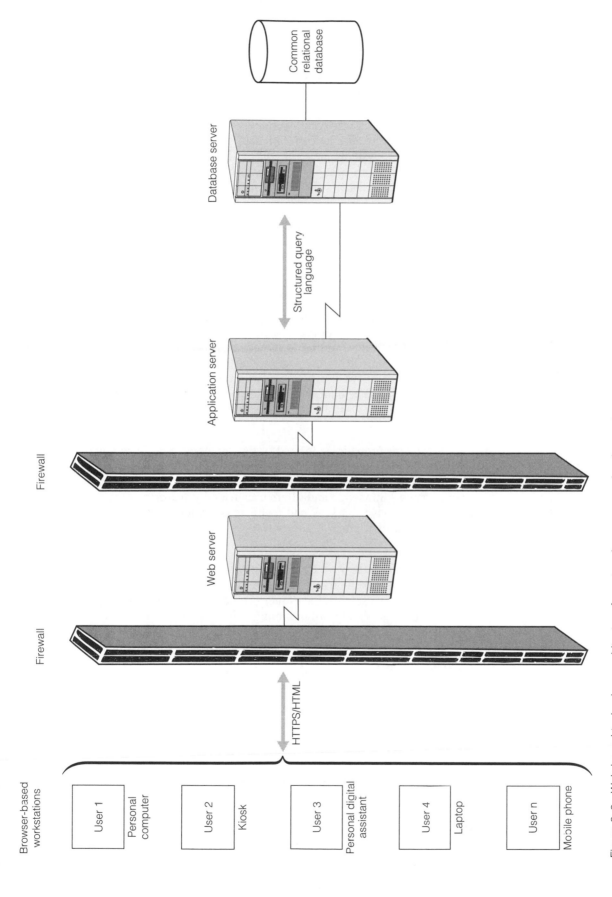

Figure 9–2   Web-based technology architecture for enterprise resource planning systems.

Database server. For efficiency and optimum performance, most database vendors and ERP firms recommend that the enterprise database reside on its own server.

Web server. When a Web interface is part of the software, a Web server is required to manage data processing between the Web browser and the software product.

Client. The end user's desktop computer, also known as the client, is the last piece of the architecture puzzle. In recent years, the number of different clients that ERP systems must support has increased significantly. Interoperability, not only with desktop computers but also with laptops, phones, and personal digital assistants (PDAs), is increasingly common.

Network operating system All the core pieces of the ERP system are tied together through an Internet-friendly network. Mainly for security purposes and to ensure efficient data transmission, the network must be based on the Internet protocol (IP) standard.

Database software ERP systems rely on relational database software to organize records into a series of tables. Under nonrelational structures, cumbersome and meticulous programming is required to navigate a database. Relational databases, by contrast, allow users to easily select files, columns, rows, and named fields using various data-access languages (such as structured query language—SQL). The database structure permits the ERP application to share data across modules within the system.

Graphical user interface Instead of the "green screens" used by older mainframe accounting systems, modern software packages use graphical user interface (GUI) for content delivery. Because GUI technology does not require programming knowledge and offers user-friendly features (such as drop-down menus and a consistent look and feel across modules), it improves productivity and decreases training requirements.

Development tool sets ERP products include powerful development tool sets that enable customers to configure their application (e.g., adding a drop-down menu that uses a logical query, creating a specialized report) without changing the underlying programming code. Since the government IT department does not need to worry about addressing customized software code, such tool sets ease software upgrades and decrease the need for maintenance and support requests.

Data warehouse software A major limitation of legacy systems was that the lack of storage space prevented the archiving of historical financial data. Governments were faced with a choice between retaining limited historical information within the system or relying on paper reports for older data. With the advent of ERP systems, even more vast volumes of data had to be archived and managed. A sharp drop in the cost of storage, combined with the increased need for storage that was associated with ERP systems, gave rise to the development of data warehouse software. Data warehouse software permits the government to combine data from different types of enterprise applications, including those outside the ERP, into one database. Most data warehouses rely on powerful query tools that enable users to mine the data.

Workflow features Workflow features, the main path to a paperless government environment, permit the electronic routing of key documents that result from a business process or transaction. Workflow routes transactions via e-mail on the basis of roles and rules. For example, a system that uses workflow features might be set up to automatically route all purchasing transactions over $500 to a purchasing supervisor who has approval authority.

Security features Security regulates who has access to information and how and when such access is granted. From an end-user standpoint, "security" means employing a user name and a password. For the technology staff, security is a broader concept that may mean ensuring the security of databases, menus, records, and fields.

Systems planning and acquisition

To acquire an ERP system, a government must evaluate several types of vendors, including ERP software firms, implementation firms, hardware companies, and software firms whose products (e.g., databases, reporting systems) may be needed to support the ERP system. Partly because of the need to coordinate a number of parties and government staff, ERP projects entail risk. A formal planning and procurement process is key to the successful structuring of an ERP purchase and installation. (Table 9–1 on page 243 lists selected local governmental units that have adopted integrated ERP systems.)

The system planning and acquisition process consists of five major steps: (1) needs assessment, (2) requirements definition and request for proposal (RFP) development, (3) vendor evaluation, (4) contract negotiations, and (5) system implementation.

Needs assessment

System replacement is often a multiyear process that will have lasting effects on staff and operating procedures. For that reason, it is important to clearly identify the nature of the local government's technology needs and to determine the best way of meeting them. A technology needs assessment attempts to identify gaps between user needs and current system capabilities; the goal is to determine whether there is a "case for action" or a "business case" for modifying, enhancing, or replacing the current system. (Another term for needs assessment is *business case analysis*.)

A well-conceived needs assessment provides decision makers with an objective evaluation of the various choices that the organization faces as it confronts technology investment decisions. Because it clearly identifies the costs, benefits, and risks of different courses of action, a needs assessment is especially valuable when there is a lack of consensus within the government about how and when to proceed with the difficult task of system replacement. By documenting and sometimes quantifying system benefits, governments can set benchmarks (e.g., days to closing, hours to process payroll, days for purchase order approval, cycle time for budget development) that can be used throughout the implementation process to gauge whether the business goals for the investment in a new system are likely to be realized.

The first step in the needs assessment process is a thorough overall evaluation of the current system. Because the elimination of stand-alone systems is one of the major benefits of ERP systems, the evaluation of existing stand-alone systems is also crucial to the evaluation process.

Financial software product choices

A number of factors differentiate the enterprise software products available to the public sector. On the basis of those factors, it is possible to distinguish four tiers in the marketplace.

Tier 1: Industry leaders   If the goal of an enterprise resource planning (ERP) system is to provide software capabilities that permit seamless integration of major processes and functions across an enterprise, only a half-dozen firms (the Tier 1 firms) can provide solutions that will meet this goal. The advantages of the Tier 1 firms are superior product performance and a focus on the use of leading-edge technology. Tier 1 companies dedicate a considerable portion of revenues—15 to 20 percent—to research and development (R&D).

A related factor is that Tier 1 firms have a clear vision that extends beyond the back office and toward a total e-government solution. Even if a given vendor does not provide every part of the solution itself, it has often forged solid partnerships with other vendors to provide the needed functionality. The main disadvantages of Tier 1 products are cost (often millions of dollars when all costs are considered) and the implementation risk that comes with the installation of complex and powerful software.

Tier 2: Climbers   Tier 2 firms are working quickly to catch up to the Tier 1 firms by adopting some of the features of ERP (e.g., Web enabling) in new software releases. Advantages associated with some Tier 2 firms include a long presence in the public sector, a reputation for cost-effectiveness, and the direct provision of implementation services. The main disadvantages are that they have narrower product offerings than Tier 1 firms and are slower to meet new technology standards.

Tier 3: Niche players   Tier 3 firms are niche players because although these firms offer basic modules (e.g., general ledger, accounts payable) that are inte-

grated to some extent, their software packages are behind those of the Tier 1 and Tier 2 firms (e.g., they offer simple databases and rudimentary reporting tools). Simply put, Tier 3 products are not nearly as robust in terms of flexibility or technology standards, or in their ability to meet more advanced or complex business requirements.

Still, Tier 3 products are a viable alternative for smaller governments that simply cannot afford the products and services of Tier 2 vendors. Tier 3 firms do provide a basic level of functionality, integration, and reporting capability, as well as a reasonable level of customer support, at a very affordable price. Their R&D efforts focus primarily on (1) not falling too far behind current technological and functional standards and (2) slowly adopting product improvements demanded by customers.

Tier 4: Pretenders   The label for Tier 4 companies may seem harsh, but some of their customers would quickly agree that many companies whose products offer poor functionality are able to sell software primarily on the basis of one factor: a lower price. Although their promotional literature may tout the benefits of advanced technology, Tier 4 firms sell software that is very narrow in functionality (e.g., general ledger only), performs poorly, is technologically obsolete (e.g., is text-based, offers poor user interfaces, relies on proprietary languages, employs rigid databases), or lacks customer support. Tier 4 firms do not direct substantial resources to R&D, nor do they have to. They face a stable market demand mainly because their price is lower than that of firms in the other tiers. Unfortunately, customers often end up looking for new software shortly after implementation.

Source: Adapted from Rowan Miranda, Shayne Kavanagh, and Robert Roque, *Technology Needs Assessments: Evaluating the Business Case for ERP and Financial Management Systems* (Chicago: Government Finance Officers Association, 2002), 40–43.

Table 9–1   Selected governmental units that have adopted integrated enterprise resource planning systems.

Government unit	Software	Population (in thousands)	Employees	Operating budget (in thousands)
Cities				
Anderson, Indiana	MUNIS	60	785	100,000
Boston, Massachusetts	PeopleSoft	589	17,000	1,800,000
Charleston, South Carolina	SunGard Bi-Tech	104	1,000	106,000
Chicago, Illinois	Oracle	2,800	36,000	4,800,000
Palo Alto, California	SAP	61	1,000	323,700
Counties				
Alameda County, California	PeopleSoft	1,400	9,600	1,900,000
Cook County, Illinois	J. D. Edwards	5,000	26,000	2,600,000
Harris County, Texas	SunGard Bi-Tech	3,500	13,300	831,700
Lake County, Illinois	Oracle	644	2,800	340,000
Multnomah County, Oregon	SAP	670	4,500	1,010,000
Washington County, Maryland	PeopleSoft	338	1,200	138,600
School districts				
Austin Independent School District, Texas	SunGard Bi-Tech	78	10,000	705,000
Chicago Public Schools, Illinois	Oracle	434	46,700	3,800,000
Houston Independent School District, Texas	SAP/PeopleSoft	211	25,000	1,400,000
Jefferson County Public Schools, Kentucky	MUNIS	96	17,500	810,000
Portland Public Schools, Oregon	PeopleSoft	53	7,000	320,000
Salt Lake City School District, Utah	SunGard Bi-Tech	25	4,500	200,000
Prince Georges County Public Schools, Maryland	Oracle	139	16,700	1,100,000
Special districts				
Boston Water and Sewer Authority, Massachusetts	PeopleSoft	589	527	231,000
Chicago Transit Authority, Illinois	Oracle	7,800	11,000	925,000
Marin Municipal Water District, California	SAP	185	230	31,500
Miami-Dade Expressway Authority, Florida	MUNIS	72,000	24	37,000
Milwaukee Metropolitan Sewerage District, Wisconsin	Lawson	1,400	230	58,000
Orlando–Orange County Expressway Authority, Florida	Eden	202,000	40	72,700
Union Sanitary District, California	Lawson	322	130	21,000

Note: Figures are for 2003.

The overall evaluation will ask questions such as the following: What are the major deficiencies in the current system? Are the problems owing to obsolete technology, ineffective organization, or poor management? What level of staff resources is required to support each subsystem? Are staff members properly trained to take full advantage of the current system's features?

For each stand-alone system, questions such as the following must be considered: Does the system support only the individual department or the organization as a whole? Does the stand-alone system hold the same information as the main financial system? If so, what level of staff resources is dedicated to reconciliation? If the data do not match, which system is correct? How much work does system maintenance require? Which department is responsible for upgrading the stand-alone system?

Requirements definition and development of the request for proposals

A business requirement is a concise statement that summarizes the need or describes the performance criteria for the new system. The accompanying sidebar provides some guidelines for establishing business requirements.

Once the requirements are developed, they become the main component of a formal solicitation from vendors known as a request for proposals (RFP). As part of the RFP process, various agencies or departments within the government (e.g., procurement, accounting) must specify the performance they expect from the new system. Often, the government will establish system requirements for each business function and then insert the requirements into the RFP so that vendors can indicate whether and how their system meets each requirement.

The use of an RFP demonstrates the government's intent to use a competitive process in which proposals are evaluated according to two principal criteria: (1) how well they meet the government's needs and (2) the bidder's qualifications and expertise. Of course, governments can, and sometimes do, simply choose a system that they like, basing the choice solely on the vendor's reputation or on the fact that a neighboring jurisdiction has had success with a particular package. While such an approach is certainly faster and perhaps cheaper than an RFP, an RFP is generally superior because it ensures a competitive environment and allows the government to explore the full range of product and service offerings.

The objective of the RFP document is to obtain the information from vendors that will enable the government to select the system that best meets its needs. The document also provides vendors with information about the government that will enable them to submit realistic proposals. Consequently, an RFP must unambiguously describe (1) the scope of the project, (2) system requirements by function, (3) process-improvement goals, (4) implementation considerations, (5) evaluation criteria, (6) business terms and conditions, and (7) legal issues.

RFPs for ERP usually include both software and implementation services. Software firms may implement their own software; large clients may use an implementation firm that is separate from the software vendor.

Vendor evaluation

The evaluation of vendor proposals entails significant internal costs, including the time spent by government staff (1) reviewing and analyzing proposals, (2) staffing demonstrations for vendors, (3) visiting other governments that are using the software products under consideration, and (4) participating in contract negotiations. Because internal costs rise with the number of vendors being considered, it is useful to short-list a select number of vendors on the basis of predefined criteria and to request software demonstrations only from those vendors. In some instances, outside consulting assistance may be needed during the procurement process, which entails external costs.

What aspects of a vendor's proposal should governments analyze? Cost is one factor that merits careful analysis, particularly since initial bids often differ significantly from final contract amounts. There are many reasons for the differences, but the principal one is that initial bids reflect the vendor's uncertainty about various factors relating to the government, such as the level of staff resources that the government is prepared to invest in implementation. The cost analysis should examine software license fees, maintenance and support fees, implementation consulting costs, hardware costs, and training costs.

The vendor's implementation approach is another factor that should be carefully evaluated. Implementation firms use different methods to put the soft-

Defining system requirements Functional and technical requirements must be stated clearly and concisely so that they can be (1) included in a request for proposals and (2) attached to software and implementation services contracts as the basis for warranty and acceptance testing. If requirements are vague, it is difficult to assess whether the system meets the government's needs. The following rules are designed to establish meaningful requirements for a new system.

Start from a baseline. Consultants often convince governments that their needs are unique and that requirements should be developed from scratch. Government employees are then asked to spend a considerable amount of time interviewing with consultants and inventing requirements. This approach simply ignores the reality that major processes across cities, counties, and states are quite similar. Some of this similarity is based on the fact that most government organizations follow authoritative standards, such as generally accepted accounting principles and the Fair Labor Standards Act. Other similarities stem from accepted industry practice.

Write requirements in clear and concise terms that permit validation. Requirements should be written clearly, simply, concisely, and without jargon. Well-written requirements make it possible to assess whether they can be met by the new system. Put differently, requirements should be testable: does the system meet them or not? If it does meet them, how does it do so (e.g., out of the box, through customization)?

Don't recreate your existing system in words. The list of requirements should not describe every detail in the existing financial system. It is more useful to focus on *needs* than on the *procedures* for how things are currently done.

Recognize that a new system will improve your current processes. ERP software already reflects best business practices. Consequently, requirements should not be written to restrict the operation of the software. In other words, governments should focus on the needs being met, even if a different process must be used to meet those needs.

Consolidate similar requirements and system-wide requirements. Instead of exhaustively listing every field that should be captured by the database, use a single requirement. For example, it is more efficient to create a single requirement, such as "the flexibility to add user-defined fields in the database or on menu panels," than to describe every field in a human resource module.

Organize requirements by function, module, or process. Use logical categories to develop the list of requirements. For example, budget and procurement requirements should be listed separately. In addition, subcategories should be used to group similar requirements (e.g., budget preparation, budget analysis, budget control). Requirements should be numbered by section for easy reference during software demonstrations, contract negotiations, and various steps in the implementation process.

Perform a preliminary fit-gap analysis. At the end of the requirements definition process, the consultant should let the government know which requirements are likely to be the most problematic for ERP systems to meet. Since the government wants a system with minimal customization, this subset of potentially problematic requirements can be used during software demonstrations to evaluate vendors more closely and to validate their initial proposal responses.

Source: Michael Madden, Rowan Miranda, and Robert Roque, *A Guide to Preparing an RFP for Enterprise Financial Systems* (Chicago: Government Finance Officers Association, 1999), 41–43.

ware into production. For each implementation phase, vendors should be asked to provide estimates of staffing effort for consultants and government staff. In addition, the government should analyze the implementation schedule for each module to determine whether it has the staffing capability to meet the expectations assumed by the vendor in the proposed implementation plan.

Governments acquiring new systems require vendors to demonstrate their software by following specific "scripts" that are organized by business function. After software demonstrations are completed, site visits should be conducted for the vendors still left in the competitive contracting process. The objective of the site visits is to evaluate the software in a "live" environment and to inquire about the lessons that other users have learned about a specific product. Vendors should be required, as part of their proposals, to submit a list of three to five sites that have fully operational ERP software on the same scale as that of the potential government client.

Once the demonstrations and site visits are complete, the evaluation team should discuss the suitability of each proposal and identify vendors for contract negotiations. The decision should be based on the overall value of the system in relation to the proposed cost. The definition of "value" in this context requires a judgment about the software's capacity to meet the government's current requirements and the vendor's viability as a long-term business partner—in particular, the likelihood that the vendor will invest in the product and keep pace with advances in technology.

Contract negotiations

Contract negotiations involve three major documents: a software licensing agreement (SLA), an implementation services agreement (ISA), and a statement of work (SOW). The SLA defines the rights and responsibilities of the software firm and the government regarding the use of the product. The ISA is a contract with a company retained to implement the software. The SOW, which is an attachment to the ISA, specifies for each major step in the implementation the roles and responsibilities of the different parties—namely, the government staff, consultants, and the implementation vendor. Since software and implementation services companies are adept at negotiating contracts but governments do so infrequently (every decade or two), an independent consultant can play a useful role in advising the government throughout the contracting process.

Implementation

Implementing enterprise software is the most challenging part of the system acquisition process. It is not uncommon to hear that a government has spent millions of dollars on a technology initiative only to abandon it entirely, or to halt it and then start over again.

One study of ERP implementation found that within one year after having fully implemented their systems, 20 percent of respondents had terminated their ERP projects and 40 percent had failed to achieve their business case. The same study also found that 25 percent of the projects were over budget and that respondents had underestimated support costs for future years by an average of 20 percent.[6]

Why do ERP projects run into difficulty even though vendors tout their products as off-the-shelf? There are many possible reasons. The software products may have just been introduced and may still have significant defects. The implementation services firm may lack experience with governmental organizations. Other possibilities concern the organization implementing the system: it may have failed to adequately test the new technology, to budget for contingencies, or to anticipate how much staff commitment would be required. Organizational readiness is another issue: senior administrators, convinced that the current system was not meeting the organization's needs, may still have failed to fully evaluate the organization's capacity to install a new system. Another possibility is that the software required radical changes in process that managers were not prepared to make. As this discussion suggests, there are many risks during the implementation process that need to be carefully managed for a project to succeed.

Selecting a qualified implementation firm, with the requisite skills in project management, software configuration, business process improvement, and change management, is an important ingredient in project success. An important criterion in the selection of an implementation firm is the firms' prior experience installing the software at other public sector sites—in particular, the firm's track record in bringing those sites into production on time and on budget.

Other factors that affect implementation success are (1) the structure of the implementation rollout and (2) the quality of the methodology used to implement the software.

Rollout structure   How should the government structure the implementation of an ERP system? Research on implementation has shown that there are two key dimensions in structuring ERP projects: speed (fast or slow) and focus (technical or strategic). In the private sector, competitive pressures may promote fast implementations (six months to a year). Another impetus for fast implementations is sustainability: lengthy implementations can lead to skepticism about the whole process, making it difficult to maintain the energy level needed for completion.

When the focus of an implementation is technical, the organization's goal is to roll out core functionality without making major changes in business process. An alternative (and generally more desirable) focus is a strategic one, which means that the goal of the implementation is to maximize organizational value through positive business process change. The sidebar on page 248 describes the different options for system rollouts in relation to these dimensions.

As ERP systems have matured, implementation time has decreased. A large government typically requires twelve to eighteen months to implement financial-related modules and the same amount of time for HR and payroll applications (assuming the software is being rolled out sequentially). Small and medium-sized governments can install an entire ERP system in less time.

Implementation methodology   Software companies and implementation consulting firms have developed their own methodologies for implementing ERP systems. These methodologies are very similar across firms and products and differ mostly in the degree of emphasis put on specific phases.

A major area of difference is in the category of services known as change management. Since a new ERP system may require an organization to reengineer its business processes to match those embedded in the software, the organization may be compelled to undergo significant change, which must be anticipated and managed. Change management means addressing the impact of systems and technologies on people: providing training in the use of the product, effectively communicating the rationales for new business processes, and facilitating the shifts in roles and responsibilities necessary under the new system. Underinvesting in change management is a common problem in ERP implementations. Too often, organizations do not recognize that systems projects are as much about people as they are about technology. An effective change management mechanism seeks to ensure that behavioral implications are identified and managed.

A typology of ERP implementations   In *Mission Critical: Realizing the Promise of Enterprise Systems,* Thomas Davenport offers a typology of ERP implementations that is summarized in the chart and text that follow.

		Focus	
		Technical	Strategic
Speed	Fast	Quick relief	Quick advantage
	Slow	Poor implementation	Long-term competitiveness

Quick relief   The goal of quick-relief implementations is to modernize legacy systems and get the improvements up and running quickly. Another reason for such an approach is to eliminate potentially crippling deficiencies associated with legacy systems (i.e., the existing system relies on a database that is no longer supported).

A quick-relief implementation is generally the least expensive strategy, and many organizations adopt it in order to give ERP a "foot in the door," with the intention of later using business process reengineering or fully rolling out other modules. It is unclear, however, whether most organizations that use quick-relief implementation eventually succeed in getting funding and completing the project.

Quick advantage   The quick-advantage option takes longer than the quick-relief method because it requires some process redesign. Because of the emphasis on speed, however, it is unlikely that enterprise-wide process changes will be implemented. This option makes sense for organizations that are satisfied with implementing one or two modules and later rolling out a full ERP system.

Poor implementation   For obvious reasons, no organization would "choose" poor implementation. But organizations can end up with poor implementation if they take a slow implementation route (four years or longer) and at the same time focus only on technical considerations.

Long-term competitiveness   When long-term competitiveness is the goal, a longer time frame is needed to implement ERP, but the rationale is to take full advantage of the system's benefits, such as process redesign, implementation of best business practices, and full use of leading technology (e.g., Web, workflow). A more leisurely strategic implementation is also likely to pay more attention to the human aspect of change management.[1]

Source: Text adapted from Rowan Miranda, Shayne Kavanagh, and Robert Roque, *Technology Needs Assessments: Evaluating the Business Case for ERP and Financial Management Systems* (Chicago: Government Finance Officers Association, 2002), 78–79. Chart is reprinted by permission of Harvard Business School Press from Thomas Davenport, *Mission Critical: Realizing the Promise of Enterprise Systems* (Boston, 2000), 14. Copyright © 2000 by the Harvard School Publishing Corporation; all rights reserved.
[1]For an excellent introduction to enterprise systems and the challenges in implementing them, see Thomas Davenport, *Mission Critical: Realizing the Promise of Enterprise Systems* (Boston: Harvard Business School Press, 2000).

Another major challenge for governments seeking to modernize their systems stems from the high cost of ERP implementation, which can be anywhere from two to twenty times the cost of the software license. The main constraints facing smaller governments in their access to upper-tier technologies are the high costs of implementation and of ongoing system support.

Implementation methodologies generally consist of the following phases: (1) project preparation, (2) design for best business practices, (3) configuration, (4) testing, (5) training, (6) production activities, and (7) ongoing system support.

Project preparation   Project preparation refers to all the activities that are needed to initiate the project, including preparing the project plan, securing work space for government staff and consultants, preparing the technology architecture needed for development and training, installing the software on the servers, and garnering staff resources from various government departments or agencies.

Design for best business practices   The purpose of the design phase is to ensure that the system will meet the government's needs. To this end, stakeholders from across the organization work with consultants in a process known as a conference-room pilot (CRP). During the CRP, the participants compare maps of current business processes with the processes embedded in the software and identify gaps between the two.

Software firms emphasize that what they learn in the course of repeated ERP installations across a broad range of industries and organizational forms, combined with their research and development efforts, allows them to embed processes in the software—"best business practices"—that are typically superior to an organization's current processes. In the context of ERP, best business practices are processes and procedures that improve the performance of an organization through the innovative use of technology. Governments can adopt best practices in two ways: (1) by using the processes embedded in the software and (2) by incorporating the technology features of the software (e.g., workflow to achieve paperless processes) into existing processes. The adoption of best practices is related to business reengineering, which emphasizes that technology should be used to *improve* as well as to *automate* processes.[7]

One potential problem, however, is that best business practices are sometimes "forced" on customers because the reverse engineering that would be required to customize the product—that is, to eliminate certain process flows— would be too costly. However, for governments that *do* want to implement the processes embedded in the system, only minor setup and configuration steps are required for best practices to be realized.

In relation to ERP software, two features of best practices are important: (1) enabling technology, which means that the software has the flexibility to allow the redesign of core business processes and functions, and (2) embedded technology, which means that certain processes that have been "refined" and "validated" through repeated implementations are embedded in the software. These two features have two practical results: first, the government can elect to use the software to perform tasks better; second, the very act of implementing the software will impose changes in some business practices.

Configuration   The implementation consulting firm will typically take the lead role in configuring the software. Configuration involves making changes to the software to develop a system that closely resembles the design documents. For example, configuration may involve adding data fields to screens, triggering workflow notices for purchase order approvals, or developing custom reports. While the implementation firm is configuring the product, the government staff typically trains on the software.

Testing   There are typically two types of testing activities: unit testing is used to test individual modules in the ERP software; integration testing is used to confirm that all the modules work together as intended. The government should insist, as part of the implementation firm's obligations, that the firm provide a good testing plan, but the government itself should take direct responsibility for overseeing the testing process.

Training   Training occurs at two levels. Project-team training, which focuses on the detailed functions of the system, occurs early in the project so that the government staff can participate in the design phase of the implementation. End-user training, which focuses on specialized areas, usually occurs just before the software is placed into production. In the "train-the-trainer" approach, which is the one ordinarily chosen, select government staff receive training from the software company and then train the end users across government departments.

Production activities   The production activities phase encompasses all the steps necessary to deploy the system, including data conversion, the transfer of transactions from the old to the new system, and final testing. The most important activity that occurs during this phase is acceptance of the system.

Acceptance is both a contractual term and a step in the implementation methodology. Conditional acceptance occurs when it has been verified that the system has been installed properly in relation to the design document and the business requirements; at the time of conditional acceptance, the system may not yet have been "turned on." Final acceptance occurs only after it has been verified that all business processes, including month-end closing activities, are working as planned (i.e., the system is actually processing transactions).

Ongoing system support   System support focuses on maintaining the system once it is put into production. For an annual fee, the software firm provides maintenance and support. The "maintenance" part of the service means that the government has access to patches and software upgrades; the "support" part gives the government access to telephone support for major problems.

Much of the real responsibility for system support, however, falls to the government's internal staff. One of the major internal support activities is the provision of an internal help desk to respond to users' questions and concerns. The government may also staff a system support team to help departments optimize their use of the system.

Some governments outsource support of the financial system to private firms known as application service providers (ASPs). ASPs provide and maintain the software and hardware, freeing the government to focus on using the system. The ASP model solves two costly problems common to small and medium-sized governments: first, it eliminates the need to procure the hardware and other technological infrastructure necessary to support an ERP system; second, and perhaps more important, it reduces the need for the government to recruit and retain IT staff to support the system.

Real-time public management

By integrating business processes and consolidating information in a single silo, ERP systems overcome many of the limitations of traditional financial management systems. Today, "real-time" government is within the reach of most public sector organizations. This section describes some of the challenging public management tasks for which ERP can provide the foundation.

Shared services

A new service-delivery model known as shared services is enabling organizations to restructure their administrative support functions. The shared-services

Tips and traps for system acquisition

Tips

Define the scope of the project early on and stick to it. "Scope creep" is one of the biggest reasons that governments fail to implement a new system on time and within budget. Given the modular nature of new systems, there is no reason to purchase and implement every module that the vendor offers today.

Define the business case for the project, clearly stating the project costs, ongoing costs, and specific improvements that will result from your new system. A well-defined business case can serve as a compass to guide you through the implementation and act as a reminder of why you took on the project in the first place.

Obtain the advice of a consultant throughout the procurement and contract negotiations process. Governments purchase systems every ten to fifteen years. A consultant who is in the market on a daily basis and who knows the unique needs of the public sector can help level the playing field between governments and vendors. Consulting fees should be no more than 10 percent of what you plan on spending on the system.

Use a competitive RFP process to select your system. The ERP systems marketplace provides a broad range of products for different needs and budgets. A competitive process increases the likelihood that you will choose the best fit for your government.

Before you sign an agreement, make sure you have clearly defined a statement of work that establishes the roles and responsibilities for both the government and the implementation consulting firm. A well-defined statement of work can reap big dividends during the implementation process if disputes arise about what was purchased, what the new system was expected to do, and how it was expected to do it.

Traps

Moving to e-government before the back-office architecture is in place. Providing services electronically is a trend that will continue to grow in government. But there is a right way and wrong way to go about it. Putting an ERP system in place that can streamline the processing of transactions should come before the development of dozens of Web sites to conduct business with the citizenry. Ideally, once the foundation of the system has been laid, a Web portal within the ERP system can provide e-government functionality.

Biting off more than you can chew. ERP systems impose significant change on organizations, and organizations differ in the amount of change that they can handle all at once. Governments can reduce the risk of implementation failure by keeping the scope of a project narrow and focused.

Using a design/build consultant. Don't hire a consultant to advise you on the procurement process and retain the same consultant to implement the software. In most cases, you will sacrifice independence and objectivity in the process.

Taking shortcuts on training and change management. Most governments that have implemented ERP systems would agree that training and change management are two areas where a significant portion of the implementation resources should be directed.

Using part-time staff to implement the system. ERP system installations are complex, and the software configuration requires experienced government personnel. A key to successfully installing the system is to have full-time staff resources dedicated to the project.

model involves consolidating and redesigning administrative processes and functions to create major service centers. By eliminating the duplication of functions across an organization, the shared-services model helps achieve economies of scale in back-office processes. For example, governments often have centralized procurement, accounts payable, and payroll functions, but these functions are found within departments as well; maintaining such functions at the departmental level increases administrative costs and burdens departments with tasks that are outside their core mission. Technology features within ERP systems—such as workflow, document management, and a number of other Web-driven capabilities—permit organizations operating under the shared-services model to preserve high-quality customer service while seizing opportunities to achieve economies of scale.

Budget reform and innovation

Information technology offers new opportunities for tackling budget reform. Past budget reforms, such as performance-based budgeting, often failed, in part, because they imposed burdens on organizational processes and staffing. In an era of manual calculations and paper-based processes, innovations such as zero-base budgeting burdened government bureaucracies with significant costs. Even simpler reforms, such as program budgeting, were prohibited by obstacles such as the inability to make indirect cost allocations. Through features such as workflow and a flexible chart of accounts, ERP systems are allowing governments to improve budgeting processes and reconsider budget reforms.[8]

The integration between ERP and the Internet is boosting citizen participation in budgeting. Through modern Web technology, governments are collecting input directly from citizens and filtering it to department heads, who can then be asked to demonstrate that budget requests are responsive to citizens' complaints and service requests.

Performance measurement

One of the challenges to governments is the adoption of performance measurement systems that will guide operations management and resource allocation. Performance measurement initiatives draw data from a disparate range of sources and also require the sharing of data; by facilitating the collection and exchange of data on inputs, outputs, and outcomes, ERP technology can play an important role in increasing the feasibility of performance measurement. In addition, enterprise data warehouses can store and organize the financial and nonfinancial data related to performance measurement. Finally, ERP systems can track performance measurement information as part of routine transaction processing.

Advanced cost-accounting systems

Obtaining access to financial information that is linked to programs, services, and activities is another challenge for local governments. Because legacy systems captured transactional data primarily for the purpose of budget control, there was too little detail to be of use to managers in their efforts to guide operations.

The chart of accounts is the most important element in determining the overall usefulness of a financial system. ERP products provide a robust, flexible chart of accounts (COA) structure with multiple levels of categorization (expenditures, revenue) within each element, which allows for greater financial control.[9] A redesign of the existing COA facilitates improved financial reporting and advanced cost management capabilities.

Auditing and internal controls

The improvement of auditing and internal controls is one of the most important benefits of ERP systems. Much of the improvement in these two areas arises from the fact that ERP systems offer electronic forms that can be stored indefinitely. Also of value are software features known as audit trails and drill-down capabilities. As noted earlier, audit trails make it possible to view the entire history of changes to a record in the database, and drill-down capabilities permit end users to reach the source document that supports a journal entry.

As ERP systems have increased the number of users (internal and external) who rely on technology, the need for internal controls has become all the more pressing. To ensure that the ERP system is subject to adequate internal controls, the government must establish policies, procedures, and technological constraints in the following areas: system access, infrastructure change, software application and process changes, and data access and integrity.[10]

Governments typically impose three types of controls: (1) preventive controls, which detect problems before they arise (e.g., segregation of duties for checks and balances); (2) detective controls, which identify control violations (e.g., reconciliation of bank statements); and (3) corrective controls, which modify systems to eliminate future problems. As part of a government's annual audit, an independent accounting firm can be engaged to provide an opinion on the adequacy of internal controls.

Comprehensive executive information systems

Most organizations would concede that ERP systems have done more to increase the efficiency of transaction processing than to improve the strategic management capabilities of higher-level managers and administrators. Because ERP systems are transaction based, they are not designed to summarize, analyze, display, and disseminate information. However, ERP vendors are now using Web-based portals to provide "dashboards" (simplified, real-time views of key performance indicators, graphically displayed on a single screen) and "scorecards" (a list of performance measures that track an organization's success at meeting goals) for strategic management. These systems, which sit "on top" of ERP software packages, are referred to as executive information systems (EIS).

EIS applications are a subset of a class of technology solutions known as business intelligence software. EIS provides a management information portal to support strategic activities such as goal setting, planning and forecasting, and performance tracking.

In essence, EIS allows both department heads and managers to have a customized Web portal that gathers, analyzes, and integrates internal and external data and summarizes it to create profiles of the key indicators that are most meaningful to them. Through a single information gateway, administrators and managers can access both historical and real-time data through ad hoc queries, and can also manage and manipulate multidimensional, or cubelike, databases. The use of multiple systems often raises the odds of contradictory information; thus, EIS technologies increase the chances that organizations can establish a single version of the truth.

Summary

This chapter describes the state of the art in technologies used to manage public organizations. Financial management systems today are linked more closely than ever to other administrative functions. ERP systems, the new breed of technologies that consolidate information and promote change in business processes to reflect best business practices, are driving down governments' overhead costs and improving responsiveness to citizens, suppliers, and employees. The integration of business processes will have a dramatic impact on the efficiency and effectiveness of government service delivery. Rising citizen expectations will challenge governments to keep pace with advances in technology.

1 For a detailed discussion of the limitations of legacy financial systems, see Rowan Miranda, "Information Technology for Financial Management," in *Handbook of Government Budgeting,* ed. Roy T. Meyers (San Francisco: Jossey-Bass, 1999), 412–438.

2 Position control refers to measures that regulate the hiring of personnel to ensure that it is consistent with the budget.

3 A blanket release is a purchase order or contract for commodities or services that has been pre-approved up to a maximum amount. Maintenance of contract items refers to the specific commodities or services that are covered by the contract.

4 The terms *integration* and *interface* have distinct meanings in the technology industry. Integration refers to applications that are tightly linked together and that were, in most cases, developed using the same programming code. (In essence, integrated applications come from the same vendor and reside in a single system.) Interface refers to the computer code used to shuttle data back and forth across applications built by different vendors.

5 Although payroll is often considered a module within a human resource management system (HRMS) suite, it is treated separately in this discussion because it is a function covered by traditional financial systems.

6 Conference Board, *ERP Trends,* Research Report 1292-01 (Washington, D.C.: Conference Board, 2001).

7 For an application of business process reengineering methods to ERP, see Rowan Miranda, "Reengineering Financial Processes," in *ERP and Financial Management Systems,* ed. Rowan Miranda (Chicago: Government Finance Officers Association, 2001), 87–100.

8 For a discussion of how technology can facilitate budget reform, see Rowan Miranda, "Technology for Financial Planning and Forecasting," in *ERP and Financial Management Systems,* 135–146.

9 The use of information technology in advanced cost accounting capabilities is discussed in Robert S. Kaplan and Robin Cooper, *Cost and Effect: Using Integrated Cost Systems to Drive Profitability and Performance* (Boston: Harvard Business School Press, 1998).

10 Joseph Thompson, "Internal Controls for Enterprise Technology," *Government Finance Review* (August 2003): 46–50.

Part three:
Revenue sources

10 The property tax

ARNOLD H. RAPHAELSON

In the early years of the twenty-first century, the property tax, the four-hundred-year-old champion of local government revenues, faced a paradox. On the one hand, real property values in many places had risen substantially, yielding the promise of a growing tax base and increasing revenues even if tax rates stayed constant. On the other hand, assessment problems and the burden of supporting increased spending, especially for education, were leading to strident calls for relief and reform. American families love their homes but hate the tax on them. Nevertheless, no one predicts the tax's demise.[1]

Between the beginning of 2000 and the end of 2002, the sharp drop in stock prices reduced the value of stock assets held by American households by nearly $6 trillion.[2] During the same period, however, continued new-home construction and rising prices for existing homes—both of which were fueled, in part, by the drop in mortgage interest rates—increased home values by $3 trillion, a figure that represents a major increase in the property tax base. In 2001, 68 percent of American families owned homes, with a median value of $122,000. But only 52 percent of families had stocks or mutual funds, most of which were in retirement plans, and these had a median value of $34,000.[3]

For a large part of the population, the combination of rising property values and falling interest rates was welcome. Many who sold or refinanced homes cashed out some of their real estate assets and used them for consumption—which, like the continued rise in construction activity, helped to sustain the economy. However, rising property values also meant that for many households, the level of assets subject to property taxation was increasing more rapidly than income. At the local level, reassessments undertaken to keep up with rising market prices met with opposition. At the state level, unwelcome increases in assessments generated promises of tax relief and reform on the part of candidates for state government.

Despite frequent calls for reform, the property tax will likely remain the most important tax on wealth in the United States and the main source of local government revenues, and it will continue to be based mainly on real property. Although state property taxes were once significant, they are no longer an important source of state revenues: since 1956, states have collected less than 5 percent of the total property tax.[4] There is no federal property tax. Because real property is the least mobile of tax bases, the property tax is especially appropriate for the local level. In 1999, property taxes raised $228.5 billion, or about 72 percent of all local taxes.[5]

Although the property tax permits local governments considerable economic autonomy, citizens have expressed growing hostility toward property taxation. In the late 1970s, after inflation caused rapid increases in the real burden of the tax, special limits on property tax increases were enacted in California (Proposition 13) and some other states. Such limits temporarily slowed the increase in overall revenues from property taxation; and as local governments turned to other revenue sources, the percentage of total revenues that were collected as property taxes decreased. Nevertheless, the property tax remains the most important source of local tax revenues, and a thorough explanation of property taxation is crucial to an understanding of local government finance policies.

The principal sections of this chapter consider the background of the property tax, property tax administration, continuing issues associated with the tax, and prospects for reform. These sections consider in detail the theoretical, practical, and equity issues associated with the use of the tax.

Background

The property tax is not a tax on all wealth; it is a tax on certain types of personal or business wealth held in the form of real or personal property. Privately owned real estate is the main element in the tax base; the property of other governments and of nonprofit institutions is largely exempt. The tax rate is applied to the assessed value of a taxable property, as determined on the assessment date. The assessed value is the gross value, not the net ownership value of the property (i.e., gross value less any outstanding debt).

Origin, development, and scope

In the colonial period, various categories of property were listed as part of the property tax base, and each category was assigned a specific tax rate. Only the types of property specifically cited by law were included. However, by the middle of the nineteenth century, the tax had evolved into a general property tax. All property (real or personal) was considered part of the tax base unless specifically exempted by law, and a uniform rate—specified by state law or constitution—had to be applied to all property within a given district. Property ownership was considered an indicator of the ability to pay taxes, a view that precluded discrimination among types of property as well as among taxpayers.

The transformation of the tax into a general property tax and the development of uniform rates were at first regarded as reform measures that would remedy the ills associated with special property taxes. By 1991, however, fourteen states had formal property tax classifications and assigned different rates to different categories of property, and many other states had statutes with special provisions for properties that were being used for specific purposes (e.g., farming) or that had special characteristics (e.g., historic structures).[6] Thus, what was initially regarded as a reform—the institution of a general property tax—was eventually regarded as a problem, which led to the *re-creation* of property tax classifications and the assignment of different rates to different categories. Some citizens regard property classifications as a reform: for example, measures assigning lower tax rates to agricultural and open land can be used to discourage development and control urban sprawl. Others, however, regard such measures as unfair; in their view, the resulting differentials in the distribution of the tax burden are inequities.

Thus, although a general property tax may be in effect in principle, rarely does it in fact cover and tax all properties at uniform rates.[7] Some states have as many as twenty-four classes of property subject to the tax, but the tax base is overwhelmingly made up of real estate—that is, land, improvements, and structures. The rest of the tax base (and only in some jurisdictions) is personal property other than real estate—including tangibles such as automobiles, household goods, inventories, and equipment, and intangibles such as stocks and bonds (see Figure 10–1).

Classes of realty usually depend on use—for example, commercial, residential, industrial, or agricultural. In 1991, the last year that the Advisory Commission on Intergovernmental Relations (ACIR) reported such information, Minnesota, with twelve classes, had the most classifications of realty. Nine

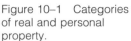

Figure 10–1 Categories of real and personal property.

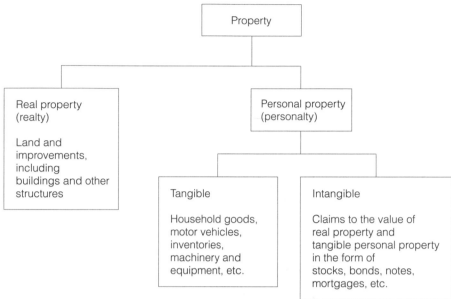

states exempted all tangible personal property; twenty-eight states and the District of Columbia included all personal property in one rate class; and thirteen states had more than one class for personal property. Residential tangible personal property was exempt in thirty-nine states and the District of Columbia; in contrast, only ten states exempted commercial and industrial personal property, such as equipment and inventories.[8]

Intangible personal property is generally exempt from taxation or taxed at low rates. Discovering, assessing, and applying a property tax to stocks or mortgages, for example, is both costly and impractical, and the tax is easy to avoid. And if, for example, a real estate mortgage and the real estate itself are both taxed, it can be argued that a tax on intangibles entails double taxation of the same property. Thus, while some economists have proposed taxing intangibles at relatively low rates, others argue that from both a practical and theoretical viewpoint it is wisest to eliminate intangible property from the property tax base altogether.[9]

In Montgomery County, Pennsylvania, the tax on intangibles was eliminated after the state supreme court ruled against excluding the stock of Pennsylvania corporations from the tax rolls.[10] In Florida, a rate of 0.1 percent is applied to personal property with a value of more than $10,000, but some intangibles (such as retirement-account assets) are exempt. Since residents are not required to file if the tax would be less than $60, an additional $60,000 in property is thereby exempted.[11]

Table 10–1 describes the 1991 tax base (the U.S. Census Bureau collected these data for the 1992 Census of Governments but has not done so since then). The table shows increasing annual growth in the base between 1956 and 1981 and continued growth, at lower rates, through 1991. By 1990 and 1991, the recession had reduced market and assessed values for certain types of properties, a change that is reflected in the lower rate of growth in assessed values between 1986 and 1991. In 1991, real estate accounted for almost 85 percent of the total of locally assessed property.

In the 1990s, the continued decline in the importance of personal property in the tax base occurred partly because several states stopped taxing such property. Real estate property values, in contrast, have grown at stable or increasing rates.

Table 10–1 Gross and net assessed property values, selected years (in billions of $).

Type of assessed value	Year							
	1956	1961	1966	1971	1976	1981	1986	1991
Total gross assessed value	280.3	365.9	499.0	717.8	1,229.1	2,958.2	4,817.8	6,924.2
Total net assessed value (net locally taxable)[a]	272.2	354.0	484.1	694.6	1,189.4	2,837.5	4,619.7	6,681.6
State-assessed property	22.5	27.8	41.6	53.5	84.7	159.0	242.8	285.8
Locally assessed property	249.7	326.1	442.5	641.1	1,104.7	2,678.4	4,376.9	6,395.8
Real property	202.8	269.7	378.9	552.7	959.1	2,406.7	3,910.7	5,806.7
Personal property	46.9	56.5	63.6	88.3	145.6	271.7	466.2	589.0

Note: Because of rounding, detail may not add to totals.

[a] Net locally taxable property value excludes property exempt from taxes.

Revenue growth

This section examines trends in property tax revenues and their underlying causes. Although a number of the trends discussed here are applicable to a great many localities, it is important to remember that the role of the property tax varies significantly by state and by region. For example, for local governments in New Hampshire in 1997, property taxes were $58 per $1,000 of personal income and $1,555 per capita, whereas in Alabama, the figures were $10 per $1,000 of personal income and $210 per capita. Clearly, the averages for all states—$31 per $1,000 in personal income and $783 per capita—do not begin to reflect the extremes of the spectrum.[12]

In 2000, the Office of the Chief Financial Officer of the District of Columbia calculated effective property tax rates for the District and for the largest city in each of the fifty states. The unweighted average of these fifty-one effective rates was 1.68 percent, or $1.68 per $100 of market value.[13] However, the calculations revealed significant differences among the cities. The highest effective rates were in Bridgeport, Connecticut; Providence, Rhode Island; and Newark, New Jersey, at 4.55, 3.52, and 3.34 percent, respectively. The lowest effective rates were in Denver, Colorado; Cheyenne, Wyoming; Birmingham, Alabama; and Honolulu, Hawaii, at 0.71, 0.71, 0.70, and 0.37 percent, respectively. The median rate for the fifty-one cities was in Columbus, Ohio, at 1.52 percent.[14]

During the period from 1957 to 1999, aggregate property tax revenues rose for both state and local governments. As Table 10–2 shows, the increase was from about $13 billion in 1957 to about $240 billion in 1999. About 95 percent of property tax revenues go to local governments. Despite the overall growth in revenues, however, the importance of the property tax in state revenues shows a pronounced downward trend through 1987, followed by a more recent small rise. In 1902, state collections of $82 million in property taxes made up 52.6 percent of total state tax revenues.[15] By 1957, the states had largely left property tax collection to local governments and had come to rely primarily on income, sales, and excise taxes. Although state property tax revenues were nearly $500 million in 1957, they were only 3.3 percent of state tax revenues. Property tax revenues continued to make up a diminishing percentage of state revenues: by 1991, state property tax collections of $6.2 billion (primarily taxes on public utility properties) were only 2 percent of total state tax revenues. However, the percentage had risen to 2.3 by the end of the 1990s.

Although they remain a high percentage of total local revenues, local government property tax collections show a similar trend. In 1932, property taxes were the source of more than 97 percent of local tax revenues.[16] By 1957, property tax revenues were $12.6 billion and 75.3 percent of local tax revenues, but only 43.4 percent of revenue from all sources—a shift that reflects the increased significance of state grants to local governments.[17] By 1991, local property tax revenues were $161.8 billion—75.3 percent of total local tax revenue. The decreasing importance of the property tax reflects, in part, public resistance to property taxation, which has led local governments to meet spending needs through other taxes and charges.[18]

Table 10–3 illustrates the effects of pressure to reduce reliance on the property tax. Between 1953 and 1990, the average annual increase in property tax revenues was 7.7 percent. In the breakdown by periods, growth (calculated on the basis of current dollars) in property tax revenues generally outstripped growth in the gross national product (GNP) and in the consumer price index (CPI). The exceptions were in the 1970s. After the limitations introduced during the "tax revolt" of 1973–78, from 1978 to 1980 the average annual increase

Table 10–2 Property tax revenues by level of government and as a percentage of total tax revenues, selected years.		Revenues (in billions of $)			As a percentage of total tax revenues	
	Year	Total	State	Local	State	Local
	1957	13.1	0.5	12.6	3.3	75.3
	1962	19.1	0.6	18.4	3.1	87.9
	1967	26.0	0.9	25.2	2.7	86.6
	1972	42.1	1.3	40.9	2.1	83.5
	1977	62.5	2.3	60.3	2.2	80.5
	1979	64.9	2.5	62.5	2.0	77.5
	1982	81.9	3.1	78.8	1.9	76.0
	1987	121.2	4.6	116.6	1.9	73.7
	1991	168.0	6.2	161.8	2.0	75.3
	1992	178.4	6.6	171.7	2.0	75.6
	1997	218.8	10.3	208.5	2.3	73.3
	1999	240.1	11.7	228.5	2.3	72.3

Note: Because of rounding, detail may not add to totals.

Table 10–3 Average annual rates of increase in local property tax revenues, the gross national product, and the consumer price index, selected periods.	Periods	Local property tax revenues (%)	Gross national product (%)	Consumer price index (%)
	1953–58	8.4	4.3	1.9
	1958–63	7.2	5.9	1.5
	1963–68	7.0	8.0	1.4
	1968–73	10.4	9.0	2.4
	1973–78	7.8	10.6	4.9
	1978–80	1.2	10.2	12.4
	1980–83	9.4	7.7	6.6
	1983–86	7.7	7.6	3.3
	1986–89	8.5	7.0	4.1
	1989–90	9.2	5.1	6.1
	1990–94	5.4	5.7[a]	3.6
	1995–99	4.2	5.6[a]	2.4

[a]Gross domestic product substituted for gross national product.

in property tax revenues fell to 1.2 percent a year. During that period, the GNP rose at the nominal rate of 10.2 percent and consumer prices rose at the rate of 12.4 percent. Property tax revenues again rose at higher rates in the 1980s, but their overall decline as a percentage of total local government revenues indicates that collections from other sources have risen even more.[19]

Despite the decline in the relative importance of the property tax, the absolute level of collections by local governments has increased. As Table 10–2 shows, local property tax collections rose from $12.6 billion in 1957 to $228.5 billion in 1999. Even after the tax-limitation measures of the 1970s, local government property tax collections more than doubled between 1982 and 1991.

Property tax administration

Property tax administration involves (1) discovery of the tax base, (2) preparation of a property list, (3) appraisal and assessment of property, (4) recognition of exemptions, (5) determination of the tax levy, and (6) collection. Fundamental to accomplishing these tasks, of course, are a highly qualified staff and organization, the necessary procedures and forms, and a system— generally computerized—for maintaining records and retrieving information on the tax base.

Discovery

Discovery of the tax base involves discovery of both real and personal property. Discovery of real property is relatively straightforward. The property exists in situ, subject to easy canvass, and there is a conventional system for recording both its description and its ownership. Discovery of personal property, both intangible and tangible, is more complicated and presents significant practical and theoretical problems.

The major practical impediment to taxing intangibles is the difficulty of finding (1) assets (e.g., cash and bank deposits) held outside the assessment district and (2) other assets for which ownership is not subject to registration or records. The discovery of intangible property is difficult and uncertain: it depends largely on (1) the candor of citizens, who may feel that by complying with the law and revealing their assets they will incur a tax burden that many others avoid; (2) other sources of information (e.g., federal income tax returns); and (3) specific legal actions (e.g., probate) that yield a property listing. Enforcement costs for full compliance are prohibitive, and the taxation of some forms of intangible property represents double taxation of underlying real property values. Abolishing the tax on intangibles, rather than attempting to improve its administration, may be the best solution to the theoretical and administrative problems associated with it.

Discovery of tangible personal property (other than automobiles) is also difficult, and assessors have tended to be cautious in enforcing this part of the tax. Some of the characteristics of movable property, such as inventory, create theoretical problems that make fair and accurate assessment difficult. First, on a given assessment date, property value may not represent an annual value: if a major delivery is delayed, for example, the assessment will be artificially low. Second, seasonal variations among industries mean that those industries that maintain high inventories during the assessment period will bear a disproportionate share of the tax burden. Third, different policies for inventory valuation can yield different values for the same property. For example, the same inventory may be valued at wholesaler's cost, wholesale price, or retail price. Finally, because they are beyond the assessor's experience and cannot be otherwise determined, some values may have to be determined on the basis of self-assessment by the property owners. Like the tax on intangible personal property, the tax on tangible personal property has been questioned: critics have argued that since such property is not served by local governments (whereas real property does benefit from local services), the tax is not justified.

In short, taxes on all forms of personal property are so burdened by controversy that any proposals for the reform of property tax administration are likely to focus on real property. The remainder of this section focuses on the issues associated with the implementation and administration of the tax on real property.

Inventory

An inventory, or property list, identifies parcels (tracts or plots of land) according to maps and a numbering system that are designed to reflect any changes that may have occurred as the result of the consolidation or subdivision of properties. Aerial photographs may be used to confirm locations, identify parcels and improvements, establish relationships among different areas, and check for changes. (Such photographs have led to the discovery of property that had been omitted from tax rolls for many years.)[20] In some areas, computer-assisted mass appraisal (CAMA) systems have been coordinated with geographic information systems for use in regional planning and other governmental efforts.[21]

Appraisal and assessment

Once discovery and inventory are complete, the property may be appraised. It is through appraisal and assessment—the heart of property tax administration—that the share of the tax burden is determined for each property owner. Both appraisal and assessment are valuations, and they are related. Conducting an appraisal means determining the market value of a property. Conducting an assessment means determining the value of a property in the context of the tax base. A tax rate is applied to the assessed value to determine the tax bill.

The assessor appraises—establishes a market valuation for—each parcel and ultimately determines the total value of the property in the district. Appraisal cannot be based on rules of thumb or arbitrary judgment; both equity and law require that each valuation be defensible. The assessor is often called on to defend the accuracy of a valuation as well as the consistency of the appraisal method.

The assessor's goal is to value the land and improvements of each parcel at the market price (variously characterized as actual, fair, true, cash, just, or money value), and then to set the assessment at some uniform percentage of market value. Determining market price is not an easy task. During any fiscal period, only a very small percentage of the property on a tax list is subject to a market transaction—and even when there is direct evidence of the sales price on a parcel, the assessor must be sure that the price reflects the market value and is not the result of a forced sale or of a transaction made under special circumstances (e.g., a gift or a transfer of property between relatives).

Because of practical difficulties, many assessors can only hope to directly appraise and reassess a fraction of the jurisdiction's taxable properties in any given year. Simply ensuring that new construction is added to the current tax list may be a major task. Consequently, most assessors do not attempt to keep pace with annual changes in market prices. Instead, they try to maintain uniformity in the fraction of current market value at which each parcel is assessed.

Assessment is complex and often controversial. Assessors carry heavy responsibilities for the equitable treatment of all taxpayers. The assessment process works best when the variables determining value and assessment classification are clearly delineated and the assessment techniques make full use of the latest statistical tools.

In some states, percentages of values for assessments are specified by law or by constitution. However, even in states where the law specifies that assessments should be at a specified percentage of market value, there is no attempt to enforce the requirement, and average assessments will vary from the required mark. The rationale is that as long as a uniform percentage is applied to all market values, all property owners bear an equitable share of the tax burden. This rationale has been countered by claims that underassessment distorts the true tax rate and complicates the administration of state equalization programs, some of which are related to assessed property values. This problem, however, is generally solved through sampling techniques: for the purposes of state programs, state equalization boards use the results of sample surveys to adjust local assessment ratios (the assessment ratio is the ratio of the assessed value to the market price).[22]

Except in Maryland and Montana, where state employees perform assessments, local officials have primary responsibility for setting and recording assessments. Dealing efficiently with individual realty parcels on a mass basis requires the use of cadastral (tax plot) maps and of computers for detailed inventory and assessment functions; it may also require state involvement in audits of the assessment process.

Local governments are creatures of the states, are governed by state laws and regulations, and have limited latitude in carrying out their programs. Property taxation is thus done under state rules, and state appeals processes and courts may be used to enforce those rules.

Although states require uniform assessment ratios within districts, they do not require uniformity among districts. Therefore, when states give grants to local governments (e.g., school districts) to supplement local property tax revenues, they must "equalize" the ratios of assessed to market value to ensure fair comparisons of various districts' ability to support local services. Thus, many states regularly supervise the assessment process in the context of grant and equalization programs.

In fact, the trend since the early 1980s has been toward increased state supervision of local property taxation.[23] State oversight allows local jurisdictions to pay more attention to the tax base as a whole and to work toward updating appraisals, and it tends to diminish local governments' tendencies to engage in "tax-rate wars" as a means of competing for economic development.

Infrequent assessments have been blamed for inequities between older and newer homes and, in general, for high coefficients of dispersion (the coefficient of dispersion is a measure of unfairness that is discussed later in this chapter). The effects of delayed reassessment include (1) long periods during which recent buyers pay higher taxes and (2) major readjustments when the new assessments are finally complete. When property owners see sharp increases in assessments or sharp drops in market prices, they are likely to challenge assessments—although property owners naturally do not appeal very low assessments.

If reassessments are very infrequent and property prices rise dramatically during a long period of inflation, "reassessment shock"—and a raft of tax grievances—are likely to result. This was the case in Nassau County, New York, in 2002, when a state court ordered the county to reassess all of its 416,000 properties, a task it had not undertaken for sixty-four years. Because state law limits assessment increases to 6 percent in any given year and to 20 percent over five years, changes in the assessments could not begin to reflect the massive changes in market value that had occurred since the last assessment. Thus, the assessment *ratio* was critical to attaining equity. According to the chairman of the assessment board, 8 percent of property owners protested, well below the "average" of 15 percent he had expected. Nevertheless, the resulting tide of tax grievances cost the county $1 billion.[24]

Another example of reassessment shock occurred in Philadelphia—where, in a politically charged atmosphere characterized by concern about rising property tax burdens, some citizens viewed reassessment as a ploy designed to increase those burdens.[25] When property owners go to an appeals hearing, they have the burden of proof in demonstrating that an assessment is too high. In Philadelphia in 2002, "too high" was defined as (1) a market value that was more than 80 percent of "true" value or (2) an assessed value that was more than 32 percent of market value.[26] To obtain a "market value," assessors were to deduct 20 to 30 percent from the true value; the assessment would then be set at 32 percent of this *discounted* market value. Thus, a house with a likely sales price of $100,000 would be assessed at about $22,400:

$$\$100,000 - (0.3 \times \$100,000) \times 0.32 = \$22,400.$$

Thus, although the assessment target appears to have been closer to 24 percent of market value (somewhat higher for lower-priced homes), a property owner who hoped to succeed in an appeal would have had to show an assessment higher than $32,000 ($100,000 × 0.32). The Board of Revision of Taxes in Philadelphia rejected about 90 percent of the 5,000 appeals filed in 2001.[27] The reassessment and appeals procedures followed in Philadelphia are likely to be similar to those used in other cities.

Some observers have asserted that although appeals of residential assessments have increased, "the system works as it does primarily because most people don't know how it works."[28] For example, even when property prices fall dramatically, they are still likely, in many areas, to be higher than assessments. Therefore, few owners will appeal their assessments. If some do submit appeals, however, the result will be to lower the total assessments—and the revenues—for that year. But the property tax for the following year can simply be adjusted to (1) restore revenue to target levels, (2) offset the overall reduction in assessments that resulted from appeals, and (3) cover anticipated delinquencies in payments.

Methods of valuation   The problem of establishing and updating the market value of property may be approached in several ways. Among the most common methods are sales data, regression analysis, replacement cost, and capitalized value. By combining these and other analytical techniques, the assessor can obtain an adequate basis for reasonable estimates of market value in all but the most extraordinary situations. In cases where customary valuation methods do not apply, various other approaches—described later in this section—are used.

Sales data   Where there is an active and competitive real estate market, market forces will establish a going price that assessors can use to estimate the value of all properties on the roll. Current market prices are the most direct evidence of property values and should be relatively accurate, even for properties that have not recently changed hands. It is important to note, however, that each property is in some way unique; thus, an estimate of its market value cannot be obtained from transactions for other parcels unless the differences and similarities between the property in question and the other parcels are accounted for. In many residential housing projects or tracts, however, differences are not major; moreover, property values tend to follow the same market trends. Therefore, the sales prices of even a small proportion of properties in a particular area during a period of observation can provide useful information on the value of other parcels in the area.

Sales data have been used by assessors and other appraisers for many decades. Some jurisdictions use a practice known as spot reassessment, in which the sale of a property automatically triggers a reassessment based on the most recent price (see sidebar below). Although the data in such cases are clear, current, and direct, unless the other properties in the district are reassessed relatively frequently—yearly, if possible—the higher prices registered for recently sold properties will place disproportionate tax burdens on those properties relative to others in the area. Thus, a lag in the reassessment of unsold parcels can—solely on the basis of the timing of sales—effectively redistribute the property tax burden. If the size of the staff or other constraints preclude annual review and reassessment of all properties, it would be more equitable to postpone the reassessment of any properties sold on the market until the number of transactions yields sufficient evidence (and there is enough time) for a general reassessment.

Regression analysis Multiple regression analysis, a somewhat more sophisticated method for placing a value on property, is essentially a statistical technique for correlating independent variables with a dependent variable to predict market value (see sidebar on facing page).

For purposes of appraisal, the characteristics of properties may be used as independent variables in an equation where the dependent variable is the estimate of property value. The coefficients for the independent variables indicate the expected changes in property value associated with a change in the independent variable (e.g., the nature of improvements).[29]

CAMA techniques have been incorporated into software packages that employ multiple linear regression analysis. Such an analysis adjusts values on the basis of comparable sales prices. According to the International Association of Assessing Officers (IAAO), the result (i.e., the coefficient of dispersion) should be between 90 and 110 percent of the median of the assessment ratio.[30] Such computer appraisal systems require adequate numbers of representative sales

---

Spot reassessment: The "Welcome, stranger" provision One of the problems associated with the property tax during a period of rapidly rising property values, such as occurred in California during the burgeoning of the tax-limitation movement, is the use of "spot reassessments" at the time a property is purchased. Unlike general reassessment, spot reassessment has been decried by critics—and in lawsuits—as discriminatory because it inhibits sales and places a disproportionate share of the property tax burden on new owners. In some states, spot reassessment has been found to be in violation of state legislative or constitutional provisions imposing tax uniformity or equal protection.[1]

In *Nordlinger v. Hahn,* the exemptions and reassessment provisions in Proposition 13 were challenged as arbitrary because they placed different burdens on owners of similar properties.[2] The U.S. Supreme Court disagreed, however, and upheld the provisions as fostering state interests in community and family stability.[3]

[1]Paul D. Roberts, "Real Estate Tax Assessment Discrimination," *Journal of Property Tax Management* 1, no. 4 (1990): 69–71.
[2]112 S.Ct. 2326 (1992).
[3]Rosemary O'Leary and Charles Wise, "A Review of 1991–1992 Supreme Court Cases Affecting Local Governments," *The Municipal Year Book 1993* (Washington, D.C.: International City/County Management Association, 1993), 94.

Multiple regressions for property values   A multiple regression for assessing property values takes the following form:

$$y = a + b_1x_1 + b_2x_2 + b_3x_3 + \cdots + x_n, \text{ where}$$

$y =$ the estimated market value of properties

$x_1, \ldots x_n =$ the values of the independent variables

$b_1, \ldots b_n =$ the coefficients or parameters for the independent variables

$a =$ the intercept value, or the estimated value if zero values were associated with the independent variables.

For this purpose, the independent variables would be the characteristics of the properties in the sample. Examples of such variables include lot size, location, front footage, type of building, type of construction, number of rooms, and square footage. The data used to estimate the property value would be the market value (dependent variable y) and the property characteristics (independent variables x) for each parcel in the sample of recorded sales.

To see how the equation would be interpreted, assume that it is related to single-family homes, that x_1 is the independent variable representing the number of bathrooms, and that b_1 (the coefficient for x_1) is $800. On this basis, with all other property characteristics or values for independent variables held constant, the estimated sales price (y) would increase by $800 for each unit increase in the value of x_1 or for each additional bathroom. If the equation is in logarithmic form, the value for b_1 would be expressed as a percentage change in the value of the estimated sales price for a given change in the value of the independent variable. This equation could be used, for example, to predict the price levels associated with different neighborhoods, or to predict the effect of lot size, size and type of structure, and other characteristics on property values within a neighborhood.

If the capitalization argument is followed, however, the tax rate also has an impact on the property value—which, in turn, has an impact on the tax. If these interrelationships are not taken into account, the estimated coefficients will be biased. Multiple regression analysis must be used very carefully.

prices, such as those that are reported to the Internal Revenue Service or to county offices when deeds are recorded.

Replacement cost   In the replacement-cost approach, an estimate is made of the value of an existing improvement or structure on the property, less a depreciation allowance for the age of the building. The estimate is based on current construction costs and specifically takes into account size, number of rooms, building materials, and similar characteristics.

The depreciation factors, classified by type of structure, permit the value of the building to be adjusted for age and condition. Subtracting depreciation from the cost of reconstruction yields a net replacement value, which may be roughly checked against current prices for comparable buildings even though the buildings may differ somewhat in construction, age, or condition.

The value of the building site is estimated separately on the basis of sales prices for parcels that are similar in general location, size, zoning, and any other factors that might affect desirability or price. Both front footage and square footage may also be taken into account. The value derived may then be roughly compared against market transactions for vacant land. Finally, in order to test the combined estimate, the total land value plus the depreciated replacement cost of the structure may be compared against recent sales prices for other properties. Although sales prices are used to confirm the estimated assessed value, the intermediate steps are required because no one property is exactly like another.

When buildings are clustered in housing developments or industrial parks, property values may be relatively easy to estimate because price differences resulting from location will tend to be minor. However, checks of market prices outside the targeted area may be used to determine whether the separate valuations assigned to the properties within the area are within a likely range.[31]

Capitalized value Yet another method of estimating the market value of property is to capitalize the estimated net income obtainable from the property: in this approach, the value of the property is based on its earning power, or its rate of return, in relation to market rates of return on investments. (Capitalized value will be discussed in detail in a later section of this chapter.) Although this approach is seldom used as the sole basis for assessment, it is useful for checking the values derived through other means. Direct capitalization is particularly helpful when the market for a type of property (e.g., hotels and theaters) is limited.

The use of capitalized value hinges on the availability of reliable estimates of annual income or rent, operating expenses, and depreciation allowances. To estimate the property value, the annual income or rent (after depreciation and operating expenses) is divided by a current discount rate. For example, if the net cash flow from a property is $100,000 and the market rate of return is 12.5 percent, then the estimated property value would be $800,000.[32]

The capitalization method may lead to underassessment if a property is not being used in a way that will yield the highest possible income—if, for example, the property is being held primarily for speculation. Such cases should be revealed when the results of the capitalization method are checked against estimates derived from sales data. In the absence of specific zoning, classification, or other provisions to the contrary, the figure that should be used is the one that reflects the capitalized value of the property at its highest, most profitable use.[33]

Exceptions In some extraordinary cases, customary valuation methods do not apply. For example, local assessment is not appropriate for an operating railroad or a public utility, properties that serve multiple jurisdictions. First, such property is rarely if ever sold, so current market value may be virtually impossible to determine. Second, if each jurisdiction served by a facility is permitted to assess the property, the whole operation may be overtaxed: estimates of the values of separate parts of a system may make little sense in relation to the value of the system as a whole. Third, it is questionable whether a locality that has a portion of the total system—the railroad yards and terminals, for example—within its boundaries should impose a tax cost that will be shifted to all riders. It is also questionable whether utilities should be required to pay a property tax in one locality when the tax is built into the utility rates for all users, including those who live outside the area. Thus, most states employ a general tax on utility revenues, and many state governments assume responsibility for the assessment of railroad and utility property. In some instances, the states apportion the centrally assessed value among the districts; in others, they collect the tax for themselves or for distribution to the localities.[34]

For some industries, alternative taxes have been developed in lieu of the property tax because the effects of the property tax could conflict with public policy. For example, property taxes on the value of forests may induce earlier cutting than would otherwise be economically justifiable. In many jurisdictions, a severance tax—which is levied on the value of timber when it is cut and sold—has replaced the property tax on timberland.[35] The advantage of the severance tax is that it does not require annual payments, which might force the owners to cut timber prematurely in order to raise cash to pay taxes. The severance tax has also been applied to extractive industries.[36]

Periodic reassessment Adjusting the assessment of each parcel of taxable property—ideally, on an annual basis—is necessary to maintain a reasonable relationship between the assessment base and market values. The problem is not simply to keep the tax base at an appropriate level but, more importantly, to keep individual properties in line with each other. A reassessment should substantially reduce the coefficient of dispersion, an index of the amount of inequity in the assessments. (The coefficient of dispersion is discussed in more detail later in this chapter.)

Although market trends may be clear for real estate prices as a whole, the rate and direction of the trends are unlikely to be uniform throughout a jurisdiction. For example, declining neighborhoods in a central city may be surrounded by exuberant suburban developments. If, during a given time period, market values are declining in one neighborhood and rising in another, reassessment must be frequent enough to reflect these changes. As noted earlier, the longer the time between reassessments, the greater the variations between the assessed and market values for particular properties, and the greater the dispersion, among properties and neighborhoods, of assessed-to-market-value ratios.

In large assessment districts with well-staffed offices, reassessment is a continuing function: every property is assessed every few years through a combination of mass appraisal, site visits, and sampling and statistical methods. Given that budgetary constraints may preclude annual reassessment of all areas and parcels, there may be some lag in the adjustments for different areas, but a carefully designed rotation system should permit an organized staff to deal with this problem. In small districts, staff limitations may preclude the frequent reassessment of existing parcels. The principal effort may be devoted to recording new properties and construction and noting the new prices reflected in transfers. In such cases, the passage of time nurtures inequity.

There are several ways to address the problem of infrequent assessments. One approach is to consolidate small assessment districts to achieve economies of scale. Where this approach has been implemented, the result is a decline in the number of assessment districts and a concomitant increase in the areas served by full-time assessors. A second, and perhaps better, solution is to contract with an outside, professional agency to undertake periodic assessments of all areas and properties in smaller districts.

Computers can facilitate frequent reassessment. The assessor can (1) code and transfer to computer files most of the information on the property records, including property descriptions and assessed values, and (2) record all property transactions, noting the sales price when the deed is recorded. In localities where the full purchase price is not required on the deed or is not reflected by transfer-tax stamps, the assessor can obtain the information by contacting the participants in the transaction.

The sales files can then be listed by the identification number of the parcel (which will also indicate its location), the date of the transaction, the assessed value, and the sales price. The assessor can then calculate the assessment ratio—the ratio between the current assessed value and the market price. Assessment ratios have been used not only by local tax bodies, such as counties or school districts, in tax calculations, but also by state tax equalization boards for the distribution of school grants; until 1992, they were also included in the

Census Bureau's Census of Governments.[37] If the assessment process has been reasonably accurate and the property market stable, the assessed-to-market-value ratio will be close to any official assessment ratio required by local or state law.

Separate samplings may be developed for different areas of the district, for different types of property, for each planning zone, or for any other relevant characteristic. The assessment ratios may serve as the basis for updating assessments in each category of similar properties. For example, if a property rises in market value, the assessment ratio can be applied to the new value to set the new assessment and tax burden, thereby preventing further dispersion from the acceptable assessment ratio. Adequate sales data should permit this procedure to be carried out annually, at a reasonable cost, with a minimum of on-site appraisals.[38]

Once property owners have been given adequate notice of the proposed new assessment values, a period of extensive review and appeal usually occurs before the results of the reassessment are used to determine the tax levy. The less frequent the reassessments, the larger the final adjustments will be and the greater the stress on individual property owners. Sharp changes in value inevitably raise opposition to the reassessment; such opposition is less likely if values change more gradually. In boom areas, for example, if an assessor tries to ensure that assessment values keep pace with rising property values, the property tax escalates faster than income, local governments ride a curve of rising revenues, and—unless local governments lower tax rates in order to hold tax bills in check—citizen protests and appeals are likely to follow. In fact, the California revolt against the property tax in the 1970s stemmed from two principal factors: (1) property prices that were rising more rapidly than local income and (2) the increasing use of computers, which made it possible for reassessment to keep pace with the market.

The difficulty of meeting sharply rising tax levies during a period of rapid change in property values may also lead property owners to call for special classification of land (e.g., for agricultural use) or for a moratorium on the implementation of new assessments on old holdings. In some older urban or suburban areas, for example, gentrification or redevelopment can increase market values and assessments. Unless the reassessment is delayed, the tax bills of longtime residents or their survivors may rise dramatically, and some may be forced (or enticed) to sell and move. Measures such as special classifications and moratoriums on reassessment may be opposed by the owners of newer homes, who pay a higher share of the total tax burden and who benefit from the equalization that occurs when older properties are reassessed.[39]

Evaluation of assessments   How is the quality of the assessment to be evaluated? Subjective methods are based on observations of tax bills and assessments, and of the differences between the assessments of specific properties. The fairness of assessments can also be tested objectively, however, by calculating the average coefficient of dispersion: that is, the deviation from the mean of the assessment ratios for individual properties or classes of property.

The coefficient indicates how fairly the assessor apportioned the property tax burden among owners of different properties according to their "true" value: a lower coefficient indicates a more consistent assessment. While more sophisticated statistical techniques can be used, historically the coefficient of dispersion has been the accepted measure of uniformity in assessment practice and probably serves its function well enough.

The coefficient is calculated in four steps, illustrated in Figure 10–2. The first step is to determine the assessment ratio for the parcels in a sample of recently sold properties. (In the figure, actual sales prices are used in place of

Figure 10–2 Illustrative table for determining the coefficient of dispersion.

Property	Recent price ($)	Assessment value ($)	Assessment ratio[a] (%)	Deviation from mean (%)[b]
Parcel A	100,000	37,000	37	55 – 37 = 18
Parcel B	80,000	40,000	50	55 – 50 = 5
Parcel C	75,000	30,000	40	55 – 40 = 15
Parcel D	70,000	42,000	60	55 – 60 = 5
Parcel E	65,000	41,000	63	55 – 63 = 8
Parcel F	60,000	33,000	55	55 – 55 = 0
Parcel G	35,000	28,000	80	55 – 80 = 25

Mean assessment ratio   55   Average deviation 10.9

$$\text{Coefficient of dispersion} = \frac{\text{Average deviation from mean assessment ratio}}{\text{Mean assessment ratio}}$$

$$= \frac{10.9}{55.0}$$

$$= 0.198 \text{ or } 19.8\%$$

[a] The assessment ratio is the assessment value as a percentage of the recent price. The average ratio for the seven parcels is 55 percent. For this illustration, the mean, or average value, is equal to the median value (Parcel F). The median value may be used as an alternative to the mean value; however, if the mean and the median differ, the results may vary.

[b] The deviation—that is, the amount by which the assessment ratio is above or below the mean or median—is an absolute value; thus, the calculation disregards the sign.

market prices.) The second step is to determine, for the sample of transactions, the mean (average) or median of the assessment ratios. The third step is to compute the average deviation of the individual property assessment ratios from the mean or median. The final step is to divide the average deviation by the mean or median. The result is the coefficient of dispersion.[40]

In Figure 10–2, the coefficient of dispersion is 19.8 percent. Although this high a coefficient could potentially be explained by imperfections in the raw data or by problems inherent in the valuation procedures, a lower coefficient would be desirable.

Bias against or in favor of some classes of property is a problem in some localities. If there are enough representative sales in each category, the assertion of bias can be tested objectively. The test is similar to the process used to determine the coefficient of dispersion, but the average assessment ratio for the properties in each *category* is substituted for the average assessment ratio for the *separate properties*. This procedure permits the calculation of a coefficient of dispersion that relates the average assessment ratios of the different classes of property to the overall ratio for the district. Even if assessment ratios are found to vary, however, the differences may not have originated with the assessor; they may reflect the accepted political view of the tax-bearing capacity of different properties, or they may be the result of successful appeals.

Another potential problem is the overassessment of lower-priced properties in relation to higher-priced properties, a phenomenon sometimes known as regressive assessment. Such overassessments may occur because the assessor is more familiar with the values of lower-priced properties, which are generally sold more frequently. Because higher-priced properties are often unique, the assessor may give the benefit of the doubt to the owner. The assessment ratios in Figure 10–2 roughly reflect regressive assessment: the average assessment is 55 percent; the properties with sales prices of $75,000 or more are assessed below the average, whereas those with lower sales prices tend to be assessed above the average.

One way to detect regressive assessment is to calculate the price-related differential in the assessment ratios. The first step is to calculate a weighted aggregate assessment ratio (the total value of all assessments divided by the total value of the parcels in the sample). The second step is to calculate an unweighted average of the assessment ratios. The unweighted average of the assessment ratios divided by the weighted aggregate assessment ratio gives the price-related differential. If the two ratios are equal, the price-related differential will be 1, or 100 percent. A price-related differential that is substantially above 100 percent suggests that higher-priced properties are underassessed; a value considerably below 100 percent indicates that lower-priced properties are underassessed. In Figure 10–2, for example, the total of the prices of parcels listed is $485,000 and the total of assessed values is $251,000. The weighted aggregate assessment ratio is 251/485, or 52 percent, while the mean (unweighted assessment ratio) is 55 percent. Thus, the price-related differential is 55/52, or 106 percent, a figure that reflects the underassessment of the higher-priced properties.

The existence of a price-related differential may be more important for properties within a given category than for properties in different categories. Problems may arise, for example, if there is a price-related bias in the assessment ratios of residences in general, or if one section of a locality or district is overassessed relative to others.[41] In a 1994 study, Andrew A. Beveridge examined sixty-one city and suburban areas and found that in 30 percent of the cities and 58 percent of the suburbs, black home owners paid more property taxes on similar homes (as valued by the owners) than did white home owners. Infrequent reassessment, spot reassessment, and other factors were cited as possible causes of the discrepancy.[42]

Lower assessments of industrial properties (versus residential or commercial properties) may result from a deliberate effort to attract industrial employment and to stimulate economic development.

Evidence indicates the need for better property tax administration in a substantial majority of districts. The IAAO recommends that the coefficient of dispersion be no more than 15 percent for heterogeneous or older properties and no more than 10 percent for newer, more similar properties.[43] Although more recent data are not available, the 1982 Census of Governments found that in only sixteen states was the median of coefficients for different assessment districts lower than 20 percent.[44] As of 1984, more than half the assessment authorities had assessment ratios above 20 percent—well above the IAAO standard.[45]

Recognition of exemptions

Exemptions, which may be partial or complete, are granted under law on the basis of property use (e.g., hospitals, homesteads, and educational or religious institutions) or of owner status (e.g., veterans, elderly or low-income residents, and firms that have been granted industrial development incentives). Examples of fully exempt properties are state and federal facilities, nonprofit hospitals, and educational or religious institutions. Shadow assessments—assessed values assigned to fully exempt properties—are often recorded to permit estimates of the subsidy cost (i.e., the lost revenues that result from the exemption).

In Philadelphia in 2001, for example, more than one-quarter ($11 billion out of $40 billion) of the real estate was exempt from the property tax. Some observers have equated the percentage of exempt property with a percentage increase in taxes for other taxpayers. For suburban counties of Philadelphia, this increased burden was as much as 15 percent, an inequity that led to a PILT (payment in lieu of taxes) program under which exempt institutions were required to compensate for some local government services.[46]

Partial exemptions are provided under laws that are separate from those that fully exempt property. In the case of partial exemptions (e.g., for homestead use, low-income property owners, or industrial development), it is important to ensure that each taxpayer receives the appropriate exemption. The assessor must receive and act on information or applications for exemptions under local or state-mandated programs. When an assessor certifies an application, the assessment is reduced in accordance with the law. An applicant who believes that an exemption was wrongly denied may appeal or sue.

In 2002, twenty-five states and the District of Columbia (1) allowed partial exemptions of assessed or market value or (2) reduced property tax rates for home owners. Some of the exemptions were homestead exemptions; others were tied to age or to veteran status.[47] A number of states have special provisions, called circuit breakers, that are tied to taxpayers' incomes and that provide partial exemptions.

Determination of the levy

The property tax levy is generally the fallback tax used to balance the final budget. To determine the required property tax levy, the budget officer usually takes the forecast amount of local government revenues derived from sources other than the property tax and subtracts it from the total estimated expenditures. The result is the required levy. The budget officer then calculates the property tax rate by dividing the required levy by the total value of property assessments and adjusting for anticipated delinquencies and estimated collections from past delinquencies. The resulting tax rate is expressed in mills (hundredths of a cent) per dollar (or tax dollars per thousand dollars) of assessed value.

Collection

The amount of tax due on each piece of property is the tax rate times the assessed value of the parcel. The tax collector sends a bill reflecting the tax assessment, tax rate, total liability, and terms of payment (dates and discount and penalty rates) to the property owner of record. In some states, billing and collection are centralized at the county level; in others, municipalities, counties, and school districts may all collect property taxes separately; that is, each may levy and collect its own property tax. The tax has traditionally been collected in one annual payment, but the use of quarterly and semiannual installments has become increasingly popular. Often, annual payments are made by mortgage companies that have held owners' monthly payments in escrow.

Penalties and interest charges for late payments are part of enforcement. In many jurisdictions, however, the penalty interest rate is below the market interest rate—which encourages delinquencies by enabling owners to, in effect, obtain relatively low-cost loans by delaying payment. Liens against the property are imposed when the tax remains unpaid for a long period. Continued delinquency may lead to seizure and eventually to the forced sale of the property to recover the delinquent taxes.

Although the tasks of the tax collector and the assessor may be separate, their functions should be well coordinated. Both should have access to the information on the tax roll, and both must be prepared to defend their actions in assessment appeals or enforcement procedures.

Continuing issues

As a local tax used to support local services, the property tax is a highly visible levy whose costs can be related directly to the benefits of local government programs. Despite its importance to local governments, the property tax has for some time been one of the least popular sources of public revenue and continues to be the subject of controversy.[48]

The eight brief sections that follow consider some of the principal issues surrounding the tax: (1) funding for education, (2) the tax-limitation movement, (3) the incidence of the tax, (4) exemptions, (5) the capitalized value of income, (6) classification by use, (7) site-value taxation, and (8) tax-base sharing.

Financing education

In a state where funding for local schools relies mainly on the local property tax, the quality of a child's education would depend on property values in the community: a child in a poor community would thus not receive as good an education as a child in a wealthy community. In 1971, the California Supreme Court ruled in *Serrano v. Priest* that a system for financing public education that discriminated among students on the basis of the wealth of the school district violated the equal protection clause of the U.S. Constitution.[49] The *Serrano* case, and others that followed elsewhere, made it clear that the wealth or income of the state as a whole, not of a particular locality, should determine the level of spending for every child in the state.

The court decisions required the end of discrimination against any definable group, called for more intrastate equalization of educational spending, and delegated to state legislatures the responsibility for bringing about more equality. The property tax was not discarded, however, as a major source of school support; nor was there any attempt or directive to equalize educational spending on a national basis, even though the reform of the system of financing public education was a matter of national concern.[50]

Among the ways that states could respond to the requirements for reform was by increasing equalization and support programs for public schools. From 1962 to 1972, the average state share for the support of public education rose from 40.5 to 42.0 percent of total local school costs. However, by the 1983–84 school year, the average state share had risen to 48.3 percent,[51] and by 1993 it had risen to 51 percent.[52] But despite growing state support for education, equalization continued to be an issue: in 1993, challenges to school financing systems were the subjects of lawsuits in twenty-nine states, including Texas and California. In Texas, after numerous other proposals had been rejected, a new method for achieving equalization was signed on May 31, 1993—under a court deadline of June 1.

In the 1970s, rising contributions from the states and from general revenue sharing temporarily decreased pressure on local property taxation for the support of schools. However, in the 1980s, the combination of continued increases in education spending and the end of general revenue sharing again focused attention on the property tax as a source of funding for schools. In the early 1990s, there was a major emphasis on school financing—how much to spend and how to provide resources—and on state equalization programs. The call for more grants, especially for poorer school districts, was designed to reduce pressure on local property taxes by increasing state support for education. However, because proposals for property tax relief were often tied to measures that would have imposed or increased sales taxes, such proposals often failed to get statewide approval. Referenda on such measures failed in Michigan and Montana, for example. In 1994, however, Michigan voters approved reductions in property taxes and offsetting increases in sales and other taxes, which would be used to finance schools. In 2003, attempts to reduce property taxes through state action failed in New Jersey; in Pennsylvania, increased state support for local schools was successfully tied to a 10 percent increase in state income taxes.

Educational opportunity continues to be an issue, and some states have elected to rely on the property tax to support statewide "adequate" education. As of 2003, Vermont was funding a state education grant to all school districts through a state component of the property tax, equivalent to $1.10 per $100 of property value. However, towns were permitted to augment the state grant through a "local share school property tax."[53]

New Hampshire initiated a state education property tax in 1999, after the state supreme court declared funding for an "adequate education" to be a state responsibility. When the tax was first initiated, the cost to the state of providing an adequate education was estimated at $825 million, about half of which was to be funded from other state revenues and about half of which was to come from the state property tax. The tax is assessed and collected by local governments. To determine what proportion of the tax must be raised by each municipality, the state multiplies the municipality's total equalized property value (not including utilities) by the uniform tax rate of $6.60 per $1,000 of assessed value. Equalization involves comparing sales data with property assessments to determine the full and true value of property in each municipality. Thus, a community that had "underassessed" by 10 percent of market value would pay 10 percent more than the $6.60 per $1,000 of local assessed property value.[54] (For further discussion of issues related to school financing, see Chapter 3.)

The tax-limitation movement

Beginning in the mid-1970s and continuing into the 1980s, there was increasing citizen support for restricting tax increases by imposing limitations on revenues, expenditures, or both. Some of the limits took the form of amendments to state constitutions; others were simply acts of the legislature. The movement had lasting and far-reaching effects: according to a compilation undertaken by the ACIR, the number of states with limits on the property tax levy increased dramatically, from three prior to 1970 to twenty-two by 1985. The number remained steady during the early years of the 1990s.[55]

The unpopularity of the property tax
Surveys of public attitudes toward various types of taxation have shown the property tax to be as unpopular as the federal income tax.

In its landmark study of school financing, the Advisory Commission on Intergovernmental Relations cited a number of reasons for the unpopularity of the property tax:

No other tax is as harsh on citizens with low incomes and so "capriciously" related to ability to pay.

When compared with both income and sales taxes, which accord housing preferential treatment, the property tax appears to be antihousing.

Because increased property values are taxed prior to increases in spendable income, the tax is on unrealized capital gains.

Administration, particularly assessment of the tax base, is more difficult and subjective (especially during periods of inflation) than it is for any other tax, and the shock of reassessment is "without parallel" among other taxes.

Requirements that stipulate infrequent payments (for those who do not pay monthly to escrow accounts) make the cost more apparent and more "painful" than the costs associated with sales and income taxes.

Source: Advisory Commission on Intergovernmental Relations (ACIR), *Financing Schools and Property Tax Relief: A State Responsibility*, A-40 (Washington, D.C.: ACIR, 1973), 30.

In California, the tax-limitation movement began with Howard Jarvis, an activist whose campaign to curtail the property tax culminated in the passage, in 1978, of Proposition 13, also known as the Jarvis-Gann Amendment. The amendment restricted the property tax rate to 1 percent of full cash value, defined as the assessed value in the 1975–76 tax year; for newly constructed property or property resold at a later date, Proposition 13 provided for spot reassessment. Despite exemptions (e.g., residents over age fifty-five were permitted to retain an old assessment value if they sold one home to buy another of the same or lower value, or if they transferred a home to a child), the provisions for spot assessment remain highly controversial.

In addition to limiting the overall tax rate, Proposition 13 limited annual increases in assessed value to 2 percent per year. Furthermore, it required new taxes or increases in existing taxes (except property taxes) to be approved by two-thirds of the state legislature (in the case of state taxes) or by two-thirds of the voters (in the case of local taxes).

Significantly, Proposition 13 was followed by Proposition 4, which restricted overall increases in government spending. Although Proposition 13 had been directed mostly against the property tax, the subsequent passage of Proposition 4 offers some evidence that voters in California were registering a general protest against the size of the public sector. From 1987 to 1997 in California, state property tax collections per capita increased by 3.4 percent, versus an average of 4.2 percent for all states (both percentage figures are based on constant dollars). During the same period, per capita local property tax collections in California grew 0.9 percent, versus an average of 2.1 percent for all states (again, both percentage figures are based on constant dollars).[56]

Meanwhile, tax limitation appeared at the local level as well. In 1991, in Illinois, the suburban counties surrounding Chicago adopted tax caps. The caps resulted in heavy losses for school districts in these counties, some of which were forced to go to the voters for referenda to balance their budgets.[57]

Tax incidence

Statistical studies show that lower-income households spend a higher percentage of their incomes for consumption (specifically for shelter) than do higher-income households. If this finding is coupled with the assumption that much of the property tax burden is shifted away from property owners to consumers through higher prices for goods and services, including housing, one would expect the property tax burden for lower-income households to be disproportionately large. As this section will make clear, however, this is a controversial assumption.

In 1982, the ACIR studied the tax burdens of families residing in the largest city in each state. For each of the four income levels studied, the median of property taxes paid was taken to represent "typical" taxes for a city family with two adults and two dependents. The ACIR found that a family with an income of $17,500 paid 2.89 percent of its income in property taxes. As income levels rose to $25,000, $50,000, and $100,000, median property taxes fell to 2.47, 1.96, and 1.44 percent of income, respectively. This finding suggests that the proportion of the property tax burden borne by households with incomes of $100,000 was typically about half the burden of those with incomes of $17,500.[58]

Economist Henry J. Aaron and others have challenged the traditional view of the regressivity of property taxation.[59] Aaron suggests that it may be misleading to measure the tax burden in relation to current annual income rather than lifetime average annual income. For example, a worker's annual income drops sharply at retirement, but his or her property tax bill does not. If the annual income of a retiree on a pension is compared with the annual income of an employed worker, the retiree seems poorer and the tax seems regressive. In Aaron's view, averaging all income over a worker's lifetime gives a more accurate view of the tax burden.

Aaron also sees the property tax as a kind of national tax on owners of capital. In his model, market forces and investment decisions effectively redistribute the burden of the property tax; thus, property taxes are borne by all owners of capital in proportion to their ownership of capital. Income level and ownership of capital are correlated: people who own capital get income from it and thus have higher incomes. In Aaron's view, the incidence of the property tax is, in the long run, progressive.

Yet another way of looking at the property tax is as an excise tax on housing. When the incidence of the tax is analyzed using this approach, the tax does not appear to be regressive: the effective incidence of the tax shows progressivity (higher percentage burdens on higher-income residents) for home owners and rough proportionality (the same percentage burdens on all income groups) for renters.[60]

The extent to which capital owners can shift the burden of the tax to others (in the form of rental fees or of prices charged for products) has been viewed as critical to determining whether the property tax is progressive or regressive. Economist Richard A. Musgrave has noted that market conditions can affect the extent to which the tax burdens for rental housing and for various types of business property can be shifted; the burden can be shifted more easily, for example, when there is a shortage of available housing units or business property. However, Musgrave agrees with Aaron that using lifetime income renders the distribution of the property tax burden less regressive.[61]

More recently, Michael Lorelli revisited Aaron's view of the property tax as a general tax on capital. According to Lorelli, because the value of land, buildings, and equipment subject to the tax is fixed in the short run, the tax is likely to remain the burden of the capital owners.[62] And since capital ownership is directly correlated with income levels, Lorelli's view suggests that those with higher incomes will bear a greater share of the tax burden, which would make the tax progressive.

Lorelli also investigates the relationship between the property tax and the benefits provided by the government programs that are financed by the tax, citing evidence that the benefits fall as income rises; this suggests another "progressive element" in the tax. Lorelli concludes that with a combination of such progressive elements, the burden of the tax appears to be "at least proportional and probably progressive" in its effects on income distribution.[63]

Nevertheless, most economists would view the property tax independently: that is, they do not link it to the benefits it funds. And although higher-income households do tend to live in more expensive homes, the correlation between income and spending on shelter is not perfect; moreover, as noted earlier, more expensive homes are likely to be assessed at a lower percentage of market value. As a result, even with uniform rates, a lower percentage of higher incomes is spent for property taxes. In this more common view, the property tax is regressive.

Exemptions

Exemptions are granted under law on the basis of either property use or owner status. Exemptions on the basis of use vary in their financial impact. If a high proportion of the land in a jurisdiction is held by religious or educational institutions, hospitals, public housing authorities, or government agencies, for example, the financial impact can be severe. Even when these organizations make payments in lieu of taxes (which may be linked to the level of community service they provide), the payments seldom equal the amount that would be obtained through property taxes.

In 1982, the Committee for Intergovernmental Tax Equity, which was formed by local officials to encourage a program of federal payments in lieu of property taxes on federal property, estimated the 1978 value of such property at $279 billion.[64] The effort failed, although similar initiatives—also unsuccessful—arose twenty years later. Of course, tax-exempt entities may return services and economic value to the community that exceed the forgone taxes. In general, though, it may be better to support socially desirable activities through direct subsidies rather than through tax exemption.

Since many exempt properties do not carry even a shadow assessment, it is impossible to determine the cost of the exemptions. There have been a number of recommendations for reform: assess exempt property; repeal permanent exemptions; use exemptions only on a limited basis; estimate the revenues lost through the exemption of certain properties, including exemptions used to attract industry;[65] and review the uses of exempt property to ensure that those uses are in the public interest.[66] Some analysts, who view the revenue loss created by exemptions as an expenditure funded by taxpayers, have recommended that exemptions be subject to the same kind of review as government spending to ensure that the benefits justify the burdens.

Many states and localities offer industrial exemptions to sustain or expand local employment. Higher employment helps maintain the value of local property and adds to the local tax base. Critics of these inducements note, however, that exemption policies invite retaliation or imitation by other jurisdictions; if many areas offer exemptions, there may no longer be any competitive advantage in doing so. As a result, some states are beginning to restrict local use of tax abatement for economic development; recent legislation in Texas, for example, bars school districts from providing tax abatements.[67]

To relieve some of the presumed regressivity of the property tax, many states have enacted homestead exemptions and circuit breakers: in a 1994 survey, the ACIR found thirty-six states with circuit-breaker provisions and forty-eight with homestead exemptions.[68] In 1975, the ACIR recommended that homestead exemptions be replaced by circuit breakers because the exemptions usually targeted particular groups (veterans, elderly residents) without regard for income and were therefore regressive. In contrast, circuit-breaker provisions are specifically designed to provide relief for lower-income home owners and for renters who may be overburdened by property taxes.[69]

Minnesota adopted the first circuit breaker in 1964. By 1991, forty-one states and the District of Columbia had adopted circuit breakers, and several other states had low-income eligibility provisions for homestead relief. Circuit breakers vary substantially among states, however. In most states, eligibility is linked to income; the amount of relief declines as income rises, and no relief is offered once the income limit is reached. Some states include only home owners in their programs; others also cover renters. Many programs are restricted to elderly residents, with eligibility beginning at sixty-two or sixty-five years of age, and some programs offer state tax rebates or credits that act as circuit breakers. In 1992, the ACIR reported that, in general, these special provisions had made the property tax less regressive.[70]

It has been argued that circuit breakers favor those whose incomes are only temporarily low, and those who own substantial property but who may not actually be in need of relief, even if their current income levels are relatively low. For example, a worker whose income level declines as a result of a lay-

New Jersey's programs for property tax relief   Some programs for property tax relief are funded by local governments, others by the states. For 2004, New Jersey's programs included (1) the NJ SAVER Rebate, which is paid by the state based on equalized home values of up to $45,000 and the effective school tax rate, and is limited to those with incomes under $200,000; (2) the Homestead Rebate, a state rebate of between $90 and $775 for home owners and tenants who are over age sixty-five or disabled and have a gross income of less than $100,000 (home owners or tenants who are not disabled or who are under sixty-five must have gross incomes of less than $40,000); (3) Property Tax Reimbursement, under which home owners who meet particular age, income, and residence requirements are reimbursed for the difference between property taxes in a base year and the reimbursement year; (4) the Property Tax Deduction/Credit, under which home owners receive a credit of $50 or are permitted to deduct from their state taxes the property taxes paid on a principal residence, and renters are permitted to deduct 18 percent of their rent (up to $10,000); (5) the Senior Citizens Annual Property Tax Deduction, which allows home owners who are disabled or age sixty-five or older and who meet specific income and residency requirements to deduct up to $250 from their property taxes; and (6) the Veterans Deduction, under which qualified veterans or their unmarried surviving spouses are permitted to deduct $250 annually from their local property taxes. These six programs are clearly meant to be circuit breakers—that is, to provide property tax relief on the basis of income and other criteria; however, coordinating them would clearly simplify the system.

Source: State of New Jersey, Division of Taxation, "New Jersey Property Tax Relief Programs," available at www.state.nj.us/treasury/taxation/.

off or a job change may soon be reemployed at high wages, and the temporary decline in income may leave overall ownership of wealth unaffected. Another argument against circuit breakers is that older residents who might otherwise liquidate or trade down the value of their homes may be induced to stay in them if their property taxes do not fully reflect market values. On the one hand, few citizens would want retirees to be forced by high property taxes to sell their homes; on the other hand, many citizens would resent subsidizing the taxes on retirees' homes so that the homes can be inherited, free of debt, by the next generation. From the perspective of the state, allowing older home owners to defer all or part of their tax liabilities until a set future date or until a future sale or transfer of property may be preferable to circuit-breaker provisions. Deferral would mean that any shift of the tax burden from older home owners to others would be temporary.

Ordinarily, when an owner improves a property, the resulting increase in property value can lead to a tax increase; this discourages owners from improving properties or bringing them up to code. Some proponents of housing for lower-income groups have proposed the use of property tax abatements or temporary tax relief to promote housing rehabilitation. In Salina, Kansas, for example, to encourage property owners in two low- to moderate-income areas to renovate or construct homes and businesses, a program was put into effect under which 25 to 100 percent of the increase in a property's value after renovation or construction is subject to a property tax rebate for up to ten years.

Capitalized value of income

Both income and property ownership can be viewed as separate bases of ability-to-pay taxation. Income, however, is viewed as a flow over a period of time, whereas capital, or property, is perceived as a stock of wealth owned on a particular date. Income and property wealth are related, however, because property is expected to yield income during a future period. Thus, one way to determine the value of an asset is to capitalize the value of its expected earnings. For example, assume that a property is expected to yield $500 a year for an indefinite period of time and that the market rate of return on capital is 10 percent a year. The capitalized value of the property is then $5,000, the same as it would be for any other asset expected to yield $500 a year given a 10 percent rate of return. The owner of that property would thus be subject to an ability-to-pay tax that is equivalent to the tax that would be paid by someone who has an income of $500 from another source. A tax of 2 percent on the property value, then, would impose an annual burden of $100, the equivalent of a 20 percent tax on $500 of other income.

However, just as the value of expected earnings can be capitalized, so can the impact of a tax on those earnings. In the given example, a property yielding $500 in income was valued at $5,000. But if the property is subject to an annual property tax of 2 percent, or $100, and nothing else changes, the effect is to reduce the after-tax income to $400. As a result, the value of the property would fall to $4,000, reflecting the capitalization of the tax.

Moreover, if the imposition of (or an increase in) a tax effectively reduces the tax base (assessed property values) by an amount that reflects the capitalization of the tax increase, a higher tax rate will be required in order to raise the same amount of revenue. In the example, a 2 percent tax rate on a property valued at $5,000 produced $100 in revenues. But if capitalization reduces the assessed value to $4,000, a tax rate of 2.5 percent would be needed to raise the same $100. Thus, the capitalization of the property tax alters the relationship between the tax rate on gross income from property and the effective property tax rate, both of which can, in turn, affect the market value of property.[71] If the income yield from a property is irregular, then it may not be as convenient to pay a property tax as to pay a tax on a flow of income.

Research suggests that differentials in taxes and services may be capitalized. For example, all other things being equal, a property is likely to have a lower value in a district where taxes are higher and where better services do not compensate for higher taxes. However, when citizens are free to choose among districts where they wish to live, a higher tax rate does not decrease property values—as long as levels of public services are higher. Thus, higher-income families may be willing to pay both higher property taxes and higher prices for homes if they feel that they are compensated by higher-quality schools.[72]

Capitalization of the property tax has been related to urban sprawl—the spread of residential and commercial development to outlying areas where taxes are lower. In many areas, a number of factors, including economic decline and higher property taxes, have driven down the value of central-city land. Despite the lower market values of city land and existing structures, however, those planning new construction may prefer to buy more expensive land in the suburbs, where taxes are lower.

Classification by use

All states and the District of Columbia have provisions that classify property and lower the tax for certain property classifications. Tax classification, which is often implemented to satisfy voters, is used to realign the tax burden by placing higher rates on business properties than on farms or homes. It is also a means of exporting some of the tax incidence: higher rates on industrial properties or hotels are assumed to shift the tax burden to buyers (through higher prices) or to shareholders who reside outside the jurisdiction.

The principal purpose of classification by use, however, is to slow urban sprawl. If, for example, land used for agriculture is taxed at a lower rate, landowners will be more reluctant to develop the land for industrial or residential use. Several states have implemented special programs to slow the conversion of agricultural land to other uses. For example, if a landowner agrees to maintain the land in agricultural use for ten years, the property tax assessment will be based on the capitalized value in agriculture rather than on the market value for other uses, such as shopping centers.[73] Critics have noted that this arrangement carries special benefits for landowners who are willing to speculate on a future price, and that it is an insufficient inducement to prevent development on the urban fringe. Some have suggested that land use zoning would be a more effective planning tool than differential property tax assessment.[74]

Another tax reform that relies on classification encourages redevelopment and renovation by providing a lower tax rate for improvements to deteriorated properties.

Site-value taxation

There has long been an argument that the property tax should be based on land values alone, regardless of buildings or improvements. Proponents of this view claim that a tax on improvements discourages capital investment. They note that because the value of land—as distinct from the value of buildings and improvements—is derived from its scarcity and from community investment in public facilities (e.g., sewers and roads), a site-value (or land-value) tax is an appropriate way to recapture some of that investment. Proponents further argue that a tax on land value is neutral: it does not favor or discriminate against any particular land use, and whatever use is most profitable before the imposition of a land tax will remain the most profitable afterward.

Some site-value taxation proposals would provide full or partial exemptions for improvements in order to encourage building, achieve more intensive land use, and foster the replacement of deteriorated buildings on valuable sites, thereby reducing urban decay and housing costs. Such exemptions would be intended to avert some of the potential negative effects of site-value taxation. For example, in Tokyo in the 1990s, high taxes on land value meant that modest dwellings situated on valuable land were taxed at very high rates. (In fact, land values were so high that older houses were viewed as no longer "deserving" the increased value of the lot. The owner would move out, replace the house with a much more expensive one, and move back in.)

In a study undertaken by Minnesota Planning, property classification, preferential valuations, and equal property taxes on land and improvements were found to contribute to inefficient land use in Minnesota. According to the study, improvements made up about 70 percent of the property tax base; therefore, if taxes were higher on sites and lower on structures, there would be an incentive to economize on the use of land. The study concluded that successful site-value taxation would require changes in a number of property tax provisions, such as classification, and in some land use regulations, such as zoning, but that it would then have the potential to promote efficient land use.[75]

Another study of the effects of a site-value tax found that it would lead, in the long run, to substantial investment in improvements.[76] In order to maintain property tax revenues at current levels while completely exempting improvements, however, either very high site-value assessments or high tax rates on land would be required. Other empirical studies have suggested that only partial exemption of improvements would be feasible, unless property tax revenues were supplemented by funds from nonproperty tax sources.[77]

Because improvements are a major part of the current tax base, proposals to tax land only have been seriously questioned on the basis of revenue adequacy. Observers have also questioned the inequities that may result from the subsequent shifts of the property tax burden. For example, landowners who paid prices based on the previous system may be penalized by a land-only tax. Assume that two buyers paid the same price for different properties, one with a wonderful mansion on a modest site and the other with a modest cottage on a wonderful site. After a site-value tax, the second property has a higher tax and thus a higher price. In addition, the need to alter state laws and constitutions imposes serious political obstacles to the adoption of land-value tax systems.

Tax-base sharing

In metropolitan areas, intergovernmental cooperation is often achieved through state-established agencies that serve a specific purpose: the Bay Area Rapid Transit Authority and the Southeastern Pennsylvania Transportation Authority are examples. Such agencies are often governed by a council made up of representatives of the municipalities that contribute to the agency's budget. Recently, some observers have called for arrangements in which tax-base sharing would be the funding mechanism for such agencies and their councils; there have also been calls for the expansion of the responsibilities of such agencies so that they can address regional problems, such as inner-city blight, middle-class flight, and suburban sprawl.

One supporter of tax-base sharing is Myron Orfield, a regional planning advocate and a former member of the Minnesota House of Representatives.[78] In Orfield's view, when differences in the wealth of the property tax base lead to disparities in service, it is more equitable to set aside a share of the commercial, industrial, or residential property tax base and to share it throughout a metropolitan region. Such an approach has the potential to reduce the disparity between needs and resources, curb incentives for sprawl, and decrease intraregional competition for the tax base. The combination of regional tax-base sharing and regional planning could also result in a "deconcentration" of poverty and an increase in affordable housing.

A report prepared by Geoffrey K. Turnbull, of the Fiscal Research Program at Georgia State University, proposed tax-base sharing for the Atlanta metropolitan area. After examining the methods and sources of authority for different types of regional cooperation, Turnbull concluded that, as a means of coordinating regional activities, joining Georgia counties and cities into metropolitan governments would be less desirable than tax-base sharing.[79]

Prospects for reform

The property tax has been and will continue to be the focus of controversy; nevertheless, it is likely to remain a principal source of local government revenue. Overall, the property tax has a number of advantages. It is an acceptable, stable, and predictable source of revenue that is particularly well suited to local administration. The annual property tax bill provides property owners with clear evidence of the costs of local government services and thus with an opportunity to evaluate those costs.[80] The tax also enables local governments to capture some of the property value created by the community at large; for example, in communities that are well kept and have good public services, real estate prices and assessments are likely to be higher.

Despite its advantages, however, there is unquestionably room for reform of the property tax. As noted earlier, research has tended to confirm that properties with higher values are assessed at lower rates than properties with lower values, which means that the property tax is more regressive than need be.[81] Because the potential for inequity and regressivity is the most serious concern associated with the property tax, most reform proposals give the highest priority to "maintaining uniform assessments through frequent and regular reevaluation of property."[82] Many reformers view such a policy as a means of reducing flight from declining areas and contributing to their revitalization: if assessments in declining areas are reduced as property values fall, lower tax bills could provide an incentive for property owners to remain and improve their properties.

Many reform proposals emphasize the role of the state in improving the administration of the tax. In the early 1960s, the ACIR recommended strong state supervision or direct state administration of the assessment system—along with professional market-value appraisals and the disclosure of assessment ratios (to allow the fairness of the system to be evaluated). The ACIR further recommended state financing of circuit-breaker provisions, state payment of some state-mandated local expenditures, and in lieu payments for state-mandated property tax exemptions. Finally, the ACIR suggested that the states (1) reform their tax laws to eliminate the taxation of intangible personal property, a form of taxation that is theoretically suspect and virtually impossible to administer; (2) review exemption laws; (3) consolidate small assessment districts; (4) improve standards for assessment personnel; and (5) provide strong state supervision, coordination, and appeal procedures.[83] The case for more active state supervision is based, in part, on the view that state oversight would improve efficiency and equity. However, more supervision involves more costs—and, in some cases, may not be welcome or worthwhile.

Other reform proposals focus on moderation in the use of and reliance on the property tax as a way of forestalling tax-limitation measures, which often bring severe restrictions and increased pressure to cut local government programs.[84] The ACIR has recommended that, where possible, alternative taxes and state support—revenue sources that are often viewed as more equitable than the property tax—be substituted for the property tax.

Some states have adopted provisions in line with the ACIR's proposals. Many states, for example, have circuit breakers and homestead exemptions that are designed to make the tax less regressive or more progressive. Some cities, including New York and Philadelphia, have local sales taxes that are piggybacked on state sales taxes, so administrative costs are minimal and there is a broader tax base. In Pennsylvania, in 1998, municipalities and school districts were given the authority to levy a tax on earned income and net profits. Municipalities can levy an earned-income tax of up to 0.5 percent, and school districts can levy a tax of up to 0.5 percent—or, with local approval, up to 1.5 percent. Thus, if a municipality were taxing at the permitted rate of 0.5 percent, the earned-income tax could rise to a total of 2 percent of earned income. The law also permits increases or reductions in property tax revenues, and allows residents who work in one taxed jurisdiction and reside in another to use a tax payment in one district as a credit in the other.[85] Thus, sales and income taxes were permitted, as recommended by the ACIR, to expand local revenue bases beyond the constraints of the property tax.[86] In 1999, of the fifty largest cities in each state, twenty levied a sales tax, as did the District of Columbia. All fifty-one of these cities levied a property tax.[87]

How does the property tax measure up? Several criteria may be used to decide whether to impose a tax as well as to judge its equity, efficiency, and long-range effectiveness. The discussion that follows describes the criteria generally used to evaluate a tax and briefly analyzes the property tax in relation to each criterion.

Fairness Either a tax should reflect the ability to pay of those who bear its burden, or the tax burden should be matched by the benefits that individual taxpayers receive. In general, unless benefits are clearly accounted for, taxes that take a higher percentage of the income of lower-income residents (regressive taxes) are considered unfair.

Although the property tax has been criticized as regressive and unfair, efforts to determine precisely which income groups bear what shares of the tax burden have come to contradictory conclusions, depending on the assumptions used. Circuit-breaker provisions, classification systems, and equalizing grants (especially for school finance) reduce some of the regressivity of the property tax. In some states, circuit breakers have wide effects. In Maryland during the 2001–02 fiscal year, for example, one in seventeen home owners qualified by income to receive tax relief, which amounted to a total of more than $49 million in state funds.[1]

Certainty The rules of taxation should be clearly stated and evenly applied. In the case of the property tax, property appraisal should reflect market value without bias.

Property tax administration has been criticized as biased and costly. Bias toward or against some classes of property continues to be a problem in some jurisdictions, as does overassessment of lower-priced properties. Excessively high coefficients of dispersion indicate that in a substantial majority of districts, there is room for improvement in the equity of administration: certainly the variations in assessment practices would not be acceptable for other state tax bases, such as the income tax. However, with increasing state involvement in property tax administration, wider use of techniques such as computer-assisted mass appraisal systems, and the implementation of specific appeal procedures, some improvement can be anticipated.

Convenience A tax should be convenient to pay, with billing dates that coincide with taxpayers' income streams.

Although the large, lump-sum payments traditionally associated with the property tax have been a source of hardship for some taxpayers, new collection procedures and provisions for more frequent payments (through lending institutions) have made payment of the tax more convenient for many citizens.

But the calls for reform continue. Sometimes, as in Michigan and Pennsylvania, the goal is to obtain property tax relief by changing the way that schools are supported. At other times, as in New Hampshire and Vermont, there are echoes of the *Serrano* decision in California. If the courts make it the state's responsibility to provide an adequate education without regard to a local government's assessments, the state can impose its own property tax. Still other states, including Minnesota and Connecticut, are considering property tax reform as one remedy for sprawl and lack of affordable housing. Reformers in some states have requested special sessions of the state legislature to address the issue of property taxes; in New Jersey, reformers called for a constitutional convention.

At both the state and local levels, some improvements in property tax administration have occurred. Some states, for example, have not only taken over the assessment of some categories of property but also extended technical and

In some states, increases in assessments take effect gradually; in Maryland, for example, the effects of an increase in assessed value are phased in over three years. Also, some local governments have the authority to permit home owners who are over age sixty-five to defer tax increases; the deferred amounts become liens on the property.[2] And cities in Pennsylvania are permitted by state law to defer payment of tax increases until a property is sold.[3] Such provisions can minimize the shock of property tax increases.

Efficiency Administration should be feasible and efficient, and the costs of administration should not be out of proportion to revenue. A tax should be appropriate for its geographical jurisdiction, and should be neither too easy to avoid nor too costly to enforce. For example, in a large state, it may be too costly for state government to assess property values, and it may be too easy to avoid sales taxes levied at various rates by small localities.

The property tax can be administered efficiently by local governments because the real property tax base is not portable. State property taxes, as in Vermont and New Hampshire, can also be administered locally with some state equalization. Generally, other major taxes, such as income and sales taxes, are difficult to enforce on a local basis: to avoid income or sales taxes, taxpayers can move from one jurisdiction to another or can make purchases in other jurisdictions.

Productivity A tax should produce sufficient stable revenue to meet locally desired levels of expenditure.

Through early 2003, new construction and rising property values in many areas had increased the tax base and, despite some fluctuations in income and employment, provided a fairly stable source of tax revenue. During the recession of the 1990s, however, changes in property incomes and market values led to decreased revenue in some areas, although sales and income taxes had sharper declines than the property tax.

Neutrality A tax should not distort the way a community would otherwise use its resources unless it is clear that such a change is socially desirable.

The property tax has been criticized for its adverse effects on housing and on capital investment. A land or site-value base would be more neutral, but it would be difficult to implement.

[1]State of Maryland, *A Homeowner's Guide to Property Taxes and Assessments,* available at www.dat.state.md.us/sdatweb/hog.html.
[2]Ibid.
[3]Tom Ferrick Jr., "Which Tax Fiend Gets the Pitchfork?" *Philadelphia Inquirer,* 15 September 2002, B1.

advisory consulting services to assessment districts. Assessment districts have been made larger through consolidation of smaller districts or through the designation of the county as the assessment unit.

Meanwhile, in the state of fiscal crisis that prevailed at the beginning of the century, some local governments began looking again to the property tax. In an effort to reduce a projected 2003 budget deficit of billions of dollars, New York City mayor Michael Bloomberg proposed, among other measures, an 18.49 percent increase in property taxes that would have affected renters as well as home owners. Because the city has significant sales and income tax revenues that make up the difference, New York's property taxes are low compared with those of many other cities. Nevertheless, there was substantial opposition to the increased burden and a threat of "political payback" for some city council members who supported the budget changes and the tax increase.[88] The increase was implemented despite the threat.

Similarly, there were angry objections in Philadelphia to a reassessment that led to an increase in the property tax burden. The city's tax rate of 2.664 percent of assessed value had been constant for years, and a rate change would have required council approval. In 2002, however, the Board of Revision of Taxes notified about 56 percent of taxpayers (about 270,000 out of 485,000) that their assessments had increased; about 11 percent (30,000) of those whose properties had been reassessed were notified that their assessments had been reduced. Objections focused not only on the increased burdens (some tax bills doubled in a one-year period), but also on the fact that some homes at lower price levels appeared to have been subject to particularly large increases.

The total estimate of the city's taxable market value rose about $1.3 billion, to $33 billion—a figure that would yield a $34 million revenue increase for the city and its schools without any increase in the tax rate. Some blamed the mayor, who attributed the increase to rising property values. The tax board said that the changes were the result of its annual reassessments.[89]

The major objections to the property tax often concern the assessment process. In the suburbs of America, reassessment may be infrequent; up to fifty-year intervals can be cited. As a result, the relationships between current market values and tax bills may be inconsistent. In cities, where reassessment may be much more frequent, regressive assessment practices have often been documented; notorious cases include the peculiarly low assessments of mayors' homes and of multimillion-dollar estates.[90] Other taxes, such as sales and income taxes, are based on current market values and rarely require assessments; moreover, such taxes are based on actual purchases and on income flows, rather than on the estimated value of an unsold asset. Finally, even where assessments are fair and accurate and the system includes circuit breakers, the property tax may still be regressive.

However, the property tax remains the main revenue source of local governments. Local knowledge can be important to tax administration even if professional consultants do reassessments. As a local revenue source, the property tax can be thought of as a grassroots source of autonomy for local judgments. There are few calls to totally abolish the property tax. Instead, both the amount of property tax collections and the volume of calls for property tax reform are likely to continue.

1 Anthony R. Wood, "Reviled Levy Has Lasted 400 Years," *Philadelphia Inquirer,* 9 December 2001, A22.

2 The decline in these stock values is not significant to the property tax base; as intangible personal property, securities are untaxed or lightly taxed.

3 Greg Ip, "As Housing Buoys Economy, It's No Surprise to Fed's Chairman," *Wall Street Journal,* 28 May 2003, A1.

4 U.S. Department of Commerce, Bureau of the Census, *Taxable Property Values,* 1992 Census of Governments, vol. 2, no. 1 (Washington, D.C.: U.S. Government Printing Office, 1994), xiv.

5 Tax Foundation, *Facts and Figures on Government Finance* (Washington, D.C.: Tax Foundation, 2002).

6 Bureau of the Census, *Taxable Property Values.*

7 Most of the older data in this section are from U.S. Department of Commerce, Bureau of the Census, *Taxable Property Values and Assessment—Sales-Price Ratios,* 1987 Census of Governments, vol. 2 (Washington, D.C.: U.S. Government Printing Office, 1989). More recent data are from Tax Foundation, *Facts and Figures.*

8 Advisory Commission on Intergovernmental Relations (ACIR), *Significant Features of Fiscal Feder-*

alism, 1992 Edition (Washington, D.C.: ACIR, 1992), 140–142.

9 J. Richard Aronson, "Intangibles Taxes: A Wisely Neglected Revenue Source for States," *National Tax Journal* 19 (June 1966): 186–187.

10 *Annenberg v. Commonwealth of Pennsylvania et al.,* Slip Opinion J-109-1997 (Penn. Supreme Court, 7 April 1998).

11 State of Florida, Department of Revenue, "Florida's Personal Intangible Property Tax: Updated Information for 2002," available at www.myflorida.com/dor/taxes/ippt.html.

12 Michael F. Lorelli, *State and Local Property Taxes,* Special Report No. 106 (Washington, D.C.: Tax Foundation, August 2001), 5.

13 This average was significantly (about 30 percent) higher than the rates that had been calculated in the 1980s on the basis of Federal Housing Administration (FHA) mortgages—a discrepancy that can perhaps be accounted for by the time gap and by the differences between urban property and all FHA properties.

14 District of Columbia, Office of the Chief Financial Officer, *2000 Tax Rates and Tax Burdens in the District of Columbia: A National Comparison* (Wash-

ington, D.C.: Government of the District of Columbia, 2001), 19.

15 Advisory Commission on Intergovernmental Relations (ACIR), *Significant Features of Fiscal Federalism, 1984 Edition* (Washington, D.C.: ACIR, 1985), 39–62.

16 Ibid.

17 Ibid.

18 Tax Foundation, *Facts and Figures.*

19 ACIR, *Significant Features, 1984,* and Tax Foundation, *Facts and Figures.*

20 Mason Gaffney, "Adequacy of Land as a Tax Base," in *The Assessment of Land Value,* ed. Daniel M. Holland (Madison: University of Wisconsin Press for the Committee on Taxation, Resources, and Economic Development, 1970), 175–176.

21 Annie Aubrey, "Issues in the Property Tax as a Revenue Source," *The Municipal Year Book 1992* (Washington, D.C.: International City/County Management Association, 1992), 44–49.

22 John Shannon, "Conflict between State Assessment Law and Local Assessment Practice," in *Property Taxation–USA,* ed. Richard W. Lindholm (Madison: University of Wisconsin Press, 1967), 39–61.

23 Lorelli, *State and Local Property Taxes,* 7, 8.

24 Bruce Lambert, "New Assessment Inequities Cited as Nassau Races to Fix Old Ones," *New York Times,* 26 November 2002.

25 See Anthony R. Wood, "Residents Have a Tough Task Appealing a Home Assessment," *Philadelphia Inquirer,* 1 September 2002. See also "How to Appeal Your Tax Increase," *Philadelphia Inquirer,* 29 August 2002.

26 The figure of 32 percent was derived from the judgments of assessors and from computer programs used to estimate sales prices.

27 Wood, "Tough Task"; and "How to Appeal."

28 Anthony R. Wood, "Figuring Out the Correct Home Assessment," *Philadelphia Inquirer,* 21 November 1993, MC1.

29 Paul B. Downing, "Estimating Residential Land Value by Multivariate Analysis," in Holland, *Assessment of Land Value,* 101–123.

30 Davis S. Jensen, "Modern Technology for the Mass Appraiser," *Intergovernmental Perspective* 19 (summer 1993): 21–23.

31 Kenneth Black, "Land Value Taxation in Light of Current Assessment Theory and Practice," in Holland, *Assessment of Land Value,* 38–39.

32 The capitalized value of income plays a special role in the evaluation of real estate, inventory, and other property and business values that are used to determine the taxes on shopping malls—a process that requires detailed analysis. See William J. Townsley and Michael J. Kelly, "Quantifying Business Value at a Regional Mall," *Journal of Property Tax Management* 2, no. 3 (1991): 19–32.

33 James M. Buchanan and Marilyn R. Flowers, *The Public Finances,* 5th ed. (Homewood, Ill.: Richard D. Irwin, 1980): 473–476.

34 James A. Maxwell and J. Richard Aronson, *Financing State and Local Governments,* 3rd ed. (Washington, D.C.: Brookings Institution, 1977), 134–165.

35 W. David Klemperer, "An Economic Analysis of the Case against Ad Valorem Property Taxation in Forestry," *National Tax Journal* 30 (December 1977): 469.

36 Tax Institute of America, *The Property Tax: Problems and Potentials* (Princeton, N.J.: Tax Institute of America, 1967), 143–204.

37 *Thirtieth Certification of the Pennsylvania State Tax Equalization Board* (Harrisburg, Pa.: 30 June 1978); and U.S. Department of Commerce, Bureau of the Census, 1982 Census of Governments (Washington, D.C.: U.S. Government Printing Office, 1984).

38 Ted Gwartney, "A Computerized Assessment Program," in Holland, *Assessment of Land Value,* 125–141.

39 *Philadelphia Evening Bulletin,* 4 August 1972, 5. This account describes the activities—including a protest march—of organizations formed in response to a reassessment in Bucks County, Pennsylvania.

40 A technical point worth noting here is that where the mean and the median are not equal, that inequality results from a skewed (asymmetrical) distribution; thus, the value of the coefficient will vary depending on whether the mean or the median is used in the calculation.

41 These issues are discussed extensively in Karl E. Case, *Property Taxation: The Need for Reform* (Cambridge, Mass.: Ballinger Publishing, 1978); Anthony R. Wood, "The Property Tax Riddle," *Philadelphia Inquirer,* 9 December 2001, A1; and "How Assessments Go Awry," *Philadelphia Inquirer,* 10 December 2001, A1. Wood's articles compare assessments and bills within and between communities in the Philadelphia metropolitan area.

42 Andrew A. Beveridge, *New York Times,* 17 August 1994, A1.

43 Jensen, "Modern Technology," 23.

44 Bureau of the Census, 1982 Census of Governments.

45 John O. Behrens, "Taxable Property Values 1 to 6: Matters of De Facto" (paper, Seventeenth Annual Conference on Taxation, Nashville, Tenn., 25–28 November 1984).

46 Anthony R. Wood, "Because They Don't Pay Taxes, You Pay More," *Philadelphia Inquirer,* 11 December 2001, A1.

47 District of Columbia, Office of the Chief Financial Officer, *2000 Tax Rates,* 5, 6, 21.

48 Advisory Commission on Intergovernmental Relations (ACIR), *Changing Public Attitudes on Government and Taxes* (Washington, D.C.: ACIR, 1992). In addition, there are frequent letters to the editor about the level and spirit of the tax.

49 *Serrano v. Priest,* 5 Cal. 3d 584, 487 P.2d 1241 (1971).

50 Advisory Commission on Intergovernmental Relations (ACIR), *Financing Schools and Property Tax Relief: A State Responsibility,* A-40 (Washington, D.C.: ACIR, 1973), 3–4.

51 Advisory Commission on Intergovernmental Relations (ACIR), *Significant Features of Fiscal Federalism, 1985–86 Edition* (Washington, D.C.: ACIR, 1986), 38–39.

52 Behrens, "Assessments and Property Taxes," 13.

53 Vermont Department of Taxes, "Major Vermont Taxes: Real Estate Taxes," available at www.state.vt.us/tax/majorvttaxes.htm.

54 State of New Hampshire, Department of Revenue Administration, "State Education Property Taxes and Adequate Education Grant Amounts for the School Year July 1, 2001–June 30, 2002 (Property Tax Year 2001)," available at www.nh.gov/revenue/municipalities/grants.htm.

55 Advisory Commission on Intergovernmental Relations, *Fiscal Federalism, 1990 Edition* (Washington, D.C.: ACIR, 1990), 102, 103; and John O. Behrens, telephone conversation with author, 11 January 1994.

56 Lorelli, *State and Local Property Taxes,* 6.

57　Mike Peddle, "The Property Tax Limitation Act: Where Do We Go from Here?" *ILCMA Newsletter,* June 1994.

58　Advisory Commission on Intergovernmental Relations (ACIR), *Tax Burdens for Families Residing in the Largest City in Each State, 1982,* Staff Working Paper 3R (Washington, D.C., ACIR, August 1984), 37–46. The Office of the Chief Financial Officer of the District of Columbia has continued to analyze the tax burdens of urban families in the largest cities in each state, most recently in 2000 (although the calculations were based on data from the 1990 census). The results of the analysis, which are sensitive to a number of assumptions on which the analysis was based, confirm that the tax is somewhat regressive, with the burden declining from 2.6 to 2.4 percent of income as income levels rise from $25,000 to $150,000. See District of Columbia, Office of the Chief Financial Officer, *2000 Tax Rates,* 5, 6, 20.

59　Henry J. Aaron, "A New View of Property Tax Incidence," *American Economic Review* 54 (May 1974): 212–221. Aaron's views are fully explained and their implications discussed in *Who Pays the Property Tax? A New View* (Washington, D.C.: Brookings Institution, 1975).

60　Aaron, *New View,* 92, 93.

61　Richard A. Musgrave, "Is a Property Tax on Housing Regressive?" *American Economic Review* 64 (May 1974): 222–229.

62　The supply is viewed as fixed because it takes time to produce capital goods, such as structures. As a result, any increase in tax rates will decrease the return to capital and will be the burden of the owners.

63　Lorelli, *State and Local Property Taxes,* 9, 10.

64　*Intergovernmental Perspective* 8 (summer 1982): 6; and Wood, "Because They Don't Pay Taxes."

65　Aaron, *New View,* 84–85.

66　Anita A. Summers, "Proposition 13 and Its Aftermath," Federal Reserve Bank of Philadelphia *Business Review* (March–April 1979): 11.

67　Objections to these tax expenditures can be found in Minnesota Planning, "Smart Signals: Property Tax Reform for Smart Growth" (St. Paul: Environmental Quality Board, March 2000); and Wood, "Because They Don't Pay Taxes," 1.

68　Joan Casey, Advisory Commission on Intergovernmental Relations, telephone conversation with author, 17 July 1995.

69　ACIR, *Financing Schools,* 40–41. Circuit breakers are more fully described in ACIR, *Property Tax Circuit-Breakers: Current Status and Policy Issues* (Washington, D.C.: ACIR, 1975).

70　ACIR, *Significant Features, 1992,* 3; 64–68; 124–131.

71　For an explanation of capitalization and formulas for relating these tax rates to each other, see J. Richard Aronson, *Public Finance* (New York: McGraw-Hill, 1985), 333–335.

72　See Wallace E. Oates, "The Effects of Property Taxes and Local Public Spending on Property Values: An Empirical Study of Tax Capitalization and the Tiebout Hypothesis," *Journal of Political Economy* 77 (November–December 1969): 957–971.

73　Cancellation of the agreement may result in a substantial tax obligation for the owner.

74　Hoy F. Carman, "California Landowners' Adoption of a Use-Value Assessment Program," *Land Economics* 53 (August 1977): 275–287.

75　Minnesota Planning, *Property Tax Reform for Smart Growth* (St. Paul: Environmental Quality Board, March 2000).

76　Richard L. Pollock and Donald C. Shoup, "The Effect of Shifting the Property Tax Base from Improvement Value to Land Value: An Empirical Estimate," *Land Economics* 53 (February 1977): 67–77. See also John E. Anderson, "Two-Rate Property Taxes," *Intergovernmental Perspective* 19 (summer 1993): 19, 20, 28.

77　Richard W. Douglas Jr., "Site Value Taxation and Manvel's Land Value Estimates," *American Journal of Economics and Sociology* 37 (April 1978): 217–223.

78　Myron Orfield, "Metropolitics: Coalition for Regional Reform," *Brookings Review* 15 (winter l997): 6–9.

79　Geoffrey K. Turnbull, *Local Tax Base Sharing: An Incentive for Intergovernmental Cooperation,* FRP Report No. 75 (Atlanta: Georgia State University, October 2002).

80　However, it may be difficult for taxpayers to determine the final destination of property tax revenues. In some places, there are three local property taxes: for the county, for the municipality or township, and for the school district. Citizens are unlikely to discriminate among the various government jurisdictions that claim pieces of their property tax: thus, a town that plans to raise its tax rate may encounter resistance because of a recent county increase—especially when the taxes for more than one jurisdiction (e.g., county and township) appear on the same bill.

81　David E. Black, "Property Tax Incidence: The Excise-Tax Effect and Assessment Practices," *National Tax Journal* 30 (December 1977): 429–434.

82　Summers, "Proposition 13," 11.

83　Advisory Commission on Intergovernmental Relations, *The Role of the States in Strengthening the Property Tax,* vol. 1 (Washington, D.C.: U.S. Government Printing Office, 1963); and Robert J. Cline and John Shannon, "The Property Tax in a Model State-Local Revenue System," in *The Property Tax and Local Finance,* ed. C. Lowell Harriss, Proceedings of the Academy of Political Science 35, no. 1 (1983): 42–56.

84　John Shannon and Carol Weissert, "After Jarvis: Tough Questions for Fiscal Policymakers," *Intergovernmental Perspective* 4 (summer 1978): 1–18.

85　"Pennsylvania Passes Complex Education–Tax Reform Plan," *Philadelphia Inquirer,* 3 May 1998, E3.

86　District of Columbia, Office of the Chief Financial Officer, *2000 Tax Rates,* 15, 22.

87　Ibid.

88　Michael Cooper, "Mayor Seeking Quick Increase in Property Tax," *New York Times,* 8 November 2002; Michael Cooper, "Council Affirms Deep Cuts and 15 Percent Property Tax Rise," *New York Times,* 26 November 2002; Jennifer Steinhauer, "Political Payback May Await Three Rebellious Councilmen," *New York Times,* 26 November 2002.

89　Linda K. Harris, Ken Dilanian, and Maria Panaritis, "Philadelphia Residents Feel Sting of Reassessments," *Philadelphia Inquirer,* 29 August 2002; Ken Dilanian and Anthony R. Wood, "Property-Tax System Still Favors the City's Rich," *Philadelphia Inquirer,* 1 September 2002; and Tom Ferrick Jr., "Which Top Fiend Gets the Pitchfork?" *Philadelphia Inquirer,* 15 September 2002, B1.

90　Wood, "How Assessments Go Awry"; Harris, Dilanian, and Panaritis, "Sting of Reassessments"; Dilanian and Wood, "Property-Tax System"; and Ferrick, "Which Top Fiend?" B1.

11

General sales, income, and other nonproperty taxes

JOHN L. MIKESELL

The property tax remains the single most important tax to local governments in the United States, yielding more than $238 billion in fiscal year 2000, but its dominance as a local tax source has generally declined. In 1960, for example, it provided almost 90 percent of local tax revenue; it now provides less than 75 percent.[1] Revenues from local sales and income taxes have increased significantly over the years, and by 2000 had reached a combined total of just over 20 percent of all tax revenues. Sales taxes include both general sales taxes (like the retail sales tax) and selective sales, or excise, taxes (like those on motor fuel). Of all revenues from sales and income taxes, those from the general sales tax are highest, although the resulting yield remains dwarfed by that of the property tax.

This chapter examines local government use of nonproperty taxes, giving greatest attention to the general sales tax and to individual income taxes—which, as the largest components of the nonproperty tax total, make the most significant contribution to local fiscal balance. The yield from corporate income taxes and selective sales taxes is modest.

Local governments use nonproperty tax sources for a number of reasons: (1) to obtain revenue to provide local services without making additional demands on the property tax base, (2) to distribute the cost of government in a way that is not related to property ownership, (3) to provide a more flexible tax structure that is better tailored to local conditions, and (4) to increase the responsiveness of the revenue system to economic growth.

Importance of nonproperty taxes in revenue structures

Table 11–1 traces the changing significance of local tax revenues as a share of local, own-source revenue between 1960 and 2000. Reliance on the property tax declined during this period, from 68.9 percent of all own-source general revenue in 1960 to 44.2 percent in 2000; the property tax share of local tax revenues fell from 88.2 to 71.6 percent during the same period. The largest decline occurred between 1970 and 1980, when states imposed limits on local authority to levy property taxes. These limits were imposed in response to (1) general concerns about the role of government in the economy and (2) specific concerns about the property tax—in particular, about the soaring value of houses during periods of inflation. Proposition 13, adopted in California in 1978, which rigidly constrained property tax revenue, is only one of many such limits imposed during the 1970s. Since 1980, reliance on the property tax has stabilized somewhat.

The importance of other taxes, particularly general sales and individual income taxes, has been rising steadily. Between 1960 and 2000, sales and gross receipts tax as a percentage of local government revenues nearly doubled, from 5.8 to 10.6 percent. During the same period, the contribution from the general sales tax increased from 3.8 to 7.5 percent (generating a total of more than $40 billion in 2000), and the contribution from the selective sales tax increased from 2 to 3 percent (generating a total of more than $16 billion in 2000). The

Table 11–1   Percentage of local government general revenue from own sources, selected years.

Revenue source	1960	1970	1980	1990	2000
General revenue, total	100.0	100.0	100.0	100.0	100.0
Taxes	78.1	75.6	66.4	62.5	61.7
Property	68.9	64.1	50.5	46.6	44.2
Sales and gross receipts, total	5.8	6.0	9.3	9.6	10.6
General sales	3.8	3.8	6.3	6.7	7.5
Selective sales	2.0	2.2	3.0	2.9	3.0
Individual income	1.1	3.2	3.8	2.8	3.2
Corporate income	—[a]	—	—	0.6	0.7
Licenses and other taxes	2.5	1.9	2.6	2.8	3.1
Charges and miscellaneous nontax revenue	21.1	24.4	33.6	37.5	38.3

Note: Because of rounding, detail may not add to totals.
[a] Indicates a negligible amount included in the individual income tax figure.

share represented by the individual income tax increased by an even greater multiple, from 1.1 to 3.2 percent (generating a total of more than $17 billion in 2000). Corporate income tax revenue contributed 0.7 percent of tax revenue in 2000 (generating a total of more than $3.5 billion), up from a negligible share in 1960. Even contributions from licenses and miscellaneous taxes rose, from 2.5 to 3.1 percent (generating a total of more than $16 billion).

In sum, the period between 1960 and 2000 was characterized by a general movement away from the local property tax and toward a variety of non-property taxes, the most significant being the general sales tax and the individual income tax. Total collections from all nonproperty taxes increased from $2.16 billion in 1960 to $94.51 billion in 1998–99, an average annual rate of increase of 9.9 percent. Over that same period, the general price level (the implicit deflator for gross domestic product) increased at an average annual rate of about 4 percent.[2] Tax collections were increasing at a rate double that of inflation, so the higher collections represented a considerable increase in government purchasing power.

In 1997 there were 87,453 local governments in the United States. Of these, 3,043 were county governments, 19,372 were municipal governments, 16,629 were township governments, 13,726 were school districts, and 34,683 were special districts.[3] Many special districts lack taxing authority; their own-source revenue comes from charges for the services they provide. The other forms of local government usually have taxing authority, although the particular taxes they are permitted to levy vary considerably from state to state. As shown in Table 11–2, the use of nonproperty taxes across types of governments varies. Counties and municipalities both raise just over 10 percent of their own-source revenue from general sales taxes, far eclipsing the percentage raised by other types of localities. Among municipalities, the use of individual income and selective sales taxes is higher than for any other units—representing, in each case, more than 6.5 percent of own-source revenue. Only municipalities receive an appreciable share of their revenue from local corporate income taxes, and that is a modest 1.9 percent of revenue. Overall, municipalities rely the most on nonproperty tax sources: the total amounts to 30.4 percent of their total own-source general revenue, which is just over what they raise from their property taxes. Reliance on nonproperty taxes is considerably greater for counties and municipalities than for any other type of local government.

The burden associated with each tax source reflects the changes in that source's overall importance as a source of revenue. The relation between revenue sources and personal income, as displayed in Table 11–3, is a good index

Table 11–2 Reliance on general revenue sources by type of local government, as a percentage of total own-source general revenue, 1996–97.

Revenue source	Counties	Municipalities	Townships	School districts	Special districts
Own-source general revenue, total	100.0	100.0	100.0	100.0	100.0
Taxes, total	56.8	59.2	78.9	83.0	23.0
Property	39.5	28.9	72.9	80.4	17.6
General and selective sales, total	12.7	17.1	0.4	0.9	3.9
General sales	10.3	10.3	0.0	0.7	3.9
Selective sales	2.4	6.8	0.4	0.2	0.0
Individual income	1.9	6.7	2.1	0.7	0.0
Corporate income	—[a]	1.9	—	—	—
Licenses and other taxes	2.9	4.7	0.6	0.9	1.5
Charges and miscellaneous nontax revenue	43.2	40.8	21.1	17.0	77.0

Note: Because of rounding, detail may not add to totals.
[a] Indicates a negligible amount included in the individual income tax figure.

Table 11–3 Sources of local government general revenue, 1960–2000.

Revenue source	Amount per $1,000 in personal income ($)				
	1960	1970	1980	1990	2000
General revenue, total	55.52	61.10	55.95	65.59	64.11
Taxes	43.70	46.17	37.17	41.02	39.58
Property	38.28	39.19	28.23	30.55	28.33
General and selective sales, total	3.24	3.65	5.19	6.28	6.80
General sales	2.12	2.32	3.51	4.40	4.83
Selective sales	1.12	1.33	1.68	1.88	1.96
Individual income	0.62	1.94	2.15	1.95	2.03
Corporate income	—[a]	—	—	0.37	0.42
Licenses and other taxes	1.37	1.19	1.43	1.87	1.99
Charges and miscellaneous nontax revenue	11.71	14.93	18.78	24.57	24.54

Note: Because of rounding, detail may not add to totals.
[a] Indicates a negligible amount included in the individual income tax figure.

of the amount of income taken from the private economy by each tax source. Between 1960 and 2000, the property tax burden fell by about 25 percent, from $38.28 to $28.33 per $1,000 of personal income, with most of the decline occurring between 1970 and 1980. The total tax burden fell as well, but by only about 10 percent, from $43.70 to $39.58. The burdens for both general sales and individual income taxes increased. For the general sales tax the burden more than doubled, from $2.12 to $4.83, and for individual income taxes it more than tripled, from $0.62 to $2.03. The corporate income tax burden increased from a negligible amount to $0.42. Burdens for selective sales taxes, licenses, and other taxes also increased, but not as dramatically.

In sum, the burden of all local taxes except the property tax increased between 1960 and 2000, and some of the increases were dramatic. Revenue from nonproperty taxes has increased at a greater rate than economic activity (as measured by personal income) and considerably faster than property tax revenue. The shift in observed burdens stems from three sources: (1) the adoption of new nonproperty taxes, (2) increases in nonproperty tax rates, and (3) the fact that, compared with the property tax, nonproperty taxes are more responsive to changes in economic activity (i.e., they have greater revenue elasticity).[4]

With respect to fiscal impact, the general sales and individual income taxes are the most significant, both in terms of total national revenues and within jurisdictions that have local taxing authority. Table 11–4 lists the states in which

Table 11–4 States with local sales and income taxes.

State	Sales tax	Income tax
Alabama	✓ (S, L)	✓ (L)
Alaska	✓ (L)	—
Arizona	✓ (S, L)	—
Arkansas	✓ (S)	Authorized but not levied
California	✓ (S)	—
Colorado	✓ (S, L)	—
Connecticut	—	—
Delaware	—	✓ (L)
Florida	✓ (S)	—
Georgia	✓ (S)	Authorized but not levied
Hawaii	—	—
Idaho	✓ (L)	—
Illinois	✓ (S)	—
Indiana	—	✓ (S)
Iowa	✓ (S)	✓ (S)
Kansas	✓ (S)	—
Kentucky	—	✓ (L)
Louisiana	✓ (L)	—
Maine	—	—
Maryland	—	✓ (S)
Massachusetts	—	—
Michigan	—	✓ (L)
Minnesota	✓ (S, L)	—
Mississippi	—	—
Missouri	✓ (S, L), ✓ (S)	✓ (L)
Montana	—	—
Nebraska	✓ (S)	—
Nevada	✓ (S)	—
New Hampshire	—	—
New Jersey	—	—
New Mexico	✓ (S)	—
New York	✓ (S)	✓ (S personal; L corporate)
North Carolina	✓ (S)	—
North Dakota	✓ (S)	—
Ohio	✓ (S)	✓ (L)
Oklahoma	✓ (S)	—
Oregon	—	✓ (L)[a]
Pennsylvania	✓ (S)	✓ (L)
Rhode Island	—	—
South Carolina	✓ (S)	—
South Dakota	✓ (S)	—
Tennessee	✓ (S)	—
Texas	✓ (S)	—
Utah	✓ (S)	—
Vermont	✓ (S)	—
Virginia	✓ (S)	—
Washington	✓ (S)	—
West Virginia	—	—
Wisconsin	✓ (S)	—
Wyoming	✓ (S)	—

Note: S indicates state administration; L indicates local administration.
[a]Business income only.

these two local taxes are currently in operation and indicates whether the tax is administered by local governments, the state, or both. Local general sales taxes are levied in thirty-four states and local income taxes in twelve. In Alabama, Iowa, Missouri, New York, Ohio, and Pennsylvania, both local general sales and income taxes are levied, although not always by the same types of government. Local administration is somewhat more prevalent for the income tax than for the sales tax.

The local general sales tax

The first local general sales taxes were adopted in the 1930s, when the Great Depression was causing significant reductions in local government revenues. New York City adopted a general sales tax in 1934 and was followed by New Orleans in 1938. (The first state sales tax had been adopted by Mississippi, in 1932.) Localities in a number of states, notably Illinois and California, adopted general sales taxes in the postwar 1940s and in the 1950s. In 1950 Mississippi became the first state to adopt a system of state-administered local sales taxes, an innovation that made the revenue source a reasonable alternative for even the smallest of jurisdictions.[5]

Most local general sales taxes are authorized by state legislation, although some are based on home rule charters or general licensing powers. The greatest expansion in the use of such taxes occurred in the 1960s: in 1963, twelve states authorized local general sales taxes; by 1970, that number had increased to twenty-five. By 2002, local governments in thirty-four states and the District of Columbia levied general sales taxes. Although the numbers change almost daily, more than 7,000 jurisdictions—municipalities, counties, and single-purpose districts (particularly transit districts)—now levy a local general sales tax.[6] Local rates range from 0.25 percent in a number of transit districts to 4 percent in New York City and other localities in New York State.[7] In some parts of Alabama and Louisiana, the combined local and state general sales tax rate reaches 9 or 10 percent because sales taxes are levied by more than one type of local government (e.g., city, county, transit district, and school district). Among the states, the number of local governments levying the general sales tax ranges from three towns in Vermont to hundreds in several states (including Alabama, California, and Texas). Local sales taxes are levied statewide in California, North Carolina, and Virginia, although not always at the same rate.

Features

Local sales taxes, like their state-level counterparts, are general taxes on the purchase or sale of tangible personal property and apply only selectively to the purchases of services. This emphasis on the purchase of commodities is a carryover from the past, which persists despite the fact that more and more expenditures are made for the purchase of services.

General sales taxes apply at nonfractional rates on the value of a transaction. Unlike selective excise taxes on products such as cigarettes, the general sales tax is not applied to the number of units purchased. In other words, sales taxes are ad valorem rather than unit taxes.

Vendors are required to collect and remit the tax owed. Most local tax ordinances require that the tax be quoted separately from the price and forbid sellers to advertise that they will absorb the tax.

The tax is intended to be indirect: vendors collect the tax from their customers and remit those collections to the tax authorities. Although vendors are not intended to bear the burden of the tax, they must bear the costs of compliance. Some jurisdictions offer discounts for prompt remittance to re-imburse vendors for a portion of these costs, but there is no discernible rela-tionship between these discounts and the actual cost to individual vendors. The actual incidence of the tax—whether the burden is on the vendor or on the consumer—depends on market conditions. Competitive conditions may be such that merchants cannot afford simply to add the tax to the current price but may need to lower the pretax price to keep the price plus tax at a level that purchasers will accept.

Sales taxes apply to the gross receipts from the transactions, with no deduc-tion for expenses associated with operating the business. Thus, vendors must remit sales taxes without regard to whether the enterprise is profitable. Nor does the tax take into account the economic or other personal circumstances of the customer; because the sales tax is not a personal levy, a millionaire and a homeless person will pay the same tax rate on the purchase of a particular item. The sales tax is thus often criticized for violating both horizontal equity (the principle that people who are equally situated should pay substantially the same tax) and vertical equity (the principle that people who are unequally sit-uated should pay appropriately different taxes).

Sales taxes apply at the retail stage; sales between businesses are removed from taxation by means of suspension certificates that, when presented by a purchaser to a vendor, suspend levy of the tax on the purchase. Applying the sales tax to pre-retail transactions would mean that the burden borne by the re-tail consumer would be considerably higher than that advertised in the statutory rate. Furthermore, levying sales taxes on the purchase of business equipment discourages economic development. Unfortunately, even with the suspension certificate system, many business purchases remain in the sales tax base; in fact, business purchases make up about 40 percent of state sales tax revenues.[8] Local taxes modeled after state taxes would show a similar pattern.

The tax structures generally exempt certain commodities (e.g., food, pre-scription drugs), certain purchasers or vendors (e.g., charitable organizations, local governments), and certain uses of purchased commodities (e.g., goods purchased for resale). More than half the states exempt food for at-home con-sumption, and virtually all exempt purchases of prescription medicines; local taxes generally follow the same exemption patterns. However, not all states re-quire local governments to adopt the same tax base as the state, and not all lo-calities within a state levy on the same tax base.[9] These differences complicate both administration and compliance.

Three critical features are of unique importance for local sales taxes: where liability is created, the use tax, and state coordination of sales taxes levied by different jurisdictions.

Whether tax liability for a particular transaction is determined by the point of sale or the point of delivery creates considerable controversy. For example, should a purchase made from a vendor in New York City for delivery in Albany be subject to New York City's local sales tax or to Albany's? If the tax is supposed to be consumption oriented and if the intent is for purchasers to support the public sector where they live, the tax should accrue to the place of delivery. However, this approach significantly complicates the operation of the tax. Vendors must determine the jurisdiction to which delivery will be made, apply the tax rate of that jurisdiction, accumulate records by jurisdiction, and file appropriately segregated returns—a difficult task given the number of ju-risdictions that levy the tax. And the task gets even bigger because the system increases demand for out-of-jurisdiction delivery by those living in jurisdic-tions that do not levy the tax or that levy at a lower rate. Some consumers may even have high-ticket items delivered to friends living in nontax jurisdictions, or attempt to have vendors record the order as a sale for delivery to a nontax area while actually taking the purchase with them. Auditing becomes more complicated because proper application of the delivery rule must be checked.

Establishing liability at the location of the vendor simplifies administration and compliance. This approach significantly eases the application of the tax: all sales, regardless of where the purchases are delivered, are taxed at the same tax rate. A disadvantage, however, is that jurisdictions with large vendors that serve a wide shopping area gain substantial revenue, as compared with jurisdictions that have similar populations but lack such vendors. Some localities that use the location of the seller to determine tax liability make an exception for motor vehicle sales, for which the location of registration applies.

To protect the sales tax base and to protect in-state merchants from competition with states in which the sales tax rate is lower or nonexistent, states levy a use tax, which requires purchasers to pay tax on items that were purchased out of state (the tax equals the difference between the in-state tax and the tax that the consumer actually paid). Although all state sales tax laws include a companion use-tax law, that is not the case for local sales taxes. Where there is no local use tax, local vendors have no protection from competition with vendors in low- or no-tax areas.[10] The use tax is difficult to administer, but jurisdictions do manage to collect the tax on items that must be registered (like motor vehicles) or when the out-of-jurisdiction vendor collects the tax on behalf of the jurisdiction.

When sales tax jurisdictions overlap—for instance, when municipalities, counties, and transit districts all have sales taxing powers—states handle the problem in various ways. Some states do nothing, which means that the combined tax rate is permitted to reach whatever level emerges from the use of local taxing authority. Other states allow only one variety of local government (e.g., the municipality or the county) to levy sales taxes, or they grant authority only to jurisdictions that do not overlap. For example, cities and counties in Virginia do not overlap, and both may levy local sales taxes; towns overlap counties, but towns may not levy sales taxes. Still other states allow the tax paid in one jurisdiction to be fully credited against the tax owed in an overlapping jurisdiction. Finally, some states establish a maximum total sales tax rate that can apply to any transaction and then establish an order of precedence for local adoption (in Kansas and Tennessee, for example, counties take precedence over municipalities in levying a local sales tax), or they mandate a particular division of the maximum between local units, as New York does.

Yield

Local governments collected $36.2 billion from their local general sales taxes in fiscal 1998–99, more than was collected from any local tax other than the property tax. Several cities with populations greater than 250,000 collect more than half their tax revenue from their local general sales tax: Albuquerque (51.1 percent); Aurora, Colorado (69.1 percent); Baton Rouge (53.0 percent); Colorado Springs (70.5 percent); Denver (52.0 percent); Mesa, Arizona (73.7 percent); Oklahoma City (80.8 percent); Tucson (67.9 percent); and Tulsa (79.2 percent).[11] The tax is also an important source of revenue for counties and special districts (particularly transit districts) in several states. The degree of reliance on revenues from local general sales taxes depends on the sales tax rate and structure and on which other revenue options are selected by the taxing government. However, local sales taxes clearly have the potential to raise a large share of local government revenue, should that be the choice of lawmakers.

The projected yield for any local government considering a general sales tax will depend on the proposed tax rate, the size of the potential tax base, and the exemptions and exclusions. The range of rates is usually set by state authorizing legislation. Because states also use general sales taxes, they are reluctant to give their local governments a free hand in exploiting this tax source, particularly since high local sales tax rates may constrain the state's political capacity to increase its own sales tax rates. But even within the range of rates allowed by the states, local governments face an economic impediment to raising tax rates: if customers make their purchases outside the taxing jurisdiction (an effect that will be discussed in detail later in the chapter), local merchants will be hurt.

The size of the potential tax base depends on the economic activity in the taxing jurisdiction. If a state sales tax is already in effect, the state may report the state sales tax revenue collected within the local jurisdiction. Adjusting this figure to reflect the intended local rate would give an estimate of potential local revenue, assuming that the bases of the local and state taxes will be the same. But not all states maintain records of their sales tax collections by jurisdiction—and, even if they do, the data may be misleading about the local tax base. For example, in the case of retailers that have branches in many jurisdictions, some states report all collections as having originated at the retailer's home office, which makes the sales tax base of the home-office jurisdiction appear much larger than it actually is.

If no reliable data on the state tax base are available, the local base may be estimated from the experience of other localities that are generally comparable in terms of economic character, retail outlets, and population. Data on the statewide per capita sales tax base and the statewide base per dollar of personal income can be used to confirm such estimates.

A broader tax base will yield more revenue than a narrow one. An exemption for food purchased for at-home consumption, for example, generally justified as a means of reducing the regressiveness of the tax, will reduce potential yield by 15 to 20 percent. Excluding services from the typical goods-driven tax base will have a similar revenue impact. However, localities usually have little direct say about the composition of their sales taxes, particularly when the tax is state administered. Because state-administered taxes usually must follow the coverage of the state tax, their prospects for a broader tax base are limited: only fifteen of the forty-five states with general sales taxes fully tax food purchased for at-home consumption, and only twenty provide extensive coverage of the purchase of services.[12] And any locality that implements a sales tax base that diverges from that of the state will, while enjoying the fiscal autonomy, make compliance more difficult for its vendors and make administration more difficult for its tax collectors. But following the state template—which generally exempts food and most services—may exclude as much as two-thirds of expenditures from the base. And because services constitute a growing share of total consumer expenditures, the exclusion of services is of increasing significance.

Over time, sales tax revenue will vary with short-term business activity and with long-term changes in the economic base. Evidence from state revenue systems (a good proxy for what could be expected from typical local sales taxes) reveals that, in the long term, the general sales tax base shows unitary elasticity in relation to state economic activity: that is, an increase of 1 percent in state personal income is accompanied by a 1 percent increase in the sales tax base. However, the sales tax base can be significantly influenced by national or regional recessions (particularly if the stabilizing force of food consumption is excluded from the base), causing it to deviate from the expected pattern. Purchases of consumer durables (e.g., automobiles, appliances, furniture), which can constitute a considerable share of a jurisdiction's sales tax base, are particularly volatile, as are purchases of business equipment. In sum, sales tax revenue can be surprisingly unstable.

Administration

Local general sales taxes may be administered by a local jurisdiction, by an overlapping local government, or by the state. Of the five states that do not levy a state general sales tax (Alaska, Delaware, Montana, New Hampshire, and Oregon), only Alaska permits local sales taxes, so in all other states with local general sales taxes, administration overlaps that of the state. The trend, however, is away from local administration. Only in Alabama, Arizona, Colorado, Louisiana, Minnesota, and Idaho are any local general sales taxes administered separately from the state—and in the first four states, some local general sales taxes are state administered (see Table 11–4). The state administers local general sales taxes in Arkansas, California, Florida, Georgia, Illinois, Iowa, Kansas, Nebraska, Nevada, New Mexico, New York, North Carolina, North Dakota, Ohio, Oklahoma, Pennsylvania, South Carolina, South Dakota, Tennessee, Texas, Utah, Vermont, Virginia, Washington, Wisconsin, and Wyoming. In Alaska, boroughs and the municipalities within them must coordinate their tax bases; in Louisiana, combined parish-city administration is required when adoptions overlap.

When administration is local, vendors must register, collect, and remit on a local cycle, thus duplicating the administrative structure and processes used for the state tax. (Alaska is, of course, an exception because it has no state sales tax.) Establishing a local administration program requires (1) registration of local vendors and of entities that will be permitted to purchase without paying the tax, (2) distribution of returns to vendors, (3) a system of accounting for revenues and returns as they are received, (4) delinquency control, (5) auditing of returns, and (6) an enforcement system. Except in the largest taxing jurisdictions, the resources available for auditing and enforcement do not even remotely approximate those used by the states. Most localities do improve administration by exchanging information with the state, but seldom is information transfer a regular step in the administrative process of either localities or the state.

The advantage of local administration is fiscal autonomy: the choice of tax structure and rates; the selection of administrative and enforcement personnel (including the freedom to award jobs); the establishment of administrative and compliance standards designed specifically for local needs and preferences; the freedom to respond to prevailing local business practices and economic conditions; and the quick and certain availability of tax revenues without any risk of redistribution or delay.[13]

Local administration also has a number of disadvantages:

1. Administration and compliance efforts are duplicated: two sets of administrators are doing essentially the same tasks, and vendors must go through two compliance procedures.
2. Tax structures and administrative procedures for the local and state tax often differ, complicating compliance and creating confusion for vendors and consumers.
3. In the absence of coordinated and unified tax laws it may be difficult to establish which jurisdiction may tax a particular transaction; as a result, some transactions will be untaxed and some will be taxed twice.
4. Because tax collections remain where they are collected, local administration effectively prevents tax revenues from being redistributed in order to respond to differing fiscal needs.
5. Many localities, particularly smaller jurisdictions, lack adequate auditing and enforcement systems and are compelled to simply accept whatever revenue is received as satisfying legal liability.

A state-administered supplement (piggyback) to the state sales tax base is an attractive means of providing local fiscal autonomy while saving localities the trouble of establishing their own administrative processes. All states except Alaska and Louisiana provide this alternative, although not all eligible localities accept it. Thirty-one states have state-administered local sales taxes: Alabama, Arizona, Arkansas, California, Colorado, Florida, Georgia, Illinois, Iowa, Kansas, Minnesota, Missouri, Nebraska, Nevada, New Mexico, New York, North Carolina, North Dakota, Ohio, Oklahoma, Pennsylvania, South Carolina, South Dakota, Tennessee, Texas, Utah, Vermont, Virginia, Washington, Wisconsin, and Wyoming. When the state administers the local general sales tax, registration, reporting, and enforcement procedures follow those for the state tax. Ordinarily, a single return will serve for both state and local tax liability; vendors with branches in more than one jurisdiction are required to report sales and liability separately for each local taxing jurisdiction.

State administration is typically characterized by the prompt remittance of collections to taxing jurisdictions and low (or no) charge for the administrative service. The laws often limit the administrative charge to the state's collection cost; only the largest localities would be able to manage administration of equivalent quality for less than the charge for state administration. In California, for example, the charge in 2001 was $0.84 per $100 of local sales tax collected. Most distributions are monthly, following the typical cycle under which larger vendors make remittance to the tax authorities. This cycle brings a steady revenue flow to localities; however, because there is a time lag between the state's receipt of the revenue and its distribution of collections to localities, the cycle also makes the receipt of particular payments to localities slower than it would be under local administration.

Experiences with state administration have led to several conclusions:

1. When local administration is the rule, switching to state administration is difficult and slow, despite the promise of free, high-quality state administration. Full autonomy, once in hand, is difficult for local governments to abandon.
2. Quick remittance is feasible and should be possible even if charges are as low as 1 percent of collections. (For the state, the most difficult task is to ensure that revenues are credited to the proper jurisdiction; ensuring proper crediting is also the primary reason for the extra administrative costs associated with a piggybacked tax.)
3. When compliance with the local tax is fully coordinated with the state tax (single registration, single return, same base, and taxability based on the location of the vendor), there is little additional compliance cost associated with the tax and therefore little justification for providing a vendor discount for complying with the local tax.
4. Local use taxes are even more difficult to administer than state use taxes, and the resulting complications are probably of greater impact than the revenue and retailer protection that the taxes are presumed to bring. State administration of local use taxes does not significantly improve their administration.
5. State revenue departments report that local sales tax administration is one of the most troublesome parts of their total administrative effort. Among the problems they report are the difficulty of keeping vendors informed of local adoptions and rate changes, and ensuring that collections are properly allocated to localities. Nevertheless, state administration is usually of higher quality than localities can manage on their own.

Remote vendors and undue compliance burdens

The growth of retail activity flowing through remote vendors (mail-order catalogs, telemarketers, and, particularly, the Internet) is challenging the viability of both state and local sales taxes, but the role of local taxes in the dispute is critical. As noted previously, to protect their sales tax base and their retailers from competitors in areas that have lower or no sales taxes, state and many local governments levy use taxes. However, such taxes are extremely difficult to collect directly from the purchaser; as a practical manner, they are collectible only from the vendor.

The U.S. Supreme Court ruled in 1992 that a remote vendor may be required to register as a tax collector only by those jurisdictions in which it has a physical presence.[14] To require a business to register and collect in all jurisdictions in which it makes sales would, the Court held, place an undue burden on interstate commerce and thereby violate the commerce clause of the U.S. Constitution.

Why would it be a burden? Because any business making sales throughout the nation would need to know the definition of the sales tax base, the appropriate tax rate, and the necessary filing regulations for every state levying a sales tax and every locality levying a use tax. Furthermore, to ensure that the appropriate amounts were being collected, the business would need to relentlessly track changes in tax rates or tax bases (there were 771 rate changes by state or local governments in 2001 alone).[15] Maintaining such information for thousands of jurisdictions would overwhelm the capacity of any shipping and billing system. Internet vendors, in particular, would be vulnerable to demands that no typical retail store would have to meet. For large multistate retailers, compliance costs under such a system have been estimated to be as high as 14 percent of sales tax collected; for small multistate retailers, estimates are as high as 87 percent of sales tax collected.[16] For single-state retailers, the cost ranges from 4 to 7 percent of collections.

In an effort to persuade Congress that requiring remote vendors to register as sales tax collectors need not be an undue burden, states are attempting to streamline the sales tax program and simplify the compliance structure. The major elements of this program are (1) uniform sales tax exemptions, (2) standardized compliance schedules, (3) a match between the base used by a state and its taxing localities, (4) state administration of all local sales taxes, and (5) application of a single local tax rate throughout the state. The hope is that enough states will adopt the streamlined sales tax package to persuade Congress that compliance is no longer burdensome—and, therefore, that businesses that make sales without a physical presence in a state can be required to register as tax collectors for that state. Unless remote vendors are required to collect state and local sales taxes, the competitive imbalance between local and remote vendors will persist, and local retailing and the sales tax base will continue to erode.

Revenue allocation and fiscal disparity

Local general sales tax revenues are not equally distributed among taxing localities: those that have a high concentration of economic activity in retail trade, particularly vendors of consumer durables, have a larger sales tax base than those that do not. Within Los Angeles County, California, for example, seventy-eight cities levy a 1 percent sales tax, but per capita collections in 2001 ranged from less than $9 in Rolling Hills to more than $50,000 in Vernon.[17]

Dramatic as the difference is within a single county, the range is even greater for California as a whole. The mean per capita collection was $33.18 for the lowest quintile of cities and $5,167.20 for the highest. For localities with a larger sales tax base—a product of the economic structure of the jurisdiction— fiscal options are much wider: such localities can support a greater array of services or levy lower rates for other taxes and charges. Thus, levying a local sales tax is vastly more productive for some jurisdictions than for others.

Local sales taxes also have an impact on land use policy. When local revenue options apart from the sales tax are limited, jurisdictions tend to favor retailing over other types of economic activity and may compete aggressively for high-value retail businesses, providing development incentives in order to take advantage of the revenue that such businesses generate. Localities are also likely to practice "fiscal zoning," which means limiting land use to those activities that yield high sales tax revenue. A bias in favor of retail development, however, works against industrial development—a form of development that can, over the long term, have a greater positive impact on the local standard of living than retail development. Exactly this bias has been found in California, where local sales taxes represent a major revenue stream for cities.[18]

Locational effects

Loss of business activity to surrounding, lower-tax areas always accompanies the adoption of a local sales tax or an increase in the sales tax rates. When the local sales tax is widespread, this effect is ordinarily minimized because there are few opportunities to shop without facing the tax. However, if a local tax rate is relatively high and consumers have access to lower-tax jurisdictions, the rate differential clearly influences shopping patterns, particularly on high-ticket items.[19]

Because the evidence shows that differences in sales tax rates may have a significant impact on retail activity (see sidebar), the use of geographically broader taxes—county or regional—may be necessary to reduce the negative economic impact of a highly localized tax. Even if wider adoption is not possible, however, the potential business impact is likely to prevent local governments from overly aggressive exploitation of the sales tax.

Equity

The traditional view of the sales tax burden is that although the tax is imposed on the vendor, it is actually paid by the consumers of taxed goods and services as an addition to the total purchase price. The reasoning is as follows: when the tax is imposed, (1) the price (including tax) of taxed goods must increase, (2) the price of production inputs must fall, or (3) the vendor must absorb the tax out of profits. There are no other alternatives. Lower prices on inputs are unlikely, especially in the long run, because the sales tax is not universal. Since many consumer goods and services, and even more goods purchased by businesses, are exempt from the sales tax, suppliers of inputs have other opportunities—and will seek them out if vendors of taxed goods try to reduce the prices they pay for inputs. If vendors absorb the tax out of profits, the resulting lower profits will reduce the number of vendors—which will, in turn, reduce supply and induce higher prices, restoring profit. If the taxed industries offer lower returns, it is more likely that product prices will rise and that consumers of those products will bear the sales tax burden.

The argument becomes more complicated, however, when the sales tax applies only to a small geographic area and consumers have the option of making purchases in nearby areas that levy no sales tax or a lower tax. Consumers

Evaluating the impact of sales taxes on retail sales A number of studies have estimated the impact of a local sales tax on local retail sales. Examining the effects of increases in the New York City sales tax rate between 1948 and 1965, William Hamovitch found that for each 1 percentage point increase in the tax rate, sales decreased by 6 percent.[1] Focusing on apparel and home furnishing sales in New York City, as measured by Census of Business data for 1929 to 1963, Henry Levin found that the sales of taxed goods decreased and the sales of nontaxed goods increased.[2] Both studies are consistent with the idea that differences in sales tax rates will have a distorting impact on the local economy and will decrease sales among vendors selling taxed commodities. Nevertheless, the New York City case may be special.

In a study of city-suburban sales tax rate differentials across the central cities of all metropolitan areas in the United States, John Mikesell found a 95 percent probability that a 1 percent increase in the ratio of the city-suburban sales tax rates will decrease per capita city sales by between 1.69 and 10.92 percent.[3] In addition to demonstrating the impact of local sales taxes on the locality where retail sales occur, this result implies that applying sales taxes to a wider area can prevent much of the sales loss: a countywide sales tax, for example, would cause a smaller decrease in sales than a city-only tax.

Analyzing the effect of differences in sales tax rates between Washington,

D.C., and the surrounding suburbs between 1962 and 1976, Ronald Fisher found no effect on total sales; however, each 1 percent increase in the rate differential led to a 7 percent decrease in revenue from food sales.[4]

In a study of the impact of a temporary (1979–82) 0.5 percentage point increase in Bay St. Louis, Mississippi, John Mikesell and C. Kurt Zorn found that a difference of 1 percentage point would have lowered sales by about 3 percent, primarily by decreasing the sales per vendor rather than by lowering the number of vendors in the city.[5] (The purpose of the rate increase was to raise revenue to satisfy a liability award against the city. Since the increase was not intended as a permanent part of the revenue structure, vendors may not have thought it worthwhile to relocate.)

[1] William Hamovitch, "Effects of Increases in Sales Tax Rates on Taxable Sales in New York City," in Graduate School of Public Administration and Social Service, New York University, *Financing Government in New York City* (New York: New York University, 1966), 619–634; and William Hamovitch, "Sales Taxation: An Analysis of the Effects of Rate Increases in Two Contrasting Cases," *National Tax Journal* 19 (December 1966): 411–420.
[2] Henry M. Levin, "An Analysis of the Economic Effects of the New York City Sales Tax," in Graduate School of Public Administration and Social Service, New York University, *Financing Government in New York City* (New York: New York University, 1966), 635–691.
[3] John L. Mikesell, "Central Cities and Sales Tax Rate Differentials," *National Tax Journal* 23 (June 1970): 206–213.
[4] Ronald C. Fisher, "Local Sales Taxes: Tax Rate Differentials, Sales Loss, and Revenue Estimation," *Public Finance Quarterly* 8 (April 1980): 171–188.
[5] John L. Mikesell and C. Kurt Zorn, "Impact of the Sales Tax Rate on Its Base: Evidence from a Small Town," *Public Finance Quarterly* 14 (July 1986): 329–338.

can thus avoid some or all of the burden, and businesses may find it attractive to locate in lower-tax areas. If businesses relocate, the demand for land in the taxing jurisdiction will decline, as will land prices. Hence, when a sales tax is levied in a small jurisdiction, landowners may bear the burden.

Most analyses of the general sales tax assume that consumers bear the burden of the tax in proportion to their purchases of taxed goods and services. Starting with this assumption, the local sales tax can be evaluated according to two basic principles of fairness: benefits received and ability to pay.

With respect to benefits received, the question is whether those who pay more sales tax obtain more benefit from local government services than those who pay less—and, if so, whether there is a good match between tax paid and benefits received. Few studies have examined the relationship between resident incomes and demand for local public services, but there is some evidence that benefits (as measured by willingness to pay) do rise with income, although not in direct proportion to the income increase.[20] Therefore, under the benefits-received principle, sales tax payments should also rise with income, but less than proportionately. Consumer expenditure data from surveys conducted by the U.S. Bureau of Labor Statistics confirm that the ratio of sales tax paid to income falls as income rises (because higher-income households spend a smaller proportion of their income on taxable purchases than do lower-income households), so it may be tentatively concluded that the distribution of the sales tax burden is at least somewhat consistent with the benefits-received principle.

Most analysts, however, evaluate the fairness of the general sales tax in terms of ability to pay, where the tax fares less well. Since, as noted, the percentage of income spent on taxed purchases falls as household income increases, the sales tax imposes a higher effective tax rate on lower-income households than on higher-income households, meaning that the distribution of the sales tax is regressive.[21] Regressivity is a problem for most consumption taxes, but especially for the general sales tax because the total burden is economically significant.

Since lower-income households spend a higher percentage of their income on food than do higher-income households, the exemption of food purchased for at-home consumption provides greater relief to lower-income households and significantly reduces the regressivity of the sales tax. However, this exemption complicates compliance because the retailer has to distinguish properly between taxable and exempt purchases and retain records to demonstrate that goods were properly sorted. In addition, verification of proper sorting must be added to the list of tasks included in tax department audits.[22] Finally, sometimes arbitrary distinctions must be made between what is considered food for at-home consumption and what is not—and regardless of what category is assigned by the tax administrators, vendors and manufacturers will complain that an item has been classified improperly (controversies have arisen over items such as takeout food, snacks, soft drinks, and candy, among others), and there will be difficulty ensuring that items have been properly classified at purchase. (Although the system relies on vendors to make the proper classification, vendors always have an incentive to treat purchases as untaxed.) Of course, the food exemption is expensive in terms of revenue loss—and because higher-income people also purchase food, a substantial amount of that revenue loss benefits people who would not ordinarily qualify for government assistance.

The credit/rebate approach is an alternative means of reducing the regressivity of the sales tax. Under this scheme, there is no food exemption, but taxpayers receive a refund—either in the form of rebate payments or as a tax credit—equal to the sales tax that would have been paid on a "minimally necessary" amount of food. Thus, if this amount is estimated to be $3,000 and the sales tax rate is 5 percent, an eligible taxpayer would be entitled to a $150 refund.

The rebate/credit approach has several advantages over the food exemption. First, it involves less revenue loss because the sales tax is relieved only on a minimum amount of food purchases. Second, it prevents tax relief from being wasted on expenditures that exceed the minimally necessary amount. Third, it targets relief to those who most need it and thus provides even sharper reductions in regressivity than does the exemption. Finally, eliminating the food exemption simplifies compliance and the administration of the tax.

Nevertheless, the rebate/credit approach has fallen out of favor with American lawmakers. To receive the tax relief, a household must file either a tax return for the tax against which the credit will apply or, if the household does not need to file that tax return, a request for a rebate. Experience has shown that as many as 5 percent of eligible households do not file for the credit/rebate for which they are eligible. If these missing households are at the upper range of the income distribution, the effective regressivity of the tax is reduced; if they are at the lower, the effective regressivity of the tax is increased. Unions and advocates for low-income groups view the food exemption as more of a "sure thing," and their arguments have led to a significant reduction in the number of rebate/credit systems.

Summary

Local general sales taxes provide local governments with valuable fiscal autonomy, allowing them more flexibility in determining the size of their budgets and in deciding how to divide the cost of government services among the citizenry.

Experience and research have yielded a number of important observations about the local general sales tax in the United States:

1. State administration can provide low-cost tax administration, coordination between state and local tax bases, and regulation of the rates applied by localities. These three elements combine to lower the cost of compliance and decrease retailers' confusion about the operation of the tax.
2. Compliance and administration are easier if the base of the local sales tax is the same as that of the overlapping state tax.
3. Establishing tax liability at the location of the vendor, rather than at the place of delivery, significantly simplifies compliance.
4. Prohibiting local use taxes, especially for purchases made within the state, significantly simplifies compliance.
5. Making rates uniform over as large a geographic area as possible (e.g., county rather than city) reduces undesirable location effects.

Local general sales taxes bring four significant problems:

1. The tax is likely to distort location decisions for retail businesses.
2. Because businesses typically purchase production inputs within the local sales tax base, the tax discourages economic development.
3. The vertical distribution of the tax burden is regressive; and because sales tax burdens are assigned according to household preferences for taxed purchases, the tax also violates the principle of horizontal equity.
4. The tax is likely to yield radically different revenues across localities, and this disparity is unlikely to be in accordance with differing needs for local government services.

The local income tax

The first modern local income tax was adopted by Philadelphia in 1938 under the 1932 Sterling Act, by which the state permitted the city to tax any non-property sources not already taxed by the state. In 1939, the state supreme court declared the Philadelphia tax unconstitutional for violating the uniformity requirement of the state constitution, which precluded a progressive income tax. (Philadelphia's flat-rate tax was considered progressive because it exempted the first $1,000 of income.) The following year, the city adopted a flat-rate tax on all income earned within its boundaries (i.e., wages, salaries, and net income from professions, partnerships, and unincorporated businesses), with no personal deductions or exemptions. Major features of this tax—a flat rate, no deductions, and the exclusion of property income—have been retained. The tax has served as a model for other local governments in Pennsylvania and for localities in a number of other states.

Between 1940 and 1962, the income taxes adopted by local governments followed the Philadelphia model. In 1962, however, Detroit introduced a broader tax levied on all forms of income, including dividends, rental income, interest, and capital gains. Two years later, Michigan adopted the Uniform City Income Tax Ordinance, which incorporated the provisions of the Detroit tax. The tax base was essentially adjusted gross income as defined in the U.S. Internal Revenue Code.

The next major development came in 1966, when New York City introduced a personal income tax that (like those of Michigan cities) was very similar to the federal levy. The New York City tax, however, was not flat rate. Income was taxed at graduated rates ranging from 0.4 to 2.0 percent, and the taxpayer was permitted to take personal deductions.

A final development occurred in Maryland, in 1967, when the state enacted a law under which the city of Baltimore and all counties were required to levy a local income tax on residents at not less than 20 percent and no more than 50 percent of the state income tax liability. Between these limits, increases or decreases in rates had to be in increments of 5 percent. Nonresidents could not be taxed. The county income taxes were piggybacked on the state income tax, filed as a section of the state return, and administered by the state comptroller in the same way as the state income tax.

Features and extent of use

Local income taxes are levied in Alabama, Delaware, Indiana, Iowa, Kentucky, Maryland, Michigan, Missouri, New York, Ohio, Oregon, and Pennsylvania; Arkansas and Georgia have authorized local income taxes, but no taxes have been adopted (see Table 11–4).[23] The taxes are particularly common in Indiana, Kentucky, Maryland, Ohio, and Pennsylvania.[24]

Not all local income taxes apply to a tax base that resembles the broad base used by the federal income tax. For individual incomes, the base generally includes, at a minimum, wages and salaries. Localities that levy an earnings tax limit their tax to this base, plus (usually) unincorporated business profits, and omit income such as capital gains, dividends, and interest.[25] When the base is this limited, it is usually because of the administrative difficulty of including the other income sources in it. Individual income taxes on wages and salaries are collected through employer withholding, so collection is simple and the revenue is available quickly, with monthly remittance to the locality. Initial enforcement is against the local employer, who is responsible for withholding; local employers are easier to pursue than nonlocal firms making nonwage payments. When the local government itself is administering the tax, it is natural to favor the earnings tax over broader taxes on all types of income because the earnings tax is much easier to administer. Income taxes apply to a broad base, typically derived from the state income tax, which is itself based on the federal tax. Indiana, Iowa, and Maryland levy broad income taxes, and in none of these states is corporate income included in the local base. Corporate income is taxed in some local jurisdictions, including some in New York, Michigan, and Pennsylvania; where this income is taxed, total corporate income is typically allocated to the locality according to a formula that averages the shares of payroll, property, and sales in the locality.

Although local income taxes are flat-rate taxes, they usually have personal exemptions; thus, the effective rate is progressive at lower income levels and becomes generally proportional at higher income levels, as the impact of the exemption is diluted.[26] Taxes on earnings have few features beyond an initial exemption and flat rates. Those that have a broader base may have nonbusiness itemized deductions, but provisions are usually simpler than those for the federal income tax.

Yield

In fiscal year 1998–99, local governments collected $16.54 billion from individual income taxes and $3.16 billion from corporate income taxes. Although as a source of nonproperty tax revenue the income tax is outranked only by the general sales tax, more than half the total comes from local taxes in two states (New York and Pennsylvania), and in only three other states (Indiana, Maryland, and Ohio) does the state total exceed $1 billion. In other words, the overall fiscal significance of the local income tax is concentrated in a relatively limited number of states, although it may be extremely important in the finances of a particular jurisdiction. Among cities with populations of 250,000 or more, several collect more than half their tax revenue from their income tax: Cincinnati (73 percent), Cleveland (72 percent), Columbus (85 percent), Louisville (64 percent), Philadelphia (52 percent), and Toledo (83 percent).[27] The income tax also represents a significant revenue source for more populous counties in Kentucky and Maryland, although it yields more than half the tax revenue only in Jefferson County, Kentucky (51 percent). Undoubtedly, the local income tax can be an extremely productive revenue source, permitting lower rates for other taxes or higher expenditures on local services.

The yield that can be expected in a particular locality depends on the rate levied, the size of the tax base, and the definition of the tax base. Some local jurisdictions, including those in Alabama, Delaware, Kentucky, Missouri, Ohio, and Pennsylvania, define the tax base to encompass earned income (wages and salaries) and the net income of unincorporated businesses. The tax base excludes property income (rental income, capital gains, dividends, and interest). The Portland, Oregon, tax base is limited to business income and excludes wages and salaries. The tax base for localities in Indiana, Iowa, Maryland, Michigan, and New York City is much broader, including roughly the same income sources as the federal income tax. At any given rate, the yield for a broader base will be greater than for a base that is limited to earned income. To estimate the revenue potential for a particular locality, it is necessary to analyze the relevant income components in the jurisdiction; records from the state income tax can normally be used as a data source. Multiplying the proposed rate by the estimated base yields an estimate of revenue.

Limiting the tax to wages and salaries reduces collection and enforcement costs because the tax is collected through employer withholding. Collecting tax on business income is much more difficult. Since property income is unevenly distributed (most is concentrated among more affluent families), excluding property income from the income tax base makes the tax both horizontally and vertically inequitable. Excluding property income is also likely to reduce the growth prospects for the tax base (i.e., the revenue elasticity), although it would also reduce the downward volatility of the tax in the face of economic recession. Extending the tax to corporate income, while broadening the base, increases its sensitivity to economic recessions because the corporate profits base is extremely sensitive to economic cycles.

Administrative issues

When administration is local, the government must (1) develop a master list of local income tax payers and of local employers, who will be expected to withhold collections from payrolls; (2) develop and distribute tax returns and instructional materials; (3) handle revenue accounting as returns come in; (4) pursue delinquent files; (5) administer an audit program; (6) arrange to exchange information with state and federal income tax administrations; and (7) apply enforcement mechanisms (liens, garnishment, seizures, etc.) against entities that do not comply. Administrative costs tend to be lower when a high proportion of the total tax comes from withholding and when the number of employers in the jurisdiction is limited. A local income tax administered by the state often appears as a line on the state tax return. While this approach makes compliance and administration simple, it does dull the transparency of the local component for taxpayers.

Because withholding is critical to any income tax, regardless of whether it is limited to wages and salaries, local tax authorities need to maintain a good relationship with employers in the jurisdiction. Employers' remittance of the tax usually follows a monthly cycle for large firms and a quarterly cycle for smaller ones; firms are also normally required to submit to each taxpayer a yearly withholding report, which the taxpayer uses to prepare his or her return. When the income tax extends beyond wages and salaries, taxpayers may be required to submit quarterly payments of estimated tax on income that has not been subject to withholding or other prepayment.

State versus local administration Local income taxes may be either self-administered or piggybacked on the state tax. Local administration is found in Alabama, Delaware, Kentucky, Michigan, Missouri, Ohio, Oregon, and Pennsylvania.[28] State administration is prescribed in Indiana, Iowa, Maryland, and New York (see Table 11–4).

When permitted, local governments themselves can arrange for central administration. One particularly successful example is the Central Collection Agency (CCA), a part of the Cleveland Department of Finance, which administers the individual income taxes (applied to wages, salaries, and other employee compensation, rental income, and unincorporated business profits) levied independently by forty-three Ohio municipalities in the northern part of that state.[29] CCA performs all the functions of a standard tax administration agency: it aggressively maintains the taxpayer list, mails returns to taxpayers, provides taxpayer assistance during filing season, processes all payments (estimated payments, reconciliations from individual taxpayers, and withholding payments from employers), bills for any tax due, assesses penalties and interest, mails delinquency notices, conducts audits of taxpayers, and distributes collections each month, transferring funds electronically to contracting municipalities.[30] The CCA contract limits the charge for its services to 5 percent of collections, but actual charges are based on expenses (the total is allocated among municipalities by a formula based on revenue share and number of transactions) and are much lower than the limit. In the CCA area, the municipalities can choose to levy the tax, can choose the rate that they levy, and can choose whether to administer the tax themselves or to contract with CCA. This range of choices gives the municipalities great fiscal autonomy and, because the municipalities can opt in or out, requires CCA to attend carefully to the quality and cost of its service.

Defining the tax base In many of the jurisdictions that levy an income tax, the tax base is gross earned income. The tax has no nonbusiness deductions or exemptions, and property income (rent, interest) is excluded. In other words, the base includes wages and salaries and, sometimes, income from unincorporated businesses. The obvious question is whether the base should be widened.

One important argument in favor of expanding the income base is equity. A narrow base violates the principle of horizontal equity because people with equal total income will have differing tax liability: for example, if two people both have total incomes of $50,000 but one person's income is entirely from wages and salaries and the other person's income is half from rents, interest, and dividends, the first person's effective tax rate is double that of the second, a clear example of horizontal inequity.

Vertical equity concerns the relationship between tax payments made by households with different levels of affluence. Because higher-income households are likely to receive a larger share of their total income from rents, interest, and dividends than are lower-income households, a tax that excludes these payments from the base is likely to cause higher-income households to pay a smaller share of their total income in taxes than lower-income households. Assume, for example, that a flat tax rate of 1 percent applies to taxable income. If one person has an income of $50,000, entirely from wages and salaries, and a second has an income of $100,000, of which 75 percent comes from property, the second person's effective tax rate (tax paid as a share of total income) would be lower, even though his or her tax-paying capacity is considerably higher. This pattern violates the typical conception of vertical equity; thus, there is obviously a strong argument, from the perspective of equity, for including all income sources in the tax base.

Another advantage of a broader tax base is that it allows the same amount of revenue to be generated by a lower tax rate, and a lower rate is always preferable because it gives taxpayers less incentive to change their behavior solely to reduce their tax liability. Such distortions of behavior create "welfare cost" or "deadweight loss" (terms that refer to the cost to society of causing people and producers to change their behavior because of the tax), and the losses increase disproportionately as the tax rate increases. A low rate also reduces the inequities that arise from omitting certain incomes from the base: the difference between taxed and total income is smaller.

Finally, a base that is as broad as the state income tax simplifies enforcement. The exchange of information, assuming that both taxing authorities are willing and that there is no legal impediment, can provide a powerful tool for collecting the tax. It also opens the door for state administration of the local tax; taxes that limit the base to earnings are predominantly locally administered.

Although the case for a broad base is strong, several jurisdictions, notably in Kentucky and Pennsylvania, continue to levy income taxes on a narrow base, principally because it is easier to administer a tax on the income that passes through employer payrolls than a tax on property (or "unearned") income. Because property income is not subject to employer withholding, the administrative costs associated with adding this flow to the tax base are considerable. Taxes on property income, instead of being collected from the employer, must be collected directly from the taxpayer, who must report the income. Moreover, the sources of property income are often outside the locality, making enforcement more difficult. Auditing is more costly because it extends to each taxpayer instead of simply requiring visits to employers. Finally, a broad-based tax puts more responsibility on the taxpayer than does a tax limited to wages and salaries. Piggybacked state administration, as is practiced in Indiana, Iowa, and Maryland, makes broad-based taxes much simpler. State enforcement powers make the local tax easier to collect and reduces the compliance burden for taxpayers. But only three states provide state administration.

Taxing nonresidents   The issue of taxing nonresidents arises when people live in one taxing locality but work in another. This situation raises three important questions: (1) Should nonresidents (i.e., commuters) be taxed? (2) If so, at what rate? (3) Should the taxes paid in one jurisdiction be credited against those owed in another?

Local government practice with respect to nonresident taxation varies. Non-residents are usually taxed, though often at a lower tax rate than residents; in fact, nonresident rates that are half the resident rate are quite common (this is the practice, for example, for Michigan municipalities). Two important exceptions to the practice of taxing nonresidents are New York City and Washington, D.C. Although the administrations of both cities would like to include nonresidents in their tax base, they can do so only after authorization (from the state and from Congress, respectively).[31] Another exception is Maryland, where income taxes are entirely residence based and do not apply to nonresident income at all.

The benefits-received principle provides some guidance regarding the taxation of nonresidents. Commuters benefit from the services provided by the jurisdictions where they work. Some payment by nonresident workers is therefore clearly justified, especially for services associated with such workers. If there is no feasible scheme for charging nonresidents directly, then income taxation provides a means of distributing the cost of services between residents and nonresidents. Determining the appropriate tax rate is more difficult, however. Although one study concluded that Detroit's 0.5 percent nonresident income tax fully compensated the city for benefits that commuters received, it is difficult to quantify the benefits received by the commuters.[32] It could be argued, moreover, that since residents bear property and other local tax burdens, their total contribution may be so large that they should pay lower income tax rates than commuters, not the other way around. Finally, taxing nonresidents at the same rate as residents, rather than at a lower rate, would eliminate the incentive to move to neighboring jurisdictions for tax savings.

Although the practice of crediting taxes paid to one jurisdiction against those owed in another (to prevent two localities from taxing exactly the same income) is virtually universal, if the benefits-received principle is followed to its ultimate conclusion, the credit would not be justified. Commuters who impose costs on or receive benefits from a jurisdiction should bear the tax without receiving a credit in their home jurisdictions. But the jurisdictions of residence want to protect their residents from bearing a double burden; extending the credit, even though it may lack logical justification, is a reflection of that protective inclination.

Locational effects

The influence of local income taxes on local economic activity has not been examined as explicitly as the impact of local sales taxes on local retail activity. Factors that are likely to affect the location choices of private individuals and businesses include (1) the size of the geographic area in which the tax is applied, (2) the rates applied in neighboring areas, and (3) the fiscal adjustments (the services provided by the revenue or the reductions in other tax rates) that accompany the income tax.

The causes of locational decisions are complex and hard to test. Although the income tax appears to have little effect on location choices, the evidence is, at best, inconclusive. Of course, the analysis is complicated by the variations in local income taxes, some of which apply to nonresident income and some of which do not. In the first instance, a move outside the locality would not end tax liability as long as the place of employment is unchanged. Moving would have an impact, however, if the tax were on residents only. It is clear, however, that regardless of the actual impact, local governments are afraid that an income tax will influence location choices, and this concern tempers their enthusiasm for the tax. In policy discussions, perception is often almost as important as evidence.

Fiscal disparity

Like the local sales tax base, the local income tax base is not evenly distributed across localities. In Maryland, for example, for fiscal year 2000, the per capita local income tax base ranged from a low of $6,257.32 in Somerset County to a high of $28,041.85 in Montgomery County. The average for the lowest quintile of counties was $8,554.54, compared with an average of $22,997.18 for the highest quintile. At a given tax rate, the base-rich counties raised just over two and one-half times as much revenue as did their base-poor neighbors.[33]

Maryland counties can choose their own tax rate, which is applied to the state-administered tax base, and those rates do differ, ranging from a low of 1.25 to a high of 3.01 percent. However, base-poor counties have not chosen to exert sufficient tax effort to counterbalance the disparity in the wealth of the base, or they are not permitted by the state to levy fully counterbalancing rates. The counties with the lowest and highest per capita tax revenues are the same as those with the lowest and highest per capita income tax base—$188.35 in Somerset County and $813.21 in Montgomery County—and the differential is roughly the same as the differential between their tax bases, the high being roughly four and one-half times as great as the low. The per capita revenue ratio is slightly lower, however, because Somerset County levies a tax rate of 3.15 percent, compared with 2.95 percent in Montgomery County. Comparing the average per capita tax revenue for the highest and lowest quintiles shows the same general pattern: $215.28 versus $558.43; again, the high is slightly more than two and one-half times the low.

The implication is clear: providing local governments with the authority to levy their own income tax delivers unequal fiscal capacity. If the state's principal concern is to ensure equal access to the services provided by local governments—that is, to ensure that local government finances are adequate to deliver equivalent services at comparable tax rates—the authority to levy income taxes has the potential to make fiscal equity more difficult to attain. If, however, the state is more concerned with providing fiscal autonomy and making local governments bear more of the political responsibility for financing the services they provide, disparity is a less serious concern.

Summary

Local income taxes have proven to be a productive and reliable source of revenue. Strong arguments can be made, on the basis of equity and efficiency, in favor of a broad-based income tax, but a tax limited to earned income can also be extremely productive and within the capacity of a local government to administer. A broad-based tax, piggybacked to allow state administration, improves the equity and administration of the tax, but it also reduces local governments' fiscal autonomy. Because the revenue potential from the income tax varies significantly across localities, the tax has considerable potential to widen fiscal disparities between jurisdictions.

Other nonproperty tax revenue

Local governments raise a modest amount of revenue from nonproperty taxes apart from those on income or general sales. Table 11–5 shows that localities generated about 5 percent of their total tax revenue from selective sales (excise) taxes and from license taxes on motor vehicles, motor vehicle operators, and certain businesses. These taxes may be levied either on an ad valorem basis (on the value of the transaction) or on a per-unit basis. Although the real revenue productivity of taxes levied on a per-unit basis lags during periods of

Table 11–5 Revenue from selected non-property taxes, 1996–97.

Classification	Revenue ($ in millions)	Percentage
Tax revenue, total	284,398	100.0
Selective sales	13,975	4.9
Motor fuel	881	0.3
Alcoholic beverages	319	0.1
Tobacco products	181	0.1
Public utilities	7,598	2.7
Other	4,996	1.8
Licenses	1,219	0.4
Motor vehicle	1,188	0.4
Motor vehicle operator	2	0.0
Corporations	4	0.0
Other	25	0.0

Note: Because of rounding, detail may not add to totals.

inflation, the unit basis sometimes makes sense. Unit-based motor fuel taxes make sense, for example, as a quasi-price for the use of roads; and, in the case of cigarettes, the health effects depend on the number of units consumed, not on their value. Despite long-term revenue consequences, the particular purpose of the tax may thus militate against the ad valorem levy.

No excise or license tax makes a major contribution to the finances of local governments. Of all the categories, ad valorem excise taxes levied on the gross receipts of public utilities (particularly electric and telephone) are the most significant, producing 2.7 percent of total tax revenue.[34] There is no particular justification for these taxes, other than that the businesses are not fugitive and the taxes can therefore be easily collected. Municipal governments receive most of the tax revenue from public utility taxes.

Virtually all localities license certain privileges and economic activities undertaken within their borders. Although localities sometimes license other activities, most of licensing revenue (0.4 percent of total tax revenue) comes from motor vehicle licensing, which is usually undertaken by counties and represents the largest source of this category of revenue.

Local governments collect modest amounts of tax revenue from the traditional "big three" excise taxes: motor fuel, alcoholic beverages, and tobacco products. However, the combined contribution to total tax revenue is modest: 0.3 percent for motor fuel, and 0.1 percent each for alcoholic beverages and tobacco products. Counties collect more revenue from motor fuel sales than from alcohol or tobacco, and municipalities collect more revenue from alcohol and tobacco sales.

A number of states permit local taxes on the transfer of real property. The taxes apply at the time of sale to the buyer, the seller, or both and are usually collected when deeds are registered. The levy may be a percentage of the sale price of the property, a flat deed-recording tax, or a combination of the two. States may levy the tax as well. Proceeds from the tax are often directed toward dedicated funds for the protection of natural resources or the acquisition of parks and open space. Total revenue from the tax can be significant in some jurisdictions, but the amounts are modest in comparison to the proceeds from broader-based taxes.

Excise taxes

Excises may be levied on either the sales price of a transaction (ad valorem tax) or the number of units purchased (unit tax). They apply to a narrow base and are thus vulnerable to criticism from the perspective of both equity and efficiency. Horizontal equity is violated because taxpayers who are otherwise equally situated will pay different amounts of tax, depending on their taste for the taxed commodities. And because the consumption of many excised items does not rise as rapidly as income, the burden is distributed regressively.

Efficiency is a problem for several reasons. First, by making the relative prices of taxed and untaxed goods differ from the relative costs of production, excise taxes mislead consumers about relative scarcities and therefore distort production and consumption choices. These distorted choices are even more significant to the local economy when consumers make purchases outside the taxing jurisdiction in order to avoid the tax. Second, excises are many times more expensive to collect (per dollar of revenue collected) than are broader-based taxes. Many administrative expenses associated with collecting any tax—registration, delinquency-control systems, auditing, accounting, and so on—do not vary with the amount actually collected. Hence, it is more productive to concentrate on more robust sources than to divert resources to lower-yield taxes.

The arguments against excises carry less weight in the case of alcoholic beverages, tobacco products, and motor fuel. Taxes on alcohol and tobacco products are often referred to as "corrective taxes" because they correct for misleading signals that emerge from the private market. Specifically, the consumption of alcoholic beverages and tobacco products may impose costs (predominantly health-related costs) on third parties. Since these costs are not reflected in market prices, excise taxes provide a means of compelling users of such products to bear more of the full costs and to adjust their consumption patterns accordingly. Motor fuel taxes, on the other hand, operate as a proxy charge for the use of streets and roads. Hence, these three taxes—although still subject to the disadvantages of excises noted earlier—do have redeeming virtues within the private market. Whether these virtues are compelling enough to justify local governments' levy of the taxes is, however, another matter. Since consumers can easily avoid all the taxes by making purchases across a border, the damage to a select group of vendors (in the form of lost sales) may make the application of the taxes unwarranted at the local level.

Revenue from public utility excise taxes is fairly stable—and, because it is collected from relatively few firms, is generally easy and inexpensive to collect. The tax burden is almost certainly shifted forward to the purchasers of the utility service. Private individuals bear the burden, both directly and indirectly, through the taxes paid on business purchases of utility services, which are embedded in the production costs and then reflected in the prices the business charges. Whether the tax burden is regressive, proportional, or progressive depends on the relationship between household income and the amount of utility services consumed by the household, both directly and indirectly.

Taxes are collected at the utility level. The taxes of users who live outside the taxing jurisdiction benefit the jurisdiction where the utility is located, not the jurisdiction where the users live. In any case, the consumption of utility service would not normally be considered a reasonable basis for the distribution of the costs of government; utility taxes are driven by convenience, not by any fundamental principles of government finance.

Licenses

Governments license activities and privileges within their borders for different reasons. Sometimes the license is used to control or limit an activity, and sometimes the license is intended to produce revenue. Although the motives are often mixed, one test is the degree of control associated with the license.

If licenses are provided to all comers, then the revenue motive is probably the most important, even though the proceeds are still likely to be modest.

Governments must be vigilant to ensure that license fees intended to produce revenue actually yield enough revenue to make the administration of those fees worthwhile. (The cost of administration is less of a concern when the primary purpose is to police an activity.) Licenses may be issued for flat fees or may be based on the gross receipts or physical size of a business. If a fee is flat rate or based on physical size, the fee structure should be periodically evaluated and adjusted to ensure that payments are in keeping with increases in the general price level.

Summary

Excise taxes and license fees make only a modest contribution to local government finances. The strongest argument for these taxes is that they support the achievement of special purposes—often purposes that are not directly related to revenue. In particular, certain activities, or the production or consumption of certain goods, may be associated with social costs that are not reflected in market prices. Excises and licenses afford a way of inducing private entities to pay attention to these social costs.

Although excise taxes and license fees would normally have but a modest role in local government finances, some local governments unfortunately lack the authority to levy more productive taxes (e.g., sales or income) and therefore seek revenue diversity by levying a long list of excise and license taxes. This practice is expensive in terms of administrative and compliance costs and almost certainly creates a bad climate for economic development. Nor do these taxes generally yield much revenue. Local governments are distinctly better served by the authority to levy a single broad nonproperty tax than by the authority to levy a large variety of taxes with a modest combined yield.

Conclusion: Diversity in the local revenue structure

Allowing local governments to impose nonproperty taxes increases their control over their fiscal destiny, giving them greater choice in determining what they will spend and how that spending will be financed from various segments of their economies. Local governments may, for example, use such authority to relieve reliance on the property tax or to increase the services provided to citizens. Such choices are important aspects of fiscal autonomy.

From the revenue side, fiscal autonomy (and responsibility) is greatest when the locality chooses what taxes it will levy, defines the bases it will use, sets the rate and preference structure for those bases, and administers the taxes. While piggybacking a local tax on a comparable state tax can provide a considerable degree of fiscal autonomy without some of the problems that full autonomy can create, local governments may not agree, if given the choice, that the autonomy thereby achieved is sufficient. In particular, they may be concerned that a government (i.e., the state) that does not receive the revenue from a tax that it administers is likely to feel less urgency about collecting the tax—or reforming it—than is a government that uses the revenue to finance its operations. Local governments may feel that, in practice, administration is inextricably tied to tax policy and that unless they have control over administrative decisions, they lack adequate fiscal autonomy.

Nonproperty taxes can give local governments alternatives for relieving their reliance on the real property tax. However, a locality that plans to administer these taxes on its own, without linking them to the administration of a comparable state tax, must have greater administrative capacity than is necessary to levy a property tax. The nonproperty tax bases are fugitive; they will not remain in the taxing jurisdiction in the same way that real property does. Nonproperty taxes require greater compliance efforts on the part of taxpayers than the property tax, and if these taxes are to be satisfactorily collected, administration must be vigorous, forceful, and focused on inducing compliance.

1 Within that total, its yield is much more important to school districts than to municipalities and counties.

2 Implicit price deflator from Bureau of Economic Analysis, "National Income and Product Accounts" tables, available at www.bea.gov/bea/dn1.htm.

3 U.S. Department of Commerce, *Government Organizations,* vol. 1 of *1997 Census of Governments* (Washington, D.C.: U.S. Government Printing Office, 1999).

4 The revenue elasticity equals the percentage change in the tax base that results when economic activity (defined as personal income) increases by 1 percent.

5 These Mississippi taxes were ultimately replaced by a system of state grants to municipalities.

6 In Louisiana, the tax has been an important revenue source for school districts, a rare divergence from school districts' almost total reliance on property taxes.

7 Combined local sales tax rates in New Orleans equal 5 percent, but this figure represents levies from three separate local governments: the city of New Orleans (2.5 percent), the Orleans Parish school board (1.5 percent), and the regional transit authority (1 percent). These local sales taxes are in addition to the 4 percent state sales tax.

8 Raymond Ring, "Consumers' Share and Producers' Share of the General Sales Tax," *National Tax Journal* 52 (March 1999): 79–90.

9 Even when the state administers the local tax, the two bases might not be identical, which creates confusion. For example, Georgia began phasing out the state tax on food purchases in 1996, but Georgia localities could not afford the revenue loss from the narrowing of the base. Here is the "clarification" provided in an information bulletin from the state department of revenue, which illustrates why most analysts believe that the state and local tax bases should be identical: "On October 1, 1998, no [state] sales tax will be charged on eligible food and beverage. Local Option, Special Purpose, Educational, and MARTA Sales Taxes will still have to be collected except for the Homestead Tax (DeKalb and Rockdale Counties) and the Local Option Tax in Taliaferro, Webster Counties and any future Local Option Tax. This change does not affect the exemption from all sales taxes when purchases are made with food stamps or WIC [women, infants, children] coupons."

10 Some localities in the following states do not levy a local use tax to accompany their sales tax: Alabama, Alaska, Arizona, Colorado, Idaho, Illinois, Iowa, Kansas, Minnesota, Mississippi, Missouri, New Mexico, Oklahoma, Pennsylvania, Vermont, and Wisconsin.

11 U.S. Department of Commerce, Bureau of the Census, *Government Finances: 1998–99* (Washington, D.C.: U.S. Government Printing Office, 2001), 129–151.

12 John L. Mikesell, "Changes in State Retail Sales Taxes: Can These Taxes Survive Prosperity?" in *Proceedings of the Ninety-Third Annual Conference on Taxation of the National Tax Association* (Washington, D.C.: National Tax Association, 2001).

13 During recessions, states frequently manage their own revenue shortfalls by delaying the distribution of local revenues collected by state authorities and delaying state transfers to local governments. The delay provides the state with sufficient cash to avoid borrowing, but the strategy simply moves the budget crisis from the state to the local level.

14 *Quill Corp. v. North Dakota,* 504 U.S. 298 (1992).

15 Rate change tally from Vertex, Inc., personal communication with author.

16 Robert Cline and Thomas Neubig, "Masters of Complexity and Bearers of Great Burden: The Sales Tax System and Compliance Costs for Multistate Retailers," *State Tax Notes* 18 (24 January 2000): 297–313. The Cline-Neubig estimates have been vigorously challenged as overestimates.

17 Paul G. Lewis and Elisa Barbour, *California Cities and the Local Sales Tax* (San Francisco: Public Policy Institute of California, 1999).

18 Ibid.

19 Some states (including Alaska, Arizona, Arkansas, Florida, North Dakota, and Tennessee) attempt to reduce this incentive by setting a cap on the amount of tax that can be collected in a single purchase. The cap complicates administration of the tax and creates an incentive to lump as many purchases as possible into a single transaction. It also complicates compliance, but retailers are apparently willing to accept the inconvenience because the cap reduces the incentive for customers to shop where the tax rate is lower.

20 Robert P. Inman, "Fiscal Performance of Local Governments: An Interpretative Review," in *Current Issues in Urban Economics,* ed. Peter Mieszkowski and Mahlon Straszheim (Baltimore: Johns Hopkins University Press, 1979), 285–292.

21 The effective sales tax rate equals sales tax paid (statutory rate times percentage of income spent on taxed purchases times income) divided by income. As the percentage of income spent on taxed items declines (as household income increases), the effective sales tax rate also falls.

22 Electronic cash registers and universal price code labels simplify compliance, but the system must still be tested to verify that items are properly categorized as taxed or exempt.

23 Taxes on employer payrolls are also levied by a few municipalities in California and New Jersey. They are not covered in this review because they differ considerably from employee-based income taxes.

24 Two studies suggest that local governments use their income tax revenue not to increase spending but to replace portions of their property tax revenue; see Elizabeth Deran, "Tax Structure in Cities Using the Income Tax," *National Tax Journal* 21 (June 1968): 152; and James D. Rogers, *Report of the Task Force on Local Real Estate Taxation to the Pennsylvania Tax Commission* (Harrisburg: Commonwealth of Pennsylvania, 1981), 50–51. The question has not been reexamined recently.

25 Some earnings taxes accompany the individual portion with a business earnings tax. The business portion includes corporate income.

26 Because the impact of the flat exemption declines as income increases, the effective tax rate (tax paid divided by household income) increases as income increases. Thus, an exemption of $1,000 has a greater relative effect for a household with an income of $20,000 than for one with an income of $100,000.

27 U.S. Department of Commerce, Bureau of the Census, *Government Finances: 1998–99* (Washington, D.C.: U.S. Government Printing Office, 2001), 129–151.

28 The Alabama taxes are occupational taxes paid by the employer but withheld from the employee's pay.

29 Other similar groups operate in Ohio. The Regional Income Tax Agency, for example, serves even more localities than the CCA.

30 A taxpayer who works or earns a profit in more than one municipality served by the CCA would file one return with the CCA and make only a single payment to the CCA, but the taxable income would be distributed among the municipalities and each would receive tax revenues in accordance with that distribution. Similarly, a taxpayer who resides in one municipality and is employed in another would owe income tax to both—a situation that, assuming both municipalities had contracts with CCA, would also be handled through a single return. Thus, the CCA arrangement provides a degree of convenience for the taxpayer.

31 New York City did tax nonresidents until 1999. Yonkers, New York, continues to tax nonresidents.

32 William B. Neenan, *Political Economy of Urban Areas* (Chicago: Markham Publishing, 1972), 147–150.

33 Data from Comptroller of Maryland, "Income Tax Summary Report, Tax Year 2000," available at www.comp.state.md.us/publications/fiscalrprts/summary00.pdf; and U.S. Department of Commerce, Bureau of the Census, "Detailed Tables," available at http://factfinder.census.gov/servlet/BasicFactsServlet.

34 These are taxes on the service provided by the utility (e.g., electric, water, telephone) and are distinct from the charges for utility service provided by a municipally owned utility. Chapter 12 discusses municipal user charges.

12 User charges and special districts

EDWARD J. BIERHANZL AND PAUL B. DOWNING

Successful management of local government finance requires the adoption of policies that are politically acceptable, economically sensible, and appropriate for local needs. Fulfilling all three of these criteria often involves the adoption of a wide variety of revenue strategies. It makes both political and economic sense that different revenue sources are appropriate for different purposes.

Since the mid-1970s, citizens have often used the voting booth to express their resistance to increases in the property tax. Local government revenue sources based on the benefits-received principle—according to which those who use a public service should pay directly for at least a part of the cost of that service—do not seem to have met with the same resistance from citizens. Thus, for the past several decades, local governments have been systematically shifting away from the property tax and toward user charges: between 1981 and 1991, current charge—the term used in the Census of Governments to refer to user charges—increased 141 percent, whereas the property tax increased only 107 percent.[1] Although the gap has narrowed recently, growth in user charge revenue still outpaces growth in property tax revenue. Between 1991 and 1996, current charges grew by 32 percent, while property tax revenue grew by 14 percent.[2] Nationwide, for 1999–2000, the total amount collected from charges and utility revenue was nearly as much as that collected from the property tax ($217 billion and $238 billion, respectively).[3] Many local governments now collect more revenue from user charges than from property taxes.

Like user charges, special districts provide a means of isolating the funding and provision of specific services. Because special districts are dedicated to a single task, the services they offer can often be more closely tailored to the needs of citizens. In fact, special districts often rely on user charge financing to ensure that revenues correspond closely with the quantity of service being provided. Furthermore, because special districts are often financially and administratively independent, their services are insulated from the budgetary trade-offs that are a necessary part of consolidated government.

This chapter opens with a general overview of user charges and user charge design. It describes how pricing principles can be used to design user charge systems that reflect variation in costs and demand, and it discusses practical considerations such as administrative costs and consumer acceptance. Next, the chapter examines the structure of charges for individual services such as water supply, sewerage, and solid-waste collection. It then discusses three important financing tools that are analogous, in their functioning, to user charges: development fees, special assessments, and tax increment financing. The chapter then compares user charges with the property tax in terms of the effect on development, on demand, and on various income groups. Next, it examines special districts, which rely heavily on user charges, and considers the relationship between the number of special districts and the cost and quality of service provision. Finally, the chapter looks at the role of privatization in the provision and financing of local services.

User charges

As defined by the U.S. Census Bureau, the category "charges and miscellaneous revenue" generally refers to all nontax, own-source revenue except that from utilities, liquor stores, and insurance trusts. More specifically, current charges are those "amounts received from the public for performance of specific services benefiting the persons charged."[4]

User charges function very much like the prices charged for privately produced goods: they represent payment for services that would not have been provided if the charge had not been paid. For example, a golfer who failed to pay the required fee would be excluded from playing on a municipal golf course; a home owner who did not pay the connection charge would not be connected to the municipality's natural gas line.

One important difference, however, between the user charges imposed by a public entity and the prices charged by private producers is that people or firms do not always have the opportunity to decline government services and thereby avoid paying the charge. Some charges, such as those for refuse collection, for example, must often be paid regardless of whether the service is used at all (although the consumer always has the option of moving outside the jurisdiction to avoid such a charge). Other user charges, such as those for electricity and water, vary with the amount of service used, which means that the consumer can avoid some (or all) of the charge by reducing consumption.

In a properly designed user charge system, price has two principal functions: (1) to ration government-supplied goods and thereby discourage excessive or wasteful consumption; and (2) to provide cost signals that enable consumers to properly evaluate the service—in other words, to decide whether the value they place on the service is in proportion to the cost of providing it.

Economic theory suggests that user charge financing should lead to more efficient service provision than property tax financing, and empirical research has confirmed this effect. In a study by Edward Bierhanzl that used sewer service as an example of a user-charge-financed system, an increase in reliance on user charges (defined as user charge revenue divided by total expenditures) was shown to reduce total expenditures.[5] This same study also involved a preliminary extension of the analysis to other services, which generally supported the findings for sewer service: not only were expenditures reduced, but the reduction occurred without a significant decrease in the quantity of service provided. This study and others suggest that the efficiency gains resulting from user charge financing can be substantial.[6] The ability to provide the same level of service for less money is a very attractive proposition for local elected officials and is surely one of the main forces driving the continued growth of user charge financing at the local level.

Figure 12–1 shows the variety and extent of user charges and fees. Local governments impose charges not only for common services such as transportation, water, and sewerage, but also (1) for overseeing private enterprise, as in the case of restaurant and building inspections; (2) to cover the expenses of special services such as police protection and crowd control at private events; and (3) to cover the cost to the local government of private activities (e.g., licenses for carnivals). In some cases, license fees are a way for a local government to capture part of the profits of a private business (e.g., a taxi service); such fees are analogous to sales or gross receipts taxes. Fees are also charged for administrative paperwork—for example, to obtain a development permit or file a tract map.

As local governments computerize their administrative operations and provide more services over the Internet, there are opportunities to collect fees for services such as geographic information systems (GIS) mapping, the provision

Figure 12–1 Types of local government charges and fees.

Sewerage
Sewerage service charges

Stormwater sewerage
Runoff fees
Recharge-basin fees

Sanitation
Trash-collection charges
Landfill charges
Refuse-hauler licenses

Public utilities
Water meter or connection charges
Water service charges
Electricity charges

Health and hospitals
Inoculation fees
Hospital charges
Ambulance charges
Concession rental fees

Parking
Meter fees
Parking lot fees

Parks and recreation
Golf course greens fees
Permit charges for tennis courts, picnic
    shelters, etc.
Rental fees for the use of stadiums and
    amphitheaters

Rental fees for the use of playing fields
Park development fees and land
    dedications

Transportation
Subway and bus fares
Bridge and road tolls
Landing and departure fees
Dockage fees

Development
Streetlight installation charges
Special fees to fund convention center
    construction
Tract-map filing fees
Special fees for services provided to
    rental properties

Police and fire protection
Charges for special events
Fire-inspection fees

Social control licenses
Merchant licenses
Animal-control tags

E-government services
GIS (geographic information system)
    map fees
Property tax information charges
Records search fees

of access to tax records, and database searches. Furthermore, in areas where, to avoid duplication of services, various local government entities specialize in providing certain services, governments can charge each other for service provision. For example, a central city may charge the local county government for providing county residents with access to the city water supply. Local governments often contract with one another to provide transit service as well.

The degree to which fees and charges cover the costs of supplying a good or service varies widely among services. Services least likely to be financed by user charges fall into two categories: (1) those that have traditionally been considered ordinary functions of government—police and fire protection, for example; and (2) those that evoke strong sentiment among citizens concerned with equity in the distribution of services: examples are education and certain recreational facilities, such as picnic areas and downtown public parks. Although school vouchers have created substantial controversy in education circles, the debate is always about how the money should be spent, not about where it should come from. The belief is widespread that charging parents directly for education would be inequitable, and there is little disagreement that the source of funds should be broad-based taxes of one form or another. For other services, such as sports facilities and sanitation, citizens feel that a mix of user charges and general revenue financing is appropriate.

At the other end of the revenue spectrum, where user charges are relied upon most heavily, are services such as air terminals and sewer service. User charges are often designed to cover most or all of the costs of providing such services; in these areas, the notion that it is equitable to charge users for the cost of service provision is widely accepted.

Finally, there are services for which user charges generate revenues that are many times higher than the cost of providing the service. In the case of municipal parking, perhaps the best example, charges serve primarily as a revenue-raising and allocation device and are not closely related to the costs of service provision. Urban downtowns, for example, typically have many more people who wish to park than there are spaces available. Municipal parking fees allocate those limited spaces to the people who value them (and are willing to pay) the most.

Table 12–1, which shows revenues from charges as a percentage of expenditures for selected services, provides some insight into the difference between the cost of services and what citizens pay. Charges for sewerage have increased substantially since 1991–92, but changes in user charges for other services have been less significant. The highway revenues shown in the table are derived primarily from toll bridges, although some toll roads are also included. Tighter federal clean-air legislation, along with increasing concern about deteriorating infrastructure, may eventually lead to greater reliance on user charges to curtail traffic, reduce pollution, and help pay the costs of road repair.

The extent to which local governments rely on user charges to finance various services depends as much on political considerations as it does on economic considerations. For this reason, even when user charge financing may be economically feasible, it may be rejected on equity grounds or because of incompatibility with the local political structure. For example, residents of a small rural town where all services have traditionally been funded through property tax revenues are likely to have a different attitude toward user charges than residents of a large, professionally managed city with a variety of fees, charges, and other revenue streams. Since trends in user charge financing will shift with the prevailing political climate, predicting the course of such trends is often difficult.

Table 12–2 compares the growth in user charges with that of other revenue sources. From 1986 to 1997, intergovernmental revenue for municipalities grew at approximately the same rate as property and sales tax revenue, with an increase of approximately 70 percent over the period. Utility charges and liquor store revenue grew at rates significantly below that. Current charges, by contrast, grew at a significantly higher rate, with nearly twice the revenue growth of the property tax.

Local government reliance on charges varies among jurisdictions. Table 12–3 shows that special districts depend the most on such charges, whereas school districts depend the least. Generally, special districts provide utility services, and taxpayers readily accept the use of charges to finance these services. Education, on the other hand, has traditionally been provided largely free of direct charges. Counties and municipalities are general-purpose governments that provide both utility and education services; thus, their relative reliance on charge revenues lies between that of special districts and school districts.

Table 12–1 User charge revenue as a percentage of expenditures for selected municipal services.

Service	1991–92	1996–97	2000–01
Airports	71.0	99.3	75.9
Highways	6.2	6.3	5.1
Hospitals	60.8	77.1	67.4
Parks and recreation	22.2	23.8	21.6
Sewerage	83.0	94.7	99.3
Solid waste	49.8	56.5	55.3

Table 12–2   Municipal revenues, 1981–82 to 1996–97 (in millions of $).

| Revenue source | Fiscal years | | | | Percentage increase, 1986–87 to 1996–97 |
	1981–82	1986–87	1991–92	1996–97	
Intergovernmental revenues	31,621	37,753	49,474	62,851	66.5
Taxes (own source)	37,077	55,566	76,385	94,395	69.9
Property taxes	19,519	27,265	40,440	45,973	68.6
General and selective sales taxes	10,174	15,654	20,254	27,244	74.0
Charges and miscellaneous[a]	22,586	37,183	49,257	64,943	74.7
Current charges	12,513	19,386	30,128	42,444	118.9
Utility charges	20,465	28,812	35,651	43,336	50.4
Liquor store revenue	275	275	284	309	12.4

[a] Includes current charges, interest earnings, special assessments, and "other and unallocable" revenue.

Table 12–3   Percentage of revenues from various sources for local governments, 2000–01.

Revenue sources[a]	All local governments	Counties	Municipalities and townships	Special districts	School districts
Intergovernmental revenue	35.2	36.1	22.6	22.9	56.9
Tax revenue	33.2	33.6	36.6	12.5	34.3
Charges and miscellaneous	21.1	26.2	22.2	38.7	8.5

[a] Additional revenue sources not listed are utility, liquor store, and insurance trust revenue.

User charge design

User charges and fees have substantial theoretical and practical advantages over taxes as a means of financing certain activities. They promote efficiency by functioning similarly to a pricing system: that is, they ration supply by allocating service to those who value it most. An increase in the flow of user charge revenues signals the need to increase the supply of a service *and* furnishes the funds to do so. However, for a user charge to achieve its goal as an allocation mechanism and a revenue source, it must be carefully designed.

Practice varies among governments, but most employ one of two pricing systems for user charges: (1) a marginal-cost, multipart system that takes into account the varying costs of production and distribution, or (2) an average-cost system that charges the same price per unit regardless of the volume of service consumed or the location of demand.[7] Often, the nature of the service will determine which system is used.

Pricing

Pricing principles applied in the private economy are relevant to a user charge system for publicly provided services. The price of gasoline, for example, reflects not only the cost of extracting and refining the petroleum but also the cost of transporting it from the production site to the place of purchase. Because private firms charge a price that includes the marginal costs of production and distribution, the retail price charged for gasoline will be higher in an area to which the cost of transportation is higher. (The state of Oregon, for example, has no gasoline refineries. All gasoline must come in from Washington or California by truck or pipeline; as a result, gas prices are generally higher than in areas closer to refining capacity.)[8]

Pricing also depends on demand. A consumer's willingness to pay for a soda, for example, depends on the satisfaction he or she expects to receive from drinking it. In general, the soda will be purchased if the consumer expects to enjoy it more than he or she would enjoy another product that costs the same amount of money. More sodas will be demanded if the satisfaction with the product increases—on hot days, for example. More sodas may also be demanded if the price goes down. The relationship between the cost of supplying sodas at a given level of output and the demand for soda determines the price. If price and cost are equal, the price paid by the consumer covers the cost to the producers of supplying the sodas.

Cost   Like prices, user charges should reflect the cost of providing additional units of the publicly provided good, a cost that often varies by location. For example, it is more costly to collect refuse in low-density areas far from a landfill site than to collect refuse in high-density areas nearer a landfill. The user charge should thus be higher for those in the low-density area. User charges can also allocate services to those users who value the good or service most highly: those who are willing to pay the "price." For example, if a higher toll is charged at peak times for the use of a bridge, those who most value the service will pay the charge; others will limit their use of the bridge to times when the toll is lower.

If user charges are to reflect the costs of providing a service, it is essential to understand both the numerous variables that affect cost and the often complex relationships between those variables. Variables include output, density of development, and customer location. The next three sections examine these variables in detail.

Output   To understand the role of output in determining cost, consider a typical utility: water supply. Water is obtained and treated at one location. The cost of producing potable water at this location depends on how much water is to be supplied to the community: larger volumes of water require larger facilities, more operating materials, and more labor. Thus, there is a positive relationship between the volume of water to be processed and total long-run costs.[9] Long-run marginal cost has been shown to decline as service provision moves from small to medium-sized water treatment plants, but to remain constant or even increase as large-capacity water treatment plants are constructed.

Although processing a given volume of water can cost more or less, depending on the size of the plant that is constructed, once the plant exists, many costs—such as those for the land, the building, and large equipment—are fixed; in other words, they do not change with the level of use. However, other costs—primarily short-run operating costs—vary with the volume of water produced each day.

As the volume of water treated in an existing plant is increased, the change in the short-run marginal costs can be calculated. The short-run marginal costs of treatment (i.e., the incremental cost of treating one more gallon of water at a given level of operation) generally remain constant (or increase only slightly) as the volume of production approaches the designed capacity of a plant. However, if the designed capacity is significantly exceeded in the short run, marginal costs may rise appreciably.

Density of development   Several studies undertaken since the late 1960s have explored the effects of development patterns on the cost of service, with primary emphasis on density.[10] These studies show that as the density of development (number of households per acre) increases, the long-run cost of service per household declines. Again, the water system can be used to illustrate this concept. Water pipe is laid down the center of a street, and individual service lines extend from the water main to each building. The higher the density, the more dwelling units are served per mile of pipe. Furthermore, the cost of laying a water main increases in proportion to its diameter, but the volume of water a main can carry increases more than proportionally, according to its square. Thus, the larger the main, the lower the average cost per unit of water carried. This simple physical aspect of service delivery suggests that a variety of services, from water and sewer service to telecommunications, can be extremely costly to provide to low-density, rural areas. Currently, this cost differential is particularly acute for high-speed, two-way telecommunications: people in many rural areas cannot be economically provided with fiber-optic cabling service.

Estimates of the relationship between the long-run cost of service and the density of development for selected services indicate that the cost of service can vary substantially by density and type of development. Low-density, single-family housing is often significantly more expensive to serve.[11]

Location   Another component of distribution cost is location: the distance from the point of use to the production site. In order for households or businesses located at some distance from the treatment plant to obtain service, water mains must be laid from the plant to each location. Clearly, the total costs will increase with the distance between the plant and the customer.

To economize on the cost of transportation and distribution, some local governments provide services at more than one site in a metropolitan area. For example, some cities have more than one wastewater treatment center or water supply tower. There is, however, a limit to the potential for cost savings: too many production sites can lead to higher output costs. For example, increasing the number of water treatment plants rather than extending the distribution area of a single plant may result in higher costs, depending on local geography and development patterns. Thus, for each public service, a different combination of number of production sites and distribution distance will minimize the total costs of supplying the service.

Demand   As is the case in the private sector, cost is only one side of the equation determining the price of services: the other side is demand. Once decisions have been made on the location and output capacity of production and distribution facilities, the demand for the service becomes an important influence on the cost (and therefore the price) of a service.

At some point at or beyond the designed capacity of the facility, the short-run marginal costs of serving additional users increase sharply. If the demand for the service varies significantly over time, the facility may periodically face a capacity constraint, commonly called *peak load*. At peak load, the incremental cost of serving one more user or providing one more unit of a good far exceeds the average cost of serving a consumer. If the facility is financed through general revenues, or if the same low, average-cost price is charged at all times, the result may be overuse of the facility during peak demand periods.

Overuse implies that the average user is subsidizing the peak-load user. Overuse also results in lower service quality and higher social and private costs (e.g., equipment failure and lost time). In the case of water supply, pressure is lost; in the case of electricity supply, brownouts occur; on highways, traffic jams occur. If during peak demand periods, however, consumers are charged a higher rate that reflects the true cost of peak output, overuse and its attendant costs can be sharply reduced.[12]

Components of an ideal user charge system

An ideal user charge system takes into account three major components:

The short-run costs of current output. Generally, a quantity charge is sufficient to recover the short-run costs of current output. A quantity charge is a single charge per unit that varies directly with the quantity consumed and is set to equal the short-run marginal cost of producing the output demanded. However, if significant peak-load demands occur, and those demands substantially increase short-run marginal costs during peak-load periods, charges during such periods should be considerably higher. A time-variable volume charge that is linked to peak demand reflects the true cost of serving residents at various times of day.

The difference between the quantity charge and the full cost of production, including full capital costs. When the quantity charge is insufficient to recover full capital costs, a capacity charge should be levied. This charge reflects the outlay for the fixed costs of the service, such as depreciation and financing. The capacity charge should be a flat fee allocated on the basis of each customer's potential use of designed capacity. Of course, where the quantity charge covers both the short- and long-run total costs of production, a capacity charge is not needed.

The long-run cost of serving residents at each location. A location charge should be levied to reflect the cost of serving each specific location at a specific density; it can be levied monthly or as a connection charge, fiscal impact fee, or special assessment when a service is initially brought into an area.

If these three components are taken into account, the result is a multipart charge that is higher for those who demand more service, for those who use the service during peak periods, and for those who live in areas that are particularly expensive to serve (because of distance, density, or both).

A well-designed user charge system can improve public service provision in two ways: first, by allocating the available supply to those who value it most; and second, by providing local officials with accurate information on the desirability of expanding a service. When the user charge system embodies the actual costs of service, residents receive price signals that help them determine how much of the service they wish to use and when they wish to use it. When services are provided free of charge or when the charges do not reflect actual costs, there is an incentive to overuse the service, and the quantity demanded does not necessarily reflect willingness to pay the full cost of providing the service.

With a well-designed user charge system, in contrast, the quantity demanded offers managers of the public facility a realistic indication of how much of the service is needed and what price users are willing to pay for it. If the quantity demanded during peak-load times at peak-load prices, for example, indicates that the revenues generated will cover the cost of expansion, it may be worthwhile to expand the facility. Finally, a well-designed charge system assists developers and prospective new residents in deciding whether the value of developing a new area is worth the cost of obtaining the required public services.

Practical considerations

A number of practical considerations add to the complexity of developing a user charge system: among these are administrative costs, consumer acceptance, equity issues, the difficulty of determining the costs of service, and the existence of merit goods.

Administrative costs   Administrative costs include the cost of collecting data on consumption, calculating service costs for each resident at that resident's volume of use, and billing for and collecting the user charge. For some services, administrative costs may be significant. Although it is relatively easy and inexpensive to install a water meter, for example, it is quite difficult and expensive to monitor the volume and noxiousness of sewage in the treatment system.

In some cases, the administrative cost of directly calculating individual usage may be so high that indirect methods should be used instead. For example, volume charges for sewer service are often based on the amount of water consumed, an indirect measure that retains the advantages of the volume charge but limits administrative costs. In the case of some services, however, indirect measurement may present its own problems. For example, since industrial sewage is much more difficult and costly to treat than household waste, a simple volume charge may not adequately reflect the true cost of treatment. Consequently, it may be necessary to obtain information on the noxiousness of industrial sewage in order to ensure that charges adequately reflect costs.

For many public services, the rate of use among residents (and thus the cost of service per resident) is relatively constant. If the administrative cost of employing variable charges based on volume are higher than the additional revenues thereby obtained, variable charges would be uneconomical. Similarly, when disparities in the cost of serving residents at different locations are small, the extra administrative costs of instituting location charges may outweigh any gains in efficiency. Finally, billing costs in a user charge system can be substantial—in some cases, high enough to prohibit periodic billing. In this age of inexpensive computers, however, a local government that prepares periodic bills for other services may be able to process another item at minimal expense.

Consumer acceptance   A second practical consideration is consumer acceptance of the user charge system. When the benefits of a public service are easily identified—consumption of water or the use of a public golf course, tennis courts, or bridges, for example—most citizens readily understand and accept user charges. However, charges that cannot be as easily related to use (e.g., a countywide "stormwater" fee) will encounter resistance. Furthermore, consumers may be concerned about the effect of a user charge system on their federal income tax payments: because local taxes are deductible from taxable income but user charges are not, a dollar paid in user charges is more costly to the local resident than a dollar paid in property taxes. (The difference between the two costs will depend on the resident's marginal income tax rate.) Thus, extensive employment of user charges can make local government services more expensive to residents, although this phenomenon will be most significant for high-income residents and for high-income communities.

Equity   The proper design of any tax or charge system requires consideration of equity issues. Although user charges are, by definition, based on the benefits-received principle of taxation, there may still be concern about the effect of a user charge system on low-income residents. Residents of public housing or residents who have very low property values, for example, would have a low tax burden if municipal services were financed entirely with property taxes. These same residents would pay a higher cost for public services under a system of user charges. And, as is the case with many tax policy issues, there may be a trade-off between efficiency and equity. Depending on the priorities of local decision makers, equity may take precedence, and some efficiency may be sacrificed to pursue equity-related goals. In the name of fairness, for example, municipalities often exempt low-income residents from paying fees for access to recreation facilities or from charges for services such as trash collection.

Costs of service   In general, user charges should reflect the full costs of service, including operation, maintenance, and the capital costs of production and distribution. These costs may not be easy to calculate, however, because (1) local government accounting systems are not necessarily designed to facilitate such calculations and (2) neither the current value nor the past cost of capital investments may be known (which is typically the case with long-lived assets such as water mains). Lack of adequate information can lead to undercharging—and, in turn, to a more rapid expansion of service than is economically justifiable.

Because it is not always practical to design a single user charge that reflects both capital and operating costs, some services are financed through two separate revenue plans. In the case of sewerage, for example, local governments typically have an operation, maintenance, and repair budget with dedicated sources of revenue, and a separate capital budget with its own dedicated sources of revenue. Because of the nature of capital investment, the initial cost of the facility is more likely to be covered, at least in part, by lump-sum charges and fiscal impact fees than by volume-based marginal cost charges. Since capital investment is a large, one-time expense, it is appropriate to fund it with large, one-time charges.

Merit goods   There are particular public goods or services—merit goods—for which it is considered counterproductive to charge the full cost of production. In the long run, consumption of these goods benefits society as a whole. Recreation, for example, improves health and fosters positive social interaction, and education improves productivity and enhances the quality of life in the community. (Precisely which public services should be included in the category of merit goods is debatable.) Thus, in most jurisdictions, user charges for certain services are set below the cost of providing the service, or services are provided free or at a discount to lower-income citizens. Consequently, the more affluent residents provide some subsidy to enable lower-income residents to consume merit goods.

User charges for individual services

Production, distribution, and administrative costs vary among publicly supplied services, and charges should vary accordingly. This section outlines user charge systems for several services. The systems described attempt to incorporate both the theoretical ideal and the practical realities of local government finance.

Water supply

The water supply of a local government closely approximates a privately produced good. In fact, many communities are served by privately owned and operated water utilities. Others are served by special districts that operate much like privately owned utilities. The major arguments in favor of a public system (or a controlled private utility) are efficiency, safety, and certainty of supply.

Municipal water service is commonly billed using a block rate charge. A block rate charge system is one that assigns different price categories—either higher or lower—on the basis of the volume used. For example, a water supply system that charged users $0.12 per hundred gallons for the first 5,000 gallons, $0.10 per hundred gallons for the next 5,000 gallons, and $0.08 per hundred gallons for anything over that amount would be using a decreasing (or declining) block rate charge.

The use of a declining block rate charge system has been justified on two bases: first, because as larger facilities are constructed, the long-run marginal costs of operation decline. When this is the case, a declining block rate will approximate the marginal costs of operation. Second, a declining block rate charge is, in effect, a subsidy to high-volume users, which has been perceived as a means of strengthening the community's employment and tax base.

But the declining block rate system simply does not reflect the current cost of obtaining, treating, and distributing water. To begin with, long-run marginal costs decline only when two criteria are met: (1) the source of supply is a river or lake, and (2) water is being drawn at a rate that is slower than the rate of replenishment. If, however, the water source is being drawn down at a rate that equals or exceeds the rate of replenishment (as is the case when highly populated areas draw water from aquifers), the appropriate short-run marginal cost is the opportunity cost of the water: that is, applying an additional gallon to one use means forgoing the opportunity to apply that gallon to another use. In this case, costs increase with quantity rather than decrease, and the model of declining costs is not applicable. Moreover, even if long-run marginal costs *do* decline, a declining block rate charge is still not appropriate because the volume charge should reflect *short-run* marginal costs: that is, the costs that vary with day-to-day changes in demand. At volumes below the design capacity of a given plant, the short-run marginal costs of producing more water are constant; as volumes at or above the design capacity are produced, the short-run costs increase.

With respect to the use of a declining block rate charge as a subsidy, such subsidies have doubtful economic impact in the long term; they also encourage waste. Nevertheless, delivering large volumes of water does reduce pipe, meter, and administrative costs, and these savings should be reflected in a proportionately lower capacity charge for high-volume users.

While population growth and the protection of some water sources for alternative uses make it advisable to increase the flat, per-gallon fee for water use, population dispersion makes distribution costs far more important. The three major variables affecting distribution costs are (1) the distance from the point of use to the source of supply or central distribution site (e.g., treatment plant); (2) the density of customers in an area; and (3) the capacity to serve each customer (usually measured in terms of the size of the lateral pipe from the water main).

It is not practical to calculate the location cost of serving individual customers. Instead, service areas can be delineated that are relatively homogeneous in terms of distance and density. The next step is to estimate the marginal costs of distribution to each area and to allocate those costs to each customer within the area in proportion to expected consumption. The second part of the distribution charge would be based on the street frontage occupied by each customer. (The cost of distributing water increases as the number of feet of pipe between customers increases.) A front-foot charge based on this cost would then be levied on each customer.

While front-foot charges are designed to cover the costs of distribution, they reflect only the density portion of distribution costs, not the distance portion. Some local governments, such as Fairfax County, Virginia, have recognized this problem and have adjusted their charges for new connections to include at least some of the distance costs. But even these distance charges include only the capital costs of distribution. Maintenance costs are not included, nor are the capital costs involved in the construction of the treatment facility.

Generally, the physical information on which charges are based will not change too rapidly, so the administrative cost of calculating and applying user charges for water service should not be excessive. With the quantity of water demanded by most residential (and probably most commercial) users so small relative to total output, the short-run marginal costs of output can be treated as constant, and a flat rate per unit of water consumed can be charged to all classes of consumers.

The most efficient way to measure use is to meter all connections and to bill users periodically. This process is not too expensive, and failure to adhere to it will increase wasteful consumption. Because marginal costs are likely to increase at peak load if the system is near capacity, peak-period users should theoretically be subject to a surcharge in addition to the average rate. However, the extra costs involved in metering peak-period use may prohibit levying such charges on all but a few high-volume users. Thus, even in cases where peak demand increases short-run marginal costs, it may not be feasible to charge a higher peak-load price. In most cases, the average customer should pay (1) a constant quantity charge based on metered use and (2) a capacity charge to help cover the fixed costs of the treatment plant.

One factor makes the design of an appropriate fee structure for water especially difficult: weather. In large portions of the country in any given year, population growth and weather patterns often conspire to create drought conditions. Local governments dealing with the resulting water shortages need to carefully review the design of their water charge systems. While peak-load pricing may be difficult to implement, many local governments use a strategy during droughts that essentially creates a de facto peak-load charge: when mandatory government rationing of residential water supplies is in place, those who violate the rationing rules are fined; thus, when demand for water is particularly high relative to supply, those who use water pay a high price. Monitoring is costly and enforcement difficult, since prohibited use is discovered only through direct observation (a green lawn or a wet driveway is often a giveaway) or through the reports of neighbors. If periods of drought rationing become common enough, municipalities may find it worthwhile to implement a permanent peak-pricing strategy. Such formal recognition may be welcomed, at least in part, by citizens who would rather be treated as high-value customers than as scofflaws.

Regardless of peak-load pricing strategy, total charges can be billed monthly or bimonthly. An alternative billing method is to levy the distribution and capacity charges (but not the use charge) as a lump sum or special assessment at the time of development. The lump-sum charge has the minor advantage of reducing the complexity of the billing procedure. On the other hand, having the distribution charge appear on the monthly bill acts as a continual reminder of the cost of the consumer's choice of location. A 1992 survey by Ernst & Young indicated that 54 percent of the water utilities surveyed billed monthly, 33 percent quarterly, and only 13 percent bimonthly.[13]

It was once common to find water charge systems that were not closely related to the cost of service, but this situation is changing. Although some users in outlying areas that are expensive to serve are still undercharged, and although some users in areas that are less expensive to serve are still overcharged, most local governments have moved to narrow the gap. Ernst & Young reports that in the early 1990s, a majority of the 145 cities surveyed employed an additional service charge (which could cover location costs), an additional volume charge (which could cover capacity costs), or both for customers outside the city.[14] This policy is an important step toward using marginal cost to differentiate customers who locate in areas that are expensive to serve.

Sanitary sewerage

The general cost characteristics of the sanitary sewerage system are similar to those of the water supply system. The average costs of collection and transmission increase with the distance between sewage production and disposal sites. The costs decrease with increases in population density because dense development reduces transmission distance.

The marginal cost of treating sewage is determined by both the strength (or pollution potential) and the volume of the sewage. For domestic and commercial customers, strength is relatively constant and need not be included as a variable in determining charges: the volume of sewage is the variable on which to base the output price. However, because it is relatively expensive to build meters to measure sewage flows from individual households, a measurement of water consumption might be better. Domestic and ordinary commercial water consumption, excluding lawn sprinkling, will generate a very close approximation of the quantity of sewage discharged. This volume can be estimated by metering water consumption during the winter months, calculating the monthly average, and using that figure as the basis of the monthly sewerage charge for the entire year.

For industrial consumers, strength of sewage may be an important variable. To reduce the burden on local systems, pretreatment could be required to bring industrial sewage down to average domestic strength. Given current law, this approach may be optimal for the industry as well as for the local government. The federal Water Pollution Control Act requires users of wastewater treatment systems to pay their full share of operation, maintenance, and repair costs. The alternative to pretreatment, therefore, would be a strength surcharge imposed in addition to the regular volume charge. The option of pretreatment allows the industry to make the most efficient decision regarding wastewater generation.

One factor that determines how industrial users pay for sanitary sewerage is the feasibility of metering. Since, for high-volume water users, there may be significant differences between metered water consumption and sewage flow, sewage meters may be justified in spite of their high cost. U.S. Environmental Protection Agency guidelines suggest that metering be used whenever possible because it is the best way to assess charges that are consistent with the costs of service.[15]

Sewer collection and transmission charges should be calculated similarly to water distribution charges. Service areas should be defined, and a charge should be established for front footage. A capacity charge should also be made on the basis of water meter or water pipe size. The potential for water consumption is a good indicator of the demand for sewer capacity.

Current practice in charging for sewage collection and treatment is somewhat more varied than for water supply. In recent years, local governments have moved increasingly toward cost-based charges for sanitary sewerage, a shift that can likely be traced to two factors: (1) the general move toward user charges as a funding source for local governments and (2) an increase in the scope of regulations (including the Water Pollution Control Act, mentioned earlier) that require sanitary sewerage users to pay the costs of the service. By 1990, only 18.6 percent of agencies responding to a survey by the Association of Metropolitan Sewerage Agencies relied on flat rates to pay for operation and maintenance, and the vast majority of sewerage agencies used volume rates (at least) to assign costs to customers. In fact, fully 100 percent of the agencies surveyed reported employing user charges as a source for some revenues, and these charges raised an average of 86.4 percent of the total revenue for agencies that used them.[16] Many agencies also use special levies and hookup fees to pay for operation and maintenance or for capital improvement. Such fees are part of an optimal charge structure that takes into account the characteristics of service provision and the distance of the consumer from the treatment plant.

Stormwater sewerage

Stormwater either percolates into the ground or flows across the surface to a body of water such as a lake or stream. Urban development tends to increase surface runoff because buildings, roads, parking lots, and other paved areas are impervious to water. Stormwater sewerage costs increase as density decreases and as paved development increases. Although stormwater sewerage costs do vary with distance, they differ from sanitary sewerage costs because the collected stormwater runoff is released untreated into nearby bodies of water rather than routed to a treatment plant. Because there is no treatment, no output charge is needed.[17]

In the past, user charges for storm sewers, if they existed at all, consisted only of service-area and front-foot charges. Thus, the charges did not reflect the percentage of impervious area in the development. A charge system that recognized the additional runoff (and related costs) generated by development would, however, more accurately reflect the costs of service. Thus, a service-area charge should be apportioned among land users on the basis of the surface area of each site and the percentage of that area covered by impervious materials. Furthermore, the charge should reflect the distance to a viable outfall site. (Note, however, that the service areas for sanitary sewerage and stormwater sewerage will not be the same, since the location of stormwater outfalls is likely to differ from the location of treatment plants.) Failure to levy appropriate stormwater charges can encourage excessive development of areas that are uneconomical to serve and can ultimately lead to higher service costs for everyone.

Stormwater runoff is an area of user charge financing that has received increased attention in recent years. With a heightened awareness of the environmental impact of development, local governments have tightened their restrictions regarding runoff, particularly the runoff associated with new construction. An increased ability to assess the economic and environmental costs of stormwater runoff, coupled with a greater willingness to have individuals bear the costs of their own actions, has led to the increased use of fiscal impact fees, which charge builders and home owners for the costs of their location decisions.

In 1992, Tallahassee, Florida, adopted a monthly stormwater user charge that applies to all types of development and is based on the amount of impervious area in the development. The charge incorporates a discount for any on-site facility (such as a holding pond) that reduces or slows runoff and increases percolation into the groundwater. The funds from the charge are used to build off-site facilities, primarily holding ponds and storm sewers. Other cities have adopted similar policies and have given developers the option of buying space in existing municipal holding ponds, building their own, or funding new facilities. Rising pressure to constrain new development and increasing support for smart growth policies have increased the appeal of such measures.

Solid-waste collection

Solid-waste collection, like water supply, closely approximates a private service. Disposal, collection, and transmission costs vary with the volume of refuse collected and the distance and density involved.[18] Because disposal sites can contribute to surface and groundwater pollution, the costs assigned to solid-waste collection may also include environmental damage.

Among individual consumers, variations in volume have only a minor effect on cost; but variations among different types of residential development (e.g., apartments versus single-family homes) and between residential and commercial consumers can cause substantial differences in the cost of service. Consequently, one part of the charge for each group of customers should be a capacity charge: a flat price per unit of refuse multiplied by the average volume of refuse for that particular group.

Cost-of-service characteristics indicate that the optimal method of allocating costs is a two-part charge system including (1) a per-unit disposal charge based on actual volume and (2) a collection and transmission charge based on the cost of serving each collection route. The second portion of the charge would be higher for areas that are less densely developed and that are situated farther from the disposal site.

Current practice typically consists of a flat fee independent of volume or location, in part because there are some practical problems associated with implementing an ideal, two-part charge system for refuse collection. One problem is the measurement of volume. On the face of it, one can easily determine volume by counting the number of full or partially full thirty-gallon (or some other standard size) trash cans collected from each resident. But how tightly may a "full" trash container be packed? If volume is really the relevant variable (e.g., if the trash were going to a landfill), then maximizing the scarce landfill space would require packing as much trash into a given volume as possible. On the other hand, proper landfill operation might require that trash not be densely packed. The answer to the question ultimately depends on the specifics of landfill operation.

Further disadvantages of a two-part charge system are the time that the collector spends recording the number of cans collected from each site, the probability of error, and a possible increase in the number of consumer complaints. However, technology is likely to eliminate at least some of these disadvantages. Many local governments now use trucks that automatically empty cans, and rapid advances in handheld computer systems and automated record keeping may increase the feasibility of metering individual refuse collection.

For the time being, however, an approximation of the volume charge should be considered. The best system for single-family residences may be to collect no more than a certain number of cans per collection day and to charge a flat fee for this maximum number of cans. More cans may be collected, or cans may be collected more often, but only at an additional charge and with prior agreement. Another approach is for the refuse-collection agency to sell specially designated plastic trash bags to residents and assess a per-bag fee at the time of sale. Any refuse that customers want collected can be put in the bags; the agency then simply collects as many of the special bags as are presented. This system has the advantage of automatically assessing a volume charge (the per-bag fee) to all participants and eliminates the need to measure volume at the point of collection.

Special collection charges may be justified for multifamily residential complexes. It takes less time to collect a given number of cans at one location than to collect the same number at different locations; therefore, the collection charge per can should be lower for apartments. Multifamily residences and commercial customers who use special containers and sophisticated handling equipment could be charged a lower collection charge per unit.

A private refuse collection company in Leon County, Florida, has developed a charge system that allows consumers to select either curb or backyard collection. A sticker attached to the mailbox post indicates which service has been selected. This company has not found it feasible to assess a volume charge for residential pickup, but it does charge large commercial customers on the basis of volume. Another innovative sanitation user charge has been adopted in Jacksonville, Florida, where firms are charged a special fee for the disposal of hazardous waste. Revenue from this fee is used to finance the area's hazardous-waste landfill. This program is a prime example of an application of the "user pays" philosophy.

Highways and bridges

The costs of providing a road or bridge are different from those of providing other public services. A road or bridge is designed to carry a specific volume of traffic at a specific speed over a specific time period. If the volume of traffic is below the design capacity, there is no congestion and the costs of accommodating one more car (including wear and tear on the road and increased risk of accidents) are minimal. When traffic exceeds the design capacity, however, congestion results, traffic slows, and travelers suffer delays, which entail implicit costs because the travelers' time is spent sitting in traffic instead of doing something more valuable.

Putting a user charge into effect during peak traffic periods might help ensure that those who use a road or bridge during such times consider the costs they are imposing on other drivers. In practice, there are two options: one is to charge a higher toll during peak periods (such as morning and evening rush hours); the other is to charge no toll during off-peak hours and to collect tolls only during peak traffic hours.[19] Unfortunately, tolls generally remain constant at all times of day—and, in many cases, discount coupons or discount tokens are sold to frequent users of the facility. The combination of a flat rate and the discount structure yields a bargain price, which serves as an incentive to use the facility and may even encourage traffic at peak times. Consequently, the level of use cannot be relied on as an accurate reflection of demand. A peak-load charge, on the other hand, would encourage the use of car pools and alternative transportation and may yield a more accurate reading of demand for both the public and private segments of the transportation system.

The adoption of user charge financing for road use has been hampered in the past by technological limitations, since manual collection of tolls and the presence of a toll plaza substantially restrict the flow of traffic. The additional wait time imposes a real economic cost on motorists that is exceeded only by the cost of the frustration generated by tollbooth congestion. Fortunately, the technology that allows automated collection of tolls is now inexpensive and widespread, allowing tolls to be collected without affecting the flow of traffic. This development has important implications both for user charge financing generally and for the implementation of peak-pricing strategies in particular.

The technological feasibility of automated toll collection has come about at the same time that the necessity of generating revenue for roads is growing. Proper road maintenance requires substantial resources. In addition, the useful life of ordinary highway surfaces is thirty to fifty years, and as the national highway system ages, replacement costs will be substantial. Critics of toll roads often refer to roads without tolls as "free roads," but since taxpayers must pay the substantial costs of repair and replacement in one way or another, roads are never free. In fact, they are generally excellent candidates for user charge financing. States and localities already routinely rely on earmarked gas taxes to fund transportation, but tolls offer two distinct improvements over this approach: first, tolls can match road use and payment precisely rather than approximately; second, electronic toll collection can maximize efficiency by making use of peak pricing.

Electronic toll collection is widespread for bridges, tunnels, and roads. Texas and California have also experimented with high-occupancy toll (HOT) lanes on ordinary highways. Unlike high-occupancy vehicle lanes, which allow multiple-occupancy vehicles only, HOT lanes allow both multiple-occupancy and single-occupancy vehicles; but the high-occupancy vehicles travel at no cost, while the single-occupancy vehicles use the lane for a fee. To encourage efficient road use, tolls are charged only during rush hours; and during toll periods, the price paid is adjusted in real time to correspond to the level of use of the lane. This is precisely the sort of peak-pricing system that characterizes an appropriately designed user charge system.

Transit systems

Like highways and bridges, transit systems have limited capacity and wide variations in peak and off-peak demand, which means that the cost of service during peak periods is high. When the costs of service are higher, economic efficiency requires that the price paid by users reflect those higher costs. (During off-peak periods, the marginal costs are much lower, but they are not zero because the transit system uses fuel and drivers as well as equipment.) Operating costs are also affected by the length of trip, suggesting that charges should be linked not only to time of day but also to distance traveled on the system. Several transit services use a practical system of zone fares: users pay an initial charge plus zone charges for each boundary crossed. In the absence of such a system, long-distance riders are undercharged and generally overuse the transit system.

The prices now charged for most public transit systems, like those for highways and bridges, fail to adequately reflect true costs. Typically, the price is the same during peak and off-peak periods. If use of the service during peak periods is sold at a discount, the peak-period prices are effectively reduced. Therefore, the excess demand generated during peak hours (because of the discounts) does not necessarily reflect genuine willingness to pay for increased capacity. At the same time, the absence of peak-load charges for highways and bridges keeps more cars on the road, thus *reducing* the demand for public transit facilities during peak periods. The result is that poorly designed pricing systems for both roads and public transit provide policy makers with inaccurate information about users' willingness to pay the true costs of capacity and use.

Parks and recreation

The cost characteristics of park and recreation facilities are similar to those of highways or bridges. Once a facility is built, the marginal cost of serving one more user is essentially zero at low levels of use. At high levels, however, crowding reduces everyone's enjoyment; like the time spent waiting in traffic, crowding generates an implicit cost. Tennis courts are a good example. In low-use periods, courts are always available, but at high-use times, the courts are filled. A charge levied during high-use periods would ensure efficient use of the courts. Those who value the use of the courts during high-use times can pay for the service, and those who can easily arrange to play at off-peak times can avoid the charge.

Many park and recreation facilities impose charges only during peak demand periods.[20] Others—public golf courses, for example—charge for all use but increase the charge on weekends. And when charges are discounted for

An example of a properly designed user charge system A properly designed user charge system serves two functions: (1) rationing government-supplied goods to discourage excessive or wasteful consumption and (2) providing information about the cost of service provision so that users can make efficient decisions about service consumption.

When the supply of a good, such as tee times on a golf course, is fixed, user charges are particularly important in rationing the limited available space. The fee structure at the North Kingstown (Rhode Island) Municipal Golf Course illustrates how a properly designed user charge can help ration a scarce good. The user charges are designed to reflect the fact that the demand for the service varies substantially by the time of day and the day of the week.

The highest fee is charged for the most popular time: morning or early afternoon, on weekends and holidays, during fair-weather months. Weekdays are cheaper during the high season, and tee times during the winter months are cheaper still.

The fee structure is also designed to address equity issues. North Kingstown residents receive a $3 discount at all times. Since user charge revenue generally does not cover all the costs associated with providing parks and recreation, some portion of the golf course is presumably financed through general tax revenue paid by North Kingstown taxpayers. Offering residents a discount places a higher cost on visitors and limits the extent to which North Kingstown residents subsidize out-of-town golfers.

Seniors also receive a $3 discount Monday through Thursday. To the extent that seniors have lower incomes, this discount introduces some vertical equity into the fee structure. Limiting the discount to Monday through Thursday further ensures that seniors are encouraged to use the course during less busy times.

	Weekends and holidays		Weekdays	
	Daytime	After 4 PM (high season) or 1 PM (low season)	Daytime	After 4 PM (high season) or 1 PM (low season)
High season (April 1–October 31)	$35	$19	$28	$28
Low season (November 1–March 31)	$21	$13	$21	$13

low-income groups, such as senior citizens, the lower prices are generally offered only during off-peak weekday hours. Although communities have historically regarded recreation as a merit good, citizens are now insisting that users of some recreation services pay their own way. Open park and picnic areas, it is generally agreed, should be available to all, but local governments are meeting increased resistance to using general revenue to subsidize the more "exclusive" activities such as golf and tennis.

E-government

With the advent of faster computers and large-scale digital storage, local governments have the capacity to maintain huge databases of the information that is collected in the ordinary course of government administration. In addition to facilitating administrative tasks, these databases have created an opportunity for local governments to obtain revenue: with little additional effort, local governments can provide access, for a fee, to property lists, tax rolls, land records, and a wide variety of GIS maps and data.

Such services are excellent candidates for user charges. Unlike services such as roads, parks, or public safety, data services provide benefits directly to specific individuals, which makes it easy to identify and charge recipients. Of course, the rules that apply to fee structures for other services apply to data services as well. For example, the fee should cover only the marginal cost of providing the service. The collection of GIS data that occurs as part of a development planning process is an ordinary expense of government that provides a collective benefit to citizens and should therefore be funded out of general tax revenue. But the time and materials involved in putting particular data on computer disks for the use of private individuals can appropriately be charged directly to the user.

Paying for growth and development

In addition to funding services for existing residents, user charges are also widely used to pay the costs of serving new development. They are particularly important when municipalities want to ensure that the residents of new developments pay for the additional services required by those developments.

A development fee is a form of user charge, often assessed directly on the developer of new property, that is designed to pay for the public infrastructure within the development (e.g., water and gas mains). Fiscal impact charges are closely related to development fees (the terms are often used interchangeably), although impact fees are often assessed to pay for additions to public infrastructure—such as the expansion of a water treatment plant—that will be shared by new development and existing residents. Special assessments, like development charges and fiscal impact fees, are based on the benefits-received principle: the purpose of special assessments is to ensure that when a particular area receives new or additional services (e.g., sidewalks, streetlights), the recipients pay for the services. Finally, tax increment financing is a way of structuring property taxes so that they act like user charges: tax assessments are based on the benefits that accrue to property owners as the result of public sector infrastructure improvements.

Development charges and fiscal impact fees

In the sense that they are charges levied on users for the purpose of financing public services, development charges can be thought of as a form of user charge. In theory, a development charge should reflect the full capital costs of providing a service, and should therefore be equivalent to the capacity charge and location charge used in an ideal, marginal-cost user charge system. In practice, however, the developer and the local government often negotiate development charges. Payment of development charges may take several forms, including in-kind contributions (such as park facilities or schools to be constructed by the developer).

Although development charges reduce the burden on general revenue, they may also increase housing costs: by making new development more costly, the charges indirectly reduce the supply of new housing, which drives up housing prices and discourages some potential buyers. Of course, this is exactly the purpose of the charges: efficiency requires that only those buyers who are willing to pay the full cost of new construction (including the cost of the new infrastructure needed to serve development) should purchase houses.

For development charges to enhance efficiency in the way that user charges do, they must be closely related to the cost of the services provided. In fact, a "rational nexus" is a common legal requirement associated with municipal development charges. Under the rational nexus requirement, development charges are legitimate when it is clear that (1) new development has created a need for new facilities and (2) the revenue is spent in a way that benefits the residents who are paying the charge. When these conditions are met, development charges will efficiently limit growth in areas that cannot be economically served and redirect that development to areas that are less expensive to serve. Development charges do not stop development, as some have argued. But by reallocating development to areas that are more economical to serve, these charges help to shape long-term land use decisions in ways that enhance economic efficiency.

The fiscal impact fee, an increasingly popular form of development charge, is a one-time fee intended as payment for the cost of off-site public facilities needed to accommodate the increased demand for public services generated by a new development. Whereas many development fees are designed to cover the costs of facilities that exclusively benefit the new development, fiscal impact fees cover the incremental costs of expanding facilities that may serve new and old areas alike. Any service that requires the expenditure of funds for capital facilities and equipment is a candidate for fiscal impact fee financing. Services for which fiscal impact fees have been imposed include roads, schools, parks, drainage, police, fire, solid waste, libraries, schools, and water. Once impact fees are adopted for one service, jurisdictions often extend them to other services as well. Fee revenues are usually segregated from the general fund (in most cases, this is part of the rational nexus legal requirement) and must be spent on land, capital improvements, and equipment that serve the development that was charged the fee.

The water system provides a good example of how a fiscal impact fee might work in practice. A large residential subdivision increases the demand for water treatment and distribution. The capital costs imposed by this new development include the portion of the treatment plant capacity used by residents of the new subdivision and a pro rata share of the capital cost of the water mains used to bring water to the subdivision. In the case of water supply, collecting a one-time impact fee (to cover capital costs) and imposing a user charge (to cover variable costs thereafter) comes close to the ideal marginal-cost user charge structure. In practice, impact fees, like other developer charges, are often subject to negotiation and usually cover far less than the full costs attributable to new developments. As noted earlier, instead of paying a fee, developers sometimes make contributions of another kind: donating land for recreational use, for example.

While impact fees have received increasing attention from a theoretical perspective, there have been few comprehensive studies on their use. In three separate surveys conducted in the mid-1980s, Paul Downing, James Frank, and Elizabeth Lines found 219 recreational impact fees, 190 sewer impact fees, and 21 fire impact fees in the United States.[21] At the time of the surveys, fees ranged from a few dollars to as much as $1,800 per single-family dwelling unit for recreation, $6,200 for sewers, and $600 for fire service; in 1985, the national averages were $377 for recreation, $689 for sewers, and $183 for fire service. In a 2002 survey, the National Association of Realtors found that impact fees for single-family homes ranged from less than a dollar to a maximum of $9,896 for roads (El Dorado County, California); $552 for libraries (El Centro, California); $3,164 for parks (East Greenwich, Rhode Island); $1,915 for fire service (El Dorado County, California); $6,500 for sewers (Fountain Hills, Arizona); and $9,050 for water (Brighton, Colorado).[22]

Fiscal impact fees have desirable economic characteristics. One of the most important costs involved in paying for a community's capital improvements is the cost of serving new residents, which can be especially high in outlying areas. Impact fees are designed specifically to ensure that those costs are paid for (at least in part) by the new developments themselves. Because impact fees strengthen the relationship between costs and benefits received, they can help to ensure that new development is undertaken only when it is economically beneficial to do so.

The political advantages of impact fees are substantial. The fees are designed to directly pay for infrastructure, allowing the local government to maintain lower property taxes and user charges. For example, if the expansion of public facilities to accommodate new development were financed by property taxes, both current and new residents would pay, and current residents would thus partially subsidize new development. If current residents do not perceive expansion as valuable, they will resist it. Under an impact fee system, the developer pays the incremental capital costs (which generally will be capitalized into house prices),[23] and there is no additional burden on current residents.

Unfortunately, political maneuvering by local elected officials and resistance from real estate developers occasionally result in impact fees that either fail to cover the full cost of development or are used to fund projects unrelated to new development. These distortions significantly interfere with the ability of impact fees to help efficiently allocate resources. Successful local government management requires that user charges follow as closely as possible the models of ideal charges described earlier.

Most local government managers view impact fees favorably because they provide an immediate source of funds to pay for capital improvements: it is not necessary to float bonds or to seek authority to raise taxes. Furthermore, if the funds are judicially constrained for use in building capital facilities, they are not subject to political wrangling during annual budget deliberations. Finally, given the growing interest in smart growth policies and the growing concern about the costs of growth, politicians can use impact fees to demonstrate that new development is paying its own way and is not being subsidized by current residents.

Special assessments

Special assessments, another form of user fee, are charges paid by a particular area of a jurisdiction for services provided to that area. For years, local governments have used front-foot and connection charges when water or sewer service is provided to areas that were previously served by private wells or septic tanks. Special assessments for curbs and gutters, paved roads, and streetlights have become more common as municipal governments annex developing rural areas.

Special assessments are similar in their function and economic effects to fiscal impact fees in that the areas served by the new facilities are required to pay the cost of any needed improvements. Also like fiscal impact fees, special assessments exemplify the benefits-received principle. Special assessments that vary with location and density function similarly to the location portion of an efficient, multipart, marginal-cost user charge. If special assessments accurately reflect the cost of service, they will give consumers correct information on costs, which consumers can then compare to the value they place on the service.

A very interesting special assessment system was developed in Riverside, California. The city wished to install streetlights in various residential areas.

But instead of requiring the areas to accept the streetlights, the city held special elections. First, each area voted for or against streetlights; each area then cast a separate vote on the quality of the lights to be installed. Voters knew that a yes vote on streetlights would cost them money; they also knew that the exact amount of money would depend on the streetlights they selected. Thus, the system enabled citizens to make informed choices, weighing the value that the streetlights had for them against the direct cost of obtaining the lights. Applied to a broad spectrum of services, this and similar systems for obtaining accurate information on citizen preferences have the potential to significantly reduce waste.

Like impact fees, special assessments are becoming increasingly important tools of growth management. In local government circles, in academic research, and in popular discussions, suburban sprawl has become one of the most important issues in land use planning for the twenty-first century. Conservation is becoming a higher priority, and environmental, community, and political activists are making sure that overdevelopment and sustainable growth get substantial attention.

While concerns about sprawl inevitably raise issues related to individual and community values, they also contain an important public finance dimension. Regardless of the perspectives or motivation of either side, conflicts over development often come down to who will pay. While the initial concern over new development may not have anything to do with economic efficiency, the policies put into place to deal with new development often do. Economists, activists, and residents can often agree that it is appropriate for new development to pay its way. This means not only paying the cost of infrastructure to serve the new development but also paying the opportunity cost that arises when environmental resources are developed rather than conserved. Fortunately, user charges, fiscal impact fees, and special assessments are becoming more widely accepted financing tools, which makes it politically easier to implement economically appropriate policies: for example, developers of a wetland area can be charged a fee, which can then be used to replace the wetlands elsewhere.

Tax increment financing

Tax increment financing (TIF) is another fiscal tool that has been gaining in popularity. What sets TIF apart from impact fees and special assessments is that it has been used most extensively to finance redevelopment rather than new development. TIF follows the same benefits-received principle as impact fees and special assessments: it allows development within a particular area to be paid for by the residents of that area.

In TIF's simplest form, a government entity designates a particular geographic area as the subject of the financing mechanism. The current taxable value of the land is established, and any revenue generated from an increase in property values (the "increment") is devoted to paying for specific improvements in the area. For example, the extension of a mass-transit line can be funded through the increased tax revenue generated by higher property values in the now more accessible—and desirable—location. A 2002 report by the Independent Budget Office of the City of New York, for example, examined the use of TIF to fund a proposed $1.5 billion subway line extension as part of a plan to expand commercial development on Manhattan's far west side.[24] While TIF is most often employed on a much smaller scale, the report cites the use of TIF to fund such large-scale projects as the San José arena and convention center, the International Spy Museum in Washington, D.C., and a University of Illinois expansion in Chicago.

The economic advantage of TIF is that payment is closely tied to benefits. One of the best ways to measure the value that infrastructure or service improvements add to a property is by observing the change in the property's actual market value. Since property tax assessments should, in principle, reflect such changes, a properly designed tax increment policy should collect additional revenue roughly in proportion to the increased value generated by the improvements.

While the mechanism used to collect the revenue is the property tax, the method of assessment and the use of the funds differ substantially from the standard property tax model. The fact that TIF collects revenue in proportion to the increase in property value, regardless of the total property value, brings it much more in line with the principles of benefit-based taxation than any standard, wealth-based property tax. In fact, the New York City report cites this as a significant political advantage: even residents who generally oppose tax increases realize that "additional property taxes paid by property owners in the TIF district [are] payment for benefits received from TIF improvements."[25]

Comparison of revenue systems

Local government finance managers weighing the advantages and disadvantages of alternative financing methods need to consider the effects of various revenue systems on private decisions and on the distribution of costs. A comparison of user charges with the property tax, the other principal source of local government revenue, is useful for financial planning. Three major issues need to be considered: the effects on land development; the effects on demand for publicly provided services; and the effects on different income groups.

Effects on development

The timing and intensity of development are influenced by two factors: (1) what is charged for publicly provided services and (2) who is responsible for paying the charge (e.g., developers, future home owners, or current residents).[26] This section first considers the effect on development of various types of user charges and fees; it then compares the effect of user charges with that of the property tax.

Depending on how a user charge system is designed, it can either limit or encourage growth. If, for example, development charges will significantly increase housing prices in a proposed new development, the developer may not proceed with the investment—meaning that growth will be discouraged. This effect is tempered, however, by legal restrictions that require the new development to pay, through fees, only for the infrastructure it needs. Even though new residents ultimately bear the cost of development fees, as long as the value of the services financed by the fees is at least equivalent to the fees themselves, new residents are no worse off. Thus, without necessarily discouraging all growth, fees can help ensure that new development occurs only in those areas where the value of the development is greater than the cost of servicing it.

Ideally, marginal-cost user charges should reflect the difficulty and cost of bringing services to the locality and should be adjusted to account for all margins along which cost varies (e.g., distance, density, volume). Thus, in areas where charges are higher, land is less likely to be developed. On the other hand, in lower cost-of-service areas, a marginal-cost user charge will not reduce potential development as much; this is actually an advantage for the local government because it allows services to be provided in the most cost-effective way.

If an average-cost user charge is employed, new, high-cost areas will pay somewhat less than full cost for public services because the average cost for the entire jurisdiction will be somewhat below the cost of serving high-cost areas. Thus, an average-cost user charge may promote growth at the expense of existing developments, creating a subsidy that will stimulate demand for further development: because new home owners will be getting a bargain on their development charges, they will be willing to pay more for a house, which will encourage developers to build more.

In low cost-of-service areas, however, the average-cost user charge will be higher than the cost of service. This disparity means that potential home owners will be willing to pay less for a house than they otherwise would, which will discourage developers from building in more centrally located, lower-cost areas. Under a properly designed marginal-cost system, in contrast, all new development pays for the full incremental costs of public services.

The impact of the property tax on development is somewhat difficult to determine because the property tax almost never occurs in isolation: there will usually be one or more user charges in effect at the same time, and the number and type of user charges will inevitably affect development as well. Nevertheless, it is probably safe to assume that financing public services through the property tax has an intermediate effect: it stimulates growth less than an average-cost user charge would, but it does not limit growth to the extent that a marginal-cost user charge would.

A closer look at the interaction between user charge systems and property values will illustrate how these effects occur. Under an average-cost user charge system, property values, and hence property taxes, tend to be higher in high cost-of-service areas and lower in low cost-of-service areas than they would be under a marginal-cost system.[27] Thus, for example, residents of high-cost areas do not pay the full costs of services through user charges, but they do pay higher property taxes.

To encourage the most economically efficient development, it is most advantageous to combine the property tax with a marginal-cost user charge system. It is probably impossible to design a marginal-cost system that captures all the differences in the marginal cost of service, but it will at least be a closer approximation than an average-cost system, and the property tax will help offset any inaccuracies. Under an average-cost system, whenever the cost of serving new residents is higher than that of serving current residents, the property tax, in effect, requires current residents to provide a partial subsidy to new residents.

Effects on demand

In addition to affecting development patterns, the different methods of financing public services also affect demand. The volume charge of a marginal-cost user charge system reflects the variable cost of increasing output; residents decide, on the basis of this cost, how much to consume. An average-cost user charge, however, will either be higher or lower than the short-run marginal cost of increasing output. Since users make consumption decisions on the basis of the average cost charge, rather than on the actual marginal cost of the service, they may over- or underconsume the service. For example, in the case of water supply, low-volume users are often charged more than the actual costs they impose on the system, an inefficiency that inhibits water consumption by this group. It is important to note, however, that even an average-cost user charge will discourage at least some consumption that is not assigned a value that is at least as high as the cost of obtaining it.

Financing public services through the property tax implies that the cost to the consumer for the use of additional units is zero. Because this is seldom the case, the property tax stimulates overconsumption of public services and increases the cost to the local government—a phenomenon that partially explains the concern at both the state and local levels about funding ever-expanding services.

Both the property tax and average-cost user charges encourage demand by failing to discourage use during peak periods. In contrast, a marginal-cost user charge that is higher during peak periods helps distribute use more evenly. Peak-load charges are appropriate for a number of services, including bridges and highways, public transit, and recreation.

Effects on different income groups

Local government managers often express concern about the effects of alternative financing systems on various income groups. In general, it is presumed that lower-income residents should pay less for public services because they have less ability to pay. But how much less? One criterion used to gauge the equity of various financing methods involves determining what percentage of income is paid for public services. A *progressive* financing system is one in which, as income increases, so does the percentage of income paid for public services; a *regressive* financing system is one in which, as income decreases, the percentage of income paid for public services increases.

Both average- and marginal-cost user charge systems are somewhat more regressive than the property tax.[28] However, marginal-cost charges are much less regressive than average-cost charges. When an average-cost user charge is employed, lower-income residents generally pay more than it actually costs to serve them; in effect, lower-income residents subsidize higher-income residents. This subsidy does not occur under a marginal-cost charge system because higher-income people tend to live in larger homes situated in more distant and less dense areas. Thus, their cost of service is higher, and they pay higher marginal-cost user charges.

In addition, because marginal-cost user charges provide important information about the value of a service, they can enhance the efficiency of service provision. Thus, it may be optimal for a government to preserve the beneficial characteristics of user charges and to assist low-income residents through other, more general programs. The presence of low-income groups should not be the deciding factor in a decision to forgo user charges in favor of an alternative revenue source.

Special districts

Special districts play a unique role in local government finance. Not only do special districts have a more narrowly defined set of responsibilities than general governments, they also often have a more restricted set of revenue sources. To a greater extent than any other government entity, special districts rely on user charges to finance their services.

The U.S. Census Bureau defines special districts as limited-purpose governmental units that exist as separate entities. In theory, special districts have fiscal and administrative independence from general-purpose governments. Fiscal independence means that a special district may determine its budget and issue debt without review by other local officials or governments, may levy taxes for its own support, and may collect charges for its services.[29] Administrative independence, according to the Census Bureau, means that a public agency has a popularly elected governing body that represents two or more state or local governments and performs functions that are essentially different from those of its creating governments.[30] In order to be considered a special district by the Census Bureau (as opposed to being simply an agency of a larger government), the district must be an organized entity, it must have a "governmental character," and it must have substantial autonomy.[31] Because school districts are unique in many respects, they are generally considered distinct from other special districts.

Although the Census Bureau definition describes them as independent, many special districts are, by law, subordinate to a parent governmental unit (or units). These so-called dependent special districts generally have one or more of the following characteristics:

The agency officers are appointed by the chief administrator or the governing body of the parent government, or both; or the officers of the district are identical to the officers of the governing body of the parent government.

The agency controls facilities that supplement or take the place of facilities ordinarily provided by the creating government.

The agency's property and responsibilities revert to the creating government after the agency's debt has been repaid.

The agency's plans or budgets must be approved by the creating government.

The parent government specifies the type and location of facilities that the agency is to construct and maintain.[32]

The range of services provided by special districts includes water supply, sewerage, refuse collection, fire protection, housing and community development, transportation, drainage, and flood control. Table 12–4 shows the number of special districts in selected categories. The Census Bureau groups special districts into single- and multiple-function categories. As Table 12–4 indicates, most types of districts increased in number between 1982 and 2002; the greatest growth was in libraries (148 percent); health (67 percent); electric power, gas supply, and transit (53 percent); and parks and recreation (39 percent). Fire protection districts were the most numerous in each year reported.

Fiscal characteristics

Most special districts in metropolitan areas have the right to levy user charges, and they often have significant power to levy property taxes as well. The property tax is the only form of general tax levied by special districts. In some categories of special district, such as fire protection, libraries, parks and recreation, and some natural resource districts, more than 75 percent of revenues may come from the property tax. On the other hand, special districts that provide utility services such as sewerage, water, and electricity rely on user charges and use little or no property tax revenue. On average, in 1996–97, special districts accounted for only 3.7 percent of local government general taxes in the United States. In contrast, during the same period, special districts accounted for 20.1 percent of local government charges.[33]

Their relatively heavy reliance on pricing mechanisms—user fees, charges, and special assessments, for example—is one of the features that distinguishes special districts from other governmental entities. In 2000–01, 38.7 percent of all special district receipts were derived from charges, compared with 26.2 percent for counties, 22.2 percent for municipalities and townships, and 8.5 percent for school districts (see Table 12–3). These figures are not surprising, since special districts frequently provide services that the public associates with user charge financing rather than with taxes.

In addition to obtaining revenue from charges and taxes, many special districts receive considerable financial aid from federal, state, and local sources. Table 12–5 outlines the revenue sources, including intergovernmental

Table 12–4   Number of special districts, selected years, by function.

Function	1982	1987	1992	1997	2002	1982–1992	1992–2002
			Years			Percentage change	
Selected single-function districts							
Cemeteries	1,577	1,627	1,628	1,655	1,666	3.2	2.3
Drainage and flood control	2,705	2,772	2,709	3,369	3,247	0.1	19.9
Electric power, gas supply, and transit	317	411	461	470	485	45.4	5.2
Fire protection	4,560	5,070	5,260	5,601	5,725	15.4	8.8
Health	451	484	584	686	753	29.5	28.9
Highways	598	621	636	721	743	6.4	16.8
Hospitals	775	783	737	763	711	−4.9	−3.5
Housing and community development	3,296	3,464	3,470	3,469	3,399	5.3	−2.0
Libraries	638	830	1,043	1,496	1,580	63.5	51.5
Natural resource districts, including irrigation and soil and water conservation	3,527	3,588	3,519	3,614	3,732	−0.2	6.0
Parks and recreation	924	1,004	1,156	1,253	1,287	25.1	11.3
School buildings[a]	960	713	757	755	518	−21.1	−31.6
Sewers	1,631	1,607	1,710	2,004	2,004	4.8	17.2
Water supply	2,637	3,060	3,302	3,409	3,405	25.2	3.1
Total	24,596	26,034	26,972	29,265	29,255	9.7	8.5
Multiple-function districts							
Natural resources and water supply	170	98	131	117	102	−22.9	−22.1
Sewer and water supply	1,095	1,168	1,344	1,384	1,446	22.7	7.6
Other	1,332	785	1,044	1,217	1,627	−21.6	55.8
Total	2,597	2,051	2,519	2,718	3,175	−3.0	26.0

[a] Dependent public school systems of county, municipal, township, or state governments.

Table 12–5   Selected revenue sources for special districts (in millions of $).

Revenue sources	1971–72	1976–77	1981–82	1986–87	1991–92	1996–97
Total revenue	6,821	14,408	30,961	50,654	68,548	91,378
Taxes	968	1,743	2,846	5,491	8,087	10,528
Intergovernmental aid	550	4,332	8,271	10,783	14,843	21,876
Charges and miscellaneous	2,672	5,275	12,687	20,847	27,502	35,249

revenues, for special districts. In the 1970s and early 1980s, intergovernmental revenue was the fastest-growing source of revenue for special districts. Although growth slowed for a time, intergovernmental revenue was again the fastest-growing source between 1991–92 and 1996–97, reflecting the continued importance of intergovernmental transfers for local governments facing overburdened budgets.

Administrative control

Special districts are governed by elected or appointed boards that are responsible for such activities as the day-to-day administration of district affairs and the employment of administrative staff. Board members often rely heavily on professional consultants and appointed committees for decision making. It is also common for districts to employ a full-time, salaried administrative officer who is responsible for carrying out the policies formulated by the board.

Special districts may be created or dissolved through a number of procedures, including petitions, public hearings, state actions, referenda, and court actions. The general trend in the United States has been for special districts to become more common and to take on more varied responsibilities. Furthermore, there has been an expansion in the number of ways that special districts can be created.

The rules governing the creation of special districts in Florida offer an example of the many possibilities for special district creation. Although in general, independent special districts may be created only by the state legislature, there are numerous exceptions. Counties can create hospital districts, and both counties and municipalities can create community development districts. Two or more counties can create regional jail districts, and two or more counties or municipalities can create regional water authorities or regional transportation authorities. The governor is also empowered to create certain independent districts. Counties and municipalities generally create dependent special districts by ordinance, but the state legislature can also create them by special legislative act.

Proliferation and efficiency

The number of special districts in the United States has grown continuously over the past several decades, but the rate of growth has been slowing. The most rapid increase in the number of special districts was in the 1950s and 1960s; the growth rate has declined substantially since then, probably because most areas now have special districts for the most appropriate services. In the five years from 1997 to 2002, the Census Bureau recorded the slowest growth in the number of districts in half a century (see Table 12–6).

The overall growth in the number of special districts seems contrary to the reform tradition of political science, which views centralization as the most logical form of local government. In the reform view, a fragmented local government environment (i.e., one made up of many units of government, including special districts) is ineffective, uncoordinated, and unresponsive.[34] The growth in the number of local governmental units is consistent, however, with the theory that competition among local governmental units leads to the best mix of public goods and services as long as there are no substantial economies of scale involved.

Among the principal criticisms offered of special districts are the following:

Districts frequently provide uneconomical services.

Districts distort the political process by competing for scarce public resources.

Table 12–6   Number of special districts and school districts, selected years.

Year	Number of special districts	Percentage change from preceding reported year	Number of school districts	Percentage change from preceding reported year
1952	12,340	—	67,355	—
1957	14,424	+16.9	50,454	−25.1
1962	18,323	+27.0	34,678	−31.3
1967	21,264	+16.1	21,782	−37.2
1972	23,885	+12.3	15,781	−27.6
1977	25,962	+8.7	15,174	−3.8
1982	28,078	+8.2	14,851	−2.1
1987	29,532	+5.2	14,721	−0.9
1992	31,555	+6.9	14,556	−1.1
1997	34,683	+9.9	13,726	−5.7
2002	35,356	+1.9	13,522	−1.5

The multiplicity of districts interferes with citizens' understanding and hence citizens' control, and the result is unresponsive government.

Districts increase the costs of government within an area.[35]

In the 1960s and 1970s, when such objections found their widest support, a limited amount of empirical work had been undertaken to attempt to evaluate the relative merits of special districts and monolithic municipal providers. Much research has been done since, and although a variety of results have been observed, some common themes have emerged from this work.[36]

In some cases, the level of efficiency achieved by special districts is comparable to that of general-purpose governments. In a California study that evaluated the economic performance of 153 sewage plants, some of which were operated by municipalities and others by districts, the special districts were found to be as efficient as general-purpose governments.[37] The nature of sewage collection suggests that special districts can be an efficient means of providing service. Because many sewage treatment districts operate with economies of scale, smaller communities often construct their own collection systems and contract with a sewage district for treatment; this arrangement allows small jurisdictions to control their own collection systems while realizing economies of scale in treatment costs.

The efficiency of special districts also stems from their ability to finance capital expansion. The Metropolitan Water District of Southern California, for example, was formed by a number of municipalities and districts in order to generate the necessary funds to transport water from the Colorado River to the Los Angeles Basin—something no single agency could have done alone. Special districts can also operate within more logical geographic boundaries than can general-purpose units of government. A flood control district that crosses several jurisdictional boundaries but serves all the residents of a particular floodplain may be more desirable than flood control services limited to areas within legally specified boundaries.

Perhaps the most important way that special districts can contribute to efficiency is by providing a mechanism for meeting diverse collective demands for public goods and services. For example, a community may consist of five distinct neighborhoods, each characterized by homogeneous preferences for local public services. Under a consolidated local government organization, it is unlikely that the quantity and quality of the services provided will match the various preferences of each neighborhood.[38] Some residents will have more goods and services than they feel are necessary, given what they currently pay; others will want more goods and services but will be unable to obtain them, irrespective of what they are required to pay.

The ability to create or dissolve special districts permits residents to create "collective consumption units" that can obtain services that more closely match the preferences of each neighborhood. The proliferation of private developments, gated communities, and neighborhood associations reflects the desire for such "tailored" services. The very nature of gated communities implies a certain homogeneity of tastes and preferences. Neighborhood associations in these and in other geographically well-defined communities have taken over many jobs, including road repair, parks and recreation, growth management, zoning, and community transportation. These services can easily be tailored to suit the preferences of the community residents.

The notion that the proliferation of special districts can increase both efficiency and responsiveness reflects an economic and public-choice view of local government that contrasts with the reform view described earlier. Charles Tiebout's famous article, "A Pure Theory of Local Expenditure," popularized the idea of citizens voting with their feet and choosing among competing jurisdictions to best satisfy their preferences for local services.[39] Tiebout and others have argued that governmental competition efficiently allocates resources to local services in much the same way that market competition allocates resources in the private sector.

Empirical tests of the effects of providing additional special districts (and thus adding choices to the range of available services) have generated mixed results. Studies of the relationship between service costs and increases in the number of special districts found that when several states effectively restricted the proliferation of special districts, local government per capita taxes and expenditures substantially increased.[40] These increases were found to be significantly greater than those that occurred in states where the rate of growth in the number of special districts was the highest.

The findings of more recent studies have been most conclusive when focusing on the effects of competition on educational outcomes. Although there continues to be strong interest in the effects of jurisdictional competition on a variety of services, research tends to focus on education because of the wealth of information on educational outcomes—information that is often difficult to collect and compare for other services. Nevertheless, the findings concerning competition among school districts should have some applicability to other services. Studies of the effects of school competition have generally been consistent in finding that competition improves educational outcomes.[41] Significant attention has likewise been devoted to the relationship between district size, absence of competition, and student performance.[42]

In Sweden, when the number of local government units was decreased by approximately 80 percent, it was found that as the local units increased in size, (1) voter participation in local elections and citizen participation in voluntary civic and service organizations declined appreciably; (2) local elected officials differed more markedly from their constituents in such characteristics as income level, social status, and level of education; and (3) local elected officials' resistance to spending programs decreased. In addition, local elected officials in larger units of local government tended to "follow the dictates of their conscience" rather than the demands of their constituents, probably because of lack of contact with constituents and lack of concern for their preferences.[43]

Other research on citizen attitudes toward local government produced the following results:

The popularity of special-district government, and the fact that its focus has shifted from providing services in predominantly rural areas to providing services in urban areas, indicates communities' preference for services tailored to their needs.[44]

Proposals for more centralized local governmental organizations, such as city-county consolidations, are rejected by voters nearly three times as often as they are passed.[45]

Citizen confidence in and satisfaction with local government increase as the size of the governmental unit decreases.[46]

In summary, the optimal size and number of special districts depend on many factors, which vary from one place to another. A general decline in number is not necessarily good, and decisions about decreasing or increasing the size or number of districts should be made on a case-by-case basis. The value of this approach is clear if one considers the important ability of special districts to address different levels of intensity in residents' preferences for local services. If, for example, a local government observes an increase in the cost of providing services when a special district is created, the cost increase may actually represent an increase in the efficiency of resource use if it signals that residents who were previously willing to pay for a higher level of service—but who were unable to obtain the level of service they desired—are now able to do so.

Privatization

User charges and fees, special assessments, development fees, tax increment financing, and special districts all have a common purpose: they are designed to create a link between the receipt of public services and the payment for those services. This link creates important incentives for efficiency by providing consumers with the information necessary to make informed decisions about the use of public services. All these revenue strategies can be understood as public sector approximations of the transactions that take place in the private sector. Logically, the next step is to examine the possibility of having the production of services actually occur in the private sector.

Privatization is an increasingly attractive option for governments that confront growing budget pressure in the face of increasing demand for public services. Like the financing mechanisms described earlier in the chapter, privatization can offer greater efficiency and reduced financial burdens.

It is not unusual for government to provide services that depend, in part, on materials or equipment provided by private firms. Municipal transit agencies, for example, use buses purchased from a private manufacturer. Municipal wastewater is treated using pipes, tanks, and equipment produced by private firms. By extension, local government services could be *provided* by the local government but *produced* by the private sector. Keeping in mind this distinction between the provision and the production of government services, it is possible to examine the variety of ways that the privatization of government services can be structured.[47]

Approaches to privatization

Instead of turning all responsibility for a service over to the private sector (which was the original, narrower meaning of the term *privatization*), local governments are more likely to delegate public services. In this approach, the government retains some responsibility for provision of the service, but production is handled by the private sector. The most common institutional structures for this type of privatization are contracting, franchises, grants, and vouchers.

Contracting   A contract relationship exists when a government entity purchases goods or services from a private producer. Such arrangements have been part of local government operations for centuries and are used throughout all levels of government to obtain the necessary supplies and materials for day-to-day government operations—everything from paper clips to fire engines.

In addition to the rather unremarkable contracts for such goods, contracts are frequently in place for government purchase of administrative services, such as computer programming and maintenance, building upkeep and landscaping, printing and publishing, vehicle maintenance, management consulting, record keeping, and communication services. Finally, local governments rely on private producers to deliver services directly to citizens in areas such as trash collection, transportation, emergency services, street cleaning and repairs, and utility installation and repairs.

What distinguishes contracting from other forms of service delegation is that the government entity, rather than the actual consumer, pays the provider. In fact, it is this characteristic of contracting that renders private participation in many contracted services invisible to citizens; citizens may not even realize that a service has been privatized.

It is appropriate for the government entity to act as sole buyer when (1) the government is the consumer of the service (as in the case of maintenance for government buildings), (2) there are "public good" characteristics that make individual purchases impractical (as in the case of road repair), or (3) the government does not wish to charge citizens on the basis of consumption (as in the case of ambulance or fire service).

Franchises In a franchise arrangement, consumers pay the service provider directly. Because franchise arrangements are therefore limited to services for which residents can be charged on the basis of consumption, franchises are often found in utility services such as electricity, gas, water, telecommunications, and trash hauling. Franchises are also becoming an increasingly popular means of providing local bus service.

A franchise arrangement can be either exclusive or nonexclusive. *Concession*—essentially a franchise arrangement—is the term used when a private company provides food service at stadiums, parks, airports, or other government-owned properties.

Grants Under a grant arrangement, consumers and the government share the payment for privately produced services. The government's role is thus not only to arrange for service provision but also to subsidize production. Commonly, the government will select one or more private organizations and provide them with a subsidy in the form of direct payments, tax exemptions, or subsidized use of public facilities. The private organization produces the services and charges consumers less than the full cost of the service.

Private firms often use government grants to subsidize their provision of hospital services and low-income housing, since these are widely regarded as services that should be available regardless of ability to pay. Government subsidies for museums, theaters, and other cultural venues are justified similarly. Such services are often provided by nonprofit groups that rely on a combination of direct monetary grants and publicly provided infrastructure.

Vouchers Voucher programs also provide a government subsidy to encourage private production and consumption; unlike grants, however, vouchers provide a subsidy to consumers rather than to producers. This difference in the structure of the arrangement changes the effect of the subsidy in two important ways. First, because the subsidy does not favor one producer over another, there is no artificial limit placed on the competition between potential suppliers. Second, because a government can place limits on who may receive the vouchers, they can be targeted to subsidize consumption by people who meet certain (usually income) requirements.

While school vouchers continue to provoke substantial debate at the local level, other local voucher programs—such as those subsidizing housing and child care, for example—have been in existence longer and with less associated controversy. The food stamp program of the U.S. Department of Agriculture, while not a local program, clearly illustrates the advantages of a voucher system over grants. Since the subsidies are paid to individuals, there is no political pressure to favor one producer over another; and since acceptance of the vouchers is widespread, consumers can exercise a substantial degree of choice. Also, since the expressed purpose of the program is to provide assistance to low-income families, the government can target qualified families in a way that a grant subsidy could not.

The decision to privatize

Privatization is, first and foremost, simply a tool—one possible institutional arrangement—that local governments can use to run their operations more efficiently and effectively. The most important question to ask when considering the use of service contracting is whether it is appropriate to the task at hand. As with user charges, development fees, and special districts, successful use of privatization requires a careful consideration of the particular circumstances. Since the goal is to harness the efficiency (or some other positive aspect) of the private market, certain conditions must be met for privatization to work. As is the case with user charges in general, cost reductions can be realized only if residents have good information about the choices that are available.

The key condition for successful privatization is competition. The private sector is not inherently more efficient or more responsive than the public sector; it is the competition that is found in the private sector that creates incentives to increase efficiency and lower costs. Creating the appropriate incentives in the public sector requires establishing a similar competitive atmosphere. Clearly, then, the presence of a competitive market (or the potential for a competitive market) should be an important factor in determining the feasibility of privatization.

As with user charges and impact fees, the design of a privatization plan is crucial. When feasible, contract terms should be shorter, rather than longer, to increase opportunities for competition and to provide alternatives in the event of unforeseen cost increases. Performance bonds, which are designed to cover the costs of replacing the contractor, are a common way to ensure that bidders submit accurate offers. A contractor who fails to conform to the requirements of the contract forfeits the value of the bond. Of course, the best way to ensure that the privatization process is not manipulated after a contract has been let is to consistently maintain a competitive atmosphere.

A detailed discussion of the broader political implications and effects of privatization is beyond the scope of this chapter; however, a consideration of past trends in privatization is useful in that it reveals where privatization has been successful and where it has not. A study of the trends in privatization for the years 1988 to 1997 shows that privatization gained in popularity during those years.[48] In 1997, the most popular use of contracting was for vehicle towing and storage, with 82.2 percent of cities and counties surveyed reporting that they used contracts for this service. Contracting was also popular in the area of health and human services, with at least two-thirds of cities and counties reporting the use of contracts for the operation or management of hospitals, day care facilities, and homeless shelters. The least common areas for contracting seemed to be spread throughout local government services. Fewer than 10 percent of local governments reported using contracts to provide prisons, libraries, or tax assessment, or to maintain title records.

The changing nature of privatization is significant as well. The study found that although contracting was by far the most widely used strategy and had been increasing in popularity, local governments were not expanding their use of franchises, and the use of subsidy programs was actually declining. Another important finding was the substantial variation in which services were contracted for. Between 1988 and 1997, the use of contracting expanded greatly in some services, grew modestly in others, and declined slightly in still others. For example, there was an increase of more than twenty points in the percentage of cities that used contracting to provide for the operation and management of each of the following categories: commercial solid-waste collection, electric and gas utilities, hospitals, homeless shelters, day care, and museums. During the same period there were declines in the reliance on contracting for airport operation, utility billing, vehicle fleet management, and maintenance. Finally, even where there was overall growth in the use of contracting, the pattern of growth varied between services and over time.

It is one thing to observe that the use of privatization is growing at the local level. It is also important to ask whether privatization actually results in more efficient service provision. Of course, increased efficiency is not always the only (or even primary) goal of privatization. But since the most important economic argument in support of privatization is increased efficiency, cost of service and other efficiency measures are an appropriate way to measure privatization's success.

A broad survey of efficiency studies shows that privatization very often leads to more efficient and less costly service provision.[49] The strongest evidence for efficiency was found in the provision of bus service, cleaning services, and refuse collection. Of thirty-one studies, twenty-six found private production (usually through a contracting arrangement) more efficient or less costly. Four studies found no significant difference between private production and government production, and only one study (from 1976, and focusing on refuse collection in Montana) found that municipal production was more efficient. Results were less supportive of privatization in the areas of electric power and water utilities, however. Of seventeen studies, seven found no significant differences and five found public production to be more efficient.

Competition may account for the differences in findings for some services. Transportation, cleaning services, and trash collection are all areas where competition is already substantial or where firms can easily enter the market and compete. In Estes Park, Colorado, for example, two private companies are authorized to collect refuse from all residential areas; because the companies compete directly on service levels and price, residents can choose the level of service they prefer and observe its direct relationship to price. Significantly, both companies find it efficient to set fees in relation to the volume of refuse collected from each customer; both companies dispose of the refuse in a county-run disposal site for a volume-based fee.

In the case of water and electricity services, the fixed costs of production are high and government monopolies are widespread; thus, there is less competition, and entry into the market is more difficult. Even with limited competition, however, evidence shows that private sector efficiency gains are possible if the privatization plan is properly structured. Careful attention to specific circumstances, along with an understanding of the conditions necessary for introducing competitive forces, can help local governments realize significant efficiency gains through privatization.

Summary

The combined forces of fiscal pressure, technological feasibility, and broader acceptance of benefit-based fees should ensure continued reliance on institutional arrangements that allow local governments to collect revenue from those who benefit from government services. In the case of utilities and similar services, the move away from the property tax and toward user charges, development fees, and franchises has been under way for some time. Reliance on charges and fees to finance other public services varies in its application but is growing nevertheless.

When correctly designed, user charges have several advantages over the property tax as a source of local revenue. Charges based on the cost of providing public services allow the consumer-taxpayer to evaluate the cost against the level of service provided. In many cases, the charges allow for optimal allocation of publicly provided goods: that is, low-cost users and off-peak users pay less, and high-cost users and peak-period users pay more. The amount of revenue obtained from user charges can provide an indicator of the need to expand or contract service supply. Simultaneously, user charges provide the revenue needed to maintain facilities and finance any needed expansion.

The primary disadvantages of user charges are regressivity and administrative costs. A marginal-cost user charge is likely to be regressive when compared with the property tax. However, a properly designed marginal-cost user charge system is likely to be decidedly less regressive than an average-cost user charge system. Since this level of regressivity is common in state sales taxes, it is not likely to be a serious problem for user charges.

Administrative costs for a properly designed user charge system can be considerable. Unlike property tax financing, a user charge system requires that a local government measure the amount (and sometimes the timing) of consumption. However, technological advances have significantly reduced the costs associated with monitoring consumption and have also lowered the costs of billing and record keeping. These cost reductions continue to increase the feasibility of adopting new user charges or other benefit-based fees.

When established under the appropriate circumstances and with the appropriate structure, special districts can improve the efficiency of production and the measurement of demand. Inappropriate creation of special districts, however, can lead to lack of responsiveness and duplication of services. User charges are used far more in special districts than in any other form of local government; however, even in special districts, the level of user charge revenue varies significantly among types of service and among states.

Privatization, especially through contracting, is a means of introducing market incentives to the provision of local services. Much like the employment of user charges, the implementation of contracting and other privatization strategies varies widely across jurisdictions and across services within jurisdictions. Like user charges, privatization has seen steady growth in many areas, which is likely to continue for the foreseeable future.

User charges, whether levied by special districts or other governmental units, are likely to play an increasing role in the future of local government finance, particularly as the unpopularity of the property tax continues to rise. Of the many advantages of user charge financing, one of the most important is the fact that user charges reflect the benefits-received principle of finance, according to which users pay for the services they consume. User charges also provide price and cost information that allows consumers to make informed choices about which services they desire, at what level, and at what price. The net result is an improvement in the functioning, responsiveness, and equity of local government.

1 U.S. Department of Commerce, Bureau of the Census, *Finances of Municipal and Township Governments,* 1987 Census of Governments, vol. 4, no. 4 (Washington, D.C.: U.S. Government Printing Office, 1988), table 1.

2 U.S. Department of Commerce, Bureau of the Census, *Finances of Municipal and Township Governments,* 1997 Census of Governments, vol. 4, no. 4 (Washington, D.C.: U.S. Government Printing Office, 2000), table 1.

3 U.S. Department of Commerce, Bureau of the Census, *Government Finances, 1999–2000* (Washington, D.C.: U.S. Government Printing Office, 2003).

4 U.S. Department of Commerce, Bureau of the Census, *Compendium of Government Finances, 1997* Census of Governments, vol. 4, no. 5 (Washington, D.C.: U.S. Government Printing Office, 2000).

5 See Edward J. Bierhanzl, "Incentives for Efficiency: User Charges and Municipal Spending," *Journal of Public Finance and Public Choice* 16, no. 1 (1999): 19–34.

6 See, for example, Edward Bierhanzl and Paul Downing, "User Charges and Bureaucratic Inefficiency," *Atlantic Economic Journal* 26 (June 1998): 175–189.

7 Marginal cost is the change in the total cost of producing and delivering a product as output is increased by a small amount.

8 U.S. General Accounting Office (GAO), *Motor Fuels: Gasoline Prices in the West Coast Market,* GAO-01-608T (Washington, D.C.: GAO, April 2001).

9 The long run is a period of time long enough to allow additional facilities to be built. The short run

is a shorter amount of time during which facilities cannot be expanded. In the short run, using the existing facilities more intensively can increase output, but this usually entails higher marginal costs per unit.

10 See, for example, Chesapeake Bay Program, *Cost of Providing Government Services to Alternative Residential Patterns* (Washington, D.C.: U.S. Environmental Protection Agency, 1993); and Real Estate Research Corporation, *The Costs of Sprawl* (Washington, D.C.: U.S. Government Printing Office, 1974).

11 Chesapeake Bay Program, *Providing Government Services.*

12 Practical considerations, including the cost of monitoring and collecting for peak use, may limit the expediency of peak charges, especially for small consumers. However, modern computer technology is making such charges more practical every day.

13 Ernst & Young, *Ernst & Young's 1992 National Water and Wastewater Rate Survey* (Washington, D.C.: Ernst & Young, 1992), 33.

14 Ibid., 39.

15 Association of Metropolitan Sewerage Agencies (AMSA), *Municipal Wastewater Treatment Agency Financial Survey 1990* (Washington, D.C.: AMSA, 1990).

16 Ibid.

17 If an effluent fee (a fee reflecting the pollution potential of the water) were charged for stormwater release, then an output charge—and perhaps some treatment—would be appropriate.

18 Núria Bosch, Francisco Pedraja, and Javier Suárez-Pandiello, "The Efficiency of Refuse Collection Services in Spanish Municipalities: Do Non-Controllable Variables Matter?" (Institut d'Economia de Barcelona, 2001).

19 Tolls are desirable only if the benefits of controlling use exceed the cost of establishing and operating the toll collection system.

20 Michael A. Pagano, "The Price of Leisure: User Fees and Recreational Facilities," in *The Municipal Year Book 1990* (Washington, D.C.: International City Management Association, 1990), 30–40.

21 See Paul B. Downing and James Frank, "Recreation Impact Fees," *National Tax Journal* 36 (December 1983): 477–490; James Frank, Elizabeth Lines, and Paul B. Downing, "Community Experience with Fire Impact Fees" and "Community Experience with Sewer Impact Fees" (Policy Sciences Program, Florida State University, 1985).

22 National Association of Realtors, "Impact Fee Study—2002," available at www.realtor.org.

23 John Yinger, "Who Pays Development Fees?" in *Local Government Tax and Land Use Policies in the United States: Understanding the Links,* ed. Helen F. Ladd (Northampton, Mass: Edward Elgar, 1998); and Yinger, "The Incidence of Development Fees and Special Assessments," *National Tax Journal* 51 (March 1998): 23–41.

24 Independent Budget Office of the City of New York (IBO), *Learning from Experience: A Primer on Tax Increment Financing* (New York: IBO, September 2002).

25 Ibid., 4.

26 The effects of charges on development are explored by various authors in *Local Service Pricing Policies and Their Effect on Urban Spatial Structure,* ed. Paul B. Downing (Vancouver: University of British Columbia Press, 1977).

27 Paul B. Downing, "User Charges and the Development of Urban Land," *National Tax Journal* 26 (December 1973): 631–637.

28 This effect is demonstrated in Paul B. Downing, "The Distributional Effect of User Charges" (Department of Economics, Virginia Polytechnic Institute, October 1974).

29 U.S. Department of Commerce, Bureau of the Census, *Finances of Special District Governments,* 1997 Census of Governments, vol. 4, no. 2 (Washington, D.C.: U.S. Government Printing Office, 2000).

30 The special district is one of the two organizational forms most commonly used in lieu of direct municipal provision of services, the other being the municipally owned utility. Another term, *public authority,* encompasses both special districts and municipally owned utilities.

31 Bureau of the Census, *Finances of Special District Governments,* 1997 Census of Governments, vol. 4, no. 2.

32 See U.S. Department of Commerce, Bureau of the Census, *Government Organization,* 1997 Census of Governments, vol. 1 (Washington, D.C.: U.S. Government Printing Office, 1999).

33 Derived from U.S. Department of Commerce, Bureau of the Census, *Government Finances,* 1997 Census of Governments, vol. 4 (Washington, D.C.: U.S. Government Printing Office, 2000).

34 A considerable number of private and public organizations have promoted the reform tradition, including the Advisory Commission on Intergovernmental Relations, the National Municipal League, and the Committee for Economic Development, which in 1966 advocated an 80 percent reduction in the number of governmental units in metropolitan areas in the United States.

35 Advisory Commission on Intergovernmental Relations (ACIR), *The Problem of Special Districts in American Government: A Commission Report* (Washington, D.C.: ACIR, 1964), 74–75.

36 A valuable overview can be found in Kathryn A. Foster, *The Political Economy of Special-Purpose Government* (Washington, D.C.: Georgetown University Press, 1997).

37 Ibid.

38 With a constitutionally imposed majority rule, the level of output of public goods will most likely correspond to the preferences of the median voter.

39 Charles Tiebout, "A Pure Theory of Local Expenditure," *Journal of Political Economy* 64 (October 1956): 416–424.

40 See Thomas J. DiLorenzo, "The Expenditure Effects of Restricting Competition in Local Public Service Industries: The Case of Special Districts," *Public Choice* 37 (winter 1981): 569–578; and Stephen L. Mehay, "The Effect of Governmental Structure on Special District Expenditures," *Public Choice* 44 (winter 1984): 339–348. On the general effects of competition among local governments on the cost of providing local public services, see Thomas J. DiLorenzo, "Economic Competition and Political Competition: An Empirical Note," *Public Choice* 40 (summer 1983): 203–209; and Richard E. Wagner and Warren Weber, "Competition, Monopoly, and the Organization of Government in Metropolitan Areas," *Journal of Law and Economics* 18 (December 1975): 661–684.

41 Jay Greene and Marcus Winters, "When Schools Compete: The Effects of Vouchers on Florida's Public School Achievement," Education Working

Paper no. 2 (New York: Manhattan Institute, July 2003).

42 Lori Taylor provides a review of the literature on education and other services in "The Evidence on Government Competition," Federal Reserve Bank of Dallas *Economic and Financial Review* (second quarter 2000): 2–10.

43 Jorgen Westerstahl, "Decision-Making Systems" (paper presented at the annual meeting of the American Political Science Association, Chicago, Illinois, 1973).

44 California Local Government Reform Task Force, *Special District Report* (Sacramento: California Local Government Reform Task Force, February 1974).

45 "New County, U.S.A.," *The American County* (February 1972): 10.

46 U.S. Congress, Senate Committee on Government Operations, Subcommittee on Intergovernmental Relations, 93rd Cong., 1st sess., *Confidence and Concern: Citizens View Americans and Government,* vols. 1 and 2 (Washington, D.C.: U.S. Government Printing Office, 1973).

47 The arrangements described here are adapted from a list in chap. 4 of E. S. Savas, *Privatization and Public-Private Partnerships* (New York: Seven Bridges Press, 2000), 66–67.

48 Elaine Morley, "Local Government Use of Alternative Service Delivery Approaches," *Municipal Year Book 1999* (Washington, D.C.: International City/County Management Association), 34–44.

49 Jeffrey D. Greene, *Cities and Privatization: Prospects for the New Century* (Upper Saddle River, N.J.: Pearson Education, 2002), 154–158.

Part four:
Financial
management

13 Economic development

TIMOTHY J. BARTIK

Local governments are becoming increasingly involved in local economic development programs: government-supported activities that seek to increase the number and quality of local jobs or the size of the local tax base by a variety of measures, such as assistance to individual businesses. This chapter provides a brief overview of local economic development policies in the United States and offers a conceptual framework that can help local officials decide on the appropriate goals, scope, and scale of those policies.[1]

Overview of local economic development policies

Local economic development may be defined as increases in the "local economy's capacity to create wealth for local residents."[2] Such increases occur if local resources, such as labor and land, are used more productively. Simply by creating more jobs, economic development enhances productivity if it uses labor or land that otherwise would be unemployed. But economic development can also enhance productivity without job growth—by shifting labor and land already in use to better jobs and more productive uses.

Although it can be argued that all local government activities affect local economic development, local economic development policy is usually defined more narrowly as special activities, undertaken by local public or private groups, to promote economic development. Economic development programs fall into two categories: (1) customized assistance targeted to individual businesses and (2) strategic initiatives to change the government's tax, spending, or regulatory policies in order to promote business in general.

Local economic development is increasingly regarded as a major local government responsibility. According to one survey of elected officials in jurisdictions with more than 100,000 in population, 86 percent believe that "bringing about economic development" is a major responsibility of local governments.[3] The "first priority" for local economic development is increasing jobs located in the city (48 percent of respondents), increasing the local tax base (18 percent), and diversifying the local economy (10 percent); the remaining 24 percent of those surveyed listed miscellaneous other first priorities.[4]

Although local governments play an important role in local economic development, the roles of other groups are at least as important. According to a survey of chief administrative officers in cities and counties conducted by the International City/County Management Association (ICMA), many organizations participate in the creation of local economic development strategies, including local chambers of commerce, private businesses, citizen advisory boards, public-private partnerships, state government, utilities, and private economic development foundations.[5] Economic development programs are also carried out by local business organizations and local universities and community colleges.

In this chapter, when reference is made to specific types of local economic development programs, it is important to remember that many such programs are not carried out by government agencies. Government at the local, state, and national levels may fund, regulate, or facilitate local economic development initiatives, but the programs themselves are often carried out by private or quasi-private entities. Furthermore, a wide variety of private and nonprofit entities are deeply involved in shaping economic development policies; such groups regard economic development as too important to abandon to the changing fortunes of electoral politics.

According to the ICMA survey, the most common barriers to local economic development include limited availability of land, lack of skilled labor, high land costs, lack of capital and funding, citizen opposition, a limited number of major employers, and traffic congestion. The survey also found that local economic development strategies focus on manufacturing, retail or service industries, technology and telecommunications, tourism, and warehousing and distribution industries. Among the most common economic development programs supported by local governments are tax incentives, job-training programs, community development loan funds, community development corporations, and microenterprise programs.

On average, between 2 and 3.5 local government staff members per 100,000 in population devote at least 70 percent of their time to economic development. Local government spending for economic development averages between $7 and $16 per capita annually.[6] This figure implies that for the entire United States, total local government spending for economic development is between $2 and $4 billion annually. However, detailed state studies suggest that local tax incentives to promote economic development exceed direct local spending on economic development. For example, a study of Michigan found that local government tax incentives for economic development were more than $40 per capita annually. Most of these tax incentives—more than $30 per capita in forgone revenue—were in the form of property tax abatements for new or expanding manufacturing plants; the rest ($9 per capita) occurred as part of tax increment financing (TIF) plans, in which the property tax increment from economic growth in a designated district is used to finance infrastructure

---

Kalamazoo's many economic developers   Like many areas, Kalamazoo, Michigan (county population about 240,000), has many different public, private, and public-private groups engaged in a variety of economic development activities. The lead economic development organization is Southwest Michigan First (SMF), a private nonprofit that receives funds from the private sector, the county, the city of Kalamazoo, the city of Portage (the largest suburban community in the metropolitan area), and local foundations.

SMF is involved in business recruitment, business retention, and high-technology development: it helps firms find new sites in Kalamazoo, sponsors a business visitation program and both a regular and a high-tech incubator, and is working with Western Michigan University to develop a research park.

A local private college runs a federally and locally funded small business development center. The local community college runs a training center, built with state funding, that provides businesses with customized training funded by employer fees or by grants from the state economic development agency.

Both Kalamazoo and Portage have their own economic development staff, who seek to promote the development of particular areas: in Kalamazoo the focus is on various brownfields, the downtown, and neighborhood business districts; in Portage the focus is on the continued health of the county's main shopping areas. Kalamazoo also supports an independent, nonprofit agency that oversees downtown redevelopment; the agency is funded, in part, by revenues from a tax increment financing district.

in that district.[7] On the basis of this and similar studies, local tax incentives for economic development provide U.S. businesses with more than $10 billion annually in tax savings.

Goals of economic development policies

Local economic development programs are often politically controversial because they involve government assistance to individual businesses, which may be perceived by political liberals as corporate welfare and by political conservatives as unwarranted government interference in private markets. Such views often motivate citizen opposition to economic development efforts—which may, in turn, inhibit the creation of effective local economic development policies. On the other hand, local economic development programs often seem difficult to constrain: once the government agrees to support a few businesses, how can it justify refusing requests to support other businesses? Local government managers need to encourage consensus about the appropriate goals of economic development policies; such consensus provides a basis for deciding what local economic development efforts should and should not do.

Public subsidies for economic development can be justified by the creation of fiscal and employment benefits. Fiscal benefits occur when the tax revenue that results from job creation is greater than the public expenditure that results from job creation (e.g., the new or expanded roads that are required when employment increases and when population increases as a result). Employment benefits occur when people who would otherwise be unemployed obtain new jobs or when people who are already in the labor force move into better-paying jobs. Economic development policies that enable local firms to add to the local economy's export base or to substitute local goods for imports are more likely to increase the total number of jobs in the local economy. (In this context, *export* refers to goods or services sold outside the local jurisdiction, and *import* refers to goods or services that are purchased by local residents or businesses but produced outside the jurisdiction.) If economic development policies lead to increased sales for assisted businesses but fail to expand local exports or substitute local goods for imports, then the sales increases for assisted businesses will be counterbalanced by lower sales in other local businesses—making it less likely that there will be an increase in total local jobs.

When economic development policies help export-base or import-substituting businesses to grow, only some of the total increase in jobs will occur in the firms that receive direct assistance; additional job growth will occur through multiplier effects. For example, in order to expand, the assisted businesses will require inputs from other businesses, some of which may be local. At the same time, the assisted businesses and their local suppliers will generate increased worker income, some of which will be spent at local retailers. Multiplier effects will be larger under the following circumstances: (1) if the local jurisdiction is larger, making it more likely that demands for supplies or for retail goods can be satisfied locally; (2) if the assisted businesses have strong links to local suppliers, which is more likely for long-established businesses; or (3) if the workers in the assisted businesses are paid higher wages, which increases demand for local retail.

Econometric models can be used to estimate the size of multiplier effects. Local government managers should be skeptical of claims of multipliers greater than 2.5 (i.e., for each job created in an assisted business, 1.5 jobs will be created in supplier and retail businesses); such multipliers require assisted businesses to have unusually strong links to local suppliers or unusually highly paid workers.

Should local economic development programs emphasize businesses that export outside the local economy or businesses that substitute local goods for

Econometric models Any model used to determine the economic, employment, and fiscal impact of new business must combine sound economic theory with area-specific information about local supplier linkages.[1] Two of the most prominent economic impact models, which are used to estimate the effects of a new plant on local production and income, are the IMPLAN model and the REMI model.

The results obtained through economic impact models can be used in fiscal impact models, which estimate how the economic impacts will affect government taxes and expenditures. Fiscal impact models require data or assumptions about (1) the effect of business growth on population growth and (2) the effect of business and population growth on service and infrastructure needs. The most prominent nationally available local fiscal impact model is the LOCI model, which was developed at Georgia Tech. Some states, including Maryland, New York, Oklahoma, and West Virginia, have their own economic or fiscal impact models. New York State's economic impact model, which includes estimates of employment benefits, is particularly sophisticated.

[1] For the best available summary of models for analyzing the economic and fiscal impact of new business on a local economy, see Kenneth Poole et al., *Evaluating Business Development Incentives* (Washington, D.C.: National Association of State Development Agencies, 1999).

imports? In theory, either approach can provide an equivalent boost to local jobs; in practice, however, it is difficult to determine whether a business expansion will actually cause local goods to be substituted for imports. In addition, import-substitution strategies that give preferential treatment to local suppliers can lead the suppliers to become less competitive in the export market.[8]

Assistance to non-export-base firms can increase local wealth if it leads to the use of land or labor that would otherwise be unusable—for example, if a firm were encouraged to use an abandoned brownfield site or to hire unemployed disadvantaged workers. In such cases, even if the growth of the assisted firm comes at the expense of other local firms, the mere fact that unusable land or labor is being put to use will free up land or labor already in use for other purposes. The greater availability of land and labor will, in turn, encourage export-base firms to expand, with consequent multiplier effects on the local economy. Nevertheless, determining whether the land or labor used by the assisted firm would otherwise be unemployable can be difficult. Land or labor that is unemployed may eventually have come into use anyway, in the normal course of economic change. The greater the obstacles to the use of a land parcel or the employment of a worker, the more likely the land or the worker would otherwise be unemployed.

One way to increase the wealth of a local economy without increasing exports or decreasing imports is by increasing productivity. For example, providing businesses with information on how to better use new technologies will increase local wealth if the value of the increased productivity exceeds the program's costs (in this case, the cost of hiring consultants who can provide businesses with advice about technology). However, because the benefits of productivity-improvement efforts are, in large part, enjoyed by the business sector, there is some question as to whether such programs should be subsidized by the general public or by taxes or fees on business. A subsidy from the general public might make sense under any of the following conditions:

1. If the program affects enough businesses to increase local competition in a given industry, resulting in increased quality and lower prices and shifting some benefits to local consumers.

North Carolina's customized training programs North Carolina is among the most active states in providing customized training programs that meet the needs of individual businesses. The state annually provides training to nearly 10 percent of its workers, at a cost per trainee of around $140. The training programs are designed to attract new branch plants and to foster business expansions, but they also encourage assisted businesses to hire disadvantaged workers, particularly for entry-level jobs.

The most intensive customized training is provided by the New and Expanding Industry Training program, under which community colleges provide training to firms that are creating at least twelve jobs in an industry that exports goods or services outside the state. The colleges place ads for potential trainees and screen applicants for trainee slots, and the firms choose trainees from among those screened. The firms provide the training equipment and the colleges pro-

vide the facilities and the trainers. The firms decide which trainees are hired.

Short-term training is provided by the Occupational Continuing Education (OCE) program, through which community colleges offer occupational training for a state-subsidized fee. A firm that has more than ten trainees is eligible to receive customized training; 60 percent of OCE courses are arranged by employers. Case studies of North Carolina's customized training programs suggest that community colleges sometimes enable welfare recipients and other disadvantaged residents to enter these customized industrial training programs and to subsequently gain employment in manufacturing.[1]

Source: Based on Timothy Bartik, *Jobs for the Poor: Can Labor Demand Policies Help?* (New York and Kalamazoo, Mich.: Russell Sage Foundation and W. E. Upjohn Institute for Employment Research, 2001), 259–260.
[1]Rosemary Batt and Paul Osterman, "Workplace Training Policy: Case Studies of State and Local Experiments," Working Paper 105 (Washington, D.C.: Economic Policy Institute, 1993).

2. If the program helps businesses or groups (such as women or minorities) whose success is socially beneficial. (Some might argue that small-business success is inherently socially beneficial.)
3. If the program enhances the productivity of workers in many jobs (e.g., by training workers in general skills) and thereby increases wages.
4. If the value of the resulting productivity increases exceeds the program's costs, and if the assisted businesses either export outside the local economy or substitute local goods for imports. Such programs may provide the same boost to the local economy as financial incentives, but at a lower cost.

Fiscal benefits

Fiscal benefits are one rationale for the public subsidy of economic development. New jobs increase local profits, wages, sales, and property values, all of which will increase local tax revenues. Although some local governments assume that increased tax revenues are the only fiscal effect of new jobs, additional factors must be considered to determine the true fiscal impact of local economic development.[9]

1. New or expanding businesses require increased public infrastructure or services. One study found that, on average, for every dollar in tax revenue paid by businesses, about sixty cents in public expenditures is required.[10]
2. New businesses and new jobs attract additional households, and the typical household consumes more in public services than it pays in state and local taxes. However, this is less true of higher-income households

than of lower-income households, and less true of childless households than of households that use public schools. Therefore, the more jobs that go to current residents rather than to in-migrants, and the greater the relative in-migration of higher-wage or childless households, the greater the fiscal benefits of economic development.

3. The fiscal benefits of new businesses and new jobs vary depending on the perspective that is being applied. If, for example, the focus is on the fiscal well-being of the local government in which a new or expanding business is located, the expansion may appear to be entirely beneficial— in part because at least some of the fiscal costs are being borne by other governmental units in the local labor market. For instance, the cost of public education for additional students, a significant part of the public service costs associated with new households, is rarely paid by the local government that attracts the business. Although the ideal is to consider the effects of economic development on all jurisdictions in the local labor market, in practice, a financially hard-pressed local government will sometimes have to focus on its narrow fiscal self-interest.

4. Economic development that does not require additional infrastructure— if, for example, the local highway system can accommodate more cars without increased congestion—will have greater fiscal benefits. Analyses that consider one business expansion at a time, rather than the cumulative impact of many business expansions, are less effective at revealing the true impact of business growth on local infrastructure. Another issue is whether, in return for business growth, a local government is willing to accept a decrease in the quality of public services (e.g., increases in travel time as local roads become more crowded). A fiscally troubled local government may downplay the costs, in the form of lower-quality public services, of additional business activity.

5. The net fiscal benefits of economic development will be greater when the assistance is decisive in inducing the new business activity. If the new activity would have occurred anyway, there is a net loss equal to the cost of the subsidy. Such subsidies should be avoided, but this is easier said than done: program managers rarely know for certain which subsidies were decisive and which were not. A complete fiscal analysis will make some assumptions about what proportion of economic development subsidies were decisive and will weigh the fiscal benefits (if any) of such subsidies against the costs of providing unnecessary subsidies.

Although an econometric model can be used to evaluate the fiscal effects of economic development, the results are only as accurate as the model's structure and the information fed into the model will permit. Thus, accurate results require (1) a model that allows for the factors just listed and (2) users who can provide information on those factors.

If a local government manager adopts a short-term perspective, considers only the well-being of his or her own jurisdiction, and ignores the effects of growth on the quality of local services, then local economic development may appear to provide sizable fiscal benefits. On the other hand, if a local government manager adopts a long-term perspective, considers the fiscal costs and benefits for all affected local governments, and takes account of the full, long-term costs of maintaining public services at a given level of quality, then the fiscal benefits of local economic development will depend on its employment benefits—that is, on whether it raises employment rates and wages. Over the long run, most public-finance literature suggests that the average cost of providing local public services, including infrastructure, of a given quality is roughly constant, per household and business, as a community grows.[11] Thus, in the long run, if employment and population both increase by the same percentage, public service costs should also increase by the same percentage. If tax revenues increase by the same percentage, long-run fiscal benefits will be nil. However, if local wages go up, tax revenue will increase by a greater percentage than employment, and if population increases less rapidly than employment, public service costs will also increase less rapidly; in other words, if economic development raises wages or employment rates (the ratio of employment to population), fiscal benefits accrue.

Employment benefits

When an unemployed local resident gets a new job, the employment benefits consist of the wages paid for that job minus whatever value the resident places on his or her time while unemployed—a value that economists refer to as the "reservation wage." The reservation wage of an unemployed person is the lowest wage at which that person would accept a job, and it can be measured by surveys of unemployed workers or by statistical analysis of how wages affect the acceptance of job offers. Assuming that the unemployment was involuntary (i.e., the worker would have preferred employment at his or her current market wage to unemployment), the employment benefit—the difference between the worker's market wage and reservation wage—is positive. However, the employment benefit will be less, perhaps considerably less, than the worker's market wage. Thus, the common practice in cost-benefit analyses of economic development programs—which is to count *all* the wages of new jobs as employment benefits, without any deduction for the reservation wages of the unemployed—is flawed. As noted earlier, employment benefits also accrue when residents who are already working move up to better-paying jobs.

Local job growth brings sizable employment benefits. An employment increase of 10 percent in a metropolitan area increases average real earnings in the same metropolitan area by about 4 percent per person.[12] Half of this increase occurs because unemployed local residents get jobs; the other half occurs because some workers get better-paying positions.

Research suggests that for every ten jobs created in a local labor market, such as a metropolitan area, about eight will go to in-migrants or to local residents who would otherwise have obtained employment in some other local economy. When an in-migrant (or a potential out-migrant) gets a new local job, even if he or she was previously unemployed or employed at a lower wage, the local employment benefits will generally be small. Migrants are, by definition, essentially neutral about moving to a new place or staying where they are—and, since migrants generally have their choice of new locations, creating more jobs in one community does not appreciably enlarge the opportunities for migrants: that is, even without economic development in a given area, a migrant could have moved somewhere else and obtained a similar job.

Local residents, in contrast, have significant attachments to their home area and therefore gain greater benefit from improved local job opportunities. In the short run, benefits occur because local employers, in the face of rapid business growth, will lower hiring requirements in order to fill vacancies, allowing local residents to get jobs that would otherwise have been unattainable. Moreover, these short-run gains will persist because the newly employed or better-employed local residents will acquire better job skills, greater self-confidence, and a better reputation with other local employers, all of which will increase their long-term wages and employability.

These employment benefits accrue to local residents throughout a local labor market, not just to the residents of the jurisdiction that develops new jobs.[13] Most people do not live and work in the same place.[14] Furthermore, even if workers do work close to home, the effects of job creation in one neighborhood or jurisdiction are still spread broadly. For example, if new suburban jobs go to suburbanites who previously commuted to the city, the resulting city vacancies will provide job opportunities for city residents. Although there are some benefits to having more jobs nearby, job availability in the metropolitan area is a greater determinant of demand for a person's labor than is the number of nearby jobs.[15]

Local government managers can increase the employment benefits of local economic development in three ways. First, economic development should be pursued more aggressively when local unemployment rates are high. Under these conditions, the average unemployed worker is more desperate for a job and the benefit from job growth is greater.

Second, local governments should use positive incentives (e.g., improved training for local job seekers, help with screening local job seekers) to encourage assisted businesses to fill a higher proportion of their job vacancies with unemployed or underemployed local residents. Studies of the low-wage job market suggest that many businesses have great difficulty finding productive workers. Six months into the job, more than one-quarter of new employees are producing less than 75 percent of what the employer anticipated upon hiring.[16] Moreover, many low-wage workers hired quickly quit or are quickly fired; studies find that half of all low-wage workers hired lose their jobs within five to nine months.[17] Given the difficulties of finding and retaining productive workers, particularly in the low-wage job market, efforts on the part of local economic development agencies to improve training and screening of local residents are likely to have significant appeal to employers.

Although many local governments require businesses assisted through economic development programs to hire local residents, the requirement is seldom enforced because of fears of discouraging economic development. A few cities, such as Portland, Oregon, with its now-defunct JobNet program, and Berkeley, California, with its First Source Employment Program (see sidebar), have designed programs that (1) helped businesses receiving economic development incentives find productive workers by training and screening prospective workers before referring them to the business and (2) avoided coercion of businesses by requiring only that referred workers be *considered*.[18]

Third, local governments should focus economic development assistance on jobs with higher wage premiums—that is, jobs that pay well relative to the skills required. Empirical studies indicate that growth in such jobs results in greater earnings benefits for local residents.[19]

Other benefits and costs

Local economic development will usually raise local housing prices, which helps home owners and other landowners but hurts renters. Local economic development may also have environmental costs, including increased pollution, urban sprawl, and traffic congestion; loss of green space; and loss of local character. Local economic development projects can be modified, however, to minimize or reverse such effects. The term *sustainable development* is often used to refer to development efforts that integrate environmental considerations into plans for economic growth.[20]

The market theory of economic development

The productivity of local businesses may be efficiently increased if "market failures"—that is, the inefficient provision of inputs to business production—

Berkeley's First Source Employment Program Begun in 1986, Berkeley's First Source Employment Program requires employers who have received direct or indirect assistance from the city to enter into "first source" agreements, which require them to promise to consider workers who are referred through the First Source Employment Program. The program draws workers from more than twenty training providers and community groups.

First Source requirements apply to virtually any city assistance: city financing, city contracts, and city permits for new, nonresidential construction of more than 7,500 square feet (in which case the requirement applies to both the construction firm and the business tenants). On the other hand, hiring is voluntary, and the program works with employers to try to find workers who meet the employers' requirements. About 250 workers are hired annually through First Source, a sizable number for a city of 100,000. About four-fifths of the workers are members of minority groups, and three-fifths are low income; one-third are hired by employers who are not subject to First Source requirements—that is, employers who have not received any other city assistance.

To succeed, the program must serve the interests of two different groups: disadvantaged job seekers and employers seeking workers. Without the voluntary involvement of both groups, the program would be unable to generate significant employment for disadvantaged workers.[1]

[1] For more information on the First Source Program, see Frieda Molina, *Making Connections: A Study of Employment Linkage Programs* (Washington, D.C.: Center for Community Change, 1998).

can be identified and redressed. Among the reasons for market failures are the following:

Insufficient information. For example, a business may have difficulty identifying a reliable consultant who can explain how best to integrate the latest technology into the production process. The available information is often unreliable and self-serving, and the claims of competing "experts" may be difficult to evaluate.

Insufficient research and development. Because the benefits of research and development (R&D) tend to accrue to other businesses that imitate any successful breakthrough, many businesses are reluctant to invest in R&D, particularly basic R&D.

Insufficient business capital. Many of the regulations that pertain to capital markets inhibit loans to business ventures that have high expected returns but high risks.

Insufficient training. Many businesses are reluctant to provide training because of concerns that well-trained workers will move to other employers. Small businesses have difficulty obtaining funds to invest in training.

Insufficient land. Because land use is heavily regulated by zoning, and because a single landowner may have the power to prevent the assembly of parcels for a sizable business development, businesses may not always be able to obtain the land that they need, at a price they can afford, for construction or expansion.

Insufficient public infrastructure. Because of the difficulty of fully charging all users of infrastructure, jurisdictions are sometimes reluctant to provide needed infrastructure improvements.

Regulatory constraints. Business regulations, such as environmental laws, may be inefficient in a number of respects: the overall level of regulation may be excessive, the regulation may be too inflexible to respond to specific needs, or the regulations may not be understood by businesses.

Programs designed to correct market failures—that is, to provide inputs more efficiently—are a valuable economic development tool. Assuming that program benefits exceed costs, such efforts are an efficient means of assisting businesses.

Specific types of economic development programs

This section discusses several different types of economic development programs: business attraction, business retention, new business development, high-tech, and development that focuses on specific types of land.

Business attraction

One of the chief goals of many local economic development programs is to attract a large branch plant that will pay good wages and have a sizable multiplier effect. At least in the short run, however, few communities will achieve this goal. In the United States during any given year, an estimated 1,500 major expansions or relocations are being pursued by an estimated 15,000 economic development organizations—a 10:1 ratio.[21]

Although the use of direct incentives to attract branch plants is the method that receives the most public attention, successful attraction involves a great deal more. Available land and appropriate infrastructure are always critical location factors. In fact, some of the most successful local economic development organizations have based their success on their control of desirable land (see the sidebar below).

Battle Creek Unlimited Battle Creek Unlimited (BCU), a private nonprofit organization sponsored by the city of Battle Creek, Michigan, was set up in 1971 to help revitalize a city economy that, during the 1960s and 1970s, lost nearly 10,000 jobs from its export base. The phasing out of the Fort Custer military base, which was complete by 1968, was one of the most serious economic losses.

The city of Battle Creek acquired more than three thousand acres of the former base and turned over management of the property to BCU. BCU then used its control of this developable land, together with long-term efforts to promote Battle Creek to existing local businesses and to new prospects from throughout the world, to attract more than seventy companies and seven thousand jobs to what is now the largest industrial park in Michigan.

A considerable part of the investment was made by Japanese auto suppliers.

The success has created a lasting financial base for BCU, which is largely supported by tax increment financing on increases in property values at Fort Custer and other targeted sites. Perhaps equally important, BCU's success has led to long-term political support and stable management, which rarely characterize local economic development organizations.

Sources: Based on James Hettinger and Janette Burland, "Battle Creek Military Base Conversion Process," *Economic Development Commentary* 19, no. 2 (1995): 18–22; and on interviews conducted by the author. The Economic Development Commentary is a publication of the International Economic Development Council (IEDC). Formed through a merger of the American Economic Development Council and the Council for Urban Economic Development, IEDC is the world's largest professional membership organization for economic developers, serving more than 4,500 members. For more information, visit www.iedconline.org or write to 734 15th Street, N.W., Suite 900, Washington, DC 20005.

The availability of labor with appropriate skills at a reasonable wage rate is also important. Modest variations in wages or skills can offset the largest direct incentives. For example, the most recent data suggest that outside enterprise zones, the median state and local incentive offered to a typical firm is equivalent to $218 in annual wages per worker; inside enterprise zones, the figure is $526. The highest incentive offers, which in some state enterprise zones eliminate almost all state and local business taxes, amount to $1,566 in annual wages per worker.[22] Even this incentive, however, could be entirely offset if labor in a competing jurisdiction were $0.79 per hour cheaper or offered the equivalent of $0.79 per hour in the form of higher productivity. (A subsidy of $1,566 annually per worker, divided by 2,000 annual work hours, is equal to $0.78 per hour of work.)

Less tangible advantages, such as the ability to solve problems for business prospects or to provide those prospects with good information, can also have substantial effects on business location decisions. Large corporations are often interested in finding a location for a plant and moving into production as quickly as possible. Local economic development agencies often help businesses save time by providing reliable information about available sites and smoothing the permitting process. According to an ICMA survey, 72 percent of local governments offered zoning and permit assistance to attract businesses, 39 percent offered one-stop permit issuance, and 23 percent offered "regulatory flexibility."[23]

Marketing Marketing experts advise communities to develop a marketing approach that emphasizes some special comparative advantage that is relevant to business needs.[24] And since large corporations locating a new plant use site consultants more than 50 percent of the time, communities should market to site consultants as well as to business prospects.[25] The ICMA survey notes that communities use a range of marketing techniques, including promotional materials, Web sites, advertising, direct mail, and visits to potential prospects.[26] (Web sites have probably become even more important since the survey was undertaken; consultants and businesses now expect communities to have reliable and relevant information available on the Web.)[27]

Direct incentives Communities continue to devote significant resources to direct incentives, and these incentives do affect business locations, albeit at a high price per job created. The national total for all state and local economic development incentives is probably more than $17 billion per year.[28] About two-thirds of these incentives are financial (tax incentives, loans, grants, and loan guarantees); the other one-third consists of customized job training (21 percent of the incentive package for the typical firm and state) and special provision of infrastructure (13 percent of the incentive package).[29] Seventy-four percent of local governments offer infrastructure improvements as an incentive, 36 percent offer training support, and 16 percent offer employee screening.[30] (Training incentives tend to be state funded but are delivered by local community colleges.) An increasingly common (and expensive) incentive is the provision of land for free or at a reduced price (offered by 39 percent of communities), or even free or reduced-price buildings (11 percent of communities).[31]

Tax increment financing The increasing use of TIF, which can be viewed as either a financial or an infrastructure incentive, is an important trend. Under TIF, the increased tax revenues (increments) generated by development are not dedicated to the general fund but to special services directly related to a designated improvement district. TIF is often used to finance new infrastructure in the TIF district, in which case bonds are issued to pay for the infrastructure, and the revenue increases that result from development are used to service the bonds. An important feature of TIF is that, typically, the TIF district captures all tax increases that would have accrued to all overlapping taxing districts, including school districts, the county government, and any special-purpose governmental units. This is a fiscal advantage for the sponsoring local government, but it may create ill will, which has led some areas to develop a formula for sharing TIF revenues. TIF is authorized in forty-eight states, and according to an ICMA survey, 50 percent of communities have used it.[32]

Locational impact of incentives   Research suggests that incentives are likely to have modest but possibly important effects on business location decisions.[33] For example, a 10 percent reduction in state and local business taxes will, in the long run, increase business activity and employment in a state or metropolitan area, or the number of new plants that locate in the state or metropolitan area, by about 2 or 3 percent. Calculations based on these figures indicate that each new job created in a state or metropolitan area requires a net loss of about $7,000 annually in business tax revenue.[34] This figure takes into account both (1) revenue gained from induced business activity and (2) revenue lost through reductions in taxes on business activity that would have occurred anyway.

Assuming that economic development incentives affect the targeted firms about as much as reductions in business taxes affect all firms, economic development incentives should, therefore, also have a net cost per job created of about $7,000 per year. This is a large cost, however, because even though the typical job will pay much more than $7,000 per year, the employment benefits from creating a job will typically be much less than what a job pays. For a worker who was already employed, the new wages will probably be close to the wages of the previous job. And even an unemployed worker would have been engaged in activities that carried a monetary value of considerably more than zero; when that worker takes a new job, the forgone opportunity to engage in those activities offsets much of the wage benefits of the job.

Because different locations within the same metropolitan area are often virtually interchangeable from a business perspective, offering similar access to labor, resources, and markets, location incentives have much larger effects within a single metropolitan area than among different states or metropolitan areas. Available evidence suggests that, within a metropolitan area, the effects of incentives are likely to be so large that, assuming that no other local communities opted to compete with the offer, a community offering incentives could gain tax revenue on net:[35] that is, enough additional tax revenue to more than offset the incentive costs. In practice, however, all communities in a metropolitan area are likely to offer incentives—a practice that, at an annual cost of $7,000 per job created, has only modest effects on the area's overall business activity and provides no competitive advantage to any one community. (A later section of this chapter considers the implications of this situation for organizing economic development.)

Timing of incentives   One way to increase the cost-effectiveness of an incentive is to offer more of the incentive up front. Evidence indicates that the executives who make location decisions have annual discount rates of 12 percent, in real terms.[36] Thus, for the average executive seeking to locate a new plant, go into production quickly, and meet profit targets, the portion of a property tax abatement that reduces property taxes ten years from now is close to irrelevant; what matters is the plant's profitability in the short and medium term. Not only do up-front incentives have a greater impact on location decisions, but they also compel local government managers to deal with the fiscal costs of incentives now, instead of passing those costs on to their successors.[37]

Clawback agreements A clawback agreement is a legally binding arrangement that affords some protection to a local government that has provided a firm with up-front incentives. Under such an agreement, the local government will recover a portion of the incentive if the company relocates, closes the plant, or does not meet other performance goals. Between 1992 and 2002, the number of states with clawback laws for some economic development incentives increased from nine to seventeen; it is generally believed that local governments have also increased their use of clawbacks.[38] According to the ICMA survey cited above, 59 percent of local governments "always" require a performance agreement as a condition for providing business incentives, and 30 percent "sometimes" require a performance agreement.[39] Even with a clawback agreement, however, some incentive costs may be unrecoverable. One way to address this problem is to shift the incentive mix toward training and infrastructure incentives, which will remain behind if the company leaves and will help the area attract new business activity.

Targeted incentives Another option is for local governments to use incentives more selectively—that is, only in cases where the benefits are likely to be great. For example, local governments may choose to restrict the use of large incentives to periods when local unemployment is high. Economic development agencies can also target businesses that are likely to offer the greatest economic benefits: firms that pay higher wages and are likely to hire local workers who would otherwise be unemployed, and firms that are more likely to use local suppliers, with consequently higher multiplier effects. Businesses that offer the lowest environmental costs or the greatest environmental benefits, such as those that use brownfield sites or create minimal pollution, can also be targeted.

Some communities attempt to restrict the use of incentives to situations in which the incentive will be decisive in tipping the location decision. Although this approach makes sense in theory, it is difficult to apply in practice. To begin with, the business has much more information about its location options and profitability than the community does, and unless the community engages in a large number of such negotiations with firms or has help from a state agency that often engages in such negotiations, it will be next to impossible to determine when an incentive will be decisive. Nevertheless, in some states, firms are ineligible for large discretionary incentive programs unless they can document the value of the incentive in the decision-making process. For example, firms that wish to participate in the Michigan Economic Growth Authority tax credit program, which provides a large refundable tax credit, must present financial data showing that the credit is needed to tip the balance in favor of a Michigan site over an out-of-state site.[40]

Business retention

A focus on business retention makes sense for several reasons. First, when existing local businesses expand, contract, or close, such decisions can have huge effects on a local economy's export base. During a typical one-year period, there are "gross flows" of job creation and job destruction in manufacturing equal to about one-tenth of total jobs in manufacturing; that is, plant contractions and closings are about one-tenth of total manufacturing employment, and plant openings and expansions are also about one-tenth of total manufacturing employment.[41] Of the jobs added through plant openings and expansions, about 85 percent are added through expansions in existing firms. Many of these expansions and contractions are large: during a typical one-year period, almost three-fifths of the manufacturing jobs created through expansions occur in firms that are increasing employment by 25 percent or more; similarly, about two-thirds of the job losses occur in firms that are decreasing employment by 25 percent or more.[42] Thus, an economic development program that affects even a modest number of decisions by local businesses can have significant effects on local employment.

Second, local businesses are strongly linked to the local area: to the local labor force, local suppliers, and other local institutions. A community that focuses on attraction programs risks wasting economic development resources on efforts to draw firms that have no compelling reason to locate there; retention programs, in contrast, take advantage of the fact that firms are *already* in the community and therefore have a number of reasons to remain. Moreover, because existing firms are likely to use more local suppliers and to know better how to hire locally, an output increase in a local firm is likely to have larger multiplier effects on the local economy, more employment benefits for local residents, and more favorable fiscal benefits (because of lower in-migration) than a comparable increase in output for an attracted firm.

Retention programs involve getting information on the needs of local businesses and then undertaking government actions that will better meet those needs—and thereby increase fiscal and employment benefits. The degree of direct government involvement in business retention varies: at the low end of the "activism" spectrum are governments that undertake business visitation and surveying programs and make some effort to improve government services, tax policies, or regulations in response to what is learned in these visits. Governments that take a somewhat more activist approach may engage in business and manufacturing extension programs that involve more direct, customized services to individual businesses. The most activist governments take a strategic role, working directly with business clusters and networks to plan the area's economic future. All three approaches can be pursued simultaneously and often overlap in practice.

Business visitation and surveying   Business visitation and surveying programs gather information through mail surveys, visits conducted by trained volunteers, visits conducted by paid economic development staff, or some combination of all three.[43] The surveys and visits may include all local businesses or target sectors of particular interest, such as businesses above a particular size threshold, export-base businesses, or businesses in a particular cluster (clusters are discussed further in a later section of this chapter).

Visits and surveys typically focus on a broad range of issues, such as the local business climate; the quality or availability of local labor; and the need for help with exporting, government procurement, financing, or local regulations. To give the community a more business-friendly image, economic development agencies often take care to ensure that such efforts are well publicized. However, if such programs are to have more than a short-term effect on public relations, effective and timely follow-up is essential. Local economic development staff must not only address the individual problems of specific businesses but also use the information to identify local policies that need to be reconsidered.

Business visitation and surveying programs are common. In 74 percent of communities, local government representatives call on local businesses in order to improve business retention. Sixty percent of local governments survey local businesses to improve business retention, and 22 percent use an ombudsman program to help local businesses overcome problems with local regulations or other issues.[44]

Extension services   Extension services provide low-cost, short- or longer-term consulting, mostly to small and medium-sized enterprises, and may also make referrals to private consulting firms. The advice covers a wide range of business issues, from technology improvement to workforce development, management improvement, and marketing. As noted earlier, private markets often fail to provide businesses—particularly small and medium-sized businesses—with access to reliable information. Extension services can help correct this particular market failure, both by playing the role of trusted advisors and by serving as honest brokers who can help businesses select private consulting services.

Because the necessary level of staff expertise is beyond what a small community can provide on its own, extension services tend to be offered by state or regional institutions. Since 1989, extension services have been funded by the Manufacturing Extension Partnership (MEP) of the National Institute for Standards and Technology. Typically, extension services are also partially supported through user fees, which provide a built-in "market test" of the usefulness of the services.

Evidence suggests that manufacturing extension services are effective in improving business productivity. In one study that asked clients of MEP-funded programs how the assistance had affected their firm, about 64 percent of respondents reported productivity improvements; business clients also reported that the assistance had led to average sales increases of $143,000 and average cost savings of $50,000.[45] In addition, a study of the seven regional Industrial Resource Centers (IRCs) funded by the state of Pennsylvania compared the productivity growth rate of assisted and unassisted firms and found that the annual rate of productivity growth in assisted firms was between 3.6 and 5.0 percentage points higher than that in unassisted firms.[46]

Pennsylvania's Industrial Resource Centers   Begun in 1988 by the state government, Pennsylvania's seven regional Industrial Resource Centers (IRCs) are funded by the state government, the federal government (through the Manufacturing Extension Partnership program), and client fees. Each regional center provides small- and medium-sized manufacturers with direct advice or third-party referrals to assist with a wide variety of issues, including human resources, business management, business systems, product quality, process improvements, and market development. The seven IRCs have more than a thousand "engagements" annually. Some involve services provided to more than one firm at a time—for example, training sessions on ISO 9000 standards.

Of the assisted manufacturers, 86 percent have fewer than 250 employees. Half the "interventions" require less than eight hours of IRC staff time; one-quarter require more than forty hours. (More IRC staff time is required when the firm's problems cannot be readily addressed by private consultants or other third parties.) Sixty percent of IRC interventions involve third parties—typically consultants, but also universities, community colleges, and state and local economic development organizations.

Source: Based on Eric Oldsman and Jack Russell, "The Industrial Resource Center Program: Assessing the Record and Charting the Future" (unpublished report prepared for the Commonwealth of Pennsylvania, 1999).

The design of extension services affects the types of economic development benefits these services can deliver. For example, when firms increase their productivity by improving their management practices or their use of technology, they may need fewer employees. In Pennsylvania, for example, although the annual rate of growth in output for assisted firms was between 1.9 and 4.1 percentage points higher than for unassisted firms, this increase was smaller than the increase in productivity: one possible conclusion is that, because of the assistance, employment was lower than it would otherwise have been. However, since the study did not account for the effects of IRCs on the survival or relocation of assisted firms, this conclusion may be misleading; if some of the firms would otherwise have gone out of business or left the state, then the overall effects on employment in assisted firms may have been positive. In addition, the increase in output in assisted firms has multiplier effects on the local economy, increasing employment among local suppliers and retailers.[47] Since, however, productivity improvement at assisted firms may somewhat reduce the benefits of extension services for the unemployed, the case for such programs may have to rely more on their fiscal benefits (positive, according to the study of Pennsylvania's IRCs) and on the value of the wage increases brought about by productivity improvements.

Other types of extension services may provide greater benefits for local unemployed workers. Some services, such as Cleveland's WIRE-Net program, combine advice to local businesses with efforts to link those businesses to local unemployed workers. The assistance package provided by WIRE-Net includes both help with technology and management and access to a "job-candidate bank" of local residents who are qualified for entry-level jobs.

WIRE-Net WIRE-Net (Westside Industrial Retention and Expansion Network) was started in 1988 by four Cleveland community development corporations to improve the retention of manufacturers, especially those with fewer than a hundred employees, in Cleveland's Westside neighborhood, and to increase the employment of neighborhood residents in those firms. WIRE-Net is funded by the city of Cleveland, the state of Ohio, federal agencies, local foundations, charitable donations, and membership fees from 150 Westside manufacturers.

WIRE-Net targets the three hundred Westside manufacturers that, together, employ more than ten thousand workers. Services include direct consulting and referrals on business management, assistance in finding new sites in the neighborhood, and lobbying efforts to obtain improved infrastructure and services.

WIRE-Net's Hire Locally program helps firms find qualified local residents for job vacancies. WIRE-Net also runs the Precision Machining Training program, which helps local residents acquire the skills that local manufacturers need. During a typical year, WIRE-Net assists about one in twenty of the area's manufacturers, that together employ about one in twelve of the area's manufacturing employees. Each year, the number of placements associated with its job-placement and training programs is equivalent to about 1 percent of the area's manufacturing employment; most placements fill preexisting openings. According to WIRE-Net staff and area firms, of all the forms of assistance WIRE-Net offers, the most valuable to firms are its Hire Locally program and its efforts to help manufacturers find new sites and get approval to build on them.

Source: Based on Neil S. Mayer, *Saving and Creating Good Jobs: A Study of Industrial Retention and Expansion Programs* (Washington, D.C.: Center for Community Change, 1998), 17; updated on the basis of information provided on the WIRE-Net Web site, www.wire-net.org.

Networks and clusters   Networks and clusters are both currently "hot" terms in local economic development policy. A network is a formal arrangement between firms in a local economy that agree to cooperate for their mutual benefit; for example, firms in the same industry may jointly sponsor a training program at a local community college, or microenterprises may share marketing or shipping expenses. A cluster is created when a number of firms in a given area (and their suppliers) specialize in a particular industry or related industries, and both information and workers flow freely among the firms, usually without any formal arrangements.[48] This flow is not the only distinguishing feature of a cluster but is an incentive for its continuation and growth: firms want to take advantage of the local economy's ample and qualified supply of specific types of local labor and of good local information about technical developments in the industry.

Regional economic analysis has traditionally theorized that the specialization of industries (e.g., autos in Detroit, software in Silicon Valley) occurs because the concentration of many firms in the same industry in the same local economy offers enormous cost advantages—which, in turn, derive from better access to specialized labor, specialized suppliers, and specialized information about industry innovations. If a local economic development agency lacks sufficient economic expertise to identify local clusters on its own, such clusters can be identified by experienced consultants.

Clusters normally occur on their own, but advocates of "cluster policy" argue that by thinking in terms of clusters, local economic development organizations can develop policy interventions that improve on what happens naturally. First, and by far most important, are efforts to increase the pool of "medium-skilled" labor for the cluster. Low-skilled labor is available in most locations, and high-skilled labor is mobile, but medium-skilled labor is often both scarce and less mobile. The availability of such labor is one of the most important reasons that clusters occur, and limits on this availability are an important constraint on the growth and development of a cluster.[49]

Although government has traditionally played a role in the provision of education and training, such efforts are not always designed to address the particular needs of local employers, including those that are in clusters.[50] An economic development agency can address this problem by improving the communication between local educational institutions and local clusters to help ensure that the skills in demand are well taught. In addition, a training program that is designed to support a cluster can target some of the training slots to people who are difficult to employ, which will increase the employment benefits of the cluster. To sustain employers' confidence in the initiative, training programs that seek to include the difficult-to-employ must ensure that program graduates can meet rigorous standards.

Public investments in local research institutions offer another means of improving a cluster's competitiveness. For example, an industry cluster may benefit if a center of excellence in a field related to that industry is created at a local public university. (Funding such a center of excellence would require successful political lobbying of the state government, which might in turn require the local economic development agency to persuade all the local political and business groups to make this project their top priority.)

Some clusters may benefit from formal networking arrangements, which can be facilitated by local economic development organizations. In addition to advocating for improved training programs and support for local research, such networks may cooperate on marketing or on efforts to address tax or regulatory issues.

Finally, various economic development programs, including those designed to attract businesses or to foster the development of new firms, may encourage

Mine Maintenance Training Program

Since the late 1980s, Great Basin College and a cluster of gold-mining companies in northeastern Nevada, the third-largest gold-producing area in the world, have run the Mine Maintenance Training Program, a cooperative education and training program. The industry has often been short of workers skilled in diesel technology, industrial plant technology, electrical technology, and welding. Under the program, the Manpower Training Cooperative (a nonprofit coordinating body of area mining companies) provides scholarships to prospective employees, typically high school seniors. Students work full time for a summer at one of the participating companies and are then awarded a scholarship to Great Basin College, where they take an intensive, year-long course of study in a mining-related field. The one-year associates' degree program brings students into the workplace in less time than was previously the case and responds to the cluster's need for more rapid training.

Program instructors have mining-related backgrounds, and industry committees advise on course design. The mining-industry cluster has also donated mining-related equipment to the college to help support the program. During a typical year, 85 percent of program graduates get a program-related job. Surveys of cluster firms report high satisfaction with the skills of program graduates.

Source: Based on U.S. Department of Agriculture, Fund for Rural America, "Great Basin College, Elko, Nevada: Mine Maintenance Training Program," a case study available at www.rtsinc.org/benchmark/profiles/profile16.php4. Printed with permission of Regional Technology Strategies, Inc.

---

the formation of new clusters.[51] For example, if a current industry cluster is declining and there is no feasible way to arrest the decline, a local economic development agency may focus on attracting new branch plants or new start-ups that will use the types of workers who have been left behind by the old cluster; this process may eventually lead to the formation of a new cluster.

The challenge in devising cluster policy is to minimize the risk of being wrong. It is difficult to predict the future of local clusters in the long term. Perhaps a particular local cluster is doomed, and specialized investments in training and research will be wasted. Perhaps the new cluster that the local economic development agency is trying to create will not be viable. Ideally, cluster investments should be adaptable to the future needs of the local economy even if the targeted cluster (actual or potential) does not develop as expected.

New business development

Claims that entrepreneurship creates a large proportion of new jobs have been exaggerated,[52] but it is true that during a typical one-year period, the number of jobs created by new firms with fewer than twenty employees is typically equivalent to slightly less than 2 percent of existing employment. (That is, the gross increase in the number of jobs attributable to new firms is equivalent to about 2 percent of existing employment. The *net* increase or decrease in total local jobs will depend on plant openings, closings, expansions, and contractions.) But will increases in small-business start-ups expand the local economy?

Because the sales of small businesses are disproportionately local, the sales of new small businesses tend to reduce the sales of other local businesses, with little net effect on the size of the local economy. However, even if a new small business sells locally, it may still expand the local economy if its sales replace imports. New small businesses may also expand the local economy by hiring people who have a harder time finding work; this is one rationale for aid to new, minority-owned businesses, which are often more likely to hire members of minority groups—who, because of discrimination, would otherwise have trouble finding work.

Support for new small businesses may also be justified as an investment in human capital: when people become entrepreneurs, they develop skills that may be useful not only in managing a new business but also in many other jobs. Government support for investment in entrepreneurship has the same rationales as government support for education—for example, that most people cannot borrow enough to pay the large up-front costs of education. Initiatives that support the development of entrepreneurial skills have benefits that go beyond increases in wages and income. Even though becoming an entrepreneur does not necessarily increase income, it may offer nonpecuniary benefits, such as the enjoyment that comes with "being your own boss." These nonpecuniary benefits may justify a small-business development program that increases successful small-business start-ups without increasing the incomes of participants. For entrepreneurs who are members of disadvantaged groups, public support may be justified as a means of increasing social equity. Relations between diverse racial and ethnic groups may improve if members of all groups feel that they have a reasonable chance of achieving positions of leadership and prestige, such as becoming successful entrepreneurs.

Programs for new small businesses include entrepreneurship training, small-business advice, business incubators, and capital market programs.

Entrepreneurship training   Entrepreneurship training programs, which are often aimed at members of disadvantaged groups (women, minorities, unemployed workers) provide training in the development of business, marketing, and financing plans. A rigorous, landmark evaluation study suggests that these programs increase business start-ups. In this study, which examined the effects of entrepreneurship training for people receiving unemployment benefits, recipients were invited to attend orientations that explained the entrepreneurship training program. The 4 percent of recipients who expressed interest in such training were then randomly assigned to either a group that received training or a control group that did not. Sixty percent of the group that received training gained some self-employment experience, versus 44 percent of the control group.[53] Because the results for the two groups should have been the same, on average, the difference of 16 percentage points can very likely be attributed to the program.

It is important to note, however, that if the entrepreneurship program had claimed credit for all business activity associated with the effort—a common practice of program managers—it would have claimed credit for the full 60 percent of the treatment group that entered self-employment, even though most of those in this subgroup would have started up a business anyway, as is shown by what happened to the control group. Moreover, the study did not investigate whether the additional entrepreneurs boosted their local economies.

Small-business advice   In the United States, small-business advice is most prominently provided by 58 small business development centers (SBDCs) and their more than 1,000 subcenters and "service locations." In fiscal year 2002, these centers and subcenters received $88 million (about half their funding) from the federal Small Business Administration (SBA); the other half came from state and local sources.[54] SBDCs counsel small businesses on business development issues and provide training in start-up and operations. Annually, about 250,000 clients (people or businesses) receive individual counseling from SBDCs, about three-fourths of whom already own existing businesses; the other one-fourth of counseling clients are those who hope to start a business.

SBDCs also provide about 330,000 clients annually with business training. Of these, 70 percent do not operate a business, and the other 30 percent already own a business.[55]

Studies that have asked clients about the impact of SBDC services suggest that the services are useful.[56] Even if SBDCs do help their clients, however, further research is needed to determine whether SBDCs boost the local economy (e.g., by reducing local imports, increasing local exports, or increasing the hiring of difficult-to-employ workers). Local governments can strengthen the effectiveness of SBDCs by providing funding and encouraging centers to focus on services that will provide greater employment and fiscal benefits to the local area.

Incubators   Business incubators provide start-up firms with cheap space, shared office support, and business development advice. In 1980 there were 12 business incubators in the United States; in 2002 there were an estimated 950.[57] Eighty-five percent of incubators are nonprofit and the other 15 percent are for-profit; the nonprofit incubators provide more intense services, including business counseling and management and technical assistance.[58] Most nonprofit incubators require operating subsidies. Forty percent of incubators focus on technology-oriented businesses, 30 percent are mixed use, and the remainder have other areas of focus.[59]

Evidence suggests that incubators improve their clients' performance. In a 1997 study, about two-thirds of incubator clients said that the incubator assistance had been "important" or "very important" to their business success. However, finding firms whose performance can be compared with that of incubator firms has been difficult.[60] Moreover, even if incubators help their tenants, it is unclear whether the assistance boosts the local economy or simply reduces employment in other (nonincubator) firms.

Capital market programs   Capital market programs use several means to increase the supply of capital to new small businesses. Direct loans to small businesses from local revolving loan funds (RLFs) are the most prevalent (and growing) method. As of 1999, the RLF industry had an estimated $8 billion in assets.[61] Many RLFs were originally capitalized with grants from federal agencies, such as the Economic Development Administration or the Department of Housing and Urban Development, but RLFs are increasingly likely to receive investments from state governments and banks.

Sometimes new nonprofit or for-profit organizations are created specifically to provide capital to new small businesses. For example, business development financial institutions (BDFIs), which provide loans to or invest in new small businesses, are supported with deposits or investments from foundations or the government; the investors and depositors in BDFIs are willing to accept below-market rates of return.[62]

New small businesses can also gain access to capital through guarantees or subsidies that encourage private, for-profit financial institutions to expand their loans to small businesses. The most long-standing example of this approach is the SBA's 7(a) program, which guarantees loans made by financial institutions to small businesses. Under Capital Access Programs, a more recent and growing approach, twenty states and two city governments subsidize "loan-loss reserve" funds for banks that lend to businesses with above-market risk.[63]

Capital market programs also differ in the type of financing provided. Most programs focus on increasing the availability of loans, but some increase the availability of venture capital and other forms of equity capital.[64] Some capital market programs are publicly funded and managed; others place public funds into privately managed venture capital organizations.

As is the case with other small-business programs, it is unclear whether increased activity on the part of assisted businesses decreases the activity of other local businesses. Another important issue is whether capital market programs are succeeding in targeting projects that are too risky to receive private-market financing, but not so risky as to outweigh the potential benefits (specifically, increasing the size of the local economy or providing greater opportunities for entrepreneurship).[65]

Ensuring that capital market programs succeed in targeting the appropriate projects requires skill in acquiring information about individual businesses and making sound judgments. And even when the staff have relevant prior experience and skills, political pressures may lead governments to avoid all risk (who wants to take the political heat for a loss?) or to finance businesses that have political clout. Although the establishment of independent financial entities and the provision of subsidies to private sector financing sources will reduce the potential for political pressure, getting the incentives right—that is, encouraging the program managers to support the right kind of loan or investment, in which above-market risks are justified by social benefits—remains a challenge. At worst, private organizations can use financing subsidies and guarantees to transfer the costs of their bad judgments to the public. Capital Access Programs, which subsidize risk but only to a limited extent, have probably been the most successful at getting the incentives right.

Capital Access Programs   Since the first Capital Access Program (CAP) was begun by the state of Michigan in 1986, CAPs have spread to twenty states and two cities. CAPs are designed to encourage banks to make business loans that are not excessively risky but that would be considered too risky under normal lending rules. When a bank makes a business loan under a CAP, it contributes 3 to 7 percent of the value of the loan (the actual percentage varies depending on CAP rules in that particular state or city and on the bank's perception of the loan's riskiness), usually charged as points to the business borrower, to a reserve fund that can be used only to cover losses from the bank's own CAP loans; the government contributes a matching amount to the fund.

Under a government loan guarantee, loan losses are absorbed by the government. Under a CAP, however, the government's exposure is limited to its reserve fund contributions, and the bank is liable for any losses that exceed the amount in the bank's loan-loss reserve fund. In a competitive banking market, bankable business borrowers will not seek loans through a CAP (because such borrowers have the option of obtaining loans that do not carry the extra points). Thus, riskier businesses make up the market for CAP loans, but because of the liability associated with CAP loans, banks will be reluctant to make loans with an expected loss rate greater than whatever percentage has been set aside for that loan in the loan-loss reserve, which varies from program to program and with the bank's decisions but is less than 14 percent.

Through CAPs, banks are making more than $200 million in loans per year, with cumulative losses of 3.7 percent of cumulative loan volume, which is greater than normal bank loss rates; this figure indicates that CAPs are inducing banks to make riskier loans but that those loans are not exceeding the program's targeted risk range. Public contributions to CAPs are only 4.3 percent of cumulative loan volume, which means that each government dollar leverages $23 of additional business loans.

Source: Based on Alan Berube, *Capital Access Programs: A Summary of Nationwide Performance* (Washington, D.C.: U.S. Department of the Treasury, January 2001).

Largely because of the difficulty of identifying companies that do not receive financing that are comparable to businesses that do receive financing, no rigorous evaluation of capital market programs has been undertaken. The financing process is designed to select businesses that have a better chance of succeeding. This selection process relies on private and confidential information that is unlikely to be available to the researcher—and that therefore cannot be used to match the financed businesses with a control group. The more adept the financing process is at using private information to pick out successful companies, the more difficult the job facing researchers in trying to find a matching "control" group of firms with which the financed firms can be compared.

Some evaluation results, however, are positive. Firms that receive SBA loan guarantees grow faster than comparable firms that do not receive such guarantees.[66] RLFs have a default rate of 5 to 15 percent, considerably higher than the default rate on normal bank loans to businesses, which suggests that the industry does indeed serve firms that would be unlikely to receive bank financing.[67] On the other hand, although the rate of employment growth is higher in counties where RLFs have higher rates of growth than in counties where RLFs have lower rates of growth, the small magnitude of the effect implies that fewer than one in twelve RLF loans encourages new business activity in a given county.[68] Case studies of BDFIs suggest that these organizations may promote modest employment growth in depressed communities.[69] Data on Capital Access Programs suggest that these programs provide financing for projects that carry above-market risk but are not excessively risky.[70]

High-technology development

High-technology industries are usually defined as those whose goods, services, or production processes involve intensive use of new scientific and technical knowledge.[71] Many local governments are interested in high-tech development: in a survey of local government administrators, more than half described high-tech as an area of focus for economic development.[72]

A focus on high-technology makes some sense because it is expected to be a high-growth area. According to the U.S. Bureau of Labor Statistics, future high-tech employment growth is expected to be over 50 percent greater than average employment growth for all industries, and high-tech firms' growth in output is expected to be more than twice the all-industry average.[73] If one includes the jobs that will be created in supplier industries when high-tech expands, the growth of high-tech industries can be expected to generate a little more than one-quarter of net new jobs in the U.S. economy. Wages in high-tech industries are also higher than the all-industry average, although high-tech firms also have higher educational requirements. Finally, many, although not all, high-tech manufacturing firms are less polluting than non-high-tech manufacturing firms.

How can local economic development agencies encourage high-tech development? All the economic development techniques described in this chapter are applicable to high-tech. Recruitment programs can target high-tech industries. There are currently more than 130 research parks in the United States, which is a targeted way to provide appropriate land for high-tech firms as part of an attraction strategy.[74] Much of the advice provided by extension services is technology related and would be useful to small high-tech firms. Many clusters are high-tech. Policies to foster new business growth can focus on high-tech: 40 percent of existing business incubators have a high-tech focus.[75]

Nevertheless, a number of significant features distinguish high-tech development from general economic development efforts. First, because high-tech growth depends heavily on new knowledge, high-technology industries require ready access to the research conducted at universities. Second, high-tech industries depend on staff who have advanced skills—yet another reason that the quality of local universities is particularly important to high-tech firms. Third, in order to attract highly skilled workers from elsewhere, high-tech firms must be able to offer a high quality of life.[76] Fourth, high-tech industries require special infrastructure, such as broadband telecommunications services. Finally, high-tech goods or services frequently require a longer development time than non-high-tech goods or services, so high-tech development requires access to "patient capital"—for example, loans with more generous repayment terms, or equity investors who are willing to wait longer in order to cash out with a large return.

Clearly, many of the sources of high-tech growth require expensive investments that go beyond what most local governments can do on their own. Short of making such investments, local governments can promote high-tech development by

Analyzing the performance of the firms in local high-tech clusters to determine whether the local area has any comparative advantage as a basis for future development. Not every community should imitate Silicon Valley, and most that try will fail.

Encouraging state governments to develop research centers at local universities that will support technology transfer to local industries or high-tech clusters.

Improving the kinds of amenities that are important to potential employees of high-tech firms. For example, such employees may be drawn to an area if local high schools have a math and science center for academically talented students.

Working with nearby universities and other institutions to attract venture capital to the area. Such efforts might include lobbying for state funding to provide equity investments to the local high-tech cluster, or setting up programs that link local high-tech ventures with wealthy local investors.

In rural areas, working with other institutions to determine whether, by aggregating the demands of various users, the region can create sufficient demand so that telecommunications companies will invest in broadband infrastructure. (The alternative of direct public investment in such infrastructure is expensive—and, given rapidly changing telecommunications technology, risky.)

Instituting training programs for entry-level jobs in high-tech firms and their suppliers. High-tech industries tend to employ many in-migrants or highly educated local residents, so special efforts to target entry-level jobs to local residents will broaden the employment benefits associated with the high-tech firms.

Few evaluations have been done of strategies for high-tech development. One evaluation, which focused on Ben Franklin Technology Partners (BFTP), a system of regional centers in Pennsylvania, found that the start-up firms that had been assisted by BFTP had a higher rate of employment growth, by five employees per year, than did similar, unassisted firms.[77] Interviews conducted as part of a case study of San Diego offer evidence that San Diego's high-tech development efforts may have been responsible for some, but not all, of San Diego's gain during the 1990s of more than 40,000 high-tech jobs.[78] In the case of both BFTP and San Diego, the high-tech strategy was comprehensive and included university research, technology transfer, business advice to start-up companies, and efforts to increase the availability of venture capital (see sidebars on next page). Comprehensive high-tech strategies may be more effective than a single program.

Ben Franklin Technology Partners

Ben Franklin Technology Partners (BFTP), a program created by the state of Pennsylvania in 1982, uses state funds to promote the creation of high-tech jobs in Pennsylvania. The funds are distributed through four regional centers (known as "partners"). BFTP provides high-tech companies with financing for research and development, and with business and technical advice and referrals. BFTP also provides funding for regional infrastructure and services that are thought to support high-tech companies, including

business incubators; research parks; university-based, technology-related research centers; and venture capital funds and other financing vehicles.

Two-thirds of the firms receiving financing have twenty or fewer employees. Assistance is provided to a wide range of industries, from high-tech manufacturing firms to companies providing high-tech services, such as software.

Source: Based on Nexus Associates, *A Record of Achievement: The Economic Impact of the Ben Franklin Partnership* (Harrisburg: Commonwealth of Pennsylvania, October 1999).

San Diego's high-technology policies

Despite defense cutbacks in the late 1980s and early 1990s, San Diego experienced rapid growth of high-tech employment in the 1990s, particularly in small, start-up firms and in the biotech, pharmaceutical, and communications industries. This growth may be attributed, in part, to local leadership, which helped to create a variety of regional services to promote high-tech. This leadership came from the University of California, San Diego (UCSD), and from local governments, foundations, economic developers, and chief executive officers of local firms.

Among other important actions, UCSD funded the establishment of several research centers and succeeded in attracting well-known professors in science and technology. UCSD also created CONNECT, a fee-based extension program that promotes networking activities for the high-tech sector,

including seminars on start-up skills, management, and marketing, and opportunities for entrepreneurs to present their business plans to venture capitalists or other investors. Another regional service that promotes high-tech is the San Diego chapter of the MIT Enterprise Forum, which also offers seminars and networking opportunities. In addition, San Diego State University offers an entrepreneurial training program; San Diego City College has an incubator and technical training programs for workers; the area's state-sponsored regional technology program provides high-tech businesses with referrals to service providers and financing sources; and a local manufacturing extension center provides technical help to local manufacturers to improve their performance.

Source: Based on Innovation Associates, *Developing High-Technology Communities: San Diego* (Washington, D.C.: U.S. Small Business Administration, April 2000).

Special types of land

Some local economic development policies target the development of specific types of land, including brownfields, economically distressed neighborhoods, and downtowns. One rationale for such programs is that they increase the effective supply of land for business development—which, according to the aforementioned ICMA survey, was a barrier to economic development in 57 percent of local jurisdictions.[79] Another rationale is that the redevelopment of certain categories of land can improve surrounding neighborhoods or an entire area. Redevelopment may occur through residential as well as business redevelopment. The best mix of business and residential redevelopment depends on circumstances: it may make most sense to emphasize business redevelopment, for example, on brownfield sites that would be difficult to market for residential uses or in neighborhood or downtown commercial districts.

Brownfields Brownfields are "contaminated industrial/commercial property that is abandoned, underutilized, or idle."[80] Brownfield sites are distinct from the relatively few Superfund sites, for which the U.S. Environmental Protection Agency (EPA) takes charge of cleanup. Although brownfields usually have lower levels of contamination than Superfund sites, brownfields still face significant barriers to development.[81] Under environmental law, landowners who have not made special agreements with federal and state environmental agencies are liable for the costs of cleaning up any contamination that might be discovered. For any entity that might otherwise be interested in redeveloping the site, this liability creates significant uncertainty, particularly since the types and scope of environmental contamination may be only imperfectly known. In addition to the problems associated with cleanup costs, many brownfields are difficult to redevelop because of aging infrastructure or the proximity of deteriorated neighborhoods. According to a 1999 survey of 231 cities conducted by the U.S. Conference of Mayors, the most frequently mentioned barriers to the redevelopment of brownfields were lack of cleanup funds (mentioned by 90 percent of respondents), liability issues (71 percent), and the need for an environmental assessment of the brownfields (60 percent).[82]

Almost all states have "voluntary cleanup programs," under which landowners and the local government come to a formal agreement with state agen-

---

The Dallas Brownfields Program
Begun in 1995 with a grant from the U.S. Environmental Protection Agency, the Dallas Brownfields Program (DBP) has promoted the redevelopment of Dallas's brownfields by providing information and education, linking property owners with groups that can provide assistance, and easing the redevelopment process. The key activity of the DBP is its sponsorship of the Dallas Brownfields Forum, a group of more than two hundred members who meet every two months; the forum's members include developers, property owners, consultants, bankers, community residents, and representatives of environmental agencies and other public agencies. The forum provides participants with information and opportunities to discuss specific projects, helps resolve project-specific problems, and develops policy recommendations to submit to the various public agencies on how to better encourage brownfield redevelopment.

The DBP also provides property owners with a free environmental site assessment, help in dealing with environmental agencies, and information on available economic development programs. Finally, under a formal written agreement developed by the DBP, the Texas state environmental agency will relieve property owners of liability if they agree to a voluntary cleanup. The DBP has been involved with the redevelopment of twenty-four sites representing more than $800 million in public and private investment. Because of the DBP, the U.S. Environmental Protection Agency has designated Dallas a Brownfields Showcase Community.

Sources: U.S. Department of Housing and Urban Development, Office of Policy Development and Research, "Dallas Brownfields Program Spurs Neighborhood Revitalization," available at www.huduser.org/periodicals/fieldworks/0402/fworks2.html; *Brownfields Redevelopment: A Guidebook for Local Governments and Communities*, 2nd ed. (Washington, D.C.: International City/County Management Association, 2001), 221; and Seth Kirshenberg and Charles Bartsch, "Brownfields: Options and Opportunities," *Management Information Service Report* 29, no. 5 (May 1997): 20–21.

cies that sets cleanup standards and limits liability. Only some states have a memorandum of agreement with EPA, under which the state can offer assurances that if the agreed-upon cleanup is undertaken, there will be no liability for current or future landowners at the federal level. Given current environmental laws and the potential cleanup costs, brownfields cannot be redeveloped without federal or state involvement. However, local government can serve as a catalyst for redevelopment by

Identifying which brownfield sites to target first for redevelopment (a site would be given higher priority if it is easier to redevelop or if its redevelopment would offer greater spillover benefits).

Encouraging state and federal agencies to provide financial support for cleanup and redevelopment—as well as assurances that if cleanup is undertaken, the property's owners will receive some protection from future liability.

Negotiating with state and federal agencies to establish cleanup standards that balance costs against the protection of public health. (Such standards can be scaled back if the landowner and local government agree to institutional controls, such as zoning and deed restrictions, that ensure that future uses of the land can tolerate higher remaining contamination levels without threatening public health.)

Distressed neighborhoods   Distressed neighborhoods have long been targeted for redevelopment through government intervention; examples include urban renewal in the 1940s and 1950s, Model Cities during the War on Poverty, and Community Development Block Grants during the era of President Nixon's New Federalism. Enterprise zones are the latest form of governmental intervention in support of the redevelopment of distressed neighborhoods. *Enterprise zone* is a generic term for an approach to revitalization that relies on tax or financial incentives or special public services to encourage business development in a designated area. Thirty-six states have created more than 2,800 such zones (under various names); however, 2,083 are in Arkansas and Louisiana, another 227 are in Ohio, and the remaining 500 are in the other thirty-three states.[83] In addition, since 1994 the federal government has designated 193 "empowerment zones," "enterprise communities," and "renewal communities"; the associated incentives have varied over time and by type of zone.[84] Enterprise zone incentives typically include tax breaks for businesses that invest or locate in the zone and hire zone residents. Improvements to infrastructure or public services (e.g., road repair and enhanced police protection) are often made within enterprise zones. In addition, the enterprise zone program may pay the local government or a nonprofit agency to assist in promoting zone development. Sometimes enterprise zones offer tax breaks for zone residents.

One concern about enterprise zones is whether the incentives and special public services will be sufficient to overcome the severity of the problems in the zone, such as crime, inadequate infrastructure, and low job skills. Another question is whether zone residents benefit. Since most Americans do not live and work in the same neighborhood, any jobs that are created will not necessarily go to neighborhood residents. And even if jobs do go to neighborhood residents, will they go to residents who are difficult to employ, or to residents who are already employed? Finally, even if the zone succeeds in increasing local property values, property tax revenues will increase and neighborhood home owners and other landowners will benefit, but some neighborhood renters may be displaced.

Some evaluations of enterprise zones have concluded that they do not work. For example, several studies compared business activity in zip codes that encompassed state-designated enterprise zones with business activity in otherwise similar zip codes that did not include enterprise zones, and found little evidence that the zones increased overall business activity.[85] Another study found no evidence that state-designated zones with high levels of incentives outperform zones with low levels of incentives.[86] This same study also found that only 10 percent of workers living in enterprise zones held jobs that were located within their zone, and that only one-fourth of jobs in zones were held by zone residents, which suggests that it is difficult to ensure that the benefits from new zone jobs accrue to zone residents. All these studies, however, were conducted in the late 1990s; the federal versions of enterprise zones, or newer state enterprise zones, with larger incentives or services, may prove to have larger benefits.[87]

Downtown development   One question raised about downtown development is whether it really *is* economic development. Will the jobs gained through successful downtown development benefit the area as a whole, or will they simply move jobs from other business centers to downtown businesses? In fact, downtown development *will* increase total local business activity if it succeeds in attracting customers who would otherwise shop outside the local economy or on the Internet; downtown development may also play an important symbolic role in attracting businesses and households to the area.[88]

Among the approaches being applied, often successfully, to encourage downtown development are the following:[89]

Restoring and enhancing unique downtown amenities, such as older buildings, waterfront areas, or pleasant spaces for walking

Developing downtown housing to create a critical mass of local retail demand, which will allow retail businesses to flourish and also attract outside shoppers

---

The Downtown Franklin Association
In the 1970s, the downtown of Franklin, Tennessee, fifteen miles south of Nashville, had severe economic problems: vacancies were over 50 percent and many of the remaining businesses were pool halls, thrift shops, and liquor stores. In 1984, the Downtown Franklin Association, a private, nonprofit organization made up of downtown merchants, property owners, public officials, and volunteers, was organized to revitalize and restore Franklin's downtown.[1] The key strategy was to undertake extensive and widespread visual improvements that would preserve the historic character of Franklin. The association successfully lobbied city hall and the state to invest more than $1 million in public infrastructure improvements, including new streets, sidewalks, and streetlights; new water and sewer pipes; and the

restoration of Franklin's historic courthouse square. Property owners were encouraged to improve building facades in order to restore their historic character—a task that was accomplished, in part, through labor donated by local volunteers. The association also organized events to attract new visitors to downtown. Franklin's efforts, assisted by the strong Nashville economy, have led property values in the downtown area to more than triple. Downtown Franklin has been designated a Great American Main Street by the National Trust for Historic Preservation.

Source: Based on Richard Moe and Carter Wilkie, *Changing Places: Rebuilding Community in the Age of Sprawl* (New York: Henry Holt, 1997), 166–172. © 1997 by Richard Moe and Carter Wilkie. Printed by permission of Henry Holt and Company, LLC.
[1]The Downtown Franklin Association merged with a broader county preservation group in 1998.

Attracting outside demand to the downtown by means of special marketing events or through expensive investments that will attract outsiders, such as museums and sports stadiums.

Downtown development is supported in a number of ways: by the local general fund, by grants from higher levels of government, and through taxes financed by the development itself. Under a tax increment financing plan, for example, all the property taxes from new development in a designated area, such as a downtown, are used to support improved public services or infrastructure in that area. TIF plans can be used to support bonds that will pay for infrastructure up front. A second alternative, available in some states, is to create a business improvement district.[90] Under this arrangement, property owners in the designated district can vote to increase their property taxes and then to devote the additional funds to the improvement of the district.

Organizing and managing local economic development

Ideally, local economic development policy should be coordinated, or even organized, within a local labor market (such as a metropolitan area), for two reasons. First, the economic development policies pursued by one jurisdiction have significant spillover effects on other jurisdictions within the same local labor market. When a jurisdiction pursues economic development on its own, most of the jobs that it attracts would probably otherwise have located somewhere else within the same labor market. Thus, although one jurisdiction gains tax revenue from increased business activity at the expense of other jurisdictions, the overall fiscal effects and effects on the labor market are similar, regardless of where the business is located.

If more and more jurisdictions enter the competitive fray, the jurisdiction that initiated the competition will lose its initial advantage in attracting new jobs, but all jurisdictions will be devoting more resources to economic development programs. Furthermore, when jurisdictions pursue economic development on their own, they tend to overinvest in attracting businesses that provide large amounts of business tax revenue to the jurisdiction of location but low employment and fiscal benefits for the entire local labor market, and to underinvest in attracting businesses that increase congestion and create environmental costs in the jurisdiction of location but offer larger employment and fiscal benefits for the entire local labor market.

Second, many economic development programs are more effective if they are coordinated across an entire labor market. A single, unified marketing campaign to attract new branch plants, for example, is more likely to succeed than a scattered, uncoordinated collection of efforts. Job-training programs work better when they target workers from throughout the local labor market for jobs throughout that same market. The firms in a cluster tend to be located throughout a local area, so cluster strategies need to be areawide.

No one metropolitan area can be described as an ideal model of regional cooperation in economic development. Virtually every metropolitan area at least gives lip service to regional cooperation on marketing and job training, and that lip service is often accompanied by actual cooperation. If an area arranges for a consultant to do a cluster study, the study is always done on a regional basis and the recommended strategies are regionally based. Nevertheless, virtually every metropolitan area is also characterized by internal competition that can undermine cooperative efforts.[91]

Successful economic development requires good communication and coordination among a wide variety of groups in the local labor market. As noted earlier, local economic development programs are carried out by a range of

Community development corporations
There are more than 1,700 community-based development organizations, usually called community development corporations (CDCs), in the United States, dating back to the War on Poverty efforts of the late 1960s and continuing today with grants and investments from organizations such as the Ford Foundation.[1] CDCs have traditionally been involved in housing development and social services but have sometimes played a significant role in economic development. Community-based organizations have some comparative advantages that may increase the effectiveness of economic development, including the following:

CDCs may be more able than other entities to effectively communicate—and advocate for—what the local community wants in economic development.

CDCs may be better able than other organizations to provide effective screening, counseling, and support services for participants in job-placement and job-training programs that are part of local economic development efforts.

CDCs may be better able to involve microbusinesses or residents who want to be entrepreneurs in programs to start up or expand small businesses.

CDC involvement may attract foundation or federal investment in an area's economic development efforts.

[1] The National Congress for Community Economic Development (NCCED) claims that there are more than 3,600 CDCs in the United States; see www.ncced.org. NCCED has assisted more than 1,700 CDCs; see www.liscnet.org.

entities: local governments, state economic development agencies, small business development centers, organizations providing business or manufacturing extension services, university centers for technology transfer, community colleges offering customized training programs, chambers of commerce, utility companies, community development corporations, and a wide variety of independent nonprofit organizations. Given all the entities involved in economic development, good communication and coordination are especially important—and may be especially difficult. Although a variety of organizational arrangements may be used, the "best" organizational arrangement will depend on the political culture and history of the area.

Private sector firms are universally involved in economic development. Private sector involvement can take a number of forms, from informal arrangements to formal public-private partnerships that are designed to administer or coordinate programs or to implement a specific project. Involving the private sector in local economic development offers both advantages and risks. For example, the private sector may provide additional funding, political clout, and leadership for local economic development and may have greater flexibility than governmental entities (in particular, the private sector may assist businesses in ways that are forbidden to local governments under state law). The risk associated with private sector involvement arises from the local government subsidies that are often provided as part of public-private partnerships: balancing public and private interests in such partnerships is sometimes difficult, and the local government must take care that the public benefit of the development justifies the subsidy.

Despite the risk of private-sector exploitation of economic development programs for narrow private goals, private sector involvement is often crucial as a source of strong, sustained leadership for local economic development—leadership with sufficient political clout to unify fragmented local efforts and to launch significant new programs or projects.[92] As a long-term process, local economic development requires sustained policies, which may be difficult for local governments—which are, after all, subject to the election cycle—to provide, particularly in the absence of ongoing private support and leadership. Traditionally, locally based banks and other large, locally controlled businesses have helped supply the funding, leadership, and political influence for local economic development. However, corporate consolidation, particularly in the banking industry, has created a "leadership gap," especially in smaller communities. Many areas must now look to other institutions for leadership on local economic development issues.

Colleges and universities are increasing their involvement in economic development and are often providing leadership to economic development programs. As worker skills, knowledge transfer, and high-tech industries grow in importance, the active involvement of higher education will become even more critical to successful local economic development.

Evaluating local economic development policies

Rigorous methodologies, such as random assignment, can be used to evaluate economic development programs.[93] However, such efforts should be financed at the federal or state level, as such evaluation is expensive and technically demanding, and most of the benefits would accrue throughout the state or nation. Local economic development organizations should not be expected to engage in expensive and complicated evaluations in order to contribute to the national debate over what works in local economic development.

What would be of value to local economic development organizations, however, are easier and less expensive evaluations that could keep local program managers and funding sources informed about how well different programs are working and how they could be improved. Regular surveys of the businesses that use various programs offer a good (and inexpensive) evaluation methodology. Such surveys should ask specific questions about how the program affected the business's location, expansion, investment, employment, and operations. To minimize bias in the responses, surveys should be administered by an organization that is independent of the program operator. Experience suggests that in the case of economic development services (such as business extension programs), where businesses lack any incentive to claim that the service was useful when it was not, such surveys provide useful information. For programs providing financial incentives, one might anticipate that, in order to keep the cash coming, businesses would claim that the incentive was decisive. But even for financial incentives, in many cases the surveyed businesses will report that the incentive had no effect. For example, the audit agency of the Colorado state legislature surveyed eighteen businesses that had located or expanded in Colorado enterprise zones, ten of which said that the zone incentive had not affected their location or expansion decisions.[94]

Survey evidence must be incorporated into local models to determine the employment, fiscal, and multiplier effects of the program. Even smaller communities can obtain reasonably inexpensive models that provide rough estimates of the ultimate effects of local economic development efforts. Information on how economic development efforts are affecting the local government's fiscal and employment goals can help improve economic development strategies. Another advantage of such information is that it helps ensure that efforts are focused on the ultimate, rather than the proximate, goals of local economic development. Increasing local business activity, for example, is not an end in itself; it is a means of achieving employment and fiscal benefits.

Conclusion

Local economic development is increasingly seen as a major local government responsibility requiring significant government resources—not least in the form of forgone tax revenues. A few common themes characterize effective economic development:

Keep your eyes on the prize. Local economic development should focus on providing employment and fiscal benefits to local residents while preserving local quality of life. Evaluations of economic development efforts should focus on how the program affects the achievement of these goals.

Maintain a broad portfolio. A comprehensive local economic development policy includes strategies focused on business attraction, business retention, new business start-ups, high-technology, and unused or underused land.

Target carefully. To increase local wealth, economic development must expand business activity that exports outside the local economy, substitutes for imports to the local economy, increases productivity, or makes better use of local resources, such as difficult-to-employ workers or contaminated land. Thus, local economic development programs should target businesses that are most likely to achieve these goals—which, in turn, implies that they will provide significant employment and fiscal benefits. Economic development efforts should also target businesses whose decisions are most likely to be affected by the assistance provided, such as those that have good alternative locations or are unlikely to receive normal bank financing. For public support for economic development to make sense, it must first make a difference in business decisions; in turn, those business decisions must provide benefits to the public, such as employment and fiscal benefits.

Link training and economic development. To effectively increase business activity and provide employment benefits, local economic development programs need to include customized training programs that can effectively serve the needs of both the business community and unemployed or underemployed workers.

Information is cheap and effective: use it. Government can subsidize the provision of basic information to businesses in order to help increase productivity and the chances of survival.

Involve the groups that will benefit and the groups that can provide special services. Economic development should be coordinated across the local labor market because that is where the benefits accrue and where businesses get most of their labor and many local supplies, as well as information from their local business cluster. Because of the special support they can provide to local economic development efforts, private businesses, educational institutions, and community organizations are among the groups that should be involved in local economic development.

There is no one best strategy for successful local economic development. Each area is different, with its own unique economic base and local institutions. However, experience has shown that efforts to broaden the market's benefits and address its failures are more likely to meet with success.

Acknowledgments: The author wishes to thank Linda Richer, Babette Schmitt, Julie Kurtz, and Claire Black for their assistance with this chapter.

1 Some other publications that give guidance on local economic development policies are National Center for Small Communities (NCSC), *Harvesting Hometown Jobs* (Washington, D.C.: NCSC, 1997); Michael J. Kinsley, *Economic Renewal Guide: A Collaborative Process for Sustainable Community Development* (Snowmass, Colo.: Rocky Mountain Institute, 1997); U.S. Department of Commerce, Economic Development Administration, *Innovative Local Economic Development Practices* (Washington, D.C.: Economic Development Administration, U.S. Department of Commerce, 1999); John Blair and Laura Reese, eds., *Approaches to Economic Development: Readings from* Economic Development Quarterly (Thousand Oaks, Calif.: Sage, 1999); Emil Malizia and Edward Feser, *Understanding Local Economic Development* (New Brunswick, N.J.: Center for Urban Policy Research, Rutgers University, 1999); Edward J. Blakely and Ted K. Bradshaw,

Planning Local Economic Development: Theory and Practice, 3rd ed. (Thousand Oaks, Calif.: Sage, 2002); Joan Fitzgerald and Nancey Green Leigh, *Economic Revitalization: Cases and Strategies for City and Suburb* (Thousand Oaks, Calif.: Sage, 2002); World Bank, "Local Economic Development: A Primer," available at www.worldbank.org/urban/led; ACCRA, *Local Economic Development Handbook* (Arlington, Va.: ACCRA, updated periodically); and Steven Koven and Thomas Lyons, *Economic Development: Strategies for State and Local Practice* (Washington, D.C.: International City/County Management Association, 2003).

2 Matt Kane and Peggy Sand, *Economic Development: What Works at the Local Level* (Washington, D.C.: National League of Cities, 1988), 4.

3 These figures are from a 1993 National League of Cities survey of elected officials in cities over 100,000 in population; see Phyllis Furdell, *Poverty and Economic Development: Views from City Hall* (Washington, D.C.: National League of Cities, 1994).

4 The author derived these percentages by dividing the percentage of respondents who selected a particular first-priority goal among the 73 percent who selected any first-priority goal (Furdell, *Poverty,* 11).

5 International City/County Management Association, "Economic Development 1999"; summary figures available at http://www1.icma.org/main/sc.asp?t=0.

6 To calculate the figures for economic development staff and spending per capita, the author used ICMA survey responses that had been broken down according to the population level of the city or county. (Most survey respondents were cities.) Per capita figures divide the average spending in a population group by the midpoint of that population category (i.e., if the population category was 25,000–49,999, the figure of 37,500 was used).

7 Timothy Bartik, Peter Eisinger, and George Erickcek, "Economic Development Policy in Michigan," in *Michigan at the Millennium,* ed. Charles Ballard et al. (East Lansing: Michigan State University Press, 2003).

8 Advocates of "local self-reliance" argue that by relying on local producers of goods and services, local areas gain more control over their economic destiny and avoid the economic shocks that can be created by changes in external markets; see Michael Shuman, *Going Local* (New York: Routledge, 2000). The mainstream opinion among economists, however, is that such a regime will significantly decrease residents' real per capita incomes because it implies forgoing both the advantages of division of labor and the comparative advantage provided by large-scale trade with other areas. In addition, many economic shocks derive from local causes, such as weather, poor management, or labor disputes at a particular local employer.

9 Bartik, Eisinger, and Erickcek, "Economic Development Policy."

10 William Oakland and William Testa, "State-Local Business Taxation and the Benefits Principle," *Federal Reserve Bank of Chicago Economic Perspectives* 20, no. 1 (January–February 1996): 2–19.

11 Ronald C. Fisher, *State and Local Public Finance* (Chicago: Irwin, 1996), 126–127; Robert P. Inman, "The Fiscal Performance of Local Governments: An Interpretative Review," in *Current Issues in Urban Economics,* ed. Peter Mieszkowski and Mahlon Straszheim (Baltimore: Johns Hopkins University Press, 1979): 270–321.

12 Ibid.

13 These arguments are presented in more detail in Timothy Bartik, *Jobs for the Poor: Can Labor Demand Policies Help?* (New York and Kalamazoo, Mich.: Russell Sage Foundation and W. E. Upjohn Institute for Employment Research, 2001), 62–66.

14 For example, according to research by Alan Peters and Peter Fisher, even though residents of enterprise zones have lower incomes and are less likely to own cars, only one in ten works within the enterprise zone. See *State Enterprise Zone Programs: Have They Worked?* (Kalamazoo, Mich.: W. E. Upjohn Institute for Employment Research, 2002).

15 Stephen Raphael, "The Spatial Mismatch Hypothesis and Black Youth Joblessness: Evidence from the San Francisco Bay Area," *Journal of Urban Economics* 43, no. 1 (1998): 71–111.

16 John Bishop, *Improving Job Matches in the U.S. Labor Market,* Brookings Papers: Microeconomics (Washington, D.C.: Brookings Institution, 1993), 335–400.

17 Most of the research on job loss of low-wage workers focuses on the employment experiences of former welfare recipients. Among the studies showing rapid job loss for former welfare recipients are Linnea Berg, Lynn Olson, and Aimee Conrad, *Causes and Implications of Rapid Job Loss among Participants in a Welfare-to-Work Program* (Evanston, Ill.: Center for Urban Affairs and Policy Research, Northwestern University, 1991); Alan Hershey and LaDonna Pavetti, "Turning Job Finders into Job Keepers," *The Future of Children* 7, no. 1 (spring 1997): 74–86; Anu Rangarajan, Peter Schocet, and Dexter Chu, *Employment Experiences of Welfare Recipients Who Find Jobs: Is Targeting Possible?* (Princeton, N.J.: Mathematica Policy Research, 1998).

18 More information on JobNet is provided in Bartik, *Jobs for the Poor,* 257–258.

19 The empirical evidence is reviewed in Bartik, *Jobs for the Poor,* 146–148.

20 The argument that the specific environmental effects of local economic development should receive consideration in local economic development policy making is uncontroversial among economists. A more controversial issue is whether increases in a local economy's use of any and all nonrenewable resources sold in the market, such as energy, should be seen as a negative external cost of economic development. That such increases should be so viewed has been argued most prominently by Herman Daly: see *For the Common Good: Redirecting the Economy toward Community, the Environment, and a Sustainable Future* (Boston: Beacon Press, 1994). The overwhelming majority of economists, however, do not believe that resources are, in general, mispriced because they are nonrenewable, although they may be mispriced in specific cases because of environmental effects (e.g., greenhouse gas emissions) or political effects (e.g., the influence of the Organization of Petroleum Exporting Countries [OPEC] over world oil prices).

21 Ted Levine, "Six Revolutions in Economic Development Marketing," *IEDC Economic Development Journal* 1, no. 1 (winter 2002): 5–12.

22 Peters and Fisher, *State Enterprise Zone Programs.*

23 International City/County Management Association, "Economic Development 1999."

24 Levine, "Six Revolutions."

25 Ibid., 9.

26 International City/County Management Association, "Economic Development 1999."

27 Levine, "Six Revolutions."

28 Bartik, Eisinger, and Erickcek, "Economic Development Policy," table 1. Incentives include all state and local tax incentives, other financial incentives, job-training incentives, and infrastructure incentives. Population estimates from the U.S. Department of Commerce, Bureau of the Census (July 1, 2002), were used to extrapolate Michigan's per capita expenditure on these incentives to the national level.

29 Figures on the share of total incentives made up of training and infrastructure were calculated from Peter Fisher and Alan Peters, *Industrial Incentives: Competition among American States and Cities* (Kalamazoo, Mich.: W. E. Upjohn Institute for Employment Research, 1998), table 4.9. The figures are simple averages based on data for the sixteen representative firms used by Fisher and Peters—which, in turn, are averages that Fisher and Peters calculated for the twenty-four leading industrial states in their sample as of 1992.

30 International City/County Management Association, "Economic Development 1999."

31 Ibid.

32 The figure for the number of states authorizing TIFs comes from Joyce Man, "Introduction," in *Tax Increment Financing and Economic Development: Uses, Structures, and Impact,* ed. Craig Johnson and Joyce Man (Albany: State University of New York Press, 2001). The book includes a number of articles that provide useful background on TIF. The ICMA survey giving the figure on the number of communities using TIFs is "Economic Development 1999."

33 This literature has been most comprehensively reviewed by Timothy Bartik and Michael Wasylenko. See Bartik, *Who Benefits?,* chap. 2; Bartik, "The Effects of State and Local Taxes on Economic Development: A Review of Recent Research," *Economic Development Quarterly* 6, no. 1 (February 1992): 102–110; and Michael Wasylenko, "Taxation and Economic Development: The State of the Economic Literature," *New England Economic Review* (March/April 1997): 37–52.

34 This calculation is as follows: the tax elasticity of private employment with respect to state and local business taxes (E) is defined as $(dJ/J)/(dT/T)$, where J is the number of jobs, dJ is the change in the number of jobs, T is the tax rate, and dT is the change in the business tax rate. The percentage change in revenue from a tax cut, $dR/R,$ will approximately equal $dT/T + dJ/J.$ Substituting and rearranging, $dR/dJ = (R/J)[1 + (1/E)].$ R/J is state and local business tax revenue per job, which was about $1,634 per job in the United States as of 1989. With a value of -0.25 for $E,$ $dR/dJ \approx $4,902.$ Updating by the change in consumer price index (CPI) from 1989 to 2002 gives a figure in 2002 dollars of (179.9/124) $4,902 = $7,112. The figure of $1,634 for state and local business taxes per private employee comes from three sources. Total state and local tax revenue in FY89 was $469 billion (U.S. Department of Commerce, Bureau of the Census, *Government Finances: 1988–89* [Washington, D.C.: U.S. Government Printing Office, 1991], 21). The most recent estimate of the business share of state and local taxes is 31 percent: see Advisory Commission on Intergovernmental Relations (ACIR), *Regional Growth: Interstate Tax Competition,* Report A-76 (Washington, D.C.: ACIR, March 1981), revised version of table A-1 (figures for 1977). Private nonagricultural employment in the United States averaged 89 million during FY89 (U.S. Department of Commerce,

Bureau of Economic Analysis, *Survey of Current Business* [January 1991]: S-10). These figures could be updated using more recent state and local data, but most of the studies estimating elasticities used earlier data, so historical data are probably more appropriate. The elasticity used is a compromise between the -0.3 preferred in the literature review by Bartik, "Effects of State and Local Taxes," and the -0.2 preferred by Wasylenko, "Taxation and Economic Development." The CPI figures come from the U.S. Bureau of Labor Statistics.

35 Bartik, "Effects of State and Local Taxes," 107–109.

36 Lawrence Summers and James Poterba, "Time Horizons of American Firms: New Evidence from a Survey of CEOs," in *Capital Choices: Changing the Way America Invests in Industry,* ed. Michael Porter (Cambridge: Harvard Business School Press, 1994).

37 For up-front incentives to have greater effects per dollar of present-value costs from the perspective of local taxpayers, the taxpayers must have an annual real discount rate of less than 12 percent.

38 Neal Peirce, "State, Local Corporate Subsidies: A New Coalition for Accountability," August 5, 2002, available at www.postwritersgroup.com/archives/peir0805.htm.

39 International City/County Management Association, "Economic Development 1999."

40 Bartik, Eisinger, and Erickcek, "Economic Development Policy."

41 All figures in this paragraph are derived from Steven Davis, John Haltiwanger, and Scott Schuh, *Job Creation and Destruction* (Cambridge, Mass.: MIT Press, 1996), chap. 2.

42 The figures on the components of manufacturing employment change are derived from Davis, Haltiwanger, and Schuh, *Job Creation.* Over a longer time frame, a greater proportion of job creation derives from new plants than from expansions. Over a five-year period, the number of jobs created in manufacturing is about 30 percent of the original base, and about 60 percent of this job creation (i.e., 18 percent of the base) comes from new plants and 40 percent (12 percent of the base) comes from plant expansions; see Timothy Dunne, Mark Roberts, and Larry Samuelson, "Plant Turnover and Gross Employment Flows in the U.S. Manufacturing Sector," *Journal of Labor Economics* 7, no. 1 (January 1989): 48–71. However, many of these new plants may be start-ups. Also, the job creation from plant expansions after five years is greater than after one year (12 percent versus 9 percent).

43 This discussion is influenced by the description of business visitation programs in Council for Urban Economic Development, "Business Visitation and Surveying," in *Local Economic Development Handbook: A Guide for Practitioners and Communities* (Arlington, Va.: ACCRA). This publication is regularly updated and is available on the Web at www.accra.org. Another source for this discussion is Christopher Allanach and Scott Loveridge, "An Assessment of Maximum-Training Business Visitation Programs," *Economic Development Quarterly* 12, no. 2 (May 1998): 125–136.

44 International City/County Management Association, "Economic Development 1999."

45 National Institute of Standards and Technology, *The Manufacturing Extension Partnership: Delivering Measurable Returns to Its Clients* (Washington, D.C.: U.S. Department of Commerce, 2002). Out of concern that respondents may find it in their inter-

ests to bias their responses, economists tend to be skeptical about survey responses to such subjective questions. In this instance, however, it is unclear why firms would want to claim that manufacturing extension services are useful if they are not.

46 Eric Oldsman and Jack Russell, "The Industrial Resource Center Program: Assessing the Record and Charting the Future" (unpublished report prepared for the state of Pennsylvania, 1999). See also Ronald Jarmin, "Evaluating the Impact of Manufacturing Extension on Productivity Growth," *Journal of Policy Analysis and Management* 18, no. 1 (1999): 99–119; and Nexus Associates, *A Record of Achievement: The Economic Impact of the Ben Franklin Partnership* (Harrisburg: Commonwealth of Pennsylvania, October 1999).

47 In addition, if any workers who left their jobs because of the productivity improvement were relatively employable, this extra supply of workers could attract additional employment to the area.

48 The discussion of clusters is influenced by two reports by Stuart Rosenfeld that provide a much more extensive analysis of the cluster approach; see *A Governor's Guide to Cluster-Based Economic Development* (Washington, D.C.: National Governors Association, 2002); *Just Clusters: Economic Development Strategies That Reach More People and Places* (Carrboro, N.C.: Regional Technology Strategies, 2002).

49 Rosenfeld, *Just Clusters,* 36; *Governor's Guide,* 10.

50 Governmental involvement in education and training stems from two major causes: first, firms tend to underinvest in training because they are afraid of losing trained workers to other employers; second, governmental provision of training offers economies of scale.

51 Rosenfeld, *Just Clusters,* 21–22.

52 David, Haltiwanger, and Schuh, *Job Creation and Destruction,* chap. 4.

53 The figures are derived from Jacob M. Benus et al., *Self-Employment Programs: A New Reemployment Strategy; Final Impact Analysis of the Washington and Massachusetts Self-Employment Demonstrations,* Unemployment Insurance Occasional Paper 95-4 (Washington, D.C.: U.S. Department of Labor, 1995). Simple averages from the two states were used to generate the figures that appear in the text. This study is regarded as a landmark study because it is the only evaluation of economic development programs ever to use random assignment, and because it led to significant changes in government policy—specifically, to greater efforts on the part of the U.S. Labor Department to allow or encourage states to run entrepreneurship training programs as part of their unemployment insurance programs.

54 Dollar figures come from www.sba.gov/gopher/ Business-Development/funding.txt. Information on the number of centers comes from www.sba.gov/ sbdc/mission.html.

55 U.S. Small Business Administration (SBA), "SBA: Small Business Development Centers—A Program Review 2001," available at www.sba.gov/sbdc/ programreview2001/SBAReport.html.

56 Many studies have been done by James Chrisman, a professor at the University of Calgary, under contract with the national Association of Small Business Development Centers or individual state programs. Chrisman's most recent study is "Economic Impact of Small Business Development Center Counseling Activities in the United States: 2000–2001." A summary of this study is available at the Web site of the Association of Small Business Development Centers, www.asbdc-us.org. A report by the SBA inspector general, however, raises some concerns about the low response rates and the wording of some of the questions in Chrisman's survey; see Inspector General of U.S. SBA, *Performance Measurement in the SBDC Program,* Inspection Report No. 98-09-01 (Washington, D.C.: SBA, 1998).

57 Dinah Adkins, *A Brief History of Business Incubation in the United States* (Athens, Ohio: National Business Incubation Association, 2002), 23.

58 Ibid., 24.

59 National Business Incubation Association, "Business Incubation Facts," available at www.nbia.org.

60 The two-thirds figure comes from Lawrence Molnar et al., *Impact of Business Incubator Investments* (Athens, Ohio, and Ann Arbor, Mich.: National Business Incubation Association and University of Michigan, 1997), 15. The difficulty of comparing firms is illustrated by this study, which was unsuccessful in finding matches and obtaining responses. This report is also described in Hugh Sherman and David Chappell, "Methodological Challenges in Evaluating Business Incubator Outcomes," *Economic Development Quarterly* 12, no. 4 (November 1998): 313–321.

61 Andrea Levere and David Wingate, "Counting on Local Capital: Evolution of the Revolving Loan Fund Industry," *Community Investments* 11, no. 1 (winter/spring 1999). *Community Investments* is a newsletter published by the Federal Reserve Bank of San Francisco.

62 John Caskey and Robinson Hollister, *Business Development Financial Institutions: Theory, Practice, and Impact,* Discussion Paper No. 1240-01 (Madison: Institute for Research on Poverty, University of Wisconsin–Madison, October 2001). Since 1994, the U.S. Department of the Treasury has provided financial and technical assistance to community development financial institutions (CDFIs), which are designed to help provide disadvantaged communities with better access to credit, including business loans. Various tax breaks are also available for investors in CDFIs. For more information, see www.cdfifund.gov/overview/index.asp.

63 Alan Berube, *Capital Access Programs: A Summary of Nationwide Performance* (Washington, D.C.: U.S. Department of the Treasury, January 2001).

64 For a report that includes twenty-three case studies of attempts to use public subsidies to expand venture capital into rural areas, see David Barley et al., *Establishing Nontraditional Venture Capital Institutions: Lessons Learned* (Columbia, Mo.: Rural Policy Research Institute, 2000).

65 One could also argue that when private financial markets fail to provide loans and investments that are financially profitable, this creates a potential opportunity for government-supported capital market programs to earn a profit. However, such programs are rarely profitable, which suggests that they must be justified on the basis of the fact that their social benefits outweigh their below-market, risk-adjusted rate of return.

66 Price Waterhouse, "Evaluation of the 7(a) Guaranteed Business Loan Program" (unpublished report prepared for the U.S. Small Business Administration, March 1992).

67 Levere and Wingate, "Local Capital."

68 Based on two sets of figures in Rutgers University, Center for Urban Policy Research, *The Impact of EDA RLF Loans on Economic Restructuring* (Wash-

ington, D.C.: Economic Development Administration, 2002). Using the IMPLAN model to derive multipliers and assuming that all RLF loans increase base economic activity, the report concludes that the average Economic Development Administration (EDA) cost per total job created is $771. However, using an econometric model that relates county employment to RLF loan volume, the report concludes that the average EDA cost per total job created is $9,000. These two figures are consistent only if one in twelve (9000/771 = 11.7) RLF loans actually increases a county's economic base.

69 See John Caskey and Robinson Hollister, "The Impact of Business Development Financial Institutions: A Review of Three Studies" (unpublished paper, Swarthmore College, April 2001), which reviews three studies that examined a particular BDFI, attempted to determine to what extent the BDFI was responsible for any subsequent business growth, and estimated the impacts of that induced business growth. The studies reviewed are Thomas Miller, "Of These Hills: A Review of Kentucky Highlands Investment Corporation; Facts, Stories, Lessons, Questions, and Return on the Taxpayers' Investment" (unpublished monograph, March 1993); Josephine LaPlante, *Evaluating Social and Economic Effects of Small Business Development Assistance: Framework for Analysis and Application to the Small Business Assistance Programs of Coastal Enterprises, Inc.* (Portland, Me.: Edmund Muskie Institute of Public Affairs, March 1996); and John Caskey and Robinson Hollister, "Final Report on the Job Impact of the Enterprise Corporation of the Delta" (unpublished paper, Swarthmore College, June 1999). Of the three, the author was able to obtain only the Caskey and Hollister study. However, according to Caskey and Hollister's 2001 review, all three studies did conclude that in a significant proportion of cases, the BDFI was decisive in inducing growth that would not have occurred "but for" the assistance. In the case of the Miller study, this conclusion is based on conversations with Kentucky Highlands Investment Corporation staff and clients. In the case of the LaPlante study, this conclusion is based on survey responses indicating that assisted firms attributed 35 percent of their firm's economic value to the assistance provided by Coastal Enterprises, Inc.; 42 percent of the firms said that they could not have obtained a loan from another source. The Caskey and Hollister study simply assumed that the intervention of the Enterprise Corporation was decisive in at least half the cases.

70 Alan Berube, *Capital Access Programs: A Summary of Nationwide Performance* (Washington, D.C.: U.S. Department of the Treasury, January 2001).

71 The Office of Technology Assessment has defined high-technology firms as those that "are engaged in the design, development, and introduction of new products and innovative manufacturing processes, or both, through the systematic application of scientific and technical knowledge"; see U.S. Congress, Office of Technology Assessment (OTA), *Technology, Innovation, and Regional Economic Development* (Washington, D.C.: OTA, U.S. Congress, September 9, 1982).

72 International City/County Management Association, "Economic Development 1999."

73 Cited in Daniel Hecker, "High-Technology Employment: A Broader View," *Monthly Labor Review* (June 1999): 18–28.

74 Figures for 1998 are from Denise Drescher, "A Brief Overview of Research Parks for Economic Developers," available at www.planning.unc.edu/courses/261/drescher/.

75 National Business Incubation Association, "Business Incubation Facts."

76 For a review of this issue, see David Salvensen and Henry Renski, *The Importance of Quality of Life in the Location Decisions of New Economy Firms* (Washington, D.C.: Economic Development Administration, 2002). Richard Florida has argued that metropolitan areas that attract a more diverse, creative population (including musicians, artists, immigrants, and gay men and women) will experience greater high-tech success. See *The Rise of the Creative Class* (New York: Basic Books, 2002). Also see Richard Florida and Gary Gates, "Technology and Tolerance: The Importance of Diversity to High-Technology Growth" (paper for the Center on Urban and Metropolitan Policy, Brookings Institution, June 2001).

77 Nexus Associates, "Ben Franklin Partnership."

78 Innovation Associates, *Developing High-Technology Communities: San Diego* (Washington, D.C.: U.S. Small Business Administration, April 2000).

79 International City/County Management Association, "Economic Development 1999."

80 For a useful brief introduction to brownfields, see Seth Kirshenberg and Charles Bartsch, "Brownfields: Options and Opportunities," *Management Information Service Report* 29, no. 5 (May 1997): 1. For a comprehensive guide to brownfields, see *Brownfields Redevelopment: A Guidebook for Local Governments and Communities,* 2nd ed. (Washington, D.C.: International City/County Management Association, 2001). Both publications influenced the discussion of brownfields in the text.

81 Kirshenberg and Bartsch, "Brownfields," 1.

82 U.S. Conference of Mayors, *Recycling America's Land: A National Report on Brownfields Redevelopment,* vol. 3 (Washington, D.C.: U.S. Conference of Mayors, February 2000).

83 Peters and Fisher, *State Enterprise Zone Programs,* 1, 19.

84 The figures were taken from "Introduction to the RC/EZ/EC Initiative," available at www.hud.gov/offices/cpd/economicdevelopment/programs/rc/about/ezecinit.cfm.

85 Robert Greenbaum, "An Evaluation of State Enterprise Zone Policies: Measuring the Impact on Business Decisions and Housing Market Outcomes" (Ph.D. dissertation, Carnegie Mellon University, 1998); Robert Greenbaum and John Engberg, *The Impact of State Urban Enterprise Zones on Business Outcomes,* Discussion Paper No. 98-20 (Washington, D.C.: Center for Economic Studies, U.S. Bureau of the Census, 1998); and Daniele Bondonio and John Engberg, "Enterprise Zones and Local Employment: Evidence from the States' Programs," *Regional Science and Urban Economics* 30 (September 2000): 519–549.

86 Peters and Fisher, *State Enterprise Zone Programs.*

87 Other studies have found some evidence of the success of enterprise zones, but they were more limited in geographic scope or methodology. Leslie Papke, for example, found that enterprise zones had some effect on unemployment in Indiana; see "Tax Policy and Urban Development: Evidence from the Indiana Enterprise Zone Program," *Journal of Public Economics* 54, no. 1 (1994): 37–49. Barry Rubin

and Margaret Wilder found that, after the zone designation, industries in the Evansville, Indiana, enterprise zone grew faster than their counterparts, but this conclusion is limited to Evansville and does not demonstrate that the zone was responsible for the differences; see "Urban Enterprise Zones: Employment Impacts and Fiscal Incentives," *Journal of the American Planning Association* 55, no. 4 (1989): 418–431. Marilyn Rubin found that one-third of new or expanding firms in New Jersey enterprise zones said that the zone incentives were the primary or only reason for their location decision, but this conclusion is specific to New Jersey's zones and relies on possibly biased survey responses; see "Urban Enterprise Zones in New Jersey: Have They Made a Difference?" in *Enterprise Zones: New Directions in Economic Development,* ed. Roy Green (Newbury Park, Calif.: Sage, 1991).

88 As noted earlier, if redevelopment causes some land to be used that would otherwise be vacant, it will increase local economic activity by increasing the effective supply of land. However, in the case of *downtown* redevelopment, the assertion that the land would otherwise stay vacant is often implausible.

89 This discussion was influenced by an excellent short research brief on downtown development: Kent Robertson, "Downtown Development: Key Trends and Practices," *Policy Brief* 8 (St. Louis: St. Louis Public Policy Research Center, University of Missouri, June 2001), available at www.cardi.cornell.edu/cd_toolbox_2/tools/downtown_trends.cfm. Additional information is available at the National Main Street Web site of the National Trust for Historic Preservation, www.mainst.org. An excellent book on downtown redevelopment in large cities is Bernard Frieden and Lynne Sagalyn, *Downtown, Inc.: How America Rebuilds Cities* (Cambridge, Mass.: MIT Press, 1989).

90 For more on business improvement districts, see Mildred Warner et al., "Business Improvement Districts: Issues in Alternative Local Public Service Provision" (working paper, Department of City and Regional Planning, Cornell University, June 2002), available at http://www.cce.cornell.edu/restructuring/.

91 Some sources that list examples of regional cooperation in economic development include Linda McCarthy, *Competitive Regionalism: Beyond Individual Competition* (Washington, D.C.: Economic Development Administration, 2000); descriptions of consulting projects undertaken by ICF Consulting on regional economic development planning and clusters, available at www.icfconsulting.com/Markets/Community_Development/edindex.asp; and Bruce Katz, ed. *Reflections on Regionalism* (Washington, D.C.: Brookings Institution Press, 2000). Usually when researchers cite models of regional cooperation, they refer to extraordinary cases such as the tax-base sharing effort in the Minneapolis–St. Paul area, the growth boundaries in Portland, Oregon, or city-county consolidations such as those in Louisville, Indianapolis, and Nashville. Although such cases may encourage or require more intense regional cooperation, it is not at all clear that such exceptions to the rule are realistic models for most local governments. In addition, healthy regional cooperation in economic development can occur without tax-base sharing, growth boundaries, or metro consolidation—although it may be more difficult.

92 The effects of corporate consolidation on local leadership for economic development and the potential for higher education to play a stronger role in local economic development are among many topics discussed in Beth Siegel and Andy Waxman, *Third-Tier Cities: Adjusting to the New Economy* (Washington, D.C.: Economic Development Administration, 2001). This insightful paper provides a good general discussion of the problems facing older, smaller cities (with populations of 15,000 to 110,000).

93 Timothy Bartik, "Evaluating the Impacts of Local Economic Development Policies on Local Economic Outcomes: What Has Been Done and What Is Doable?" (paper presented at a conference on Evaluating Local Economic and Employment Development, organized by the Local Economic and Employment Development Programme of the Organization for Economic Cooperation and Development, Vienna, Austria, November 20, 2002), available at www.upjohninst.org.

94 Sara Hinkley and Fiona Hsu, *Minding the Candy Store: State Audits of Economic Development* (Washington, D.C.: Good Jobs First, 2000). For a useful guide to surveys of business clients of economic development programs, see Harry Hatry et al., *Monitoring the Outcomes of Economic Development Programs* (Washington, D.C.: Urban Institute Press, 1990).

14 Debt management

Paul A. Leonard

At the end of 2001, the amount of tax-exempt securities and loans outstanding in the United States totaled $1.69 trillion; in 2001 alone, state and local governments sold more than $285 billion in long-term bonds and an additional $56 billion in short-term notes. Many of the more than 17,000 state and local government issuers were selling securities for the first time or had not sold debt in many years. Such issuers may be unfamiliar with the procedures, parties, and processes involved in the issuance of new debt. Because a poorly designed or poorly managed bond issue can burden taxpayers with excess interest costs over the life of the issue, it is important for issuers to have a thorough understanding of the process.

This chapter provides local government managers and finance officers with an overview of debt issuance and management. It covers the basics of a capital improvements program and a debt management policy; provides an overview of the tax-exempt securities market; and describes the debt issuance process, including the members of the financing team and the factors considered in the evaluation of credit quality. Finally, the chapter considers municipal bond defaults, the process of refunding a bond issue, and recent controversies in municipal debt financing.[1]

Capital financing

State and local government expenditures can be classified as current or capital expenditures. Current expenditures are those made for goods and services that will be used within a year, and are reflected in the operating budget. Typical current expenditures are wages and salaries, fringe benefits (e.g., medical insurance, retirement contributions), data processing, consumable supplies, maintenance, and travel. Capital expenditures represent spending on fixed assets (capital improvements) that will provide services over a number of years. Because most jurisdictions are prohibited from using the proceeds of long-term bond issues to finance current expenditures, virtually all long-term debt financing is used to fund capital improvements.

Most local governments use a capital improvements program (CIP) to manage their capital financing needs. A CIP is, in effect, a blueprint that identifies the capital projects to be funded over the next five or six years.[2] The CIP is updated annually; the first year of the CIP serves as the current year's capital budget. In addition to identifying planned capital projects, the CIP also serves as a financial planning and management tool: it (1) establishes priorities that balance capital needs with available resources; (2) pairs projects with their potential internal and external funding sources; (3) ensures the orderly improvement or replacement of fixed assets; and (4) provides an estimate of the size and timing of future bond sales.

Once the local government's capital needs have been determined, the next step is to decide how the projects will be funded. The two basic choices are pay-as-you-go financing (paying for capital projects out of current revenues) or pay-as-you-use financing (issuing debt that will be repaid over the economic life of the capital project). The pay-as-you-go approach has several advantages: it saves interest expenditures, preserves debt capacity for future borrowing, and does not encumber future budgets with mandatory debt service expenditures. Pay-as-you-use also has advantages: users pay for a capital project as they receive the benefits, and the local government need not accumulate funds before undertaking a project.

Debt policy

Along with a CIP, each government should have a written debt policy establishing guidelines for the use of debt. The policy should specify (1) the maximum amount of debt that can be issued; (2) the purposes for which debt can be issued; (3) the types of debt that can be issued; and (4) the debt maturity structure.[3] These components are discussed briefly in the three sections that follow.

Amount and purpose of debt

The maximum amount of debt that can be issued will depend, in most instances, on constitutional or statutory limits on the amount of full faith and credit (general obligation) debt that an issuer can sell. Such limits are often expressed as a percentage of a jurisdiction's assessed valuation. In addition to taking legal debt limits into account, the issuer must determine the practical limits of debt service capacity by assessing the effect of debt service outlays on future budgets. Moreover, as discussed later in the chapter, there are federal limits on the amounts of private-purpose debt that can be sold by issuers in each state.

The purposes for which debt can be issued reflect local taxpayers' views on the acceptable uses of debt financing. Examples of capital projects commonly financed through debt are schools; parks and recreational facilities; roads and bridges; hospitals; and public facilities such as libraries, museums, and office buildings.

Types of debt

There are two basic types of long-term debt: general obligation (GO) bonds and revenue bonds.[4] Unlimited-tax GO bonds, which are secured by the full faith, credit, and taxing powers of the issuing government, legally obligate the local government to levy taxes on all assessable property within its jurisdiction at whatever level is necessary to meet the debt service payments on the bonds. Limited-tax GO bonds are backed only by special taxes, such as a sales tax; by specific revenue sources; or by a maximum property tax millage rate.

Unlimited-tax GO bonds are an appropriate financing vehicle for capital projects that benefit the community as a whole. One limitation of such bonds, however, is that the amount issued is generally subject to constitutional or statutory restrictions. In addition, because unlimited-tax GO bonds normally require voter approval, which requires significant planning, GO financing does not allow an issuer to issue debt quickly to take advantage of favorable interest rates.

In part because of the difficulty of obtaining voter approval for GO bonds, many governmental units have turned to other forms of financing, including a variety of revenue-backed bonds (see the accompanying sidebars). Because revenue bonds are secured by the revenues of the project being financed, their credit quality depends on the financial strength of the underlying capital project. Moreover, since revenue bonds are secured by specific revenue sources rather than by an issuer's unlimited taxing power (and despite the fact that many carry an implicit or explicit governmental guarantee), some investors may view them as having lower credit quality than similarly rated GO bonds; as a result, revenue bonds may require a somewhat higher interest rate. Revenue bonds typically do not require voter approval.

What type of bonds a local government chooses to issue will depend on a number of factors, including

The direct and indirect benefits of the project

The timing of the benefits from the project

The issuer's legal authority to sell GO bonds

The probability of voter approval for the issuance of GO bonds

The availability of revenues from other sources, such as user charges, and the cost-effectiveness of such sources (e.g., the cost of collecting user charges versus the amount of revenues raised)

The total cost (interest costs plus all issuance costs) of each type of bond

The need to maintain flexibility for future financing.

There is no easy way to balance all these factors. As noted earlier, GO bonds generally require voter approval, whereas revenue bonds do not. Therefore, GO financing may be more appropriate for projects that have greater public appeal, and revenue bond financing may be more appropriate for projects with less public appeal.

Common types of revenue bonds

Airport revenue bonds   Secured by traffic-generated fees (e.g., landing, concession, fueling) or by lease revenues from airlines.

College and university revenue bonds   Secured by dormitory-room rentals or tuition.

Hospital and nursing home revenue bonds   Secured by federal and state reimbursements, third-party payments, and patient charges.

Industrial development revenue bonds   Secured by payments from businesses that use the facilities; sold to finance the construction of commercial facilities (e.g., manufacturing plants, shopping malls).

Multifamily revenue bonds   Secured by mortgage payments and federal subsidy payments; sold to finance housing for low-income or senior residents.

Public power revenue bonds   Secured by revenues from electric power plants.

Resource recovery revenue bonds   Secured by tipping fees, revenues from energy generated, and revenues from the sale of recoverable materials; sold to finance facilities that convert refuse into recoverable products or commercially salable energy.

Single-family mortgage revenue bonds   Secured by payments on residential mortgage loans.

Sports complex and convention center revenue bonds   Secured by revenues from events held at the facilities and by earmarked funds from other revenue sources, such as local motel and hotel room taxes.

Student loan revenue bonds   Secured by payments on federally insured or state guaranteed student loans.

Toll road revenue bonds   Secured by revenues from the tolls on the road, bridge, or tunnel being financed.

Water and sewer revenue bonds   Secured by connection fees and user charges.

Other types of long-term financing vehicles   State and local governments use other types of long-term financing vehicles in addition to traditional general obligation and revenue bonds. These financing options include bonds, leases, and bonds secured by leases.

Double-barreled bonds   Secured by the issuer's general taxing power and by specific revenues from outside the general fund.

Special assessment bonds   Issued to finance capital improvements that benefit a specific area within a community; a user fee is levied on the properties, households, or businesses benefiting from the improvements.

Tax increment financing bonds   Used to promote economic development in a specific area; paid from the increase in tax revenues generated as a result of economic growth in the targeted area.

Mello-Roos bonds   Issued by California local governments to finance public facilities in developing areas; secured by revenues from the specific development.

Leasing in lieu of a debt issue   Used to secure assets that are too expensive to purchase or that may be needed for only a short period of time.

Certificates of participation (COPs)   Collateralized by leases between a lessor and a government; paid from the annual appropriations made by the government to the lessor. Typically used for capital leases for large projects where the financing exceeds $10 million.

Short-term notes   In addition to long-term bonds, governments may issue short-term notes, which have maturities of less than thirteen months. The following list includes the most common types of notes.

Bond anticipation notes (BANs)   Issued in anticipation of the issuance of long-term bonds; secured primarily with the proceeds of the bond issue, although some BAN issues are also backed by the issuer's general obligation (full faith and credit) pledge. The credit quality of BANs is determined primarily by the issuer's ability to secure long-term bond financing.

Tax anticipation notes (TANs)   Issued in anticipation of the collection of taxes; secured by the taxes for which they were issued. Many TAN issues are tied to the collection of property taxes.

Revenue anticipation notes (RANs)   Issued in anticipation of the collection of revenues; secured by the revenues for which they were issued.

Grant anticipation notes (GANs)   Issued in anticipation of the receipt of grant funds (e.g., from the state or federal government); secured by the grant for which they were issued.

Tax and revenue anticipation notes (TRANs)   Issued in anticipation of the collection of taxes and revenues.

Tax-exempt commercial paper (TECP)   A type of short-term (30 to 270 days), uncollateralized borrowing; often backed by an irrevocable letter of credit, a revolving credit agreement, or a line of credit issued by a commercial bank.

TANs, RANs, GANs, and TRANs are generally used to smooth out governmental cash flows. Many current government expenditures—such as payroll costs, maintenance, and insurance—are incurred at regular intervals, whereas revenues, taxes, and grants are received at irregular intervals. As a result, many governments must borrow funds temporarily to cover cash deficiencies.

Some projects (e.g., water and sewer systems) provide benefits to specific users or property owners, and others (e.g., public roads, fire and police protection) provide essentially equal benefits to all taxpayers. Although equity considerations would suggest that the beneficiaries should pay the cost of a capital project, such an arrangement is unfortunately not always possible. For example, a local government may wish to finance a civic center with revenue bonds that are to be paid solely from the revenues generated by the center (e.g., event fees, concessions, parking). However, if the revenues from the center were insufficient to entirely cover the costs of the facility or varied widely from year to year, the revenue bonds would be viewed as risky, which would make the financing expensive. As an alternative, the local government could levy taxes on motel and hotel rooms (on the assumption that the civic center will attract additional business for these enterprises); another alternative would be to issue unlimited-tax or limited-tax GO bonds.

Debt maturity structure

The maturity structure of a debt issue is determined by several factors, including the type of project being financed, the financial position of the issuer, and constitutional and statutory constraints. A basic principle is that the maturity of an issue should not exceed the useful life of the project being financed. Limiting the maturity of an issue also reduces the total amount of interest paid over the life of the bonds.

A bond is a single security, typically with a principal amount of $5,000. A bond issue consists of many bonds. For example, a $1 million bond issue consists of two hundred bonds, each with a principal amount of $5,000. In a serial bond issue, portions of the total issue mature in different years. Most GO bonds are sold in serial form, meaning that each bond issue consists of bonds with more than a single maturity. The maturities of most GO bond issues range from one to fifteen years, and may be longer.

GO bonds are commonly issued with a "level debt service" structure, which is similar to that of the amortized loans used for most consumer borrowing. Under such a structure, the principal amount that matures each year increases over time; and since the amount of interest being paid declines each year (as bonds are retired), the total of principal and interest payments remains the same. Thus, a level debt service structure simplifies budgeting in future years.

An alternative is to structure debt service so that the project's costs and benefits are equal each year (where project costs include operating and maintenance expenses as well as debt service payments). Under this structure, the debt service schedule (the sum of principal and interest) may increase or decrease over time. For example, if a project generates equal benefits each year over its useful life and if operating and maintenance expenses are expected to increase as the facility ages, then debt service would decline over time.

In contrast to GO bonds, many revenue bonds are sold as "term" bonds, all of which have the same maturity date. However, term bonds are usually subject to a mandatory sinking-fund provision, which requires a fixed principal amount of bonds to be called and retired each year—effectively transforming the term bond structure into a serial structure. In an alternative type of sinking fund, an "invested" sinking fund, the issuer makes annual or semiannual payments to a third party (often the bond trustee), who then invests the payments so that there are sufficient funds to retire the bonds at the maturity date. Current U.S. Treasury regulations prohibit the investment of sinking-fund moneys in taxable securities, so arbitrage opportunities do not exist.[5]

The tax-exempt securities market

The volume of tax-exempt debt sold by state and local governments has grown substantially since the 1970s. During that decade, the average annual amount of long-term debt issued was $30.7 billion; during the 1980s, average annual volume more than tripled, to $106 billion. This significant increase resulted largely from the financings that took place during 1985. In that year, in anticipation of the more stringent limitations scheduled to take effect under the Tax Reform Act of 1986 (TRA), state and local governments issued $206 billion in long-term bonds. (The TRA is discussed in more detail in a later section of this chapter.) By the 1990s, average annual issuance of long-term bonds had grown to $207 billion.

Table 14–1, which traces the volume of tax-exempt securities issued from 1992 to 2001, shows that the volume of long-term, tax-exempt debt surged in 1993 to more than $292 billion; this increase was in response to sharply lower interest rates. Table 14–1 also indicates that revenue bonds have become the dominant form of financing, accounting for $184 billion, or 64.4 percent, of new issues in 2001. In 1970, revenue bonds constituted only 33.5 percent of long-term, tax-exempt debt volume; the proportion had increased to 47.4 percent by 1975 and to 70.0 percent by 1980. There are several reasons for the increased use of revenue bonds since the 1970s: principally, the increase in the use of tax-exempt debt to finance private-purpose projects; voters' reluctance to approve—or officials' reluctance to request approval for—GO issues; and restrictions on the use of GO debt.[6]

Table 14–2 presents data on the composition of long-term, tax-exempt debt. Columns 1, 2, and 3 give the breakdown of new-money issues, refundings, and combined issues. The table shows a sharp increase in refundings in 1993 and 1998—years that saw declining interest rates in the tax-exempt securities market. *The Bond Buyer,* a daily trade publication that covers the municipal bond market, publishes several indexes of interest rates in the municipal market. During 1990, *The Bond Buyer*'s "index of 20 bonds," a widely used measure of long-term interest rates in the tax-exempt market, averaged 7.27 percent; the index declined to 6.44 percent during 1992 and to 5.59 percent during 1993. Between 1990 and 1993, local governments took advantage of lower interest rates to refund debt that had been issued at high interest rates during the 1980s. A similar drop in rates occurred in 1998, when the average level of *The Bond Buyer* 20 index fell to 5.09 percent, its lowest annual rate since 1968.

Table 14–2 also shows the breakdown of fixed-rate and non-fixed-rate debt (non-fixed-rate debt includes variable-rate bonds, zero-coupon bonds, linked-rate bonds, and convertible bonds). From 1992 to 2001, there is a clear overall pattern of increased use of non-fixed-rate debt.

Table 14–3 shows the breakdown of new, long-term, tax-exempt debt by purpose for 1993, 1997, and 2001. The dollar amounts of bonds issued for education, housing, and transportation had the largest increases during the period shown; bonds sold to finance electric power, environmental facilities, and health care declined the most.

Issuers sometimes use credit enhancements to improve the credit quality of their bonds and thereby reduce interest costs; credit enhancements also reduce the cost to investors of obtaining information about the bonds. Investors, especially individual investors, do not have the time or expertise to evaluate the credit quality of governmental issuers: evaluating the quality of the third-party enhancement is easier and less expensive. If the cost of the enhancement is lower than the present value of the savings in interest costs over the life of the bond, a credit enhancement is worthwhile for an issuer.

Table 14–1 Volume of tax-exempt securities issued, 1992–2001 (in billions of $).

Year	General obligation bonds	Revenue bonds	Total long-term bonds	Short-term notes	Total long-term bonds and short-term notes
1992	80.5	154.2	234.7	42.9	277.6
1993	91.5	200.7	292.2	47.4	339.6
1994	55.8	109.2	165.0	40.3	205.3
1995	60.4	99.6	160.0	38.3	198.3
1996	64.3	120.7	185.0	41.7	226.7
1997	72.3	148.2	220.5	46.4	266.9
1998	93.5	192.7	286.2	34.7	320.9
1999	70.2	157.2	227.4	36.6	264.0
2000	65.5	134.7	200.2	41.0	241.2
2001	101.6	184.1	285.7	56.2	341.9

Table 14–2 Composition of long-term, tax-exempt debt, 1992–2001 (in billions of $).

Year	(1) New money	(2) Refunding	(3) Combined	(4) Fixed-rate	(5) Non-fixed-rate
1992	111.4	92.4	30.8	209.4	25.2
1993	96.7	150.2	45.3	262.3	29.9
1994	114.6	38.6	11.8	140.8	24.2
1995	111.7	33.8	14.4	133.9	26.1
1996	123.8	45.9	15.2	158.5	26.5
1997	137.6	60.2	22.7	182.6	37.9
1998	160.2	82.0	44.0	249.1	37.1
1999	157.3	38.3	31.8	186.4	41.0
2000	164.9	19.4	15.9	146.6	53.6
2001	197.7	62.9	25.0	227.8	57.9

Note: Because of rounding, totals for columns 1, 2, and 3 may not equal totals for columns 4 and 5.

Table 14–3 Purposes of tax-exempt bonds, selected years (in billions of $).

Purpose	1993 Amount ($)	1993 Percentage	1997 Amount ($)	1997 Percentage	2001 Amount ($)	2001 Percentage
Education	47.8	16.4	46.0	20.9	71.6	25.1
Electric power	27.8	9.5	6.5	3.0	11.4	4.0
Environmental facilities	13.1	4.5	7.5	3.4	6.1	2.1
Health care	32.0	11.0	26.2	11.9	23.3	8.2
Housing	14.7	5.0	19.6	8.9	21.8	7.6
Industrial development	8.8	3.0	7.8	3.5	7.4	2.6
Public facilities	16.8	5.8	11.0	5.0	10.9	3.8
Transportation	28.6	9.8	24.3	11.0	32.0	11.2
Utilities	36.6	12.5	21.8	9.9	28.8	10.1
Other	65.9	22.6	49.7	22.5	72.4	25.3
Total	292.2	100.0	220.5	100.0	285.7	100.0

Note: Because of rounding, detail may not add to totals.

Bond insurance and letters of credit are the two most common types of credit enhancement in the tax-exempt securities market. Under a standard bond insurance policy, the insurer agrees to pay investors the scheduled principal and interest over the life of the bonds if the issuer fails to make payments in full and on time. As reported by *The Bond Buyer,* the major bond insurers in 2001 were Financial Security Assurance, Inc. (1,590 issues totaling $34.5 billion), the MBIA Corporation (1,253 issues totaling $32.5 billion), the AMBAC Indemnity Corporation (1,072 issues totaling $32.3 billion), and the Financial Guaranty Insurance Company (1,349 issues totaling $30.8 billion).[7] From 1992 through 1998, the proportion of bonds sold with insurance increased steadily, beginning at 34.4 percent and peaking at 50.7 percent. The proportion of bonds sold with insurance declined slightly in 1999 to 46.3 percent, and much more steeply in 2000 to 39.7 percent. The proportion of insured bonds rebounded in 2001 to 46.3 percent.[8]

Letters of credit (LOCs) are most often used to support variable-rate issues that include a put option, which allows the investor to redeem the bond at its par value at regular intervals that may be as frequent as every seven days. The LOC provides investors with a direct claim against the issuing bank in the event that the issuer is unable to make the required payments.

Because both bond insurance and LOCs substitute the credit of the third-party enhancer for that of the issuer, credit-enhanced bonds are granted the same rating as that of the enhancer. All the major bond insurers have the highest rating given by the major rating agencies (Moody's Investors Service Aaa and Standard & Poor's AAA). The rating granted to LOC-enhanced issues is the same as that of the issuing bank.

Tax aspects of municipal bonds

Municipal bonds are sometimes referred to as tax-exempt because the interest income on such bonds is exempt from federal income taxes; many states also exempt the interest income on municipals issued by in-state jurisdictions. Since investors seek to maximize after-tax income for a given level of risk, the before-tax (or nominal) yield on a municipal bond will be less than that on a comparably risky taxable security.

Assuming that the level of risk is the same, the general relationship between taxable and tax-exempt yields is as follows:

Tax-exempt yield = taxable yield × (1 − marginal tax rate).

For example, an investor in the 31 percent income tax bracket would view a yield on a municipal bond paying 5.52 percent as equivalent to a yield of 8 percent on a taxable security; both bonds have the same after-tax yield. The higher the tax rate paid by an investor, the greater the value of the tax exemption for municipal bonds. Table 14–4 shows the relationship between the yields on ten-year, tax-exempt, Aaa-rated state bonds and taxable, ten-year Treasury bonds for 1992 to 2000 (yields on state bonds are often used as a benchmark for rates in the municipal market). Because of the tax exemption on municipal bonds, before-tax yields on municipals are always lower than before-tax yields on comparable taxable securities. The ratio of the tax-exempt yield to the equivalent taxable yield increased from 75.6 to 91.2 percent between 1992 and 2000.

The unique tax aspect of municipal bonds makes them attractive to investors who face high marginal tax rates. As shown in Table 14–5, the primary purchasers of tax-exempt securities are individuals (both directly and through mutual funds), property and casualty insurance companies, and commercial

Table 14–4 Yields on tax-exempt state and taxable U.S. Treasury bonds, 1992–2000.

Year	Ten-year Aaa-rated state bonds (%)	Ten-year U.S. Treasury bonds (%)	Ratio of state bond yield to Treasury bond yield
1992	5.15	6.81	75.6
1993	4.55	5.67	80.3
1994	6.10	7.74	78.8
1995	4.66	5.70	81.8
1996	4.99	6.28	79.5
1997	4.44	5.81	76.4
1998	4.08	4.64	87.9
1999	5.07	6.28	80.7
2000	4.78	5.24	91.2

Note: Yields are for December of each year.

Table 14–5 Ownership of outstanding tax-exempt debt, selected years (in billions of $).

		Percentage of total outstanding debt held by					
	Total outstanding debt ($)	Individual investors			Commercial banks	Property and casualty insurance companies	Other
Year		Direct holdings	Mutual fund holdings	Total			
1985	743.0	40.9	9.4	50.3	31.2	11.9	6.7
1986	789.6	38.2	16.4	54.6	25.8	12.9	6.7
1992	1,302.8	45.0	23.3	68.3	7.5	10.3	13.9
1993	1,377.5	40.0	26.8	66.8	7.2	10.6	15.4
1994	1,341.7	37.3	27.9	65.2	7.3	11.5	16.0
1995	1,293.5	35.2	30.7	65.9	7.2	12.5	14.4
1996	1,296.0	33.4	32.3	65.7	7.3	13.5	13.5
1997	1,367.5	34.3	30.5	64.8	7.1	14.0	14.1
1998	1,464.3	33.3	34.0	67.3	7.2	14.2	11.3
1999	1,532.5	34.2	34.0	68.2	7.2	13.0	11.6
2000	1,567.8	34.1	34.7	68.8	7.3	11.7	12.2
2001	1,685.4	33.0	36.0	69.0	7.1	11.3	12.6

Note: Because of rounding, detail may not add to 100 percent.

banks. As discussed in the next section, after 1986 there was a significant decline in the purchase of municipal bonds by commercial banks because of a change in the effective tax rate paid by banks on interest income from municipals. Between 1992 and 2001, the proportion of tax-exempt debt held by each major investor group remained relatively constant. Note, however, that while the overall proportion of tax-exempt debt held by private individuals fluctuated very little during that period, there was a significant increase in the share of that debt held through mutual funds rather than through direct ownership.

The Tax Reform Act of 1986

The Tax Reform Act of 1986 (TRA) was one in a series of attempts by the U.S. Treasury to define what types of state and local government debt are tax-exempt. The federal government views the interest on tax-exempt securities as a tax expenditure (i.e., a loss of federal revenue attributable to the federal tax code). The Treasury estimated that the revenue loss from tax-exempt debt increased fourfold (to $16.4 billion) between 1976 and 1984. The TRA generally avoided restricting traditional, public-purpose government financing, targeting instead tax-exempt bonds used to finance private purposes. The TRA had a significant impact on both the supply of and demand for tax-exempt securities.

Effect on supply   On the supply side, the law significantly restricted the issuance of private-purpose bonds, tightening the limitations on volume and expanding the types of issues subject to such limitations. According to the TRA, a bond is private purpose (nongovernmental) if it meets two criteria:

Persons or entities other than state or local governments use 10 percent or more of the bond proceeds (or $15 million, in the case of electric and gas facilities) in a trade or business.

Ten percent or more of the debt service is secured by revenues or property used in such trade or business.

Bonds are considered private-purpose bonds if an amount equal to the lesser of $5 million or 5 percent of the proceeds is used to make loans to nongovernmental parties (e.g., for home mortgages). Under the TRA, the interest income on bonds that meet the tests for private activity is subject to taxation unless it is provided with a specific exemption. The TRA also repealed tax-exempt status for several categories of bonds, including the industrial development bonds (IDBs) used for pollution control facilities; sports, convention, and trade show facilities; parking facilities; industrial parks; and hydroelectric facilities. Private-activity bonds that retained tax-exempt status included those for multifamily rental housing; publicly owned airports, docks, and wharves; sewerage and solid-waste disposal facilities; water supply systems; local gas and electric facilities; mass-commuting facilities; and IDBs used for hazardous waste and qualified redevelopment projects.

The TRA also placed a more restrictive cap on the volume of industrial development, student loan, and mortgage revenue bonds that can be issued. Previously, student loan bonds and most IDBs were limited on a state-by-state basis to the greater of $150 per capita or $200 million; mortgage revenue bonds were restricted to the greater of $200 million or 9 percent of the prior three-year average of mortgage originations. The new, consolidated cap was the greater of $75 per capita or $250 million in 1987 and $50 per capita or $150 million thereafter. Exempt from the cap were solid-waste disposal facilities and government-owned airports, docks, and wharves. Nonprofit entities other than hospitals were permitted $150 million per borrower of total tax-exempt debt but were otherwise exempt from the consolidated volume limits. In 2002, the volume limits on private-purpose bonds totaled $23.9 billion for all states.[9]

The TRA drastically reduced the arbitrage profits available to issuers of tax-exempt debt. (Arbitrage profits are earned when the proceeds from tax-exempt securities are invested in higher-yield taxable securities, such as U.S. Treasury notes.) Prior to the TRA, arbitrage profits were available from three sources. First, the "temporary period" rule allowed borrowers to invest the proceeds from a tax-exempt issue at unlimited yields for up to three years after the offering date. Second, borrowers could invest up to 15 percent of the proceeds from an issue in "reasonably required reserve and replacement funds" for the life of the issue. Third, the yield on an issue was defined as the discount rate that equated the net proceeds of the issue (par value less all underwriting expenses) to the present value of future debt service payments. If net proceeds were used in the yield calculation, an issue's "yield" was often as much as 50 basis points—or 50 percent—higher than the true interest cost.

The TRA effectively required that all arbitrage profits be rebated to the federal government. Arbitrage profits not subject to rebate were permitted for only six months after the date of sale and only if all bond proceeds were expended for the intended purpose. For issues of less than $5 million, issuers were permitted to continue investing for the three-year "temporary period." The definition of an issue's yield was also changed to the issue's true interest cost, further reducing the permitted yield on investments. Finally, reserves were limited to 10 percent of bond proceeds, and investment earnings were not to exceed the yield on the issue.

The TRA also restricted bonds sold after January 1986 to a single advance refunding and limited to 2 percent the level of proceeds from private-purpose bonds that could be used to pay for issuance costs.

Effect on demand   The TRA had a significant impact on the demand for tax-exempt securities. In the case of individual investors, the effects were mixed. On the one hand, the act reduced marginal federal income tax rates, thereby reducing individual demand for tax-exempt securities. In addition, interest on private-purpose bonds sold after August 7, 1986, was to be included in the calculation of an individual investor's alternative minimum tax liability—meaning that for some investors, the interest income on these bonds would not be fully exempt from federal taxation. On the other hand, demand for tax-exempt securities was strengthened by the elimination of other tax shelters that had been used widely by individual investors: for example, deductions on individual retirement account and 401(k) plans became subject to new restrictions. Moreover, the increase in the tax rate on long-term capital gains made tax-exempt securities more attractive investments.

The TRA's impact on the demand for tax-exempt securities was greatest for commercial banks.[10] Prior to the TRA, commercial banks could deduct as an expense 80 percent of the cost of funds used to purchase tax-exempt securities, which made tax-exempt securities attractive on an after-tax basis. For example, with a marginal corporate income tax rate of 46 percent (the top rate prior to the TRA) and 80 percent deductibility, a bank that paid 4 percent for deposits and used the funds to invest in high-quality tax-exempts yielding 3.75 percent could earn an after-tax return of 1.22 percent. This return is calculated as follows:

$$3.75\% - \{4\% \times [1 - (0.80)(0.46)]\} =$$
$$3.75\% - \{4\% \times [1 - 0.368]\} =$$
$$3.75\% - \{4\% \times [0.632]\} =$$
$$1.22\%.$$

The TRA eliminated the 80 percent deduction for interest expenses on funds used to purchase tax-exempts after August 7, 1986, and it lowered the top marginal federal corporate income tax rate to 34 percent. The elimination of the deductibility of interest expenses for banks was equivalent to increasing the tax rate on interest income from municipal bonds. The effect was to virtually eliminate commercial banks' demand for tax-exempt securities. As noted earlier (see Table 14–5), beginning in 1986 there was a pronounced reduction in the holdings of commercial banks; as tax-exempt bonds held by commercial banks matured, they were not replaced in bank portfolios (with the exception of bank-qualified issues). By 1992, commercial-bank holdings of tax-exempts were 7.5 percent of the outstanding stock of tax-exempts, and they have remained roughly at that level. Individual investors, both through direct purchases and through the purchase of tax-exempt mutual funds and money-market mutual funds, have filled the void left by the exit of commercial banks. At the end of 2001, combined holdings by individuals accounted for 69 percent of the outstanding stock of tax-exempts.

The TRA allowed the bank interest deduction to be retained for purchases of public-purpose bonds from issuers of less than $10 million in new debt each year. This category of bonds is referred to as bank qualified. In 2001, the volume of bank-qualified bonds was $16.8 billion.[11]

Issuing debt in the primary market

Bonds issued by state and local governments are sold to investors through the underwriting process. An issuer sells the bonds to a group made up of investment banks, commercial banks, or both; the group of banks is called the underwriting syndicate. The members of the underwriting syndicate then resell the bonds to investors. The underwriters earn a profit if they can sell the bonds to investors at a price that is higher than what they paid to the issuer. This section describes how an underwriting syndicate is selected and the services that it provides.

Selling debt to the public involves three elements: origination, underwriting (risk bearing), and distribution. Origination includes all activities necessary to prepare a new issue for sale. The underwriting syndicate performs a risk-bearing service when it purchases the bonds from the issuer at a fixed price; this protects the issuer from the effects of any decreases in price that might occur during the time that the bonds are being sold to investors. Distribution involves selling and delivering the securities to investors.

Origination

Most government issuers use an independent financial advisor to assist in preparing securities for sale. The financial advisor provides a wide range of services: he or she may evaluate the issuer's financial plans and debt policy, offer technical assistance in structuring the new issue, monitor the activities of other members of the financing team, and disseminate information to potential investors. Table 14–6 summarizes the results of a survey investigating the range of services that state and local government issuers received from financial advisors.

Financial advisory services are provided by commercial banks, investment-banking firms, and independent advisory firms. Table 14–7, which lists the top twenty-five financial advisory firms for 2001, shows that these firms are generally independent firms or regional investment-banking firms. The table also shows that business strategies and clientele vary among firms: for example, some firms advised on a large number of small issues (e.g., Springsted Incorporated), while others advised on a small number of large issues (e.g., Lamont Financial Services Corp.).

Preparing a new securities issue for sale involves the services of many other specialists. The sidebar on page 404 lists the most commonly used specialists.

During the origination phase, several important documents are prepared: the official statement (OS), the bond resolution, the bond indenture, and the notice of sale. The OS contains all the information that investors require to evaluate the bonds being offered. Although state and local governments are not subject to Securities and Exchange Commission (SEC) disclosure provisions, SEC Rule 15c2-12 requires underwriters to review an issuer's OS before purchasing bonds from that issuer (disclosure is discussed in more detail later in this chapter). Failing to follow the requirements of this rule may lead to suspension or revocation of an underwriter's broker-dealer license. Because state and local

Table 14–6 Services provided by financial advisors.

Service	Number of governmental units using service
Prepares official statement	746
Recommends maturity schedule	708
Recommends registration procedures	536
Conducts investor relations meetings	363
Aids in rating agency presentation	676
Verifies bids and aids negotiations	684
Analyzes bond sale results	620
Analyzes capital budget	98
Analyzes debt position	320
Analyzes financing options	416
Reviews debt management	147
Reviews investment management	108
Prepares annual financial report	110
Performs other services	19
Total	806

Table 14–7 Top twenty-five financial advisory firms, 2001 (in billions of $).

Rank	Name of firm	Par value of bond sales ($)	Number of bond sales
1	Public Financial Management Inc.	25.8	514
2	Public Resources Advisory Group	19.3	121
3	First Southwest Company	11.2	467
4	Lamont Financial Services Corp.	5.5	43
5	Evensen Dodge Inc.	5.4	296
6	RBC Dain Rauscher Inc.	5.0	169
7	P. G. Corbin & Co.	4.6	48
8	Seattle-Northwest Securities Corp.	3.2	38
9	Estrada Hinojosa & Co.	2.7	51
10	Government Finance Associates Inc.	2.7	23
11	Arimax Financial Advisors Inc.	2.7	35
12	Robert W. Baird & Co.	2.6	90
13	Ponder & Co.	2.5	45
14	CSG Advisors Inc.	2.4	131
15	First Albany Corporation	2.4	20
16	Government Development Bank for Puerto Rico	2.4	9
17	Springsted Incorporated	2.3	279
18	Montague DeRose & Associates	2.3	17
19	William R. Hough & Co.	2.2	39
20	A. C. Advisory Inc.	2.1	11
21	Carnegie Morgan Partners LLC	2.1	13
22	Kaufman Hall & Associates Inc.	2.1	23
23	Morgan Keegan & Co.	2.1	58
24	Stauder, Barch & Associates Inc.	2.0	136
25	A. G. Edwards & Sons Inc.	2.0	39

government issuers are subject to the general antifraud provisions of SEC regulations, they must disclose all material information in the OS.

The guidelines prepared by the Government Finance Officers Association to assist local governments in complying with SEC requirements recommend that the following sections be included in the OS:

Cover page describing key features

Introduction

Description of credit enhancements

Specialists involved in preparing a bond issue for sale

Consulting engineer   Prepares a feasibility study and detailed design specifications for capital projects, and coordinates construction activities.

Bond counsel   Determines whether there is legal authority to issue the proposed securities and certifies that the securities qualify for exemption from federal and state income taxes; also drafts the bond documents, including the official statement and resolutions authorizing the issuance of the securities.

Trustee   Acts as an agent for bondholders to enforce the terms of the bond indenture; takes legal action against the issuer in the event of nonperformance by the issuer.

Paying agent and registrar   Maintains a record of the bondholders and distributes scheduled principal and interest payments to bondholders.

Securities depository   For securities issued in "book entry" form (book entry securities have no physical certificates), maintains a record of the bondholders.

Description of the issuer (name, location, type of governmental unit)

Description of the debt structure

Documentation (bond resolution, bond indenture)

Financial information about the issuer (revenues, debt burden, tax rate, budget figures)

Legal matters (material legal matters that may affect the bonds—e.g., is the issuer being sued or otherwise involved in litigation?)

Other information deemed material.[12]

The bond resolution, the document approved by the issuer to authorize the issuance of the bonds, includes the following information:

Amount of bonds to be issued

Maturity dates of the bonds

Security for the bonds (source of funds to pay the bonds)

Approval of the preliminary official statement and official statement

Approval of the terms of the bond sale to the underwriting syndicate

Approval of the bond indenture.[13]

The bond indenture, the legal contract between the issuer and the trustee, establishes the responsibilities of the issuer and the rights of the bondholders. The bond indenture provides detailed information about the bond covenants and other features that protect the bondholders.

The notice of sale (NOS) is an issuer's official notice of intention to sell an issue by competitive bidding. The NOS must be advertised prior to the bid opening date in accordance with state or local statutes. Smaller issues may be advertised in local or statewide newspapers; larger issues or those with regional or national appeal may be advertised in *The Bond Buyer*. An NOS should contain at least the following information:

Total par value of the bonds to be sold

Amount of bonds in each maturity

Maturity dates

Call provisions, if any

Maximum interest cost permitted

Minimum dollar bid permitted

Time, date, and place for receipt of bids

Basis on which the issue will be awarded

Constraints on the bids

Size of the good-faith deposit

Name of the bond counsel

Name of the person to contact for further information.[14]

Underwriting and distribution

The sale of new issues occurs in one of three ways: through private placement, competitive bidding, or negotiation. In a private placement, the securities are placed directly with the investor and are not offered for sale to the general public. Private placement allows the issuer to tailor the terms of the offering to meet the issuer's particular needs; private placement is also used when the issue has a complex structure or the issuer has unusual circumstances (e.g., a past default). The use of private placements in the tax-exempt securities market is very limited, generally constituting less than 3 percent of new-issue volume.

Competitive bidding and negotiation are the methods used for the public sale of securities. Under competitive bidding, the issuer conducts the origination activities, such as preparing the OS and other documentation, evaluating the issue for bond insurance, obtaining a rating, and scheduling the issue date.[15] Once the terms of the offering are established, the bidding is advertised through an NOS. On the sale date, sealed bids are accepted and opened simultaneously, and the securities are awarded to the underwriting syndicate that bids the lowest interest cost. The underwriting syndicate then resells the securities to investors. The terms of the offering (bond yields and underwriter compensation) are established through the bidding process.

There are two commonly used measures of interest cost: true interest cost (TIC) and net interest cost (NIC). The TIC (which is also referred to as the Canadian method of determining interest cost) is the more conceptually correct measure: it is the interest rate that matches the bond proceeds to the present value of the debt service payments. Computer software is available that will quickly calculate the TIC on an issue. (A computer is necessary because calculation of the TIC requires an iterative trial-and-error algorithm; in addition, because many issues are in serial form, numerous cash flows must be valued.)

The NIC, the traditional means of determining interest cost in the municipal market, was developed as an easy-to-calculate measure long before computers were invented. The NIC is calculated as follows:

NIC = [total coupon interest + bond discount (or − bond premium)]/bond-year dollars, where bond-year dollars is the sum of the par value of each bond times the number of years to maturity.

Because the NIC does not consider the time value of interest payments (i.e., a dollar of interest, whether paid next year or twenty years in the future, has the same value), the NIC may not give bids the same ranking as the TIC. Thus, the NIC could appear more favorable to an issue that is front-loaded—that is, an issue that has high coupon rates on the bonds that mature in the early years. Front-loading is the practice of putting higher coupon rates on shorter-maturity bonds and lower coupon rates on longer-maturity bonds. Lower apparent interest costs may encourage the underwriters to front-load the issue.

In a negotiated underwriting, the issuer first selects a firm to serve as managing (or senior) underwriter, evaluating potential firms according to several criteria, including expertise, financial resources, and experience. The selected firm then assembles an underwriting team (syndicate) to structure, underwrite, and distribute the securities. The terms of the offering are established through negotiation between the issuer and the managing underwriter.

Each method of sale has advantages and disadvantages. The advantages of competitive bidding include the following:

Competitive bidding provides an incentive for underwriters to submit their best bid, resulting in the lowest possible borrowing cost given market conditions.

Historically, gross underwriter spreads (discussed later in this chapter) have been lower on issues sold by competitive bidding.

A competitive sale avoids the appearance of unfairness or impropriety in the selection of an underwriter.

The disadvantages of competitive bidding include the following:

Since bidders do not know whether they will be awarded the bonds, they do not conduct as much research before the sale as they would for a negotiated sale; as a result, underwriters may include a risk premium in their bid to compensate for uncertainty about market demand for the securities.

Competitive bidding allows issuers less flexibility to change the timing or structural characteristics of a scheduled offering.

The issuer loses control over which underwriter is selected and thus cannot affect the distribution of bonds to specific types of investors; this may be an important consideration if an issuer is attempting to include regional or minority-owned firms in the underwriting syndicate.

The advantages of a negotiated issue include the following:

Because the underwriter performs the tasks associated with origination, the issuer is spared the time and expense.

The negotiating underwriter can conduct more extensive presale efforts to assess investor demand; this service is especially valuable for occasional and first-time issuers.

A negotiated issue permits the underwriter to time the sale of the securities in response to changes in market conditions.

The flexibility of a negotiated sale allows the structure of an issue to be changed in response to market conditions or to meet the needs of investors.

A negotiated sale provides an issuer with more control over the composition of the underwriting syndicate.

The disadvantages of a negotiated issue include the following:

Since the terms of an offering are established through negotiation, issuers must keep themselves informed to ensure that prices reflect current market conditions.

Since underwriters provide such a wide range of services in a negotiated issue, it may be difficult to determine whether the gross underwriter spread charged is appropriate for the level of services rendered.

Selection of an underwriter through negotiation may leave the issuer more open to charges of favoritism.

The choice of bidding method will be influenced by several factors, such as the size and complexity of the issue, the credit quality of the issuer, investors' familiarity with the issuer, and market conditions. The size of the issue influences both the level of investor demand and the market's ability to absorb the issue. Issues that are too small may not attract sufficient bidding interest, while very large issues may not be easily absorbed by the market. Thus, unusually large or small issues may benefit from negotiation.

When bond issues have complex or unusual structures, underwriters may need to educate potential investors about the issue's features. Consequently, issues with commonly used and widely understood structures may be floated successfully by competitive bidding, whereas issues with complex security structures or innovative structural features (e.g., put options, variable rates, interest rate swaps) may benefit from a negotiated underwriting. In addition, since negotiation provides the flexibility to respond to changing market conditions, it may be the preferred method in an unstable market; this is particularly true in the case of refunding issues, when the cost-effectiveness of the deal may be sensitive to small changes in market rates.

Since investors generally prefer high-quality issues, issuers may be wise to use competitive bidding for issues with investment-grade ratings (those rated Baa or BBB and above). Because investors are generally more familiar with the credit quality and credit history of more frequent issuers, less additional marketing activity is necessary for a new issue. Therefore, frequent issuers may achieve good results through competitive bidding, whereas less frequent issuers may benefit from the additional marketing efforts associated with a negotiated sale.

Negotiation is the preferred method of sale for issuers of tax-exempt bonds. The dominance of negotiated underwritings dates back to the mid-1970s and can be attributed to two factors: the growing volatility of interest rates in the municipal bond market and the increasing use of more complicated revenue bond structures.

There is a strong association between method of sale, type of bond (GO versus revenue), and purpose. For example, during 2001, of the $21.8 billion in housing issues sold to investors, $21.2 billion were revenue bonds and $19.4 billion were floated by negotiation. There was a similar relationship for electric power, health care, and environmental issues. On the other hand, many governments are required by statute to use competitive bidding for GO bond issues.

Underwriters are compensated for their services through the gross underwriter spread. The gross spread is the difference between the gross proceeds received by the underwriter from the sale of the bonds on the market and the price paid to the issuer. The spread is generally expressed in terms of dollars per $1,000 of par value. The gross spread has four basic components:

The takedown, or sales commission, is compensation to the underwriters for selling the bonds to investors; the takedown is normally the largest component of the spread.

The management fee compensates the underwriter for origination and advisory services.

The expense component reimburses the underwriter for outlays incurred on behalf of the issuer, such as those for legal counsel, bond printing, mailing and printing of official statements, and the services of rating agencies.

The underwriting fee is compensation for the market risks in a fixed-price underwriting.

Gross underwriter spreads declined significantly between 1992 and 2001, from an average of $9.62 per $1,000 of par value to $6.64—a decline of

31 percent.[16] This pattern is a continuation of a decline that began in the early 1980s (in 1981, the average spread on all long-term tax-exempt securities was $23.93 per $1,000 bond). The overall decline in spreads is consistent with an increase in competition between underwriters. During the period from 1992 to 2001, the differences in underwriter spreads between bonds sold by negotiation and those sold by competitive bidding remained small, averaging about $0.50 per $1,000 bond.[17]

The secondary market for municipal bonds

After the issuer makes the initial sale of the bonds to investors, subsequent trades between investors take place in the secondary market, whose primary purpose is to provide liquidity to investors. Unlike the stocks and bonds traded on the New York Stock Exchange and the American Stock Exchange, municipal bonds have no central securities exchange. Instead, the secondary market for municipals is an over-the-counter market that consists of a network of dealers and brokers; this network includes local and regional brokerage firms and commercial banks as well as large Wall Street firms. Dealers provide immediacy of execution to investors by standing ready to buy (at their posted bid price) and sell (at their posted ask or offer price) on demand; dealers maintain an inventory of bonds in which they make a market. Brokers facilitate trading by providing information to buyers about potential sellers and to sellers about potential buyers; brokers do not maintain an inventory of bonds.

Because the number of outstanding bonds is small, most municipal bonds do not have an active secondary market and are considered illiquid securities. The standard denomination of a municipal bond is $5,000; thus, a $3 million bond issue contains only six hundred bonds. If the bonds are a serial issue with equal maturities over fifteen years, only forty bonds will mature each year. With such a small number of bonds, it is not profitable for a firm to maintain an inventory and continuously make a market. If an investor wants to sell a bond that is not handled by a dealer, the investor usually hires a local firm to serve as a broker to locate a potential buyer. There is, however, an active secondary market for some large issuers. Well-known market "names" (e.g., New York City, the state of California) are supported by numerous dealers, many of whom have an investment-banking relationship with the issuer.

For retail investors, a standard lot (i.e., the minimum standard trading volume) is $25,000 (i.e., five $5,000-par-value bonds); anything less than $25,000 is considered an "odd lot." The dealer spread (the difference between the dealer's asking and bid prices) for retail investors ranges from one-quarter of one point (0.25 percent of par value), or $12.50 per $5,000 bond for large blocks of actively traded bonds, to four points (4 percent of par value), or $200 per $5,000 bond on odd lots of an inactive issue. For institutional investors, an odd lot is anything below $100,000 of par value. Spreads for institutional investors generally do not exceed one-half of one point (0.50 percent of par value), or $25 per $5,000 bond.

There is no central public information repository where all sellers can list the securities they have for sale and all buyers can indicate their interest in purchasing securities.[18] There is, however, comprehensive information on the transaction prices of actual trades. Municipal Securities Rulemaking Board (MSRB) Rule G-14 requires brokers and dealers to report information on transactions to the MSRB. Although the reporting requirement initially covered only transactions between dealers, since 1998 it has also included transactions with customers.[19]

A report released by the MSRB in January 2000 provides insights about the level of trading of municipal bonds in the secondary market.[20] The study analyzed the trading activity of all bonds sold between May 1, 1998, and June 30, 1998; the trading period analyzed was from May 1, 1998, to April 30, 1999. The study found that virtually all trading occurred within the first four days after issue. Of the total par value of bonds issued, only 19.0 percent traded on the day of issue; 18.1 percent traded on the following day. Two days after issue, only 4.1 percent traded, and by the fourth day after sale, only 1.6 percent traded. These data show that less than 20 percent of all bonds trade in the secondary market at all, and by four days after the sale date, virtually no bonds trade.

Credit quality

The issuer's credit quality is one of the most important determinants of the interest rate that the issuer will pay on its debt. The stronger the issuer's perceived ability to pay the principal and interest on time and in full, the lower the interest rate that investors will require to purchase the securities, and the lower the issuer's interest cost.

Contributing factors

Credit quality varies with the type of bond being issued. GO bonds, for example, are backed by the full faith, credit, and general taxing powers of the issuer; thus, the issuer's ability to meet the debt service obligations depends on whether the tax base can generate sufficient revenues—which depends, in turn, on four factors: debt burden, budgetary soundness, tax burden, and the overall condition of the economy.[21]

Debt burden　An issuer's debt burden depends on the gross amount of outstanding debt, the amount of direct net debt (gross outstanding debt less sinking funds and reserve accounts dedicated to repayment of the debt), and the amount of overall net debt (direct net debt plus overlapping debt of other issuers that is supported by taxes levied in the issuer's jurisdiction). Debt burden is usually evaluated on a per capita basis.

Although there are no fixed standards for assessing an issuer's debt burden, the following circumstances may indicate too much debt burden:

Overall net debt exceeding 10 percent of assessed value

Overall net debt exceeding $1,200 per capita

An increase of 20 percent or more over the previous year in overall net debt as a percentage of market valuation (the market value of real property in the jurisdiction)

For overall net debt as a percentage of market valuation, an increase of 50 percent or more over the figure for four years earlier

Net direct debt exceeding 90 percent of the amount authorized by state law

Overall net debt exceeding 15 percent of per capita personal income.[22]

Other factors to consider include key measures of debt burden in comparison to median figures for all issuers; debt service payments as a percentage of estimated tax revenues; unused debt capacity; and the history of voter approval for new taxes and bond issues.

Budgetary soundness　Several factors must be considered in determining budgetary soundness. One factor is the reliability of an issuer's budgeting and accounting records, and a good indicator of reliability is whether an independent accounting firm regularly audits the financial accounts. Another factor is an issuer's history of producing balanced budgets, maintaining adequate reserve accounts, and using short-term financing to cover budgetary deficits. Finally, an assessment must be made of the way in which an issuer has dealt with constituent demands for more services and with employee demands for higher wages and benefits.

Tax burden An assessment of tax burden considers the diversity and stability of the issuer's primary revenue sources and the overall level of taxes. Ideally, an issuer would have well-diversified revenue streams and would not rely heavily on any single source; issuers with one large revenue source are more vulnerable to the effects of sudden economic change. A related factor is the presence of a single large taxpayer in the jurisdiction. The level of taxation must also be considered: a low current tax burden may indicate that taxes can be raised in the future to meet unanticipated revenue shortfalls.

Overall condition of the economy Key indicators of overall economic health include the level and growth rate of per capita personal income, trends in population growth, the age distribution of the population, the diversity of industry, the age and condition of the housing stock, and the level of new building activity.

For GO bonds, factors that signal a decline in an issuer's ability to pay its debt service include

Declining property values and increasing taxpayer delinquency

Annual increases in the tax burden that are higher than those of adjacent areas

An increasing property tax rate and a declining population

Declines in the number and value of permits for new buildings

Actual revenues consistently falling below budgeted revenues

Increases in the size or frequency of year-end deficits

Annual increases in expenditures that exceed the rate of inflation

Increasing unfunded pension liabilities

Increasing GO debt in conjunction with stagnant property values

Increasing unemployment and declining personal income.[23]

Bond ratings

Because substantial expense and time are required to evaluate the credit quality of an issuer of tax-exempt securities, many investors use an issue's bond rating as their primary guide to credit quality. When they issue new securities, state and local governments generally request and pay for one or more bond ratings because they realize that unless they obtain a rating, many potential investors will not consider purchasing their bonds; in addition, some institutional investors are restricted to purchasing bonds rated as investment grade.

Bond ratings are obtained during the origination phase of the new-issue process so that the bonds will be rated at the time of sale. The three major bond-rating firms are Moody's Investors Service, Standard & Poor's (S & P), and Fitch Ratings. Letter designations indicate the rating firms' evaluation of an issuer's credit quality. The top four rating categories (Baa or BBB and above) are considered investment grade. Figure 14–1 shows the bond-rating designations for Moody's and S & P.

Rating agencies rate bonds upon the request of the issuing government for an agreed-upon fee, which is usually based on the time and effort needed to carry

Figure 14–1 Bond-rating designations, Moody's Investors Service and Standard & Poor's.

Moody's Investors Service		Standard & Poor's	
Rating	Description	Rating	Description
Aaa	Best quality	AAA	Highest quality; extremely strong capacity to pay
Aa	High quality by all standards	AA	High quality; very strong capacity to pay
A	Upper-medium grade	A	Strong capacity to pay principal and interest
Baa	Medium grade	BBB	Adequate capacity to pay principal and interest
Ba	Has speculative elements	BB	Least degree of speculative characteristics within the speculative grade category
B	Generally lacks character-istics of a desirable investment	B	Speculative
Caa	Poor standing; may be in default	CCC & CC	Highly speculative; vulnerable to nonpayment
Ca	Speculative in a high degree; often in default	C	Subordinated debt and preferred stock that is highly vulnerable to non-payment
C	Extremely poor prospects	D	In payment default

out the analysis.[24] Once the rating agency rates the new bond issue, it continues to maintain and renew the rating until the bond has been fully redeemed.

Although many investors believe that all rating agencies grade all types of bond issues according to the same criteria, this is not quite accurate. Moody's and S & P, for example, take slightly different approaches to rating municipal bonds: Moody's focuses more on the issuer's debt level, and S & P focuses more on the issuer's economic base.

A bond rating affects marketability and bond financing costs. If a bond receives an investment-grade rating, several underwriters will enter bids, which will keep the pricing competitive and the bond financing costs down. If a bond receives a speculative or low investment grade, however, fewer underwriters will be interested in bidding. The price will be higher to compensate for the additional risk, and the end result will be higher bond financing costs.

There are three principal reasons that a local government may decide not to obtain a rating for a bond issue. First, if the local government anticipates receiving a poor rating, the effort may not be worth the investment: a bad rating will only damage the marketability of the bond and increase the financing costs. Second, if the issue is to be marketed locally, potential investors may already have sufficient information about the creditworthiness of the issuer, obviating the need to obtain a rating. Third, the amount of debt being issued may be so small that the potential interest savings resulting from a good rating will not offset the cost of obtaining one.

A bond rating is necessary to attract nonlocal or institutional investors. In the case of a small bond issue, the lack of a rating may not significantly influence the bond financing costs or marketability. But a large bond issue without a rating sends a message that the issuer's creditworthiness is poor.

Bond insurance

Once a local government has obtained a rating for a particular bond issue, it may purchase private bond insurance to improve the bond's rating.[25] As noted earlier in the chapter, the insurance company agrees to stand behind the debt obligations of the issuer, and this financial assurance results in a higher rating for the bond issue that is based on the credit quality of the insurance company.

Insurance premiums are based on an assessment of the financial condition of the issuer and the associated risk of default. Because each insurance company uses its own assessment criteria, a preliminary rating from a rating agency is not necessarily required. The insurance premiums are typically quoted as basis points for negotiated bond issues and converted into a flat dollar amount for competitive issues. To calculate the total premium, the basis-point price is multiplied by the total principal and interest of the bond issue. As of March 2002, a $20 million bond with an underlying (preliminary) A rating had an average premium of between 15 and 25 basis points.[26]

A local government would choose to purchase bond insurance only if the higher rating would reduce the overall cost of financing the bond (taking into account the cost of the insurance premium). Even when local officials believe that purchasing insurance would be in the government's best interest, however, insurance will not necessarily be available. Because bond insurance is a long-term commitment and the insurer cannot change the guarantee once it has been issued, insurance companies evaluate creditworthiness more critically than do the rating agencies.[27] If the preliminary rating is below investment grade, it is unlikely that any reputable insurance company will be willing to underwrite the policy. It may also be difficult to purchase bond insurance if the issue is too small, because insurance companies may be unwilling to undertake the risk associated with an unsuccessful marketing of the bond issue.

As noted earlier, the four leaders in the municipal bond insurance market are the Financial Security Assurance, Inc., MBIA Corporation, the AMBAC Indemnity Corporation, and the Financial Guaranty Insurance Company.

Analyzing credit quality

An analysis of the credit quality of a revenue bond focuses primarily on whether the project being financed can generate sufficient revenue to meet debt service payments. Important factors to evaluate are the debt service coverage ratio (the portion of the debt service that projected revenues will cover), projected customer demand for the product or service produced by the facility, and the quality of the enterprise's management. In addition, the bond documents should provide investors with detailed information in the following areas: (1) limitations on the basic security, (2) flow-of-funds structure, (3) rate or user charge covenants, (4) priority of revenue claims, (5) additional-bonds test, and (6) other covenants.[28]

Limitations on the basic security Revenues available to pay the bonds should be clearly identified, as should any limitations on those revenues stemming from federal, state, or local laws or procedures.

Flow-of-funds structure The bond indenture should state clearly the order in which revenues flow through the accounting funds and the priorities for the use of funds. A net revenue structure is one in which debt service is paid to bondholders immediately after basic operating and maintenance funds are paid but before other expenses are paid. A gross revenue structure is one in which bondholders are paid before operating and maintenance expenses are paid.

Rate or user charge covenants The bond indenture should indicate what the issuer is legally obligated to do with respect to setting rates or user charges. For example, an issuer may be obligated only to set rates or charges that are sufficient to meet all expenses (including debt service), or an issuer may be obligated to set rates or charges at sufficiently high levels to maintain specified reserves. The indenture should also indicate whether the issuer needs prior approval from other governmental units before rates or charges can be changed.

Priority of revenue claims   The legal opinion should indicate whether other parties can legally claim the revenues securing the bonds before the revenues enter the flow-of-funds structure.

Additional-bonds test   The bond documents should describe the circumstances under which additional bonds can be issued that have an equal claim on the securing revenues. A commonly used additional-bonds test requires projected revenues to cover by some multiple the sum of the maximum annual debt service on the current and additional bonds (e.g., projected revenues must be two times the maximum annual debt service of the old and new bonds).

Other covenants   The bond documents should indicate whether there are other covenants that provide protection to bondholders. Examples include covenants to maintain adequate insurance on the facilities, to have an annual audit by an independent accountant, and to keep the facilities in good operating condition.

Municipal bond defaults

Although the overall credit quality of municipal bonds is quite good, defaults do occur. Between 1982 and 1996, the relative level of defaults was very low: less than 0.5 percent of outstanding indebtedness.[29] In 1996, of the sixty-nine issues that defaulted, twenty-four were housing issues that totaled $179 million, or 22 percent of the total dollar amount of defaults. The states with the largest defaults in 1996 were California (twenty-six issues totaling $274 million) and Kentucky (two issues totaling $142 million).

The large increase in the dollar amount of defaulted bonds in 1983 was caused by the default of a single issuer: Washington Public Power Supply System (WPPSS), commonly referred to as "Whoops." WPPSS, a wholesale power authority in Washington State, initially planned to construct five nuclear power plants to generate electricity. Projects four and five were backed by "take-or-pay" purchase contracts signed by participating private and public utilities in the Northwest.[30] In 1982, after issuing $2.25 billion in tax-exempt revenue bonds backed by the anticipated revenues from these contracts, WPPSS stopped construction on projects four and five: not only had WPPSS experienced huge cost overruns on these plants, but it had also determined that the power from these facilities was not needed to meet anticipated demand. In 1983, when the Washington Supreme Court ruled that the public utilities in the state had no authority to repay the outstanding debt of projects four and five, WPPSS defaulted on the $2.25 billion in revenue bonds. The bondholders sued WPPSS and the participating utilities in an attempt to force them to make the promised debt payments. In December 1988, a $753 million settlement was reached. Under the terms of the settlement, bondholders received between ten and forty cents per dollar invested in the WPPSS bonds. WPPSS remains the largest default in the history of the municipal market.

Refunding a bond issue

Most long-term bonds include an optional redemption provision, commonly referred to as a call option, that permits the issuer to redeem the bonds at a preset price, usually slightly above par, on certain dates prior to the stated maturity. Should interest rates fall substantially after issuance, the call option allows the issuer to redeem the old bonds at a preset price and issue new bonds at a lower interest rate. Thus, the call option gives an issuer the flexibility to refinance a debt to take advantage of lower interest rates.

As noted earlier in the chapter, issuers of tax-exempt securities have refunded substantial amounts of debt in recent years, and the volume of new issues sold for refunding purposes tends to rise when interest rates decline and to fall when interest rates increase. A refunding will be beneficial to an issuer if the costs of issuing the new bonds and redeeming the old bonds (e.g., under-writing costs on the new issue plus the call premium on the old issue) are less than the present value of the interest savings that will be realized over the remaining life of the old bonds.

A call provision is detrimental to the owners of the bonds (i.e., to investors) because bonds are generally called for early redemption during a period of declining interest rates. As a result, investors have to reinvest their funds at a rate lower than that on the called bonds. Since a call provision benefits the issuer but is harmful to investors, callable bonds have higher coupon rates. Thus, a call feature gives an issuer future financing flexibility, but in return for a higher borrowing cost.

One way to offer some protection to investors, and also reduce borrowing costs, is to include a provision in the bond indenture that prohibits an issuer from redeeming bonds under the call option for a certain period—often five to ten years—from the date of original issue. This period of time is called the period of call protection, or the deferment period. Including a deferment period ensures investors that promised coupon payments will continue for a minimum period. In addition, most bond indentures require the issuer to pay a call premium to investors when the bonds are called. In the tax-exempt bond market, these premiums range from 2 to 5 percent of par value. The call premium is another way to compensate investors for the loss of their bonds.

An advance refunding can be used to issue new bonds to take advantage of lower interest rates prior to the date of first call of the old bonds—in other words, during the deferment period of the old bonds. There are two types of advance refundings: standard defeasance, or net cash defeasance, and crossover refunding. A defeasance of an outstanding bond issue involves a formal release of the lien of the bondholders on the pledged assets or revenues, in exchange for the pledge of cash or securities sufficient to repay the bonds. In a standard defeasance, the proceeds of the new bonds are used to purchase a portfolio of U.S. Treasury securities. Treasury regulations limit the yield on these securities to the yield on the new tax-exempt bonds. The Treasury securities are held in an escrow account, and the escrow account is structured so that the income and principal meet all debt service payments on the old bonds until the first call date. On the first call date, the funds in the escrow account are used to call the old bonds at the call price (par value plus call premium).

In a crossover refunding, the proceeds from the new issue are not used to defease the debt service obligations on the old bonds. Instead, an escrow account is established sufficient to pay only the call premium and the principal amount of bonds to be redeemed at the call date. During the time prior to the first call date, the escrow funds are used to pay the debt service on the new tax-exempt bonds. On the call date, the escrow funds are used to redeem the old bonds. After the call date, the issuer pays the debt service on the new bonds.

Recent controversies in the tax-exempt securities market

Three areas of concern in the securities industry have been at least partially addressed by federal and state laws: inadequate disclosure of information to investors about the creditworthiness of issuers, political contributions by municipal securities businesses to government officials, and yield burning. Each is discussed below.

Disclosure

The full disclosure to investors of information about the creditworthiness of issuers is essential for the efficient operation of securities markets. When potential investors are unable to gauge the ability of an issuer to make promised bond payments, they may not participate in the market or they may bid low prices that assume the worst about an issuer's ability to pay. In either case, issuers' interest costs will be higher than they would have been if investors had been fully informed.[31] It is thus in the best interests of issuers (i.e., issuers will receive the lowest possible borrowing costs) to disclose complete information about their current financial condition and future prospects. In securities markets, disclosure occurs at the time of issue through the preparation and distribution of an official statement; after issuance it occurs through the periodic reporting of financial data and other material events.

The Securities Act of 1933 and the Securities Exchange Act of 1934 are the two principal laws that govern the securities industry in the United States. The Securities Act of 1933 (1) requires that investors receive financial and other significant information concerning securities being offered for public sale (primary market disclosure) and (2) prohibits deceit, misrepresentations, and other fraud in the sale of securities. The Securities Exchange Act of 1934 created the Securities Exchange Commission (SEC) and gave the SEC the power to register, regulate, and oversee brokerage firms, transfer agents, and clearing agencies, as well as the nation's securities self-regulatory organizations (SROs). SROs include the New York Stock Exchange, the American Stock Exchange, and the National Association of Securities Dealers, which operates the NASDAQ (National Association of Securities Dealers Automated Quotation) system. The 1934 act also empowered the SEC to require periodic reporting of information by companies with publicly traded securities (secondary market disclosure).

Issuers of tax-exempt securities are exempt from the registration and periodic disclosure requirements of these acts. However, in the early 1970s, as the size of the tax-exempt securities market grew and the number of participants expanded, concerns developed about the lack of a formal regulatory mechanism. Congress responded by passing the Securities Acts Amendments of 1975, which created the Municipal Securities Rulemaking Board. The MSRB develops rules to regulate securities firms and banks involved in the underwriting, trading, and selling of municipal securities. Its mission is to protect investors and to foster a fair and efficient municipal securities market. The board consists of fifteen members: five representatives of bank dealers, five representatives of securities firms, and five public representatives not affiliated with any bank dealer or securities firm. The MSRB is self-funded through fees and assessments paid by the dealer community.[32]

The Securities Exchange Act of 1934 specifically prohibits the SEC from imposing a presale filing requirement on issuers of municipal securities, and neither the 1933 nor the 1934 act requires issuers to periodically provide financial information after securities are issued. However, issuers have voluntarily adopted disclosure guidelines for official statements (which have been published by the Government Finance Officers Association),[33] and issuers may be subject to state disclosure requirements under so-called blue sky laws. Fourteen states (Arizona, Delaware, Florida, Idaho, Illinois, Kansas, Massachusetts, Michigan, Nebraska, North Carolina, Oregon, Rhode Island, Tennessee, and

Texas) require full disclosure; issuers in these states must file official statements, disclose specific information in those statements, and obtain approval from a state regulator.[34] In fifteen states (Alabama, Alaska, Colorado, Hawaii, Iowa, Maine, Maryland, Mississippi, Missouri, Nevada, New Mexico, North Dakota, South Dakota, Wisconsin, and Wyoming), issuers are not subject to any disclosure requirements and need not obtain approval from a state regulator.[35] The remaining twenty-one states have various filing and approval requirements.

Since there is no legal mechanism to force mandatory disclosure by issuers, disclosure regulation in the tax-exempt securities market occurs indirectly, through requirements on underwriters. SEC Rule 15c2-12 requires underwriters to (1) obtain and review a final official statement (OS) prior to purchase, (2) send a preliminary OS to a potential customer who requests one, (3) contract with the issuer to obtain a final OS, and (4) send a final OS to any potential customer who requests one.[36] Amendments to Rule 15c2-12 require the disclosure of annual financial data and timely updates on material events that may affect issuers' ability to make promised bond payments. Since Rule 15c2-12 prohibits dealers from underwriting tax-exempt securities unless they have determined that issuers have agreed to make these disclosures to investors, disclosure is thus an indirect requirement for issuers.[37]

The MSRB has also adopted rules intended to improve disclosure practices. Rule G-32 requires underwriters to provide investors with copies of official statements that issuers have voluntarily supplied. Rule G-17 requires underwriters to disclose to investors, at the time of trade, all material facts concerning the transaction. Rule G-19 requires that underwriters have "reasonable grounds" to believe that the securities they sell are suitable for investors. Rule G-36 requires underwriters to provide the MSRB with copies of official statements that issuers have voluntarily provided.[38]

Although the level of disclosure in the tax-exempt securities market has improved dramatically in recent years, the market still lacks (1) standardized disclosure requirements that would apply to all issuers and (2) a single, centralized repository for such information.

Political contributions and prohibitions on municipal securities business

MSRB Rule G-37, entitled "Political Contributions and Prohibitions on Municipal Securities Business," took effect on April 25, 1994. It (1) prohibits brokers, dealers, and municipal securities dealers from engaging in municipal securities business with issuers if they have made political contributions to officials of the issuers and (2) requires dealers to record and disclose certain political contributions, as well as other information, to allow public scrutiny of their political contributions and municipal securities business. The prohibition on engaging in municipal securities business does not apply to municipal finance professionals who are entitled to vote for the officials of issuing entities, as long as their total contributions to each official per election do not exceed $250.

Rule G-37 was enacted in response to concerns, on the part of regulators, public finance professionals, and the media, that public officials' decisions about contracts with financial advisors, bond lawyers, underwriters, and other finance professionals were being improperly influenced by political contributions made to those officials. (The practice of requiring, either expressly or implicitly, political contributions from those who wish to be considered for an award of underwriting, advisory, or related business is referred to as "pay-to-play.")[39]

In 1995, William B. Blount, then chairman of the Democratic Party in Alabama and a principal in the securities firm Blount, Parrish & Roton, challenged Rule G-37 on two grounds: first, that it violated his First Amendment rights to free speech and free association; second, that it violated the Tenth Amendment by attempting to regulate state election campaigns, which was a usurpation of the states' power to control their own elections. In upholding Rule G-37, the Court of Appeals for the District of Columbia Circuit stated that the rule was a constitutionally permissible restraint on free speech because it served a compelling governmental interest in rooting out corruption in the market for municipal securities.[40] The U.S. Supreme Court declined to review the case.[41]

In July 2001, the MSRB issued a formal request for comments on Rule G-37.[42] Several organizations, including the Association for Investment Management and Research, the Bond Market Association, the Democratic National Committee, the Government Finance Officers Association, the Investment Company Institute, and the Republican National Committee, urged that Rule G-37 be revised, noting that its broad application unduly circumscribes the constitutional rights of individual employees and creates unnecessary burdens for municipal securities firms.[43]

Yield burning

As discussed in the section on refunding, issuers can take advantage of declining interest rates by advance refunding of an outstanding bond issue. To prevent issuers from earning arbitrage profits, Internal Revenue Service (IRS) regulations state that the yield on the Treasury securities used to fund the escrow account may not materially exceed the yield on the new tax-exempt bonds.[44] If arbitrage profits are earned, these profits must be rebated to the U.S. Treasury; if arbitrage profits are not rebated, the bonds will be considered "arbitrage bonds" and will lose their tax-exempt status.

In the early 1990s, the IRS began exploring regulations that would specify how the fair-market value of securities used in refunding escrow accounts would be determined. The issue became front-page news in 1995, when an employee of a major investment-banking firm claimed that he had been fired for telling federal authorities about his firm's policy of overvaluing escrow-account securities. The practice—in which investment bankers excessively mark up the prices of Treasury securities sold to issuers for refunding escrow accounts—is referred to as "yield burning" because the inflated prices "burn down" the securities' yields to give the appearance of compliance with arbitrage regulations. Yield burning also creates excess profits for the securities firms—in effect, shifting arbitrage profits from the issuer to the investment banker.

Because the disclosure of widespread yield burning threatened to make billions of dollars of tax-exempt debt taxable, it had a tremendous impact on the tax-exempt securities market.[45] In response to the allegations about yield burning, the IRS issued Revenue Procedure 96-41, which outlined a voluntary closing agreement program for pre-refunded bond issues. Under the program, issuers could make payments to the U.S. Treasury for the difference between the amount paid for escrow-account securities and their fair-market value. Concurrently, the SEC began its own investigations, which resulted in civil administrative charges of fraud against a large number of investment-banking firms. In April 2000, the SEC announced that as part of a global settlement agreement involving 3,603 bond issues, seventeen firms would pay a total of $120 million to the U.S. Treasury and $18 million to issuers.

If previous settlements are included, more than $170 million has been paid to the U.S. Treasury and issuers.

Conclusion

The market for tax-exempt securities continues to evolve in several respects; many new types of debt securities are becoming available, including debt securities packaged with other financial instruments, such as interest rate swaps. In addition, investors and market professionals are making increasing demands for state and local government issuers to disclose more information about their financial condition on a continuing and timely basis. To understand the many financing alternatives available and to be responsive to disclosure requirements and other regulations, local government finance officers must make a continuous effort to stay up-to-date.

1 For a comprehensive treatment of capital finance and budgeting, see A. John Vogt, *Capital Budgeting and Finance: A Guide for Local Governments* (Washington, D.C.: International City/County Management Association, 2004).

2 See J. B. Kurish and Patricia Tigue, *An Elected Official's Guide to Debt Issuance* (Chicago: Government Finance Officers Association, 1993).

3 Ibid., 114.

4 See Sylvan G. Feldstein and Frank J. Fabozzi, "Municipal Bonds," in *The Handbook of Fixed-Income Securities,* ed. Frank J. Fabozzi (Homewood, Ill.: Business One Irwin, 1991).

5 An arbitrage opportunity exists when sinking-fund monies can be invested at a rate that is higher than the interest rate on the bonds.

6 George G. Kaufman and Philip J. Fischer, "Debt Management," in *Management Policies in Local Government Finance,* 3rd ed., ed. J. Richard Aronson and Eli Schwartz (Washington, D.C.: International City Management Association, 1987), 293–294.

7 Thomson Media, *The Bond Buyer/Thomson Financial 2002 Yearbook* (New York: Thomson Media, 2002), 65.

8 Ibid.

9 Ibid., 27.

10 For an empirical analysis of the impact of commercial bank demand on state and local government borrowing costs for bank-qualified issues, see Ronald W. Forbes and Paul A. Leonard, "Bank-Qualified Tax-Exempt Securities: A Test of Market Segmentation and Commercial Bank Demand," *Municipal Finance Journal* 14 (winter 1994): 18–31.

11 Thomson Media, *Bond Buyer/2002 Yearbook,* 214.

12 Government Finance Officers Association (GFOA), *Disclosure Guidelines for Offerings of Securities by State and Local Governments* (Chicago: GFOA, 1991).

13 See Kurish and Tigue, *Elected Official's Guide,* 31.

14 See Kaufman and Fischer, "Debt Management," 307.

15 See Paul A. Leonard, "Negotiated versus Competitive Bond Sales: A Review of the Literature," *Municipal Finance Journal* 15 (summer 1994): 12–36.

16 Thomson Media, *Bond Buyer/2002 Yearbook.*

17 Ibid.

18 For many years *The Blue List,* a weekly publication of Standard & Poor's Corporation, listed municipal bonds and notes offered for sale and their asking prices, but it is no longer published.

19 This information is available by subscription through the Web site of the Municipal Securities Rulemaking Board (MSRB), www.msrb.org, or by subscription through Thomson Financial Corporation's Municipal Market Monitor (www.tm3.com/tm3home/). The Thomson site allows the user to search for the trading history of specific securities.

20 Municipal Securities Rulemaking Board, Muni Price Reporting/Transaction Reporting System, "Release of Certain Statistical Information on Transaction Patterns in the Municipal Securities Market, Report on Frequently Traded Securities," available at www.msrb.org/msrb1/TRSweb/MarketStats/Statistical1_19_00.htm.

21 See Sylvan G. Feldstein, "Guidelines in the Analysis of General Obligation and Revenue Municipal Bonds," in Fabozzi, *Fixed-Income Securities.*

22 See Karl Nollenberger, ed., *Evaluating Financial Condition: A Handbook for Local Government* (Washington, D.C.: International City/County Management Association, 2003).

23 See Feldstein, "Guidelines," 466–467.

24 The remainder of the section entitled "Bond Ratings" was contributed by Mary H. Harris.

25 The section entitled "Bond Insurance" was contributed by Mary H. Harris.

26 These averages were quoted by an insurance industry official in a telephone conversation with Mary H. Harris.

27 Unlike insurance companies, rating agencies can downgrade bond ratings if a jurisdiction's creditworthiness deteriorates.

28 Feldstein, "Guidelines," 445–447.

29 Thomson Media, *Bond Buyer/2002 Yearbook.*

30 The take-or-pay contracts obligated the purchasing utilities to make payments whether or not they actually received any electric power.

31 The classic article on market failure is George A. Akerlof, "The Market for 'Lemons': Quality Uncertainty and the Market Mechanism," *Quarterly Journal of Economics* 84 (August 1970): 488–500.

32 Further information about the MSRB can be found at www.msrb.org.

33 GFOA, *Disclosure Guidelines.*

34 See Lisa M. Fairchild and Timothy W. Koch, "The Impact of State Disclosure Requirements on Municipal Yields," *National Tax Journal* 51 (December 1998): 733–753.

35 Ibid.

36 Lisa M. Fairchild and Nan S. Ellis, "Rule 15c2-12: A Flawed Regulatory Framework Creates Pitfalls for Municipal Issuers," *Journal of Urban and Contemporary Law* 55, no. 1 (1999): 9–17.

37 Ibid.

38 Municipal Securities Rulemaking Board, "MSRB Discussion Paper on Disclosure in the Municipal Securities Market," *MSRB Reports* 21, no. 1 (May 2001).

39 Robert E. Plaze, "Pay-to-Play and Public Pension Plans" (speech, annual joint legislative meeting of the National Association of State Retirement Administrators, the National Conference on Public Employee Retirement Systems, and the National Council on Teacher Retirement, Washington, D.C., 26 January 1999).

40 *Blount v. Securities and Exchange Commission,* 61 F.3d 938 (1995).

41 *Blount v. SEC,* 61 F.3d 938 (1995); cert. denied, 517 U.S. 1119 (1996).

42 Municipal Securities Rulemaking Board, "MSRB Review of Rule G-37," *MSRB Reports* 21, no. 2 (July 2001).

43 Bond Market Association, "The Bond Market Association Says Application of Rule G-37 Too Broad; Makes Recommendations to the MSRB to Narrow and Avoid Infringement on Rights" (press release, 15 October 2001).

44 Interest income on municipal securities is exempt from federal income taxes; as a result, yields on municipal bonds are lower than those on otherwise comparable U.S. Treasury securities. Therefore, it would be possible for state and local government issuers to issue low-cost municipal bonds and use the proceeds to purchase higher-yielding Treasury securities. The issuer would earn an arbitrage profit equal to the difference between interest earned on the Treasury securities and interest paid on the municipal bonds.

45 Because the affected issues would be classified as arbitrage bonds, the debt would become taxable.

15 Procurement

KHI V. THAI

The importance of the procurement function in local government stems from four principal sources.[1] First, for the government to fulfill its mission, goods and services have to be obtained in a timely fashion. Second, because government resources are limited, public procurements have to be conducted efficiently (by minimizing administrative costs) and effectively (by obtaining goods and services at a fair and reasonable price). Third, because corruption in public procurement is a potential problem, local officials need to ensure that procurement is conducted with integrity, fairness, and openness. Finally, the sizable procurement expenditures of public entities make it possible to use governmental purchasing power to achieve broader socioeconomic goals—including economic development, environmental protection, and social equity.

To ensure that the multiple goals of the procurement function are achieved, governmental entities operate under strict laws and regulations governing procurement and have established systematic processes with which procurement officials must comply. These processes vary depending on the type of goods or services being purchased.

This chapter provides an overview of local government procurement. As used in this chapter, *procurement* refers both to a distinct *function* of local government (like budgeting or human resource management) and to all *administrative activities* that are necessary to that function. Thus, public procurement means "buying, purchasing, renting, leasing, or otherwise acquiring any supplies, services or construction,"[2] and it also encompasses the development of requirements and specifications, the selection of vendors, the solicitation of sources, the preparation and award of contracts, and all phases of contract administration.[3] (Because purchasing is defined here as just one of many procurement alternatives, the term *procurement* rather than *purchasing* will be used throughout this chapter.)

Historical development of local government procurement

Municipal procurement in the United States predates that of the state and federal governments.[4] In the colonies, for example, printing was one of the services contracted out by government. But there were no professional procurement officials; whatever goods or services government needed were supplied by commissaries, which received a commission on what they bought for government. Although state legislatures had begun, by the late 1800s, to create boards or bureaus responsible for purchasing, centralized procurement was hardly standard practice at that time.

In 1810, Oklahoma became the first state government to create a central procurement board for all state departments and agencies,[5] and many local governments eventually followed Oklahoma's example.[6] Baltimore, Chicago, Cleveland, Los Angeles, Minneapolis, New York City, and Philadelphia all took steps to centralize their purchasing function before 1920.[7]

During the past century, centralized procurement has gradually become common in local government. However, the trend toward centralization has recently come under challenge, with many practitioners and researchers contending that decentralized procurement is more responsive to end users, eliminates bureaucratic obstacles to the achievement of program goals, improves interdepartmental coordination, and empowers service delivery managers to obtain what they need.

The middle part of the twentieth century saw the creation of the first uniform government procurement code. The American Law Institute and the National Conference of Commissioners on Uniform State Laws, with the endorsement of the American Bar Association (ABA), put forth the Uniform Commercial Code (UCC) in the fall of 1951. Pennsylvania was the first state to enact the UCC, and by 1980, all the states except Louisiana had adopted most of its provisions.[8] In 1979, after five years of intensive effort, the ABA issued *The Model Procurement Code,* which was updated in 2000 and renamed *The 2000 Model Procurement Code for State and Local Governments.*[9]

Goals of public procurement

The goal of public procurement is to satisfy the internal customer by obtaining exactly what is needed, exactly when it is needed, and at a fair and reasonable price; at the same time, the procurement office must serve the government's long-term interests by minimizing business and technical risks, maximizing competition, maintaining procedural integrity and transparency, and accomplishing socioeconomic objectives. Because the procurement office is but one of the many jurisdictional units that are involved in the procurement process, the goals of the acquisition system should be conceived broadly and should encompass the contributions of all stakeholders.

Cost

The cost of supplies and services is more than just the price—the dollar amount—of the contract. For example, when the contract provides for free on board (FOB) origin, the buyer pays the cost of shipping and risk of loss during transportation, and that additional cost is not covered in the contract price. In the case of capital assets, a comprehensive cost analysis—known as life-cycle costing—should include (1) the initial acquisition price offered by bidders, (2) the total operational costs of the capital asset, and (3) the final disposal cost or repurchase price. It is essential to clearly specify all costs for the whole cycle of the capital asset in the invitation to bid or request for bids. (For an example of life-cycle costing, see the accompanying sidebar.)

Quality

Quality in procurement refers to the extent to which the end users' specified requirements are met. To ensure that the procurement office has a clear understanding of these requirements, end users must

Define the need in functional terms

Describe the performance or design characteristics that are necessary to satisfy the need (e.g., height, weight, energy usage, reliability, useful life)

Prescribe standards for determining whether a deliverable is acceptable (i.e., meets the need as defined in the contract) and, when appropriate, establish inspection and testing procedures for measuring the deliverable against those standards.

When competing contractors are being evaluated, among the factors to be considered are past performance (including compliance with schedules),

Example of life-cycle costing The following table shows an example of costs submitted by three vendors who bid on a piece of heavy equipment with an expected life of five years.

Bidder	Equipment price ($)	Annual guaranteed operational and maintenance cost ($)	Repurchase price (-) or disposal cost ($)	Total bid price ($)
A	45,000.00	4,500.00	1,000.00	68,500.00
B	52,000.00	3,400.00	(7,000.00)	62,000.00
C	46,000.00	4,000.00	(3,000.00)	63,000.00

If the procurement evaluation team attends only to the initial acquisition price, Bidder A, with an initial price of $45,000, would be awarded the contract. When the annual guaranteed maintenance cost and the repurchase price are taken into account, however, Bidder B offers the lowest cost: $62,000.

But what happens if interest costs are taken into account? Assuming an overall interest rate (discount rate) of 10 percent, the present-value cost (true economic cost) of the bids is determined as follows:

> The initial purchase price, minus the present value of the repurchase price (or plus the present value of the disposal cost), plus the present-value cost of maintenance.

The annual maintenance costs are constant; thus, their present value can be obtained by multiplying the annual costs by 3.791, the present value of a five-year annuity at 10 percent (the figure of 3.791 can be obtained from a table of annuities).

The present value of the disposal costs or repurchase price is given by

$$\frac{s}{(1 + \lambda)^n} \quad \text{or in this case} \quad \frac{s}{(1.10)^5}, \text{ where}$$

n = the estimated economic life of the capital asset in years
λ = the appropriate discount or interest rate for a local government
s = the scrap value or remaining value of the capital asset at the end of its economic life in year n.

In terms of present value, the life-cycle costs proposed by the three bidders are as shown the following table.

Bidder	Equipment price ($)	Present value of annual operational and maintenance cost ($)	Present value of repurchase price (-) or disposal cost ($)	Present value of bid ($)
A	45,000.00	17,059.50	621.00	62,680.50
B	52,000.00	12,889.40	(4,347.00)	60,542.40
C	46,000.00	15,164.00	(1,863.00)	59,301.00

Thus, the inclusion of interest costs would dictate award of the contract to Bidder C, whose bid offers the lowest present-value life-cycle cost: $59,301.[1]

[1] Annualized costs, which are obtained by dividing the total costs by the present-value annuity factor for the given number of years, are useful for comparing bids when the number of years for the life of the equipment varies: the annualized costs for Bidders A, B, and C, respectively, are $16,534.03, $15,970.03, and $15,642.57.

technical excellence, management capability, personnel qualifications, and prior experience.

Timeliness

Like quality, timeliness in procurement is defined as meeting the end users' needs. Because good planning is essential for timeliness, part of the task of the procurement office is to ensure that all the necessary steps are taken into account in establishing a schedule for the delivery of goods or services or for oversight of a capital project. (Of course, forecasts of the time required for an acquisition should also incorporate the probable risk of delay.)

When the requirement is for supplies, the procurement office must factor in time for shipping and distributing the supplies to the designated location, receiving and inventorying the supplies, and physically distributing supplies to the end users. In the case of projects, the following steps will need to be taken into account: (1) preparing specifications and purchase descriptions; (2) obtaining funding and administrative approvals for purchase requests; (3) soliciting offers, selecting providers, and awarding contracts; and (4) inspecting and accepting the work.

Risk avoidance

In a contractual relationship, both the jurisdiction and the contractor want to achieve their desired objectives: the jurisdiction wants to achieve its mission within budget, and the contractor wants to maximize profit. Both parties recognize that a contractual relationship carries certain risks, and both will try to minimize them. When the risks are perceived as being too high or unfairly apportioned, either or both parties will probably be unwilling to enter into a contract.

There are three types of risk: business, financial, and technical. Unfortunately, no contractor can forecast, with absolute certainty, the cost of doing work under a contract. Unpredictable perils can arise at any time—from strikes to equipment malfunctions (business risk), general inflation (financial risk), and defective parts (technical risk). To minimize the effect of risk, bidders may inflate their proposed prices to cover worst-case scenarios.

For a government entity, the main financial risk is payment of an inflated price: that is, a price that is designed to protect against worst-case scenarios that may never materialize. Thus, on the one hand, procurement offices need to protect against unreasonably inflated prices. On the other hand, they need to understand the supplier's situation, which is subject to unpredictable perils. It is in the local government's interest to avoid the risk of an unsigned—or unfulfilled—contract. For that reason, it may be necessary to consider allowing certain clauses in the contract that will help protect the contractor from the consequences of unpredictable perils.

For standard commercial (off-the-shelf) supplies and services, the business and technical risks tend to be minimal. However, for more complex and uncertain undertakings—such as developing a new computer program, building to a structural specification, or conducting research and development—risk may be a significant factor in establishing the terms and conditions of the contract. For the contractor, technical risks are strongly related to financial risks: any difficulty in meeting technical requirements may require more effort (labor and material costs) than was contemplated at the time the price was agreed to. The contractor may even discover that the work is impossible at any price. For the government entity, business and technical risks may lead to unexpectedly higher budget allocations and possible failure of the entire project.

Competition

Competition is defined as the effort of two or more vendors to secure the business of a third party by offering the most favorable terms (price, quality, promptness of delivery, or service). Competition provides significant incentives to reduce cost and increase quality. Moreover, in the area of high technology, competition is critical to innovation. A sound procurement system promotes full and open competition in soliciting offers and awarding government contracts; "full and open competition" means that all responsible sources are permitted to compete.

When procurement officials acquire goods, services, capital assets, and supplies, they need to comply with statutory requirements for competition. They also need to take all necessary actions to promote a competitive environment, including ensuring that contractors themselves foster effective competition for major and critical products and technologies, and that qualified international sources are permitted to compete. Occasionally, in order to establish or maintain alternative sources for goods or services, government entities may *exclude* a particular source from a contract action. This is most likely to occur if the government entity determines that such an exclusion would increase or maintain competition and thereby reduce costs.

The usual requirements for competition are also inapplicable when

Contracts are awarded using simplified acquisitions, emergency procurement procedures, or sole-source procurement

Contracts are awarded using contracting procedures that are expressly authorized by statute

Contract modifications are made (such modifications may include, for example, the exercise of pricing options that were evaluated as part of the initial competition and that are within the scope and under the terms of an existing contract)

Orders are placed under definite-quantity contracts.[10]

Integrity and transparency

As discussed in detail later in this chapter, procurement protests are common. The best way to avoid protests is to ensure that the procurement process is characterized by integrity and transparency. In practical terms, this means (1) dealing with all vendors fairly and in good faith, (2) maintaining impartiality and avoiding preferential treatment (except in the case of certain legally required preferences, such as those for local vendors or minority-owned businesses), and (3) avoiding any appearance of conflict of interest and any actions that would compromise public trust in the procurement system.

Public policy objectives

As mentioned earlier, the magnitude of government outlays creates opportunities for implementing public policies, particularly with regard to environmental protection and socioeconomic goals. In order to meet such goals, government entities can, for example, use green procurement, require contractors to use fair employment practices, provide safe and healthful working conditions, and pay fair wages. Public entities may also give preference to local contractors, to small businesses, or to businesses owned by women or members of minorities. Finally, governmental procurement may be used to promote the rehabilitation of prisoners and to support the independence of handicapped citizens.

The procurement function

Public procurement consists of five core elements: policy making and management, procurement regulations, authorization and appropriations, the procurement function in operations, and feedback (see Figure 15–1).

At the local level, organizational structures for procurement vary from the simple to the complex, depending on the size of the governmental unit. In small towns and villages, for example, which have no procurement structure, the manager is responsible for all administrative functions of government, including budgeting, accounting, and procurement. Most larger local governments have procurement divisions within their finance or administrative services departments. Even within large local governments, however, very few departments—except perhaps transportation or public works—have their own procurement office. In all but the smallest local governments, each level of management within the procurement structure must have well-defined authorities and responsibilities—from the issuance of policies, regulations, and standards of performance to the supervision and management of the workforce.

Public procurement is conducted within a democratic framework, under the checks and balances powers of the three branches of government: legislative, judiciary, and executive. Public procurement in most local governments is under the authority and responsibility of the executive—the administrator or manager. Elected officials (the legislative branch) are also involved in procurement through the establishment of procurement policies and the appropriation of funds for procurement projects. In very small local governments, it is not uncommon for elected officials to be involved in the selection of vendors. Although the courts are not directly involved in setting procurement policies, they try all cases that involve contract disputes, and their decisions become a source of procurement regulations.

Because public procurement is a very complicated process, sound procurement regulations are needed to maintain public confidence in procurement procedures and to ensure fair and equitable treatment of all parties who deal with the procurement system. In many small local governments, procurement budgets are limited and procurement statutes hardly exist; nor is there a pro-

Figure 15–1   Public procurement system.

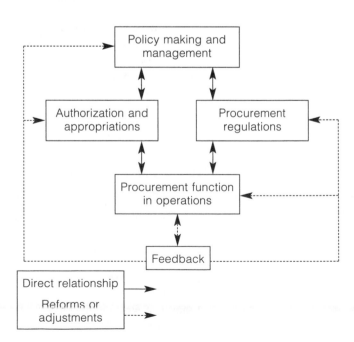

curement code. Since the absence of a procurement code, regulations, or manual may create serious legal or financial problems, however, it is wise for even the smallest local government to develop a code, even if it is only a simple one. (Exemplary local procurement codes can be found in *The 2000 Model Procurement Code for State and Local Governments.*)

Procurement professionals have dual responsibilities: they ensure that user agencies comply with procurement regulations, and they are directly involved in procuring goods, services, and capital assets as authorized and funded. Feedback is crucial to a sound procurement system. By continuously evaluating what is required for successful procurement, elected and appointed local government officials can make adjustments or reforms where needed. In some cases, feedback may indicate that procurement regulations, policies, or standards are no longer current or suitable. In other cases, feedback may show that the procurement cycle does not work effectively—for example, that payment is too slow or that technological improvements, such as e-procurement or purchase cards, are needed. Feedback may come from procurement professionals, legislative bodies or committees, oversight bodies (e.g., internal auditors or evaluators, or a specially created team), or user agencies. Feedback may also come from contractors or vendors, industry and professional organizations, and the public.

The procurement process

For any procurement project, the governmental entity must first determine whether there is a need for goods or services; if a need exists, the governmental entity will identify alternative means of meeting the need and will select the best one. There are four basic alternatives for the provision of goods or services: in-house provision, contracting out, leasing, and privatization.

If privatization is selected, the goods or services will be privately financed and provided, and no procurement will occur. If the governmental entity authorizes provision of the goods or services, the end user will request the necessary funding. If the requested funding is appropriated, procurement will proceed. If the request for funding is rejected, there will be no procurement. In principle, the procurement process does not start until funding is secured (see Figure 15–2).

Acquisition planning phase

Ideally, a local government's strategic plan will anticipate changes in its requirements for technological capabilities and identify goods, services, and capital assets that are critical to implement the plan. Common goods and services that government entities need include low-dollar-value, commercial items (such as paper and paper clips); laptop or desktop computers; office equipment; routine maintenance; and travel. Budget requests and decisions regarding such basic goods and services are usually based on the previous year's level.

For large capital acquisitions (such as information technology and construction projects) that require major funding, the process is more complicated. As part of the capital budgeting process, all local government departments evaluate their needs for capital assets and then prepare requests—commonly known as a "wish list"—for submission to the budget office. All capital projects on this list have to be assessed in terms of (1) functionality; (2) full life-cycle costs, including all direct and indirect costs for planning, procurement, operations, maintenance, and disposal; (3) affordability (full life-cycle costs relative to expected funding levels); (4) risk; and (5) the local government's

Figure 15–2 Circumstances under which procurement occurs.

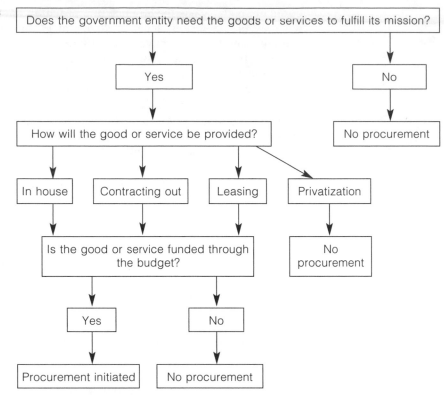

capacity to manage the asset. (For a discussion of capital planning and budgeting, see Chapter 6.)

Procurement funding phase

The formal beginning of the budgeting phase occurs when a departmental budget proposal is submitted to the budget office or local government manager. Proposals for the acquisition of capital assets must be justified in a number of ways, primarily through a cost-benefit analysis that includes life-cycle costs. In addition, the budget office must receive assurances that all known costs have been identified and that cost, schedule, and performance goals for the procurement have been set and will be monitored. Once submitted, proposals for the acquisition of capital assets may have to be defended formally or informally. After carefully reviewing with staff all such requests, the manager (or mayor) determines which ones will be included in the proposed capital budget and submits the proposed budget to the governing body.

The funding phase ends when the operating and capital budgets are approved. In practice, procurement officials are rarely involved in the acquisition planning and funding phases; most view the procurement phase as their principal area of responsibility. This situation is unfortunate, as procurement officials could provide valuable assistance in assessing the local government's needs, generating procurement requirements, and making decisions about procurement funding.[11]

Procurement phase

Once the capital and operating budgets have been approved for the coming year, procurement can proceed. Each procurement requires (1) the development of a contract with a vendor and (2) administration of the contract. Both steps comprise several discrete tasks; in order to manage those tasks well, the finance or procurement office must do some preliminary planning first.

Procurement planning   Procurement planning is an administrative action whose purpose is to effectively implement all funded procurement programs and to obtain all funded procurement items.[12] There are actually two types of procurement plans: the central procurement office's procurement plan and a procurement plan for a specific funded good, service, or capital asset.

Even before the fiscal year begins, the procurement officer must develop a timetable for the overall conduct of all procurement within the local government. In many cases, the procurement office knows for sure, even during the budget decision phase, that certain procurement requests will be funded, and can therefore create a plan that will allow the procurement process to start immediately after the formal approval of the budget. A well-designed procurement plan will make it possible for procurement to be undertaken in a timely and orderly fashion, and will spread the workload evenly throughout the year. As the budget year progresses, the procurement office must monitor the number of procurement projects, the purchase dollars available, and the timing of contract decisions.

The second type of procurement plan, which concerns specific goods, services, or capital assets rather than the overall conduct of the procurement function, is focused largely on contracts because most, if not all, goods, services, and capital assets are procured through contractual arrangements. Thus, the term *contract planning* is often used for the second type of procurement planning. The essence of contract planning is the creation of a comprehensive plan that coordinates the efforts of all staff responsible for procurement projects or programs. The plan requires the following actions:

Ensuring that all social, economic, and environmental requirements (set-asides, small business, energy efficiency, etc.) are met

Checking the local government's inventory records to determine whether supplies can be obtained from existing stock

Determining whether a procurement request can be "bundled" with other requests to obtain volume discounts

Identifying sources of supplies

Selecting a procurement method

Identifying opportunities for cooperative purchasing

Processing purchase requests

Certifying the availability of funds

Deciding whether to use term contracting (see sidebar)

Preparing a timetable for the procurement program or project cycle.[13]

Term contracting   Term contracting establishes a source for supplies or services to be delivered over a period of time and can be arranged in any of the following ways: (1) definite quantity for a definite period; (2) indefinite quantity for a definite period; or (3) indefinite quantity for an indefinite period. In purchasing office equipment, materials, supplies, and services, most local governments use indefinite-quantity contracts, which are also referred to as *open-ended contracts, blanket contracts, requirement contracts, blanket orders,* and *term contracts;* of these, *term contracts* is the most general term.

Inventory management, the selection of procurement methods, cooperative purchasing, and green procurement (to meet environmental requirements) are discussed in more detail later in this chapter.

Contract formulation   Contract formulation, also called pre-award phase procurement or tactical procurement, includes five major activities: preparation of the solicitation documents, solicitation of offers, evaluation, negotiation, and contract award (see Figure 15–3). (It is important to note that the procurement process described in this section varies depending on whether the contract results from simplified acquisition, sealed bidding, or negotiation—topics that will be discussed later in this chapter.)

Preparation of solicitation document   Once needs and requirements have been identified, procurement officials have to prepare a solicitation document—an invitation to bid (ITB), a request for bids (RFB), a request for information (RFI), a request for quotations (RFQ), or a request for proposals (RFP). Because the requirements generated during the strategic planning and capital budgeting phases are not specific enough, procurement officials must specify in detail all requirements with which vendors must comply.

In general, there are three types of specifications: functional, performance, and design. Functional specifications focus on the need or intended use and allow for flexibility in the supplier's response: for example, functional specifications for a water-purification system would allow the local government to entertain proposals for a chemical additive system, a filtration system, a distillation system, or any other approach that would achieve the government's goal for water purity. Performance specifications describe the capabilities that the product or service must possess. Performance requirements for a water-purification system might specify, for example, level of purity, throughput, and power use. Design specifications detail the specific physical characteristics that the product or service must possess. Thus, design requirements for a water-purification system might (1) specify the materials to be used for each component of the system and (2) include blueprints for the casting, valves, impellers, filters, and power module.

There may be other specifications as well, such as (1) brand name, model number, or other designations that identify the level of quality desired; (2) logistical requirements (where and when delivery should be made); (3) maintenance requirements (what level of maintenance is to be provided); or (4) packaging requirements (e.g., environmentally friendly packaging). Many local governments save time and expense by tailoring specifications that other agencies have developed for similar products.[14] In addition to specifications, the solicitation document may cover many other aspects of the vendor's and the local government's responsibilities and the relationship between the two (see Figure 15–4).

Solicitation of offers   To maximize competition, procurement officials are required to provide public notice in advance of a solicitation. Typically, such notice is published for a prescribed period of time in newspapers and trade journals. Electronic solicitation is becoming more and more common in public procurement.

Figure 15–3   Steps in contract formulation.

Figure 15–4   Contents of a typical request for proposals.

Cover page
Table of contents
Description of purpose
List of objectives
Description of existing environment (i.e., a description of the existing conditions under which goods or services are delivered)
Description of how to submit inquiries
Description of source selection method
Information on where and when the pre-proposal conference will be held
Description of the minimum criteria—such as experience, qualifications, and financial capacity—the government will use to determine whether prospective offerors qualify as responsible.
Timetable identifying the projected milestones for completion of the solicitation, contract negotiations, and project startup. For example:

Request for proposal issued	January 1
Cutoff date for submission of written questions	January 14
Pre-proposal conference and site visit	January 15
Deadline for amendments or additions to the submitted proposal	January 18
Proposals due	January 28
Evaluation of proposals	February 14
Contract negotiations	March 1
Contract execution	March 15
Notice to proceed	April 1

Description of services, goods, systems, or other solution to be provided
Description of constraints on the successful offeror (e.g., security requirements, conditions at the work site that could affect the offeror's performance)
Description of personnel requirements for successful offeror
Description of the responsibilities of the governmental entity
Description of reporting requirements for successful offeror
Terms and conditions of agreement
Description of insurance requirements for successful offeror
Description of bonding requirements for successful offeror
Statement specifying the importance of complying with all requirements
Statement specifying how to deal with ambiguity, conflict, or errors
List of implied requirements
Statement that the jurisdiction will not be liable for any costs incurred by the offerors in the preparation or presentation of their proposals or in any discussions or negotiations
Description of process for rejection of proposals
List of allowable exceptions to requested format
Statement stipulating that the jurisdiction's requests for clarification of proposals will be in writing, and that such requests will not affect the offeror's proposed price
List of characteristics that will determine a proposal's validity
Description of the proposal submission format.

During the solicitation-of-offers phase, procurement officials answer informal inquiries from prospective offerors about specifications, terms, or conditions. It may also be important to conduct a formal pre-solicitation or pre-proposal conference for any of the following reasons:

To give potential offerors an opportunity to inspect a work site or government property

To explain complicated specifications and requirements

To explain revisions to requirements

To address inquiries from a large number of offerors.

Evaluation   After offers (bids, quotations, or proposals) are solicited and received, they are evaluated. To ensure that all bidders are treated fairly and equitably, the local government must include the criteria for evaluation in the original solicitation documents and must strictly follow the criteria. The evaluation process must also be well documented.

Negotiation   A good contract negotiation is a long process. To be prepared for it, procurement officials must (1) have a technical understanding of what is being negotiated and of each side's negotiating position; (2) determine how much competition there is for the provision of a particular product or service; (3) prepare a thorough cost and price analysis; and (4) ensure that all negotiation issues have been identified (these include, but are not limited to, terms, conditions, prices, dates, quantities, and liabilities).

All parties to the negotiation must be treated fairly, and the results of the negotiation must be able to withstand public scrutiny. Purchasing officials must always conduct themselves according the highest standards of ethical conduct. They must also be familiar with various negotiation tactics and be able to use them in ways that meet the ethical-conduct test. Effective negotiators have the ability to listen, to question, and to maintain control of their emotions.

To demonstrate that a fair and reasonable price was obtained, the negotiation must be documented. A complete negotiation record is both a means of protecting the public trust and a document that can assist in the interpretation of the agreement in the event of a dispute. The record may also lay the foundation for future negotiations. The negotiation is not complete until the contract is written and executed.

Contract award   The last major step in contract formulation is the contract award. This phase consists of preparing and issuing the award, determining the responsibilities of the various parties, and dealing with possible irregularities (such as mistakes and protests). As soon as possible after the contract is awarded, unsuccessful vendors must be notified of the decision; most jurisdictions notify unsuccessful vendors in writing, indicating the vendor's score, the results of the evaluation, the total score of the winning bid, and the value of the contract.

Contract administration   For commercial items, contract administration consists of ordering the items, monitoring their quantity and quality, paying invoices, and keeping a good accounting record. For construction projects, contract administration is more structured and more complicated; the major phases, shown in Figure 15–5, are (1) initiating work and/or modifications to work (for a construction project or a major system), or ordering (for acquisitions of materials and supplies), (2) contract monitoring, (3) payment and accounting, and (4) contract closeout (termination).

It is important to note that not all phases of contract administration receive equal attention; in practice, some phases are occasionally omitted. The attention given to each phase depends on a number of factors, such as the nature of the good or service and the specific contractual arrangements. In the procurement of capital assets, the contract award and the ordering phase often coincide: once the contract has been signed, the goods have, in effect, been ordered. In the case of blanket orders for office supplies, new orders can be

Figure 15–5   The contract administration process.

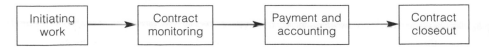

placed (the ordering phase) at the same time that invoices for previous orders are being paid (the payment phase).

Preparatory work   After a contract is awarded, the contract administrator issues a notice to proceed that sets the contract administration in motion. Although most local governments do not require a formal contract administration plan, procurement officials are responsible for ensuring that the parties comply with all terms and conditions of the contract. (The decision to conduct a post-award conference depends on the size and complexity of the project, the contract type, the urgency of the project, and the contractor's performance history.)[15]

Monitoring   The procurement official or contract administration team needs to carefully monitor the contract to ensure that both parties meet their responsibilities as outlined in the contract; among the areas to be monitored are quality, adherence to the budget and schedule, acceptance of deliverables, contract disputes, contract changes, and timely and appropriate payment.

Payment   There are three types of payment: advance payments, or prepayments (an extension of credit to the supplier by the organization); interim payments (often used in the case of construction, capital equipment, certain professional services, and other labor-intensive or capital-intensive contracts); and final payments (issued after the work or product has been delivered, tested, inspected, and installed). All payments must be authorized by the procurement official, as he or she is the one who knows when a contract needs to be paid.

Closeout   The final payment is authorized only when the contract is closed out, or terminated. A contractor who fails to perform according to contractual provisions is legally in breach of contract, which usually results in termination—that is, cancellation—for default. In the case of a purchase order, receipt of the items and subsequent payment constitutes closure.

   Before a contract can be closed out, however, the procurement official must verify that

All contractual requirements have been met.

All changes have been incorporated into the final contract document.

All deliverable items (hardware, data, and reports) have been received.

All bailed (borrowed) equipment and all classified documents have been returned.

Final payment has been made.

Once these requirements have been met, the procurement official or contract administrator writes a formal closure document that describes the contractor's strengths and weakness in the performance of the contract. If disputes subsequently arise, the document is invaluable; it may also be useful in the review of potential contractors for subsequent projects.

Selecting a procurement method

Many local government procurement regulations require competitive sealed bidding (also known as invitation to bid or request for bids). However, this procurement method is not the most appropriate for all circumstances. Selection of a procurement method is determined by two major factors: the type of good or service to be purchased, and the market uncertainty and risk associated with that type of good or service.

Types of goods and services to be purchased

Government entities purchase five major types of goods and services: commercial items, major systems, construction and architectural or engineering services, general services, and utility services. These goods and services can, in turn, be classified into three types, on the basis of market availability:

Commercial items, such as office supplies and equipment, that are customarily available in the commercial marketplace

Items that are customarily available in the commercial marketplace but that have been modified for government use (e.g., police cars and snowplows)

Items used exclusively for governmental purposes (e.g., fire engines, street signs, and certain types of information technology).

Depending on the supplies or services to be purchased, requirements should be stated in terms of functions to be performed, performance required, essential physical characteristics, or a combination of the three.

Commercial items   Commercial items are those that are sold competitively in the marketplace. For this category of goods or services, requirements for almost all acquisitions should be defined in terms that enable and encourage vendors of commercial items to respond to solicitations. To ensure that only those provisions necessary to satisfy specific needs are included, local governments should use market research to develop specifications in such a way as to promote full and open competition.

Wherever possible, standard commercial items should be used to prepare specifications; this approach allows the local government to obtain lower prices, reduce handling costs, carry smaller inventories, and avoid problems with quality. Excessive standards will not guarantee the integrity of goods or services and may contribute to higher costs. Ordinarily, requirements should not specify a particular brand name, product, or feature that is peculiar to one manufacturer unless the following conditions apply:

The particular brand name, product, or feature is essential to the government's requirements, and market research indicates that similar products from other companies do not meet, or cannot be modified to meet, the agency's needs.

The authority to contract without providing for full and open competition is supported by the necessary laws, justifications, and approvals.

The justification for the use of simplified acquisition procedures (i.e., procedures that do not provide for maximum practicable competition) is documented in the file when the contract is awarded.

Major systems   A system acquisition is normally designated as "major" when it meets the following criteria: the acquisition (1) is critical to enabling a user agency to fulfill its mission; (2) entails the allocation of relatively large resources for the particular end user; and (3) warrants special management attention, including decisions from department or agency heads. For local governments, major systems are most often information technology systems.

Construction and architectural or engineering services   Professional architectural or engineering services are performed or approved by a person who is licensed, registered, or certified; such services may include general consultations; surveying and mapping; program management; value engineering; soil engineering; construction-phase services; drawing reviews; studies, investigations, tests, or evaluations; the development of comprehensive plans, conceptual designs, or plans and specifications; and the preparation of operating and maintenance manuals.

In local governments, construction procurement may consist of design, construction, operation, or maintenance. The ABA recommends the use of competitive sealed bidding when the delivery method includes all aspects of the project (i.e., both construction and architectural and engineering services); examples of such delivery methods are design-build, design-build-operate-maintain, and design-build-finance-operate-maintain.[16]

Services   Some of the services that local governments normally contract out include

Maintenance, overhaul, repair, servicing, rehabilitation, salvage, modernization, or modification of supplies, systems, or equipment

Routine recurring maintenance of real property

Housekeeping

Advisory and technical assistance services

Operation of government-owned equipment, facilities, or systems

Communications services

Architectural and engineering services

Transportation and related services.

Depending on the type of service, either sealed bidding or negotiated contracting may be used.

Utility services   Utility services include electricity, natural gas, water, and sewer service. For this type of purchase, negotiated contracting—particularly sole-source contracting—would be most appropriate.

Market uncertainty and risk

Vendors who work with governmental entities have to consider a number of risk factors:

Complexity. Complex requirements, particularly those unique to the government, usually require the government to assume a greater share of risk. This is especially true for complex contracts, where uncertainties or the likelihood of changes can make it difficult to estimate development costs in advance. (One study found that the uncertainty and risk created by unclear specifications led vendors to add an average of 20 percent to most fixed-price contracts.)[17] When a requirement is recurring, or if quantity production begins, the cost risk should shift to the contractor, and a fixed-price contract should be considered.[18]

Urgency. If urgency is a primary factor, the government may choose to assume a greater proportion of risk or offer incentives to ensure timely performance.

Extended performance period. In times of economic uncertainty, contracts extending over a relatively long period should include terms that allow for price adjustments, which are usually based on economic indicators.

Size of contract. The dollar value of purchases adds to the level of market uncertainty and risk. In general, the more specific the type of good or service, the higher the dollar value, the greater the complexity, the more urgent the procurement, and the longer the period of performance or the production run, then the higher the risk and the higher the cost to the local government.

Procurement methods

The ABA lists eight procurement methods: small purchases (also known as *micro purchases,* the term used by the federal government), simplified acquisition, emergency procurement, limited-competition procurement, sole-source procurement, competitive sealed bidding, request for proposals, and architectural and engineering services procurement.[19] The procurement method chosen depends largely on the amount of the expenditure. The remainder of this section describes the first seven of these procurement methods; discussion of the procurement of architectural and engineering services is beyond the scope of this chapter.

Small purchases

Because it is not cost-effective to use a long procurement process for small purchases, most, if not all, government entities allow small purchases to be handled through purchase orders, petty cash (buyers pay in cash and submit receipts for reimbursement), or purchase cards. In determining an optimal threshold for small purchases, transaction costs—the costs involved in the competitive process—are one factor that must be taken into account. Although governmental units sometimes attempt to avoid a time-consuming and costly competitive process by dividing a larger purchase that exceeds the threshold into several smaller purchases (e.g., dividing a $19,000 purchase, which would have required a formal RFB, into two $9,500 purchases to sneak it in under the $10,000 rule), this practice is unethical and may be illegal.

A number of approaches can be used for small purchases. For example, blanket contracts, which allow staff to quickly obtain low-cost replacement items, save time and money by eliminating (1) purchase orders, (2) the tasks involved in receiving the goods, and (3) the need to deal with individual invoices. Under such an arrangement, the supplier sends the jurisdiction a monthly invoice for draws against a set amount established in the blanket contract. Purchase cards (P-cards), another approach, permit the quick purchase of low-cost, frequently used items and enable jurisdictions to obtain detailed information about what items are purchased and by whom. P-cards do not compromise control any more than an open purchase order would (an open purchase order allows people to pick up supplies as needed). In fact, P-cards can be obtained with smart chips embedded in them that limit what can be purchased.

There are three important points to understand about small-value procurements: (1) each local government has its own rules for such procurements; (2) blanket contracts can be awarded with minimal competition; and (3) the local government is still required to demonstrate that the process was fair and open and that reasonable value was obtained.

Simplified acquisition

Simplified acquisition procedures are generally used to acquire commercial items whose expected price is above the maximum for small purchases but below the threshold for competitive procurement. Simplified acquisition is used to reduce administrative costs; improve government contracting opportunities for small businesses, disadvantaged businesses, and businesses owned by women or members of minorities; promote efficiency and economy; and avoid unnecessary burdens for local governments and contractors.

Under simplified acquisition, the procurement official will generally take the following actions:

Publicize the proposed acquisition

Solicit and evaluate quotations (technically and in terms of price)

Negotiate, if necessary, with one or more of the bidders

Select a firm on the basis of price and any other evaluation factors

Issue a purchase order (which, upon acceptance by the vendor, becomes a contract).

Emergency procurement

With the increasing threat of natural and manmade disasters, emergency procurement plans are much more prevalent than they were in the past. Emergency procurements are expedited procurements that ordinarily result from a catastrophic situation such as a flood, fire, epidemic, or failure of critical equipment. Emergency procurement should be used only when there is a threat to public health, welfare, or safety—not because a contract with an incumbent vendor is expiring and there is not enough time to issue an RFP. Although time is of the essence, emergency procurements must be carefully documented because they are subject to audit and public scrutiny. Typically, reliable suppliers with whom the local government has already worked are contacted to provide required goods and services. Ideally, local governments should establish potential contracts in advance and then implement them whenever conditions dictate.

The key element in emergency procurement is a set of established guidelines or regulations that clearly define and govern such procurements. These may include a provision for the mayor or other official to issue an executive order prohibiting vendors in the affected area from increasing prices more than 10 percent above their pre-emergency levels. Such a provision prevents unscrupulous businesses from profiting from an emergency at the expense of the public and the jurisdiction.

Limited-competition procurement

When there are a large number of responsible suppliers, some local governments use limited-competition procurement to reduce the cost of the process. If, for example, a local government needs approximately $50,000 worth of project management services and invites two hundred suppliers to submit proposals, forty suppliers may respond, each of whom may spend $10,000 on its proposal; collectively, the industry would have spent more than $400,000 to obtain one $50,000 contract.

Under limited-competition procurement, competition would be restricted to, say, twenty suppliers whose names would be selected randomly or according to some rotational system; an alternative is to issue twenty RFPs on a first-come, first-served basis. Whatever procedures are used for limited-competition procurement, they must be equitable and transparent.

Sole-source procurement

Sole-source procurement, an award made to a supplier without any competition, should be used only when justified—that is, when the necessary goods or services can be obtained only from a single supplier—and not to reduce competition. Sole sourcing is commonly used to obtain additional equipment or spare parts from an existing source, to acquire maintenance services for proprietary software, and to acquire an expert when there is only one source of the expertise. It may also be used to acquire innovative products for evaluation. Since it can be difficult to defend, sole sourcing is (and should be) used rarely, and then only with the approval of upper-level managers. (Requiring such approval prevents end users from lobbying procurement staff.)

Before sole sourcing is used, a reasonable amount of market research must be undertaken to attempt to locate competing suppliers. And before the contract is awarded, user agencies must carefully document their determination of need and the justification for their use of sole sourcing. Finally, to ensure that any abuse of the process can be detected, the procedures used for sole sourcing must be clearly defined and strictly audited.

Some government entities advertise their intent to award a sole-source contract by issuing an RFP; the advertisement typically identifies the amount of the contract and the nature of the procurement. By announcing the intent, the local government hopes to identify any suppliers it may have overlooked, and also to avoid complaints. Contracts resulting from sole-source awards are often published in a public register or on an annual basis.

Competitive sealed bidding

As the dollar value of potential contracts goes above a certain threshold ($10,000 in many local governments and $100,000 in the federal government), the procurement methodology becomes formalized; to preserve the integrity of the bidding system, competitive sealed bidding—also known as invitation to bid (ITB) or request for bids (RFB)—is used. The purpose of this procurement method is to identify the vendor (1) whose bid conforms in all material respects to the requirements and criteria set out in the RFB, (2) who submits the lowest price, and (3) who has been in business long enough to provide the required goods or services.

Competitive sealed bidding is a simple, straightforward procurement process whose three key concepts are present in its name:

Competitive: Multiple suppliers with known capabilities are invited to submit bids.

Sealed: The bids are all opened at the same time, and no changes are permitted once they are opened.

Bidding: Each vendor's bid is based on the government's statement of mandatory, objectively measurable requirements.

Sealed bids must be used when

There is sufficient time for the solicitation, submission, and evaluation of sealed bids.

The award will be made on the basis of price or price-related factors.

It is not necessary to discuss the bids with the respondents.

There is a reasonable expectation of receiving more than one sealed bid.

Request for proposals

The other major type of "full and open" procurement is a request for proposals, which is more formally known as competitive sealed proposals. Essentially, an RFP is used when an RFB is not appropriate: for example, when the requirements are not fully known or are qualitative rather than quantitative, or when selection will be based on a combination of factors other than price (see sidebars on pages 439 and 440–441).[20]

Cooperative purchasing

Cooperative purchasing is not new: its origins can be traced at least to the 1930s, when the Michigan Municipal League bought fire hoses for member

---

Requests for information, requests for letters of interest, and pre-solicitation conferences An RFI—request for information—is a little-used procurement strategy that simply involves requesting information from known and qualified firms. It is used in the purchase of new or complex items for which user agencies cannot develop comprehensive specifications. Usually, potential suppliers will provide enough information to enable the local government to consider several possible solutions to their needs and to develop a short list of firms that are capable of providing the necessary goods and services. Although devising an RFI and analyzing the resulting information takes time, the value of the approach should never be underestimated.

If a local government has no plan to purchase goods or services but is simply interested in learning about products and services available in the market-place, it can use another method: a request for letters of interest. In this approach, the local government identifies the types of problems it has or the types of services in which it is interested and invites suppliers to provide information.

Still another approach is to call up two or three vendors and invite them to present information about their products or services. Vendors will gladly do so and will welcome the opportunity to learn more about an organization's problems and requirements. Nor is there any conflict or impropriety in inviting vendors to present their credentials, although inviting only one firm to present its credentials may raise some concerns about favoritism. Inviting several competing suppliers to brief an agency on their capabilities, however, is not favoritism but good business—a matter of keeping up-to-date with a changing marketplace. This process is commonly referred to as a pre-solicitation conference.

---

cities in large quantities at substantial savings. Now a widespread practice, cooperative purchasing offers the following advantages: lower prices (because of the economies of scale that can be obtained through larger-volume purchases), lower administrative costs, increased competition, and more favorable terms and conditions. Cooperative purchasing takes three principal forms: cooperative bidding, consolidated purchasing, and piggyback cooperatives.

Cooperative bidding

Under cooperative bidding arrangements, two or more public procurement agencies agree on specifications and contract terms and conditions for a given item and combine their requirements in a single request for competitive sealed bids. Once bids have been received and discussed by the participants, each agency issues and administers its own purchase orders, contracts, or both. Cooperative bidding requires a sponsoring entity or "lead agency"; for example, several cities or towns may issue a joint bid for an asphalt contract.

Consolidated purchasing

To undertake consolidated purchasing, local government entities sign formal agreements with their fellow participants to create a consolidated purchasing agency. For example, the city of Fort Lauderdale and Broward County, Florida, initiated a cooperative purchasing agreement in 1956; after almost half a century, twenty-four governmental entities are participating. This formal cooperative arrangement offers numerous opportunities to participate in joint bidding, and all members have a say in the development of specifications; the inclusion of special terms and conditions; the makeup of the bid list; the development of

Request for bid or request for proposal? In the field of procurement, a competitive sealed bid, or request for bids (RFB), and a competitive sealed proposal, or request for proposals (RFP), are the two accepted methods for the formal procurement of goods or services that meet a fairly high cost threshold. The objective is the same, but the method varies depending on the need.

Generally, an RFB is used when

The local government can describe its needs clearly and specifically enough so that potential bidders can adequately and competitively respond

There are enough potential bidders to ensure fair and open competition

All the requirements are mandatory.

Award is made to the lowest responsive and responsible bidder. This is an objective bid.

RFPs are more costly and more time-consuming, and are used to meet a complex need that is difficult to specify. Specifically, the RFP is used when an organization wants to

Use a contract that is not fixed-price

Discuss technical or price aspects of proposals with offerors

Give offerors the opportunity to revise their proposals

Compare proposals in terms of price, quality, and other contractual factors

Make an award in which price is not the determining factor.

To initiate an RFP, the local government creates a statement or scope of work describing what needs to be done and specifies the criteria it will use to evaluate responses from potential offerors. An evaluation committee reviews the proposals and may discuss them with individual offerors, which may lead to the submission of "best and final" offers. Using established criteria, the members of the evaluation committee will rate each proposal; the proposal that receives the highest rating will receive the award. Unlike the RFB, which is strictly an objective award, the RFP is somewhat more subjective.

The RFB is generally the preferred method. It is simpler, cheaper, faster,

---

a qualified-products list (if applicable); the selection of receiving locations; packaging preferences; and decisions related to transportation, payment, and liability.

Piggyback procurement

Piggyback procurement (sometimes referred to as hitchhiking) is a "permissive" form of cooperative arrangement that is less formal than cooperative bidding or consolidated purchasing arrangements. In a piggyback cooperative, a large purchaser requests competitive sealed bids, enters into a contract, and arranges, as part of the contract, for other public procurement units to purchase from the selected vendor under the same terms and conditions. The members of the cooperative then order from contracts awarded by the sponsoring agency. Members choose to participate independently, after the award by the sponsoring entity, and place their orders with the consenting supplier. The quantities required by the smaller entities are normally assumed to have little or no impact on the bid pricing.

In 1994, Congress established a cooperative purchasing program that authorized the General Services Administration to allow state, local, Indian tribal, and the Puerto Rican governments access to more than four million services and products and direct buying relationships with many commercial suppliers. In and more objective than the RFP. And since the RFB process does not ordinarily permit negotiations or discussions, and since all the requirements are mandatory, the RFB does not produce many protests from suppliers.

The accompanying table highlights the differences between an RFB and an RFP.[1]

	Request for bids	Request for proposals
Specifications	Specific as to performance and design	Focus is on end results; proposer must develop and provide solution
Opening	Public: all information is available to other bidders and the public	Public, but only the names of the proposers are read; no pricing or other information is made available
Evaluation	Based strictly on technical specifications; no material changes allowed	Based on quality; elements of each proposal are assigned weighted values, and evaluation is conducted by committee
Discussion	None	Individual discussions with each proposer
Changes	None	Each proposer is allowed to submit a "best and final" offer that may change the solution, the price, or both
Award	Lowest responsive and responsible bidder	Proposal awarded the highest ranking by evaluation committee; not necessarily the least expensive

[1]The table was adapted from National Institute of Governmental Purchasing (NIGP), *Intermediate Public Procurement* (Herndon, Va.: NIGP, 2000), 93.

many states, including Massachusetts, Oregon, and Washington, a qualified political subdivision within a state (e.g., a county, city, or school district) is automatically allowed to purchase through the state's contracts. The Western States Contracting Alliance, established in 1993, is a cooperative purchasing arrangement that benefits member states and other public entities, including cities, counties, public schools, and institutions of higher education. A fee of 0.1 percent on all sales, built into the contractor's price for the products and services, goes into a separate fund to support cooperative procurement efforts.

Innovations in procurement

In an effort to cope with changes in public policy, management, and technology, public procurement has initiated a number of innovations in the past two decades. This section briefly describes four such innovations: green procurement, e-procurement, purchase cards, and reverse auction.

Green procurement

According to a 1998 survey, 18 out of 26 randomly selected large cities and 8 out of 18 randomly selected large counties have either statutes or administrative decisions that require a preference for recycled products. Recognizing that recycled products are not always the least expensive, most municipal and county governments that have required preferences for recycled products allow the price of such products to exceed by no more than 10 percent the lowest complying bid received. The city of Los Angeles, for example, places a cap of $2,500,000 per fiscal year on additional costs resulting from application of the preference. The city council, however, may authorize additional increments of $25,000 beyond the cap.[21]

The principal role of a procurement official in promoting the use of recycled products is to develop specifications that include recyclable materials and products; when bid awards are made, to give preference to recycled or recyclable products; and to draft or revise specifications to require recycled or recyclable materials. In addition to buying recycled and recyclable products and materials, local governments can use equipment that is compatible with recycled products and require contractors to use recycled or recyclable products.

The city of Escondido, California, provides a good example of commitment to recycling. In early 1990, the city adopted a purchasing policy for recyclables that started with paper products of all kinds and was eventually expanded to include recycled oil, recapped tires, recycled latex paint, recycled wallboard, re-inked ribbons, and recycling bins made of 25 percent postconsumer waste. Rounding out its commitment, the city joined a statewide program to establish forty "recycling market development zones" by 1996.

Green procurement extends beyond recycling to include several broader goals:

Reducing operation and maintenance costs by saving energy and water

Cutting disposal costs by improving purchasing decisions and reducing waste

Improving indoor air quality

Reducing the level of toxic substances entering the environment

Reducing the level of the emissions that contribute to climate change.

A few local governments, including Des Moines, Iowa; Cook County, Illinois; and Seattle, Washington, already follow green procurement guidelines developed by the U.S. Green Building Council for facilities construction. Known as the Leadership in Energy and Environmental Design (LEED) standards, these guidelines cover a host of issues, from site selection to the design of heating and cooling systems.

E-procurement

E-procurement is conducted online. According to a 2002 survey conducted by the International City/County Management Association, 43 percent of local governments purchase equipment online, and 52 percent purchase office supplies online.[22]

In July 2002, the city of Fort Lauderdale rolled out its new Direct Purchase System, which allows for Web-enabled requisitioning and payment authorization; the system also has tracking capabilities, an online bidder selection feature, and a commodity and services search engine. After inputting a purchase requisition electronically, a user can route it through the approval path—including finance and budget—to procurement, where the purchase order, ITB, or RFP is issued. The status of a requisition can be checked online at any time.

Many local governments in the United States have the capability to accept proposals online and issue purchase orders electronically, and many local governments post their RFPs online.[23] The purchasing division of Allegheny County, Pennsylvania, posts all ITBs and RFBs with an expected price of more than $30,000 on the county's Web site.

Purchase cards

Purchase cards (or P-cards) are credit cards issued to corporate or government users so that they can conduct small-value purchases—usually under $1,000—for their organizations. The use of P-cards has increased significantly since the early 1990s. The advantages of the P-card approach are that it speeds up processing and delivery and saves on the labor costs associated with paper processing.

   To ensure that P-cards are not abused, the U.S. General Accounting Office recommends that government entities establish sound internal control systems; improve and enforce compliance with purchasing requirements; prevent wasteful and questionable purchases; and control the purchase, recording, and safeguarding of assets.[24]

Establishing a sound internal control system   A sound internal control system includes the following characteristics:

Policies designed to ensure that when P-cards are used, duties for all phases of the purchasing process are segregated: that is, no one individual should be able to take all the steps needed to request, purchase, pick up, and receive goods and services purchased. Such policies should also require segregation of the responsibilities of cardholders, approving officials, funds certification officers, and property custodians.

Detailed procedures that specify the type and extent of reviews by approving officials. At the very least, these procedures should (1) describe the types of supporting documentation that the cardholder has to provide (such as an invoice or credit card receipt, certification of funds availability, and documentation of best value); (2) list the purchasing requirements (e.g., spending limits) against which the P-card bills should be checked for compliance; and (3) require that, as evidence of review, the approving official sign the cardholder's monthly billing statement.

A systematic process to ensure that P-card holders and approving officials receive training before being granted purchase cards or approval authority, and that they receive timely, periodic refresher training afterward.

A records retention policy for P-card transaction files.

Policies that limit the number of cardholders assigned to any one approving official.

Policies and procedures that will identify cardholders who have multiple P-cards, cancel the additional cards, and prohibit the future issuance of multiple cards to cardholders.

Procedures for periodically assessing whether each cardholder continues to have a valid need for a P-card and whether the individual's spending limits are appropriate.

In case of missing invoices, procedures for following up on transactions to (1) determine what was purchased and whether the items were for legitimate government needs and (2) take disciplinary actions as warranted.

Procedures to ensure that when cardholders leave the government entity, are reassigned, or no longer have valid needs for the cards, P-cards are canceled and the purchase files are retained.

A government-wide P-card monitoring system that (1) calls for the development and use of analytical tools to evaluate overall program results and (2) assigns specific responsibility for following up on the effectiveness of actions to address the findings that emerge from audits or management reviews.

Detailed procedures for conducting annual reviews of the activities of cardholders and approving officials (e.g., which population to use when selecting the sample, which internal controls to assess, which techniques to use in the analysis of bank electronic data).

Enforcing compliance with purchasing requirements   To ensure that compliance with purchasing requirements is enforced, the government entity should (1) revoke or suspend the purchasing authority of cardholders who frequently or flagrantly fail to comply with policies and procedures (e.g., cardholders who make split purchases, obtain cash advances, or exceed established dollar thresholds); and (2) take appropriate disciplinary action against supervisors or approving officials who direct or approve purchase transactions that fail to comply with policies and procedures.

Preventing wasteful and questionable purchases   To prevent wasteful and questionable purchases, the government entity should take the following actions:

Establish policies that describe (1) when it is permissible to purchase items, such as gift cards and foods, that should be controlled or restricted and (2) what justifications and approvals are required for such purchases.

Establish procedures for determining best value, including types of acceptable documentation.

Establish policies and procedures to control payment by third-party online payment companies. Such policies might include requiring documented advance approval from the approving official to help ensure that the item is needed and that the online payment company is the only viable method of payment, as well as a subsequent verification to help ensure that the item or service was in fact received.

Recording and safeguarding purchased assets   To establish controls over the purchasing, recording, and safeguarding of assets, the government entity should

Require centralized receiving and acceptance of purchased assets

Establish required time frames for completing and submitting property input forms (forms on which received property is recorded) and for recording accountable assets in the property management system

Establish procedures to ensure that appropriate disciplinary action is taken against cardholders, approving officials, or property custodians who are unable to account for purchased assets under their responsibility

Establish procedures to ensure the physical security of computer-related equipment (e.g., placing the items in locked storage until they can be entered into the property management system and assigned to users)

Require purchases of certain assets, such as computer equipment, to be coordinated centrally to take advantage of economies of scale, standardize the types of equipment purchased, and better ensure bona fide government need for each purchase.

Reverse auction

In the mid-1990s, a new sourcing technique known as reverse auction emerged in the private sector, where it has had a profound impact on the purchase of goods and services.[25] This technique has now been introduced in the field of public procurement: Miami-Dade County, for example, conducted three reverse auctions in 2002.

Reverse auction, also called "electronic reverse auction" or e-RA, is an on-line, real-time, dynamic bidding process that allows a group of prequalified suppliers to bid competitively during a scheduled time period (usually about an hour, although brief extensions are often allowed if bidders are still active at the end of the set time period).

In a traditional auction, buyers submit successively higher bids and the highest bid wins; in an e-RA, in contrast, *sellers* submit successively *lower* bids and the lowest bid is the winner. Through the use of a special Internet system, bidders can place their bids and see their competitors' bids, but they do not know who the actual competitors are. This mechanism ensures confidentiality until all bidding is complete.

A reverse auction can be successfully conducted only when certain conditions are met:

Goods or services can be clearly specified (with respect to design, terms, and conditions), and those specifications can be translated into prices that a supplier will commit to.

There is a strong likelihood that the current price exceeds the market price by a sufficient amount to ensure that the e-RA will be cost-effective.

A change in suppliers would be acceptable (e-RAs cannot be used, for example, when a switch in suppliers would result in unacceptably large change costs).

A sufficient number of qualified, competitive suppliers exist in the marketplace and are willing to participate in an e-RA.

The value of the goods or services being purchased is high enough so that the potential savings will cover the cost of holding the event.

Instead of investing in a do-it-yourself system to conduct an e-RA, it is most cost-effective for a local government to hire an Internet portal provider, who will train the bidders before the event to ensure that they know how to access and use the system, and who will be available during the event to answer questions (other than those relating to the solicitation document).

E-RAs have a number of benefits:

They can reduce the cost of purchasing goods and services.[26]

By increasing competition, they may be more effective at getting a fair market price than traditional RFBs or RFPs.

Because they offer a quick and effective search mechanism, e-RAs have faster cycle times than traditional sourcing processes and thus may enlarge the pool of qualified suppliers.[27]

As information is revealed through e-RA events, governmental entities can gain insight about price levels, market prices, and market elasticity or rigidity.

To ensure the success of an e-RA, procurement officials should

Carefully plan the event beforehand

Develop clear specifications for items

Develop clear auction rules

Ensure before the actual event that both buyers and suppliers are adequately trained in the use of the e-RA system

Ensure that only qualified bidders participate

Select only commodities that are appropriate to an e-RA.

In addition, local governments should make a point of reading the market accurately: if the reserve (maximum) price is set too far below the market price, no bidders will respond. Local governments should avoid awarding business at a price that is so low that it will threaten the supplier's survival or prevent the supplier from delivering as specified. Finally, local governments should resist the temptation to hold repeated e-RA events for the sole purpose of pressuring incumbent suppliers to reduce their prices, and they should not use e-RAs at all if there is a risk of damaging the local government's relationship with a key supplier.

Inventory management

An inventory is usually thought of as a stockpile of commodities—paper supplies, books, food, chemicals, or hardware. But the cash in the local government treasury, the machines a local government owns, and the amount of operating space are also types of inventories. This section of the chapter covers the management of both materials inventories and current assets or properties.

Managing materials inventories

Although materials inventory management is a common practice in the private sector, where it is essential to the timely production of goods, it is not common in local governments because their mission is to provide services rather than to produce goods. However, for those local governments that choose to purchase in bulk and have stores or warehouses, sound inventory management helps minimize total costs. Costs associated with inventory fall into the following categories:

Ordering and receiving costs: the labor cost (clerical and correspondence) of placing the order and receiving the item into stock. (Discounts on larger purchases may lower ordering costs.)

Carrying costs, or holding costs: costs associated with deterioration, obsolescence, storage, insurance, and imputed financing (i.e., the opportunity cost of tying funds up in inventory). Generally estimated as a percentage of the cost of the inventory, carrying costs may be as high as 20 to 30 percent per year.

Stockout, or shortage costs: the costs of service interruption and losses to citizens if a product or service is not available. Because some stockout costs are imputed or implicit, they are easily underestimated. The imputed cost of a stockout may include, for example, citizens' resentment when service is delayed or interrupted. Although it is not possible to obtain a precise accounting of the political or social cost of such resentment, a rough dollar cost (including an estimation of citizens' inconvenience) can be calculated for a stockout.

The two basic inventory models are the safety stock model and the economic ordering quantity (EOQ) model (see sidebar on pages 448–449). The safety stock model can be used to arrive at an inventory size that minimizes the costs of stockouts relative to carrying costs; the EOQ model can be used to determine the optimal size and frequency of orders. These two models are not mutually exclusive but complementary: in fact, various dynamic models combine the safety stock and EOQ approaches into one model.

Managing current assets or properties

Sound inventory management not only prevents the loss of assets or properties but also uncovers surplus property for timely disposal. Surplus property includes scrap, waste, rubbish, and obsolete, worn, or damaged stock or equipment.[28] Damage, normal wear and tear, and obsolescence are the principal sources of surplus goods in local government inventories. Obsolete items may be brand-new, used but serviceable, or reparable. Damaged items may also be reparable. Procurement officials must be aware of the condition of these items to determine their approximate market value.

Materials in use—motor vehicles, office furniture, computer hardware and software, machine-shop tools, and hundreds of other classes of materials—usually represent the largest single group of a local government's current assets. Generally, disposal becomes necessary when materials can no longer be used or when it is no longer economical to continue to use them. In some cases, there are built-in indicators of disposal, and action is taken when predetermined conditions, such as the following, are met: a damaged or obsolete item is not operating at all, a worn-out or damaged item is not economical to repair, an item is no longer needed, or an item is no longer used because of technical changes or market trends.

Conclusion

A sound procurement system has two types of goals: procurement and nonprocurement. Procurement goals include quality, timeliness, cost (in the broadest sense), minimizing risk, maximizing competition, and maintaining integrity. Nonprocurement goals include economic goals (e.g., preferring domestic or local firms), environmental protection, and social goals (e.g., assisting minority- or woman-owned business concerns).

For many local governments, maintaining integrity and transparency are of particular importance. Increased scrutiny on the part of taxpayers and competing vendors, among other factors, has led to the perception that public procurement is characterized by waste and corruption. Whether procurement is the single most corrupt aspect of governmental operations is in question, but it is almost certainly the most publicized. Hardly a day goes by without the revelation of another major scandal in public procurement somewhere in the world. The only way to combat the potential for corruption is to establish a procurement system with clearly stated goals and policies.

But such goals and policies can have other purposes as well. Thus, in a community where corruption is a concern, procurement policies may focus on integrity or transparency; where discrimination is a concern, however, procurement policies may focus on equity. And if the local economy is ailing, procurement may be used as a tool for economic development or stabilization. It is the job of policy makers and public procurement professionals to make trade-offs among the various goals of procurement.

Two basic inventory models

The safety stock model   Safety stocks are carried because the patterns of supply and demand can be somewhat erratic and independent of one another. Obviously, the more supply and demand can be synchronized, the smaller the need for safety stocks. The function of the safety stock is to avoid the losses caused by stockouts—that is, when a shortage of materials causes a slowdown or shutdown in service or in the construction of a project. Slowing or closing down an operation incurs costs, and bringing a service or project back up to speed after the shortage is made good usually entails even more costs. In general, maintaining service at a consistent level by means of a safety stock inventory minimizes operating costs.

Establishing a safety stock involves a careful analysis of activity patterns: that is, how erratic and how large are surges in demand, how dependable are suppliers, and how quickly do new shipments come in? The next step is to estimate the costs of stockouts. What are the costs of failing to serve citizens, and what are the costs of shutdowns and of the startups that follow a stockout? The answers to these questions are combined into a stockout cost probability function, which relates the size of the inventory to the probability of a stockout. To translate the function into monetary terms, the probability of a stockout is then multiplied by the estimated costs. Clearly, the larger the inventory in relation to normal patterns of demand, the smaller the probability of stockouts; the smaller the inventory in relation to normal patterns of demand, the larger the probability of stockouts.

From the point of view of avoiding stockouts, a large inventory is desirable, but holding costs, or stock losses— deterioration, obsolescence, storage, insurance, and imputed financing costs— increase directly with inventory size. Because holding costs are proportional to inventory size, they can be converted into an inventory holding cost function.

The optimal safety stock level can also be determined through marginal analysis. The minimum cost is the point at which the first derivative of the holding costs equals the derivative of the stockout loss function—that is, where the marginal costs of the two functions are equal. This would be expressed as

$$\frac{\partial SO}{\partial X} = \frac{\partial HC}{\partial X}, \text{ where}$$

∂ = changes
SO = stockout losses
HC = holding costs
X = inventory size.

Note that since the cost of capital is an important part of the holding cost function, a rise in the interest rate would move managers to economize on inventory holdings and run a greater risk of stockouts. On the other hand, a decrease in holding costs would allow managers to maintain a larger inventory.

Because the theoretical model just illustrated requires fairly complex and expensive computer modeling systems, it may make more sense, particularly for smaller local governments, to substitute rules of thumb that approximate the ideal solution. (However, with the development of less expensive computers, it may pay to move toward the more sophisticated models.) The rules of thumb, which have been developed for various kinds of activities and supplies, are stated in terms such as the following:

Certain inventories should be sufficient to cover about fifteen days' worth of demand.

Raw material stocks should cover thirty days of normal service.

General inventories should be turned over at least six times a year.

Since inventories absorb funds (i.e., they must be stored and financed), the efficiency with which inventories are controlled is of considerable interest to the procurement officer who wishes, while providing good service, to minimize governmental outlays.

The economic ordering quantity model

Once the safety stock level has been established, it is necessary to determine the optimal size and frequency of orders. The economic ordering quantity (EOQ) problem arises because of the ordering costs—that is, the clerical and correspondence costs associated with preparing and placing an order and checking it in once it is received.

It is generally assumed that a portion of the ordering costs is fixed for each order (i.e., does not vary with the size of the order). Thus, when orders are placed for larger quantities, the average ordering cost *per unit* decreases. If the supplier offers quantity discounts, these also, in effect, lower the ordering costs. However, when orders are placed for larger quantities, the size of the average inventory goes up, as do holding costs. Thus, the optimal amount and frequency of orders must be determined within the constraints created by ordering costs on the one hand and holding costs on the other.

The purpose of the EOQ model is to determine the optimal size of an order—the size that will minimize ordering costs in relation to holding costs. If there is an assured supply nearby and/or if usage rates are so stable that stockout losses are unlikely (i.e., the required safety stock is zero), the EOQ model solves the whole of the inventory problem. If these conditions are not met, the EOQ model is generally combined with the safety stock model.

Solving the EOQ problem involves three variables:

1. Predicted demand, or usage, for the applicable planning period
2. Holding costs as a percentage of inventory size
3. Ordering, or transaction, costs (i.e., the costs of placing an order and checking an item in, and getting it into stock).

The idea is to set the size of orders so as to minimize the total of holding and ordering costs for a given period. If, given the rate of usage, smaller orders are placed, the average inventory will be low and holding costs will be held down. On the other hand, small orders must be placed more often, which raises ordering costs.

The optimal EOQ is obtained when the marginal holding costs and the marginal ordering costs are equal. In the simple case, the mathematical solution yields the following formula:

$$EOQ = \sqrt{\frac{2SO}{HU}}, \text{ where}$$

S = estimated demand or usage in dollar terms for the period
O = ordering costs per order
H = holding costs as a rate for the given period (e.g., 24 percent for a year or 12 percent for six months)
U = costs per unit.

The formula as given will solve for the optimal EOQ in terms of units. If U is dropped from the equation, EOQ will be the optimal dollar amount of the order; however, when quantity discounts are offered, it is useful to have a unit cost and to be able to see the effect of various unit costs on optimal order size.

In this analysis, the problems of ordering quantity and safety stock have been treated separately. The average inventory resulting from the EOQ (one-half of the EOQ) has been solved independently and, presumably, simply placed on top of the safety stock. In theory, however, the EOQ and safety stock problems should be solved simultaneously because a larger EOQ policy results in higher *average* inventories and reduces the probability of stockouts. There are more complex computer models that do solve the EOQ and safety stock problems simultaneously.

Source: Adapted from Eli Schwartz, "Inventory and Cash Management," in J. Richard Aronson and Eli Schwartz, eds., *Management Policies in Local Government Finance,* 4th ed. (Washington, D.C.: International City/County Management Association, 1996), 390–394.

1   This chapter is based, in part, on the author's forthcoming book, *Introduction to Public Procurement* (Herndon, Va.: National Institute of Governmental Purchasing, 2004).

2   American Bar Association, *The 2000 Model Procurement Code for State and Local Governments* (Chicago: American Bar Association, 2000), 7.

3   Ibid.

4   Khi V. Thai, "Public Procurement Re-examined," *Journal of Public Procurement* 1, no. 1 (2001): 11–13.

5   Harry R. Page, *Public Purchasing and Materials Management* (Lexington, Mass.: D.C. Heath and Company, 1980).

6   Arthur G. Thomas, *Principles of Government Purchasing* (New York: D. Appleton and Company, 1919).

7   Ibid.

8   Page, chap. 2.

9   American Bar Association, *2000 Model Procurement Code.*

10   Definite-quantity contracts provide for the purchase of definite or known quantities of materials or services. Because the quantities are known, it is possible to obtain very favorable prices under such contracts.

11   For further information about public procurement, see Khi V. Thai, "Public Procurement Process: A New Perspective," *Journal of Public Procurement* (forthcoming).

12   National Institute of Governmental Purchasing (NIGP), *Advanced Public Procurement* (Herndon, Va.: NIGP, 1999), 137.

13   See Thai, "Public Procurement Re-examined," for in-depth explanations of these activities.

14   Because federal, state, and local governments acquire many similar items, including information technology and equipments, the Federal Acquisition Regulation, posted by the U.S. General Services Administration at www.gsa.gov, is an excellent source for specifications.

15   See John Cibinic Jr. and Ralph C. Nash Jr., *Administration of Government Contracts* (Washington, D.C.: National Law Center, George Washington University, 1995).

16   American Bar Association, *2000 Model Procurement Code,* article 3-203.1.c.

17   Carol Pettijohn and Yuhua Qiao, "Procurement Technology: Issues Faced by Public Organizations," *Journal of Public Budgeting, Accounting, and Financial Management* 12 (fall 2000): 441–461.

18   Ibid.

19   American Bar Association, *2000 Model Procurement Code,* 22.

20   For more information on RFPs, see Michael Asner, "Bulletproof RFPs," *IQ Report* 35, no. 9 (September 2003).

21   National Institute of Governmental Purchasing (NIGP), *NIGP 1998 Preference Report* (Herndon, Va.: NIGP, 1998).

22   Evelina Moulder, "Inside E-Government: Applications for Staff," *Special Data Issue* no. 6 (2002).

23   See, for example, Shreveport, Louisiana (www.ci .shreveport.la.us/Bid/bids.asp#HeaderTop); Cleveland, Ohio (www.city.cleveland.oh.us/business_ center/RFP/rfp2.asp?type=Bid); and Walla Walla, Washington (www.ci.walla-walla.wa.us/departments/ public-works/bids-rfps.cfm).

24   U.S. General Accounting Office (GAO), "FAA Purchase Cards: Weak Controls Resulted in Instances of Improper and Wasteful Purchases and Missing Assets," GAO-03-405 (Washington, D.C.: GAO, March 2003).

25   Stewart Beall et al., *The Role of Reverse Auctions in Strategic Sourcing* (Tempe, Ariz.: Center for Advanced Purchasing Studies, 2003).

26   Beall et al. report prices between 10 and 20 percent below historical prices. In a September 19, 2003, e-mail message to the author, Amos Roundtree, director of strategic acquisition planning, Miami-Dade County Department of Procurement Management, estimated that in the three e-RAs the county had conducted in 2002, Miami-Dade had achieved cost savings of $181,083, or about 10 percent of the prices it had previously been paying for the auctioned goods and services.

27   Beall et al. report that e-RAs can reduce cycle time by as much as 40 percent when compared with traditional sourcing processes.

28   Scrap consists of materials that do not meet requirements or standards and cannot be economically reworked. Waste is nonmetallic scrap that has some market value. Rubbish is refuse that has no market value but must nevertheless be disposed of.

16 Cash and investment management

M. Corinne Larson

In the public sector's continuing effort to do more with less, one area of financial management that is all too often overlooked is the management of cash and investments. Through effective cash management, local governments can produce significant additional revenue with little additional cost. This chapter discusses various tools and techniques that can be used to manage a local government's cash resources.

Objectives of cash management

In local government, the cash management function falls under the purview of the finance director or the treasurer, depending on the structure of the organization. In a small local government, the finance director will typically have complete responsibility for day-to-day cash management duties. Larger local governments have staff dedicated to the cash management function and may have a designated finance officer who handles the local government's investments on a full-time basis.

Public sector cash management offers many challenges. Local governments must perform a delicate balancing act: on the one hand, they need enough liquidity to meet operating expenses and other cash demands; on the other, they need to invest their funds to earn as much revenue as possible. To further complicate matters, local governments must maximize revenue without putting their funds at risk and must conduct their affairs under the watchful eye of the public.

The first step in improving cash management is understanding what cash management means. Cash management is more than investing funds. The cash management function begins when the government receives monies owed, ends when the payers' checks clear, and includes all activities in between. The following is a list of the objectives of a sound cash management function.

Managing liquidity. The main objective of cash management is liquidity management. The finance officer must make sure that enough cash is on hand to meet the government's financial obligations.

Accelerating collections. A central part of liquidity management is to collect all monies owed and to do so in the most efficient way possible. (The next major section of this chapter discusses collection systems.)

Maximizing investment earnings. Once funds have cleared the banking system and are available for use, the government must decide what to do with those funds until they are needed. Because investing exposes governments to risk, it is important for local governments to familiarize themselves with investment tools and techniques that can help minimize exposure to risk while maximizing investment earnings potential.

Reducing the need to borrow. Private sector finance managers can draw on bank lines of credit to cover temporary shortfalls of cash. Although some local governments can do so as well, most rely on internal transfers from other funds or issue tax anticipation notes (TANs) to cover temporary shortfalls. Careful cash management—collecting all monies owed and making efficient use of those funds until needed—may help local governments minimize the need for frequent fund transfers or reduce the need to borrow. How disbursements are managed will also influence how much cash will be available for investment.

Managing disbursements efficiently. Instead of delaying disbursements, local governments can employ certain techniques to manage disbursements efficiently and effectively. A good cash management policy will specify how disbursements will be handled, whether to take advantage of discounts, and what types of bank products will be used to manage disbursements.[1]

Providing accurate and timely reporting. Knowing how much cash is on hand is a very important part of the cash management function. Governments need to have accurate reporting systems in place. Many banks offer real-time balance reporting information. Governments can use these services to check their internal records against the bank's records to make sure all incoming and outgoing cash is recognized and accounted for correctly.

Collections

Governments receive cash from a variety of revenue sources, including taxes, special assessments, intergovernmental revenues, licenses, permits, and fees. Most local government collection systems strive to achieve three goals: (1) to accelerate the receipt of available funds, (2) to safeguard the government's cash, and (3) to keep banking costs to a minimum. Some approaches to dealing with cash receipts, such as lockboxes, accelerate the receipt of available funds and help safeguard cash. Others, such as concentration accounts, help the local government centralize its cash management and thereby reduce banking costs.

Collection systems vary among local governments depending on the size of the jurisdiction, the nature of the revenues received, and the payment methods allowed. By conducting a cost-benefit analysis, a government can determine which payment methods would be most effective for the types of revenue it collects.

This section (1) describes the principal payment types and collection methods, (2) explains the importance of accelerating the availability of funds and implementing an accurate and timely reporting system, and (3) discusses the determination of collection rates and the pursuit of delinquencies.

Payment types and collection methods

How a local government handles cash receipts will affect its ability to achieve the overall goals of the collection system. This section focuses on the payment types that local governments accept and on the collection methods that they use.

Payment types   Cash receipts take a number of forms: coin and currency, paper checks, credit card charges, Fedwires (a wire system operated by the U.S. Federal Reserve), or Automated Clearing House (ACH) transactions.

Coin and currency   Over-the-counter payment of coin and currency ensures that the government will receive "good" funds (funds available for immediate use because they do not have to go through a check-clearing system), but staff are required to count, wrap, and deposit the cash into a local bank. Such deposits may also require the use of armored car services, which are an added expense.

Paper checks   Although paper checks are the most common means of paying obligations, the acceptance of checks delays the receipt of good funds. An out-of-town check is not available for use until it clears the Federal Reserve System, a process that can delay the receipt of usable funds for up to three days. The government also runs the risk of accepting a "bad" check and must then contend with costly collection efforts and possible legal action.

Local governments typically accept checks over the counter and by mail. Some governments arrange with local financial institutions to accept over-the-counter payment of taxes and other amounts owed. This approach can speed up the availability of funds, help reduce the local government's workload, and tighten the government's internal controls by keeping the checks and cash out of the local government's office.

Sound cash management practice dictates that all checks received be deposited in the bank that same day. Checks received after banking hours may have to be deposited at a night depository.

Credit card and electronic transactions   Credit card and online payments allow a local government to receive good funds in one day and are becoming more common for fees and taxes.[2]

Credit cards offer significant flexibility: they can be used for over-the-counter collections, telephone transactions, mail-in payments, and electronic transactions. Many local governments that have recreation centers, civic centers, golf courses, and other similar public services find it cost-effective to accept credit card payments even though they must pay credit card companies a fee. Credit cards can also help to reduce the number of bad checks governments receive.[3] Credit card payments can benefit citizens by making payments more convenient and by saving time, particularly when citizens can handle a number of transactions online, such as renewing permits and licenses and enrolling in recreation programs. One disadvantage of credit card payments is that if a taxpayer challenges a charge, the government may lose its funds if the credit card company reverses the transaction through a charge-back.

Online payment offers several benefits to local governments, including reducing the staff time needed to provide face-to-face service, reducing the incidence of bad checks, and speeding up the availability of funds.

Fedwire   Fedwire is a method of electronic transfer operated by the Federal Reserve System. Funds sent by Fedwire are available for immediate use. Because of the cost, such transfers are generally reserved for larger dollar payments: receiving a wire typically costs between five and ten dollars, and sending a wire costs between five and twenty dollars, depending on whether the transaction is conducted via telephone or personal computer and is repetitive or nonrepetitive.[4]

Automated Clearing House transactions   An ACH transaction is an electronic funds transfer that moves through a network of automated clearinghouses that operate similarly to the Fedwire system but at a fraction of the cost. ACH transactions take one day to become available and are a very cost-effective means of collection: the national average cost of an ACH debit is thirteen cents, and the national average cost of an ACH credit is twelve cents.[5]

For corporate tax payments, ACH credits offer benefits to both the government and the corporation. The corporation can keep its funds longer and know for certain when the tax payment will clear. The government will know that it is receiving funds on the due date and that those funds will be good within one day.

Collection methods　The local government's approach to handling payments will affect the safety and availability of funds. As noted earlier, lockboxes safeguard cash and accelerate the availability of funds. Zero-balance accounts help minimize banking costs and facilitate investment.

Lockboxes　A lockbox is simply a post office box used to collect checks that are retrieved by a bank and processed around the clock, to reduce float. Citizens mail payments to a post office box that is emptied daily by the bank. Receipts are deposited immediately, and a record is sent to the government either by mail or by courier. To reduce mail float, most lockboxes are located in major cities. Ideally, lockboxes would be situated in the city or cities that are closest to the customers who are remitting the greatest number of checks or the greatest amount of dollars.

A lockbox enables a local government to keep the checks out of its physical office and reduces processing time for staff. For example, a lockbox would eliminate the need for employees to open envelopes, remove and copy the checks, make out deposit slips, and make daily bank deposits. Some lockbox users prefer to receive a listing of the dollar amounts of deposits and to have copies of checks sent by regular mail. Others prefer to pay extra for courier service and receive the information the next day. More sophisticated users have the bank electronically update their accounts-receivable records.

A lockbox can speed up collections because checks are collected twenty-four hours a day, seven days a week, and are sent through the check-clearing process faster. For several reasons, however, lockboxes are less common in the public sector than in the private sector. First, most taxpayers are located in the same or in a nearby geographic area, so the benefit of around-the-clock collection is lost. Second, because many governments are restricted to using in-state banks, a government that has large taxpayers in another state cannot set up a lockbox in that state but must continue to deposit out-of-state checks in its local bank. Third, statutes or ordinances may require the government to physically receive tax payments.

Depending on the nature of the local government's collections, it may use a retail lockbox, a wholesale lockbox, or both. A retail lockbox is used to collect a large volume of checks made out for small amounts. For example, a public utility may contract with a bank or third-party provider to collect checks from retail customers, which are generally small dollar amounts, and process the payments electronically, using scannable documents that are mailed to the customers with their invoices. A wholesale lockbox processes a smaller volume of payments made out for larger amounts. A government might use a wholesale lockbox for property taxes or other large payments (e.g., rents, payments from vendors at airports or convention centers).

Zero-balance accounts　Many governments use zero-balance accounts (ZBAs) to collect funds. The balances on these accounts are brought to zero at the end of each day and transferred to a general checking account, commonly referred to as a concentration account. ZBAs are especially useful for governments that need to segregate funds in different bank accounts, and for government agencies at outlying locations (such as community recreation centers, parks departments, and civic centers) because they can deposit their funds into a branch of the government's bank. At the end of the day, the bank will automatically transfer those funds into the government's concentration account. A ZBA structure reduces the government's banking costs and allows funds to be automatically transferred into a single account for investment.

Accelerating receipts and obtaining timely and accurate records

The two cornerstones of an effective collection system are (1) accelerating the availability of funds and (2) implementing a reporting system that provides accurate and timely information.

Availability of funds   The faster funds can become available, the sooner the government can make use of them. Improved technology, in the form of electronic funds transfers, allows finance officers to maximize the availability of funds. For example, local governments that collect property taxes through an escrow agent acting on behalf of a home owner can receive funds electronically and thus speed up the availability of funds. Some governments accept credit card payments for fees, services, taxes, and licenses and get next-day availability on those funds. Many states use the ACH system to pay local governments, an approach that is cost-effective for both sender and receiver and allows next-day availability of funds.

Accuracy and timeliness of reporting   Ensuring quick receipt and availability of funds will not benefit a local government if the finance office has no idea that funds have been received. Finance officers need daily information on bank balances, cash receipts, and other transactions that will affect their cash positions. Online reporting systems from banks are a cost-effective means of ensuring that the finance office knows exactly how much cash has been collected, how much is available for immediate use, and how much has a one- or two-day float (see sidebar on next page).

A balance-reporting system is of more value to governments that receive out-of-state checks than to governments whose collections are confined to the immediate geographic area. If a government's taxpayers are located in the same geographic area and there are only one or two banks in town, most of the funds will be available immediately or within one day. In these cases, effective cash management will require less expensive and less sophisticated bank products.

When bank-account balances are reported through an electronic connection, finance staff can update the daily cash position worksheet, track check clearings, monitor automated payments (such as debt service payments), and record any electronic deposits. This type of information greatly improves the accuracy of record keeping and allows the government to manage its cash more effectively.

Collection rates and delinquent revenues

To be fair to taxpayers, a local government should strive for high collection rates for all revenues owed and keep the payment process simple and easy. In addition, delinquent revenues should be pursued.

A target collection rate is part of the design of any collection system. A local government should determine its average collection rate over a defined time period and monitor its progress toward the target rate. For example, if a government has $10 million in property tax budgeted and collects $9 million that year, its collection rate is 90 percent. Is that an acceptable rate? If not, the government should review its collection methods and take remedial action. If

Float   Float is the amount of time it takes for a payee (the government) to receive usable funds from a payer (the taxpayer). There are many types of float:

Mail float is the length of time it takes for a check mailed by the payer to be received by the payee.

Processing float is the period between the time a check is received and the time it is deposited in a bank.

Check float is the delay between the time an invoice is received or a payment is due and the time it takes the check to clear the payer's bank account.

Collection float is the period between the time the payer mails a check and the time the payee receives available funds.

Availability float is the time it takes for a deposited check to become usable funds.

How does float affect the collection process? Because a local government cannot benefit from funds received until the funds clear the processing system and become usable, float can cost a local government money.

The following example demonstrates the benefit of reducing float: Assume that a local government collects $15 million in property taxes and that its return on investments is 2.5 percent. By reducing float by two days, the government benefits by $2,082 annually ($15 million × 2 days × 0.0250/360 = $2,082).

When a local government deposits a check from a taxpayer that is drawn on the same bank, it will receive same-day credit for the check, assuming that the check is deposited before the bank's cutoff time. (Checks drawn on the same bank where they are being deposited are referred to as "on-us" checks.)

If a taxpayer writes a check from a different bank in the same city, the local government's bank will typically receive one-day availability on this check because it must go through a local clearinghouse before it becomes available. If the taxpayer is a corporation that uses an out-of-state bank, the corporation's check may take one or two days to become available funds, depending on which bank it uses and that bank's relationship to the government's bank. For example, if the two banks have a correspondent relationship with one another, they will literally swap bundles of checks and give one-day credit on the funds, thereby bypassing the Federal Reserve clearing process. If the two banks do not have such a relationship, then the out-of-town check will have to clear through the Federal Reserve System and be presented at the drawee's bank to become available funds. When this happens, the check may have one- or two-day availability, depending on which Federal Reserve district the banks are located in and on the availability schedule of the government's bank. (An availability schedule is a listing of how soon a bank will give credit for checks drawn in certain Federal Reserve districts.)

collection rates were even lower in previous years, a 90 percent collection rate may be acceptable. There is no industry standard for collection rates, but local governments should monitor the effectiveness of their collection programs and implement changes as needed.

Local governments should devote serious effort to collecting delinquent revenues and should pursue to the full extent allowed by state law all delinquent taxpayers and other parties whose payments are overdue. However, governments should not engage in aggressive collection practices unless they have the full support of their governing bodies.

When in-house efforts fail, some local governments contract out the collection of past-due accounts. Private collection agencies offer a variety of services, from sending collection letters to referring accounts to national credit-reporting bureaus to pursuing legal action. The benefits of using a collection agency include (1) reduced staffing requirements for the local government, (2) access to state-of-the-art computer equipment for the automatic generation of letters, and (3) access to the agency's experience and expertise. Drawbacks to using a collection agency include (1) the possibility of antagonizing citizens, (2) cost (the agencies take as their fee a percentage of the past-due amount that is collected), and (3) record-keeping problems that occur when the agency records are maintained separately from the government's internal records.

Concentrating funds cost-effectively

A local government should maintain as few bank accounts as possible. Sometimes, however, a government must maintain separate bank accounts for a variety of reasons—for example, to segregate monies designated for specific funds or to make it easier to account for different fund types. When separate bank accounts are used, a local government will often move the funds from those accounts into a concentration account, commonly referred to as a general account, in order to make the most effective use of its cash. Concentrating funds only makes sense, however, if it is done cost-effectively.

How funds are concentrated will depend on the number and types of accounts a government maintains and the number of banks it uses. It is important not only to move funds as inexpensively as possible, but also to ensure that once funds are concentrated, they are invested immediately. Leaving idle balances in a concentration account creates an opportunity cost in the form of lost earnings.

Generally, the concentration account is maintained with the primary bank. Depending on how a government has its accounts structured, its disbursement accounts may be funded by the concentration account, and any deposits made at outlying locations may be transferred at the end of the day to the concentration account.

Local governments can use a number of bank products to concentrate funds. As technology improves, bank products are becoming increasingly sophisticated and more affordable for smaller governments.

As noted earlier, ZBAs are a cost-effective means of concentrating funds. One drawback of a ZBA, however, is that the finance officer will not know how much activity occurred in the account until the next business day. For outlying locations, the government must set up an internal reporting system so that the main office is notified of any deposits; or the main office may need to get deposit information the next day through a bank reporting system.

Governments also can move funds by ACH, a method that is both cost-effective and particularly useful for governments that use more than one bank. For example, banks charge, on average, thirteen cents to initiate an ACH debit using bank software, and a nominal fee (typically fifteen cents) to credit an account where the funds are deposited.[6] Funds moved by ACH will have one-day availability unless the accounts are in the same bank, in which case the funds will have same-day availability.

Fedwire assures the government of same-day use of the funds but can be very expensive and should be used only for large dollar amounts. Initiating a repetitive outgoing wire can cost an average of $6.94, and receiving an incoming wire can cost an average of $8.65.[7] Fedwire is useful for transferring funds to and from investment accounts.

To calculate the break-even cost of a wire transfer, simply take the total cost of the wire (i.e., as an outgoing wire from one bank and an incoming wire to another) and divide it by a daily investment rate, which will be the overnight investment rate divided by 360. In the example that follows, the total cost of the wire is $15.59, and the government receives 1.5 percent on overnight investments. The break-even cost of the wire is $374,760.

Cost of wire/(annual interest rate/360) = $15.59/(0.015/360) = $374,760

An automatic sweep account is essentially a ZBA in which the government's available funds are automatically swept into an investment vehicle, such as an overnight repurchase agreement or a money-market mutual fund, at the end of the business day. At the beginning of the next day, the funds are returned to a concentration account. Sweep accounts often have a balance threshold and will sweep funds over the amount of the threshold. Figure 16–1 shows how a sweep account can be structured.

Sweep accounts can cost anywhere from $50 to $175 per month, depending on the bank and the investment vehicle used. Collateralized repurchase agreements are the most expensive type of sweep investment. Governments that have large bank balances would find that sweep accounts are cost-effective. Governments that have liquidity problems might find that sweep accounts cost more than the interest earned on the account. The accompanying sidebar offers an example of a cost-benefit analysis of a sweep account.

Ensuring the safety of deposited funds

For a finance officer entrusted with the care of public funds, ensuring their safety is the primary goal. The only way to fully guarantee the safety of public funds on deposit with financial institutions is by requiring the bank to pledge securities, such as U.S. Treasury securities and government agency securities, for any amounts above the Federal Deposit Insurance Corporation (FDIC) limit of $100,000.

The bank failures of the late 1980s and early 1990s prompted many state legislatures to pass laws requiring the collateralization of public deposits. These laws specify the level of protection required and the types of collateral that banks may pledge to protect public deposits. State laws still vary widely, however. In those states where no laws govern public deposits, local governments may be permitted to have their deposits collateralized according to local ordinances and practices. Some states have collateral pools. Many local

Figure 16–1
Sweep account.

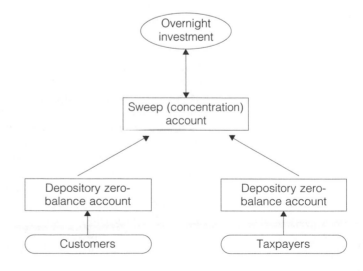

Cost-benefit analysis of a sweep account In this example, the local government has a sweep account at its primary bank and pays for banking services through direct fees rather than through compensating balances. The investment vehicle is a collateralized overnight repurchase agreement with a monthly fee of $175. The threshold balance is $25,000, so any funds over $25,000 are swept into an overnight repurchase agreement at the end of the day. A sweep account paid for by direct fees allows the local government to realize a net benefit of $10,587.87.

Service month	Net interest earned ($)	Sweep fee ($)	Gain ($)	Bank fees ($)	Net position ($)
January	10,008.81	175.00	9,833.81	9,814.53	19.28
February	10,307.22	175.00	10,132.22	10,370.54	(238.32)
March	10,518.84	175.00	10,343.84	10,421.37	(77.53)
April	12,009.13	175.00	11,834.13	10,537.29	1,296.84
May	11,400.74	175.00	11,225.74	9,737.06	1,488.68
June	12,223.25	175.00	12,048.25	9,596.52	2,451.73
July	10,300.87	175.00	10,125.87	10,132.23	(6.36)
August	12,057.54	175.00	11,882.54	10,113.20	1,769.34
September	11,354.45	175.00	11,179.45	9,874.60	1,304.85
October	10,256.55	175.00	10,081.55	10,482.79	(401.24)
November	12,575.14	175.00	12,400.14	10,912.35	1,487.79
December	11,009.25	175.00	10,834.25	9,341.44	1,492.81
Total	134,021.79	2,100.00	131,921.79	121,333.92	10,587.87

governments that are not required by law to collateralize their deposits do so anyway to protect their funds against default on the part of financial institutions.

Even though banks are stronger today than they were in the past, finance officers must still pay careful attention to the financial health of the banks that hold public funds. Financial institutions hold millions of dollars in demand deposits (checking accounts) and in time deposits (such as certificates of deposit—CDs). And, given the frequency of mergers and acquisitions, a smaller number of banks are holding larger shares of public funds. Governments should implement risk control measures that include (1) the development of a formal risk management policy, (2) routine credit analysis of financial institutions, and (3) the use of fully secured investments.[8]

To monitor the exposure to risk, the finance officer should study the daily and average monthly balances of all the local government's bank accounts, particularly if a block of collateral securities is used for demand deposits. One way to help eliminate excess balances on deposit—and thereby reduce the government's exposure—is through sweep accounts that have a fully collateralized repurchase agreement as the investment vehicle. Governments that use non-interest-bearing CDs as compensating balances to pay for bank services should ensure that the bank pledges securities to collateralize those CDs. The government should also ensure that the pledged securities are in amounts large enough to cover the government's balances during high points in its cash flow cycle.

Some states permit financial institutions to pledge securities at face value rather than at market value. If the market value of the security is less than par, the deposits may be undercollateralized and thus exposed to some risk. Finance officers should recognize this risk and require deposits to be secured (1) by short-term, high-quality securities such as U.S. Treasury notes or

(2) by securities whose value is greater than the amount of exposure (e.g., 102 percent). Some states have specific laws regarding the percentage of coverage required and the types of securities that can be pledged.

Disbursement

A disbursement system is designed to safeguard the government from incorrect claims and to keep spending within budgetary guidelines. State statutes and local ordinances often outline general disbursement procedures, including methods of approval and the responsibilities of government officials. Cash management is concerned with the most effective and efficient way to pay disbursements that have already been approved.

The main objectives of a disbursement system are (1) to pay the government's obligations in a timely and cost-effective manner, (2) to provide the finance officer with information on funding requirements, (3) to take the guesswork out of managing the government's liquidity, and (4) to reduce or eliminate opportunities for fraud and theft. Knowing the local government's disbursement requirements enables the finance officer to make effective investment decisions, to know with certainty whether there will be any funding shortfalls, and to make the necessary arrangements to cover those shortfalls cost-effectively. In designing a disbursement system, a local government should (1) review the timing of its disbursements to determine whether a centralized system is needed, (2) determine which disbursement method will be most efficient, and (3) ensure that appropriate protections against fraud are in place. Internal controls, which ensure that only authorized payments are made to authorized parties, are an important part of any disbursement system.

Centralized versus decentralized disbursement

Local governments may have either a centralized or a decentralized disbursement system. The main advantage of a centralized system is timing: bill paying can be matched to cash inflows, which is particularly important for local governments that have large expenditures and seasonal cash flows. Centralized disbursement also allows local governments to process payables in time to take advantage of vendor discounts when offered. Finally, a centralized system allows local governments to implement a disbursement schedule that eliminates frequent check runs but ensures that bills are paid on time. Many governments issue checks once a week or even twice a month; issuing checks in batches enables local governments to manage their cash flows more effectively and save on bank transaction costs, check supplies, and postage.

Disbursement float Disbursement float is the length of time between the preparation of a payment (e.g., a check) and its presentation for payment at the government's bank. Many factors can affect disbursement float, including (1) mail time for a check to reach the payee, (2) the time it takes the payee to deposit the check, (3) the Federal Reserve district where the check is initially deposited and the Federal Reserve district where the check is drawn, (4) the relationship between the receiving and the paying banks, and (5) the type of payment method being used. If a government pays by ACH credit, for example, there would be a one-day disbursement float, meaning that the government would have use of those funds for one additional day. Funds transferred by wire are available immediately, so there would be no disbursement float.

Disbursement methods

A government may pay its debts by wire transfer, ACH credit, or check. Because wire transfers are expensive, they are rarely used for vendor payments. Local governments generally use wires when they are required to by contractual obligations or when the dollar amounts are very large. As noted earlier, paying by wire allows the government to hold on to its cash until the payment due date.

The use of ACH credits is becoming increasingly common, especially for federal tax payments and employee and benefit-related pay. Most governments offer direct deposit and encourage employee participation, and many employees are taking advantage of the option. There are many advantages to direct deposit, including reductions in (1) check-processing charges; (2) staff time spent preparing checks, replacing damaged checks, and making special arrangements for absent employees; (3) employee time for cashing checks; (4) account-reconciliation time; (5) storage costs for canceled checks; and (6) the incidence of lost or stolen checks.

Checks remain the most common payment method. However, the single largest drawback to paying by check is the uncertainty about when a check will actually clear the government's account. Another problem with using checks for disbursements is that they are frequently stolen or altered. Many of the protections against fraud that a local government must establish as part of its disbursement system are focused specifically on the risks associated with checks.

Protections against fraud

The revised Uniform Commercial Code (UCC) places the burden on employers to keep their check stock secure. Local governments can take a number of general steps, outlined in the following section, to protect their check stock; they can also ensure that duties are properly segregated and that impress accounts are handled appropriately. Finally, they can make use of a bank service called positive pay.

General precautions To ensure the safety of their check stock, local governments are advised to take the following general precautions:

Undertake a background check on all employees who will have access to the government's financial assets, and require drug screening. Many fraudulent activities are undertaken because employees have financial problems.

Use standardized, prenumbered forms that require the approval of a supervisor before a file can be established for a vendor or an employee. Such forms not only make it more difficult to set up bogus vendors or ghost employees but also help guard against collusion.

Restrict access to vendor and employee files to protect against unauthorized tampering.

Require passwords to access accounts payable and payroll systems, and distribute passwords only to those employees who have responsibility for those functions. Employees should not post their passwords or access codes on the monitors of their personal computers or on bulletin boards. Passwords should be kept simple so that employees can memorize the code and then discard the written password.

Create automated audit trails. Software should automatically track any changes made to vendor and employee files, and the tracking records should not be accessible to users of the software. Reports, such as accounts payable check runs, should be generated periodically and reviewed by a supervisor for reasonableness.

To discourage tampering, use high-quality, secure check stock with safety features (e.g., watermarks, a "void" pantograph, and unique colors and background designs). Color copiers and laser printers make check tampering and duplication easy for criminals. Checks with safety features are nearly impossible to alter or duplicate.

Keep check stock in a secure place and limit access to those employees who print accounts payable and payroll checks. Facsimile signature plates should also be kept in a locked drawer accessible only to those employees who are authorized to use the plates.

If checks are signed on a check-signer, maintain a log of the beginning and ending check numbers, dates, and the number and type of checks.

Segregation of duties   Segregation of duties is crucial to ensuring the integrity of the disbursement system. Duties such as payment authorization and disbursement processing, for example, should be segregated: the employee who enters disbursement requests into the accounts payable system should not distribute checks. Although this level of segregation may be difficult to achieve for smaller entities in which one person oversees the finance function, any level of segregation that can be achieved will provide added protection to the organization.[9]

Impress accounts   Many local governments set up impress accounts for minor expenditures such as postage and petty cash. These accounts are established at a certain dollar amount (e.g., $500) and are replenished at the end of an accounting cycle for the amount of funds used, bringing the cash back to the established amount. Impress accounts are an effective internal control because checks cannot exceed the established dollar limit for the account. If the account is overdrawn, management would be alerted to a potential problem immediately.

Positive pay   Because check fraud has become a multibillion-dollar business, banks have come up with a service called *positive pay,* which helps reduce check fraud. Banks typically offer two types of positive pay services. Standard positive pay requires the government to transmit to the bank a file of legitimate checks that have been issued. When a check is presented for payment, the bank's software attempts to match the presented check to the issue file. Checks that match the issue file are paid; those that do not are returned to the issuer unpaid. Some banks will notify the government of rejected checks and allow them time (usually twenty-four hours) to research the item and advise the bank on whether to accept the check. With this service, the bank retains the responsibility for handling exceptions.

The other type of positive pay service is *reverse* positive pay. Under this arrangement, when a check is presented for payment, the bank transmits to the designated contact at the government entity an image of the check or the check's MICR (magnetic ink character recognition) line. The government then has to notify the bank within a specified time period whether the check should be paid or returned. With this service, the government, as the issuer of the check, is responsible for handling exceptions.

Banking relationships

Local governments use a variety of banking services, which can be very costly. Because banks are an integral part of a cash management program, it is essential for a local government to establish and maintain a good working relationship with its banks. To develop such relationships, local governments need to

(1) initiate competitive bidding and negotiation for banking services; (2) insist on written contracts for services; (3) evaluate paying by direct fees, compensating balances, or a combination of both; and (4) conduct a cost-benefit analysis of services.

Before preparing an RFP (request for proposal) for banking services, the finance officer should have in mind what types of services are required and should also inquire about new products and services that banks may have to offer. Governments that routinely issue RFPs for banking services can determine whether they are receiving competitive pricing from their banks. How often an RFP is issued depends on three factors:

Quality of current service. A government might consider issuing an RFP sooner if its bank is making a lot of errors, if the availability of deposited checks seems to be less favorable than what other banks offer, or if the bank's financial condition deteriorates.

Mergers and acquisitions. A bank that has merged with or been acquired by another bank may not offer the same level of service or type of products that it previously provided. In such cases, the government may consider bidding out its banking to find a more compatible business partner.

Level of competition. A local government may find (particularly if it is required to do business with banks only in its geographic area) that because of mergers and acquisitions, few banks can qualify to respond to its RFP. In such circumstances, the government might enter into longer contracts with the winning banks and issue RFPs less often, perhaps every four to five years. RFPs are labor- and time-intensive projects that can tie up staff time for several months.

To help local governments develop an RFP, many professional associations offer sample documents that describe the key components.[10] A well-developed RFP will include minimum qualifications to bid, a description of the current account structures and services used, a description of the services desired, and a standardized response form or a list of specific guidelines for responding to the request. Particularly if the government has significant amounts of cash, the RFP should also include minimum size requirements for eligibility. A government with $10 million may need only one local bank to handle all its needs, whereas a government with $100 million may need a bank for custodial safekeeping, a bank for depository services, and a bank or brokerage firm for investment services. Credit qualifications should also be specified, and should be limited to banks in the top two tiers assigned by a nationally recognized bank-rating agency.[11] Qualifications to bid may also include geographic restrictions, ability to handle special conditions, collateral requirements, or a Community Reinvestment Act rating (a federal measure of how well banks meet the credit needs of the communities they serve).

An evaluation matrix can make it easier to compare RFP responses. The evaluation criteria should be weighted to reflect what is most and least important to the government but should be kept fairly simple to avoid unnecessarily complicating the evaluation process. Once an RFP is awarded, a written banking services contract formalizes the relationship. Figure 16–2 on the following page is a sample evaluation matrix.

Cash flow forecasting

A cash flow forecast is a schedule of expected receipts and disbursements for a given time period. Although accurately predicting the peaks and valleys of cash flows is one of the most difficult aspects of cash management, a timely and accurate cash flow forecast is the basis for a sound investment program.

Figure 16–2 Evaluation matrix.

Evaluation category	Weight	Bank A		Bank B	
		Rating	Score	Rating	Score
1. Meets needs	3	4	12	4	12
2. Stability	3	4	12	4	12
3. Pricing	3	5	15	3	9
4. Level of service	2	3	6	4	8
5. Quality of relationship	2	4	8	3	6
6. Technology	2	5	10	4	8
7. Implementation plan	2	4	8	3	6
8. Professionalism	2	4	8	4	8
9. Growth potential	1	4	4	3	3
10. Reputation	1	5	5	4	4
Total weighted score		42	88	36	80

An accurate forecast can strengthen an investment program by allowing the finance official to determine (1) how much money will be available for investment, (2) when this money will become available, and (3) how long it will be available for investment. These considerations are important because yields are often linked to the size and maturity of an investment. Accurate cash flow forecasts can also help government officials to make prudent decisions about the timing of major purchases and to estimate if and when short-term borrowing, in the form of revenue anticipation or tax anticipation notes (TANs), may be necessary. Many local governments prepare an annual cash flow forecast for the current fiscal year and the next two to three fiscal years, depending on the maximum maturities of their investments. Updating the annual forecast monthly or quarterly helps to improve the forecast's accuracy.

Developing and monitoring cash flow forecasts

To prepare the forecast, the finance officer needs to identify the major types of routine transactions—such as accounts-receivable collections, accounts-payable disbursements, payroll and related expenses, and debt service payments—and to note the schedule of these payments, by month, throughout the fiscal year. The current annual budget document can provide an estimate of anticipated revenues and expenditures, and historical data from the general ledger will help identify peaks and valleys in the government's bank balances, recurring receipts and disbursements, and infrequent receipts and disbursements. This information will allow the government to identify those times during the year when it has excess cash that can be invested in a higher-yielding investment than the government's bank account.

A comparative analysis of data over the course of two to three years can help pinpoint trends in cash flows. For example, if a local government typically collects 95 percent of revenues owed, the forecasted receipts should be 95 percent of the projected revenues, not 100 percent.[12] However, it is important to take account of any factors—such as changes in economic or demographic conditions, federal or state aid, local tax levies or tax laws—that may have affected (or that will affect) the patterns of receipts and disbursements.

When considering receipts, for example, the finance officer should analyze typical payment patterns. Some citizens will pay as soon as they receive the bill, while others will wait until the due date; most fall somewhere in between. By determining the percentage of bills paid between thirty and forty-five days after mailing, the finance official can get a more accurate idea of when to expect the tax receipts. Similarly, if the expected inflation rate is 5 percent for the coming year, estimates for disbursements such as utilities and supplies will need to be adjusted upward. Thus, if a government spends a yearly average of $1,000,000 on office supplies, the forecasted amount should be $1,005,000 for the new year. If these purchases are spread evenly throughout the year, the forecast would show a monthly expense of $87,500. Labor agreements that will change the pay structure of government employees will also require an adjustment. If a contract calls for a 4 percent pay raise in the first year, a 5 percent pay raise in the second year, and a 4.5 percent pay raise in the third year, estimated payroll and related employee benefits need to be adjusted accordingly.

Throughout the year, the finance official should adjust the cash flow forecast as needed, keeping the data as current as possible and revising the forecast on the basis of any new information that may become available. Monitoring of the cash flow forecast has a number of benefits: it can (1) help identify cash flow patterns and increase the accuracy of future forecasts, (2) allow early identification of problems in the annual budget estimates, (3) reveal inaccuracies in record keeping, and (4) assist with internal control by isolating collection problems or missed deposits.

Many local governments find that all they need to project their cash flows is a simple spreadsheet program and a good handle on historical cash flow patterns in their jurisdiction. Figure 16–3, a sample cash flow forecast that was prepared using an electronic spreadsheet, depicts the cash flows for a small local government whose main revenue source is the property tax. Property taxes are due at the end of January and July. Other revenues are light in January but come in steadily throughout the rest of the year. For illustrative purposes, the figure shows the government's actual cash flows for the first quarter of the year and its projected cash flows for the remainder of the year. The government would prepare a forecast for the current fiscal year and for the next one to two years, depending on its investment horizon.

This type of forecast is useful for determining the net change in cash position by month. If the projected net change is positive, the government can expect to receive more cash than it pays out; if it is negative, the government can plan for those shortfalls and schedule investment maturities to cover them.

Occasionally, disbursements may bulge at a time when revenues (such as property tax collections or a state or federal grant) are insufficient to cover them. TANs, often floated with a major bank, can be used to bridge such a gap. Because the notes are short-term and tax-exempt, the interest rate should be quite low. If all goes well, when the revenue comes in, it will suffice to retire the notes and there will be a considerable reserve left over.

Using a cash flow forecast for investment purposes

In the forecast shown in Figure 16–3, the government has investment maturities of $1,525,000 coming due in May, and in June it expects to pay out $1,366,000 more than it plans to collect. Given the projected shortfall in June, the government can invest the $1,525,000 for only one month or less. In July, the government expects to collect $1,268,000 more than it will spend. According to the cash flow forecast, these funds can be invested to cover the next projected shortfalls, which occur in September, October, and December. Alternatively, the funds can be invested to cover shortfalls in the following year, since the investment maturities that will come due in September, October, and December will be sufficient to cover the shortfalls for these months.

The purpose of preparing a cash flow forecast is twofold. Governments need to have enough liquidity on hand to cover anticipated and unanticipated cash needs, and governments need to invest idle funds to generate interest income. When a cash flow forecast is used for investment purposes, a government's

	January	February	March	April	May	June	July	August	September	October	November	December	Total
Beginning balance	15,650												
Property tax revenue	1,340	900	500	20	5	5	1,340	900	500	20	5	5	5,540
Other revenues	254	770	1,130	951	937	770	848	959	840	1,048	985	852	10,344
Payroll and payables	(416)	(924)	(416)	(921)	(416)	(924)	(416)	(924)	(416)	(924)	(416)	(924)	(8,037)
Other expenses	(403)	(874)	(1,753)	(508)	(401)	(1,217)	(504)	(475)	(1,150)	(530)	(480)	(1,100)	(9,395)
Projected net change	775	(128)	(539)	(458)	125	(1,366)	1,268	460	(226)	(386)	94	(1,167)	(1,548)
Portfolio income and maturity	0	0	0	250	1,525	250	1,575	250	2,500	550	2,350	2,100	
Projected portfolio balance	16,425	16,297	15,758	15,300	15,425	14,059	15,327	15,787	15,561	15,175	15,269	14,102	
Actual portfolio balance	15,650	15,967	15,878	16,032									
Actual net change in portfolio balance		317	(89)	154									

Figure 16–3 Sample cash flow forecast, 2003 (in thousands of $).

idle funds may be broken down into two categories: liquid funds (those that will be needed to cover immediate cash needs) and core funds (those that will not be needed to cover immediate cash needs). Liquid funds are invested in local government investment pools, money-market mutual funds, or short-term instruments, such as commercial paper, CDs, or Treasury securities with maturities under one year. Core funds, on the other hand, are invested in instruments whose maturities are greater than one year.

A government can use its cash flow forecast to determine how much of its portfolio is core funds and how much is liquid funds. The cash flow forecast depicted in Figure 16–3 reflects a core fund balance of $14 million. This balance can be determined by identifying the projected portfolio balance. The projected portfolio balance in this example never falls below $14 million. This government knows that it can invest up to $14 million of its portfolio and still maintain adequate liquidity to meet its operating needs. Any funds above $14 million would be needed for liquidity purposes and would be invested in short-term instruments.

Each month, the finance officer would enter the portfolio's actual balance and calculate the net change. This information helps gauge the accuracy of the forecast and will alert the government to any budgetary problems or concerns.

Optimal cash and security holdings

Bank balances and service charges should be analyzed carefully. If the local government's average deposits are in excess of the bank's required offsetting balance, funds may be tied up unnecessarily. However, before the finance officer can decide whether excessive cash is being carried, he or she must first determine the optimal cash balance. It may well be that the local government would do best to maintain a cash balance in excess of the offsetting amount, if this saves some transaction and supervision costs.

Determining cash and security positions

The finance officer must decide on the optimal transaction cash balance and on the excess liquidity balance that may be held in money market funds or marketable securities. Let us assume that the local government's holdings of total liquid funds, comprising both cash and marketable securities, has been set. This amount consists of funds appropriated for capital improvements but not yet spent; funds set aside for debt service and other special purposes; and funds that have accumulated through the seasonal collection of taxes or the flotation of TANs. Given the total amount of liquid assets, transaction cash, and marketable holdings, the finance officer must decide how much of each type of asset to hold.

The simplest guidelines are the rules of thumb still used by many smaller local governments. One rule is to hold a certain number of days' expenditures as the transaction balance. For example, the cash balance might be one week's expenditures. If average weekly expenditures are $125,000, this amount would be held in cash at the bank, and the residual liquid funds would be invested in marketable securities. Whenever the cash balance falls below $125,000, securities would be sold to restore the cash balance to that amount. On the other hand, any cash in excess of $125,000 would be invested in marketable securities.

Other rules of thumb based on expenditure patterns can easily be devised: such rules are particularly useful for smaller local governments, which may be unable to justify the additional effort and expense of administering the more sophisticated models. The decision whether to use a more complex model often depends on the amount of funds involved and the level of prevailing interest rates versus the extra administrative costs.

There are analytical models that permit the optimal cash balance to be accurately determined, and computer use has resulted in some fairly complex systems. However, the relatively simple model analyzed in the accompanying sidebar—the economic ordering quantity (EOQ) model—is useful for illuminating most of the variables contained in the more complex programs.

Consolidating cash accounts

Economies of scale are possible in cash management. This fact argues against the proliferation of special cash funds, for it follows that the combined transactions of two activities can be covered by a smaller balance than the sum of two separate funds. Of course, the segregation of funds is often required by law, but since cash management efficiency can be improved through the consolidation of separate accounts, revisions to such laws would save local governments money. Transacting all banking business through a single account, or through as few as possible, permits the release of extra funds for portfolio investment.

To improve cash management, the Advisory Commission on Intergovernmental Relations (ACIR) has recommended the use of ZBAs; under such a system, there would be only one general account—but for control purposes,

---

The economic ordering quantity model　One common cash model is derived from the economic ordering quantity formula also used in inventory management. In this model, the carrying cost of holding cash (i.e., the interest forgone on the cash balance) is weighed against the estimated fixed cost per transaction of transferring funds from the marketable securities portfolio to cash transaction holdings. The costs of carrying transaction funds are directly proportional to the average cash balance held (i.e., the greater the cash balance maintained, the greater the earnings forgone from the potential investment of those funds in the security market). On the other hand, the total transaction costs vary directly with the number of transactions, and the number of transactions will be lower if a higher average cash balance is maintained. What is involved, therefore, is a trade-off between potential lost interest earnings on the one hand and transaction costs on the other.

A simple problem can be used to illustrate the application of the EOQ formula. Consider a local government with estimated total cash payments *(T)* of $6 million for a three-month period. These payments are expected to be steady over the period. The total of explicit and implicit costs per transaction *(b)* is $100, and the interest rate advantage on marketable securities *(i)* is approximately 3 percent per year, or 0.75 percent per quarter. The use of the following EOQ equation determines *C,* the optimal initial cash balance:

$$C = \sqrt{\frac{2bT}{i}} = \sqrt{\frac{2(100)(6,000,000)}{0.0075}}$$
$$= \$400,000$$

The optimal initial cash balance is $400,000, and over the period, the average cash balance will be one-half of $400,000, or $200,000. This means that the local government should make fifteen transfers from marketable securities to cash for the period ($6,000,000 ÷ $400,000).

The optimal number of transfers will be larger if transfer costs are relatively low and interest rates relatively high. On the other hand, the higher the cost per transfer and the lower the interest rate, the higher the optimal average cash

there would be separate clearing accounts for different departments. A zero balance would be maintained in the clearing accounts, but the bank would automatically transfer funds from the master account when checks are presented for payment. Such a system economizes on the size of the cash balances by consolidating them, while still allowing the finance officer control over the individual accounts.[13]

Investing

Effective cash management practices can enhance a local government's revenue stream by producing interest earnings, which often become an important revenue source. As noted earlier, finance officers must try to earn the best return possible without sacrificing the safety of the funds. They must also work within the constraints of state statutes; local laws, ordinances, and charters; and internal policies and procedures. In short, they must base their decisions on the principles of safety, legality, liquidity, and yield.[14]

Investing can be thought of as a three-step process. In the first step, which is undertaken before any investment purchases are made, the investor must become familiar with and understand the various risks. In the second step, the investor purchases an investment instrument that (1) complies with the government's written policies and procedures and (2) results in a market rate of return on the government's funds. In the third step, the investor

---

balance held over the period and the smaller the number of transactions.

In the given illustration, the unavoidable total cost of cash management for the period under the optimal solution is

Transaction costs	15 × $100	= $1,500
Forgone interest multiplied by the average balance	$200,000 × 0.0075 =	1,500
Total costs		= $3,000

For comparison, here are two contrary examples. If this local government set an initial cash balance of $200,000 instead of $400,000, it would have had thirty transfers for the period and held $100,000 as an average cash balance:

Transaction costs	30 × $100	= $3,000
Forgone interest multiplied by the average balance	$100,000 × 0.0075 =	750
Total costs		= $3,750

In this case, the smaller cash balance creates lower opportunity losses, but these are overwhelmed by the higher level of transaction costs.

If, however, the initial cash balance had been $500,000, there would have been only twelve transfers but a larger-than-average balance of $250,000.

Transaction costs	12 × 100	= $1,200
Forgone interest, multiplied by the average balance	$250,000 × 0.0075 =	1,875
Total costs		= $3,075

In this case, transaction costs are reduced, but the amount of lost interest is increased, more than offsetting the savings on transaction costs.

Although local government expenditures are usually sufficiently predictable to make the EOQ approach feasible, the flow of cash payments is seldom completely certain. To cover a modest degree of uncertainty, however, one need only add a precautionary balance so that the transfer from marketable securities to cash is triggered before the cash balance reaches zero. Nevertheless, in general, the EOQ model gives the finance officer a fairly good benchmark for judging the optimal cash balance. The model does not have to be used as a precise rule; it simply suggests what the optimal balance would be under a given set of assumptions.

produces investment reports that summarize the government's investment program, display the performance results, and recap economic activity for the period. Furthermore, a government must decide if it will, or even can, concentrate funds from various bank accounts, internal funds, or both to take advantage of economies of scale when making investments. There are several reasons that larger pools of cash typically generate higher investment returns: (1) higher dollar investments generally pay more favorable returns, (2) transaction costs are reduced because fewer transactions are necessary, and (3) higher dollar amounts render more investment options available.

Risks of investing

Some risk is associated with even the safest, most conservative investment. When investing public funds, it is imperative that the finance official understands the risks of a particular investment option.

Credit risk Credit risk, also known as default risk, refers to the possibility that the issuer will be unable to redeem the investment at maturity. Local governments can control credit risk by carefully screening and monitoring the credit quality of issuers, limiting investments to those of the highest credit quality, and holding collateral with a third-party custodian against certain investments, such as CDs and repurchase agreements.

Liquidity and marketability risk Liquidity risk refers to the investor's ability to sell an investment before maturity. A nonnegotiable CD is an example of a commonly used investment with high liquidity risk. Closely related to liquidity risk is marketability risk, which refers to the investor's ability to sell an investment before maturity without incurring a significant loss in price. Local governments can limit their exposure to liquidity risk and marketability risk by purchasing investments for which there is an active secondary market (the market where securities are traded after they have been issued).

Market risk On high-grade securities with a fixed rate of return and minimum default risk, market risk—that is, a change in the market price—is largely confined to interest rate risk. If the market interest rate falls during the holding period, the market price will increase. (The price of the security at maturity is always the same.) However, if the market interest rate rises, the security price will fall, and an investor might incur a loss if the security is sold prior to maturity. Because of the effects of the discount rate over time, when there are changes in the market rate, the price of longer-term securities varies more than the price of shorter-term securities. Therefore, in an environment characterized by a normal yield curve, longer-term securities generally carry a higher yield than shorter-term issues. When the yield curve is inverted, shorter-term securities have a higher yield than longer-term securities. Figure 16–4 on page 472 illustrates this point. (Typically, the yield curve is normal during an economic expansion and is inverted at the peak of the expansion.)

Criteria for investments

Because of the investment losses suffered by public entities in the mid-1990s, most local governments are required to have a formal investment policy. Such a policy (1) identifies investment objectives, (2) defines risk tolerance, (3) assigns

An investment warning A local government may, at times, have considerable funds in excess of transaction balances. It is common for the finance officer to invest these funds in recognized securities that offer the highest yield when compared with other investment alternatives. Although it may be tempting, particularly in times of lower interest rates, to invest in innovative financial products that promise a high yield, investors of public funds should use caution, and should avoid venturing into such areas without carefully investigating the volatility of the security, its potential downside loss, the reliability of the issuer, and the reputation and character of the purveyor of the instruments.

In the mid-1990s, the financial news was filled with stories of local governments that had made risky investments and suffered subsequent losses. These losses offered local governments plenty of examples illustrating why they should stay clear of exotic investment instruments. The most highly publicized example was Orange County, California, which suffered a $1.7 billion loss when it invested in exotic securities and leveraged its portfolio. In December 1994, the news that Orange County would be forced into bankruptcy rocked the public sector. Unfortunately, Orange County was not the only government that sustained losses when interest rates rose rapidly in 1994; many other local governments learned a painful lesson on interest rate risk.

In the early 2000s, governments were reminded of the importance of evaluating credit or default risk. The Arizona State Investment Pool suffered a $131 million loss when National Century Financial Enterprises, a health care finance firm, defaulted on its asset-backed debt amid a federal fraud investigation.[1]

These losses highlight the need for finance officers to use caution when investing public funds, especially when interest rates are low. Between January 2001 and June 2003, the Federal Reserve cut short-term interest rates from 6.5 to 1.00 percent. Because interest rates had dropped to levels not seen in more than forty years, many local governments failed to reach their budgeted interest income and responded by investing in higher-yielding securities that had high credit risk, or by investing in callable securities that were called as interest rates fell. Those governments whose portfolios had a high concentration of callable securities found that they had to invest the proceeds from those called securities in investments with even lower yields. Governments that failed to lock in rates as they were falling earned investment returns of less than 2 percent—an example of reinvestment risk.

In general, placing funds in recognized securities with maturity dates that match disbursement dates minimizes financial risk. Although even sophisticated investors can be taken in by what appear to be attractive investment opportunities, finance officers have a fiduciary obligation to exercise a high level of care and to make prudent investment decisions. Going back to the basics of understanding the characteristics of each investment alternative, analyzing the financial markets, and making investment decisions based on cash flow needs is the only way to ensure the safety of public funds.

[1] Jonathan Sidener, "Public Funds Suffer Hit," *Arizona Republic*, 11 January 2003.

responsibility for the investment function, and (4) establishes control over the investment process.

Even the best investment policy, however, does not tell the finance officer what investment instruments to purchase or how much to invest and for how long. Finance officers typically base investment decisions on cash flow needs. In many cases, idle funds are deposited in interest-bearing accounts (such as a local government investment pool) or are invested in overnight repurchase

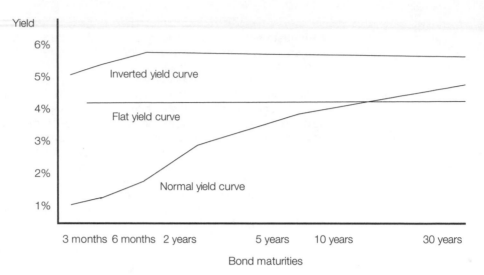

Figure 16–4   The shapes of the yield curve. The inverted yield curve occurs when short-term interest rates are higher than longer-term rates. This type of yield curve is common when the economy has reached its peak, and it portends lower rates in the future. The flat yield curve occurs when the economy is making a transition from an economic expansion to a slowdown. The normal, upward-sloping yield curve occurs when the economy is expanding, and it portends higher rates in the future.

agreements until needed. When large amounts of cash will be available for a substantial period of time, the finance officer may choose to invest in longer-term investments, such as CDs or Treasury bills.

Investment options should be evaluated on the basis of legality, safety, maturity, liquidity, and yield—in that order of priority.

Legality   Is this investment an allowable investment option? Most state statutes specifically outline what types of securities are allowable investment options for local governments; others are less clear and leave room for interpretation. Finance officers must understand applicable state statutes and the local government's investment policy and ensure that investment decisions comply with these requirements.

Safety   How safe is the investment? What is the credit risk? Is there any possibility that the government might lose its principal? Generally, the higher the yield, the greater the risk. Therefore, high-yield instruments with a great degree of credit risk are not suitable investments for local governments.

Maturity   How long will the investment be held? The longer the investment is held, the higher the credit and interest rate risk. Many finance officers rely on their cash flow forecasts to determine how long idle cash will be available for investment. If cash is needed before an investment matures, the investment may have to be sold, which could result in a loss of earnings and principal. To provide a natural hedge against changes in interest rates, local governments should consider investing in instruments with varying maturities.

Liquidity   How easily can invested funds be converted to cash without a significant loss in price? The more liquid an investment, the easier it will be to obtain funds if unanticipated cash needs arise. Some investments, such as nonnegotiable CDs, are highly illiquid. If a government does not have a good handle on its cash flow projections, such investments should be avoided. Many local governments keep a portion of their portfolios in readily available assets, such as investment pools, to ensure that they have cash on hand to meet unexpected needs, and, in a normal yield-curve environment, invest a portion of their portfolio in longer-term securities, such as Treasury notes, to take advantage of higher yields.

Yield   What is the return on the investment? Finance officers should seek to earn the highest return possible after balancing the concerns for legality, safety, liquidity, and maturity. By establishing a benchmark for performance, investment officers can evaluate the effectiveness of their investment program. (Benchmarks will be discussed later in this section.)

Investment options

When local government finance officers evaluate investment options, they must consider all aspects of the investment transaction. As noted earlier, some investments are more liquid than others, some are subject to more price volatility, and some are more expensive relative to other options. In addition, the attitudes of the citizens and the governing body should be taken into consideration before an investment purchase is made. If the jurisdiction has a low tolerance for risk, only conventional, relatively stable investments should be made.

Instruments that are typically allowable for local governments include local government investment pools, certificates of deposit, repurchase agreements, Treasury securities, government agency securities, and corporate securities.

Local government investment pools   Local government investment pools can be state sponsored or organized as joint-powers pools, in which local governments pool their cash for investment purposes. A state investment pool consolidates excess cash from local governments—often with state excess cash—to create one large sum of money. The advantage of an investment pool is that the funds can be invested at a higher yield than if each participant invested individually. Periodically, each participant receives a share of the interest earned. Most pools allow participants to make daily deposits or withdrawals.

Investing in a pool often makes the most economic sense (1) when funds are invested for a short period, (2) if the local government lacks the staff to administer a more aggressive investment program, or (3) if interest rates are expected to be volatile.

Certificates of deposit   Nonnegotiable CDs are bank time deposits that pay a fixed rate of interest and have a set maturity date that can range from one week to several years. Early redemption of a nonnegotiable CD can result in significant penalties, so investors should view these investments as highly illiquid. Also, because CDs are only insured up to the FDIC limit of $100,000, governments need to conduct a credit analysis of the bank offering the CD and buy only collateralized CDs. Collateralized CDs typically pay a lower interest rate than other investment options because banks factor in the cost of tying up collateral for these investments.

Nonnegotiable CDs make sense if investors can lock in a favorable interest rate and are confident that they will not need the funds for the term of the deposit. Smaller governments that have a limited number of investment options and wish to diversify their portfolios may find that, in certain interest rate environments, CDs can be a good complement to investment pools.

Governments that invest in negotiable CDs should be aware that these deposits cannot be collateralized because the bank will be unable to determine that the CD is owned by a public entity and will therefore be unable to pledge collateral securities against the deposit. In fact, for this very reason, many states do not allow local governments to invest in negotiable CDs. If a local government wishes to invest in a negotiable CD, it should evaluate the financial strength of the bank and obtain short-term and long-term debt ratings from a nationally recognized rating organization such as Standard & Poor's, Moody's Investors Service, or Fitch Ratings. A local government will have exposure to a bank's credit risk when it purchases a negotiable CD. However, smaller local government entities might note that CDs under $100,000 in aggregate are covered by FDIC deposit insurance.

Repurchase agreements   A repurchase agreement ("repo") is a simultaneous transaction between a buyer of securities (the investor) and a bank or securities dealer. In a repo transaction, the investor exchanges cash for temporary ownership of securities, with the agreement that the securities will be "repurchased" on a certain date and at a specified interest rate. Overnight repos are common cash management tools that allow local governments to make effective use of excess funds. A sweep account will often rely on a repo as its investment mechanism.

A government can protect its interest in the repo by (1) insisting on delivery versus payment for all transactions,[15] (2) safekeeping purchased securities with a third-party custodian, and (3) entering into a written master agreement that specifically outlines the responsibilities and liabilities of the buyer, the seller, and the custodial bank. It is especially important to outline how underlying securities will be liquidated in case of default by the seller.

The agreement also should specify what types of securities will be used as collateral. Treasury bills are the most liquid and stable instruments, and therefore the most preferred by investors. Other commonly used instruments include Treasury notes and bonds and government agency securities. In addition, to avoid market risk, shorter-term instruments are preferable. The riskier the underlying securities, the higher the collateralization ratio should be. The pledging requirement for repos is typically 102 percent, which means the collateralization ratio is 2 percent. Thus, if the repo is $100,000, the pledged securities should have a market value of $102,000; the margin, $2,000, protects the investor from changes in the market value of the underlying securities.

Treasury securities   Treasury securities are commonly used investment instruments in the public sector. They are highly liquid, marketable securities whose principal and interest are fully guaranteed by the U.S. government. The Treasury securities used by public sector investors are bills and notes: bills are short-term, marketable securities that are issued on a discount basis, meaning that the investor pays less than face value at the time of purchase and receives full face value when the Treasury bill matures. Treasury bills are issued in maturities of one, three, or six months. Notes are coupon-bearing securities, meaning that the investor will receive interest payments semiannually. Treasury notes have maturities of at least one year and less than ten years.

Treasuries are auctioned by the U.S. Treasury Department on a regular schedule. Investors can purchase newly offered securities directly from the Treasury, through its Treasury Direct program, or from the secondary market (the market where securities are sold after their initial issuance) through a financial institution or broker.

Because Treasury securities have an active secondary market, investors can often sell them before maturity without suffering a significant loss in price, and they may even make a gain on the sale. Another advantage is that Treasury securities that meet almost any maturity requirement can be purchased on the secondary market. Because there is such an active market for these securities, bid–offer spreads are generally narrow, so investors can easily determine whether they are receiving a fair price for the investment.

Securities from government agencies and government-sponsored enterprises Some investors do not understand the difference between a government agency security and a security issued by a government-sponsored enterprise. The only government agency that issues money-market securities is the Government National Mortgage Association (Ginnie Mae). Other government agencies issue long-term securities in smaller quantities that are unsuitable investments for local government operating funds.

Government-sponsored enterprises—the Federal National Mortgage Association, the Federal Home Loan Mortgage Corporation, the Federal Home Loan Bank, and the Federal Farm Credit Bank—issue larger blocks of securities on a more frequent basis and in shorter maturities. These securities are rated by nationally recognized rating organizations and do not carry the full faith and credit guarantee of the U.S. government. However, these securities tend to have more active secondary markets than government agency securities and are in most cases appropriate for operating funds.

Corporate securities Many local governments, particularly larger governments, invest in corporate securities such as commercial paper and corporate notes. Commercial paper is a short-term investment, issued on a discount basis, with a maturity under 270 days. Corporate notes are coupon-bearing securities with various maturities. These securities often offer higher returns than the investment alternatives discussed previously. However, local governments considering corporate securities should analyze the issuers' short- and long-term debt ratings. Most state statutes have very specific guidelines on the use of corporate securities.

Evaluating and reporting on investment performance

Governments need timely and accurate reports to monitor the performance of their investments. Performance should be measured against an established benchmark, and regular investment reports should be prepared for review by the governing body.

Performance benchmarks Choosing a benchmark can be a frustrating experience for a finance officer, who must place a higher priority on protection of principal than on yield. The benchmark should be set at a level that is achievable within the constraints of the investment policy; in other words, the benchmark must be realistic and attainable.

To be most useful, a benchmark should closely match the portfolio in terms of risk, maturity, and investment management style. So, for example, a government with a weighted average portfolio maturity of ninety days should measure its performance against a benchmark such as the three-month Treasury bill. Similarly, a government that invests only in a pool with a weighted average maturity of thirty days should measure its performance against a short-term benchmark such as the one-month Treasury bill, a money-market index, or an investment-pool index.

For portfolios with a mix of investment instruments, the finance officer can develop a composite benchmark that reflects the government's model portfolio, as defined by the investment policy, in terms of credit quality, maturity restrictions, and diversification requirements. The yields for the securities in the portfolio model could be tracked, weighted accordingly to the desired portfolio mix, and averaged to come up with a composite benchmark. For example, assume an investor must maintain a weighted average maturity of one year or less and that allowable investment instruments consist of overnight repurchase agreements and Treasury bills and notes. A composite benchmark yield can be created by taking the average monthly yield for each of these securities, weighting the yield on the basis of the percentage each contributes to the total portfolio, and averaging the weighted yields. In the example shown in Figure 16–5, the composite benchmark return is 1.318 percent for a portfolio consisting of short-term securities with a weighted average maturity of 360.4 days, or approximately one year. To determine how well its portfolio performed for the month, the government would compare its weighted average return against the benchmark return.

Investment performance reports　Since reporting is such an important part of the investment process, reports are often required to be sent regularly to the governing body, the investment oversight committee (if one exists), and others as deemed appropriate. The following information is typically included:

A list of investments by type and as a percentage of the portfolio

A list of investments by maturity date

The cost of each investment, its yield, and its accrued interest

The market value of each investment

Comparative returns for prior periods, such as the prior quarter or fiscal year.

The investment report might also include other information, such as the following:

A comparison of current income with forecast or budgeted income

A comparison between the portfolio's average weighted yield to maturity and the benchmark

The percentage of the total portfolio held by each institution

The principal and type of investment by fund

Figure 16–5　Derivation of a composite benchmark.

Assumptions
Portfolio composition: Overnight repurchase agreement and Treasury securities.
Weighted average maturity target: One year.

Instrument	Days	Weight (%)	Weighted days	Yield (%)	Weighted contribution
Overnight repurchase agreement	1	10	0.1	1.25	0.00125
Three-month Treasury securities	90	25	22.5	1.11	0.00278
Six-month Treasury securities	183	25	45.8	1.10	0.00275
Two-year Treasury securities	730	40	292.0	1.60	0.00640
			360.4		0.01318

Notes: Weighted average maturity of benchmark:
　360.4 days. Benchmark return: 1.318%.

Market and economic information

An interest rate outlook

Trend graphs of interest rates over a specified time period, such as the last five years.

Some state statutes have very specific reporting requirements for local governments; others allow a local government to determine its own reporting requirements, which are typically outlined in the government's investment policy.

Conclusion

Prudent investment decisions can increase a local government's investment revenue. Cost-effective methods for undertaking collections and processing receipts and disbursements can reduce a local government's cash management costs and ensure the collection of all monies owed. A well-run cash management program protects a government's funds and makes the most effective use of them.

1 For information on writing cash management policies, see Association for Financial Professionals (AFP), *AFP Manual of Treasury Policies: Guidelines for Developing Effective Control* (Bethesda, Md.: AFP, 2001).

2 According to a 2002 survey by the International City/County Management Association, at least one-quarter of all local governments with populations of 250,000 or more offer citizens the option of paying their taxes online, and most others plan to offer this service. Among smaller local governments, the numbers are much lower, but a few are offering online payment of taxes and fees, and many more plan to do so. See "E-Government: What Citizens Want; What Local Governments Provide," *Special Data Issue* 5 (2002).

3 Many local governments accept credit cards; however, some are not allowed to because of the discount fee that credit card companies charge. A cost-benefit analysis must be performed to determine whether it makes sense to accept payments by credit card. Some local governments have negotiated special arrangements with credit card companies to reduce or eliminate discount fees. The Government Finance Officers Association of the United States and Canada was actively involved in evaluating whether it is appropriate for governments to incur the cost for accepting credit card payments. For more information, see Betsy Dotson, "Hearings Held on Credit Card Charges," *Public Investor* 13 (March 1994).

4 "Executive Summary," in Phoenix-Hecht, *The Blue Book of Bank Prices 2002–2003* (Research Triangle Park, N.C.: Phoenix-Hecht, 2003).

5 Ibid.

6 Ibid.

7 Ibid.

8 For a detailed discussion of collateralization practices and safeguards, see M. Corinne Larson, *An Introduction to Collateralizing Public Deposits for State and Local Governments* (Chicago: Government Finance Officers Association, 1996).

9 For an in-depth discussion of internal controls for local governments, see Stephen J. Gauthier, *Evaluating Internal Controls: A Local Government Manager's Guide* (Chicago: Government Finance Officers Association, 1996).

10 The Association for Financial Professionals (AFP) maintains a library of articles on RFPs and banking relationships and has a number of RFPs available electronically. See also AFP, *Standardized RFPs: Effective Tools for Selecting Cash Management Banks,* 2nd ed. (Bethesda, Md.: AFP, 2003).

11 On its Web site, www.fdic.gov, the FDIC maintains a list of bank-rating and analysis services, along with a description of the services offered by each.

12 The collection rate can be determined by dividing cash received by revenues billed. If a local government has $80 million in property tax due in a given year and historical analysis shows an average collection rate of 95 percent, the estimate for tax receipts for the coming year should be 95 percent of $80 million, or $76 million.

13 Advisory Commission on Intergovernmental Relations (ACIR), *Understanding State and Local Cash Management* (Washington, D.C.: ACIR, May 1977).

14 For an in-depth discussion of public sector investing, see Girard Miller with M. Corinne Larson and W. Paul Zorn, *Investing Public Funds*, 2nd ed. (Chicago: Government Finance Officers Association, 1998).

15 In a delivery versus payment transaction, the buyer's funds are released when delivery of the seller's securities (or collateral) is received. Both parties send their respective cash and securities to a third-party custodian, who sends a written confirmation of the transaction when it is successfully completed. This arrangement protects the buyer from any fraudulent activities or credit risk on the part of the seller. If the seller were to default or go bankrupt, the buyer would have ownership of the securities.

17 Risk management

PETER C. YOUNG AND CLAIRE LEE REISS

Risk pervades every aspect of governmental activity and exacts a cost—known as the *cost of risk*—on local governments.[1] Even if the finance department does not directly perform risk management functions, it has an interest in how those functions are undertaken: the cost of risk affects the government's financial status, which the finance department is responsible for managing. Thus, local government finance officers can better protect the government's financial position if they understand the day-to-day functions that make up local government risk management.

Large local governments often employ a professional risk manager who has specialized training and experience in the risk management field. In very large local governments, the risk manager may supervise a staff of employees who perform risk-related functions, including claims management, safety programming, and risk financing. Smaller local governments are unlikely to have full-time risk management staff. In these jurisdictions, risk management functions fall to one or more employees who have other responsibilities and who usually lack formal risk management training.

The finance department is involved in risk management regardless of whether the local government has a professional risk management staff. If there is such a staff, it is often housed in the finance department, and the finance director or another senior finance employee directly oversees the risk management function. If there is no professional risk management staff, finance department employees often have responsibility for various risk management functions, especially those associated with risk financing.

Historically, the purchase of insurance has been a risk management function, and the management of insurance is still central to the typical public entity's risk management program. However, the responsibility for purchasing insurance has gradually drawn risk management into a number of related areas that might be collectively referred to as "the management of insurable risks." For example, the responsibility for buying workers' compensation insurance almost inevitably compelled risk management staff to address workplace health and safety. Health and safety responsibilities, in turn, widened the scope of risk management to include matters such as training, equipment maintenance, and the integration of employee benefits (e.g., the coordination of workers' compensation with group health and disability benefits). Responsibility for purchasing property and liability insurance led to similar expansions in the risk management function. As a consequence of such changes, typical local government risk management functions now include the following:[2]

Risk financing, including the purchase of insurance

Management of insurable risks

Occupational health and safety programs

Workers' compensation management

Compliance with regulatory and legal requirements

Cost of risk Cost of risk has two elements: (1) the cost of losses that occur and (2) the cost of uncertainty. The cost of losses, in turn, includes direct and indirect components. The direct costs of loss, such as payment of claims, loss of property, insurance premiums, and legal expenses, are an obvious potential expense for governmental entities. The indirect costs of loss can be more difficult to identify. For example, the indirect costs of a major fire at a school building are likely to be many times higher than the direct costs of fire damage to the building and its contents. Alternative locations may have to be acquired; new and more expensive computers and equipment may have to be purchased; future insurance costs may rise; the school year may have to be extended; there may be expediting costs; and, of course, community relations may be affected. Estimates of the total costs of such events rarely include indirect costs; thus, the cost of losses for governmental entities is much higher than conventional estimates suggest.

The cost of uncertainty—the effect of the possibility of losses, even when they do not occur—is even more difficult to measure. Of course, fear and worry can exact a toll on decision making, but most risk managers focus on the misallocation of resources as the more important cost of uncertainty. Uncertainty produces doubt about the future, and this means that decision makers may be guessing as to the best deployment of resources. For example, allocations made to programs with high levels of uncertainty often include "fudge factors" to account for the unknown and the unexpected. Measures that local governments take to control risk (e.g., buying investment management software, hiring a risk manager, providing safety training for employees) are also costs of uncertainty because they would not be necessary in a world of certainty. There is no escaping the cost of risk. Nevertheless, one of the principal goals of risk management is to minimize the cost of risk.

Catastrophe planning

Contract review

Security

Risk assessment

Public policy research

Some involvement in employee benefits

Some involvement in the management of financial risk.

Even this broader description of typical risk management functions does not reflect, however, the continued expansion of risk management in the direction of addressing all organizational risks, not just those traditionally insured. Since the 1990s, risk management has been gradually transformed from a relatively narrow technical function focused on the management of insurable risk into a general management function concerned with assessing and addressing *all* organizational risk. Thus, risk management may now encompass financial risks (such as interest rate and credit risks), political and regulatory risks, and even competitive risks (such as competition between public and private schools). This new, emerging view of risk management increases the need for top management guidance in setting risk management policy and blending risk management into general management functions.

Where the latest trends will ultimately take public risk management is unknowable at this point; nevertheless, it is possible to delineate a general risk management framework that accommodates both the traditional and emerging views of risk management. The next section of the chapter presents such a framework; the second major section of the chapter covers risk financing in detail, including risk financing options, risk financing decision factors, and the implementation of a risk financing program.

Elements of a risk management framework

Risk management incorporates five distinct elements:[3] (1) mission identification, (2) risk and uncertainty assessment, (3) risk control, (4) risk financing, and (5) program administration.

Mission identification

The purpose of mission identification is to determine risk management goals and objectives (i.e., the mission of the risk management function) and to ensure that they align with and advance the overall purposes of the organization. Thus, risk management is described as mission driven.

Risk and uncertainty assessment

Risk and uncertainty assessment involves three overlapping activities: (1) risk and uncertainty identification, (2) risk analysis, and (3) risk measurement.

Risk and uncertainty identification   Risk and uncertainty identification is the systematic process of discovering an organization's risks and exposures to risk. Because local government activities are continually evolving, creating new exposures and reducing others, identification is a continuous process. Local government risks generally fall into two broad categories: asset exposures and liability exposures. Asset exposures concern physical, financial, human, or intangible assets. Liability exposures include both legal liability and exposures related to moral responsibilities.

Physical assets are tangible—for example, police vehicles, school buildings, computers, roads, waste treatment facilities, and business records. When the loss of a physical asset occurs, the impact stems not only from the cost of repair or replacement but also from the costs associated with the loss of use until repair or replacement occurs.

Financial assets include stocks, bonds, letters of credit, money, and other such instruments. Because they both hold and issue assets (e.g., hold short-term investments and issue bonds), local governments are subject to financial exposures on two fronts. Exposures include mismanagement of investments; default; embezzlement; theft; and fluctuations in interest rates, prices, and currency exchange rates.

Human assets are the staff members, elected officials, volunteers, and others who work in a local government and are critical to the government's ability to fulfill its mission. They are subject to numerous types of physical and economic risk: injury, illness, death, and unemployment, for example. Insufficient pay, unpleasant working conditions, or an inadequate pool of potential employees may hinder the government's ability to assemble and retain a qualified workforce—and, in turn, its ability to fulfill its mission. A major local disaster may prevent employees from coming to work, which will interfere with local government operations just when they are most important.

Intangible assets include the community's reputation (i.e., its desirability as a place for businesses and households to locate) and attributes such as the community's credit and bond ratings.

Protecting against theft and embezzlement   A local government is as vulnerable to theft and embezzlement as any business. Local governments often conduct cash transactions with citizens; in addition, because local governments work with many contractors and purchase large amounts of goods and services, they are vulnerable to manipulation by dishonest employees, who may set up dummy accounts and contracts to siphon off public funds. A local government with these and similar exposures needs a system of carefully considered and well-enforced internal controls, including documentation of financial transactions; surprise audits; and separate contracting, ordering, and accounts-payable functions.

Because losses from theft or embezzlement are not covered by common property insurance policies, local governments should—regardless of how much they trust their employees—evaluate their need for crime or employee dishonesty coverage. In some cases, state law may take this decision from local governments by imposing bonding requirements for certain public officials, including the finance director.

Local governments' exposure to legal liability generally falls into the following categories:

Premises liability: for injuries on government premises, such as slips and falls

Contractor liability: for the actions of private or nonprofit contractors performing services for the government

Volunteer liability: for the actions of volunteers working for the government, even for a day, and for negligent injury to those volunteers

Employee liability: direct or vicarious liability for the actions of the government's employees

Product or service liability: for goods or services provided by the government (e.g., firefighting services)

Environmental impairment liability: for environmental damage arising from governmental operations (e.g., leaks in a water treatment facility or in an underground storage tank)

Employment practices liability: for actions occurring in the course of the management of employees (e.g., harassment and discrimination)

Workers' compensation and employers' liability: for work-related injuries and illnesses

Motor vehicle liability: for injuries involving government-operated vehicles (e.g., police cars hitting other cars or pedestrians)

Professional liability: for errors by professionals such as doctors, lawyers, architects, or engineers (e.g., a medical error on the part of a doctor employed at a county hospital)

Errors and omissions liability: for wrongful acts of public officials and employees (e.g., land use planning decisions); also known as public officials' liability

Police and law enforcement liability: for wrongful arrest, excessive use of force, civil rights violations, and other wrongful actions taken in the course of an officer's duties.

Many other types of exposure may apply to specific types of public entities. For example, school systems have significant exposure to liability for child abuse, water and sewer authorities have significant exposure to liability

Law enforcement liability Law enforcement liability is one of the exposures that distinguishes local government risk management from that of other types of business. Police are vulnerable to allegations of excessive force, false arrest, breach of confidentiality, and violation of citizens' constitutional rights, to name just a few. And they operate in environments that can be dangerous, where rapid response is required and there may be little time to analyze the situation, and where the use of deadly force may occasionally be required. Because sworn police officers are sometimes (although not usually) legally considered to be on duty even when they are not on shift, and because they are obligated to intervene if they are able to do so, if a law is being broken that is within their jurisdiction, potential local government liability for police actions may extend outside of work hours—to include, for example, the off-duty security assignments police officers often take on for private businesses and organizations. The unique nature of police liability exposure means that a local government must carefully review its liability coverage to ensure that both the government itself and its police officers are appropriately covered. Many local governments have recognized that control of the off-duty employment of police officers, and financing the associated liability risks, can be a special challenge.

for environmental damage, and electrical utilities face potential liability for electrical injuries.

Moral responsibilities reflect values and ethical standards to which elected public officials and local government employees—as demonstrated through their actions—are expected to adhere.[4] Although more difficult to identify than legal liability, exposures related to moral responsibilities may be equally important. For governments, the consequences of failing to live up to moral responsibilities can include unfavorable publicity, loss of reputation, voter dissatisfaction, excessive turnover among elected officials, and, ultimately, a shrinking tax base. For example, abuses of the zoning decision-making process or perceived unfairness in the allocations of program resources may undermine citizens' support of the government and may also, more broadly, call into question all the decisions and actions undertaken by public officials. In other words, failure to adhere to community values can lead not only to direct problems for community leaders but also to a loss of trust in public institutions.

Risk analysis Risk analysis, the second step in the risk and uncertainty assessment process, involves examining risks to determine how hazardous conditions lead to actual losses. Governments with substantial resources for risk management may use systems and engineering analysis to analyze their risks. Methods derived from behavioral psychology may also be useful. However, many local governments will not have access to such sophisticated tools. Small local governments can investigate their exposures through a variety of means, including the following:

Analyzing the causes of previous losses

Consulting with neighboring local governments about their losses

Consulting with the risk control staff at the local government's risk pool to identify common local government vulnerabilities

Conducting brainstorming sessions with staff at every level of the organization

Consulting with the government's insurance broker or risk management consultant

Identifying and analyzing "near miss" incidents that did not produce losses, but might have.

Increasingly, risk analysis also involves the study of "positive risk"—that is, situations in which risk factors can give rise to opportunities as well as to exposures. Evaluation of investment risk, before making the investment, is an obvious example.

Risk measurement Risk measurement, the third step in the risk and uncertainty assessment process, determines the impact of risk on the local government's resources and on its ability to continue providing services. Measurement may focus on the impact of risk on specific objects or on the organization as a whole. By identifying those exposures that may have the greatest financial or operational impact, risk measurement provides a basis for choosing which exposures to address first.

Risk measurement approaches vary with the needs and capabilities of the government. For example, large local governments with substantial resources and a significant number of past losses may conduct a quantitative analysis of their loss history to determine the frequency, severity, and financial or operational impact of different types of losses. Smaller local governments may have to rely on intuitive estimates of the effects of what they believe to be their greatest exposures. In such cases, "measurement" may be limited to categorizing risks according to frequency (how often losses occur) and severity (the financial and other impact of losses when they do occur).

Risk control

Risk control, the third element of the risk management framework, focuses on avoiding, preventing, reducing, transferring, or neutralizing risks and uncertainties. Risk control measures can range from the simple (wearing hard hats) to the complex (catastrophe management plans). The major categories of risk control are risk avoidance, loss prevention, loss reduction, uncertainty reduction, and contractual risk transfer.

Risk avoidance, which involves simply avoiding the activity that produces a risk of loss, is a difficult risk control strategy for many local governments because they must provide certain services to their citizens, either because they are legally mandated to do so or because their citizens have strong expectations of receiving those services. An example of risk avoidance would be to close the local public swimming pool to avoid potential liability for injuries to divers.

Loss prevention measures are designed to prevent losses from occurring. Examples include workplace safety procedures designed to prevent accidents, and internal controls designed to prevent embezzlement. Loss reduction measures are designed to reduce the losses from accidents that do occur. Examples include sprinklers that turn on automatically in case of fire, and eyewash stations where employees can wash toxic or caustic materials out of their eyes. Uncertainty reduction measures are designed to reduce the misallocation of resources that comes from lack of knowledge about the effects of risk. An example is an analysis of a local government's loss history and current exposures to help it direct loss prevention and control efforts where they can be most useful.

Contractual risk transfer involves contracting with a third party to perform the risk-producing activity and to assume responsibility for any resulting losses; responsibility is generally assumed through a combination of contractual indemnification, hold-harmless agreements, and insurance requirements. For example, a local government may contract with a hospital management company to manage its hospital, or with a waste management company to collect its refuse. Because such transfers are subject to public procurement requirements and because the enforceability of indemnification and hold-harmless clauses may be limited by state law, a financial and legal review of such contracts is important.

The range of possible risk control methods is almost unlimited. The choice of risk control measures will depend largely on the scope of the local government's activities. Some risk control methods are mandatory, such as the state OSHA workplace safety standards that apply to local governments. Others may be optional, such as installing video monitors in local government offices where cash is handled. Line employees and neighboring local governments can be valuable sources of information and suggestions about risk control measures.

Risk financing

Risk financing, the fourth element of the risk management framework, enables an organization (1) to obtain reimbursement for losses that occur and (2) to fund programs that reduce uncertainty and risk or enhance positive outcomes. Qualifying with the state as a self-insured entity, buying insurance, establishing a letter of credit, and participating in a public risk pool are all examples of risk financing measures. A less obvious measure would be the use of earmarked taxes to fund a highway safety and maintenance program.

All risk financing techniques belong to one of two categories: (1) risk retention, in which a local government assumes all or part of a risk or loss, or (2) risk transfer, in which one organization (such as an insurance company or public risk pool) agrees to pay for the losses of another organization (such as a local government) in exchange for a premium. Governments often use a combination of financing alternatives. Risk financing options will be discussed in more detail in a later section of this chapter.

Program administration

Program administration, the fifth element of the risk management framework, involves a range of technical and general management activities, such as buying insurance, administering claims, developing hedging arrangements, and implementing loss control programs and safety training. An effective risk management program requires staff with both technical competence and solid management capabilities. In a large local government, such staff may have professional backgrounds in risk management. In a small local government, risk management staff may have the requisite skills but have other responsibilities as well.

A closer look at risk financing

This section of the chapter focuses on the financial aspects of risk management. Five related subjects are explored: (1) changes in the risk financing market, (2) risk financing options, (3) factors in risk financing decisions, (4) implementation methods for risk financing programs, and (5) the characteristics of a typical risk financing program.

Changes in the risk financing market

During the early years of the new century, the global insurance market was in deep crisis, and no solutions had appeared on the horizon. The "soft market" of the late 1990s, which had been characterized by low premiums and easy insurance availability, had disappeared. A number of factors contributed to the situation, including the following:[5]

Inadequate pricing that, until 2001, relied excessively on investment income to ensure sustainability. For example, from 1975 through 2001, all U.S. insurers selling property and casualty insurance obtained, collectively, a net underwriting profit (where premiums collected and retained exceeded claims paid) in two years only: 1977 and 1978.

The significant downturn in the global equity and bond markets. Benfield Grieg, the global reinsurance broker, estimates that in the first three quarters of 2002, the global insurance market suffered a loss of $90 billion in the global equity markets alone. This sum is considerably larger than the loss of $70 billion that the destruction of the World Trade Center, in September 2001, is estimated to have cost the industry.[6]

The general increase in the frequency and severity of losses and the greater frequency of catastrophic losses, both natural and man-made, of which the loss of the World Trade Center was just one example.

The greater propensity on the part of insurance companies to accept more pessimistic scenarios in relation to the performance of their portfolios. During 2002, for example, a number of major companies had to strengthen their balance sheets to deal with adverse developments relating to past liability claims, such as those for asbestosis.

In the early years of the new century, the stock market continued to be depressed and the global economic outlook remained bearish—conditions that would not support a return to a "soft market." Rating agencies took a more aggressive stance toward the credit rating of insurance companies, many of which found that their ratings for ability to pay claims had been revised downward. In the hard market, insurance companies withdrew, voluntarily and involuntarily, from certain sectors and coverages. Premiums increased sharply, often without any relation to the insured's loss experience, and other terms and conditions of insurance policies were tightened. For example, some policies that had previously covered an insured for defense expenses (including attorneys' fees) in addition to the policy limits began to include attorneys' fees within the limits of coverage. As a result, the insured may exhaust coverage limits defending the claim before a judgment is even entered. In addition, the total amount of insurance available for sale has been reduced, so limits of coverage offered to the insured are lower. The tightening of the reinsurance market has contributed to many of these changes.

One problem in the insurance market is the continuing difficulty of insuring against losses resulting from terrorist attacks. After September 11, 2001, many insurers excluded terrorism as a covered cause of loss or raised premiums for terrorism coverage to unaffordable levels. The Terrorism Risk Insurance Act (TRIA) of 2002 sought to remedy this situation by (1) providing federal government support for insurance coverage for acts by foreign terrorists and (2) requiring commercial insurance companies to offer terrorism coverage for an additional premium. Many organizations, however, have not opted to buy the terrorism coverage offered under TRIA, either because the coverage is too narrow or too expensive, or because those who are in charge of such decisions do not believe that the entity is at risk for a terrorist attack. Another area posing significant challenges is professional liability coverage for physicians: increases in premiums and lack of coverage availability have made it difficult for some physicians to continue practicing, especially in high-risk areas such as obstetrics.

Dire times in the insurance industry produce problems for all buyers of insurance. However, managers within governmental entities face two particularly vexing challenges. First, hard insurance markets tend to be extremely severe for public entities. And even if insurance is available and affordable, risk managers may wonder whether it is wise to trust the protection of the local government's assets to companies whose financial ratings are lower than those of the local government itself. Second, local government risk managers may wonder whether the past ills of the insurance industry should be allowed to increase the costs of future protection for public entities. These challenges may lead some local governments to question whether traditional insurance is the best tool available for financing their risks.

Observers of the insurance industry are beginning to detect a trend that first manifested itself in the hard insurance markets of the mid-1970s and mid-1980s: the development of alternative risk financing solutions—substitutes for, or complements to, traditional insurance that include risk pools, risk retention groups, captive insurance companies, banking arrangements, and capital market arrangements. Despite the fact that traditional insurance continues to dominate the risk financing world, it is probably more appropriate to consider it as one of a growing array of financial strategies for dealing with risk.

Although no action by a local government can restore the pricing and coverages of a soft market, local governments that face sudden, significant increases in their insurance expenses because of the hard insurance market can take some steps to try to manage this additional cost. First, the local government should be certain it is working with a reputable agent or broker who is familiar with the government's risks, and is making an effort to keep costs down and to obtain terms, conditions, and limits that are as beneficial to the public entity as possible. Second, if public risk pools within the state provide similar coverage, the local government should compare their offerings with its current coverages to determine whether pool coverage would be more reliable and cost-effective. Third, the government should participate actively in framing the presentation of its risk to the insurance carrier to ensure that the carrier fully understands the government's risk management efforts and loss history. Finally, the local government may consider whether an increase in deductibles or a decrease in limits would yield significant premium savings without creating exposure to unmanageable loss.

Risk financing options

This section briefly describes the principal approaches to risk financing used today.

Risk retention　There are two forms of risk retention: unplanned retention and planned retention, which is also referred to as self-insurance. Unplanned retention, which occurs when the risk assessment process fails to identify a risk that later produces a loss, is almost unavoidable.

Some governments self-insure by choice because they prefer to pay for and manage their losses directly, rather than through an insurance company. Of those governments that self-insure, some do so to reduce costs; others seek greater control over the management of their programs, especially their claims. If the state has a special interest in promoting secure risk financing arrangements—in the area of workers' compensation, for example—local governments and other organizations may be compelled to meet specific requirements before they are permitted to self-insure rather than buy commercial insurance.

Although many local governments make a deliberate decision to self-insure certain risks, others self-insure because they cannot buy commercial insurance. Insurance may be unavailable in an unusually hard insurance market, where carriers stop writing certain types of coverage or charge prohibitive premiums. Insurance may also become unavailable when insurance carriers decide that a certain type of risk is uninsurable, as they did for terrorism coverage for a period after September 11, 2001.

Very few local governments, except those with large budgets, can self-insure all their exposures, but most can find benefits in retaining some risks. Large local governments can self-insure a significant part of their losses and buy excess coverage as protection from catastrophic loss. Medium-sized and larger governments can sometimes reduce their premiums by accepting large deductibles as a form of partial self-insurance. Typically, however, small local governments cannot afford the possible consequences associated with large deductibles.

Commercial insurance   Local governments have traditionally protected themselves from a variety of risks by purchasing insurance policies from commercial insurance companies. The local government pays premiums; should a covered loss arise, the insurance company settles the claim up to its limits of coverage, in addition to providing other services such as legal defense. At the end of the policy period, usually one year, coverage is updated and a new premium is calculated. The cost to the local government is generally the premium and a deductible (if one is present and a loss occurs). Larger public entities may also have access to more sophisticated commercial insurance arrangements, such as retrospectively rated policies, which may offer some premium reduction to entities with good loss histories.

A commercial insurer's contractual promise to pay is only as good as its financial status. Each state has its own insurance regulations, which are designed to ensure that insurers have the financial ability to satisfy their obligations to policyholders. Nonadmitted (or "surplus lines") carriers—insurers not licensed in a particular state but permitted in some circumstances to sell insurance in that state—are usually not subject to the same regulatory requirements as admitted carriers. The financial status of any insurance carrier (admitted or surplus lines) should be investigated by any local government that plans to rely on that carrier for part of its risk financing plan. Information should be available from the local government's insurance broker or agent, from its risk management consultant, or through industry resources that rate insurance carriers for various factors, including financial strength and claims-paying ability.

Intergovernmental risk pools   Many local governments secure risk financing through intergovernmental risk pools, cooperative risk financing vehicles that provide public entities with an alternative to commercial insurance. Pools reinforce their financial stability through various mechanisms, including reinsuring portions of their exposure through commercial carriers or through specialized captive insurance companies established to reinsure pool losses. Pools currently exist in all states, and it is estimated that 40 percent of all local governments in the United States participate in one or more pools.

Intergovernmental risk pools come in various forms. Risk transfer pools are much like insurance companies. An indemnity agreement transfers the risk from a member local government to the pool. Member local governments (1) support the pool by making premium payments (or contributions) that cover the members' covered losses and the pool's operating costs, and (2) submit their covered claims to the pool for payment. As with commercial insurance companies, the risk transfer is only as good as the pool's financial ability to pay losses under the indemnity agreement. The local government remains liable to third parties for covered losses and will have to pay those losses if the pool cannot do so.

Other types of pools bear less resemblance to commercial insurance. Some are group insurance-buying arrangements in which members pool their purchasing power to buy commercial insurance. In a banking pool, members make contributions that the pool uses to pay its administrative expenses and establish reserve funds for extraordinary losses, but each member has a separate account out of which its losses are paid. A risk management pool provides risk management services for member local governments. Interestingly, most of the successful pools that began as risk financing pools are evolving into variations of the risk management pool.[7]

Pools offer local governments some potential advantages over commercial insurance:

Because they are established specifically to serve the insurance needs of local governments, pools offer local governments more consistent coverage than commercial insurance carriers. Commercial insurance carriers are established to make a profit, and they may withdraw from a market if it becomes less profitable.

Although the primary purpose of public risk pools is not to lower costs, member contributions may nevertheless be lower than insurance premiums. Member contributions may also remain more stable in a hard market than commercial insurance costs, although contributions will necessarily rise if the pool's cost for reinsurance increases.

Pools can respond more directly to the needs of their members, providing both broader coverage and valuable risk management services that are targeted to member needs.

Because membership in a pool is viewed legally as a special form of retention, pools enjoy important tax and regulatory benefits that lower the costs they must pass on to members.

A disadvantage of pools is that if the pool's losses far exceed expectations, the pool can demand payments in addition to premiums. Local governments contemplating pool membership should understand in advance their potential obligations for additional assessments.

Other risk financing tools   Other risk financing options may be employed in special cases. For example, a risk retention group (a private sector version of an intergovernmental risk pool) is sometimes used in public health care settings where public, nonprofit, and private issues entwine. A captive insurance company (an insurance company that insures only one client, its parent organization) is sometimes used for joint ventures between a public entity and a private entity that has access to a captive insurance company. Banking arrangements to secure credit commitments in advance of a loss (such as lines and letters of credit and other lending programs) are sometimes used for special ventures or as a basis for securing self-insurance arrangements.

Among the most interesting developments in risk financing have been recent efforts to apply financial risk management tools and strategies to other organizational risks. Finance officers have long used forwards, futures, options, and other secondary financial instruments to hedge interest rate risks, credit risks, currency exchange risks, and certain price risks. For example, a futures contract for heating oil can help lock in a price for a future delivery. Since the mid-1990s, investment banks have begun to experiment with (and offer) financing products that provide "coverage" for a range of nonfinancial risks.

Thus, risk managers today may use weather bonds, multiple-trigger products (policies that provide coverage against multiple causes of loss), or even options contracts to protect against important risks. Weather bonds, for example, allow an issuing government to obtain financial resources based upon unusual weather events, such as too much snow. Although the development of such products abated somewhat as a result of the economic slowdown of the early 2000s, experimentation with such products has had a critical result: the advancement of the notion that risk financing products can be created to address the impact of risk on organizations, regardless of the cause of loss.

Finally, risk financing is occasionally handled through arrangements with different levels of government. For instance, some local or regional authorities will extend their risk management and financing services to other entities within their region of service.

Risk financing decision factors

This section identifies and explains a range of general factors that influence risk financing decisions. Although most risk financing programs ultimately involve many different tools—some retention, some transfer, some alternative strategies—the following factors tend to influence their form and function:[8] (1) the state of the risk financing market, (2) limitations on risk control, (3) local government financial capacity, (4) the level of uncertainty that characterizes the risk, (5) possible tax or regulatory considerations, and (6) the possibility of catastrophic loss.

State of the risk financing market   A local government's control over the structure of its risk financing program is strongly influenced by the state of the risk financing market. In the 1990s, the insurance market was highly competitive with respect to price, and risk managers were able to dictate the form of their financing program. Beginning in 2000, difficulties in the insurance market transformed the situation: insurance companies began to dictate terms, prices, and levels of coverage. This restrictive environment, while offering little latitude to risk managers in terms of insurance program design, has served as a strong motivation for the consideration of alternative financing strategies.

Limitations on risk control   It is axiomatic in risk management that uncontrollable risks should be transferred whenever possible. "Uncontrollable" means that a governmental entity has no reasonable means of avoiding, preventing, reducing, or mitigating a potential risk and is therefore left to the vagaries and whims of misfortune. If, for example, a self-insured risk produces wildly unpredictable loss results—no losses for some years, disastrous losses in others—this instability can play havoc with budgets. A local government may also have limited control over risks that arise from the activities of contractors who are performing work on its behalf.

Local government financial capacity   Because most local governments have little margin for financial error, unpredictable risks render retention unattractive. Nevertheless, a large and financially secure public entity can reasonably absorb some surprises, and may be comfortable assuming a certain level of risk even when predictability is not high. Any local government that is evaluating its financial capacity to retain a risk should consider the cumulative effect of many small losses, as well as the effect of infrequent large losses, on its financial condition. Obviously, trends in demands, revenues, and the economy can change the financial risk-bearing capacity of a local government over time.

Level of uncertainty   Regardless of a local government's ability to control a risk or its financial capacity to bear a risk, predictability is a significant factor in risk financing decisions. Can a local government accurately estimate the frequency and the potential magnitude of losses arising from a risk, which it must do in order to project its probable losses from that risk? How secure are the assumptions on which the statistical estimates are based? Are there interdependencies with other risks that can lead to catastrophic losses? Is the local government considering not just average expected losses but also the potential variation around that average, which reflects what exceptionally good and bad years may look like? These are important issues, especially when a local government considers self-insurance.

Tax or regulatory considerations   Although tax considerations do not appear to be a common concern among local governments, they may occasionally become an issue. For example, because pool premiums are not taxed and are not subject to the same regulatory costs as commercial insurance premiums, pool premiums will tend to be lower than commercial insurance premiums, everything else being equal.

Regulatory issues can present problems, especially when insurance may be required by law—such as workers' compensation, motor vehicle liability, professional liability, public officials' (directors and officers) liability, and certain performance bonding requirements. All other factors may argue for self-insurance, but if there is a regulatory requirement mandating the purchase of insurance, that ends the debate.

Possibility of catastrophic loss   In local government risk management, there is no objective set of criteria for determining when a loss becomes catastrophic. Whether a loss is catastrophic depends on its effect on the local government and the government's ability to continue serving its citizens. A loss that severely impairs that ability is probably catastrophic to that government and its citizens. A loss that is catastrophic for a small local government with few resources may not be catastrophic for a large, well-funded local government.

The potential for catastrophic loss often arises from exposures such as natural disasters, where the level of predictability is low and the level of uncertainty about the outcome is high. For example, it is very difficult to predict an earthquake in advance—and if one does occur, it can produce losses ranging from the negligible to the catastrophic.

But exposure to catastrophic loss is not limited to events that are unpredictable or that have uncertain effects. Some risks, especially in the financial area, present the possibility of catastrophic loss even though they are predictable and produce relatively certain outcomes. Dramatic shifts in interest rates would be an example. For that reason, an important rule of thumb in risk financing is that risks that may produce catastrophic loss (however they are defined by a particular entity) should be transferred.

Summary: Risk financing decision factors   Taken together, the factors just discussed form a landscape in which the following generalizations apply: insurance becomes less attractive to local governments when (1) markets are hard, (2) the risks in question offer ample opportunity for risk control to be practiced, (3) the financial capacity of the entity to absorb unexpected losses is high, (4) the risks in question are well-known and measurable, (5) tax or regulatory considerations are low, or (6) the chance of catastrophic loss is negligible. Since risks rarely have all these characteristics, it may be more useful to think of risks as existing along a continuum: at one end would be the environment just described, and at the other end would be an environment in which insurance is essential.

Evaluating the cost of risk   One of the practical problems with measuring the success of risk management programs is the challenge of proving a negative. In other words, the fruit of many risk management initiatives is that nothing happens: losses do not occur. How can it be clearly established that a $10,000 safety program directly prevented injuries? Or, for that matter, that spending $10,000 for an insurance policy was a good idea when no claims occurred? Determining the efficacy of risk management efforts is further complicated by the fact that results may be very long in coming (e.g., a stop-smoking campaign will not affect health care costs for years). Finally, many of the costs and benefits of risk management are indirect and difficult to measure.

It is nevertheless important to look critically at risk management from a financial perspective. The Public Risk Management Association (PRIMA) conducts periodic studies that are designed to determine the potential impact of risk on governmental entities; the most recent was in 1998.[1] The definition of "cost of risk" used in the studies plainly illustrates the difficulties associated with such measurements. PRIMA defines the cost of risk as the sum total of property costs (property insurance costs plus retained property losses), liability costs (liability insurance costs plus retained liability losses), and workers' compensation costs (workers' compensation insurance costs plus retained losses and safety and loss control expenses). Omitted from this definition are any costs not related to property, liability, or workers' compensation. For instance, financial risks (interest, currency, default, inflation) have a huge impact on public pension funds and health care costs but appear nowhere in PRIMA's computation. Nor,

for that matter, is there any recognition of indirect costs, inefficiencies in resource allocation, loss of reputation, or even the psychological costs of risks.

Thus, when the most recent PRIMA report indicates that the average cost of risk for local governments is 3.23 percent of total average local government budgets, it is reasonable to assume that this number accounts for only one part of the total cost of risk. Moreover, because the study was conducted in 1998, the results do not reflect current changes in the economy generally; nor do they reflect the changes in the cost of insurance since the market hardened in 2000 or the impact of the stock market collapse. Information gathered since 2000 suggests that insurance rates have climbed anywhere from 75 percent to several thousand percent, depending on the type of insurance. Collapsing stock prices have placed extraordinary pressure on pensions and savings programs, and double-digit inflation rates for health care have seriously affected group health plans, workers' compensation costs, and, indirectly, liability coverages such as motor vehicle insurance.

Without accurate data, it is impossible to estimate the actual cost of risk for local governments. Moreover, the variations in impact on small, medium, and large entities cannot be known with any certainty. However, the results of PRIMA's study were viewed as accurate within the narrow confines of its focus, so it is probably accurate to say that the cost of risk is some multiple of 3.23 percent of total local government budgets.

[1]Public Risk Management Association and Deloitte & Touche LLP, *Cost of Risk Evaluation in State and Local Government, Second Biennial Survey* (Washington, D.C.: Public Risk Management Association and Deloitte & Touche LLP, 1998).

Implementing a risk financing program

A thorough risk assessment should allow the local government to array its risks according to the factors described in the previous section and to develop a general sense of the best structure for its risk financing program. Some risks will obviously require transfer, and others will obviously meet retention criteria. A third group of risks will offer no choice at all because insurance is either unavailable or required by law.[9] Risks in the fourth and final category, which have some characteristics that call for retention and others that call for transfer, are the most difficult to address. A close financial analysis is required to identify the appropriate mix of financing strategies for such risks.

The factors described in the previous section provide little guidance on how much risk to retain and how much to transfer. A local government may have a general sense that it can retain some risk but may wish to transfer larger losses to a pool or insurance company. But how much retention is too much? In principle, a number of techniques can be used to analyze the impact of various combinations of loss outcomes. The techniques can be very sophisticated (Monte Carlo simulations, for example, use computer-generated random numbers to predict a range of loss outcomes) or more basic (information on past losses can be used to develop a probability distribution indicating the likelihood and size of a range of possible losses). A probability analysis of its own loss history may, for example, show a government that 95 percent of the time its losses are below $10,000, and that losses ranging from zero to $10,000 can be handled by the operating budget and are therefore retainable. Using this information, the government could purchase insurance only for losses that exceed $10,000.

Unfortunately, very few risks present decision makers with statistically reliable information. Smaller local governments, in particular, may not have sufficient loss experience to develop a reliable probability distribution. And dependence on shaky statistical assumptions can be a risk in its own right. Therefore, for the vast array of risks faced by local governments, the decision to retain or transfer risk is political, budgetary, and highly subjective.

Public sector administrators considering retaining risk should ask themselves the following questions:

Will the government be comfortable with the potential impact of variability on its budget?

Will the government be risking significant losses to save a small premium expense?

Can the government proactively control retained risks in a way that will allow it to minimize its out-of-pocket costs?

Is the government confident that its exposures to catastrophic loss are covered?

Public sector administrators considering transferring risk should ask themselves the following questions:

If a covered loss occurs, is the government confident of the risk bearer's financial capacity to pay for the loss according to the contract terms?

Does the government understand the limitations, terms, and conditions of the risk transfer?

These questions have technical aspects that require both risk management and financial expertise not found in most local governments. Fortunately, resources are available that can assist local governments to analyze their risks and structure and implement a risk financing program. Independent risk and actuarial consultants are one resource. Independent consultants work on a fee-for-service basis and generally should not be involved in selling to the local government the risk financing products that they recommend. Insurance agents and brokers, who are part of the insurance industry, are another resource. The advantage of using insurance agents and brokers is that they are capable of analyzing a government's risk financing needs and assisting in the placement, implementation, and ongoing management of a risk financing program. The disadvantage is that insurance brokers and agents often have close ties and contractual relationships with the same insurers that they will recommend to the local government. It is crucial to select a reputable broker or agent who can provide objective risk financing advice to the government, regardless of his or her relationship with potential insurers.

Selecting a broker or agent   There are two broad approaches to selecting an insurance broker or agent for a public entity.[10] One is to use a single-stage process in which the entity sets specifications for a package of services and insurance and then selects a broker on the basis of the package he or she proposes in response to the entity's specifications. In the other approach, the public entity uses a competitive process to select a broker to provide risk management and insurance placement services and then works with that broker to secure the risk financing program. Although the advantages and disadvantages of these approaches are vigorously debated, the second, two-stage approach is more practical and therefore preferable. In the one-stage approach, unless the local government has sufficient knowledge of the market to divide it between competing brokers (or can hire an independent consultant to do so), the competing brokers have to visit the same insurance companies; such duplication of effort is highly inefficient and is commonly cited as one of the reasons the insurance industry views the public sector as a difficult market.

Selecting a broker in one stage and then working with that broker to develop a financing program makes logical sense. A local entity wants the broker on its side of the table. And to develop the best possible risk financing strategy, the broker needs inside knowledge of the local government, which is rarely possible when the broker is developing a program as a competing outsider.

Brokers ordinarily are compensated by commissions, which are paid by insurers for business placed. This practice has its supporters, but from the standpoint of a local government, there is a potential conflict of interest: Is the broker working in the government's best interest or the insurer's? Local governments can address this issue by negotiating broker services on a fee-for-service basis (in which the buyer pays the broker directly for services received); this arrangement allows the broker to shop for insurance and risk financing on a "net of commissions" basis. (Since insurers typically pay brokers a commission of between 10 and 15 percent for bringing the business, that amount would be subtracted from the premium that is quoted.) Such an approach may result in an overall lower cost for insurance and brokering services, but the main benefits are (1) to ensure that the broker is working in the government's interest and (2) to obtain a clear understanding of the services being provided and the price for those services.

Selecting an insurance and risk financing program   A local government may work with a broker, with an independent risk consultant, or through its own staff to decide how to configure its risk financing program. The decision will include how much risk the local government can afford to retain, how much risk it needs to transfer, what limits of coverage it will need for transferred risk, and what risk financing strategies will be used for both retained and transferred risk.

Once a local government has decided how to configure its risk financing program, it needs to place insurance with one or more carriers or other financial vehicles for the risk it plans to transfer. For a public entity, the process of purchasing insurance is generally subject to legal requirements, meaning that insurance may be placed through either competitive sealed bidding or competitive negotiation. Under competitive sealed bidding, which is generally used to obtain the lowest possible premium, the local government prepares detailed specifications for a package of coverages and services and then awards the contract to the responding insurer that submits the lowest bid. Under competitive negotiation, which is generally used when factors other than price—such as terms, conditions and scope of coverage, level of professional service, and financial strength of the insurer—are important, negotiation is permitted between the public entity and potential providers.

Many local governments have achieved significant savings in premiums by calling for competitive sealed bids, although this is highly unlikely in a hard market. Competitive sealed bidding is not always easy, however. It is difficult and time-consuming to write detailed specifications and prequalify bidders—and, until the local government has gained experience with the process, it may be costly as well. Many local governments that use competitive bidding hire independent risk consultants to help with the process, which reduces the savings.

Competitive sealed bidding works best when financial, loss-experience, property inventory, and other records provide potential bidders with trustworthy information about the local government's risk status before they submit bids. Underwriters also consider the quality of the local government's financial management practices, the local government's commitment to safety and loss control, and the local government's record of compliance with insurers' loss control recommendations. With such information, the underwriter can gain a realistic view of the local government's exposure to risk and submit a more responsive bid.

In general, bidding (both for broker services and for insurance) should be conducted only once every three to five years for each major classification of insurance. Instead of dealing with anonymous buyers of a commodity, insurers prefer to have long-term relationships with local governments. Nevertheless, in the current climate, insurers are likely to commit to arrangements for no more than one year.

A typical risk financing program

The term *risk financing portfolio* is important to understand because it reflects the fact that, in order to obtain an acceptable level of coverage, a public entity must carefully select a combination of insurance and risk retention strategies. The combination of policies, programs, and tools that the local government selects represents its integrated portfolio of risk financing arrangements.

Selecting the right financing vehicles requires an understanding of both the public entity's risks and its available risk financing options. While it is possible to imagine a local government employing a range of conventional and exotic financing options, the vast majority of local governments will rely heavily on risk pools and commercial insurance policies. Indeed, even when exotic tools are employed, they tend to supplement or support the coverage that is provided by insurance or pools.

Before considering the types of coverage that constitute the typical local government's risk financing portfolio, several matters are worth mentioning. First, although a single insurance company is unlikely to offer all the coverages a local government needs, a single independent agent (who represents multiple insurance companies) *is* likely to be able to help a local government find all the coverages it needs. Second, large governments have some ability to modify the insurance policies they buy, but for small local governments, buying insurance means buying "off the rack": seldom can small local governments negotiate or customize their insurance coverages. Finally, pools provide many, if not all, of the coverages described in this section. Thus, this discussion applies equally to communities that participate in pools and to those that buy insurance commercially.

The average insurance portfolio for a local government will likely contain most of the following insurance policies or pool coverages:[11]

Property insurance Property insurance covers most fixed and movable property that the local government owns, or for which it may be legally liable, against the risk of direct physical loss or damage. It is generally wise to assume that such insurance does not cover property while it is not on its usual premises. Since property insurance typically excludes a number of different types of property and causes of loss, local governments must be certain that they know whether their policies cover their major exposures. For example, property in transit generally requires special types of coverage known as "floaters." Standard property policies may exclude most losses caused by floods, hurricanes, and earthquakes, and electronic data processing equipment (computers and associated equipment and data storage media) may not be adequately protected by the terms of the local government's property policy.

Income interruption and extra expense insurance Coverage for income interruption and extra expenses (1) protects revenue streams derived from government activities and (2) funds additional expenses the government must incur to continue providing essential services after a major loss. Such coverage is activated only by a direct physical loss that is covered under the standard property policy, which means that it cannot technically be purchased alone.

A local government should know whether its income interruption insurance covers losses caused by direct physical loss at other premises, such as the premises of a key supplier. Another important concern is whether the government's extra expense insurance covers expenses that help the local government restore operations more quickly but that do not directly reduce a loss from income interruption. For example, expenses to expedite the reconstruction of a damaged building may or may not be covered under such policies.

Boiler and machinery insurance Boiler and machinery insurance provides protection for the sudden and accidental breakdown of insured boilers, large machinery, air conditioning and refrigeration equipment, and the like. Large equipment is usually excluded from standard property policies because damage to such equipment often results in collateral damage to other property, and insurance companies therefore like to treat the risk separately. Because of the catastrophic potential, boiler and machinery insurance also includes business interruption coverage and extensive loss control services (frequent inspections of equipment, advice on and servicing of equipment).

General liability insurance Although many governments buy special governmental (or public entity) liability policies, all are related to the commercial general liability (CGL) policy, which is the standard liability policy available in the market. A CGL policy provides coverage mainly for bodily injuries and property damage to third parties caused by, or arising out of, a covered accident that occurs during a local government's operations. Protection is provided for all sums, including legal expenses, that the local government is legally obligated to pay. The CGL policy also covers liability for personal injury, including false arrest, defamation, invasion of privacy, wrongful eviction, discrimination, and civil rights violations.

Public officials' liability insurance   Public officials' liability coverage is sometimes known as "errors and omissions" coverage because it provides protection for any mistakes or oversights committed by an employee or official, including wrongful acts—breaches of duty that may arise from the actions of elected officials. Following illegal procedures in making a zoning decision would be an example.

Law enforcement liability insurance   Owing to the particular characteristics of public safety activities, the public officials' liability policy is inadequate for the needs of law enforcement officials. Sometimes the general liability policy, when combined with public officials' liability coverage, can adequately address this risk, but the issue should be raised with the local government's insurance agent.

Motor vehicle insurance   Coverage provided under auto policies is dictated in part by the laws of particular states (e.g., no-fault laws). In general, coverage is provided in two areas: the government's liability to third parties arising out of the operation of its vehicles (i.e., the damage government drivers cause to others) and property damage to the local government's vehicles.

Special events liability insurance   Parades, fairs, conventions, and other special events, including those hosted by third parties on public property, present a number of coverage problems that are not addressed by standard policies.

Aviation and airport liability insurance   While aviation and airport liability would not seem to be an issue for small local governments, many communities do have small airports that are controlled by the government. And some communities may borrow or rent aircraft for specific purposes, such as aerial photography or surveys. Therefore, aviation-related risks, which are not covered elsewhere, might prompt consideration of this coverage.

Professional liability insurance   Professionals (doctors, lawyers, engineers, and architects) tend to be excluded from other liability coverages, at least for acts that they undertake within their profession. Professional liability coverage (sometimes called malpractice insurance) protects professionals and their employers (or clients, if they are contracted consultants) against claims that they violated professional standards. Such coverage is very important for local governments that have hospitals, nursing homes, or health care clinics. It may also be needed when attorneys, architects, accountants, engineers, or other professionals advise the local government. Logically, such professionals would likely have their own liability insurance, but it is not always certain that their coverage would protect the local government.

Workers' compensation insurance   Workers' compensation insurance covers the costs arising out of the deaths of or injuries to employees. Most states require employers to purchase workers' compensation insurance or to obtain formal permission from the state to self-insure.

Umbrella liability insurance   Umbrella liability insurance provides increased limits for the other policies that are purchased. Most liability policies provide coverage only up to some limit—a limit that is too low even for small local governments. Umbrella insurance allows the government to extend coverage to a dollar level that provides adequate liability protection.

Other coverages   Local governments may also consider some of the following, less common coverages:

Employment practices liability insurance. Employment practices liability insurance covers employers for liability arising out of employment practices; common allegations include discrimination and sexual harassment. Employment practices liability may be covered by some public officials' liability policies or purchased as stand-alone coverage with separate limits.

Cyber and media liability. Local governments that publish documents or operate Web sites may be liable to third parties for defamation, disclosure of confidential information, invasion of privacy, violation of intellectual property rights, or errors and omissions. The local government's general liability and public officials' liability policies may offer some coverage for these exposures, but it may not be sufficient to address the needs of public entities with complex exposures. Local governments with such exposures should discuss the limits of their existing coverage with their insurance advisor to determine whether they need more comprehensive coverage.

Fidelity and public official bonds. State law may require certain local government officials who are in a position of trust to be bonded before taking office; the bond protects the local government from theft of funds on the part of the official. The bond may be purchased for a specific official, for specific positions, or as part of a crime insurance policy, which provides expanded protection against dishonest acts by other people, including third parties.

Conclusion

Risk management is a rapidly evolving field that uses an expanding number of innovative approaches to address a wider variety of risks than ever before.

A successful risk management program has never been more essential to the financial position of local governments than it is today. In the post–September 11 environment, everyone is more acutely aware of risk and its potentially catastrophic consequences. Although more demands are being placed on local governments to address risk of every type, a combination of declining tax revenues and increasing cost of risk may actually reduce the resources available to meet these demands. To meet the challenges of this environment, local governments must reach out and involve all levels of their operations in risk management activities. The keys to doing so effectively are information, communication, and collaboration.

Information is indispensable for effective risk control. The government must know what its risks are, how likely they are to produce adverse events, how those events will affect the government's ability to continue to serve its citizens, and what cost-effective actions can be taken to control those risks. Information technology has greatly increased local governments' ability to obtain, record, manipulate, and transfer the information that is needed to effectively manage risk.

Communication is the flow of information, and it flows in multiple directions: to and from the risk manager and the operational departments that deal with risk daily, and to and from the local government's upper-level management and governing body. The risk manager needs information from the operational departments to help design an effective approach to risk control, and operational staff need information from the risk manager to know what the local government expects of them. Senior management and the governing body need information about the local government's risk management needs so that they can provide both overall direction for the risk management program and the visible support that will be indispensable to the program's success.

Collaboration is a crucial part of the risk control process. Operational staff will be much more receptive to risk control programs that they have helped design. And the programs will be much more effective if created in collaboration with operational staff, who know the risks best because they face them every day.

Information, communication, and collaboration are equally important to risk financing decisions. A local government needs information to identify both the risks it must finance and the available risk financing vehicles. The process of applying for coverage requires the local government to provide extensive information about its operations, loss history, and exposures. And the process of developing risk financing relationships, whether with commercial carriers, pools, or other parties, requires communication and collaboration among the local government's risk manager, insurance agent, and the potential carrier or pool.

No amount of effort will retrieve the soft insurance market of the 1990s. However, a local government that uses information, communication, and collaboration to create a pervasive culture of risk management is likely to substantially improve its risk management results and reduce its overall cost of risk in the process.

1 C. Arthur Williams Jr., Michael L. Smith, and Peter C. Young, *Risk Management and Insurance,* 8th ed. (New York: Irwin McGraw-Hill, 1999), chap. 2.

2 Peter C. Young and Martin Fone, *Public Sector Risk Management* (Oxford, U.K.: Butterworth Heineman, 2000), chap. 2.

3 Williams, Smith, and Young, *Risk Management,* chap. 8.

4 Young and Fone, *Public Sector Risk Management,* chap. 6.

5 "Global Nonlife Insurance in a Time of Capacity Shortage," *Sigma,* no. 4 (2002).

6 Benfield Grieg, *First Quarter Report* (London: Benfield Grieg, 2003).

7 Young and Fone, *Public Sector Risk Management,* chap. 7.

8 Peter Young and Steven Tippins, *Managing Business Risk* (New York: Amacom Books, 2001), chap. 7.

9 Ibid., chap. 11.

10 Ibid.

11 National Center for Small Communities (NCSC), *Limiting Small Town Liability: A Risk Management Primer for Small Town Leaders* (Washington, D.C.: NCSC, 2002).

18 Public employee pension funds

John E. Petersen

By the turn of the twenty-first century, approximately twenty million people, or one out of every fourteen U.S. citizens, were covered by state or local government pension plan programs—as current employees, inactive members, or beneficiaries. Almost all of the 1.2 million state and local government employees were covered by some form of pension plan, and a growing army of retirees and survivors depended on benefit payments for all or part of their livelihood. Because pensions affect so many people and involve so much money, concerns about them will continue to be at the forefront of public financial administration: Will pension benefits promised to employees today be adequate in the future? Are the programs being managed in the most secure, efficient, and economical manner? And, most crucial of all, will benefits promised today be affordable for contributing local governments tomorrow?

Severe reversals in the fiscal health of state and local governments in the early 2000s have made these questions all the more pertinent and pressing. The recession of 2001—which was, in large part, a product of the financial bubble of the late 1990s—and the exceedingly slow economic recovery that followed vividly illustrate the fact that pension system finances can be drastically affected by changing financial markets and unsettled economic conditions. In an aging economy in which future growth is uncertain, the ability of retirement systems to meet future claims cannot be taken for granted. Accordingly, major public policy issues surround the continued health of all retirement systems, public and private, in the United States, including those of state and local governments.

It is estimated that state and local governments pay nearly $50 billion a year in contributions, accounting for about six cents out of every tax dollar they collect. In addition, employees belonging to contributory plans pay an average of 4.4 percent of their wages to help finance their retirement plans. But these contributions are only the first part of the financing story. Managers of public pension systems are ever mindful of the need to accumulate sufficient resources to meet future obligations. As the growth in public sector employment levels off, the number of beneficiaries and the level of benefit payments will increase in relation to both tax collections and the current public payroll. Unless enough money is set aside and productively invested today, the public sector could face underfunded pension obligations tomorrow. Over the years, this sobering prospect has increased the emphasis on the management of state and local government retirement programs.

Historically, retirement benefits were enriched without adequate provision for funding. Thus, the mounting costs of public pensions were caused, in part, by the absence of a forward-looking policy concerning their design, financing, and administration. In the 1970s, the realization that many plans were inadequately funded led to a rude awakening. Although subsequent trends in pension finances—actuarial funding, high investment earnings, lower inflation rates, and a tightening of benefits—have produced great improvement, the financial soundness of most pension plans and the real worth of the benefits depend on the ability of the funds to continue to earn good returns and to stay abreast of cost-of-living increases. Failure to do so will mean either a reduction in the real worth of benefits, increased contributions to meet retirement goals, or some combination of the two.

As this chapter will show, pension practices have reformed. But vigilance is still required; problems will become more difficult in time because pension obligations, by their very nature, can leave a legacy of financial and administrative burdens. Furthermore, as recent events have shown, market conditions can dramatically change the value of assets and the credibility of assumptions about earnings, leaving the adequacy of funding veiled in uncertainty.

Another realm of concern is the great economic power of pension funds as investors. Pension fund investments have diversified, the types of investments have expanded, and legal impediments have been relaxed. To best handle the funds within his or her control, the pension fund manager will usually seek the advice of professionals. But the financial markets can be volatile, and crystal balls can become cloudy. Furthermore, as powerful investors that often have substantial equity interests, the funds have a major role to play in ensuring the integrity of the financial markets and the quality of corporate governance. Finally, as retirement systems continue to rapidly accumulate assets (amounting to nearly $2 trillion by the early 2000s), there continue to be calls for investment policies that are directed toward "socially useful" objectives. Adding such responsibilities to the primary objective (or, some would contend, the sole objective) of financing and protecting employee benefits presents difficult challenges to the legislators who enact retirement programs and the pension fund trustees and managers who oversee them.

The universe of public pensions

In 1997, the U.S. Census Bureau reported 2,276 public employee pension systems with a combined membership of 15.2 million (of which 12.8 million were active employees and 2.4 million were inactive) and 5.2 million current beneficiaries.[1] The Census Bureau excludes the following systems from its count of public retirement systems: (1) those that forward contributions to private insurance companies as premiums paid for the purchase of annuity policies, (2) those that make direct payments of benefits from annual appropriations of general funds, and (3) those that have members who belong to the Teachers Insurance and Annuity Association and do not have any supplemental state or local coverage. Thus, only systems administered by a sponsoring state or local government are included in the Census Bureau number.[2]

Membership at state and local levels

Retirement systems for public employees are administered at both the state and local levels. As shown in Table 18–1, 88.9 percent of the covered employees in 1997 belonged to state-administered systems, which also accounted for 82.5 percent of the financial assets. Local governments accounted for 90.6 percent of the total number of systems but had direct responsibility for only 11.1 percent of the employee membership. Based on the underlying census data for individual state systems, it is estimated, however, that approximately 70 percent of the members of the state-administered systems are local government employees.

Table 18–2 shows the growth in pension plan coverage from 1950 through 1997. During this period, the ratio of active pension plan members to full-time-equivalent employees increased from about 68 to about 90 percent. In view of the wide coverage that already exists and the slowing growth in government employment, it is unlikely that active membership in plans will increase very

Table 18–1   Key measures of state and local retirement systems, 1997.

A. Numbers and dollar values.

	Number of systems	Total membership (in millions)	Current beneficiaries (in millions)	Annual receipts (in billions of $)	Annual payments (in billions of $)	Investments (in billions of $)
Total	2,276	15.2	5.2	227.5	76.2	1,478.9
State	212	13.5	4.3	188.4	58.9	1,220.5
Local	2,064	1.7	0.9	39.1	17.3	258.4

B. Composition.

	Percentage of total number of systems	Percentage of membership	Percentage of current beneficiaries	Percentage of annual receipts	Percentage of annual payments	Percentage of assets
Total	100.0	100.0	100.0	100.0	100.0	100.0
State	9.4	88.9	81.6	82.8	77.3	82.5
Local	90.6	11.1	18.4	17.2	22.7	17.5

Table 18–2   State and local pension active membership and full-time-equivalent employment, 1950–97.

Year	(A) Number of full-time-equivalent employees (in millions)	(B) Number of active pension members (in millions)	Coverage: (B) as a percentage of (A)
1950	3.8	2.6	68.4
1960	5.5	4.5	81.8
1970	8.5	7.3	85.9
1982	10.9	10.1	92.7
1992	13.2	12.0	90.9
1997	14.2	12.8	90.1

rapidly in the future. However, as the membership matures, the number of beneficiaries will continue to grow.

At the local level, 81 percent of all systems are administered by municipalities, 7 percent by townships, 7 percent by counties, and the remainder by school districts and special districts. Membership in county government systems tends to be considerably larger (3,200 members, on average) than membership in municipal government systems (620 members).[3]

Most member employees belong to a relatively small number of the plans: 67 percent of all members (10.2 million) belong to the 96 largest of the 2,276 plans. Thus, the remaining 2,180 plans have approximately 5 million members; of those, nearly 1,500 plans have fewer than 100 members—only 0.3 percent of total membership. These very small systems predominate at the local level.[4]

Among states, there are great contrasts in the number of systems: in Hawaii, one plan covers all state and local government employees, whereas Pennsylvania has 337 plans—and this figure may be understated.[5] Plans vary in size as well, particularly when the very largest systems are considered: three statewide systems—in California, New York, and Texas—include more than 600,000 active members each, and the largest ten systems account for one-third of all state and local employees who belong to retirement systems.[6]

Membership is increasingly concentrated in the largest systems: the portion of employees covered by systems with more than 100,000 members grew from 50 to 70 percent between 1972 and 1997.[7] This consolidation has many advantages in terms of administering and standardizing plans, especially among potentially competing jurisdictions and groups of employees. On the other hand, greater concentration can diminish the power of individual governments to control their personnel policies and pension costs.[8]

Financial flows and assets

Retirement funds are financed from three sources: government employer contributions, employee contributions, and investment earnings. In contrast to most private sector retirement programs, state and local retirement plans are contributory: that is, they rely on employee contributions. As would be expected, as pension plans move toward financial maturity and continue to increase their assets, the importance of employee and employer contributions relative to fund earnings is diminishing. Table 18–3 provides an overview of the financial operations of state and local retirement systems from 1967 through 1997. Between 1977 and 1997, investment earnings rose from 30.6 to 71.0 percent of all receipts, a dramatic sign of the growing maturity of the funds and the higher rates of return that were available on investments during the period.

Another indicator of the growing maturity of public pension systems is the growth in payments to retiring employees, survivors, and disabled beneficiaries. Payments increased more than sevenfold between 1977 and 1997, from $9.8 billion to $76.2 billion, as is shown in Table 18–3. Payments in 1997 nevertheless amounted to only 5.3 percent of assets, largely because the recent annual growth rate of disbursements for benefits and other payments (9.5 percent between 1992 and 1997) was lower than the growth rate of assets (11.5 percent). However, barring a resurgence of rapid growth in public sector employment, benefits paid out should continue to grow in relative importance. Since the early 1990s, the effect of these payments has been muted by the absence of inflation and offset by strong investment earnings. But as

Table 18–3   Financial data on state and local employee retirement systems, 1967–97.

	1967	1977	1987	1992	1997
Receipts ($)	6.6	25.4	99.4	147.8	227.5
Annual growth rate (%)	—	14.4	14.6	8.3	9.0
Government contributions ($)	3.1	12.4	30.4	35.8	45.0
Annual growth rate (%)	—	15.1	9.4	3.3	4.5
Percentage of receipts	46.4	48.8	30.6	24.2	19.8
Employee contributions ($)	2.0	5.2	11.2	16.8	20.9
Annual growth rate (%)	—	10.3	8.0	8.4	4.5
Percentage of receipts	29.8	20.6	11.3	10.8	9.2
Investment earnings ($)	1.6	7.4	57.8	96.0	161.6
Annual growth rate (%)	—	16.9	22.7	10.7	11.0
Percentage of receipts	23.8	30.6	58.1	64.9	71.0
Benefit and other payments ($)	2.7	9.8	30.5	48.4	76.2
Annual growth rate (%)	—	13.8	15.3	9.7	9.5
Percentage of receipts	40.8	38.5	30.6	32.7	33.5
Percentage of assets	6.8	7.9	5.9	5.6	5.3
Financial assets ($)	39.3	123.5	512.9	859.0	1,479.0
Annual growth rate (%)	—	12.1	15.3	10.9	11.5

Notes: All dollar figures are in billions.
(—) indicates not applicable.

the sharp market reversals of the early 2000s illustrate, long-term projections are difficult to make. As is discussed later in this chapter, if benefit payments accelerate and investment earnings fail to increase at the assumed rates, it may be necessary to increase employer and employee contributions to prevent the level of assets (and future earnings) from eroding.[9]

Not shown in Table 18–3 is the present value of the future benefits that will need to be paid and the relationship between those benefits and the market value of existing assets and contribution levels. The adequacy of assets to offset forecasted future benefits and the ability of current contribution rates to accumulate needed reserves are the major factors in determining the financial viability of pension funds and the funds' long-term costs to government. These topics are considered later in this chapter.

Defined-benefit and defined-contribution plans

Most public pensions are defined-benefit plans, which means that benefit payments are usually set by some formula based on (1) years of service and (2) salary level toward the end of the employment period. Under a defined-benefit plan, the governmental employer is committed to this level of benefits regardless of whether the pension fund assets can support it. However, a growing number of employees are enrolled in defined-contribution plans, in which the participant's benefits are based not on a fixed formula but on the level of benefits that can be sustained by (1) the total amount contributed by the employer and employee and (2) the accumulated income earned from these contributions. As of the mid-1990s, only about 5 percent of all public employees were covered solely by defined-contribution plans, but an additional 10 percent were covered by plans that combined both defined-benefit and defined-contribution elements.[10]

State and local governments may continue to move toward plans that are characterized by defined contributions and variable benefits. One advantage of a defined-contribution plan is that the government's liabilities are clearly delineated. In a defined-benefit plan, if the total of contributions and accumulated funds turns out to be inadequate to cover the promised benefits, the governmental sponsors of the plan must raise the needed funds or renege on their promises. This problem does not occur in a defined-contribution plan because the required funds have already been contributed and the sponsor has no further obligation. Nor can a defined-contribution plan be used as a political device to pledge a high level of benefits, the cost of which will be borne by future residents of the community. Moreover, since the need for actuarial projections is minimal, administrative costs are considerably lower.

Defined-contribution plans can also present certain advantages to the employee, although these are not always obvious at first glance. First, although they are not guaranteed, adequate retirement benefits should be ensured through a sufficiently high contribution level. Second, if the funds are invested in a balanced portfolio, the safety of a recipient's pension does not depend solely on the fiscal safety and probity of the sponsor. Thus, there is not likely to be a failure or a cutback in benefits if, for example, the employer goes into bankruptcy. Finally, since the benefits are fully funded at the start, there need be no delay in vesting the employee, and there is no difficulty in making the sums already contributed portable if the worker changes employers.

But there are also drawbacks to the fixed-contribution approach. The greatest is that the employee bears the full risk of future retirement income. A worker who makes poor investment decisions may end up destitute at retirement. However, this problem can be alleviated by restricting the funds into which the defined contribution may be placed.

Deferred-compensation and defined-contribution plans   More and more public sector employees have joined deferred-compensation and defined-contribution plans, either to augment or to replace their defined-benefit plans. In some cases, employers contribute to the plans; in other cases, the point is primarily to improve before-tax retirement savings. Among the options for deferred compensation are voluntary salary-reduction plans—that is, the Section 457 plans that permit state and local government employees to defer up to $7,500 of their annual income.

Unlike defined-contribution retirement plans, deferred-compensation plans do not belong to the employees in trust; instead, they are merely promises from the employer to pay in the future (which is why they are not currently taxable income for the employees). If a financial emergency occurs—such as the one in Orange County, California, in the mid-1990s—the savings are at risk, which is something that few participants understand.[1]

About 7 percent of public employees are estimated to be using the 401(a) and 407(k) defined-contribution plans. Since an estimated 22 percent of these also have defined-benefit plans, it appears that only somewhat more than 5 percent of all state and local employees rely solely on defined-contribution plans for their retirement.[2] Available information about defined-contribution plans is limited, but it is likely that they will continue to grow as governmental employers prohibit or curtail entry of new employees into defined-benefit plans.

In the private sector, the growth in defined-benefit plans during the 1990s was steadily eclipsed by that of defined-contribution plans, as corporations shifted to the individual accounts the responsibility for meeting retirement payments. As of 1997, slightly less than half of full-time private sector employees had defined-benefit plans, and about half had defined-contribution plans (with about half of the latter group also being covered by some form of defined benefit). Workers in large firms were more likely to be covered by defined-benefit plans and those in small firms less likely.[3]

By the early 2000s, corporate pension plans in the United States were in increasing trouble as their investment values saw large declines in the financial markets and as the plans faced a swelling number of retirees. Efforts to economize by redefining benefit schemes in ways that reduced payouts (through the cash-balance method, for example, which has benefits accrue evenly over an employee's career) were challenged in court by older workers whose benefits would have been reduced. A growing number of companies were contemplating filing for bankruptcy just to get rid of burdensome fixed-benefit plans (as airlines and steel producers had done), while other firms simply stopped offering these plans to newly hired employees.[4]

[1]Mary Rowland, "A Retirement Plan with No Guarantee," *New York Times*, 26 January 1995, 31.
[2]Ann Foster, "Public and Private Defined-Benefit Pensions: A Comparison," *Compensation and Working Conditions* (summer 1997): 37–43.
[3]Ibid.
[4]Janice Revell, "Pensions May All Be in Peril," *Fortune*, 1 September 2003, 44.

Another possible difficulty with a defined-contribution plan is that the final investment of the funds may not carry the "insurance" framework that is embodied in the defined-benefit plan, in which benefits for a large number of people with different life expectancies are combined in an actuarial system that can provide each individual with benefits over his or her lifetime. In contrast, the defined-contribution account is not protected against the "risk" of a long postretirement life. This problem can be avoided by requiring that the major part of the accumulated defined-contribution benefits be placed in lifetime annuities upon retirement.[11]

History, legal setting, and budgetary impact

Public pensions arose earlier than those in the private sector, with the establishment, in the late nineteenth century, of limited-benefit programs for firefighters, police officers, and teachers. The number of plans accelerated rapidly in the 1930s and 1940s, particularly during the period when public servants were not eligible for social security coverage. Approximately one-half of the largest state and local systems were founded between 1931 and 1950.[12]

Over time, the evolution of plans in different states at different times under different pressures has resulted in a heterogeneous mixture of administrative structures, benefit provisions, and funding techniques. Because changes have occurred at both the state and the local levels without benefit of a consistent policy or legal framework, attempts to rationalize or restructure public employee retirement plans are often bogged down in a maze of legal and philosophical conflicts. In most states, legal provisions governing defined-benefit plans are bewildering in their variety and complexity.

Provisions of great substantive importance (benefit levels, contribution formulas, eligibility, funding requirements, and allowable investments) are often tucked away in nooks and crannies of various state statutes and shaped by various judicial interpretations. Home rule local governments may establish their own systems as they please; those subject to "bracket laws" (specialized legislation that pertains to only one or a few jurisdictions) may be hemmed into antiquated and conflicting requirements. Frequently, common-law interpretations of particular issues are relied on in the absence of specific action by a legislative body.

The patchwork of laws characteristic of defined-benefit plans can lead to uncertainty and confusion for the employee and the employer. For example, some states have constitutional provisions that treat public employee pension rights, once they are conferred, as fundamental matters of contract that cannot be altered except through amendment to the constitution. Other states view such rights as basic statements of policy, but as lacking any contractual element. Still others view the public servant's pension as tantamount to a gratuity, giving the employee little comfort as to the security of the plan's provisions. About 50 percent of pension plans carry a constitutional or statutory restriction against any decrease in benefits once they have been granted.[13]

Because of the technical complexity and long-range cost effects of laws governing pension provisions and their financing, state and local legislative bodies carry a heavy burden in assessing the condition of retirement funds and the implications of pension-related decisions. In an effort to develop expertise in these matters, many states have created permanent legislative bodies to screen bills and recommend reform measures. Others have attempted, with varying degrees of success, to provide for formal state supervision of local government pension systems. According to recommendations of the Advisory Commission on Intergovernmental Relations (ACIR), such regulatory entities should have the power to provide technical assistance, maintain information, and review and comment on proposed changes in state and local retirement systems.[14]

A consideration of their importance in the overall government budget offers yet another perspective on public pension systems. According to figures from the U.S. Census of Governments, in 1967 state and local government contributions to pension systems represented less than 7 percent of their payroll costs and 4 percent of their total tax collections. In 1982, the respective figures were 11.5 percent of payroll and 8.2 percent of tax collections. But by 1997, the ratios had fallen to 9.5 and 6.2 percent, respectively.[15] It should be borne in mind that approximately three-quarters of state and local government employees belong to plans that also include social security coverage; these figures do not include the employer contribution rates for social security. By 2002, social security rates had climbed to 6.2 percent (or a combined rate of 12.4 percent for employees and employers) of the $84,900 maximum taxable wage base, substantially increasing the overall retirement-related costs for government employers and employees. In addition, governments and their employees pay 1.65 percent of wages to Medicare, which is not capped.

Public pension system organization

Establishing retirement policies, administering contributions and benefits, and managing investments are all part of operating a pension program. But, as is so often the case in state and local government, form does not necessarily follow function: the relationships among the various elements of pension plan operations are so varied that they defy easy generalization. Although each public employee pension plan was at one time or another established primarily to provide postretirement payments to employees, the details of a particular plan's relationship to the contributing government, to employees, and to a host of public and private entities that may also be involved in the pension process are subject to great variation.

The prototypical state or local retirement system is a special trust fund created under the laws of the state or local government to provide government employees with pensions and other employment-related benefits. Usually, such laws—be they generic (applicable to all systems in the state) or specific (applicable only to certain units)—provide that administration of the system shall be the responsibility of a retirement board, a board of trustees, or a particular department or office in the government sponsoring the system. Within the statutory framework, however, the details of practice can vary greatly from one jurisdiction to another.

The statutes themselves differ a great deal as well. Some spell out the operations in detail, while others let the retirement board or responsible department work out the particulars through bylaws and regulations. Some legislative bodies retain close control over the plan's administrative budget through an appropriation process, and may see fit to delegate investment and other administrative functions to government departments and offices that are independent of the retirement board.

Retirement boards provide general oversight and governance. They may be granted either broadly or narrowly defined power and may be either aggressive or passive about setting policy. In some large systems, these boards make legislative recommendations, set investment policy, establish rules of benefit entitlement, review and approve the budget, and hire internal staff and outside consultants to carry on daily operations. At the other extreme, retirement boards may be left with relatively little to do but review disability and retirement claims.

Pension fund organization generally follows one of three models; the model chosen determines the structure of the organization, its level and range of responsibility, and its degree of independence from the sponsoring or contributing governmental unit. In the most prevalent model, the retirement board retains the ultimate authority to make operating decisions, which it will either implement itself or delegate to staff or private agents acting on its behalf. In the second model, there is a separate retirement board, but some aspects of the system's operation are entirely beyond the board's control. For example, the investment function may be assigned to a government official (such as a controller, treasurer, or finance officer), or it may be the responsibility of a separate investment board that invests the pension fund's money along with the monies of other state or local government agencies. In the third model, the administration of the retirement plan is part of the government's internal activity, and no separate board exists to oversee it. The governing body sets policy, and local government departments or officials carry out the administrative duties. In this model, frequently found in smaller systems, an outside private trustee (such as a bank or insurance company) is often delegated responsibility for executing investment policy. Not infrequently, a private trustee for the plan handles other services relating to the payment of pension benefits.

Multi-employer systems, in which several local governments (and, perhaps, state agencies) jointly sponsor and finance a plan, are usually set up under an umbrella of special state authority. The contributing governments share in the policy making through representation on a board of trustees. Members of such boards are appointed, elected, or statutorily defined in such a way as to represent the various types of government and, not infrequently, active employees and retirees who are members of the system.

Retirement boards usually consist of seven or more members, a number specified under enabling legislation that sets up the retirement fund. In a 1992 survey of 291 systems, the average board had eight members, with three elected by the employees, three appointed by the governmental employer, and two serving ex officio (usually a finance officer, treasurer, or chief executive). The boards typically were responsible for investments (87 percent of the cases), benefits (71 percent), and actuarial assumptions (85 percent).[16]

Professional knowledge of pensions, personnel policies, or finance is usually not a prerequisite for serving on a retirement board. As a result, most boards—and probably most elected officials who find themselves responsible for retirement system administration—must rely heavily on inside administrators and outside advisors to help set policy and carry on day-to-day operations.

Pension fund administration

Day-to-day administration of a retirement plan may be lodged in several different places and entail a variety of duties.

Role of the administrator

Large systems with broad powers usually have a full-time plan administrator to provide leadership, deal with professional services and the public, and oversee the staff. In smaller systems, municipal clerks, finance officers, local government managers, police chiefs, or fire chiefs may find themselves serving as part-time pension plan administrators and investment officers. In many cases, consultants or insurance companies may carry out all or a major part of administrative and investment responsibilities.

Generally speaking, the plan's chief administrative officer should operate under a statement of policy that sets forth his or her responsibilities and authority. These may include overseeing compliance with the laws that control the plan, hiring staff, maintaining records and executing transactions, keeping the retirement board informed, and carrying out policy directives.

A major part of the administrator's job involves dealing with the various technical consultants used to support pension activities. Particularly important to most funds are actuaries, investment advisors, and accountants, whose specialized services either are not affordable on a full-time basis or are of greatest value when rendered on a contractual basis.

Accounting and financial reporting

The duties of investment advisors and actuaries will be discussed later, but at this juncture it is important to emphasize that a strong accounting and reporting system is central to sound pension administration. For many years, the absence of widely followed standards and the failure to offer timely and useful disclosure caused the accounting and reporting practices of public pension systems to be the focus of considerable concern.

Although different methods for displaying the financial statements continue to be permitted (including different techniques for valuing future employee salaries and asset holdings), the 1980s brought greater uniformity to public pension accounting. Regardless of the displays used, however, all public pension systems have been required since 1986 to provide a common set of disclosures, as specified in the Governmental Accounting Standards Board (GASB) Statements 5, 25, and 27, which concern disclosure of pension information by public employee retirement systems and state and local government employers.[17] The required disclosures include a description of the plan, a list of significant accounting principles, a statement on funding status, a funding progress report, and a statement of annual contributions required and made.

Although there have been threats of direct federal regulation, state and local government employee pension systems are not directly subject to federal regulation. They are, however, influenced by the federal government in two important ways: through the Internal Revenue Code (IRC) and the Employee Retirement Income Security Act (ERISA) of 1974. The IRC is important because it promulgates certain plan provisions that pension systems and pension investors must meet in order to qualify for federal tax-exempt status. In addition to addressing benefit qualification and benefit design, the IRC also requires that investment be for the exclusive benefit of the system members. Although this stipulation might be interpreted as limiting the investments that might be made, for example, to promote economic development or various social objectives, the interpretations have been broad enough to allow state and local governments to retain tax-exempt status while making investments that presumably benefit members and also serve social purposes.

The prudent-investor and diversification requirements found in ERISA are the other mechanism by which the federal government indirectly influences pension systems. Although public employment systems are exempt from the act, many state and local statutes echo ERISA's prudent-investor requirements: assets should be invested solely for the benefit of plan participants, and investments should be selected with care, skill, and diligence, using diversification where it is prudent to do so.[18]

Benefits design and adequacy

The primary purpose of a pension plan is to provide compensation to employees after they stop working. This normally occurs through monthly benefit payments that begin when the employee leaves the labor force—usually when he or she goes into normal retirement after having completed a certain number of years of service and having reached a specific age. In state and local plans, the prevailing requirements for retirement are that employees attain an age of between sixty-two and sixty-five and that they serve for at least five to ten years. However, as the following sections will show, a variety of factors and formulas are used to calculate the level of benefits, altering both eligibility for retirement and the size of the benefit payments. Only after the characteristics of a particular plan are examined can the adequacy of the pension as a source of retirement income be determined.

Benefit calculations

As noted earlier, in defined-benefit plans, which cover approximately 85 percent of all state and local government employees, benefits are determined by a formula that takes into consideration an employee's salary and years of service.[19] Benefit formulas are grouped into two classes: flat benefits and unit benefits. Flat benefits are paid out either as fixed dollar amounts or as a percentage of a salary base, and years of service do not enter into the calculation. Flat-benefit plans are of diminishing importance in the state and local sectors and are usually found in small local plans, such as fire and police pension plans.

Unit benefits are tied to length of service: the employee accumulates units of benefit credit for each year of employment. Two factors of particular importance in the unit-of-credit calculation are (1) the credit for service used in the formula and (2) the compensation base. The units of credit are typically expressed as a percentage of the employee's compensation. Take, for example, an employee who has attained retirement age and has worked for thirty years. If a 2 percent unit credit is used for each year of service, the monthly benefit payment would be 60 percent of the employee's base monthly compensation as calculated at the time of retirement.

The compensation base involves two subsidiary components: (1) the definition of employee compensation and (2) the time period over which compensation is measured. Most retirement plans use the employee's base pay as the compensation figure for calculating the pension, but a large number of plans also include overtime pay, sick pay, and longevity pay. Clearly, the more income elements that are included in the compensation base, the larger the monthly benefit payments for any given unit of service.

Regarding the time period used to set the level of benefits, the majority of state and local workers are members of plans that take the average compensation for the last three to five years. However, in a large percentage of plans, the compensation figure is based on one year or less (either the last year of employment or the year of highest salary).[20] When a very short time interval (such as the last day of employment) is used for the formula and the compensation base is expanded to include overtime and other pay, there is a great possibility of abuse. For example, retiring workers may be given last-minute promotions or opportunities to work excessive overtime to enlarge their compensation base and thus increase monthly retirement benefits.

Most employee retirement plans include benefits other than those associated with normal retirement, including disability benefits, death benefits, and survivor benefits. By far the most controversial—and, in many ways, the most difficult to administer—are those related to disability. Excessive disability claims have long been associated with certain locally administered pension plans, especially those for firefighters and police. An example of the potential for abuse is New York State's 1970 Heart Law, which presumes that every heart ailment suffered by fire or police employees is job related, entitling such employees to a tax-free disability pension at three-quarters pay.[21]

Cost-of-living adjustments

The need to keep pension benefits in line with the cost of living has understandably received much attention. In an inflationary environment, retirees' benefits can erode quickly as increases in consumer prices lower the real purchasing power of monthly retirement checks. Although few plans attempt to fully match rising prices, most state and local employees are covered by plans that make some effort to keep pace with inflation.

Cost-of-living adjustments can take several forms. For some plans, ad hoc adjustments are legislated from time to time, as the legislative body that controls benefits sees fit. Other plans have formal requirements that benefits be increased at a constant percentage over time, and still others gear benefits in some way to increases in the consumer price index. Most plans, however, limit the percentage increase in any given year. A fairly large number of plans also gear benefits to the level of investment earnings: for example, payments increase when earnings exceed the actuarial assumed rate of return.[22]

Table 18–4 illustrates the importance of cost-of-living adjustments to the preservation of purchasing power. At a 6 percent rate of inflation (roughly the average rate for the 1970s), a fixed-dollar pension benefit would have only 75 percent of its original purchasing power at the end of five years and only 31 percent at the end of twenty years. By the early 2000s, inflation rates had dropped to between 2 and 3 percent, making purchasing power easier to maintain.

In periods of high inflation, cost-of-living adjustments can be prohibitively expensive, and many such provisions carry a cap. Compared with a plan in which benefits are not tied to the cost of living, a plan with cost-of-living adjustments may cost 140 percent more annually if the rate of inflation is assumed to be 4 percent, and 170 percent more if inflation is assumed to be 6 percent.[23]

Early retirement

Most retirement plans permit employees to retire with reduced benefits before the normal retirement age. Eligibility for early retirement is determined by a combination of age and service (e.g., fifty-five with at least twenty years of service). The cost to the fund of early retirement can be considerable if benefits are not actuarially adjusted, not only because benefits need to be paid out over a longer period of life expectancy but also because the income from the assets, which would otherwise have been set aside, has less time to accumulate.

Not infrequently, benefits under early retirement are reduced by some rule of thumb that permits the retiree to receive a percentage of the benefit that would have been paid at normal retirement (a typical discount reduces benefits by half a percent for each month before the normal retirement age). However, because such rough guides usually understate the true cost to the employer of providing early retirement, early benefits should be actuarially computed so that their total cost over the expected benefit period will equal the cost of providing the unreduced benefit at the normal age.

Early retirement may be more than a nice "fringe." It may also help encourage employees to leave service when they are not capable of doing the required work or when their skills are no longer needed. However, unless the reduction in benefits is actuarially computed, the plan may end up heavily subsidizing early retirements.

Table 18–4 Purchasing power of a fixed dollar amount of benefit as a percentage of original (first-year) purchasing power.

Time period (years)	Annual rate of inflation (%)			
	0	2	4	6
5	100	91	82	75
10	100	82	68	56
20	100	67	46	31
30	100	55	31	17

Income replacement levels

The ultimate objective of retirement benefits should be to give the retiree a level of income sufficient to maintain a reasonable postretirement standard of living. Unfortunately, state and local retirement plans seldom design the benefit package rationally to accomplish this objective. On the contrary, the package of retirement benefits tends to grow in a crazy-quilt fashion, as various employee groups try to catch up with or get ahead of one another.

Pension adequacy can be described as the relationship between an employee's income at the time of retirement and the benefits received thereafter; determining this relationship calls for complex calculations involving the retiree's changing circumstances and need for discretionary income. For example, a retired person no longer pays social security taxes (and usually receives social security benefits), has a different tax status, has completed his or her savings program, and no longer has work-related expenses. Of course, he or she may have offsetting medical costs or other expenses associated with growing older, but these may be covered by Medicare or postretirement medical benefits. By and large, the cost of maintaining a given standard of living is lower upon retirement. Thus, the amount of replacement income needed to gain equivalency may be considerably less than the gross income the worker was receiving prior to retirement. However, lengthening postretirement life spans, surging health care costs, and increasing demands for medical services late in life have raised questions regarding income adequacy for retirees.[24]

The benefit income needed to provide an equivalent standard of living is computed by taking the pre-retirement gross income and subtracting federal, state, and local taxes; social security taxes; any employee contributions to the pension plan; certain work-related expenses; and personal savings. It is important to take into account the fact that most employees will receive social security benefits in addition to their income from the pension plan. Among actuarial consultants, the current thinking is that retirement benefits from all sources (including social security, defined-contribution, and defined-benefit plans) should aim to provide between 70 and 80 percent of pre-retirement earnings.[25]

As the preceding discussion indicates, social security benefits can significantly affect overall postretirement income. Furthermore, because employer and employee contribution rates have risen and could go higher, participation in social security represents not only a significant cost for both employers and employees at present, but one that is clouded with uncertainty in the future.

Historically, exclusion from social security coverage was a major deterrent to the growth of public pension systems. In the 1950s, a series of amendments to the social security laws made it possible for public employees to join social security, and a large number of systems elected to do so. As of the mid-1990s, about 76 percent of active plan members belonged to retirement systems in which active members were covered by social security.[26] However, rarely does the design of retirement plans formally taken into account the social security benefits to be received by participants; only about 13 percent of all public employee plans formally integrate pension and social security benefits to arrive at a total retirement income package.

Nevertheless, the integration of pension benefits with anticipated social security payments evidently occurs on an informal basis. As of 2002, one large-scale survey found that for plans whose members do not have social security coverage, the average unit benefit tended to be materially higher (2.43 percent) than that of plans that do have social security coverage (2.11 percent).[27]

Concerns about social security   As of the mid-1990s, more than half of retired citizens got half their income from social security, but there is ongoing concern about the system's ability to live up to its promises for future retirees.[1] Some remedial steps have been taken: contribution rates were increased under 1983 legislation (creating a surplus in the system's revenues over expenditures), and changes were introduced in 1986 and in 1994 that subjected more of the social security benefits to federal taxation. In the mid-1990s, a congressional commission on entitlement found that because of demographic changes, the trust fund would begin running out of money early in the twenty-first century.[2] According to the commission, when the huge baby boom generation begins to retire in 2010, the benefits paid out will soon overtake the contributions, ultimately emptying out the fund.

As inflation cooled in the 1990s and early 2000s, the sense of desperation was somewhat reduced, and the focus shifted to privatizing some or all of the social security system. Although consideration of the privatization alternative is beyond the scope of this discussion, implementing it would not cure the basic funding problem for those now in the system. Moreover, the transition to such a system would be hobbled by the need to fund the benefits of existing members while allowing future enrollees private options.

With or without privatization, the options available for bringing social security to an even keel are politically unpleasant: they involve some combination of boosting the retirement age, raising the contribution rate (which in 2002 was at 12.4 percent of payroll), or reducing benefits, including limiting the extent to which benefits are adjusted to reflect inflation. However, with many retirees and organized labor strongly in opposition (and with the privatization issue further complicating the debate), policy changes have yet to surface. In 2001, President Bush appointed the Commission on Strengthening the Social Security System, whose members were specifically asked to look at privatization options while preserving benefits for existing and near-term retires. However, the commission, reporting in December of 2001, was unable to make a recommendation. Poor stock market performance likely dulled much of the enthusiasm for a national system of self-directed individual accounts.[3]

[1]Eric Pianin and Spencer Rich, "Balancing Social Security and the Budget," *Washington Post,* 21 February 1995, A6.
[2]J. Robert Kerry and John Danforth, *Final Report: Bipartisan Commission on Entitlement and Tax Reform* (Washington, D.C.: U.S. Government Printing Office, January 1995).
[3]American Association of Retired Persons, "Social Security Reform," available at www.aarp.org/socialsecurity.

Pension costs and financing techniques

The determination and financing of pension costs are difficult and controversial issues that must be addressed by the policy makers and managers of retirement systems. Because state and local governments have been slow to recognize the full financial consequences of benefit promises, future generations of taxpayers have often been left with the burden of paying the costs. To the extent that future taxpayers are unable or unwilling to meet these obligations, the security of the pension promise is in jeopardy.

In passing, it should be noted that the selection of funding techniques is primarily a problem for defined-benefit plans, which entail a commitment to pay a certain level of benefits whether the fund has sufficient assets or not. In the case of a defined-contribution plan, the government, once having made its contribution, is free of future liability: future benefit payments depend on how large a contribution has been made and how well the investments have performed. Thus, in a defined-contribution plan, the costs of providing retirement benefits do not depend on the techniques chosen to finance the plan.

In the case of defined-benefit plans, there are two systems for financing benefits and determining their costs: (1) a system that recognizes the cost at the time the liability for future benefits is created (when the worker earns an increment of the future benefit payment) and (2) a system that recognizes the pension benefit only at the time a cash payment is made (when the worker collects the benefit). The first approach, which recognizes accrued liabilities, is called advance (or reserve) funding; the second is called pay-as-you-go funding. Because the pay-as-you-go approach does not recognize costs and liabilities when they are being created, governments that use this method do not account for the full costs of the plan at the time they are incurred, and liabilities that accumulate are not offset by assets set aside to help pay for future benefits through their principal and earnings.

There are variations on the themes of advance and pay-as-you-go funding, and some financing methods combine the two. For example, a technique popular at one time (but little used now) is terminal funding, under which a lump sum is set aside for the employee at the time of retirement. This sum, together with the investment earnings on it, provides benefit payments throughout retirement. In this approach, unlike that of pay-as-you-go funding, some assets are set aside, but not nearly as early as in the case of advance funding.

Although there have been no recent, large-scale surveys of the use of advance-funded (actuarially determined) versus unfunded, pay-as-you-go methods, it appears that the great preponderance of public employers do attempt to use some actuarial method to set aside assets as benefits accrue. According to the surveys done by the Public Pension Coordinating Council, 90 to 95 percent of plans have an actuarial basis for determining funding needs.[28]

Actuarial funding techniques

Although the objectives of an actuarially funded plan are relatively clear, the application can be complex and require the skills of an actuary. To calculate the present value of an uncertain future outflow of benefit payments, the actuary needs to assume future events and behavior, such as salary rates, retirements, deaths, and the rate of earnings from investments. On the basis of probabilities, a stream of future benefit payments is projected and converted into present values. Then a scheme is devised to determine the amount and timing of funds that must be set aside in order to ensure the system's ability to meet future payments. Although a detailed discussion of actuarial terminology and methodology is beyond the scope of this chapter, some fundamental concepts are discussed in this section.

Typically, the actuary is concerned with determining two types of costs that need to be funded: normal and supplemental. The normal cost is the present value of those obligations incurred as a result of employee services in the current period. Supplemental liabilities may be incurred as a consequence of a number of circumstances or events: unfunded past service for which contributions were not received at an earlier date, changes in actuarial assumptions, and the introduction of a new plan or the modification of an old one. If the plan is to be fully funded, supplemental as well as normal costs must be amortized over a period of time, typically thirty or forty years. It is important to note that the distinction between normal and supplemental costs is not absolute and depends on the particular assumptions and the cost-of-benefit allocation being used by the actuary.[29]

Pension costs can be allocated in a variety of ways, but the two major methods are the accrued-benefit and the projected-benefit methods. In the first case, the normal cost is the value of benefits accruing in the current year, and the actuarial liability is equal to all benefits accrued to date. This method tends to establish low initial costs for young entrants and immature pension funds, because interest has a longer time to accumulate and to be reinvested. At the same time, it establishes relatively high costs for older workers and mature plans.[30]

In the projected-benefit method, the normal cost is projected to remain constant over an employee's career (usually as a constant percentage of wage) if the given assumptions hold. To project benefits, future salary levels must be assumed. Various methodologies can be used in applying the projected-benefit technique. In the popular entry-age normal method, one determines the constant amount (or percentage of payroll) that must be set aside each year to accumulate the desired amount by retirement.

Pension liability and condition

Because there is no single way to determine the precise costs or required contribution rates of public pension plans, there has been much confusion over liability, unfunded liability, and the general financial condition of the plans. Because both liability and unfunded liability are basically matters of definition that depend on the actuarial methods used to determine costs or allocate benefits, the liability or unfunded liability of a particular fund, given the assets on hand, may vary greatly; and liability or unfunded liability may not be comparable among funds. Whatever the precise definitions being used, the measure of a system's funding status will usually be some ratio of assets to liabilities, and the trend in this ratio will be more important than the actual dollar amounts of assets and liabilities.

The most popular way of looking at the adequacy of a plan's funding is to look at the funding ratio: that is, the ratio of fund assets to fund liabilities at a given point in time. Although a fund is said to be fully funded when the ratio of plan assets to estimated accrued liabilities is 100 percent, professionals do not agree on the necessity of funding at the 100 percent ratio. What they do agree upon, however, is that the funding ratio should be constant or increasing; thus, trends in the funding ratio are a good indication of the relative health of funding. However, as discussed later, whatever methods are employed to determine funding adequacy, the credibility and timeliness of the actuarial assumptions are of utmost importance since they, in fact, determine the final value of a plan's liability.

Because the costs of benefits that have already accrued to employers and the costs of additional benefits that may arise in the future depend on the actuarial methods used to compute them, accrued liability cannot be compared across plans that use different actuarial methods. However, pension systems began reporting a standard measure of plan liability in 1987, when GASB mandated that the uniform pension benefit obligation (PBO) be disclosed in the footnotes to the financial statements for public employee retirement systems.[31]

Generally speaking, the PBO method of determining liability recognizes the benefits due to current retirees; the benefits due to inactive members who are not yet retired but who are vested; and the benefits due to, and likely to be due to, current active employees under given assumptions as to future salary increases as they relate to service rendered to date. The PBO does not include any benefits that will accrue as a consequence of future services to be rendered.[32] While differing assumptions about investment earnings, inflation, wage increases, and demographics can still muddy direct comparisons among different plans, the time frame and major benefit components of a plan's liability are uniform under the PBO method, which greatly improves the legitimacy of broad comparisons of funding status.

Bearing in mind the limitations of the PBO (primarily because of the variation in key underlying assumptions), it nonetheless provides a reasonably unambiguous measure of the unfunded liability of plans—that is, the difference between the PBO and fund assets. With the advent of the PBO, it has become possible to get a more consistent measure of the funding ratio (but, again, note that the credibility of the underlying assumptions is crucial). According to a 2002 survey by the Public Pension Coordinating Council, public plans appeared to be in very good health: the average value of assets as a percentage of PBO was 102 percent.[33] While the overall health of the plans appeared to be exceedingly strong, it should be borne in mind that individual systems can be seriously underfunded and that key actuarial assumptions, including earnings on assets, may be questionable.[34]

Actuarial assumptions

Whatever methods are used to determine and pay for pension costs and liabilities, the plausibility of the underlying actuarial assumptions is extremely important in judging the condition of a pension system. Because of the long time periods involved in actuarial analysis, slight changes in assumptions can cause great variation in projections of liability and required contribution rates, although the effect of a change in any one assumption is not always immediately evident.

Generally, the most important assumptions affecting the condition of a pension fund concern economic trends, interest rates or earnings (used to discount future benefits to present values), future salary levels (since most plans use a final average salary as the basis for benefits), and rates of inflation (for plans with cost-of-living escalators built into benefits). Assumptions concerning member characteristics can also be important. For example, high rates of early retirement and disability retirement can have severe consequences if they are not reflected in the actuarial assumptions. Other assumptions—regarding employee turnover and mortality, for example—appear to be less critical in the determination of pension costs.[35]

In practice, outworn assumptions may remain in use because of infrequent reevaluations. Assumptions may also be used to offset one another; for example, an assumption of a low interest rate may be used to adjust for a low assumption regarding future salary increases. Yet it is important that each significant assumption used in actuarial calculations be a realistic and explicit projection of the plan's future. Only assumptions that conform to the real world will shed light on the condition of a pension plan.[36] Unfortunately, however, the real world is a dynamic place, and assumptions can work for or against the funding status (and the required contributions) of a retirement system.

Retirement contributions often represent a major part of a state or local government's budget, amounting to 10 to 15 percent of payroll costs. (Of course, if the government's system has a substantial unfunded liability and few assets in comparison to the benefits to be paid, the necessary current contributions may be proportionately higher.) Actuarially determined contributions, which are used to ensure advance funding of benefits, depend on the assumptions used to determine the amount that needs to be contributed in order to meet the plan's normal costs and to accrue the funds necessary to cover present unfunded liabilities.

Although the real-world calculations are complex, the primary factors in determining annual costs and contributions, given a package of benefits, will be the assumptions regarding the rate of salary increases and the projected return on investments. When faced with a choice between projections, it is tempting to assume that salaries will increase more slowly and that investment returns will be more generous. For example, in the early 1990s, New Jersey governor

Actuarial assumptions and balancing a budget   The following table, which shows required annual contributions under alternative assumptions regarding salary growth and investment returns, reveals the power of assumptions in influencing the impact of pension contributions on a government's annual budget. This influence can best be demonstrated by examining the interplay between two major assumptions: the rate of salary increases and the rate of investment returns.

Investment return (%)	Annual salary growth (%)		
	6	5	4
6	$2,718	$2,250	$1,857
7	$2,439	$2,018	$1,666
8	$2,185	$1,808	$1,493

The table indicates the annual payment amounts required to reach a future value of $100,000 (assuming an annual salary growth rate of 6 percent); $82,731 (assuming an annual salary growth rate of 5 percent); or $68,320 (assuming an annual salary growth rate of 4 percent).

Assume that for each member of a group of employees, a target level of assets must be accumulated by the end of twenty years in order to fund benefit payments that have been calculated to replace a certain percentage of the retirees' final salaries. The first column of the table assumes (1) that salaries will increase at 6 percent annually during the twenty-year interval and (2) that the target level of assets to meet benefit needs is $100,000. If the annual rate of return on investment is likewise assumed to be 6 percent, the annual contribution must be $2,718 per employee. However, if the investment return is assumed to be 7 percent, the annual contribution is $2,439; and if it is 8 percent, the contribution need be only $2,185. Thus, by assuming a rate of return that is two percentage points higher than the assumed rate of salary growth, it is possible to reduce the required contribution by approximately 20 percent.

By the same token, assuming lower rates of salary increase means that benefits will be calculated on the basis

Christine Todd Whitman was able to finance the dramatic tax cuts that had been promised during her campaign by refiguring the funding assumptions for the state's public employee pension system ($36 billion in assets), thereby generating $1.3 billion in savings on contributions.[37] In the late 1990s, the New York State Common Retirement Fund used its investment gains to reduce employer contributions from 3.7 percent of payroll in 1997 to 0.6 percent in 1999 and was in hopes of soon dropping the contribution to zero.[38] It is a matter of opinion whether such strategies were ill-advised fiscal slights of hand or simply astute efforts to take advantage of the buoyant markets. What is clear is that they were motivated by temporary windfalls. As is discussed in the next section, aggressive investments in the 1990s led to impressive returns (and equally impressive assumptions regarding rates of returns on investments). But the early twenty-first century brought a sharp reminder that markets are volatile and assumptions can be wrong.

Investment of pension fund assets

In the 1990s, the meteoric rise in the assets of public pension funds made them increasingly active and sophisticated investors. As in the private sector, the trend in the public sector has been toward expanding the types of investments that may be made. Spurred by a desire to generate greater earnings on their investments, pension funds have diversified their portfolios into new investment of lower final salaries. And if final salaries are lower, the ultimate funding target will be lower as well—which also reduces the level of annual contributions. As is shown in the second column of the table, if the rate of salary increase is lowered from 6 to 5 percent, the annual contribution can be lowered from $2,718 to $2,250; a 4 percent rate of increase allows the contribution to be lowered to $1,857—an overall reduction of about 32 percent.

But by far the most attractive result, from the perspective of required contributions, is obtained when the investment assumption is increased and the salary assumption is decreased, thus increasing the spread between the two. If, instead of a 6 percent salary increase and a 6 percent investment return, one assumes a 4 percent salary increase and an 8 percent investment return, the result is a $1,493 contribution, as opposed to the original $2,718— a 45 percent reduction in the amount of the annual contribution.

If it were possible to lower by $1,000 the annual employer contribution for 10,000 employees, the result would be a savings of $10 million—enough to brighten many a local government budget. Of course, it is rarely possible, at one time, to vary assumptions to such an extent. But for major plans, where retirement contributions can amount to 10 percent or more of a government's outlays, altering assumptions has an undeniable impact. In the late 1990s, for example, when salary levels were held in check by a lack of inflation and investment returns spiraled, just such a situation occurred. Many governments, on the basis of the growth in the value of their fund's investments, were able to dramatically reduce or even cease making annual contributions. Unfortunately, circumstances had changed by the early 2000s, when the combination of an economic slowdown and reversals in the securities market led to large erosions in asset values—which, in turn, applied downward pressure to investment earnings assumptions.

areas. The use of new investment media has often required the relaxation of legal impediments that have traditionally limited pension investments to high-grade corporate bonds or to federal, state, or local government securities.

Types of investments

The basic choice in pension investment policies has typically been between (1) debt instruments, which are fixed-income obligations that—barring default— return a steady stream of interest payments, and (2) equity securities (common stock), which may or may not pay dividends and whose primary attraction is appreciation in capital value. Within these broad classifications, investments may vary by the nature of the issuer, the maturity of the obligation, or the specifics of the security (such as priority of payments to investors and the ability to convert from one form of obligation or ownership to another).

But the simple divide between debt and equity securities has been blurred by the burgeoning growth in alternative forms of investment. Although pension systems have tended to stick to basic investment types, many of the larger systems have pressed on into other investment areas, such as direct ownership of real estate and other business ventures, various forms of derivatives and options, and investment in foreign stocks and bonds.

Tables 18–5 and 18–6 display, respectively, the growth in size and the changing composition of the financial assets of state and local retirement systems from 1960 through 2000. The composition of assets, as will be discussed

Type of investment	1960	1970	1980	1990	1995	2000
Total	19.7	60.3	196.6	820.4	1,302.6	2,289.2
Deposits and currency	0.2	0.6	4.3	12.1	31.5	45.3
Corporate equities	0.6	10.1	44.3	296.1	678.9	1,335.1
U.S. government	5.7	5.1	20.9	142.4	191.7	177.4
U.S. government agencies	0.2	1.5	19.1	82.3	99.4	188.3
State and local obligations	4.4	2.0	4.1	0.4	1.8	1.4
Corporate bonds	7.1	35.0	92.2	169.3	189.2	351.2
Mortgages and miscellaneous	1.5	5.9	11.7	117.9	110.1	190.5

Note: Because of rounding, detail may not add to totals.

Type of investment	1960	1970	1980	1990	1995	2000
Total	100.0	100.0	100.0	100.0	100.0	100.0
Deposits and currency	1.0	1.0	2.2	1.5	2.4	2.0
Corporate equities	3.0	16.7	22.5	36.1	52.1	58.3
U.S. government	28.9	8.5	10.6	17.4	14.7	7.8
U.S. government agencies	1.0	2.5	9.7	10.0	7.6	8.2
State and local obligations	22.3	3.3	2.1	*	0.1	0.1
Corporate bonds	36.0	58.0	46.9	20.6	14.5	15.3
Mortgages and miscellaneous	7.6	9.8	6.0	14.4	8.4	8.3

Note: Because of rounding, detail may not add to totals.
*Less than 0.05 percent.

later in this section, has been influenced by a combination of factors, including an expansion in the types of investment vehicles available, the loosening of investment restraints, and the growing sophistication and diversification characteristic of portfolio design and management. However, rapid growth in equities also entailed more risk—and the early 2000s saw, for the first time in decades, a decline in the total market value of investments held by state and local pension systems, as will be discussed later.

Government bonds   Traditionally, state and local pension assets were largely invested in the obligations of the federal government and in those of the state or the sponsoring local government. The rationale behind such investments was security: the federal government's debt represented the greatest safety and liquidity, even if it offered a low rate of return. By 1960, however, as the higher yields on corporate bonds attracted greater attention, the proportion of pension fund assets invested in U.S. government securities began to decline. Also, the years after 1970 saw increased interest in the obligations of U.S. agencies. Such securities could serve two functions: first, they provided good yields, liquidity, and long-term investments of the highest quality. Second, several of the agency securities financed activities that were seen as socially useful (such as housing, small businesses, and rural development) but that did not entail the risk and bother that would be involved in individual direct investments.

Toward the end of the 1990s, the U.S. government briefly ran a surplus and stopped making frequent visits to the capital markets to borrow long-term. Nonetheless, the obligations of U.S. agencies have continued to be a major investment vehicle for public pension systems—and, with a return to federal deficit spending, it is likely that the U.S. Treasury will again issue long-term bonds.

Corporate bonds   Corporate bonds are especially appealing to state and local pensions. By and large, the chosen securities are part of larger listed issues that yield relatively high rates of return in comparison with government securities. (Listed issues are those listed on the exchanges.) After World War II, many of the fears about the credit quality of private debt dissolved, and plenty of high-grade industrial and utility issues were available. These securities are generally listed in secondary markets, thereby easing trading and pricing and making the market value of the securities easy to follow. The extensive use of ratings and the fact that the Securities and Exchange Commission (SEC) regulates the market provides a certain reliability to these securities. In the early 2000s, however, there were problems akin to those in equity securities: some major corporate obligations defaulted, victims of overborrowing.

Corporate equities   State and local pension systems had just begun to invest in the fixed-income securities of corporations when yet another investment frontier presented itself: the common stock. Studies undertaken in the 1960s found that, in terms of total return, investments in equities had outperformed all other securities over the long run (1926 through 1960) and that this phenomenon was likely to continue.[39] Thus, starting in the 1960s, state and local pension systems became major purchasers of corporate equities. Pension fund managers and trustees knew that the entry into common stocks presented new problems and greater uncertainty. Yet given the pressures of the times—the need to cope with inflation and to maximize the earnings on assets—prudent investment in securities with long-term growth potential was regarded as necessary in order to offset the lackluster performance of fixed-income assets.

The move to common stocks could not be accomplished without liberalization of the many restrictions governing allowable investments for state and local governments. In the early 1960s, most public pension systems that did permit equity investments allowed them to make up no more than 10 percent of total assets. Subsequently, as the potential benefits of equity investments became more evident and memories of the Great Depression and the stock market crash of the 1930s faded, such restrictions on equities were relaxed substantially, and in some cases were totally lifted.

The entry into the stock market by state and local pension plans was not accompanied by speculative excesses. Typically, the systems were partial to widely held blue-chip securities with proven dividend records. The performance of the stock market has been volatile, however. After doubling in value during the 1960s, the market averages slumped badly during the mid-1970s, when erratic stops and starts replaced once robust growth. The 1980s, however, brought a renewal of sustained growth that rocketed upward during the 1990s. By 2000, the market value of equities held by public pension funds was, in percentage terms, twice that of any other category of asset; for several large funds, the percentage of assets held in equities approached three-quarters of total holdings.[40]

Real estate   Investment in real estate is important for some pension funds, but it has never been a major factor in the aggregate. As Table 18–6 shows, between 1960 and 1990, mortgage and miscellaneous holdings grew slowly, from 7.6 to 14.4 percent of total investments, only to fall back to 8.3 percent by 2000.

Mortgages have not been a favored investment because of their illiquidity and the difficulties of servicing them (i.e., collecting the periodic mortgage payments). In addition, pension managers have been reluctant to be in the position of selecting among mortgage purchases (for fear of showing favoritism) or of having to foreclose on properties in the case of default (for obvious public relations reasons). Still, several state and some local systems have made an effort to acquire mortgages, usually showing a definite preference for in-state or in-town properties.

Public pension investment in the real estate market was given a considerable boost by the creation of several new capital-market instruments, backed directly by government guarantees or by private securities based on participation in a pool of conventional mortgages. Special pools were formed that used the mortgages of one state to appeal to those who wished to "keep the money at home" by investing within the state. Interest has not been confined to residential real estate, however. Comparisons among commercial mortgage yields, yields on equity interests in real estate, and yields available on common stocks showed the real estate market to be a consistent winner in the 1970s and 1980s.

Many pension fund systems, in search of new avenues for investment, undertook sophisticated investments in real estate, often taking positions in syndicates (a group of investors formed to make a particular investment) and selling off depreciation rights to private investors who could use the shelter. However, in the late 1980s and early 1990s, when the values of land and commercial, industrial, and hotel properties fell by 50 percent or more, some aggressive public pension systems, along with many other institutional investors, took a beating in the real estate market.[41] The importance of real estate investment in pension fund portfolios dropped after 1990—but when positive returns began to reappear, pension systems again sought to diversify their portfolios with real estate debt and equity holdings.

The "Mortgages and Miscellaneous" category shown in Tables 18–5 and 18–6 also contains various alternative investments, the exact character and composition of which can vary from fund to fund. However, these investments are notable for their lack of liquidity and, being direct placements, rarely enjoy a ready market. While these special investments can be lucrative, they can also carry high levels of risk and have been subject to considerable discussion among pension investment professionals.[42] Alabama's retirement system, to take an example, has invested aggressively in "special situations"—complicated transactions that often involve substantial risks as well as large potential gains. The system made headlines when it took a controlling 38 percent equity interest in U.S. Airways, which had gone into bankruptcy. With strong representation on the airline's board, the Alabama retirement system became heavily involved in trying to bring the carrier out of bankruptcy.[43]

Those who have general oversight of public pension funds must take care, however, especially when it comes to making alternative investments in so-called private equity transactions—equity interests that are not traded on the stock exchanges. Such investments are often made in less-than-transparent circumstances and may involve high transaction costs and potential conflicts of interest. For example, the money managers and investment advisors hired by a pension fund to put deals together may have an interest (or multiple interests) in where the fund decides to place its money. Such potential conflicts, and the risks involved, need to be thoroughly vetted when fund assets are privately placed.[44]

Derivatives   Starting in the late 1980s and early 1990s, other alternative investments became more popular with pension systems and had varying degrees of success. Although the practice was not widespread, some funds invested in derivatives (investments whose value is based on that of an underlying security or index). These investment media could be used either to hedge (protect against) future price and interest rate movements or to speculate on (take advantage of) those movements.

The rapid increase in interest rates in the mid-1990s led to large losses on the part of certain investors, both corporate and public, that were using derivatives to speculate rather than to hedge, and that had leveraged their positions by borrowing funds. Of these, the outstanding example is Orange County, California, which filed for bankruptcy after speculating with highly leveraged derivatives. (Orange County was not a pension fund but a cash management disaster.) Although some public pension systems were stung, none fell into serious trouble through the overuse or misuse of derivatives.

By the end of the 1990s, many retirement funds were investors in private-placement hedge funds, unlisted and unregulated investment entities that are usually highly leveraged and that make large investments based on predicted market changes. Depending on the style and the degree of leverage, these funds may be conservative hedging operations that buffer market fluctuations or aggressive speculative operations that bet on them.

Investment management

Faced with a broad range of potential investment media and changing markets, not to mention greater exposure to official and public scrutiny, the typical pension system manager has turned increasingly to professional help. The many forms of investment advice available to the pension administrator or board fall into three principal categories. First, a large system may elect to develop its own internal staff capability, not only to manage day-to-day operations and investments but also to advise the board of trustees. A second option is for the board to delegate investment responsibilities to an investment committee, a state investment board, or other governmental entity. The third and most popular option is for the fund to contract with outside investment professionals to manage and advise on its investment decisions. These professionals may be given broad responsibility and decision-making power not only over the general composition of the portfolio but also in the day-to-day selection and sale of specific securities; or they may serve as advisors who help set policy but have no responsibility for particular investment decisions. Another important role for outside advisors is to monitor the investment performance of the fund. The relationship between private investment advisors and the board of trustees is often controlled by statutes governing the degree to which—and to whom— the fund may delegate investment responsibilities.

There are typically three types of investment managers and counselors: bank trustees, insurance companies, and independent firms of investment counselors, many of which specialize in pension system investments. The services rendered by any one type can vary greatly. For example, a bank trustee may administer an individual fund established solely for the client, or it may combine the client's investments with those of other investors in a commingled fund. Likewise, insurance companies offer a variety of annuity packages.

Investment restrictions   State and local retirement systems operate in an environment in which most of their activities, including pension investment, are subject to direct or indirect state and local legal constraints. Legal restrictions on investments fall into two major categories: (1) specific statutory and constitutional restrictions that detail the kinds and composition of investments that pension systems can make and (2) general legal doctrines dealing with the prudence of pension fiduciaries or their agents (e.g., investment counselors). Since the mid-1970s, there has been a move away from "laundry lists" of specific types of permissible investments toward a more expansive notion of discretion as defined by a broad "prudent-person" rule.

Under the traditional prudent-person rule of state and common law, the duty of a trustee in administering a trust was to exercise such skill as a man or woman of ordinary prudence would exercise when dealing with his or her own property—with a view toward preserving the estate and the amount and regularity of the income to be derived. Under the influence of federal fiduciary standards, the prudent-person rule has evolved into a "prudent-investor" formulation that incorporates skill, care, and diligence into the definition.[45]

Placing the fiduciary responsibilities of managing public pension fund investments under a prudent-investor rule has helped to diminish the detailed constraints often found in state law, but state courts have developed different applications of the rule. Some states have adopted "legal lists," which allow only a percentage of assets to be invested according to the prudent-investor standard. Such legal lists may apply to fiduciaries in general, including pension fund trustees, and can be just as restrictive as (and perhaps even more difficult to interpret than) legal lists drawn specifically with public employee pension systems in mind.

Risk and return measures   For the most part, pension funds can be thought of as long-term investors with well-defined inflows and predictable outflows. Their stability and long-term planning horizons give them a low preference for liquidity and the ability to withstand substantial short-term risk. Given a wise portfolio policy and sufficient diversification, pension funds should be able to weather the storms of short-term market fluctuations in order to achieve higher long-term returns. However, the extrapolations used in planning pension fund investment strategies over such long periods of time necessarily involve uncertainty as to future price levels and interest rates.

The standard analysis used to assess risk and return in the pension area has relied heavily on historical trends in the rates of return for broad aggregates of investments. One set of general benchmarks (based on studies of long-term rates of return between 1945 and 1998) is that common stocks have, on average, returned a compounded annual rate of 13.4 percent; long-term corporate bonds, 5.8 percent; long-term U.S. government bonds, 5.0 percent; and short-term U.S. notes, 4.7 percent.[46] Of course, the historically higher rates of return on stocks have not been without risks. Maintaining any portfolio involves risk—both of price fluctuations and of possible default. But the long-term record shows that the biggest risk has been the loss of purchasing power caused by inflation. During the period from 1945 to 1993, the annual rate of inflation averaged 4.4 percent. From 1993 through 1998, stocks yielded an annual rate of return of over 20 percent and long-term corporate bonds 8 percent; during that period, the rate of inflation was only 2 percent.[47] During the late 1990s, it appeared that a period of fabulous wealth accumulation was ahead for the pension funds, and that their members and sponsors would see their contribution requirements minimized. But the boom was soon to end.

Pension trustees and managers have the impulse, if not the responsibility, to keep close track of results in order to judge the value of investment counsel, to see how well investments are performing in comparison to those selected by similarly situated systems, and to see how well investments are meeting the system's objectives. Many private services produce performance measures, often comparing a particular fund's performance to a widely used market index, such as the Standard & Poor's 500.

Overall, public pension systems have performed as well as other institutional investors, especially considering their historical propensity to invest more heavily in debt instruments. A study of pension investment behavior undertaken in the late 1970s showed that once the composition of assets was taken into account, there was little to distinguish public from private pension investment results.[48] In years when the stock market has done well, private pension systems have tended to do better than their public sector counterparts. When the stock market has done less well (especially when bond prices have been rising or stable), public funds have performed relatively better. By the late 1990s, the asset mix in public pension systems had moved to more closely reflect that of the equity-heavy private pension funds. As a result, when stock prices dropped in the early 2000s, the loss of market value in the portfolios of public funds was roughly in proportion to that of private sector funds.

Portfolio theory and asset allocation   Public pension systems participate in financial markets that have become increasingly sophisticated and complex, in part because of the systematic study of the relationships among the various alternative instruments. The most important development that has resulted from this systematic study is modern portfolio theory, which has two driving principles: diversification and asset allocation. Modern portfolio theory holds that depending on the degree of relationship in price movements, two risky securities can be combined to form a less risky portfolio because the fluctuations in their prices tend to cancel each other out. Thus, diversification can be used to smooth out and enhance returns, given a level of acceptable risk. The principle of asset allocation is based on the fact that families of securities within a market category tend to move sympathetically; thus, an investor is better off diversifying holdings by consistently allocating assets among families of securities rather than trying to pick individual "winners" or trying to increase returns by timing transactions.

These theories of diversification and allocation, among other influences, increased interest in assets outside the conventional markets. In addition to moving toward real estate investments and the sometimes dangerous derivatives previously discussed, public pension systems have also expanded their interest

---

Diversification and globalization

Investing abroad has been of growing interest to U.S. public pension investors. The theory was that if business conditions and markets sagged in the United States, they would be on the uptick somewhere else—and, also, that emerging economies, in particular, presented opportunities for stellar growth that were less likely to occur in the more mature economies of the United States and Europe. In the early to mid-1990s, the theory worked out pretty well. But with the back-to-back international financial crises of 1997 and 1998, the foreign securities markets were swamped with pessimism, leading to widespread currency devaluations, equity market collapses, and bond defaults.

Research indicates that the international markets are increasingly tied together

and that they can move in lockstep, especially when on the way down. In the 1980s, the correlation among the international equity markets was only about 0.40: that means, roughly, that about 40 percent of the change in any one market "could be explained" by changes that were common to all markets. By the late 1990s, that coefficient had climbed to 0.80. And by 2001, market prices for international equities were almost perfectly synchronized: of the thirty-seven national exchanges, thirty-three had seen prices drop and the percentage drop in the respective indexes had been large—on the scale of 20 percent or so in most cases. In other words, when it came to worldwide decline in the financial markets, international asset allocation failed to work.[1]

[1]John E. Petersen, "Angling for Big Returns," *Governing*, June 2001, 74.

in international investments, both fixed-income and equity. This investment strategy is used, in part, because international markets do not move systematically with those found in the United States (thus allowing for benefits from diversification), and also because returns on international investments have tended to be somewhat higher. According to a survey done in the early 1990s, a little over 3 percent of pension assets were in foreign securities, including both equities and debt.[49] By 1996, the share had risen to 10.5 percent.[50] In an increasingly global economy, the attraction is strong to further diversify holdings and exploit investment opportunities elsewhere.

The challenges of declining markets   After a decade of strong growth, public pension systems got a firsthand view of the "risk" side of the risk-and-return equation. The early 2000s proved to be a turbulent period for all investors as the market indexes dropped sharply and numerous scandals related to corporate governance and accounting broke out. The public pension systems, many heavily affected by the declining markets of the "Enron era," were in the forefront of demanding reforms in the reporting of financial results and in the governance of corporations in which they had become major investors.

Table 18–7 summarizes the impact of market reversals on the financial assets of state and local retirement systems between 1999 and the third quarter of 2002. After peaking in early 2000, the stock market indexes plunged downward. Starting that year, rates of return on stocks went into what would prove to be a sustained decline. Although pension systems' returns were somewhat insulated at first by an increase in the price of bonds (caused by rapidly declining interest rates), the erosion in stock prices began to take its toll in 2002. By the end of the third quarter of that year, despite continuing contributions to the funds, the market value of public employee pension assets was estimated to be 15 percent lower than it had been three years earlier, dragged down by the 30 percent decline in the market value of corporate equities. Meanwhile, the funding picture was made bleaker by the fact that the economic slowdown of the early 2000s had left state and many local governments in the worst fiscal situation they had experienced in more than fifty years.[51]

Pension bonds   The fiscal plight of state and local governments was caused by a combination of factors: first, a lingering recession and the steep decline in the stock markets led to a decline in tax revenues; second, new spending programs, enacted in better times, proved hard to eliminate. The decline in the value of pension portfolios further intensified state and local governments' fiscal difficulties: although governments had fewer revenues with which to meet their contribution requirements, the requirements escalated rapidly because of the need to cover funding gaps that had been opened up by the large portfolio losses.

One response that became increasingly popular in the early 2000s was to "double up" on the market bets by selling pension bonds. The proceeds of the bond issues were invested in investment portfolios (usually stock) on the theory that, over time, the annual increases in value would exceed the inter-

Table 18–7   Assets and investment performance of state and local public retirement systems.

	1999	2000	2001	2002[a]
Financial assets (in billions of $)	2,227	2,290	2,179	1,894
Equities (in billions of $)	1,343	1,335	1,222	937
Rate of return (%)				
Stocks	21.0	−9.1	−11.9	−17.2
Bonds	−1.3	11.7	8.4	7.7

[a] Through the third quarter of 2002.

New York City looks at losses In 2000, the New York City pension fund administration, riding high on substantial returns from the fund's investments in stock, projected that its pension contributions would be a bit under $800 million in 2003 and would decrease in the years that followed. Instead, the required contribution in 2003 was $2 billion, with more needed on the horizon. Robert North, the fund's chief actuary, summarized the city's predicament: "It comes down to two things: we gave lots of benefits and we had bad investments."[1] As benefits go up and earnings go down, contributions must increase, and those contributions come out of the city taxes.

The sources of the city's investment problems were not hard to find. New York City was highly exposed to stocks, with nearly 70 percent of its assets invested in equities (compared with the 32 percent it had in equities in 1986).

The high exposure was beneficial as the markets surged upward in the 1990s, but costly when the slump came. But the downturn in stocks was only part of the problem. Another part was that the state, over the city's objections, had granted additional cost-of-living benefits to retirees, something that seemed politically astute at the time but that later created a substantial drag on the city's pensions. The pension systems, aggressively invested in equities, lost more than $9 billion in 2001, and the rate of return sank to a dismal −8 percent. As a result, the city had to contribute almost an additional billion dollars to keep the fund actuarially sound. The amount of the increase alone exceeded the amount that the city was spending each year on its parks.

[1] Michael Cooper and Eric Lipton, "New York Pension Funds Suffering from a Dual Blow," *New York Times*, 3 April 2002, A1.

est rate paid on the bonds. In effect, the *internal* obligation of the government sponsor to provide funding for its pension fund was converted into an *external* obligation to pay debt service to bondholders. A complication was that according to the U.S. Internal Revenue Code, the interest on pension bonds is taxable for federal income tax purposes—meaning that, in order to be advantageous, such investments need to earn an even higher return.

As governments exhausted various temporizing measures in an effort to balance their budgets, the sale of pension bonds became increasingly attractive. In the first nine months of 2003, several states and a number of cities and counties sold more than $13 billion in pension bonds, which represented almost 5 percent of all new municipal bond issuances for the period.[52] Despite the argument that equity investments could be expected to yield much more over the long haul than the interest rates on the bond issues (which had sunk to historically low levels by 2003), immediate gains were by no means assured, and losses were a distinct possibility. And a government that suffered severe and sustained losses would face the unpleasant prospect of owing both future employer contributions and the debt service on the bonds.

The outcome depended greatly on timing. In late 2000, for example, the city of New Orleans sold $171 million in bonds and invested in stock to fund its firefighters' pensions. The city, which had to borrow at an interest rate of more than 8 percent, anticipated a yield on its investments of nearly 11 percent. But that prediction was based on the returns of 1983 to 1999, when there was a historic bull market in stocks. Instead of earning that rate, the fund suffered losses; by June 2003, the value of the assets purchased with the bond proceeds had melted to $98 million.[53]

Despite some setbacks, with both interest rates and stock prices low, the pension-bond bet appeared worth taking to many governments, although there were complaints about the risks and high transaction costs involved in the strategy. Ultimately, regardless of the short-term behavior of the investments, the scheme gave cash-hungry governments yet another reason to borrow and to receive injections of much-needed funds into their coffers.[54]

Targeted investments   Decisions about how to invest the enormous assets of state and local pension systems have been complicated by the view that public monies should be put toward substantive accomplishments at home, in addition to simply producing earnings. Some observers have argued, for example, that these funds should be used to promote "targeted" or "socially useful" investment, whether by directly supporting certain activities (such as local housing or development projects) or by withholding funds from businesses that engage in undesirable activities (such as those that pollute, promote tobacco products, or are located in countries with poor human rights records).

Although demands for such targeting have been enduring, surveys taken in the late 1970s and 1980s indicated that despite the talk about socially useful investing, there was relatively little action: most of the targeted investment that occurred was confined to purchasing the securities of U.S. agencies that

---

Targeting pension fund investments
Whenever a socially desirable purpose needs funding, the brimming portfolios of state and local employee retirement funds are sure to come under scrutiny. Public retirement funds are especially attractive because federal law grants them broad latitude in making investment decisions.[1] This, together with the huge flow of income, has made pension funds tempting resources for meeting policy objectives.

Pension investments are often being pulled in several directions: Will they be directed toward infrastructure, inner-city investment, or regional economic targets? Will they be used to cope with budget shortfalls of the sponsoring government, or will they be used exclusively to provide (and protect) employee pensions?

Inducements to invest, especially in the form of federal guarantees, can make bottom-line sense for higher-yielding investments found in the private sector; much of the federally sponsored agency debt does exactly that for housing. But putting pension investments into government-owned infrastructure presents a more complicated picture. Since state and local governments are already able to borrow at tax-exempt

rates, attracting investment involves finding ways to further compensate non-taxpaying pension investors, who would otherwise have no interest in holding low-yielding assets.

There may also be pressure on state and local governments to use pension investments to cover budget deficits, either directly (by having the fund lend money to the sponsoring government) or indirectly (by lowering or omitting employer contributions). While the mechanics differ, in both cases the government is racking up additional liabilities that taxpayers may need to cover in future years, unless the financial markets ride to the rescue. There are, of course, traditionalists who view the social mobilization of public pension assets with alarm, believing that the sole purpose of investments is to maximize returns and protect the promises made to present and future pensioners. To the extent that the fund's earnings are maximized, the money needed for governmental contributions can be spent on other things, including social and economic programs.

[1]Paul Zorn, "Public Employment Retirement Systems and Benefits," in *Local Government Finance: Concepts and Practices,* ed. John Petersen and Dennis Strachota (Chicago: Government Finance Officers Association, 1991), 385.

---

assisted the mortgage market. For example, a survey of 130 systems (representing about 89 percent of all public pension assets) found that only 19 actually targeted any investments to promote what might be viewed as socially responsible activities. Setting aside the special case of New York City, where pension funds were used to assist a local government in financial difficulty, the systems directed only $2.4 billion in assets (less than 2 percent of the total) to targeted uses. Various forms of locally directed housing investments (typically federally guaranteed) constituted half the targeted amount, with the remainder going to a scattering of programs in the broad areas of local economic development and renewal. As of the early 1980s, most funds with any targeting at all were limiting such investments to a minor fraction of their portfolios (2 to 5 percent).[55] Nonetheless, even at those small percentages, the rapid escalation in pension assets has made large pools of capital available.

Most funds do not target investments, for the simple reason that their managers do not believe that targeted investments can earn equivalent returns at the same level of risk. Without specific legislative direction, most investment officers are unwilling (and usually unable) to make concessions in terms of lowered returns or greater risks to support preferred activities. Furthermore, there is always the selection problem: of the many claimants to such assistance, which are to be selected, and on what preferential terms and softer conditions?

Nevertheless, state and local officials have their own means of directing pension capital into "strategic areas." Public pension systems can steer resources by designating part of their investment portfolio for selected purposes, weighing factors other than return on assets, and favoring in-state investments. But targeting investments can be difficult and potentially dangerous. Consider, for example, the experience in Kansas, where state officials lost more than $100 million by targeting in-state investments to risky business ventures. In contrast, New York City pension systems have placed nearly $1 billion of long-term capital for small business and housing.[56]

Have targeted investment practices actually reduced public pension plans' returns? Some research has been undertaken to attempt to answer this question. The results have been mixed, ranging from some decrease in returns on investments, to no significant impact, to—in some cases—even increased returns.[57]

In the early 1990s, California's giant CalPERs fund designated a share of its portfolio to in-state investment in venture capital. During that decade, as the California economy prospered and the high-tech bubble began to emerge, the venture capital program grew by leaps and bounds. However, as the economy slowed and the markets crashed, both the returns and the promising investment opportunities dwindled. Nonetheless, the giant system has a reputation for both risk taking and activism in its support of investments designed to achieve various social purposes and in its support of improved corporate governance.[58]

Corporate governance and accountability   As state and local pension systems became major holders of stocks, there came the growing realization that they were both legal and effective owners of the corporations in which they had invested. As such, they were responsible for seeing that corporate management was prudent, truthful, and faithful in its duty to protect the growth in earnings and the value of investments. The revelations surrounding the major corporate scandals of the early 2000s—exemplified by the spectacular collapse of Enron and its accounting firm, Arthur Andersen—led to investor calls for reform, a movement in which many large state pension systems took a leadership role.

The roughly $1.5 billion in losses from Enron securities experienced by state and local systems mobilized the funds to take legal action. Several state funds, including those of California, Ohio, and Washington State, filed suits against the company. The fallen corporation was not the only target. The pension board that oversees Florida's $94 billion fund authorized the fund directors to sue one of its investment advisors over the $282 million the fund lost on its Enron holdings. The advisor had bought $2.7 million in Enron shares for the state fund during the six weeks before Enron filed for bankruptcy on December 2, 2001. In all, the fund was left holding $7.6 million in Enron shares, which were sold for $0.28 each. The retirement funds, along with the attorneys general of several states, were active supporters of a number of lawsuits against offending corporations and their management. They were also proponents of congressional action that led to the passage, in 2002, of the Sarbanes-Oxley Law, which strengthened corporate governance and financial reporting and led to stiffer oversight of the financial markets by the SEC.[59]

Enron was not the only offender; moreover, in addition to individual companies whose accounting procedures and ill-begotten management practices got them into trouble, the entire securities market—stressed by a worldwide recession and a series of scandals regarding the operations of mutual funds, banking firms, and the securities exchanges—suffered withering losses. For example, CalPERS reported that the market value of its portfolio had slumped from a peak of $172 billion as of June 2000 to $128 billion by September 2002.[60] It is little wonder that the giant state system was at the head of the parade of state and local pension funds clamoring for restitution for past misdeeds and for the reform of future practices in the securities market.[61]

Conclusion

As the twenty-first century began, state and local employee retirement systems encountered a new world of active oversight of the hundreds of billions they had invested both domestically and abroad. The public pension funds and their governmental sponsors, thanks to a generation of expanded investment opportunities and greatly increased funding, were dominant players in the financial markets, with great stakes in the markets' future health. The benefits of funds' huge asset holdings brought enlarged responsibilities as well, which need to be vigorously exercised if the pension benefits promised to millions of present and future retirees are to be secure.

1 U.S. Department of Commerce, Bureau of the Census, *Finances of Employee Retirement Systems of State and Local Governments,* 1997 Census of Governments, vol. 4 (Washington, D.C.: U.S. Government Printing Office, 2000), 19. In 1975, a special census by the Pension Task Force of the U.S. House of Representatives counted nearly 5,800 separate public employee retirement systems covering more than 12.5 million employees. (U.S. Congress, House Committee on Education and Labor, *Task Force Report on Public Employee Retirement Systems* [Washington, D.C.: U.S. Government Printing Office, 1978], 51–97.) This study included in its definition of a pension plan any arrangement that provided postretirement income (e.g., deferred compensation and life insurance contracts), whether administered by a government entity or by the private sector. However, for purposes of local government financial management, the definitions used by the U.S. Bureau of the Census and the corresponding numbers are more useful.

2 For an explanation of the Census Bureau definitions, see Bureau of the Census, *Employee Retirement Systems,* v–viii.

3 Bureau of the Census, *Employee Retirement Systems,* 16.

4 Ibid.

5 Ibid., 22–24.

6 Ibid.

7 Ibid.

8 See Thomas P. Bleakney, *Retirement Systems for Public Employees* (Philadelphia: University of Pennsylvania, 1972), 20–23.

9 See Charles Ruffel and Nevin Adams, "America's Pension Funding Crisis: The Perfect Storm," *Plan Sponsor* (November 2002): 92–96. In the view of the authors, as defined-benefit plans are shifted to defined-contribution plans, more risk will be shifted to employees.

10 Paul Zorn, *Survey of State and Local Government Employee Retirement Systems* (Washington, D.C.: Public Pension Coordinating Council, June 1994), B-31.

11 Workers can use some or all of their retirement assets to purchase a lifetime annuity with an insurer. The Teachers Insurance and Annuity Association offers such a group lifetime annuity program.

12 House Committee on Education and Labor, *Task Force Report,* 61–62.

13 Zorn, *Survey,* B-31.

14 Advisory Commission on Intergovernmental Relations, *Information Bulletin: State and Local Gov-*

ernment Pension Reforms (Washington, D.C.: U.S. Government Printing Office, March 1979).

15 It should be borne in mind that the aggregate statistics do not reflect the actual contributions to individual systems. According to survey information of the Public Pension Coordinating Council, actual employer contributions were most likely on the order of 9 percent, being higher in the case of small systems and lower in the case of large systems. See Zorn, *Survey,* 56–58.

16 Zorn, *Survey,* 20.

17 Governmental Accounting Standards Board (GASB), *Disclosure of Information by Public Employee Retirement Systems and State and Local Government Employers,* Statement No. 5 (Stamford, Conn.: GASB, 1986). The statement was subsequently updated by Statements Nos. 25 and 27 on the same subject, which were issued in 1994.

18 Paul Zorn, "Public Employee Retirement Systems and Benefits," in *Local Government Finance: Concepts and Practices,* ed. John Petersen and Dennis Strachota (Chicago: Government Finance Officers Association, 1991), 385.

19 In defined-contribution plans, there is no benefit formula (aside from basic eligibility rules) since the employer's sole obligation is to contribute to the plan; the level of benefits depends on the amount contributed and the investment performance of the assets during the years of contribution and retirement.

20 According to a 1993 survey by the Public Pension Coordinating Council, 43 percent of the reporting plans used the average of the last three years; 19 percent used the average of the last five years; and 12 percent used the last year or less in figuring the base for the unit-service retirement. See Zorn, *Survey,* 31.

21 Ester Fuchs, "Sure, Cut New York's Fat: But Cut It Fairly and Wisely," *New York Times,* 22 February 1995, A19.

22 According to a 1993 survey by the Public Pension Coordinating Council, most systems tie postemployment benefits to some variety of cost-of-living adjustment: 35 percent make the adjustment on an automatic basis and another 42 percent make it on an ad hoc basis. Evidently, only 22 percent of plans have no cost-of-living provisions. See Zorn, *Survey,* B-28.

23 Howard E. Winklevoss and Dan M. McGill, *Public Pension Plans: Standards for Design, Funding, and Reporting* (Homewood, Ill.: Dow Jones–Irwin, 1979), 144.

24 The rate of inflation for health care plans, after holding fairly steady at 2 to 5 percent in the mid-1990s, rocketed upward at the end of the decade. For 2000 through 2003, the increases were about 20 percent per year for retirees. See Sanford Barth, "Tackling Rising Health Care Costs," *Government Finance Review* (February 2003): 32–34.

25 See National Retirement Income Policy Committee, *National Retirement Income Policy Papers* (Arlington, Va.: American Society of Pension Actuaries, 1994).

26 U.S. Department of Labor, Bureau of Labor Statistics, *Employee Benefits in State and Local Governments 1994* (Washington, D.C.: U.S. Government Printing Office, 1996), 80.

27 Jennifer Harris, *2001 Survey of State and Local Employee Retirement Systems* (Washington, D.C.: Public Pension Coordinating Council, March 2002), 6.

28 Ibid.

29 Winklevoss and McGill, *Public Pension Plans,* pt. 2.

30 Ibid., chap. 6.

31 GASB, *Disclosure of Information.*

32 Harris, *Survey,* 6.

33 Ibid.

34 Steve Hemmerick, "State Fund Returns Lag Actuarial Rates," *Pensions and Investments,* 20 March 1995, 1.

35 Howard Winklevoss, *Pension Mathematics* (Philadelphia: Pension Research Council, 1978).

36 In 1994, Wilshire Associates compared actuarial assumptions and annual expected rates of return by asset class for eighty-two state pension plans. They found that in the case of several funds, the actuarial assumption was 1 to 1.5 percentage points higher than the actual historical rates of return for that distribution of assets. In other words, the fund was asserting that it would "best" the market. See Hemmerick, "State Fund Returns," 37.

37 Rodd Zelkos, "A Guide to New Pressures on Pension Plans," *Governing,* November 1994, 68.

38 Mark Sarney, "State and Local Pension Plans' Equity Holdings and Returns," available at www.ssa .gov/policy/docs/ssb.

39 An influential study showed that a buy-and-hold policy for stocks returned 9 percent, versus 3 percent for bonds. See Lawrence Fisher and James Lorie, "The Return in Investments in Common Stock," *Journal of Business* (June 1976): 1–26.

40 Sarney, "Equity Holdings," 8.

41 Real estate returns for commercial, industrial, and retail properties (measured both by change in capital value and rental income) declined throughout the late 1980s and early 1990s. According to the National Real Estate Index, the price per square foot of prime commercial properties declined by 30 percent nationwide from the second quarter of 1988 to the second quarter of 1993. Rents per square foot also declined by 15 percent during the same period. In overbuilt local markets, the declines were much sharper.

42 See "Alternative Investments: Policy for Public Employee Retirement Systems," in *Recommended Practices* (Chicago: Government Finance Officers Association, March 2000), 145.

43 David Rynecki, "Pension Plan Gambler," *Fortune,* November 2002, 17.

44 By the mid-2000s, public pension systems were increasingly directing money into private equity investments, primarily to achieve higher earnings on investments. While some funds were using such investments simply to diversify, others were taking major stakes (more than 10 percent of their assets) in an effort to improve investment performance in the face of large funding gaps. Wilshire Associates estimated that as of early 2004, about 5 percent of public retirement fund assets (or $100 billion) was invested in private equity. See Mary Walsh, "Concerns Raised over Consultants to Pension Funds," *New York Times,* 21 March, 2004, 1.

45 Zorn, "Retirement Systems," 385.

46 Kathryn Engelbretson, "A Multi-Asset Class Approach to Pension Fund Investments," *Government Finance Review* (February 1995): 11 (updated by the author on the basis of index averages for 1993 through 1998). Not surprisingly, the higher-yielding investments showed the greatest variability, with stocks being the riskiest (as measured by standard deviation in yield) and short-term U.S. Treasuries being the least risky.

47 Ibid.

48 See John Petersen, *State and Local Pension Investment Performance* (Washington, D.C.: Municipal Finance Officers Association, 1980).

49 Zorn, *Survey,* 66.

50 Ibid., Table I-t.

51 Robert Pear, "States Are Facing Big Fiscal Crises, Governors Report," *New York Times,* 26 November 2002, A1.

52 Mary Walsh, "States and Cities Risk Bigger Losses to Fund Pensions," *New York Times,* 12 October 2003, 1.

53 Ibid., 16.

54 For a discussion of opportunities for the artful use of borrowing to close gaps in the current budget period, see John E. Petersen, "Changing Red to Black: Deficit Closing," *National Tax Journal* 56 (September 2003): 567–577. For example, placing high-interest-rate coupons on bonds allowed them to be sold at a premium over the face value being paid to the issuer; this added amount could be used to supplement the cash in the general fund. The trade-off was that future debt service payments would be higher—but that was for the next administration to worry about, in what was hoped to be better times.

55 Paul Zorn, *Public Pension Investment Targeting: Survey of Practices* (Washington, D.C.: Government Finance Officers Association, 1983), 42–43.

56 John E. Petersen, "The Push to Leverage Public Pension Funds," *Credit Week,* 14 December 1992, 1.

57 Julia Coronado, Eric Engen, and Brian Knight, "Public Pension Funds and Private Capital Markets: The Investment Practices and Performance of State and Local Pension Funds," *National Tax Journal* 56 (September 2003): 582–584.

58 Thom Weidlich, "CalPERS Wears a Party, or Union, Label," *New York Times,* 13 October 2002, Business 1.

59 John E. Petersen, "Pension Fund Follies," *Governing,* June 2002, 64.

60 CalPERS, "Facts at a Glance: Investments," available at www.Calpers.gov.

61 In December 2003, CalPERS sued the New York Stock Exchange and several specialist securities firms for improper trading practices that, it alleged, had cost CalPERS and other investors millions. CalPERS and other state and local pension systems also sued many mutual fund managers for practices that had given advantages to hedge funds and to the mutual funds' owners and employees at the cost of fund investors. See Ben White, "Pension Fund Sues NYSE, Specialist Firms," *Washington Post,* 17 December 2003, B1.

19 Unions and collective bargaining

ROBERT J. THORNTON

One of the most significant economic developments in the public sector since the 1960s has been the growth and spread of public employee unionism. With the spread of unionism have also come collective bargaining and militant activity on the part of unions of public employees, particularly at the state and local government levels.

This chapter first describes the extent of unionism in the local government sector and the principal labor organizations involved. It then examines the legal context of local government bargaining, giving special attention to those aspects of bargaining—coverage, scope, union security, and dispute settlement—that most directly affect the local finance function. The chapter next addresses local government employee compensation, particularly the effect of collective bargaining on compensation and on the local government budgetary process. The chapter concludes with an analysis of comparable worth (or pay equity) and contracting out, two of the most controversial issues related to public sector unionism.

Public sector unionism today

As of 2002, approximately 16.1 million wage and salary workers in the United States were union members, or about 13.4 percent of all employed workers. (Economists often refer to this percentage as the "union density.")[1] In comparison, in 1973, approximately 18 million wage and salary workers were union members, and the corresponding union density was nearly twice as high.[2] The decline in these figures results largely from a drop in *private* sector union membership over the past several decades, both in absolute numbers and as a percentage of all wage and salary workers.

The decline in private sector unionism stands in marked contrast, however, to the trend in *public* sector unionism. As of 2002, 37.5 percent of public sector workers at all three levels of government combined (federal, state, and local) were union members, compared with fewer than 10 percent of all private sector wage and salary workers.[3] The figure of 37.5 percent is significantly higher than the comparable figure for 1973, which was 23 percent.[4]

Although organizations of public employees in the United States are not a new phenomenon, their growth before 1960 was unspectacular, in part because local governments generally resisted demands for collective bargaining. Such resistance was possible largely because until about 1960, public employees at all three levels of government lacked statutory rights to bargain collectively. From 1960 to the mid-1970s, however, the growth in public sector union membership was explosive, with total membership increasing by more than 500 percent.[5] Since then, public sector union membership rates have held steady.[6]

As of 2002, 42.8 percent of all local government employees were members of labor organizations. However, the percentage of organized local government employees varies substantially by function, with teachers, firefighters, and police officers having the highest unionization rates.[7]

Organizations of public employees

In contrast to private sector unions, public employee unions are relatively heterogeneous, with diverse memberships, organizational structures, and recruitment patterns. Some labor organizations are active at only one level of government—local, state, or federal—while others are active at all three levels. Some are quite restrictive in their recruiting efforts, choosing to represent public employees only in certain occupations; others will organize public employees of any type. Some labor organizations actively recruit workers in both the private and the public sectors.

Traditionally, unions and professional associations have operated with separate and distinct goals: unions concerned themselves more with wages, benefits, and working conditions, while associations focused on professional matters and the quality of services delivered. Today, however, as professional associations have become increasingly concerned with the economic well-being of their membership, the differences between the two types of organization have diminished. Many associations have become as militant as their union counterparts and have even participated in strikes; some have merged with labor unions.[8]

The following five sections briefly examine some of the major organizations that currently represent significant numbers of local government employees. It should be noted, however, that this list is far from complete. A considerable number of smaller independent organizations are active in representing local government employees, but it is impossible to create a detailed listing of all such groups because they are exempt from federal regulations requiring the reporting of financial and other information.

The American Federation of State, County, and Municipal Employees

The American Federation of State, County, and Municipal Employees (AFSCME) is one of the largest unions of public employees. Much of AFSCME's growth has occurred through the absorption of other organizations—including, for example, employee associations in Arizona, Michigan, New York, and Ohio, and part of the National Union of Hospital and Health Care Employees. In all, about sixty associations have joined AFSCME through affiliation or merger. AFSCME's membership as of 2003 totaled about 1.3 million, about half of whom are local government employees, and its ranks include almost all types of state and local government employees, from office workers and public works employees to school, social services, and health care workers.

Police and firefighters' organizations

Police are one of the most highly organized groups in the local government sector today, and police officers are represented by a number of different unions. Many are independent local organizations, while others are affiliated with a state or national association.[9] The Fraternal Order of Police (FOP), the oldest and largest body, includes both police officers and supervisors in its ranks. The order's constitution prohibits strikes, but this ban has not prevented local affiliates from sometimes striking. As of 2002, the FOP included approximately 280,000 members.

The International Union of Police Associations (IUPA), an affiliate of the American Federation of Labor–Congress of Industrial Organizations (AFL-CIO), claimed as of 2003 to represent more than 100,000 law enforcement personnel. In addition to police officers, IUPA also represents deputy sheriffs, corrections officers, and law enforcement support personnel. Like the FOP,

IUPA does not endorse strike action, preferring legislation that calls for binding arbitration.

The FOP and IUPA include only police officers within their ranks, but several other unions with diverse memberships have also been active in organizing police—principally, the Service Employees International Union (SEIU), AFSCME, and the International Brotherhood of Teamsters.

The International Association of Fire Fighters (IAFF) is the major organization representing firefighters. The IAFF is affiliated with the AFL-CIO, and its membership of 184,000 (as of 2001) includes uniformed firefighters and management (officers) as well as emergency medical workers. The IAFF is the only public employee union without substantial competition in its organizational efforts. The IAFF has not openly espoused the use of the strike, but this has not deterred some of its locals from striking.

Teachers' organizations

Two major organizations represent most of the nation's teachers: the National Education Association (NEA) and the American Federation of Teachers (AFT). As of 2002, the NEA included about 2.7 million members and the AFT approximately 1.3 million.

The NEA, which dates back to the mid-1800s, is the oldest and largest employee organization at any level of government. Most members are classroom teachers at the elementary or secondary level, but the organization's ranks also include school support personnel (e.g., teaching assistants, bus drivers, and cafeteria workers) and faculty at institutions of higher education. Until the 1960s, the NEA concerned itself almost exclusively with professional and educational matters. But then, faced with growing competition from the AFT, the NEA began actively promoting collective bargaining among its constituent local associations.

The AFT, a national teachers' union affiliated with the AFL-CIO, has grown rapidly in recent decades, largely by organizing workers in many different occupations. In addition to teachers, the AFT's ranks include paraprofessionals and other school-related personnel, as well as nurses and other health care professionals.

There have been periodic movements to merge the two national teachers' organizations, and several local and state NEA and AFT affiliates have combined. However, for the NEA, the AFT's affiliation with the AFL-CIO has been one of the major obstacles to a national merger.

Hospital and health care workers' organizations

Hospital and health care workers had for a long time been one of the least organized groups of public sector workers, but in recent years unions have made significant inroads in this sector. The biggest reason is the rapid growth of the health care industry. A large number of unions represent workers in this industry. The union with the largest number of health care workers is the SEIU, which is in fact a "mixed" union: its ranks include both public and private sector workers. The SEIU, which has been described as being "as close to an industrial health care union as exists in the United States today,"[10] includes workers in almost all professional and nonprofessional health care classifications, such as hospitals, nursing homes, clinics, and home care. Furthermore, through its Nurse Alliance affiliate, the SEIU has the largest nurse membership of any U.S. union, representing 110,000 nurses.[11]

The American Nurses Association (ANA) is the dominant professional organization representing nurses exclusively. Through its constituent state and local organizations, the ANA has long engaged in collective bargaining. Since 1968, when the ANA rescinded its no-strike policy, it has made no distinction between strikes in the public and private sectors. In 1999, the ANA created the United American Nurses (UAN) as an autonomous body within the ANA. The UAN is the labor arm of the ANA, and its goal is to organize and represent nurses across the country in collective bargaining efforts. In 2001, the UAN affiliated with the AFL-CIO; it currently represents more than 100,000 nurses through its various constituent nursing associations.

A third organization, the United Nurses of America (UNA), is affiliated with AFSCME and also actively represents nurses in collective bargaining. As of 2003, the UNA represented about 60,000 registered and licensed practical nurses. Overall, AFSCME (including its affiliated National Union of Hospital and Health Care Employees) represents a total of 375,000 health care employees of all types.

Because of the substantial potential for membership gains, the recruiting efforts of organized labor in the health care industry have become intensely competitive in recent years. Along with those already mentioned, a number of other unions have succeeded in organizing public sector health care workers. These include the United Food and Commercial Workers, the United Auto Workers, the United Steelworkers of America, and the Teamsters. In these unions, however, the proportion of membership made up of public sector health care workers is not as high as for the unions described earlier.

Mixed unions

A number of major organizations include large numbers of both public and private sector employees within their ranks. The two such unions with the largest numbers in local government are the SEIU and the Teamsters.

As of 2002, the SEIU had a membership of approximately 1.5 million and represented a cross section of building maintenance workers, hospital workers, food service workers, clerical workers, and various other groups. About half the SEIU's members are public employees. In recent years, the SEIU has been the fastest-growing labor organization in the AFL-CIO, in part because of a number of mergers with formerly independent public employee organizations. It is now the largest union within the AFL-CIO.

Within its overall membership of 1.4 million, the Teamsters union includes more than 100,000 municipal and county government workers. Much of the Teamsters' organizational success has been among street and sanitation department employees, but the union has also organized other groups of public employees, such as police officers, nurses, and clerical personnel.

To the list of significant mixed unions should be added the Laborers' International Union (LIU) and the Communications Workers of America (CWA). Both of these AFL-CIO–affiliated unions represent substantial numbers of local government workers. The LIU represents mostly maintenance and unskilled construction workers, and the CWA represents a wide variety of white-collar workers in schools, libraries, hospitals, and social service agencies.

The principal unions representing bus drivers and other local transit workers are the Amalgamated Transit Union (ATU) and the Transport Workers Union (TWU). As of the early 2000s, the ATU had a membership of more than 170,000, compared with the TWU's 125,000. Both unions have members in the public and private sectors.

The legal context of public employee bargaining

Government employees were specifically excluded from the National Labor Relations Act (NLRA) of 1935 and the Labor Management Relations Act

(LMRA) of 1947, which bestowed on private sector employees the rights to form unions and to bargain collectively. Consequently, unions of local government employees have had to depend on state or local laws, executive orders, or other avenues to participate in collective bargaining. However, several bills have been introduced in Congress—including the Public Safety Employer-Employee Cooperation Act, introduced in 1999—that would require all states to allow police, firefighters, and other public safety employees to bargain collectively over wages and working conditions.[12]

In 1959, Wisconsin became the first state to grant collective bargaining rights to local government employees. A surge of legislation in other states soon followed, and more than thirty states now grant bargaining rights to some or all government employees.[13] Two states (Georgia and Kansas) have what are called "opt in" laws, whereby local governments can decide whether they wish to be covered by the state statutes.[14] Several other states have statutes requiring employers to "meet and confer" with certain groups of public employees. In all, only nine states currently lack any statutory authorization for some form of collective bargaining for public employees.[15] Even so, unions of public employees exist in these states, and collective bargaining sometimes occurs (on occasion as the result of gubernatorial orders or attorney general opinions), especially in urban areas and school districts.[16]

Despite the near universality of some form of legal authorization for collective bargaining, the state laws are extremely varied. The four sections that follow briefly discuss major features—coverage, scope of bargaining, union security, and dispute settlement procedures—that have implications for local finance.

Coverage and duty to bargain

There is considerable variation among state statutes concerning the types of public employees that the statutes cover. Some state laws, like those of Hawaii, Michigan, and New York, are comprehensive and cover virtually all local public employees. Other states, such as North Dakota and Wyoming, have restricted their coverage to certain groups, such as teachers or firefighters.

The types of negotiation required also vary across states. As noted earlier, a number of states, such as Missouri, require only that the public employer meet and confer with employees, while most others mandate collective bargaining. The difference between the terms is more than semantic. Meet-and-confer statutes typically require only that the public employer inform employees of issues pertaining to terms and conditions of employment and give employees the opportunity to comment on proposed actions regarding such terms and conditions. Whatever agreement is reached may be written as a memorandum of understanding rather than as a collective bargaining contract. Under a meet-and-confer statute, the employer is not legally bound to negotiate or even to abide by the terms of the agreement. Under collective bargaining, in contrast, public employer and public employee representatives are equal parties in the negotiating process. Most collective bargaining statutes require good-faith bargaining, prohibit certain unfair practices, and prescribe procedures to be followed in the event of impasse. The end result of collective bargaining is an agreement that is usually binding on both parties.

Scope of bargaining

The scope of bargaining refers to the range of issues that are subject to negotiation. The scope of collective bargaining is an important concern from the perspective of both management and the union. If the scope is extremely broad, management may feel that its operating flexibility is weakened. If the scope is extremely narrow, the union may feel that its collective bargaining efforts will have little impact. As in the private sector, subjects are generally classified according to whether they are mandatory (must be bargained), permissive (may be bargained), or prohibited (cannot be bargained).

The NLRA defines the mandatory scope of bargaining for employees in the private sector as "wages, hours, and other terms and conditions of employment."[17] In the public sector, many state laws have borrowed this language.

Where there are restrictions, the scope of bargaining may be limited by listing management rights and prerogatives, and by making exemptions for the civil service system, the merit principle, and cases where conflicts with other statutes would arise.[18] Even so, there has been much controversy about which items are to be considered mandatory for bargaining purposes. Some statutes, for example, contain specific lists of items that may or may not be subject to bargaining. According to the Pennsylvania Public Employee Relations Act (Act 195),

Public employers shall not be required to bargain over matters of inherent managerial policy, which shall include but shall not be limited to such areas of discretion or policy as the functions and programs of the public employer, standards of service, selection and direction of personnel. Public employers, however, shall be required to meet and discuss on policy matters affecting wages, hours, and terms and conditions of employment as well as the impact thereon upon request by public employee representatives.[19]

The great specificity with which some state statutes define the scope of bargaining is a legislative effort to protect public managers' operational flexibility, which can be curtailed by excessively broad scope. Nevada's public employee bargaining statute contains one of the more detailed listings of mandatory bargaining subjects:

Salary or wage rates or other forms of direct monetary compensation; sick leave, vacation leave, holidays; other paid or nonpaid leave of absence; insurance benefits; total hours of work required of an employee on each work day or work week; total number of days of work required of an employee in a work year; discharge and disciplinary [actions]; recognition clause; method used to classify employees in the negotiating unit; deduction of dues for recognizing labor organizations consistent with the provisions of this chapter; no-strike provisions consistent with the provisions with this chapter; grievance and arbitration procedures for resolution of disputes relating to interpretation or application of collective bargaining agreements; general saving clauses; duration of collective bargaining agreements; safety; teacher preparation time; procedures for reduction in workforce; employee safety; safety of the public.[20]

No matter how specific the statutes, however, disagreements inevitably arise as to whether particular topics are subject to mandatory bargaining, and state and local governments have relied heavily on the courts and on administrative agencies to make these determinations. Although the net effect of legislation and court and agency decisions has generally been to limit the scope of bargaining in the public sector, there is considerable variation among the states: mandatory bargaining subjects in some states may be permissive in others. Class size, for example, is a permissive subject of teacher bargaining in some states but is mandatory in others. Manning (e.g., of police cruisers) and drug testing are two subjects that are also classified differently from state to state.[21]

Furthermore, although wages are typically the most important subject of public sector bargaining, in most states some wage-related items, such as pensions, are not subject to bargaining and may instead be decided by legislative bodies. Similarly, the scope of bargaining is often circumscribed with respect to teachers' hours of work: by setting a minimum number of days for instruction, most states effectively fix the teachers' work year. On matters not subject to negotiation, unions frequently use lobbying and other tactics in efforts to achieve their demands.

The classification of subjects as mandatory or permissive is further compli- cated by an overlap problem, which occurs when statutes specify both condi- tions of employment and management prerogatives. The most well-known example is in education, where class size is both a condition of employment and an element of educational policy subject to the determination of manage- ment. In some states—Illinois and Pennsylvania, for example—a "balancing test" has been used to determine whether class size is a mandatory bargaining subject. The balancing test weighs the effect of class size on teachers' em- ployment against the effect of class size on educational policy. In Illinois, bal- ancing tests led to one decision for police in Chicago and to another for corrections officers in an Illinois prison where there was a serious drug prob- lem: in the first case, drug testing was deemed a mandatory bargaining subject, and in the second, it was classified as permissive.

The statutory, judicial, and administrative treatment of the scope of bar- gaining is not only varied but also continuously changing. As B. V. H. Schneider explains:

Decades of controversy have attended the gradual creation of a definition of, and means for further defining, legal scope in the private sector; the process is still going on. Given the variety of statutory frameworks and the complications created by the government's being the employer, it is not surprising that the process in the public sector has had a kaleidoscopic quality.[22]

What is more, a number of states have recently begun to further restrict the scope of public sector bargaining, largely in response to taxpayer concerns. For example, a 1995 amendment to Oregon's public employee collective bargain- ing law eliminated a number of mandatory bargaining items, such as staffing levels, criteria for performance evaluation, and assignment of duties. Amend- ments in 1995 to Michigan's Public Employer Relations Act also eliminated a number of items formerly subject to bargaining, including the setting of the starting day for the school year and the privatization of instruction.[23]

Union security

Unions negotiate for union security provisions to ensure that workers whose interests are represented by a union are obliged to contribute to the support of that union. The most common union security provisions found in the local government sector are the following:

Agency shop (or fair share) provisions, which require employees in the bargaining unit who are not union members to pay a fee to the union. This fee ordinarily equals the union membership dues or is designed to cover the costs of union representation and bargaining.

Maintenance-of-membership provisions, which require all employees who become union members to remain union members as a condition of employment.

Union shop provisions, which require all employees in the bargaining unit to become union members within a specified period after becoming employed.[24]

There are other forms of union security provisions, such as the closed shop and preferential hiring agreements, but such provisions are not usually found in the public sector.

Opponents of union security provisions have argued against them on two principal grounds: first, that discharging an employee for failing to join a union or pay union fees violates the constitutionally guaranteed right of freedom of association; and second, that the security provisions violate the merit principles of civil service laws.[25] However, in the 1977 decision *Abood v. Detroit Board of Education,* the U.S. Supreme Court upheld the legality of public sector agency shop agreements that imposed a service fee on nonunion members to cover the costs of collective bargaining.[26] The Court ruled, though, that nonunion workers could not be required to support certain union expenditures not associated with collective bargaining—those for political activities, for example. In 1991, in *Lehnert v. Ferris Faculty Association,* the Supreme Court devised a set of tests to determine more precisely which union expenses may legitimately be covered by service fees for nonmembers. The Court disallowed expenses for lobbying, electoral, or political activities outside the limited context of bargaining, but approved expenses germane to collective bargaining, such as those related to strike preparation and to state and national conventions aimed at coordinating bargaining strategy.[27]

As of the late 1990s, about half the states permitted agency shop, maintenance-of-membership, or union shop provisions for at least some groups of public employees.[28] Some states have circumvented the problem associated with union security by providing by statute for the automatic deduction of fees for the union upon certification, thereby eliminating union security as a bargaining item.[29] A number of states (at least eight, as of 2003) have also spelled out procedures under which employees who object to union security provisions can determine and recover the portion of their dues that is not related to bargaining, as stipulated in the *Lehnert* decision.[30] For example, according to New Jersey law, "the representation portion of agency shop fees cannot exceed 85 percent of the regular membership dues, fees, and assessments."[31] The Ohio public employee bargaining law requires public sector unions to develop procedures for determining and rebating the non-bargaining-related portion of union dues to nonmember objectors. The Ohio law also provides an appeals mechanism for employees who dispute the determination made by the union.[32]

Strikes and dispute settlement procedures

Traditionally, there had been a universal ban on the use of the strike by state and local government employees. Strikes have been flatly prohibited in many state statutes, and severe penalties sometimes have accompanied the statutory ban. New York's Taylor Law, for example, prescribes forfeiture of tenure and double loss of pay for striking government workers. Even when the statutes do not refer specifically to strikes, common law has usually held public sector strikes to be illegal. Over the past several decades, however, the traditional ban on public sector strikes has softened somewhat. As of the early 2000s, ten states permitted some groups of public employees to strike under certain conditions, and courts in four other states have also ruled that public sector strikes are legal.[33]

Although the specific provisions of the statutes authorizing strikes vary widely across states, most prohibit public safety employees such as police officers, firefighters, and correctional employees from striking, and most states require that detailed dispute resolution procedures be exhausted before employees can legally strike. In Oregon, for example, a legal strike cannot occur until (1) both mediation and fact-finding procedures have been exhausted and (2) thirty days have elapsed after the fact finder's report has been made public.[34]

Despite fears that legalizing strikes would greatly increase their incidence among state and local government employees, most studies have found that such legislation has had little or no effect on strike incidence. The exception is Pennsylvania, which experienced a considerable increase in teacher strike activity after the passage of permissive legislation. At the same time, nationally, the number of major public sector strikes (i.e., strikes involving at least 1,000 workers) has shown a slight decline in recent years.[35]

Instead of permitting public sector disputes to be resolved by means of strikes, many states have provided various types of alternative resolution procedures; the most common are mediation and fact-finding. Under mediation, a third party assists management and the union in reaching agreement. Fact-finding, a more formal process, often follows if mediation is unsuccessful. The fact finder is a neutral party who listens to evidence from both sides and then makes recommendations for settling the dispute.

A major limitation of both mediation and fact-finding is that the resulting agreement or recommendation is nonbinding; thus, the impasse may remain after both procedures have been exhausted. Consequently, twenty-three states now provide for compulsory binding arbitration as the final step in the impasse resolution process for some or all government employees (most often for police and firefighters).[36] The two major types of arbitration are conventional arbitration, in which the decision-making authority of the arbitrator is unrestricted, and final-offer arbitration, in which the arbitrator must select the terms of one of the parties. One disadvantage of conventional arbitration is its alleged chilling effect on the negotiation process: if the parties feel that the arbitrator is likely to simply split the difference between the labor demands and the management offer, then neither party has an incentive to compromise. Rather, it is in each party's interest to hold to its initial demands, which may be considerably different from what it might ultimately agree to, or even to inflate its demands, in the belief that the arbitrator will split the difference.

Under final-offer arbitration, the arbitrator selects the terms of one of the parties—the terms that are, in the arbitrator's judgment, the most reasonable. Some statutes permit the arbitrator to select the terms issue by issue, while others require that the most reasonable package be accepted in its entirety. In either variant, the effect is to encourage both labor and management to formulate more reasonable initial demands and to offer counterproposals during the collective bargaining process.

Despite its increasing use as a means of settling impasses in the public sector, arbitration is not without its critics. In the view of some, giving a nonelected individual the power to determine the terms and conditions of employment constitutes an illegal delegation of governmental authority. Supporters, on the other hand, argue that legislatures may legally delegate authority in order to attain certain policy objectives, such as the prevention of strikes, and that arbitration constitutes a delegation of legislative authority. In any case, when court challenges to public sector arbitration statutes have occurred, the constitutionality of the statutes has generally been upheld.[37]

Another controversy surrounding the use of arbitration is the fear that it produces a "narcotic effect"—in other words, that parties who submit to arbitration will become increasingly dependent on it. Although considerable research has been undertaken on this question, the findings are inconclusive. Despite the controversies surrounding its use, it is clear that arbitration has succeeded in reducing the incidence of strikes in the public sector.

Some policy makers have been reassessing the appropriateness and adequacy of the conventional methods discussed earlier for dealing with disputes in the public sector, all of which are designed mainly to avoid strike outcomes. Consequently, there is increasing interest in alternative, cooperative approaches to dispute resolution. The state of Wisconsin, for example, provides training in what has been called "consensus bargaining," which is a problem-solving approach to negotiations and conflict resolution. Some public sector employers have also tried grievance mediation (the application of voluntary mediation techniques in grievance disputes) and preventive mediation (a means of providing information or counsel to prevent existing disputes).[38]

Unionism and earnings

The level of earnings of workers in the public sector is an important issue. An unreasonably high level means that the government may not be using its resources efficiently and may therefore be unable to address other public sector needs while maintaining moderate tax burdens. Too low a level of earnings may prevent the government from attracting and retaining workers of sufficient quality and can create a sense of unfairness if public sector workers feel that they are being paid less than similar workers doing comparable work in the private sector.[39]

This section of the chapter examines wage trends in the public and private sectors, pay determination in local governments, and the impact of unionism on public employee compensation. It also addresses a highly controversial question—namely, whether local government workers are "overpaid."

Wage trends in the public and private sectors

The level of public employee pay has been a controversial issue for many decades, and has become even more so in recent years because of increased pressure on government budgets. Experts have also sometimes strongly disagreed about whether government employees are "overpaid," a subject that will be treated later in the chapter. One important fact, however, must be stressed in this regard: the composition of occupations and industries in the public and private sectors is quite different. Thus, there is no reason to suppose that either average pay levels or average pay increases in the two sectors ought to be the same. This difference must be kept in mind in any effort to examine pay trends in the two sectors.

Comparisons of wage and salary changes may be made using the U.S. Department of Labor's Employment Cost Index (ECI). This index is the only measure of wage and salary changes available both for the private sector and for state and local governments. Using the ECI to track changes for the 1980s and 1990s, Albert Schwenk found that during the 1980s, pay increases were consistently greater in state and local governments than in the private sector. During the 1990s, however, the rates of pay increase in both the public and private sectors slowed substantially, especially within state and local governments. But overall, despite different rates of increase, pay gains in the two sectors have been similar over the long term.[40]

It is important to remember that since the mix of industries and occupations in the two sectors differ, variations in the rates of wage change should not be surprising. In particular, white-collar occupations comprise a larger proportion of the state and local government workforces. This being the case, pay comparisons will be most accurate if they are undertaken only for narrowly defined industries and occupations.[41]

Pay determination in local governments

Pay policy at the local government level is determined by the complex interaction of a number of factors: collective bargaining, minimum-wage laws, equal-pay statutes and other antidiscrimination legislation, prevailing wage requirements, and merit-pay practices.

As Harry Katz and David Lewin have noted, public pay-setting procedures are probably best viewed as falling along a spectrum bounded by two ideal types, or models.[42] At one end of this spectrum is the civil service model, according to which wages are set at levels that prevail in comparable private sector jobs. At the other end of the spectrum is the collective bargaining model, according to which labor and management jointly negotiate compensation levels that reflect the relative bargaining power of the two groups. The next two sections consider each of these models in detail.

The civil service model   In the civil service model, management possesses unilateral power to set pay but ordinarily delegates this authority to an independent commission or agency, which usually determines pay on the basis of prevailing rates for comparable jobs in the private sector. This standard, known as the prevailing-wage principle, is widely followed by state and local governments. In theory, the practice seems reasonable: it ensures fairness and efficiency by enabling the government employer to attract workers of acceptable quality. In practice, however, adherence to the prevailing-wage principle may sometimes lead to public sector pay levels that are in fact higher than those in the private sector.[43]

There are several reasons for this potential upward bias in public sector pay. First, because surveying smaller firms is costly, local governments often limit their wage surveys to large and medium-sized firms. Thus, smaller firms, which have been found to pay significantly lower wages than larger firms, are systematically excluded from local government surveys.[44]

Second, public employers sometimes react inconsistently when confronted with private sector wage scales that have been rendered "out of line" by unusual market forces. On the one hand, it is not uncommon for government employers to match private pay levels that may be unusually high because of the exercise of union power. On the other hand, if private pay levels happen to be unusually *low* because of monopsony (when a single firm employs a high percentage of the area's labor force), government employers rarely move their pay scales *downward* to match those in the private sector.[45] The overall effect of such inconsistency in response to prevailing wage rates may be an upward bias in public sector wages.[46]

Finally, government policy in setting wages for certain jobs that are unique to the public sector (such as police and fire protection, for which no private sector equivalents exist) can lend a further upward bias to public sector pay. For example, many local governments follow a system of pay parity for police officers and firefighters, whereby the salaries of the two groups are tied by some sort of formula. Because of the difference in the attractiveness of the two occupations, however, such policies have sometimes resulted in firefighters being "overpaid"—as evidenced by substantial waiting lists for firefighter positions in some jurisdictions.[47] In recent years, however, wage parity between police and firefighters has eroded somewhat, as a growing number of municipalities have allowed disparities (in favor of police salaries) to develop.[48]

Thus, even in the absence of a union, adherence to the prevailing-wage principle may cause public sector pay levels to exceed those in the private sector. This potential, it should be added, seems to be present for all public sector occupations except high-level managerial and professional positions.[49]

The collective bargaining model   In the collective bargaining model, labor and management jointly negotiate compensation levels. One of the major arguments supporting the right of workers to organize and to bargain collectively through unions hinges on the concept of bargaining power.[50] A worker facing management alone may be at a substantial disadvantage in negotiating terms of employment, whereas workers acting collectively may be able to achieve a more equitable distribution of bargaining power.

What is meant by bargaining power? Neil Chamberlain has suggested a simple yet useful definition: the ability of one party (e.g., labor) to secure the agreement of another party (e.g., management) on the first party's terms. Labor's ability to secure an agreement depends, in turn, on the costs to management of agreement versus disagreement.[51] For management, the costs of agreement include the possibility of obtaining a lower wage settlement by holding out for a longer period of time, while the costs of disagreement include incurring or prolonging a strike. Obviously, the higher the ratio of the relative costs of disagreement and agreement to one party, the higher the bargaining power of the other.

Applying Chamberlain's definition of bargaining power to public sector collective bargaining is a straightforward matter. If collective bargaining is to be a viable method of determining wages and other terms of employment for public sector workers, then neither unions nor management should possess excessive bargaining power. Most economists would define "excessive" bargaining power in the public sector as a level substantially greater than the norm in the private sector.

Do the characteristics of local government employment give public employee unions excessive bargaining power? Several features of public employment would seem to support such a contention. First, the elasticity of demand for many types of public employees is low.[52] Because many of the services that public employees perform (e.g., police, fire protection, and sanitation) are both essential and without close substitutes, the public usually has neither the desire nor the option to demand fewer services should they become more expensive (through increases in taxes or user fees). In the private sector, in contrast, when the cost of a high wage settlement is passed on to the consumer, demand for the goods or services in question may decline. Because a decline in demand can result in job loss, the private sector market tends to exert restraint on union wage levels.

Some economists contend that public sector unions, however, are often able to obtain higher wage levels without fear of job loss. Returning for a moment to the Chamberlain model, this means that disagreeing with a given set of union demands could prove very costly for the public employer. Moreover, costs may not be confined to the local government budget. A transit strike, for example, may so inconvenience local residents that enormous political pressure to settle the dispute may be brought to bear on local officials.

The fact that many public services are both essential and without close substitutes can raise the bargaining power of public sector unions by making the cost of disagreement to the public employer high. But there are also forces operating in the public sector that can make the immediate cost of *agreement* with a union's demands lower than might be the case in the private sector. This is likely to be true, for example, when the full budgetary consequences of a particular union demand might not be felt until several years later, as in the case of a multiyear contract, or even until several generations have passed, as in the case of a change in a local government pension plan.[53]

On the other hand, not all arguments and evidence support the notion that the bargaining power of public employee unions is necessarily greater than that of most private sector unions. First, some economists point out that although public employers have not often (until recently, at least) had to face competition as providers of government services, they are still subject to the "discipline of the budget."[54] Second, local governments must be concerned, in the long run, with the possible exodus of residents and businesses. Third, private sector unions are generally free to make full use of the strike—but, as has been noted, most states still prohibit public employee unions from striking to achieve wage demands. Finally, many public employers are now feeling the same pressures as private employers to restructure and downsize. Consequently, with privatization and contracting out of government services becoming commonplace in the public sector, the bargaining power of some public sector unions is no longer as strong.

Unions and public employees' wage levels

As the preceding section indicates, the question of whether the bargaining power of public sector unions exceeds that of private sector unions cannot be answered a priori. In numerous studies that have used diverse statistical techniques and have considered many different occupations over varying periods of time, economists have attempted to measure the effects of unionism on the wages of local government workers. It must be stressed that although union workers may receive pay levels that are higher than those received by nonunion workers, the difference might be the result of factors other than unions. Such factors might include differences in occupations, the mix of full-time and part-time workers, geographic location, cost of living, and employer size. Therefore, it is necessary to first control for the possible influence of these other factors when calculating the effects of unions on wages.

What does the empirical evidence show? Taken together, the studies have found that the estimated effects of unionism on the wages of local government employees vary by occupation. On average, however, most of the findings indicate that the impact of public sector unions has not been extraordinarily large: the wage differentials estimated have typically been less than 10 percent and often considerably less. In fact, the wage effects attributed to public sector unionism seem to be somewhat smaller than those observed for private sector unions, where research suggests that the average union-nonunion wage differential has been about 15 percent.[55]

Nevertheless, there is some evidence that the wage effects of public sector unions (particularly teachers' unions) may have increased somewhat in recent years. According to H. Gregg Lewis, the latest estimates show that the average union-nonunion pay gap in the public sector is now about 8 to 12 percent, certainly not negligible but still below most estimates of union effects on private sector wages and salaries.[56] Lewis also adds that although union impacts on wages in the public sector are still typically lower than in the private sector, there are important exceptions: public school teachers, refuse collectors, local transit bus drivers, and licensed practical nurses.[57]

Most studies of the impact of public employee unions have estimated their effects on wages rather than on fringe benefits or total compensation. In the private sector, there is evidence that unions have been even more successful at raising the level of fringe benefits than the level of wages.[58] Is the same true for public sector unions? There are reasons to suppose that this may be the case: for one thing, as noted earlier, the long-run costs of generous fringe benefit settlements made at the public sector bargaining table can sometimes be hidden (this is particularly true for pensions, which may be underfunded for years before the consequences become apparent). There is also some empirical evidence: one study of firefighters, for example, found that unionism's effect on fringe benefits was several times larger than its effect on wages.[59] Similarly, a study of sanitation workers found a considerably larger impact on fringe benefits than on wages.[60] Finally, a study of police, fire, sanitation, and other municipal departments (excluding those related to education) found that the average effect of bargaining on wages (3.6 percent) was dwarfed by the effect of bargaining on pensions and paid time off.[61]

Pay levels of government employees

The question of whether government employees are overpaid—that is, whether their average compensation levels exceed those of their private sector counterparts—has been the subject of much discussion over the past several decades. In fact, the taxpayer revolts of recent years and the growth in contracting out and the privatization of public services have been, in part, manifestations of the concern about labor costs in the public sector. The concern has been fueled by a number of factors, including the high levels of union penetration and activism in the public sector and the fact that payroll costs often make up more than 60 percent of state and local government expenditures.

Comparing wages and salaries Efforts to determine whether public employees are overpaid have proceeded along two principal lines: (1) comparisons of public and private compensation for identical or very similar jobs (comparability studies) and (2) comparisons of public and private compensation for similar workers (human capital studies). There are difficulties with each approach, however. Many occupations are unique to either the public or private sector, and many other occupations that appear to be comparable may not be so upon closer inspection. (Similar job titles do not always indicate similar job content.) Determining whether workers are similar requires judgment about precisely which worker characteristics are relevant for the purpose of comparing pay.[62]

Unfortunately, the evidence from the recent literature is mixed, with some studies finding that state and local governments pay higher wages than private industry and others finding the reverse. For example, basing their analysis on aggregate data from the U.S. National Income and Product Accounts, Wendell Cox and Samuel Brunelli claimed that state and local government workers were indeed overpaid.[63] For the year 1991, for example, their data showed that the average annual pay of state and local government workers was 5.4 percent higher than the average pay received by private sector workers. And when fringe benefits were taken into account, the differential nearly doubled, to 10.3 percent. Cox and Brunelli used their findings to encourage legislators and local government managers to reduce costs by contracting out and privatizing certain government services.

However, because the mix of occupations and industries differs in the private and public sectors, *aggregate* comparisons that fail to control for these differences can be misleading. For example, professional workers—a relatively highly paid group—make up more than 40 percent of all local government employees but less than 10 percent of workers in the private sector. Government employees are also more than twice as likely to possess college degrees than are workers in the private sector.[64]

Another pair of researchers, Dale Belman and John Heywood, used Current Population Survey (CPS) data for 1989 to compare public and private sector earnings while controlling for both demographic and occupational differences. They concluded that average pay for state government employees was actually comparable to that in the private sector, while average pay for local government employees was between 4 and 5 percent below that in the private sector.[65] In the most recent study shedding light on the question, Michael Miller used occupational pay data for 1993 from the Occupational Compensation Survey of the U.S. Bureau of Labor Statistics. Miller concludes the following for thirty-five occupations:

At the low end of the pay scale, state and local governments paid higher wages than the private sector did.

For white-collar jobs, the private sector paid higher salaries than state and local governments.

Pay differences were mixed for technical, clerical, and blue-collar jobs.

For virtually all professional and administrative occupations, the private sector paid substantially higher salaries than did state and local governments.[66]

It is also important to note that there are sizable variations in pay levels across occupations. As Belman and Heywood point out in a later study:

> Occupation by occupation, the results can be dramatic. In 1992 private sector psychologists in Wisconsin earned nearly twice what their counterparts earned in the public sector, but the private sector paid a third less than the public sector for groundskeepers. Overall, the modest 2.9 percent local sector advantage in Wisconsin was actually the result of one set of occupations with a nearly 25 percent advantage being offset by a slightly larger group of occupations with a 20 percent disadvantage.[67]

And in a study of metropolitan transit workers, William Moore and Robert Newman found that Houston transit authority bus drivers were paid, on average, 68 percent more than their private sector counterparts and 24 percent more than truck drivers in the local labor market.[68]

Of those studies that compare public and private sector pay levels for workers with similar characteristics, the most widely cited findings are those of Sharon Smith, who first found in 1975 that men employed by local governments earned slightly less than their private sector counterparts, while women earned slightly more. When Smith analyzed new data several years later, she found that both men and women government employees were at a slight pay disadvantage.[69] A study by Alan Krueger found that as of the mid-1980s, state and local government employees (combined) were still earning slightly less than similar workers in the private sector.[70]

Substantial variation in public-private pay levels for comparable workers also exists across cities and states. In their later study of seven states (California, Illinois, Indiana, Michigan, Mississippi, Ohio, and Wisconsin), Belman and Heywood found (after controlling for worker characteristics and occupations) that the local government sector tended to pay lower wages than the private sector in all states except California. The differentials ranged from 3 to 10 percent.[71] More important, though, the sizable variation that Belman and Heywood found in the pattern of differentials across the states led them to conclude that aggregate comparisons of public and private sector pay differentials can be misleading.[72]

Overall, the evidence seems to indicate that although some municipal workers in certain occupations and localities may be more highly paid than their private sector counterparts, municipal workers are not, in the aggregate, "overpaid."

Comparing fringe benefits   Compared with those in the private sector, are fringe benefits in the public sector higher, more widespread, or both? As Daniel J. B. Mitchell points out, even before the emergence of widespread public sector unionism, all levels of government tended to pay a greater share of the compensation dollar in the form of fringe benefits than did the private sector.[73] Data from the CPS for 1997 show that 88 percent of full-time state and local public employees participated in employer-provided health care plans, versus only 66 percent of full-time private sector employees.[74] Also for 1997, CPS data show that 87 percent of all full-time state and local public employees participated in an employer-provided retirement plan, versus only 50 percent of full-time employees in the private sector.[75] In their comparison of public and private pension plans, Alicia Munnell and Ann Connolly found that public plans have also typically been more liberal, even though most public plans, unlike private sector plans, require employee contributions. Munnell and Connolly point out further that public plans are much more likely to have cost-of-living adjustments and to offer retirement at earlier ages than private plans.[76] (For a discussion of public pension plans, see Chapter 18 of this volume.)

Why have fringe benefits tended to be more generous in the public sector than in the private sector? The occupational mixes of the two sectors account for some of the differences. As already noted, the private sector includes a larger proportion of lower-paying occupations that are likely to have low fringe benefits as well (e.g., restaurant workers). But even after controlling for occupational differences, public sector fringe benefits are, on average, more widespread.[77] Successful bargaining by public sector unions is another reason for the differences. In the state and local public sector, union workers are more likely than nonunion workers to participate in employer-provided health care plans (as of 1997, 93 versus 83 percent) as well as in employer-provided retirement plans (as of 1997, 93 versus 82 percent).[78]

Finally, it should be noted that in the absence of collective bargaining, public sector wages are often set at prevailing levels in the private sector, whereas fringe benefits ordinarily are not. Decades ago, when pay levels in the public sector were often much lower than those in the private sector, higher fringe benefits and greater job security were considered to be trade-offs for lower wages. But the fact that queues of job applicants now exist for some local government jobs is evidence that these jobs today sometimes provide total compensation packages—wages, benefits, and job security—that are superior to those of private sector jobs.[79] To ensure that their employees are neither underpaid nor overpaid, local governments would therefore be well advised to apply prevailing standards to the *total* compensation package rather than to wages alone.

Collective bargaining and the budget

Although unions may not have had an inordinately large effect on pay in the public sector, it is generally still agreed that they have placed additional pressure on local government budgets. This pressure takes two forms: first, higher wage and benefit levels require larger budgets; second, the budget process itself has become subject to limitations imposed by collective bargaining.

In many jurisdictions, the timing and general procedures of the budget formulation process were developed when the local government exercised sole control over employee compensation. But these traditional practices may not be compatible with collective bargaining. For example, if negotiations continue through the date set for completion of the budget, the budget timetable breaks down. Budget makers cannot determine their final expenditure allocations, and they may have to reorder their funding allocations, find additional revenue sources, or risk a budget deficit. In short, bargaining is generally associated with a lessening of the public employer's ability to control the budget process and the budget schedule.

Local governments use a variety of techniques to cope with this diminished control over the budget. Ideally, contract talks should begin far in advance of the date set for final submission of the budget (some local governments begin the bargaining process as early as nine months before the beginning of the new fiscal year). In some states, legislation assists local governments to coordinate the collective bargaining and budget schedules. A Rhode Island statute, for example, requires advance notice for collective bargaining:

Whenever wages, rates of pay, or any other matter requiring appropriation of money by any city or town are included as a matter of collective bargaining . . . , it is the obligation of the bargaining agent to serve written notice of request for collective bargaining . . . at least one hundred twenty (120) days before the last day on which money can be appropriated by the city or town to cover the contract period which is the subject of the collective bargaining procedure.[80]

A Massachusetts statute stipulates that the employer and the exclusive bargaining representative "shall meet at reasonable times, including meetings in advance of the employer's budget-making process."[81] A number of other states also require collective bargaining to begin at a certain time in advance of budget setting, and some even link impasse procedures to dates in the budget schedule.

According to at least two studies, however, attempts to coordinate the budget and bargaining schedules are sometimes unsuccessful. In an early study, Milton Derber et al. found that although most of the Illinois governmental units that they studied linked the expiration dates of their bargaining contracts to the fiscal year, more than half of those units failed to reach agreement with the unions before the final budget date.[82] In a survey of Iowa municipalities, Richard Kearney reported similar problems with efforts to legislate coordination of the budget and bargaining schedules. Even though a provision in the Iowa Public Employee Relations Act sets a March 15 deadline for the completion of negotiations, many of the cities analyzed reported at least one existing contract dispute after the deadline.[83]

Another approach to synchronizing the bargaining and budget processes is to adopt budgets that include estimates of wage and salary levels that are still to be negotiated. In their survey of public bargaining practices in Illinois, Derber et al. found this practice to be fairly common.[84] Of course, if an estimated wage allowance proves to be too low, additional funds may have to be provided. In Derber's survey, such funds were normally obtained through supplemental appropriations, borrowing, tax increases, or transfers within or between funds. Adopting a budget that includes estimates of future wage settlements also raises questions about overbudgeting, or padding—that is, hiding within various budget categories funds that can be used to finance a higher-than-anticipated wage settlement. Although overbudgeting is used on occasion, the practice has disadvantages. Many public employers feel that skillful union negotiators can usually detect padded items in the budget-search process.[85] In fact, if union negotiators discover the overbudgeted amount and make it a target for additional bargaining demands, the tactic may even backfire.[86]

The long-term contract is another technique for limiting the frequency of clashes between collective bargaining and the budget schedule. Long-term contracts not only reduce the number of opportunities for negotiation impasses to interfere with the budgetary process, but also save the time and expense of yearly contract negotiations. The average duration of collective bargaining contracts in state and local governments is about two years, but contracts of three, four, and even five years are sometimes negotiated.[87] State bargaining statutes may limit contract duration, however; in Kansas, Maine, and Massachusetts, for example, contracts may not exceed three years.

Although unionism places pressure on both the size of local government budgets and the budget-making process, both bargaining and budget making are fairly flexible processes that can be adjusted somewhat if they do not initially mesh.[88] For the public employer, an informed and well-thought-out negotiating strategy is the principal requirement for a successful, and relatively swift, negotiation process. Included in such a strategy should be a set of positive proposals regarding wages, salaries, and fringe benefits. These proposals should be based on information such as pay levels in other communities, conditions in the local labor market, and changes in the consumer price index.

Among the most important elements of the public employer's negotiations strategy is a detailed costing of all union demands, not only to prevent later budget overruns but also to inform the union negotiators, who may be unaware of the true costs of a proposal. Labor is the most costly item in the operation of local governments, and unless the public employer can estimate the financial impact of potential changes in wages, fringe benefits, and other provisions of a collective bargaining agreement, it is difficult to evaluate and respond to union proposals or to make informed counterproposals.[89] A careful costing of union proposals should consider in particular the following elements:

The current level of base compensation costs. All proposals and counterproposals must be evaluated with reference to existing compensation costs.

Ripple effects. Increases in wages and salaries will often result in increases in other components of compensation, such as overtime and vacations. Furthermore, agreements with one group of workers may have an impact on what is demanded by or offered to other groups of union and nonunion employees. A city that offers its police officers a substantial pay increase may well find its firefighters demanding a similar increase.

Health insurance. With the substantial increases in health care costs in recent years, public employers should not only carefully evaluate the impact of union proposals on existing health care plans but also investigate ways of containing or reducing plan costs (e.g., through employee contributions).

Pensions. Pension plans are complex, and it is essential to obtain the advice of experts when costing out the impact of union demands and counterproposals relating to pensions. Changes to pension plans, of course, can have a substantial impact not only during the life of the collective bargaining agreement but also for many years down the road.[90]

It is also important to cost out each element of a union proposal separately and to do so from management's viewpoint, rather than from that of the union. For example, a proposal to increase the number of vacation days must also consider either the cost of going without the services performed or the cost of replacing those services.[91]

Finally, the effects of the compounding of pay increases should not be overlooked. Although a union might claim that its demand of a 4 percent pay raise each year for three years amounts to an overall 12 percent increase, the actual increase over the contract period would be approximately 12.5 percent.[92]

Controversial issues in public sector bargaining

The next two sections consider the subjects of comparable worth and contracting out, two controversial issues that have major implications for public sector bargaining.

Comparable worth

Comparable worth, or pay equity, emerged in the mid-1980s as a significant issue in public sector compensation and union-management bargaining. Comparable worth is not by its nature restricted to the public sector, but the implementation of its principles has so far occurred largely within the state and local government sector.

According to the principles of comparable worth, two jobs that are dissimilar but can be shown to be of comparable worth, or value, to an employer, deserve equal compensation. The concept of comparable worth developed because of disparities in the pay of men and women. Despite nearly four decades of enforcement of civil rights and equal-pay laws, the average earnings of full-time female employees are still only about 75 percent of the earnings of full-time male employees. As both proponents and opponents of comparable worth agree, the problem does not derive primarily from wage discrimination: the Equal Pay Act of 1963 prohibits employers from paying women less than men for the same jobs. Instead, much of the wage disparity arises from the fact that female workers are heavily concentrated in a small number of occupational categories that tend to pay low wages (e.g., secretarial work, nursing, and teaching).

In *County of Washington v. Gunther,* the U.S. Supreme Court opened the door to judicial consideration of sex-based discrimination charges involving interoccupational wage differences.[93] The case concerned female prison matrons (guards), whose pay was only 75 percent of that of male prison guards, although a job evaluation had determined that the matrons' jobs were worth 95 percent of the male guards' jobs. Although the Court refused to endorse the comparable worth theory as such, it did rule that the county had discriminated against the matrons, and it ordered pay remedies.

Since the *Gunther* decision, many additional comparable worth suits have been filed. A number of unions have been active in pursuing such litigation—mainly AFSCME and the SEIU, but also the American Nurses Association, the Communications Workers of America, and others. Although for the most part the courts have not been very receptive to the concept of comparable worth, a considerable number of out-of-court settlements have resulted in pay adjustments for public employees in occupations dominated by women.

In addition, at least twenty states have established pay-equity programs that affect some state employees—and, in Minnesota, local government employees as well. Furthermore, many other states have set up task forces, authorized pay-equity studies, or appropriated funds to eliminate pay differences. Finally, a growing number of local government collective bargaining contracts contain provisions concerning pay equity—allowing, for example, for the upgrading of positions or the commissioning of pay-equity studies.

Comparable worth/pay-equity policies have met with a considerable amount of criticism. Opponents have argued, for example, that (1) such policies ignore existing labor market conditions (i.e., market forces of demand and supply); (2) most of the gap between the earnings of men and women is caused by factors other than discrimination; and (3) job-evaluation techniques, which are central to comparable worth systems, are greatly influenced by the choice of factors and weights. Proponents of comparable worth policies, on the other hand, argue that many jobs are still earmarked for one sex or the other and that businesses have successfully used job evaluation techniques for many decades.[94]

Whatever the merits of the arguments of either side, comparable worth continues to be one of the most important compensation issues of the last several decades. Although comparable worth has established a legal foothold in the public sector, it has yet to do so in the private sector. Interestingly, however, Ontario, Canada, enacted a comparable worth policy (the Pay Equity Act) in the late 1980s that applies to both public and private sector jobs—the first such policy in North America. And in the United States, several bills with very similar language to that of the Ontario legislation have been introduced in Congress. One such bill, the Fair Pay Act, would outlaw discrimination in the workplace in "equivalent jobs." The act would also require employers to provide equal pay for work of equivalent value—that is, for jobs that may be dissimilar but that require equivalent skills, effort, responsibility, and working conditions.[95]

How should public employers respond to the considerable level of interest in comparable worth? It is not clear whether employers who do not currently have job-evaluation systems should initiate them. Some legal advisors contend that undertaking job-evaluation studies may provide potential plaintiffs with ammunition for future pay-equity suits. Some human resource professionals, on the other hand, suggest that a carefully designed pay study may be useful in dealing with comparable worth claims.[96]

According to the American Society for Personnel Administration (ASPA), public employers should consider a number of questions in deciding whether to undertake a pay study. If the answers to the questions are yes, ASPA suggests that a pay study is probably appropriate:

Is there a need to bring coherence to a wage structure that has developed in an ad hoc fashion over the years?

Are managers spending a considerable amount of time determining salaries for new positions or adjusting individual wages?

Do employees view the wage system as haphazard or unfair?

Would a job-evaluation system show that some employees' wage demands are inconsistent with the worth of their positions to the organization?[97]

Contracting out

In recent years, many local governments have experienced fiscal stress and increasing taxpayer demands for greater efficiency in public service provision. One of the most controversial responses to these pressures has taken the form of contracting out, or privatizing, government services. Although the terms are often used synonymously (as will be done here), there is a slight distinction between the two. *Privatization,* the broader term, has generally been defined as any process aimed at shifting functions in whole or in part from government to the private sector. *Contracting out* refers to the hiring of private sector firms to provide goods or services to the government. Under this arrangement, the government remains the financier and also retains management and policy control over the type and quality of goods and services provided.[98]

Contracting out is not a new phenomenon: many state and local governments have long contracted out for certain services. Since the early 1990s, both state and local governments have increased the extent of their privatization efforts, with many long-standing government services now being provided by the private sector. A 2002 survey conducted by the International City/County Management Association found that 50 percent or more jurisdictions contracted out vehicle towing and storage; the operation of day care facilities, homeless shelters, drug and alcohol treatment programs, mental health programs and facilities, and hospitals; legal services; and cultural and arts programs. It also found contracting out to be prevalent in the areas of utility operation and management; job training programs; museums, disposal of hazardous materials; commercial and residential solid waste collection and disposal, and fleet and vehicle maintenance.[99]

Public sector unions have generally been strongly opposed to contracting out. In addition to citing the obvious effects on local government employment, unions complain that contracting out is not necessarily cheaper or more efficient. AFSCME, one of the strongest opponents, has argued that the transfer of services to the private sector often results in lower quality and a loss of accountability. Calling privatization of government jobs "the most important issue facing the union,"[100] AFSCME president Gerald McEntee has also charged that many private sector contractors "lowball" their initial service contracts only to raise them later.[101] Other opponents have claimed that privatization may not only result in higher costs and lower service quality but also engender corruption and employment discrimination.[102]

Although the arguments of AFSCME and other public sector unions may primarily reflect self-interest, the fact remains that privatization efforts have not always been successful. According to a report by the National League of Cities, 54 percent of elected officials surveyed reported that contracting out had been "somewhat successful," with the remainder split between calling such efforts "very successful" and "not at all successful."[103] In some cases, projected cost savings in fact turn out to be simply cost-shifting, with costs shifted either to another budget or to the future.[104]

It is also sometimes difficult to make valid cost comparisons between public and private sector service provision. Refuse collection provides a case in point. As Stanley Wisniewski points out, differences in objectives can obscure cost differences. For example, local government trash collection may have multiple goals: to pick up garbage, to keep streets and alleys free of refuse, and even to provide employment opportunities for disadvantaged workers.[105] Therefore, comparisons based solely on trash pickup costs may be misleading. In any case, before private suppliers are engaged, it is important for the public manager to provide a clear specification of both the quantity and quality of the services to be provided.

Other costs associated with switching to private suppliers may also not be immediately obvious. For example, contracting out may cause morale problems, adversely affecting the productivity of the current workforce. In the case of professional services, contracting out may leave the local government employer without a core of experienced employees for future needs. According to Wisniewski, engineers, for example,

may find it difficult to maintain their skills or may never develop certain important skills due to the lack of opportunity to work on significant complex projects. This means that current government understaffing due to contracting out may well lead to higher contractor-associated costs in the future, particularly given the likelihood of a viable competitive alternative in-house.[106]

And, as Robert Kuttner has put it, the specialized knowledge that formerly resided in the government "flips over to the vendor."[107] Overall, though, it is important to keep in mind that the primary purpose of privatization is greater efficiency. Therefore, if a function or service is more effectively provided by public employees, as will sometimes be the case, that function or service should remain public.[108]

Must privatization plans and efforts be negotiated with unions? Whether contracting out is a mandatory subject of collective bargaining depends on the jurisdiction. Some states (e.g., New York) have held contracting out to be a mandatory bargaining subject while others have not, with contracting out sometimes ruled to be a matter of managerial policy. As Marvin Levine points out, there has also been significant variation in arbitration awards dealing with contracting-out disputes.[109]

What additional advice for dealing with workers and unions might be given to the public manager who is considering contracting out certain public services? According to management attorney M. Joan Foster, public employers considering privatizing should give workers plenty of notice, keeping them informed at every step. Public employers should also involve workers in privatization discussions and give them the opportunity to retrain and adapt to change.[110] Finally, arbitrator Francis X. Quinn warns that even though a collective bargaining contract might not contain specific language limiting the right to contract out, doing so may still violate the contract if it is found to be "contrary to the spirit of the contract as a whole." Quinn notes that in the view of arbitrators, certain contract provisions, such as layoff clauses, have, in effect, been "rendered a nullity" in the event of contracting out.[111]

Conclusion

What does the immediate future hold for unionism and collective bargaining in the local government sector? In all likelihood, union density—the percentage of local government employees who are unionized—will grow, although probably at a relatively slow rate. A favorable legal environment is a very important determinant of whether public sector employers bargain collectively with their employees, but the rate at which new public employee bargaining legislation has been passed has slowed considerably since the early 1980s. There are still a number of states without such legislation, and several proposals to enact a federal law authorizing public sector collective bargaining have not generated widespread support. On the other hand, union density in the public sector will continue to dwarf that in the private sector, just as it has over the past several decades. Moreover, public sector unions will continue to rank among the largest and most influential unions in the country.[112]

With many public employers facing tight budgets and feeling increased pressures to restructure, downsize, and privatize, it is also unlikely that the impact of public sector unions on either wages or fringe benefits will increase in the future. Yet unions are likely to continue to play an active role on the comparable worth front, where their efforts have thus far had a sizable impact on the pay of women workers in the municipal sector.

1 U.S. Department of Labor, Bureau of Labor Statistics, "Union Members in 2002," *USDL News,* USDL 03-88, 25 February 2003, 1.

2 Barry Hirsch and David Macpherson, *Union Membership and Earnings Data Book* (Washington, D.C.: Bureau of National Affairs, 2002), 10.

3 Bureau of Labor Statistics, "Union Members," 1.

4 Hirsch and Macpherson, *Union Membership,* 16.

5 Leo Troy and Neil Sheflin, "The Flow and Ebb of U.S. Public Sector Unionism," *Government Union Review* (spring 1984): 1–2.

6 Bureau of Labor Statistics, "Union Members," 1.

7 Ibid.

8 Sar Levitan and Frank Gallo, "Can Employee Associations Negotiate New Growth?" *Monthly Labor Review* 112 (July 1989): 12–13.

9 John Delaney and Peter Feuille, "Police," in *Collective Bargaining in American Industry,* ed. David B. Lipsky and Clifford Donn (Lexington, Mass.: Lexington Books, 1987), 280.

10 Paul F. Clark, "Health Care: A Growing Role for Collective Bargaining," in *Collective Bargaining in the Private Sector,* ed. Paul F. Clark, John T. Delaney, and Ann C. Frost (Chicago: Industrial Relations Research Association, 2002), 104.

11 Ibid.

12 See "Police, Firefighter Unions Testify in Favor of Bill Setting State Bargaining Standards," *Government Employee Relations Report* (16 May 2000): 598. In addition, several unions (including AFSCME) have lobbied for federal legislation to give all public employees collective bargaining rights.

13 Joyce Najita and James Stern, "Introduction and Overview," in *Collective Bargaining in the Public Sector: The Experience of Eight States,* ed. Joyce Najita and James Stern (Armonk, N.Y.: M. E. Sharpe, 2001), 5; B. V. H. Schneider, "Public Sector Labor Legislation: An Evolutionary Analysis," in *Public Sector Bargaining,* 2nd ed., ed. Benjamin Aaron, Joyce Najita, and James Stern (Washington, D.C.: Bureau of National Affairs, 1988),

190–191; and John Lund and Cheryl Maranto, "Public Sector Labor Law: An Update," in *Public Sector Employment in a Time of Transition,* ed. Dale Belman, Morley Gunderson, and Douglas Hyatt (Madison, Wis.: Industrial Relations Research Association, 1996).

14 AFL-CIO, Public Employee Department, *Public Employees Bargain for Excellence: A Compendium of State Public Sector Labor Relations Laws* (AFL-CIO, 1997), 2.

15 As of 2002, the nine states were Arizona, Arkansas, Colorado, Louisiana, Mississippi, North Carolina, South Carolina, Virginia, and West Virginia. Public employee bargaining bills have been introduced, although unsuccessfully, in several of these states. Lund and Maranto, "Public Sector Labor Law," 52–54.

16 Schneider, "Labor Legislation," 192.

17 *Labor Management Relations Act,* title 1, sec. 8(d) (1947).

18 Najita and Stern, "Introduction and Overview," 10.

19 Pennsylvania, *Public Employee Relations Act,* sec. 702 (1970). In 1992, Pennsylvania passed Act 88, which changed certain bargaining provisions for public school employees. However, the scope-of-bargaining provisions in Act 88 remain virtually identical to those of Act 195.

20 Nevada, *Local Government Employee-Management Relations Act,* 288.010 et seq., as summarized in Public Employee Department, *Compendium,* 41.

21 *Government Employee Relations Report* 31 (26 April 1993): 574.

22 Schneider, "Labor Legislation," 211.

23 "Conference Report: NPELRA" *Government Employer Relations Report* (22 April 1996): 606.

24 Robert Allen and Timothy Keaveny, *Contemporary Labor Relations,* 2nd ed. (Reading, Mass.: Addison-Wesley, 1988), 466–467.

25 Schneider, "Labor Legislation," 220.

26 *Abood v. Detroit Board of Education,* 431 U.S. 209; 95 LRRM 2411 (1977).

27 *Lehnert v. Ferris Faculty Association,* 500 U.S. 507 (1991).

28 Public Employee Department, *Compendium.*

29 Schneider, "Labor Legislation," 224.

30 Lund and Maranto, "Public Sector Labor Law," 45–46.

31 Ibid.

32 Ibid.

33 The ten states and the dates of statutory authorization are Alaska (1974 and 1992), Hawaii (1970), Illinois (1983), Minnesota (1975), Montana (1969), Ohio (1983), Oregon (1973), Pennsylvania (1970 and 1992), Vermont (1967), and Wisconsin (1977). The four states where courts have ruled that public sector strikes are legal are California, Colorado, Idaho, and Louisiana. See Najita and Stern, "Introduction and Overview," 13, 20.

34 *Oregon Revised Statutes,* sec. 243.650 et seq., as summarized in Bureau of National Affairs, *Government Employee Relations Report,* Digest of State Public Employee Bargaining Statutes, reference file 254 (Washington, D.C.: Bureau of National Affairs, 16 November 1987).

35 Robert Hebdon, "Public Sector Dispute Resolution in Transition," in Belman, Gunderson, and Hyatt, *Public Sector Employment,* 85; and Michael Cimini, "1982–87 State and Local Government Work Stoppages and Their Legal Background," *Compensation and Working Conditions* (fall 1998). Data for 1999–2002 are unpublished data provided to the author by Ann Foster, U.S. Bureau of Labor Statistics.

36 Najita and Stern, "Introduction and Overview," 15.

37 Schneider, "Labor Legislation," 208.

38 See Hebdon, "Dispute Resolution."

39 Dale Belman and John Heywood, "The Structure of Compensation in the Public Sector," in Belman, Gunderson, and Hyatt, *Public Sector Employment,* 127.

40 Albert E. Schwenk, "Compensation Cost Trends in Private Industry and State and Local Governments," *Compensation and Working Conditions* (fall 1999): 13–18.

41 Ibid.

42 Harry Katz and David Lewin, "Efficiency and Equity Considerations in State and Local Government Wage Determination," in *Proceedings of the Thirty-Third Annual Meeting of the Industrial Relations Research Association* (Champaign, Ill.: Industrial Relations Research Association, 1980), 90–91.

43 Walter Fogel and David Lewin, "Wage Determination in the Public Sector," *Industrial and Labor Relations Review* 27 (April 1974): 411–414.

44 Charles Brown and James Medoff, "The Employer Size-Wage Effect," *Journal of Political Economy* 97 (October 1989): 1027–1059.

45 Employer monopsony (literally, one buyer) will generally lead to lower wage levels than would exist in a competitive labor market.

46 Fogel and Lewin, "Wage Determination," 417–423. Note that the presence of a potential upward bias in public sector pay (compared with private sector pay) does not necessarily mean that public sector pay levels tend to be *unfairly* high. For example, the pay levels of some women workers in the private sector may be lower because of discrimination.

47 David Lewin, "Wage Parity and the Supply of Police and Firemen," *Industrial Relations* 12 (February 1973): 77–85.

48 Larry Hoover, Jerry Dowling, and Eugene Bowley Jr., "The Erosion of Police and Firefighter Wage Parity," *Monthly Labor Review* (April 1996): 13–20.

49 According to Fogel and Lewin ("Wage Determination," 416), public employees in managerial and professional jobs tend to be more "visible" to a public that is largely skeptical of the value of highly paid employees.

50 For example, according to the Labor Management Relations Act (title 1, sec. 1), the "inequality of bargaining power between employees . . . and certain employers" was one of the justifications for implementing the policies of the act.

51 Neil Chamberlain and James Kuhn, *Collective Bargaining* (New York: McGraw-Hill, 1965).

52 The elasticity of demand for labor can be defined as the percent change in the quantity of labor demanded given a 1 percent change in the wage.

53 For a classic discussion of the arguments concerning the bargaining power of public sector unions, see Harry Wellington and Ralph Winter, "The Limits of Collective Bargaining in Public Employment," *Yale Law Journal* 78 (June 1969).

54 Richard B. Freeman, "Unionism Comes to the Public Sector," *Journal of Economic Literature* 24 (March 1986): 51.

55 H. Gregg Lewis, "Union Relative Wage Effects," in *Handbook of Labor Economics,* ed. O. Ashenfelter and R. Layard (New York: North Holland, 1986).

56 H. Gregg Lewis, "Union/Nonunion Wage Gaps in the Public Sector," *Journal of Labor Economics* 8, no. 1, pt. 2 (January 1990): s321.

57 Lewis, "Wage Gaps," 323.

58 Richard B. Freeman, "The Effect of Unionism on Fringe Benefits," *Industrial and Labor Relations Review* 34 (July 1981): 489–510. The most detailed survey of local government fringe benefits is the annual *Municipal Employee Benefits Survey* prepared by Workplace Economics, Inc., in Washington, D.C. The survey presents detailed information on fringe benefits for police officers, firefighters, and sanitation workers in approximately two dozen large cities. The cost of benefits is not averaged across the cities, however.

59 Casey Ichniowski, "Economic Effects of the Firefighters Union," *Industrial and Labor Relations Review* 33 (January 1980): 198–211.

60 Linda Edwards and Franklin Edwards, "Public Unions, Local Government Structure, and the Compensation of Municipal Sanitation Workers," *Economic Inquiry* 20 (July 1982): 405–425.

61 Jeffrey Zax, "Wages, Nonwage Compensation, and Municipal Unions," *Industrial Relations* 27 (fall 1988): 314.

62 Belman and Heywood, "Structure of Compensation," 136–144.

63 Wendell Cox and Samuel Brunelli, "America's Protected Class III, the Unfair Pay Advantage of Public Employees," *The State Factor* (April 1994): 1–34. The Cox-Brunelli studies have been the object of some criticism. See, for example, "Compensation for Public Employees Said to Rise Faster than Private Compensation," *Government Employee Relations Report* (16 May 1994): 529–531.

64 Michael Miller, "The Public-Private Pay Debate: What Do the Data Show?" *Monthly Labor Review* (May 1996): 20.

65 Ibid. Miller refers to Dale Belman and John Heywood, *The Truth about Public Employees: Underpaid or Overpaid?* Briefing Papers (Economic Policy Institute, April 1993).

66 Miller, "Pay Debate," 18.

67 Belman and Heywood, "Structure of Compensation," 139.

68 William Moore and Robert Newman, "Government Wage Differentials in a Municipal Labor Market: The Case of Houston Metropolitan Transit Workers," *Industrial and Labor Relations Review* 45 (October 1991): 148.

69 Sharon Smith, "Are State and Local Government Workers Overpaid?" in *The Economics of Municipal Labor Markets,* ed. W. Z. Hirsch and A. M. Rufolo (Los Angeles: Institute of Industrial Relations, University of California at Los Angeles, 1983).

70 Alan Krueger, "Are Public Sector Workers Paid More?" in *When Public Sector Workers Unionize,* ed. Richard Freeman and Casey Ichniowski (Chicago: University of Chicago Press, 1988), 237.

71 Belman and Heywood, "Structure of Compensation," 147.

72 Dale Belman and John Heywood, "State and Local Government Wage Differentials: An Interstate Analysis," *Journal of Labor Research* 16 (spring 1995): 199.

73 Daniel J. B. Mitchell, "Collective Bargaining and Compensation in the Public Sector," in Aaron, Najita, and Stern, eds., *Public Sector Bargaining,* 141.

74 Diane Herz, Joseph Meisenheimer, and Harriet Weinstein, "Health and Retirement Benefits: Data from Two BLS Surveys," *Monthly Labor Review* 123 (March 2000): 8.

75 Ibid., 13. Estimates from the Department of Labor's Employee Benefits Survey (EBS) put this percentage even higher: at 95 percent for 1994. It is not clear why the CPS and EBS estimates should vary by this much, but one possible explanation is that many respondents to the household-based CPS lack accurate knowledge about their retirement plans.

76 Alicia H. Munnell and Ann M. Connolly, "Comparability of Public and Private Compensation: The Issue of Fringe Benefits," *New England Economic Review* (July/August 1979): 29–45.

77 Bradley Braden and Stephanie Hyland, "Cost of Employee Compensation in Public and Private Sectors," *Monthly Labor Review* 116 (May 1993): 19–20.

78 Herz, Meisenheimer, and Weinstein, "Health and Retirement Benefits," 13.

79 John Heywood and Madhu Mohanty, "Testing for State and Local Job Queues," *Journal of Labor Research* 14 (fall 1993): 464.

80 *Rhode Island General Laws,* Labor and Labor Relations, title 28 at 28-9 (1992), 1–13.

81 *Massachusetts Ann. Laws,* ch. 150E at 6.

82 Milton Derber et al., "Bargaining and Budget Making in Illinois Public Institutions," *Industrial and Labor Relations Review* 27 (October 1973): 49.

83 Richard C. Kearney, "Monetary Impact of Collective Bargaining," in *Handbook on Public Personnel Administration and Labor Relations,* ed. Jack Rabin et al. (New York: Marcel Dekker, 1983), 368.

84 Derber et al., "Bargaining," 57.

85 Ibid.

86 David Stanley, *Managing Local Government under Union Pressure* (Washington, D.C.: Brookings Institution, 1972), 83.

87 Charles Muhl, "Collective Bargaining in State and Local Government, 1994," *Monthly Labor Review* 116 (June 1995): 15.

88 Derber et al., "Bargaining," 61.

89 Sam Ashbaugh, "The Art and Science of Costing Labor Contracts," *Government Finance Review* 18 (December 2002): 33.

90 Ibid.

91 Fred Lunenberg, "Collective Bargaining in the Public Schools: Issues, Tactics, and New Strategies," *Journal of Collective Negotiations in the Public Sector* 29, no. 4 (2000): 265–266.

92 The compounded percentage change is calculated as $(1.04)^3 - 1 = 0.125$, or 12.5 percent.

93 452 U.S. 161 (1981).

94 Barbara Bergmann, "Does the Market for Women's Labor Need Fixing?" *Journal of Economic Perspectives* 3 (winter 1989): 43–60.

95 "Clinton Asks Employers to Consider Using 'Fair Pay Equity' Policies," *Government Employee Relations Report* (22 April 1996): 598.

96 "Plan Compensation Studies Carefully Due to Pay Equity Climate, ASPA Says," *Government Employer Relations Report* 23 (20 May 1985): 750.

97 American Society for Personnel Administration (ASPA), *Sex and Salary: A Legal and Personnel Analysis of Comparable Worth* (Alexandria, Va.: ASPA Foundation, 1985).

98 U.S. General Accounting Office (GAO), *Privatization: Lessons Learned by State and Local Governments,* GAO/GGD-97-48 (Washington, D.C.: GAO, 1997), 26, 28.

99 Mildred Warner and Amir Hefetz, "Pragmatism over Politics: Alternative Service Delivery in Local Government, 1992–2002," *The Municipal Year Book 2004* (Washington, D.C.: International City/County Management Association, 2004), 11.

100 "McEntee Calls Privatization Biggest Issue," *Government Employee Relations Report* (29 March 1999): 362.

101 "AFSCME Calls for Partnerships between Public Sector Employers and Employees," *Government Employee Relations Report* (18 November 1996): 1608.

102 AFL-CIO, Public Employee Department, *America . . . Not for Sale* (Washington, D.C.: Public Employee Department, AFL-CIO, 1989).

103 "Cities Remain Skeptical of Success of Privatization, League Survey Says," *Government Employee Relations Report* (20 January 1997).

104 "Extent of Contracting Out May Be Overstated, Task Force Says," *Government Employee Relations Report* (17 June 1996): 883.

105 Stanley C. Wisniewski, "A Framework for Considering the Contracting Out of Government Services," *Public Personnel Management* 21 (spring 1992): 102.

106 Ibid., 109.

107 "Disadvantages of Privatization Not Readily Apparent, Author Says," *Government Employee Relations Report* (23 January 2001): 105.

108 "Workshops Offer Tips on Managing Privatization, Workforce Reductions," *Government Employee Relations Report* (22 April 1996): 608.

109 Marvin J. Levine, "Subcontracting and 'Privatization' of Work: Private and Public Sector Developments," *Journal of Collective Negotiations in the Public Sector* 19, no. 4 (1990): 280.

110 "Advice on Privatization in New Jersey Offered NJELRA by Management Attorney," *Government Employee Relations Report* (16 October 1995): 1322–1323.

111 "Bargaining Rights in Downsizing," *Government Employee Relations Report* (31 March 1997): 436.

112 "Continuing Influence Predicted of Unions in Public Employment," *Government Employee Relations Report* (22 April 1996): 604.

Glossary

account   A separate financial reporting unit for budgeting, management, or accounting purposes. All budgetary transactions, whether revenue or expenditure, are recorded in accounts. See also *fund, chart of accounts.*

accounting standards   The generally accepted accounting principles, promulgated by the Governmental Accounting Standards Board, that guide the recording and reporting of financial information by state and local governments.

accrual basis of accounting   A method of accounting in which revenues are recorded when measurable and earned, and expenses are recognized when a good or service is used. See also *cash basis of accounting, modified accrual basis of accounting.*

activity   A departmental effort that contributes to the accomplishment of specific, identified program objectives

allotment   The distribution of budget authority by an agency to various subunits.

apportionment   The release of funds on a quarterly or project basis by the budget office.

appropriation   Legal authorization to make expenditures or enter into obligations for specific purposes.

assessed property value   The value assigned to property for the purpose of levying property taxes.

audit   An examination, usually by an official or a private accounting firm, that reports on the accuracy of the annual financial report.

balanced budget   A budget in which current revenues equal current expenditures; may be required by state law or local ordinance.

benefits-received principle   A principle under which users or those who benefit from a service pay for at least a portion of the cost of providing that service.

biennial budget   A budget that covers a two-year period.

bond   A promise to repay borrowed money on a particular date, often ten or twenty years in the future; most bonds also involve a promise to pay a specified dollar amount of interest at predetermined intervals.

bond covenant   A legally enforceable agreement with bondholders that requires the governmental agency selling the bond to meet certain conditions in the repayment of the debt.

budget   A spending plan that balances revenues and expenditures over a fixed time period (usually a year) and that includes, at least by implication, a work plan.

budget calendar   A timetable showing when particular tasks must be completed in order for the governing body to approve the spending plan before the beginning of the next fiscal year.

budget cycle   The recurring process—either annual or biennial—in which a government prepares, adopts, and implements a spending plan.

callable bonds   Bonds that may be redeemed at the option of the issuer on the call date at a price equal to the call price. The specific conditions under which the bonds may be called are identified in the bond indenture.

capital assets   Items that cost a considerable amount of money and that are intended to last a long time (e.g., buildings, land, roads, bridges, and water treatment plants). Also known as fixed assets.

capital budget   A spending plan for the acquisition of (or improvements to) land, facilities, or infrastructure.

capital improvements program (CIP)   A plan that identifies the capital projects to be funded during the planning horizon (usually five years). The CIP is updated annually, and the first year of the plan serves as the current-year capital budget.

capital outlay   Spending on fixed assets; generally, such expenditures exceed a specified amount or are for purchases intended to last more than one year.

capital projects funds   Governmental funds established to account for resources used for the acquisition of large capital improvements other than those accounted for in proprietary or fiduciary funds.

cash basis of accounting   A method of accounting in which revenues are recorded only when cash is received and expenditures are recorded only when payment is made. See also *accrual basis of accounting.*

cash flow   The net cash balance at any given point.

chart of accounts   A chart that assigns a unique number to each type of transaction (e.g., salaries or property taxes) and to each budgetary unit in an organization.

comprehensive annual financial report (CAFR)   A report that summarizes financial data for the previous fiscal year in a standardized format.

contingency account   An account set aside to meet unforeseen circumstances.

coupon rate   The interest rate that will be paid to the bondholders.

credit enhancement   A guarantee provided by a third party to pay the interest and principal on a bond if the issuer is unable to make the required payments.

debt policy   A policy that establishes the guidelines for an issuer's use of debt.

debt service   Annual or periodic principal and interest payments on debt; can sometimes include certain other fees (e.g., annual renewal fees for letters of credit).

debt service funds   One or more funds established to account for expenditures used to repay the principal and interest on debt.

default   Failure to make a debt payment (principal or interest) on time.

defeasement   The legal release of the bondholders' lien on the assets or revenues pledged by the issuer, which is given in exchange for the pledge of cash or securities sufficient to repay the bonds.

deterministic forecasting techniques   Revenue projection methods that rely on a simple mathematical formula.

Dillon's Rule   A rule under which local governments have only those powers specifically delegated to them by state law.

disbursement   Payment for goods or services that have been delivered and invoiced.

earmarking   Legal limitations on the revenue from fees, licenses, taxes, or grants that determine how the funds may be spent.

econometric forecasting   A revenue projection technique in which (1) the yield from a particular revenue source is assumed to be affected by a number of factors (such as per capita income, inflation, and population change), (2) historical data are used to estimate the weights for each factor, and (3) a statistical model is developed that determines the effect of the various factors on a given revenue source.

economies of scale   The cost savings that usually occur with increases in output; economies of scale result when fixed costs are divided among more units, resulting in lower costs per unit.

encumbrance   Budget authority that is set aside when a purchase order or contract is approved. Also known as an obligation. See also *purchase order.*

enterprise fund   A separate fund used to account for services supported primarily by service charges.

enterprises   Government-owned services, such as utilities, that are supported primarily by fees rather than by tax revenues.

entitlement program   A program in which funding is allocated according to eligibility criteria: any agencies or individuals that meet the criteria specified in law receive the benefit.

executive budget   A proposed budget put together by the chief executive or his or her designees for review and approval or modification by the governing body.

face value   See *maturity value.*

fiduciary funds   Funds that account for resources that governments hold in trust for individuals or other governments.

financial report   See *comprehensive annual financial report.*

fiscal year   A designated twelve-month period for budgeting and record-keeping purposes.

fixed assets   See *capital assets.*

floating-rate bond   See *variable-rate bond.*

full-time equivalent The number of hours per year that a full-time employee is expected to work.

fund A self-balancing set of accounts. Governmental accounting information is organized into funds, each with separate revenues, expenditures, and fund balances.

fund balance The difference between a fund's assets and its liabilities.

general fund The major fund in most governmental units; accounts for all activities (especially tax-funded functions, such as police and fire protection) not accounted for in other funds.

general obligation (GO) bond A bond that is backed by the government's unconditional ability to raise taxes. See also *revenue bond*.

generally accepted accounting principles (GAAP) Uniform minimum standards used by state and local governments for financial recording and reporting; established by the accounting profession through the Governmental Accounting Standards Board (GASB).

Governmental Accounting Standards Board (GASB) The body that sets accounting standards specifically for governmental entities at the state and local levels.

grant A payment of money, often earmarked for a specific purpose or program, from one governmental unit to another or from a governmental unit to a not-for-profit agency.

gross underwriter spread The compensation earned by the underwriting syndicate for selling bonds to investors; specifically, the difference between the sale price received by the underwriting syndicate and the amount paid by the underwriting syndicate to the issuer; usually stated as a dollar amount per $1,000 of par value.

home rule The power granted municipalities and counties to draft their own laws and control purely local matters without intervention from the state legislature.

impound To restrict spending; impoundments are generally at the discretion of the chief executive.

income-elastic revenue Revenue that increases or decreases at a greater rate than the economy expands or contracts; general sales tax revenue is an example.

incremental budgeting A budgeting process in which precedent determines how funds will be allocated among departments and programs; thus, increases in allocations usually occur in small increments over past levels.

independent auditor An accounting firm (or, occasionally, a state or local official not associated with the local government) who reviews the comprehensive annual financial report and compares it with a sample of financial transactions in order to certify that the report accurately represents the fiscal condition of the governmental unit.

interfund transfer The transfer of money from one fund to another in a governmental unit; such transfers usually require the approval of the governing body and are subject to restrictions in state and local law.

interim financial reports Quarterly or monthly comparisons of budgeted with actual revenues and expenditures to date.

internal rate of return A criterion used to calculate the desirability of capital projects: the rate of return from the project should be higher than the cost of capital to pay for the project.

internal service funds Funds that account for the goods and services provided by one department to another on a fee-for-service basis.

judgmental forecasting A method of projecting revenues that relies on the judgment of experts. Also known as a professional guess.

limited-tax general obligation bond A type of bond that is backed by special taxes, specific revenue sources, or a maximum property tax millage rate.

line-item budget A budget format in which departmental outlays are grouped according to the items that will be purchased, with one item or group of items on each line. See also *objects of expenditure*.

line-item veto A rejection by the executive of one item or group of items in a line-item budget. See also *veto*.

mandate A requirement from a higher level of government that a lower level of government perform a task, usually to meet a particular standard, and often without compensation from the higher level of government.

marginal cost The additional cost of providing service to one more consumer.

maturity date The date at which the issuer is obligated to repay the principal amount of the bond to the bondholder.

maturity value   The dollar or principal amount of a bond; this amount is used to determine the periodic interest payments and is repaid to the bondholder at maturity. Also known as par value or face value.

modified accrual basis of accounting   A form of accrual accounting in which (1) expenditures are recognized when the goods or services are received and (2) revenues, such as taxes, are recognized when measurable and available to pay expenditures in the current accounting period. See also *accrual basis of accounting, cash basis of accounting.*

net present value (NPV)   A method used to calculate the economic desirability of capital projects; under this approach, a discount rate is used to take account of the discrepancy between the present costs of undertaking a project and its future stream of benefits.

objects of expenditure   Items to be purchased in an operating budget. The line items in a budget are sometimes called objects of expenditure. See also *line-item budget.*

obligation   See *encumbrance.*

operating budget   That portion of a budget that deals with recurring expenditures such as salaries, electric bills, postage, printing and duplicating, paper supplies, and gasoline. See also *capital budget.*

operating deficit   The amount by which this year's (or this budget period's) revenues are exceeded by expenditures for the same period; does not take into account any balances left over from prior years that may be used to pay off shortfalls.

par value   See *maturity value.*

pay-as-you-go financing   A method of paying for capital projects that relies on current tax and grant revenues rather than on debt.

pay-as-you-use financing   A method of paying for capital projects that relies on debt rather than current revenues to pay for capital projects.

payments in lieu of taxes (PILTS)   Compensation from tax-exempt institutions in return for local government services.

performance budget   A budget format that includes (1) performance goals and objectives and (2) demand, workload, efficiency, and effectiveness (outcome or impact) measures for each governmental program.

performance measures   Indicators used in budgets to show, for example, (1) the amount of work accomplished, (2) the efficiency with which tasks were completed, and (3) the effectiveness of a program, which is often expressed as the extent to which objectives were accomplished.

planning-programming-budgeting system (PPBS)   A budget reform that links budgeting with planning and evaluation on a program-by-program basis; now generally known as program budgeting.

productivity   The cost per unit of goods or services when quality is held constant.

professional guess   See *judgmental forecasting.*

program   A set of activities with a common goal.

program budget   A budget format that organizes budgetary information and allocates funds along program rather than along department lines. See also *planning-programming-budgeting system, program budgeting.*

program budgeting   A budget reform that links budgeting with planning and evaluation on a program-by-program basis: under program budgeting, the benefits and costs of each program are determined, and funds are allocated to those programs that provide the greatest net benefits.

progressive tax   A tax that is relatively more burdensome on higher-income households than on lower-income households.

public hearing   An open meeting regarding proposed operating or capital budget allocations that provides citizens with an opportunity to voice their views on the merits of the proposals.

purchase order   An agreement to buy goods and services from a specific vendor, with a promise to pay on delivery. See also *encumbrance.*

put option   The right of holders of debt to sell it back to the issuer.

rainy-day funds   Reserves that provide resources when tax revenues temporarily decline as the result of a recession, the loss of a major taxpayer, or other similar circumstance.

refunding bond issue   A bond issue whose proceeds are used to redeem a currently outstanding bond issue; usually sold to achieve savings on interest costs (i.e., the interest rate on the refunding bonds is lower than that on the bonds to be refunded).

regressive tax   A tax that is relatively more burdensome on lower-income households than on higher-income households.

reserves   Money accumulated for future purposes.

revenue bond   A bond issued to finance either a project or an enterprise that is secured by the revenues to be generated by the project or enterprise.

revenue elasticity   The percentage change in revenue associated with a percentage change in an independent variable.

special-revenue fund   A fund used to account for revenues legally earmarked for a particular purpose.

tax expenditures   Abatements, partial or full exemptions, tax credits, deductions, or other forgone tax revenues.

time-series techniques   Revenue projection methods that use past values as the basis for future estimates. Also known as time-trend techniques.

time-trend techniques   See *time-series techniques.*

trust fund   A fund established to receive money that the local government holds on behalf of individuals or other governments.

unlimited-tax general obligation bond   A bond secured by the full faith, credit, and taxing power of the issuer.

unreserved fund balance   Money left over from prior years that is not committed for other purposes and that can be allocated in the upcoming budget.

variable-rate bond   A bond whose coupon rate can change over the life of the bond issue; the variable rate is generally linked to an interest rate index. Also known as a floating-rate bond.

veto   The power of an elected chief executive to override all or a portion of an act or ordinance passed by the governing body; in the case of the budget, the executive may have the power to veto specific lines in a line-item budget. See also *line-item veto.*

zero-base budgeting   A budget process under which (1) departments prepare decision packages representing various service levels and rank them; (2) departmental rankings are merged across the whole governmental unit to form a single, ranked list; and (3) funding is allocated to each successive item in the list until the money runs out.

Further readings and resources

1 The finance function in local government

Bland, Robert L., and Irene S. Rubin. *Budgeting: A Guide for Local Governments.* Washington, D.C.: International City/County Management Association, 1997.

Castells, Manuel. *The Informational City: Information Technology, Economic Restructuring, and the Urban-Regional Process.* Cambridge, England: Blackwell, 1989.

Garreau, Joel. *Edge Cities: Life on the New Frontier.* New York: Doubleday, 1991.

Judd, Dennis R., and Susan S. Fainstein, eds. *The Tourist City.* New Haven: Yale University Press, 1999.

Lang, Robert E. *Edgeless Cities: Exploring the Elusive Metropolis.* Washington, D.C.: Brookings Institution Press, 2003.

Mikesell, John L. *Fiscal Administration: Analysis and Applications for the Public Sector.* 4th ed. Belmont, Calif.: Wadsworth, 1995.

Morgan, David R., and Robert E. England. *Managing Urban America.* 5th ed. New York: Chatham House, 1999.

Rubin, Irene S. *The Politics of Public Budgeting: Getting and Spending, Borrowing and Balancing.* 4th ed. New York: Seven Bridges Press, 1999.

Ruchelman, Leonard I. *Cities in the Third Wave: The Technological Transformation of Urban America.* Chicago: Burnham, 2000.

Rusk, David. *Cities without Suburbs: A Census 2000 Update.* Washington, D.C.: Woodrow Wilson Press, 2003.

Sassen, Saskia. *Cities in the World Economy.* 2nd ed. Thousand Oaks, Calif.: Sage, 2000.

————. *The Global Cities: New York, London, Tokyo.* 2nd ed. Thousand Oaks, Calif.: Sage, 2000.

Savitch, H. V., and Ronald K. Vogel, eds. *Regional Politics: America in a Post-City Age.* Thousand Oaks, Calif.: Sage, 1996.

Squires, Gregory D., ed. *Urban Sprawl.* Washington, D.C.: Urban Institute Press, 2002.

2 Fiscal structure in the federal system

Bennett, Robert J., ed. *Decentralization, Local Governments and Markets: Towards a Post-Welfare Agenda.* Oxford: Clarendon Press, 1990.

Bird, Richard M. *Federal Finance in Comparative Perspective.* Toronto: Canadian Tax Foundation, 1986.

Bird, Richard M., and Francois Vaillancourt, eds. *Fiscal Decentralization in Developing Countries.* Cambridge: Cambridge University Press, 1998.

Ferejohn, John, and Barry Weingast. *The New Federalism: Can the States Be Trusted?* Stanford, Calif.: Hoover Institution Press, 1997.

Fischel, William A. *The Homevoter Hypothesis: How Home Values Influence Local Government Taxation, School Finance, and Land-Use Policies.* Cambridge, Mass.: Harvard University Press, 2001.

Fisher, Ronald C. *State and Local Public Finance.* 2nd ed. Chicago: Richard Irwin, 1996.

Gamkhar, Shama. *Federal Intergovernmental Grants and the States: Managing Devolution.* Cheltenham, U.K.: Edward Elgar, 2002.

Inman, Robert P., and Daniel P. Rubinfeld. "The Political Economy of Federalism." In *Perspectives on Public Choice: A Handbook,* ed. Dennis Mueller, 73–105. Cambridge: Cambridge University Press, 1997.

Kenyon, Daphne A., and John Kincaid. *Competition among States and Local Governments.* Washington, D.C.: Urban Institute, 1991.

Oates, Wallace E. "An Essay on Fiscal Federalism." *Journal of Economic Literature* 37 (September 1999): 1120–1149.

————. *Fiscal Federalism.* New York: Harcourt Brace Jovanovich, 1972.

Rivlin, Alice M. *Reviving the American Dream: The Economy, the States, and the Federal Government.* Washington, D.C.: Brookings Institution, 1992.

Sjoquist, David L. *State and Local Finances under Pressure.* Cheltenham, U.K.: Edward Elgar, 2003.

3 Public school finance

Anderson, Amy, John Augenblick, John Meyers, and Julie O'Brian. *Making Better Decisions about Funding School Facilities.* Denver, Colo.: Education Commission of the States, April 1998.

Association of School Business Officials International. "Financing School Facilities." *School Business Affairs, Supplement* (1999).

Chaikind, Stephen, and William J. Fowler, eds. *Education Finance in the New Millennium: Aefa 2001 Yearbook.* New York: American Education Finance Association, 2001.

Education Commission of the States (ECS). "Finance-Capital Construction." *1999–2000 Selected State Policies.* Denver, Colo.: ECS, December 2000.

Fernandez, Raquel, and Richard Rogerson. "Education Finance Reform and Investment in Human Capital: Lessons from California." *Journal of Public Economics* (December 1999): 327–350.

Fisher, Ronald C. *State and Local Public Finance.* 2nd ed. Chicago: Irwin, 1996.

Gold, Steven D., David M. Smith, and Stephen B. Lawton. *Public School Finance Programs of the United States and Canada 1993–94.* Vols. 1 and 2. Albany: American Education Finance Association and Center for the Study of the States, 1995.

Honeyman, David S. "School Facilities and State Mechanisms That Support School Construction: A Report from the Fifty States." *Journal of Education Finance* (fall 1990): 247–272.

Inger, Morton. "Year-Round Education: A Strategy for Overcrowded Schools." *ERIC/CUE Digest* No. 103 (1994). Available at www.ericfacility.net/ericdigests/ed378267.html (May 3, 2004).

Lautenberg, Frank R. "A Tax Credit Is the Best Way to Modernize Local Public Schools." Tax Foundation's *Tax Features* (May 1999): 4–5.

National Center for Education Statistics. "Statistics in Brief: Overview of Public Elementary and Secondary Schools and Districts: School Year 1997–98" (May 1999). Available at nces.ed.gov/pubs99/1999322 (May 3, 2004).

National Conference of State Legislatures (NCSL). "School Finance." NCSL Education Program, January 8, 1999. Available at www.ncsl.org/programs/educ/sclfin1.htm (May 3, 2004).

National Education Association. "President Clinton and Vice President Gore: Modernizing America's Schools." *What's New* (December 2000).

Quindry, Kenneth E, and William F. Fox. "The Effects of State-Local Fiscal Constraints on Education Financing." *Educational Evaluation and Policy Analysis* 5 (summer 1983): 173–183.

Romer, Thomas, and Howard Rosenthal. "Bureaucrats versus Voters: On the Political Economy of Resource Allocation by Direct Democracy." *Quarterly Journal of Economics* 93 (November 1979): 563–587.

Sharp, Donna S. "Funding Options for School Facilities: A Discussion of National School Facility Funding Programs and Trends Impacting Construction." Delaware Office of State Planning Coordination, February 25, 2000.

4 Local government expenditures and revenues

Aaron, Henry J. "Incidence of the Property Tax." In *Who Pays the Property Tax?* 18–55. Washington, D.C.: Brookings Institution: 1975.

Fisher, Ronald C. "Pricing of Government Goods: User Charges." In *State and Local Public Finance,* 2nd ed., 174–201. Chicago: Richard Irwin, 1996.

McGuire, Therese. "Alternatives to Property Taxation for Local Governments." *State Tax Notes,* 15 May 2000, 1715–1723.

Mikesell, John L. *Fiscal Administration: Analysis and Applications for the Public Sector.* Fort Worth, Tex.: Harcourt Brace, 1999.

National Conference of State Legislatures (NCSL). *Critical Issues in State-Local Fiscal Policy: A Guide to Local Option Taxes.* Denver, Colo.: NCSL, November 1997.

Netzer, Dick. "Will the Property Tax Become an All-but-Forgotten Relic of an Earlier Fiscal Age?" *State Tax Notes,* 7 July 2003, 30–37.

O'Sullivan, Arthur, Terria A. Sexton, and Steven M. Sheffrin. "Proposition 13: Unintended Effects and Feasible Reforms." In

National Tax Journal 102 (March 1999): 99–112.

Wallace, Sally. "Changing Times: Demographic and Economic Changes and State and Local Government Finances." In *State and Local Finances under Pressure,* ed. David L. Sjoquist, 30–59. Cheltenham, U.K.: Edward Elgar, 2003.

---

5 Forecasting local revenues and expenditures

Armstrong, Jon Scott, ed. *Principles of Forecasting: A Handbook for Researchers and Practitioners.* Boston, Mass.: Kluwer Academic Publishers, 2001. See also the "Principles of Forecasting" Web site maintained by Professor Armstrong at http://www.marketing.wharton.upenn.edu/forecast.

Cirincione, Carmen, Gustavo A. Gurrieri, and Bart van de Sande. "Municipal Government Revenue Forecasting: Issues of Method and Data." *Public Budgeting & Finance* 19 (spring 1999): 26–46.

Groves, Sanford M., and Maureen Godsey Valente. *Evaluating Financial Condition: A Handbook for Local Government.* 4th ed., rev. Karl Nollenberger. Washington, D.C.: International City/County Management Association, 2003.

Gujarati, Damodar N. *Basic Econometrics.* 4th ed. Boston: McGraw-Hill, 2003.

Hy, Ronald John. "Economic Modeling and Local Government." *International Journal of Public Administration* 20 (1997): 1447–1467.

MacManus, Susan A. "Forecasting Frustrations: Factors Limiting Accuracy." *Government Finance Review* 8 (June 1992): 7–11.

Maki, Wilbur, and Richard W. Lichty. *Urban Regional Economics: Concepts, Tools, and Applications.* Ames: Iowa State University Press, 2000.

Makridakis, Spyros G., Steven C. Wheelwright, and Rob J. Hyndman. *Forecasting: Methods and Applications.* 3rd ed. New York: John Wiley and Sons, 1998.

Meier, Kenneth J., and Jeffrey L. Brudney. *Applied Statistics for Public Administration.* 5th ed. Fort Worth, Tex.: Harcourt College Publishers, 2002.

Pindyck, Robert S., and Daniel L. Rubinfeld. *Econometric Models and Economic Forecasts.* 4th ed. Boston: Irwin/McGraw-Hill, 1998.

Rubin, Marilyn, Nancy Mantell, and Michael Pagano. "Approaches to Revenue Forecasting by State and Local Governments."

Proceedings of the Ninety-Second Annual Conference of the National Tax Association, 205–221. Atlanta, Ga., October 1999.

Siegel, Michael. "Forecasting in the 90s: It's Not Like It Used to Be." *Government Finance Review* 8 (April 1992): 40–41.

Wong, J. D. "Local Government Revenue Forecasting: Using Regression and Econometric Forecasting in a Medium-Sized City." *Public Budgeting and Financial Management* 7 (fall 1995): 315–335.

---

6 Cost-benefit analysis and the capital budget

Aronson, J. Richard. "Cost Benefit Analysis and the Social Cost of Capital." Chap. 9 in *Public Finance.* New York: McGraw-Hill. 1985.

Aronson, J. Richard, and John Hilley. *Financing State and Local Governments.* 4th ed. Washington, D.C.: Brookings Institution, 1986, chap. 9.

Aronson, J. Richard, and Eli Schwartz. "Capital Budget Finance." *Management Information Service (MIS) Report* (February 1971).

———. "Forecasting Future Expenses." *Management Information Service (MIS) Report* (November 1970).

———. "Forecasting Future Revenues." *Management Information Service (MIS) Report* (July 1970).

Brent, Robert J. *Applied Cost-Benefit Analysis.* Cheltenham, U.K.: Edward Elgar, 1996.

Groves, Sanford M., and Maureen Godsey Valente. *Evaluating Financial Condition: A Handbook for Local Government.* 4th ed., rev. Karl Nollenberger. Washington, D.C.: International City/County Management Association, 2003.

Liu, Ligun. "The Marginal Cost of Funds and the Shadow Prices of Public Sector Inputs and Outputs." *International Tax and Public Finance* (January 2004): 17–29.

Miller, Girard, comp. *Capital Budgeting: Blueprints for Change.* Chicago: Government Finance Officers Association, 1985.

Schwartz, Eli. "The Cost of Capital and Investment Criteria in the Public Sector." *Journal of Finance* 25 (March 1970): 135–142.

Williams, Alan, and Emilio Giardina. *Efficiency in the Public Sector.* Cheltenham, U.K.: Edward Elgar, 1993.

7 Budgeting

Ammons, David N. *Municipal Benchmarks, Assessing Local Performance and Establishing Community Standards.* 2nd ed. Thousand Oaks, Calif.: Sage, 2001.

Bland, Robert L., and Wes Clarke. *Budgeting for Capital Improvements.* Chap. 26 in *Handbook of Government Budgeting,* ed. Roy T. Meyers. San Francisco: Jossey-Bass, 1999.

Bland, Robert L., and Irene S. Rubin. *Budgeting: A Guide for Local Governments.* Washington, D.C.: International City/County Management Association, 1997.

Blom, Barry, and Salomon Guajardo. "Multi-year Budgeting: A Primer for Finance Officers." *Government Finance Review* 16 (February 2000): 39–43.

Boardman, Anthony E., David H. Greenberg, Aidan R. Vining, and David L. Weimer. *Cost-Benefit Analysis: Concepts and Practice.* 2nd ed. Upper Saddle River, N.J.: Prentice Hall, 2001.

Brent, Robert J. *Applied Cost-Benefit Analysis.* Cheltenham, U.K.: Edward Elgar, 1996.

Bryson, John M. *Strategic Planning for Public and Nonprofit Organizations: A Guide to Strengthening and Sustaining Organizational Achievement.* Rev. ed. San Francisco: Jossey-Bass, 1999.

Freeman, Robert J., and Craig D. Shoulders. *Governmental and Nonprofit Accounting: Theory and Practice.* 7th ed. Englewood Cliffs, N.J.: Prentice Hall, 2003.

Gianakis, Gerasimos A., and Clifford P. McCue. *Local Government Budgeting: A Managerial Approach.* Westport, Conn.: Praeger, 1999.

Gosling, James J. *Budgetary Politics in American Governments.* 3rd ed. New York: Routledge, 2002.

Government Finance Officers Association (GFOA). *Governmental Accounting, Auditing, and Financial Reporting.* Chicago: GFOA, 2001.

———. *Governmental Accounting, Auditing, and Financial Reporting.* Chicago: GFOA, 2002.

Hatry, Harry P. *Performance Measurement: Getting Results.* Washington, D.C.: The Urban Institute Press, 1999.

Kearney, Richard C., and Evan M. Berman, eds. *Public Sector Performance: Management, Motivation, and Measurement.* Boulder, Colo.: Westview, 1999.

Koteen, Jack. *Strategic Management in Public and Nonprofit Organizations: Managing Concerns in an Era of Limits.* 2nd ed. Westport, Conn.: Praeger, 1997.

Lee, Robert D., Jr., and Ronald W. Johnson. *Public Budgeting Systems.* 5th ed. Baltimore: University Park Press, 2000.

McCafferty, Jerry. "Features of the Budgetary Process." In *Handbook of Government Budgeting,* ed. Roy T. Meyers. San Francisco: Jossey-Bass, 1999.

Meyers, Roy T. *Strategic Budgeting.* Ann Arbor: University of Michigan Press, 1994.

Mikesell, John L. *Fiscal Administration: Analysis and Applications for the Public Sector.* 5th ed. Belmont, Calif.: Harcourt Brace College Publishers, 1999.

Mueller, Dennis C. *Public Choice II: A Revised Edition of "Public Choice."* Cambridge: Cambridge University Press, 1989.

Nice, David C. *Public Budgeting.* Stamford, Conn.: Wadsworth/Thomason Learning, 2002.

Rabin, Jack, Gerald Miller, and W. Bartley Hildreth, eds. *Handbook of Strategic Management.* 2nd ed. New York: Marcel Dekker, 2000.

Reed, B. J., and John W. Swain. *Public Finance Administration.* 2nd ed. Thousand Oaks, Calif.: Sage, 1997.

Rubin, Irene S. *The Politics of Budgeting: Getting and Spending, Borrowing and Balancing.* New York: Seven Bridges Press, 1999.

Steiss, Alan Walter, and Emeka O. Cyprian Nwagwu. *Financial Management in Public Organizations.* New York: Marcel Dekker, 2001.

Wilson, Earl R., Susan C. Kattelus, and Leon E. Hay. *Accounting for Governmental and Non-Profit Entities.* 12th ed. Boston: McGraw-Hill Irwin, 2001.

8 Financial accounting, reporting, and auditing

American Institute of Certified Public Accountants (AICPA). *Audits of State and Local Governments (GASB 34 Edition).* AICPA Audit and Accounting Guide. New York: AICPA, 2002.

Comptroller General of the United States. *Government Auditing Standards.* Rev. ed.

Washington, D.C.: U.S. General Accounting Office, 2003.

Engstrom, John, and Paul A. Copley. *Essentials of Accounting for Governmental and Nonprofit Organizations*. 7th ed. New York: McGraw-Hill Professional, 2004.

Freeman, Robert J., and Craig D. Shoulders. *Governmental and Nonprofit Accounting: Theory and Practice*. 7th ed. Englewood Cliffs, N.J.: Prentice Hall, 2003.

Governmental Accounting Standards Board (GASB). *Guide to Implementation of GASB Statement No. 34 on Basic Financial Statements—and Management's Discussion and Analysis—for State and Local Governments: Questions and Answers*. Norwalk, Conn.: GASB, 2000.

Mead, Dean Michael. *An Analyst's Guide to Governmental Financial Statements*. Norwalk, Conn.: Governmental Accounting Standards Board, 2001.

Wilson, Earl R., Susan C. Kattelus, and Leon E. Hay. *Accounting for Governmental and Non-Profit Entities*. 13th ed. Boston: McGraw-Hill Irwin, 2004.

9 Enterprise resource planning systems

Davenport, Thomas. *Mission Critical: Realizing the Promise of Enterprise Systems*. Boston: Harvard Business School Press, 2000.

Hammer, Michael, and James Champy. *Reengineering the Corporation: A Manifesto for Business Revolution*. New York: Harper Business, 1993.

Linden, Russell M. *Seamless Government: A Practical Guide to Re-Engineering in the Public Sector*. San Francisco, Calif.: Jossey-Bass, 1982.

Miranda, Rowan. *ERP and Financial Management Systems: The Backbone of Digital Government*. Chicago: Government Finance Officers Association, 1999.

Miranda, Rowan, and Natalee Hillman. "Reengineering Financial Management." *Government Finance Review* 11 (August 1995): 7–10.

Miranda, Rowan, Shayne Kavanagh, and Robert Roque. *Technology Needs Assessments: Evaluating the Business Case for ERP and Financial Management Systems*. Chicago: Government Finance Officers Association, 2002.

Sandlin, Roscoe. *Manager's Guide to Purchasing an Information System*. Washington, D.C.: International City/County Management Association, 1996.

10 The property tax

Aaron, Henry J. *Who Pays the Property Tax?* Washington, D.C.: Brookings Institution, 1975.

District of Columbia, Department of Finance and Revenue. *Tax Rates and Tax Burdens in the District of Columbia: A National Comparison*. Washington, D.C.: Government of the District of Columbia, various years.

Facts and Figures on Government Finance. Washington, D.C.: Tax Foundation, 2002.

Fisher, Glenn W. *The Worst Tax? A History of the Property Tax in America*. Lawrence: University Press of Kansas, 1996.

Lorelli, Michael F. "State and Local Property Taxes." *Special Report No. 106*. Washington, D.C.: Tax Foundation, August 2001.

11 General sales, income, and other nonproperty taxes

Cline, Robert, and Thomas Neubig. "Masters of Complexity and Bearers of Great Burden: The Sales Tax System and Compliance Costs for Multistate Retailers." *State Tax Notes*, 24 January 2000, 297–313.

Commerce Clearing House. *CCH Internet Tax Research Network*. Available at tax.cchgroup.com/primesrc/bin/login.asp (May 3, 2004).

Due, John F., and John L. Mikesell. *Sales Taxation: State and Local Structures and Administration*. Rev. ed. Washington, D.C.: Urban Institute Press, 1994.

Fisher, Ronald C. *State and Local Public Finance*. 2nd ed. Chicago: Irwin, 1996.

Fox, William F., ed. *Sales Taxation: Critical Issues in Policy and Administration*. Westport, Conn.: Praeger, 1992.

Mikesell, John L. "Changes in State Retail Sales Taxes: Can These Taxes Survive Prosperity?" *Proceedings of the Ninety-Third Annual Conference on Taxation of the National Tax Association* (2000).

———. *Fiscal Administration: Analysis and Applications for the Public Sector*. 6th ed. Belmont, Calif.: Wadsworth, 2003.

Ring, Raymond. "Consumers' Share and Producers' Share of the General Sales Tax." *National Tax Journal* 52 (March 1999): 79–90.

12　User charges and special districts

Bailey, Steven James. "Charging for Local Government Services: A Coherent Philosophy." *Public Administration* 72 (autumn 1994): 365–384.

Bird, Richard M. "User Charges in Local Government Finance." In *The Challenge of Urban Government: Policies and Practices*, ed. Mila Freire and Richard Stren, 171–182. Washington, D.C.: The World Bank Institute, 2001.

Bird, Richard M., and Thomas Tsiopoulos. "User Charges for Public Services: Potentials and Problems." *Canadian Tax Journal* 45, no. 1 (1997): 25–86.

Dewees, Donald. "Pricing Municipal Services: The Economics of User Fees." *Canadian Tax Journal* 50, no. 2 (2002): 1–15

Downing, Paul B. "The Revenue Potential of User Charges in Municipal Finance." *Public Finance Quarterly* 20 (October 1992): 512–527.

Foster, Kathryn A. *The Political Economy of Special-Purpose Government.* Washington, D.C.: Georgetown University Press, 1997.

Kolo, Jerry, and Todd J. Dicker. "Practical Issues in Adopting Local Impact Fees." *State and Local Government Review* 25 (fall 1993): 197–206.

McCabe, Barbara Coyle. "Special-District Formation among the States." *State and Local Government Review* 32 (spring 2000): 121–131.

National Conference of State Legislatures (NCSL). *The Appropriate Role of User Charges in State and Local Finance.* Denver, Colo.: NCSL, July 1999.

Nelson, Arthur C., ed. *Development Impact Fees: Policy Rationale, Practice, Theory, and Issues.* Chicago: Planners Press, 1988.

Porter, Douglas R. "Financing Infrastructure with Special Districts." In *Financing Growth: Who Benefits? Who Pays? And How Much?* ed. Susan G. Robinson, 149–155. Chicago: Government Finance Research Center, Government Finance Officers Association, 1990.

Slack, Enid, and Richard M. Bird. "Financing Urban Growth through Development Charges." *Canadian Tax Journal* 39, no. 5 (1991): 1288–1304.

Wagner, Richard E., ed. *Charging for Government: User Charges and Earmarked Taxes in Principle and Practice.* London and New York: Routledge, 1991.

Yinger, John. "The Incidence of Development Fees and Special Assessments." *National Tax Journal* 51 (March 1998): 23–41.

13　Economic development

Bartik, Timothy J. "Evaluating the Impacts of Local Economic Development Policies on Local Economic Outcomes: What Has Been Done and What Is Doable?" Paper presented at the Local Economic and Employment Development (LEED) Programme of the OECD (Organization for Economic Cooperation and Development) Conference, Vienna, Austria, November 20, 2002. Available at www.upjohninstitute.org/publications/wp/0389wp.html (May 3, 2004).

———. "Incentive Solutions." Paper presented for a conference at the Humphrey Institute of the University of Minnesota, Minneapolis, Minn., February 27, 2004. Available www.hhh.umn.edu/projects/prie/bartik_paper.pdf (May 3, 2004).

———. "The Market Failure Approach to Regional Economic Development Policy." *Economic Development Quarterly* 4, no. 4 (1990): 361–370.

———. "Who Benefits from Local Job Growth: Migrants or the Original Residents?" *Regional Studies* 27, no. 4 (1993): 297–311.

———. *Who Benefits from State and Local Economic Development Policies?* Kalamazoo, Mich.: W. E. Upjohn Institute for Employment Research, 1991.

Blair, John, and Laura Reese, eds. *Approaches to Economic Development: Readings from Economic Development Quarterly.* Thousand Oaks, Calif.: Sage, 1999.

Blakely, Edward J., and Ted K. Bradshaw. *Planning Local Economic Development: Theory and Practice.* Thousand Oaks, Calif.: Sage, 2001.

Fisher, Peter, and Alan Peters. *Industrial Incentives: Competition among American States and Cities.* Kalamazoo, Mich: W. E. Upjohn Institute for Employment Research, 1998.

Hatry, Harry, Mark Fall, Thomas Singer, and Blaine Liner. *Monitoring the Outcomes of Economic Development Programs.* Washington, D.C.: Urban Institute Press, 1990.

Koven, Steven, and Thomas Lyons. *Economic Development: Strategies for State and Local Practice*. Washington, D.C.: International City/County Management Association, 2003.

Mayer, Neil. *Saving and Creating Good Jobs: A Study of Industrial Retention and Expansion Programs*. Washington, D.C.: Center for Community Change, 1998.

Molina, Frieda. *Making Connections: A Study of Employment Linkage Programs*. Washington, D.C.: Center for Community Change, 1998.

National Center for Small Communities (NCSC). *Harvesting Hometown Jobs*. Washington, D.C.: NCSC, 1997.

Poole, Kenneth, George Erickcek, Donald Iannone, Nancy McCrea, and Pofen Salem *Evaluating Business Development Incentives*. Washington, D.C.: National Association of State Development Agencies, 1999.

Rosenfeld, Stuart. *Just Clusters: Economic Development Strategies That Reach More People and Places*. Carrboro, N.C.: Regional Technology Strategies, 2002.

Siegel, Beth, and Andy Waxman. "Third-Tier Cities: Adjusting to the New Economy." Somerville, Mass.: Mt. Auburn Associates, 2001.

Wasylenko, Michael. "Taxation and Economic Development: The State of the Economic Literature." *New England Economic Review* (March/April 1997): 37–52.

14 Debt management

Akerlof, George A. "The Market for 'Lemons': Quality Uncertainty and the Market Mechanism." *Quarterly Journal of Economics* 84 (August 1970): 488–500.

The Bond Buyer/Thomson Financial 2002 Yearbook. New York: Thomson Media, 2002.

Brucato, Peter F., Jr., Ronald W. Forbes, and Paul A. Leonard. "The Effects of State Tax Differentials on Municipal Bond Yields." *Municipal Finance Journal* 12 (fall 1991): 59–77.

Fabozzi, Frank J., ed. *The Handbook of Fixed Income Securities*. 6th ed. Homewood, Ill: Business One Irwin, 2000.

Fabozzi, Frank J., and T. Dessa Fabozzi. *Bond Markets: Analysis and Strategies*, 154–159. Englewood Cliffs, N.J.: Prentice Hall, 1989.

Fairchild, Lisa M., and Nan S. Ellis. "Rule 15c2-12: A Flawed Regulatory Framework Creates Pitfalls for Municipal Issuers." *Journal of Urban and Contemporary Law* 55, no. 1 (1999): 9–17.

Fairchild, Lisa M., and Timothy W. Koch. "The Impact of State Disclosure Requirements on Municipal Yields." *National Tax Journal* 51 (December 1998): 733–753.

Forbes, Ronald W., and Paul A. Leonard. "Bank-Qualified Tax Exempt Securities: A Test of Market Segmentation and Commercial Bank Demand." *Municipal Finance Journal* 14 (winter 1994): 18–31.

Government Finance Officers Association (GFOA). *Disclosure Guidelines for Offerings of Securities by State and Local Governments*. Chicago: GFOA, 1991.

Groves, Sanford M., and Maureen Godsey Valente. *Evaluating Financial Condition: A Handbook for Local Government*. 4th ed., rev. Karl Nollenberger. Washington, D.C.: International City/County Management Association, 2003.

Heide, Susan C., Robert A. Klein, and Jess Lederman, eds. *The Handbook of Municipal Bonds*. Chicago: Probus Publishing, 1994.

Hopewell, Michael H., and George G. Kaufman. "Costs to Municipalities of Selling Bonds by NIC." *National Tax Journal* (December 1974): 531–541.

Kaplan, Robert S., and Gabriel Urwitz. "Statistical Models of Bond Ratings: A Methodological Inquiry." *Journal of Business* 52 (April 1979): 231–261.

Kurish, J. B., and Patricia Tigue. *An Elected Official's Guide to Debt Issuance*. Chicago: Government Finance Officers Association, 1993.

Lamb, Robert, and Stephen P. Rappaport. *Municipal Bonds: The Comprehensive Review of Tax-Exempt Securities and Public Finance*. New York: McGraw-Hill, 1980.

Leonard, Paul A. "Negotiated versus Competitive Bond Sales: A Review of the Literature." *Municipal Finance Journal* 15 (summer 1994): 12–36.

Lipnick, Linda Hird, Yaffa Rattner, and Linda Ebrahim. "The Determinants of Municipal Credit Quality." *Government Finance Review* 35 (December 1999): 35–41.

Litvack, David. "Measuring Municipal Default Risk." *Government Finance Review* (December 1999): 19–21.

Moon, Choon-Geol, and Janet G. Stotsky. "Municipal Bond Rating Analysis: Sample Selectivity and Simultaneous Equations Bias." *Regional Science and Urban Economics* 23 (March 1993): 29–50.

Municipal Securities Rulemaking Board. "MSRB Discussion Paper on Disclosure in the Municipal Securities Market." *MSRB Reports* 21, no. 1 (May 2001).

———. "MSRB Review of Rule G-37." *MSRB Reports* 21, no. 2 (July 2001).

———. *Notice of Interpretation of Rule G-37.* Washington, D.C., May 24, 1994.

Perry, Larry G. "The Effect of Bond Rating Agencies on Bond Rating Models." *Journal of Financial Research* 8 (winter 1985): 307–315.

Petersen, John E., and Ronald W. Forbes. "The Impact of Tax Reform on the Tax-Exempt Securities Market." In *Investment Banking Handbook*, ed. J. Peter Williamson. New York: John Wiley, 1988.

Simonsen, William, and Mark D. Robbins. "Does It Make Any Difference Anymore? Competitive versus Negotiated Municipal Bond Issuance." *Public Administration Review* 56 (January/February 1996): 57–69.

Sorensen, Eric H. "An Analysis of the Relationship between Underwriter Spread and the Pricing of Municipal Bonds." *Journal of Financial and Quantitative Analysis* 15 (June 1980): 435–447.

Stevens, Glenn L., and R. Patrick Wood. "Comparative Financing Costs for Competitive and Negotiated Pennsylvania School District Bonds." *Journal of Public Budgeting, Accounting and Financial Management* 9 (winter 1998): 529–551.

Williams, Bruce D. "The Bond Financing Puzzle: Fitting the Pieces Together." *School Business Affairs* 60 (October 1994): 10, 12–17.

Ziebell, Mary T., and Mary Jean Rivers. "The Decision to Rate or Not to Rate: The Case of Municipal Bonds." *Journal of Economics and Business* 44 (November 1992): 301–316.

15 Procurement

Callender, Guy, and Darin Mathews. "The Economic Context of Government Procurement: New Challenges and New Opportunities." *Journal of Public Procurement* 2, no. 2 (2002): 216–236.

———. "Governmental Purchasing: An Evolving Profession?" *Journal of Public Budgeting, Accounting & Financial Management* 12, no. 2 (2000): 272–290.

Daly, John L., and Michael A. Buehner. "P-Card Utilization in Municipal Government: Advantages and Concerns." *Journal of Public Procurement* 3, no. 1 (2003): 75–94.

Gianakis, Gerasimos A., and Xiao-Hu Wang. "Decentralization of the Purchasing Function in Municipal Government: A National Survey." *Journal of Public Budgeting, Accounting & Financial Management* 12, no. 3 (2000): 421–440.

Gordon, Steve B., Stanley D. Zemansky, and Alex Sekwat. "The Public Purchasing Profession Revisited." *Journal of Public Budgeting, Accounting & Financial Management* 12, no. 2 (2000): 248–271.

Heijboer, Govert, and Jan Telgen. "Choosing the Open or the Restricted Procedure: A *Big* Deal or a Big *Deal?*" *Journal of Public Procurement* 2, no. 2 (2002): 187–215.

Herbold, Darla H. "County Use of the RRP Process to Select Joint Venture Developers of Water-View Property: A Case Study." *Journal of Public Procurement* 2, no. 2 (2002): 252–260.

Larson, Stephen J., and Armand Picou. "The Market's Response to Contract Award Announcements: Government versus Corporate Contracts." *Journal of Public Procurement* 2, no. 2 (2002): 237–251.

Lawther, Wendell C. "Invitation to Negotiate: Determining the Boundaries of Innovative Source Selection." *Journal of Public Procurement* 3, no. 3 (2003): 301–319.

Lightfoot, P., and R. G. Kauffman. "Controlling Warehouse Performance with Statistical Process Methods." *Journal of Public Procurement* 3, no. 1 (2003): 29–42.

MacManus, Susan A. "Understanding the Incremental Nature of E-Procurement Implementation at the State and Local Levels." *Journal of Public Procurement* 2, no. 1 (2002): 5–28.

Martin, Lawrence L. "Performance-Based Contracting for Human Services: Lessons for Public Procurement?" *Journal of Public Procurement* 2, no. 1 (2002): 55–72.

McCue, Cliff P., and Gerasimos A. Gianakis. "Public Purchasing: Who's Minding the Store?" *Journal of Public Procurement* 1, no. 1 (2001): 71–95.

McCue, Cliff P., and Jack T. Pitzer. "Centralized vs. Decentralized Purchasing: Current Trends in Government Procurement Practices." *Journal of Public Budgeting, Accounting & Financial Management* 12, no. 3 (2000): 400–420.

New, Steve, Ken Green, and Barbara Morton. "An Analysis of Private versus Public Sector Responses to the Environmental Challenges of the Supply Chain." *Journal of Public Procurement* 2, no. 1 (2002): 93–105.

Pettijohn, Carol, and Yuhua Qiao. "Procurement Technology: Issues Faced by Public

Organizations." *Journal of Public Budgeting, Accounting & Financial Management* 12, no. 3 (2000): 441–461.

Qiao, Y., and Glen Cummings. "The Use of Qualifications-Based Selection on Public Procurement: A Survey Research." *Journal of Public Procurement* 3, no. 2 (2003): 215–249.

Sinclair, Thomas A. P. "Governmental Purchasing in the Public Policy Process: Orienting Theory and Practice." *Journal of Public Budgeting, Accounting & Financial Management* 12, no. 2 (2000): 291–306.

Snider, Keith F., and Michael F. Walkner. "Best Practices and Protests: Toward Effective Use of Past Performance as a Criterion in Source Selections." *Journal of Public Procurement* 1, no. 1 (2001): 96–122.

Taylor, Thomas K. (2002), "A Strategy for Firms Facing Offset Obligations: A Case of Maryland." *Journal of Public Procurement* 2, no. 2 (2002): 157–186.

16 Cash and investment management

Allan, Ian J. *Revenue Collection Administration: A Guide for Smaller Governments.* Chicago: Government Finance Officers Association, 1993.

Association for Financial Professionals (AFP). *AFP Manual of Treasury Policies: Guidelines for Developing Effective Control.* Bethesda, Md.: AFP, 2001.

———. *Standardized RFPs: Effective Tools for Selecting Cash Management Banks.* 2nd ed. Bethesda, Md.: AFP, 2003.

The Blue Book of Bank Prices 2002–2003, Executive Summary. Research Triangle Park, N.C.: Phoenix-Hecht, 2003.

Bort, Richard. *Corporate Cash Management Handbook.* Boston: Warren, Gorham, and Lamont, 1995.

Gauthier, Stephen J. *Evaluating Internal Controls.* Chicago: Government Finance Officers Association, 1996.

Government Finance Officers Association (GFOA). *An Introduction to Treasury Management Practices.* Chicago: GFOA, 1998.

Larson, M. Corinne. "Evaluating Investment Options: What to Look For, What to Look Out For." California Special Districts Association's *CSDA Finance Corporation Money Matters* (spring 2000): 2.

———. *An Introduction to Collateralizing Public Deposits for State and Local Governments.* Chicago: Government Finance Officers Association, 1996.

———. "Managing Your Investment Program in Today's Market." *Government Finance Review* (June 2002): 40.

———, ed. Government Finance Officers Association's *Public Investor* 13, no. 3 (March 4, 1994).

Larson, M. Corinne, and Olga Spaic. *Collecting Delinquent Revenues.* Chicago: Government Finance Officers Association, 1995.

Masson, Dubos J., and David A. Wikoff. *Essentials of Cash Management.* 6th ed. Bethesda, Md.: Treasury Management Association, 1998.

Miller, Girard, with M. Corinne Larson and W. Paul Zorn. *Investing Public Funds.* Chicago: Government Finance Officers Association, 1998.

Schwartz, Eli. "Inventory and Cash Management." In *Management Policies in Local Government Finance.* 4th ed., 389–410. Washington, D.C.: International City/County Management Association, 1996.

Vukhac, Dung, and Rosemarie S. Teta. "How Efficient Is Your Cash Management and Investment Process?" Treasury Management Association's *TMA Journal* (March–April 1999): 62.

17 Risk management

Adams, J. *Risk.* London: UCL Press, 1998.

Barton, Laurence. *Crisis in Organizations: Managing and Communicating in the Heat of Chaos.* Cincinnati, Ohio: South-Western Publishing Co., 1993.

Bernstein, Peter L. *Against the Gods: The Remarkable Story of Risk.* New York: John Wiley and Sons, 1996.

Brown, Gregory W., and Donald H. Chew, eds. *Corporate Risk: Strategies and Management.* London: Risk Books, 1999.

Culp, Christopher L., and Merton H. Miller, eds. *Corporate Hedging in Theory and Practice: Lessons from Metallgesellschaft.* London: Risk Books, 1999.

Doherty, Neil A. *Integrated Risk Management: Techniques and Strategies for Reducing Risk.* New York: McGraw-Hill, 2000.

Dorfman, Mark S. *Introduction to Risk Management and Insurance.* Englewood Cliffs, N.J.: Prentice Hall, 1997.

Fone, Martin, and Peter C. Young. *Public Sector Risk Management.* Oxford: Butterworth-Heinemann, 2000.

Geman, Hélyette, ed. *Insurance and Weather Derivatives: From Exotic Options to Exotic Underlyings*. London: Risk Books, 1999.

Head, George L. *Essentials of Risk Control*. Vols. 1 and 2. Malvern, Pa.: Insurance Institute of America, 1995.

Head, George L., and Stephen Horn II. *Essentials of the Risk Management Process*. Vols. 1 and 2. Malvern, Pa.: Insurance Institute of America, 1997.

Head, George L., Michael W. Elliott, and James D. Blinn. *Essentials of Risk Financing*. Vols. 1 and 2. Malvern, Pa.: Insurance Institute of America, 1996.

Marshall, John F., and Vipul K. Bansal. *Financial Engineering: A Complete Guide to Financial Innovation*. New York: Allyn and Bacon, 1992.

Pfaffle, Anton E., and Sal Nicosia. *Risk Analysis Guide to Insurance and Employee Benefits*. New York: Amacom Books, 1999.

Public Risk Management Association (PRIMA). *State of the Profession 2000*. Arlington, Va.: PRIMA, June 2000. Web site: www.primacentral.org.

Reiss, Claire Lee. *Risk Identification and Analysis: A Guide for Small Public Entities*. Fairfax, Va.: Public Entity Risk Institute, 2001. Web site: www.riskinstitute.org.

Risk and Insurance Management Association, Inc. (RIMS). *Annual State of the Profession Survey*. New York: RIMS, annually.

———. *Cost of Risk Survey*. New York: RIMS, annually.

Trigeorgis, Lenos, ed., *Real Options and Business Strategy*. London: Risk Books, 1999.

Trimpop, Rudiger M. *The Psychology of Risk Taking Behavior*. Amsterdam: North-Holland Publishing Company, 1994.

Vaughan, Emmett J., and Therese Vaughan. *Essentials of Insurance: A Risk Management Perspective*. 2nd update ed. New York: John Wiley and Sons, 2003.

Williams, C. Arthur, Jr., Michael L. Smith, and Peter C. Young. *Risk Management and Insurance*. 8th ed. New York: Irwin McGraw-Hill, 1998.

Young, Peter C. *Managing Risk in Local Government*. Austin, Tex.: Sheshunoff Information Services, 1999.

Young, Peter C., and Steven C. Tippins. *Managing Business Risk: An Organization-Wide Approach to Risk Management*. New York: Amacom Books, 2000.

Zagaski, Chester A., Jr. *Environmental Risk and Insurance*. Chelsea, Mich.: Lewis Publishers, 1992.

18   Public employee pension funds

Barth, Sanford. "Tackling Rising Health Care Costs." *Governmental Finance Review* (February 2003): 32–34.

Coronado, Julia, Eric Engen, and Brian Knight. "Public Pension Funds and Private Capital Markets: The Investment Practices and Performance of State and Local Pension Funds." *National Tax Journal* 56 (September 2003): 582–584.

Engebretson, Kathryn J. "A Multi-Asset Class Approach to Pension Fund Investments." *Government Finance Review* 11 (February 1995): 11–14.

Foster, Ann. "Public and Private Defined Benefit Pensions: A Comparison." *Compensation and Working Conditions* (summer 1997): 37–43.

Governmental Accounting Standards Board (GASB). *Disclosure of Information by Public Employee Retirement Systems and State and Local Government Employers*, Statement No. 5. Stamford, Conn.: GASB, 1986.

Government Finance Officers Association (GFOA). "Alternative Investments Policy for Public Employee Retirement Systems." In *Recommended Practices*. Chicago: GFOA, March 2000.

Harris, Jennifer. *2001 Survey of State and Local Government Employee Retirement Systems*. Public Pension Coordinating Council. March 2002. Available at http:ppcc.grsnet.com.

Kerry, J. Robert, and John Danforth. *Final Report: Bipartisan Commission on Entitlement and Tax Reform*. Washington, D.C, January 1995.

National Retirement Income Policy Committee. *Policy Papers*. Arlington, Va.: American Society of Pension Actuaries, 1994.

Petersen, John. "Angling for Big Returns." *Governing* (June 2001): 74.

———. "Pension Fund Follies." *Governing* (June 2002): 64.

———. "The Push to Leverage Public Pension Funds." Standard and Poor's Corporation *Credit Week,* 14 December 1992, 1.

———. *State and Local Pension Investment Performance*. Washington, D.C.: Municipal Finance Officers Association, 1980.

Planin, Eric, and Spencer Rich. "Balancing Social Security and the Budget." *Washington Post,* 21 February 1995, A6.

Ruffel, Charles, and Nevin Adams. "America's Pension Funding Crisis: The Perfect Storm." *Plan Sponsor* (November 2002): 92–96.

Rynecki, David. "Pension Plan Gambler." *Fortune,* November 2002, 17.

Sarney, Mark. "State and Local Pension Plan's Equity Holdings and Returns." Washington, D.C.: U.S. Social Security Administration, 2000. Web site: www.ssa.gov/policy/pubs.

U.S. Bureau of the Census. *Finances of Employee Retirement Systems of State and Local Governments,* various numbers. Washington, D.C.: U.S. Government Printing Office, 2002, 19.

U.S. Congress. House Committee on Education and Labor. *Task Force Report on Public Employee Retirement Systems.* Washington, D.C.: U.S. Government Printing Office, 1978.

---

19   Unions and collective bargaining

Ashbaugh, Sam. "The Art and Science of Costing Labor Contracts." *Government Finance Review* 18 (December 2002): 33–34.

Belman, Dale, Morley Gunderson, and Douglass Hyatt. *Public Sector Employment in a Time of Transition.* Madison, Wis.: Industrial Relations Research Association, 1996.

Braden, Bradley, and Stephanie Hyland. "Cost of Employee Compensation in Public and Private Sectors." *Monthly Labor Review* 116 (May 1993): 19–20.

Bureau of National Affairs. *Government Employee Relations Report.* Washington, D.C., weekly.

Coleman, Charles J. *Managing Labor Relations in the Public Sector.* San Francisco: Jossey-Bass, 1990.

Freeman, Richard, and Thomas Kochan, eds. *When Public Sector Workers Unionize.* Chicago: University of Chicago Press, 1988.

Journal of Collective Negotiations in the Public Sector. Amityville, N.Y.: Baywood Publishing Company, quarterly.

Lewin, David, Peter Feuille, Thomas Kochan, and John Delaney. *Public Sector Labor Relations.* 3rd ed. Lexington, Mass.: D. C. Heath, 1988.

Miller, Michael. "The Public-Private Pay Debate: What Do the Data Show?" *Monthly Labor Review* (May 1996): 18–29.

Najita, Joyce, and James Stern, eds. *Collective Bargaining in the Public Sector: The Experience of Eight States.* Armonk, N.Y.: M. E. Sharpe, 2001.

Public Employee Department. "Public Employees Bargain for Excellence: A Compendium of State Public Sector Labor Relations Laws." Washington, D.C.: AFL-CIO, 1997.

Schwenk, Albert E. "Compensation Cost Trends in Private Industry and State and Local Governments." *Compensation and Working Conditions* (fall 1999): 13–18.

Siegel, Gilbert B. *Public Employee Compensation and Its Role in Public Sector Strategic Management.* New York: Quorum Books, 1992.

Workplace Economics, Inc. *Municipal Employee Benefits Survey.* Washington, D.C.: Workplace Economics, annual.

List of
contributors

J. Richard Aronson (Editor and Chapter 6) is the William L. Clayton Professor of Business and Economics at Lehigh University, where he has been on the faculty since 1965. He has also served as director of the university's Martindale Center for the Study of Private Enterprise since 1980. Prior to joining the Lehigh faculty, he was assistant professor of economics at Worcester Polytechnic Institute. In 1973 he was a visiting scholar at the Institute for Social and Economic Research, University of York, England; and in both 1978 and 1996, he was selected as a Fulbright Research Scholar to the United Kingdom. While at Lehigh he has received four teaching awards, the Hillman Award for service to the university, and the Libsch Award for research. Specializing in public finance, Dr. Aronson coedited the previous edition (1996) of this volume, and his articles have appeared in such publications as the *Journal of Finance, National Tax Journal, Economic Journal,* and *Journal of Economic Literature.* He is a member of the American Economic Association, the American Finance Association, the National Tax Association, and the Royal Economic Society, and he was appointed by Governor Thornburgh to the Pennsylvania Employee-Pension Commission. Dr. Aronson received his BA from Clark University; his MA from Stanford University, where he was a Rockefeller Fellow; and his PhD from Clark, where he received special honors in economics.

Eli Schwartz (Editor and Chapter 6) is Professor Emeritus of Economics and Finance at Lehigh University. He has taught at Michigan State University, the London School of Economics, and the Autonomous University of Madrid. In addition to publishing extensively in the areas of economic policy and public and private finance, he has had wide experience as a consultant with attorneys and private and public organizations. He has a bachelor's degree from the University of Denver, a master's degree from the University of Connecticut, and a doctorate from Brown University.

Roy W. Bahl Jr. (Chapter 4) is dean of the Andrew Young School of Policy Studies and professor of economics and public administration at Georgia State University. He has consulted widely with public and private agencies on economic development and state and local government finance issues, was staff director for both the Georgia and the Ohio Tax Reform Commissions, and has advised many other states and local governments on tax policy issues. He is the author of numerous books, monographs, and scholarly papers and has served on the editorial boards of a number of journals. He received his master's degree and his doctorate from the University of Kentucky.

Timothy J. Bartik (Chapter 13) is senior economist at the W. E. Upjohn Institute for Employment Research, a nonprofit and nonpartisan research organization in Kalamazoo, Michigan, where he is responsible for research on state and local economic development policies, local labor markets, and urban poverty. Before joining the institute, Dr. Bartik was assistant professor of economics at Vanderbilt University from 1982 to 1989. He received his PhD in economics from the University of Wisconsin–Madison in 1982.

Edward J. Bierhanzl (Chapter 12) is an economist and associate professor at Florida A&M University. His work focuses on the areas of local government finance, the application of user charges to services at all levels of government, and the relationship between institutions and economic performance. He holds a PhD in economics from Florida State University.

Paul B. Downing (Chapter 12) is Professor Emeritus in the Department of Economics, Florida State University. While at the university, he was a member and director of the Policy Sciences Program, and he received a university teaching award for his honors program class. Along with Ed Bierhanzl, he received a national award for research on the efficiency of user charges. He has published extensively on user charges for the finance of local government. He earned his doctorate in economics from the University of Wisconsin.

Mary H. Harris (Chapter 4) is assistant professor of finance at Cabrini College in Radnor, Pennsylvania. She earned her PhD from Lehigh University in January 2002 and was awarded the 2001 AEFA/NCES New Scholar's award for her dissertation topic of school district state funding programs and bond finance for capital expenditures; this work was partially published in the *Journal of Education Finance* (summer 2002). Prior to earning her doctorate, she spent thirteen years in the banking industry specializing in the areas of accounting and finance. Her research interests are school finance and education policy.

William Wallace Holder, DBA, CPA (Chapter 8) serves as the Ernst & Young Professor of Accounting at the University of Southern California (USC). He is director of the Securities and Exchange Commission and Financial Reporting Institute in the Leventhal School of Accounting, Marshall School of Business at USC. He is also a member of the Governmental Accounting Standards Board. Professionally he has chaired the Professional Ethics Committee for the California Society of CPAs, the Public Service Sector of the American Accounting Association, and audit committees, and he has served on a number of boards of directors. He has also been a member of the American Institute of Certified Public Accountants' Accounting Standards Executive Committee and Special Committee on Financial Reporting, and he is currently vice chair of the AICPA's board of examiners. A frequent consultant to a wide range of business enterprises, including large public accounting and professional service firms and the U.S. Securities and Exchange Commission, Professor Holder has coauthored several books and has published a number of research monographs and more than fifty articles in professional and academic journals. He recently provided invited testimony to Congress as part of their deliberations of the Sarbanes/Oxley Act. *Accounting Today* has named him one of the accounting profession's 100 most influential individuals in 2001 and 2002. He received his doctorate from the University of Oklahoma and is a CPA in Oklahoma and California.

M. Corinne Larson (Chapter 16) is a vice president for MBIA Municipal Investors Service Corporation, where she is responsible for servicing client relationships as well as for providing technical and educational services in cash management. She formerly served as an assistant director in the Research Center of the Government Finance Officers Association of the United States and Canada, where she managed the association's cash management programs, providing technical support in cash management to the association's membership and developing technical publications on cash management and investment topics. A frequent speaker and instructor on cash management topics, she has also authored numerous publications on cash management and investing. In addition, she has more than ten years of experience in corporate treasury management. Ms. Larson is a Certified Treasury Professional through the Association for Financial Professionals, where she sits on the editorial advisory board for the association's journal, *AFP Exchange*. She earned a BA in English from Indiana University and an MBA from the University of Notre Dame.

Paul A. Leonard (Chapter 14) is interim dean and professor of finance in the School of Business, State University of New York (SUNY) at Albany, where he teaches undergraduate and MBA courses in financial management, bank management, and capital markets. He has more than twenty years of experience as a university teacher, researcher, and consultant in the areas of financial management, capital markets, and financial institutions. Dr. Leonard has taught in the Itochu Corporation Management Development Program in Tokyo, Japan; in addition, he has conducted management development seminars for the University of California at Berkeley Extension, and he teaches in the school's joint MBA program with the Graduate School of Business Administration Zürich and at the Universidad del Salvador in Buenos Aires, Argentina. In recognition of his excellence in teaching, Dr. Leonard has received the Dean W. Warren Haynes Memorial Award for Outstanding Graduate Teaching, the Harold Cannon Memorial Award for Outstanding Undergraduate Teaching, the President's Award for Excellence in Teaching, and the Chancellor's Award for Excellence in Teaching, as well as several teaching awards from the Graduate School of Business Administration Zürich; and in 2003 he was named a Collins Fellows in recognition of his many years of service to SUNY Albany. Dr. Leonard has also conducted executive development seminars for senior New York State bank examiners in New York City and KeyBank of New York, and he has completed consulting reports on contemporary public policy and capital markets issues for the New York State Banking Department, the Public Securities Association, Donaldson, Lufkin & Jenrette Securities Corporation, Asset Guaranty Insurance Company, Merrill Lynch Asset Management, and the Municipal Finance Officers Association. His articles on topics relating to financial analysis, capital markets, and banking have appeared in numerous journals, including the *Journal of Financial Services Research*, *Journal of Banking and Finance*, *Journal of Economics and Business*, *Journal of Business Research*, *Journal of Applied Business Research*, *American Business Review*, and *Healthcare Financial Management;* he also serves on the editorial advisory board of the *Municipal Finance Journal*. Dr. Leonard earned his PhD at the University of Oregon, and his MBA and BS at SUNY Albany.

John L. Mikesell (Chapter 11) is professor of public and environmental affairs at Indiana University and director of professional graduate programs for the School of Public and Environmental Affairs. He is editor-in-chief of *Public Budgeting & Finance*. He has served as chief fiscal economist and chief of party for the U.S. Agency for International Development (USAID) Barents Group/KPMG Peat Marwick fiscal reform project with the government of Ukraine, and as Moscow-based director for assistance in intergovernmental fiscal relations with the USAID Georgia State University Consortium Russian fiscal reform project. He has worked on fiscal studies for several states, including New York, Minnesota, Indiana, and Hawaii; served on the Revenue Forecast Technical Committee of the Indiana State Budget Committee for almost thirty years; worked as consultant on World Bank missions to the Kyrgyz Republic, Kazakhstan, Azerbaijan, Tajikistan, and Turkmenistan; and been visiting scholar at the U.S. Congressional Budget Office and at the Department of Public Administration, Erasmus University Rotterdam. A member of Phi Beta Kappa, Dr. Mikesell received the 2002 Wildavsky Award for Lifetime Scholarly Achievement in Public Budgeting and Finance from the Association for Budgeting and Financial Management. He holds a BA from Wabash College and both an MA and a PhD in economics from the University of Illinois, where he specialized in public finance and taxation.

Rowan A. Miranda (Chapter 9) is an associate partner in Accenture's Finance and Performance Management Global Service Line, where he consults for public sector and higher education organizations seeking to improve their finance operations. He is also on the faculty of the Irving B. Harris Graduate School of Public Policy Studies at the University of Chicago. Formerly the director of research and consulting at the Government Finance Officers Association (GFOA), Dr. Miranda established GFOA's technology consulting practice. He is the author of several books, monographs, and articles on topics of technology, outsourcing, and public budgeting. He holds a PhD in public policy analysis from the University of Chicago.

Vincent G. Munley (Chapter 3) is the Iacocca Professor of Business and Economics at Lehigh University. He began his academic career at Lehigh in 1980 after serving for two years as a staff economist for the President's Council on Wage and Price Stability. He also spent ten years as a member of the Pennsylvania Department of Environmental Resources' Air and Water Quality Technical Advisory Committee. He was a visiting scholar at the Advisory Commission on Intergovernmental Relations in Washington, D.C., and a Fulbright Scholar at the National University of Ireland, Galway. He received a BA in economics and a BS in electrical engineering from Lehigh University, and he earned his PhD in economics from the State University of New York at Binghamton.

Wallace E. Oates (Chapter 2) is professor of economics at the University of Maryland at College Park. Following completion of his PhD from Stanford University, he joined the economics department at Princeton University, where he taught for fourteen years before moving to College Park in 1979. Much of his research and teaching has focused on issues in public finance in a federal government setting. He has worked on these issues with state governments, various federal government agencies, the Organization for Economic Co-Operation and Development (OECD), and, most recently, the European Union. He has served as president of the Eastern Economic Association (1989–1990) and of the Southern Economic Association (1993–1994), received an honorary degree of Doctor of Economics from St. Gallen University in Switzerland (2000), received the Daniel Holland Medal from the National Tax Association (2002), and has been awarded several teaching prizes.

John E. Petersen (Chapter 18) is professor of public policy and finance at George

Mason University in Fairfax, Virginia. Prior to joining George Mason, he was president and division director of the Government Finance Group/ARD, a financial research and advisory firm located in Arlington, Virginia. In that capacity, he worked as a financial advisor and consultant both domestically and internationally. Earlier, Dr. Petersen served from 1977 to 1991 as senior director of the Government Finance Research Center, a division of the Government Finance Officers Association. A graduate of Northwestern University, the Wharton School, and the School of Arts and Sciences of the University of Pennsylvania, he writes the "Finance" column for *Governing* magazine. He also serves on the editorial boards of several professional journals, including *Public Budgeting & Finance, Municipal Finance Journal,* and *Public Works Management and Policy.*

Arnold H. Raphaelson (Chapter 10) is professor of economics at Temple University. He has taught at the University of Maine and has served as professional staff member and consultant to the U.S. Senate Subcommittee on Intergovernmental Relations. He has written a number of papers on state and local finance and on health economics, and he has edited and written chapters for a volume on restructuring state and local government services. He served as a consultant on state and local taxation for the speaker of the Pennsylvania House of Representatives in 2003. His educational background includes a bachelor's degree from Brown University, master's degrees from Columbia and Clark Universities, and a doctorate from Clark University.

Claire Lee Reiss, JD, ARM (Chapter 17) is deputy executive director and general counsel for the Public Entity Risk Institute in Fairfax, Virginia. She previously served as risk manager for the city of Alexandria, Virginia, and as vice president of H.F.I.C. Management Co., Inc., in Vienna, Virginia. Prior to joining H.F.I.C., she was a defense attorney in private practice. She earned her bachelor's degree *summa cum laude* from Washington University in St. Louis and her law degree from the University of Pennsylvania. She is the immediate past president of the Potomac chapter of the Risk and Insurance Management Society (RIMS).

Leonard I. Ruchelman (Chapter 1) is professor of urban studies and public administration at Old Dominion University, where he teaches graduate courses in public ad-

ministration. He has published widely in the areas of local government and urban affairs and has worked extensively with local government agencies in southeastern Virginia. He received a bachelor's degree from the City College of New York and a doctorate in political science from Columbia University.

Larry D. Schroeder (Chapter 5) is professor of public administration at the Maxwell School, Syracuse University, where he also holds the title of Maxwell Professor of Teaching Excellence. He previously taught at both Georgia State University and the University of Indiana. His research focuses on state and local government finance, intergovernmental fiscal relations, and financial management. He has worked on these issues both in the United States and in a large number of developing countries. He holds a doctorate in economics from the University of Wisconsin as well as degrees from Central College in Iowa and Northern Illinois University.

Paul L. Solano (Chapter 7) is an associate professor in the School of Urban Affairs and Public Policy and is also the associate director of the Health Services Policy Research Group in the College of Human Services, Education, and Public Policy at the University of Delaware in Newark. He has held a long-standing academic appointment in the MPA program with specializations in public finance, financial management, and health policy. In addition to serving on numerous advisory boards, commissions, and committees for state and local government agencies, he has participated in the Initial Grant Review IGR process for the National Institute of Drug Abuse and has been a reviewer for general economic and health economic journals. Earlier he held professional positions as a budget analyst for county government and a program evaluation analyst for the U.S. Agency for International Development. He holds a bachelor's degree from Northeastern University and a doctorate from the University of Maryland.

Khi V. Thai (Chapter 15) is a professor in the School of Public Administration and has served as director of the Public Procurement Research Center at Florida Atlantic University. Previously he taught and served as director of the Bureau of Public Administration at the University of Maine in Orono. He has published widely in public budgeting and public procurement and is currently on the editorial boards of five journals, including the *International Journal* *of Public Administration* and the *Journal of Contemporary Issues in Business & Government* (Australia). He is also editor-in-chief of the *Journal of Public Procurement;* editor of the *Journal of Public Budgeting, Accounting & Financial Management;* and managing editor of *International Journal of Organization Theory and Behavior.* He has served as a faculty advisor of the Government Finance Officers Association's Budgeting and Financial Management Committee and as a nonvoting member of the National Institute of Governmental Purchasing's research and education committees.

Robert J. Thornton (Chapter 19) is Mac-Farlane Professor of Economics at Lehigh University. He formerly served as a research assistant with the Brookings Institution. He has published widely in the area of labor economics, and he currently serves on the editorial boards of the *Journal of Collective Negotiations in the Public Sector,* the *Journal of Forensic Economics, Perspectives on Work,* and *Litigation Economics Review.* He holds a PhD from the University of Illinois.

Peter C. Young (Chapter 17) occupies the E. W. Blanch, Sr. Chair in Risk Management at the University of St. Thomas College of Business in Minneapolis, Minnesota. In that capacity, he is responsible for the MBA Concentration in Risk and Insurance Management, a program recently ranked fourth in the United States by *Best's Review.* Prior to joining St. Thomas in 1994, Dr. Young was a professor of risk management at St. Cloud State University, where he developed the undergraduate program in risk management and insurance, a program now recognized as one of the top undergraduate programs in the United States. He has been a visiting professor to City University in London and Aoyama Gakuin University in Tokyo; currently he is a distinguished visiting professor at Glasgow Caledonian University in Scotland as well as a visiting professor and senior advisor at the European Institute for Risk Management in Copenhagen, Denmark. Considered a leading expert on risk management, particularly in public sector organizations, Dr. Young has written extensively on the subject of risk management and has been published extensively in academic and practitioner journals. He is also a consultant to and advises numerous organizations in the insurance and risk management fields. Most recently he has worked with Munich American Risk Partners, the Association of Small Business Development Centers, the Public Risk Management Association, the Association of Local Authority Risk Managers (UK), the National Center for Small Communities, and the Association for Governmental Risk and Insurance Pools (AGRIP). Dr. Young holds a PhD in risk management from the University of Minnesota and a master's degree in public administration (state and local government) from the University of Nebraska–Omaha.

Illustration and table credits

Figure 1–1: Data from the U.S. Bureau of Labor Statistics as presented in *Governing* magazine, *State and Local Sourcebook* (Washington, D.C.: Congressional Quarterly, Inc., 2002), 48. Figure 1–2: Data from the U.S. Bureau of Labor Statistics as presented in "Fifteen Years of Change," *Governing* magazine (October 2002): 38. Figure 1–3: National League of Cities (NLC), *City Fiscal Conditions in 2002* (Washington, D.C.: NLC, 2002), 5. Figure 1–4: Bureau of the Census, *Demographic Trends in the 20th Century,* Census 2000 Special Report (Washington, D.C.: Bureau of the Census, U.S. Department of Commerce, November 2002), 33, at www.census.gov/prod/2002pubs/censr-4.pdf. Figure 1–5: Alan Berube and William H. Frey, *A Decade of Mixed Blessings: Urban and Suburban Poverty in Census 2000* (Washington, D.C.: Center on Urban and Metropolitan Policy, Brookings Institution, 2002). Reprinted with permission of the Brookings Institution. Figure 1–6: Brookings Institution, Center on Urban and Metropolitan Policy, *Racial Change in the Nation's Largest Cities: Evidence from the 2000 Census* (Washington, D.C.: Center on Urban and Metropolitan Policy, Brookings Institution, April 2001). Reprinted with permission of the Brookings Institution. Figure 1–7: David Firestone, "The New Look Suburbs," *New York Times,* 17 April 2001, A1, A4. Figure 1–8: Center for the Study of the States, *State Fiscal Brief* (Albany: Center for the Study of the States, Nelson A. Rockefeller Institute of Government, State University at New York at Albany, 1998), 8. Reprinted with permission of the Fiscal Studies Program, Nelson A. Rockefeller Institute of Government, Albany, N.Y., www.rockinst.org. Tables 1–5 and 1–7: Edward L. Glaeser and Jesse M. Shapiro, *City Growth and the 2000 Census: Which Places Grew and Why* (Washington, D.C.: Center on Urban and Metropolitan Policy, Brookings Institution, May 2001). Reprinted with permission of the Brookings Institution. Table 1–1: U.S. Department of Commerce, Bureau of the Census, *Statistical Abstract of the United States: 2002* (Washington, D.C.: U.S. Government Printing Office, 2002), 260. Tables 1–2 and 1–3: "Inside the *Year Book,*" in *The Municipal*

Year Book 2004 (Washington, D.C.: International City/County Management Association, 2004), xii and xiii. Table 1–4: Bureau of the Census, *Ranking Tables for Metropolitan Areas, 1990 and 2000,* PHC-T-3 (Washington, D.C.: Bureau of the Census, U.S. Department of Commerce, 2000). Table 1–6: U.S. Department of Commerce, Bureau of the Census, "State of the Cities Census Data 2000," available at www.socds.huduser.org/.

Tables 2–1, 2–2, and 2–3: David Hoffman, ed., *Facts and Figures on Government Finance,* 36th ed. (Washington, D.C.: Tax Foundation, 2002), 51 and tables C4, C11, D7, and F8. Table 2–4: U.S. Department of Commerce, Bureau of the Census, *Statistical Abstract of the United States, 2001* (Washington, D.C.: U.S. Government Printing Office, 2001), 258.

Figure 3–1 and Tables 3–1, 3–2, and 3–4 (for 1999–2000 data): U.S. Department of Education, National Center for Education Statistics (NCES), *Digest of Education Statistics 2002* (Washington, D.C.: U.S. Department of Education [DOE], November 2002), tables 1, 156, 158, and 168. Figures 3–2 and 3–3 and Table 3–5: Catherine C. Sielke et al., eds., *Public School Finance Programs of the United States and Canada: 1998–99,* NCES no. 2001309 (DOE, 2001). Table 3–3: U.S. Department of Commerce, Bureau of the Census, Governments Division, Elementary-Secondary Education Statistics Branch, *Annual Survey of Government Finances* (Washington, D.C.: U.S. Department of Commerce, 2000), tables 6 and 9. Table 3–4 (for 1959–60 and 1979–80 data): U.S. Advisory Commission on Intergovernmental Relations (ACIR), M-175 (Washington, D.C.: ACIR, December 1990). Table 3–5: U.S. Department of Commerce, Bureau of the Census, *Government Organization,* 1997 Census of Governments (Washington, D.C.: U.S. Government Printing Office), table 10.

Tables 4–1 and 4–4: Based on data in U.S. Department of Commerce, Bureau of the Census, *Statistical Abstract of the United States: 2002* (Washington D.C.: U.S. Government Printing Office [GPO], 2002), 308 and table 422; and Bruce Baker, "Receipts and Expenditures of State Governments and of Local Governments, 1959–2001," *Survey of Current Business* 83, no. 6 (June 2003): 36–53. Table 4–2: U.S. Department of Commerce, Bureau of the Census, www.census.gov/govs/estimate/97stlotypesummary.html, table 2. Table 4–3: In general, U.S. Department of Commerce, Bureau of the Census, www.census.gov/govs/www/estimate.html. For 1996–1997, www.census.gov/govs/estimate/97censusviewtabss.xls, table 45; 1999–2000, www.census.gov/govs/estimate/00sl00us.html, table 1. Federal own-source revenues (total receipts less social security), U.S. Department of Commerce, Bureau of the Census, *Statistical Abstract of the United States: 2002* (GPO, 2001), 305. Other federal data, *Statistical Abstract of the United States: 1999* (GPO, 1999), table 504. Employment data, www.census.gov/govs/www/apesloc.html; *Statistical Abstract of the United States: 1999* (GPO, 1999), table 504; *Statistical Abstract of the United States: 1994* (GPO, 1994), table 494; and www.census.gov/govs/www/apes.html. Table 4–5: Based on data in Bruce Baker, "Receipts and Expenditures of State Governments and of Local Governments, 1959–2001," *Survey of Current Business* 83, no. 6 (June 2003): 36–53.

Figure 8–2: U.S. General Accounting Office (GAO), *Government Auditing Standards* (Washington, D.C.: GAO, 2003).

Table 9–1: Research and Consulting Center, Government Finance Officers Association.

Table 10–1: For 1956–81, U.S. Department of Commerce, Bureau of the Census, *Taxable Property Values and Assessment–Sales Price Ratios,* 1982 Census of Governments, vol. 2 (Washington, D.C.: U.S. Government Printing Office [GPO], 1982), x. For 1986–91, *Taxable Property Values,* 1992 Census of Governments, vol. 2, no. 1 (Washington, D.C.: GPO, 1994), xiv. Table 10–2: For 1957–82, Advisory Commission on Intergovernmental Relations (ACIR), *Significant Features of Fiscal Federalism, 1980–81* (Washington, D.C.: GPO, 1981), 42–44; and ACIR, *Significant Features of Fiscal Federalism, 1984* (Washington, D.C.: ACIR, 1985), 48–51. For 1987 and 1991, Bureau of the Census, *Taxable Property Values,* 1992 Census of Governments, vol. 2, no. 1 (Washington, D.C.: GPO, 1994), xiv. For 1992–99, Tax Foundation, *Facts and Figures on Government Finance* (Washington, D.C.: Tax Foundation, 2002), 202–205, 279–281. Table 10–3: For 1953–90, Advisory Commis-

sion on Intergovernmental Relations (ACIR), *Significant Features of Fiscal Federalism, 1992,* vol. 2 (Washington, D.C.: ACIR, 1992), 129. For 1990–99, local property tax revenues were calculated from data in Tax Foundation, *Facts and Figures on Government Finance* (Washington, D.C.: Tax Foundation, 2002), 281; consumer price index and gross national product rates came from U.S. Department of Commerce, Bureau of the Census, *Statistical Abstract of the United States: 2002* (Washington, D.C.: GPO, 2002), 417, 451.

Table 11–1: Calculated from U.S. Department of Commerce, Bureau of the Census, *Governmental Finances in 1960,* G-GF60, no. 2 (Washington, D.C.: U.S. Government Printing Office [GPO], 1961), table 1; *Governmental Finances in 1969–70,* GF 70, no. 5 (GPO, 1971), table 4; *Governmental Finances in 1979–80,* Series GF 80, no. 5 (GPO, 1981), table 4; *Government Finances: 1989–90,* GF 90-5 (GPO, 1991), table 6; and *Government Finances, 1999–2000* (GPO, 2003), table 1. Table 11–2: Calculated from U.S. Department of Commerce, Bureau of the Census, *Finances of Municipal and Township Governments,* in 1997 Census of Governments, vol. 4, GC 97 (4)-4 (GPO, 2000), table 4; and "Compendium of Government Finances," in *Government Finances,* vol. 4 of *1997 Census of Governments,* GC 97 (4)-5 (GPO, 2000). Table 11–3: Calculated from U.S. Department of Commerce, Bureau of the Census, *Governmental Finances in 1960,* G-GF60, no. 2 (GPO, 1961), table 1; *Governmental Finances in 1969–70,* GF 70, no. 5 (GPO, 1971), table 4; *Governmental Finances in 1979–80,* GF 80, no. 5 (GPO, 1981), table 4; *Government Finances: 1989–90,* GF 90-5 (GPO, 1991), table 6; and *Government Finances, 1999–2000* (GPO, 2003). Personal income data are from Bureau of Economic Analysis, "National Income and Product Accounts" tables, www.bea.gov/bea/dn1.htm. Table 11–4: Commerce Clearing House, "CCH Internet Tax Research Network" (proprietary access only). Table 11–5: U.S. Department of Commerce, Bureau of the Census, *1997 Census of Governments* (GPO, 2000).

Figure 12–1: Adapted from Selma J. Mushkin and Charles L. Vehorn, "User Fees and Charges," *Governmental Finance* (November 1977): 48. Table 12–1: U.S. Department of Commerce, Bureau of the Census, *Finances of Municipal and Township Governments,* 1992 Census of Governments, vol. 4, no. 4 (Washington, D.C.:

U.S. Government Printing Office [GPO], 1997), tables 4 and 6; *Finances of Municipal and Township Governments,* 1997 Census of Governments, vol. 4, no. 4 (Washington, D.C.: GPO, 1997), tables 4 and 6; and "State and Local Government Finances 2000–2001," table 2, available at www.census.gov/govs/www/estimate01 .html. Table 12–2: Bureau of the Census, *Finances of Municipal and Township Governments,* 1997 Census of Governments, vol. 4, no. 4 (Washington, D.C.: GPO, 1997), table 1; and *Finances of Municipal and Township Governments,* 1987 Census of Governments, vol. 4, no. 4 (Washington, D.C.: GPO, 1990), table 1. Table 12–3: Bureau of the Census, "State and Local Government Finances 2000–01," tables 1, 2, and 3, available at www.census.gov/govs/ www/index.html. Table 12–4: Bureau of the Census, *Government Organization,* 2002 Census of Governments, vol. 1, no. 1 (Washington, D.C.: GPO, 2002), table 9; *Government Organization,* 1997 Census of Governments, vol. 1 (Washington, D.C.: GPO, 1997), table 9; *Government Organization,* 1992 Census of Governments, vol. 1, no. 1 (Washington, D.C.: GPO, 1994), table 15; *Government Organization,* 1987 Census of Governments, vol. 1, no. 1 (Washington, D.C.: GPO, 1990), table 11; and *Government Organization,* 1982 Census of Governments, vol. 1, no. 1 (Washington, D.C.: GPO, 1983), table 9. Table 12–5: Bureau of the Census, *Finances of Special Districts,* 1987 Census of Governments, vol. 4, no. 2 (Washington, D.C.: GPO, 1990), table 1; *Finances of Special Districts,* 1997 Census of Governments, vol. 4, no. 2 (Washington, D.C.: GPO, 1997), table 1; and Bureau of the Census, "State and Local Government Finances 2000–01" (revised 19 August 2003), table 3, available at www.census. gov/govs/www/index.html. Table 12–6: Bureau of the Census, 2002 Census of Governments, Preliminary Report (Washington, D.C.: GPO, 2002).

Figure 14–1: Moody's *Bond Record.* © Moody's Investors Service, Inc. and/or its affiliates. Reprinted with permission; all rights reserved. Standard & Poor's, "Ratings Definitions" (released 4 March 2003). © Standard & Poor's Rating Services, a division of The McGraw-Hill Companies, Inc. Reprinted with permission; all rights reserved. Tables 14–1, 14–2, 14–3, and 14–7: Thomson Media, *The Bond Buyer/Thomson Financial 2002 Yearbook*

(New York: Thomson Media, 2002). Table 14–4: *Moody's Municipal and Government Manual* (New York: Moody's Investment Service, 2001). © Moody's Investors Service, Inc. and/or its affiliates. Reprinted with permission; all rights reserved. Table 14–5: Board of Governors of the Federal Reserve System, *Flow of Funds Accounts,* various issues. Table 14–6: Government Finance Research Center, *The Price of Advice* (Chicago: Government Finance Officers Association), 1987.

Table 18–1: U.S. Department of Commerce, Bureau of the Census, *Finances of Employee Retirement Systems of State and Local Governments,* 1997 Census of Governments, vol. 4 (Washington, D.C.: U.S. Government Printing Office [GPO], 2000). Table 18–2: U.S. Congress, House Committee on Education and Labor, *Task Force Report on Public Employee Retirement Systems* (Washington, D.C.: GPO, 1978); U.S. Department of Commerce, Bureau of the Census, *Public Employment in* [various years] (Washington, D.C.: GPO); and *Finances of Employee Retirement Systems of State and Local Governments* [various years] (Washington, D.C.: GPO). Table 18–3: U.S. Department of Commerce, Bureau of the Census, *Employee Retirement Systems of State and Local Governments,* 1967 Census of Governments (Washington, D.C.: GPO, 1968); *Employee Retirement Systems of State and Local Governments,* 1977 Census of Governments, vol. 6, no. 1 (Washington, D.C.: GPO, 1978); *Employee Retirement Systems of State and Local Governments,* 1982 Census of Governments, vol. 6, no. 1 (Washington, D.C.: GPO, 1983); and *Finances of Employee Retirement Systems of State and Local Governments, 1997,* 1997 Census of Governments, vol. 4 (Washington, D.C.: GPO, June 2000). Table 18–4: Howard F. Winklevoss and Dan M. McGill, *Public Pension Plans: Standards for Design, Funding, and Reporting* (Homewood, Ill.: Dow Jones–Irwin, 1979), 140. Tables 18–5 and 18–6: Board of Governors of the Federal Reserve System, *Flow of Funds Accounts* [various years] (Washington, D.C.: Federal Reserve). Table 18–7: Asset data, Board of Governors of the Federal Reserve System, *Flow of Funds Accounts* (Washington, D.C.: Federal Reserve, 2003). Rate of return on stocks, Standard & Poor's 500 Index. Rate of return on bonds, Lehman Brothers Aggregate Corporate Bond Index.

Index

Municipal Management Series

**Management Policies in
Local Government Finance**

Text type
Times Roman, Helvetica, Trump Mediaeval

Composition
Circle Graphics
Columbia, Maryland

Printing and binding
Edwards Brothers
Ann Arbor, Michigan

Design
Herbert Slobin